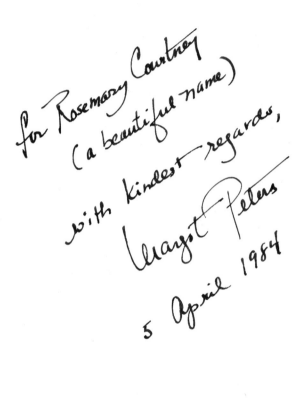

for Rosemary Courtney
(a beautiful name)
with kindest regards,

Margot Peters

5 April 1984

# Mrs. Pat

# MRS·PAT

*The Life of Mrs. Patrick Campbell*

*by* MARGOT PETERS

ALFRED A. KNOPF  NEW YORK  1984

THIS IS A BORZOI BOOK
PUBLISHED BY ALFRED A. KNOPF, INC.

Copyright © 1984 by Margot Peters

Library of Congress Cataloging in Publication Data
Peters, Margot.
Mrs. Pat: the life of Mrs. Patrick Campbell.
Bibliography: p.
Includes index.
1. Campbell, Patrick, Mrs., 1865–1940.
2. Actors—Great Britain—Biography.
I. Title.
PN2598.C23P47   1984   792'.028'0924   83-48860
ISBN 0-394-52189-7

Manufactured in the United States of America
First Edition

*For Elsie Merkel McCullough,*

*my mother*

# Contents

*Illustrations follow pages 150, 246, and 342*

# Mrs. Pat

# *Prologue*

IN THE WINTER of 1921 a young war widow living in Chelsea noted in a newspaper that a Mrs. West of Ashfields, Ormskirk, Lancashire, needed an assistant for some literary work. Although ignorant of proof-correcting, Mrs. Whittall answered the notice and soon was on the train to Ormskirk, feverishly studying the Clarendon Method as the fields and factories of the Midlands flashed by. At Ormskirk she was met by car and driven out of town into the country, past the imposing gates of Lathom Park and into the drive of a large cottage set behind a privet hedge at the edge of the Lathom estate. The door was opened by a tall and handsome woman with dark masses of hair, a deep and resonant voice, and two griffon dogs yapping at her heels. These, Mrs. Whittall learned immediately upon stepping into the entrance hall, were Georgina and Sally. It was not until some moments later that she realized that the resident of Ashfields was not "a Mrs. West" at all, but the renowned actress Mrs. Patrick Campbell.

The literary work turned out to be the actress's autobiography; but that was not the immediate task. Mrs. Campbell was leaving at once to give a lecture at Brighton. Would Mrs. Whittall mind spending the night at Ashfields alone? More important, could she be relied upon to give Georgina and Sally the delicate attentions they required? Sally would sleep in a basket, but Georgina (worth £100, confided Mrs. Campbell) preferred her mistress's pillow, or—in an emergency—Mrs. Whittall's. Furthermore, Sally had suffered a heart attack: it might be necessary to get up in the middle of the night and dose her with brandy. "God bless my soul!" exclaimed Mrs. Whittall under her breath, wondering what other duties might be extorted from her by the demanding Mrs. Campbell. But she had come a long way, she needed the money, she had mastered the Clarendon Method, and so she stayed.

Mrs. Campbell soon returned to Ashfields, and Mrs. Whittall's trials began in earnest. It became apparent, for example, that her employer

3

needed less sleep than other mortals. She would rise in the dark winter mornings full of enthusiasm, wrap herself in an old dressing gown, rouse her sleeping secretary, and, as the sun struggled over Parbold Hill, pace up and down the room dictating, her disheveled hair cascading down her back, Georgina draped around her neck like a bedraggled fur. Frequently she would stop to laugh approvingly at her own anecdotes; on the other hand, she was fully conscious that what she had already committed to paper was full of barbarous errors, and welcomed Mrs. Whittall's corrections. If toward late afternoon she happened to note that her secretary was tiring, she would graciously call a halt and, choosing a book of poetry from a shelf (Keats was a favorite), soothe her by reading aloud in her deep, mysteriously beautiful voice.

On occasion Mrs. Whittall would be pressed into service in the kitchen to make coconut icing. If there was anything Mrs. Campbell enjoyed more than a good Havana cigar, it was food—the richer and more plentiful the better. In the village it was whispered that Mrs. Campbell had even more abandoned tastes: that nude parties and who knew what other iniquities went on at Ashfields. "How disgraceful," protested Mrs. Whittall, feeling the unfairness of local gossip, but Mrs. Campbell only threw back her head and laughed: "My dear, I *love* a good disgrace!" Mrs. Whittall was denied the opportunity of witnessing any debauches; she was, however, entertained with stories of the lavish and risqué parties thrown by Ned Lathom at Blythe Hall. To these events Mrs. Campbell would go on foot, leaving by the lych gate at the bottom of the garden and walking across the fields and park to the Renaissance manor hall. Young Lord Lathom was an extravagantly generous man, a *bon vivant* who took up actors as friends and entertained them lavishly. Mrs. Campbell was a favorite of his for her audacious wit; she adored "Ned" in return. And so Mrs. Whittall was entertained with stories of the crystal balustrades, the swimming pool, the champagne and oysters, and tried to enjoy the delights vicariously, since she herself was never asked.

There were more sober moments in her employer's life, of course. Bills came with amazing regularity, bills with which Mrs. Campbell did not seem to know how to cope, except by ordering two or three new gowns from her London dressmaker to console herself. Then there were the letters from Bernard Shaw that January and February of 1922, each one refusing more firmly to allow Mrs. Campbell to publish in her autobiography the most interesting passages of the love letters he had written her nine years before when he, a married man of fifty-seven, had fallen head over heels in love. Mrs. Campbell would sit down at her typewriter to answer these in person. Her pleas to publish turned to threats. She *would* publish everything—his modesty and cowardice be damned. But the book was already in proof and Shaw adamant, so Mrs. Campbell in great indignation was forced to give in. The autobiography, she was able to announce on March 6, was finished. The very next day she left for London with profuse thanks to Mrs. Whittall for her proof-correcting and coconut frosting, but without paying her the £50 she owed her in overtime salary.

Since they were the memoirs of a famous actress, *My Life and Some Letters* created a good deal of stir. Yet the real life of Mrs. Patrick Campbell was far more romantic and tragic than the story she allowed herself to tell.

# ONE

# 1865–1881

BEATRICE ROSE STELLA TANNER was born at Forest House, Kensington, on February 9, 1865, the sixth and last child of John and Louisa Tanner. The fact of Forest House meant that John Tanner was currently in funds; it was a good house standing on the fashionable and busy Kensington Road directly across from the Palace Gardens: a good address in a city, London, where a good address was everything. There had been other good addresses, but these had been in Bombay, where John Tanner met and married in July 1852 Maria Luigia Giovanna Romanini, the seventeen-year-old daughter of Angelo Romanini, an Italian political exile. It had been love at first sight: John Tanner spoke not a word of Italian, Louisa (as she was called) not a word of English. The marriage at St. Thomas Cathedral created some excitement in Bombay, since John was the son of a wealthy Anglo-Indian army accoutrement manufacturer, and Louisa the handsome daughter of an exiled adventurer.

Three children were born to them in Bombay: John Angelo in 1853, Regina Constance (Nina) in 1857, and Louisa Leonora (Lulo) in 1858. Between the births of John and Louisa, however, the fortunes of John Tanner suffered the first of many blows. In May 1857 the long-fermenting unrest among the Bengal native army finally erupted at Meerut into a full-fledged mutiny that moved quickly to Delhi, where the city walls and then the palace were stormed, all Europeans and Christians massacred, and the former king of Delhi restored as monarch. It took months before combined British forces were able to fight back to the cantonment of Delhi. When more men, guns, and ammunition arrived to reinforce those troops in late August, the siege batteries immediately opened intense fire on the gate and bastion; and after days of heavy fighting Delhi was again in British hands.

John Tanner's army accoutrement factory in the Bellasis Road, Byculla, provided many of the guns that besieged Delhi. In fact, as Tanner later wrote to his daughter Beatrice Stella, it was on record and could be found in the Archives of the War Office that "but for the celerity and magnitude of Mr. Tanner's Ordnance Supplies the guns could not have been brought into position or the capture of Delhi effected." Far from being rewarded, however, John Tanner lost some £50,000 and, although he spent years pressing his claim, the British government never did compensate him for valuable services and losses sustained during the Indian Mutiny.

This temporary setback and the hopes of redress may have been the cause of his moving his family to England. He maintained his ordnance works in India, returning to London often enough, however, to father three more children: Edwin, Edmund (Max), and a third daughter, Beatrice Rose Stella. A man of great vigor and optimism, Tanner managed to accumulate nearly half a million pounds sterling by 1864, but, as his wife, Louisa, now knew well, half a million pounds was no guarantee that they would not be penniless a year later. And in fact shortly after 1864, as he reported cryptically to his daughter many years afterwards, he was "overtaken in his vast expectations by two severe crises in London."

This marriage of opposites—the buoyant Englishman and the quiet, artistic Italian girl—suffered the not uncommon fate of those unions which began with finding an alien character attractive and end with discovering it simply alien. John Tanner had unquenchable spirits; Louisa tended toward melancholy. The husband found his greatest pleasure in enterprise and speculation; the wife found hers in music, birds, and flowers, the poetry of Dante, Tasso, and Ariosto. John was a cheerful Darwinian; Louisa a devout Roman Catholic. John was large-handed and gregarious; Louisa was quietly devoted to her family.

Beatrice Rose Stella preferred her mother. "My Italian mother and her beautiful sisters," she wrote, "were invested for me with great romantic glamour that has remained with me. . . . My life appeared to me to have sprung from a magical past, in which Italy, Persia, India—white houses with flat roofs, white-robed Arabs, and lovely Arab horses—and my beautiful aunts—were all seen through a mist of childish imaginings; built upon stories I was told, photographs and letters I had seen, my mother's sweet singing voice, her delicious Italian accent, her guitar, and the many languages she spoke, among them Greek and Arabic." From her mother she learned a love of beauty, an artistic sensibility, a devotion to music and poetry—the melody of language, whether spoken or sung. She admired her mother's long white delicate hands; she hung upon her tales of the fortunes and misfortunes of the beautiful aunts; she was mystified by her mother's perpetual sadness. There was no harshness, no bitterness, yet she never heard her mother laugh. The melancholy did not alienate her, however.

"My father in these early days I do not recall," she wrote in her auto-biography. "I neither remember being caressed by him nor having any sense of his love for me; my whole adoration was for my mother."

Yet Stella (Beatrice, the family always called her; Stella, she would call herself) was also her father's child. From him she inherited a restless na-ture, high spirits, and acute nervous energy. From him she absorbed a love of enterprise and speculation. Like him, she had stamina, optimism, cour-age. And, like him, she would be extravagant, foolishly generous, unable to hold on to the great sums of money she would eventually earn.

Not many childhoods, perhaps, are remembered as happy. Certainly Stella remembered more sorrow than joy. She recalled clearly, for example, the occasion of her first grief: a Christmas party given by her father, with a band playing and a tree sparkling with stars and topped with a diamond-crowned fairy doll holding a golden sceptre. At the foot of the tree huge crackers, bigger than herself, which contained, she was told, costumes—kings' trains, queens' dresses, princes' and princesses' robes. She herself, wild with excitement, wondering whether her cracker would contain the dress of a princess or queen. Someone putting one of the crackers into her arms and saying, "This one is yours." Her breathless whisper, *"What is it?"* And the answer: "A cook's dress." The hours afterwards shut in a room alone, the adults having grown tired of telling her, "Stop crying" and "Don't be a silly girl."

When she was an infant, her nurse, holding the squalling thing, had told her mother, "She is not a baby; she is a tiger." Her noise and energy bewildered her brother Max, ten months older than she, whom she ter-rorized in the nursery. Though she liked to dress her prettily and teach her notes on the piano, her eldest sister, Nina, found her a difficult charge. Her passions, moods, and tears puzzled her mother, as did her scorn for dolls. Strangers terrified her: "They do not say what their faces say," she tried to tell her nurse. She was full of strange fancies and committed terrible mis-chiefs which disgraced her. Yet if there was one thing certain, it was that she was destined to be a princess, not a cook.

The absent father, the sad mother. The deaths of two of the beautiful aunts deepened Louisa Tanner's sadness. Then came an even more mel-ancholy event. The oldest child, John Angelo, had been sent to school at Brighton, as were later Nina and Lulo. John Angelo liked cricket and regattas; he liked schoolwork less, for, as he reported in a note enclosing his first certificate of good work, "properly I ought to send you one every week but some-how I cannot get any." He was punctual, however, in visiting his sisters at the Sussex Gardens School run by Miss Blackmore—"the chil-dren," he called them from his eminence as elder brother; he was an affectionate son, thoughtful of his mother and always glad to hear that his father had returned safely to Bombay. His death at school in 1868 when he was fifteen naturally came as a great shock to his parents. Stella was three, and her first memory of her mother dated from that year. She remembered her, tall and pale, dressed in black, mourning the son who had died suddenly at school.

The family had shifted residences several times since Forest House, living for a while at Ramsgate, then just around the corner from Forest House at Number 2 Kensington Gate. It depended on whether John Tanner's ordnance business, his investments in Mexican silver mines, or his dozens of small speculations were prospering or failing. In 1872 he returned to England "very rich," so rich that he carelessly destroyed the documents that might have proved his claim against the British government for the £50,000. Two years later, when Stella was about nine, the family was humbled enough to move into Tulse Dale Lodge, a house belonging to Katherine Bailey, a close friend of Louisa, and located south of the Thames between Tulse Hill and Dulwich in what was practically open country. Stella remembered it as a low gray stone house with a porch, standing in the middle of a garden and surrounded by fields and fine trees and stables. Its occupants were less congenial: one of the beautiful aunts, Dora, had also come to live there with her five children, cousins who had been wretchedly spoiled, thought the wilful Stella, by their Indian *ayahs*. Her chief impulse was to escape; her chief amusement to sit alone high up in a tree in the garden, talking to herself and to the leaves that seemed like little friends. She developed early an impatience with people who were unintelligent; she often thought grown-ups silly, their voices harsh, their movements awkward. On the other hand, if anyone had a beautiful speaking voice or fine manners, she was that person's slave.

In the absence of a father she turned to an uncle. Henry Ward Tanner was the second youngest of the nine children born to John Tanner, Senior, and Anne Mary Davis in Bombay. Twenty-one when Stella was born, endowed with the Tanner dark good looks and high spirits, yet gentle and devoted to his nieces and nephews (he would never marry), Uncle Harry, remembered Stella, was the one person in her childhood who never frightened her or made her shy. Whenever he came into the room, she would run to him instinctively and take his hand. She thought him handsome, despite disfiguring scars of smallpox, and furiously insisted that she—not Nina nor Lulo—was going to marry Uncle Harry when she grew up. She could not know, but perhaps could sense, how little Harry shared John Tanner's taste for speculation, though he patiently went along with his elder brother's endless schemes. She did know he was at heart a scholar, that he studied

French, Italian, and Latin, and that he was a great reader who imparted much of his enthusiasm for books to her as she grew older. He was a part of the household as her father never seemed to be: not an authoritarian figure, but a wise friend whose eyes always looked at her, the difficult child, with love and understanding.

Whatever she learned she learned most from the Italian mother and her Uncle Harry: like the education of most girls in the 1860's and 1870's, her formal schooling was haphazard. Even if it had not been, she hated authority from the beginning, and her resentment of rules made school for her at best dull, at worst useless. Of course, none of the Tanner children seemed particularly keen about school—Max would not return to his after the first day because he claimed the boys were disgustingly rude and vulgar. Stella joined her sisters at Sussex Gardens when she was ten. "Nothing remains in my memory but a dull monotony," she later wrote. "Governesses that made me feel shy; learning that I found difficult; and the stiffness of school discipline that hurt my sensitive mind. Walking out two by two had a tragically depressing effect upon me." She did not make friends, but amused herself with strange games and fancies. On walks, for example, she would lag behind to hide pennies in odd places, then make up stories about how beggars would find them and think God had sent the coins in answer to their prayers. The inevitable scolding for breaking ranks seemed a small price to pay for escape into fantasy.

Eventually Miss Blackmore's attention was drawn to this odd creature. She called her to her private sitting room and prescribed a cure for girlish morbidity—a certain gray powder dissolved in a cup of black coffee. Stella had no choice but swallow it; the dose made her very ill. Her father was sent for and came, looking so serious as he bent over her bed that she thought she had angered him by getting sick, and felt all the more miserable. She had forgotten, though he was remembering, that her oldest brother, John, had died suddenly at school.

After her sisters left Sussex Gardens, Stella also returned to London and spent "wretched terms" at Belsize Gardens in Hampstead. "The mistress had cold blue eyes that stared at me," wrote the dark-eyed Stella, "whether in admiration or disgust it was difficult for me to tell. She either painted or wore false eyebrows, which made her face funny to me. I know I was afraid to look at her—then I would have to laugh, and then she would frighten me. When she took the class and asked me a question, my mind became a blank. I do not remember learning anything at this school, or making any school friends." There was one vivid impression at least: a conversation with a sad-faced, kindly governess. Had she a sister? Stella asked her one day. "Yes," replied the governess, her small, pinched face very solemn, *"and her beauty was her curse."* "This answer filled me with awe," said Stella, who had been equally awed by the unhappy fates of her mother's beautiful sisters and was on her way to becoming a beauty herself, "and for a long while gravely troubled me."

Schooldays were unhappy, yet her memories of life at Tulse Dale Lodge during these years when she was growing into adolescence were scarcely happier. She could remember vividly the time a cousin came to visit during the holidays with her very small baby, which Stella begged to hold. "If you drop her, it will kill her, but if you sit on the ground I will put her on your lap," said the cousin. Stella sat down and the baby was put into her arms. But her imagination had seized upon the words "drop her . . . kill her"; she grew terrified and swayed with giddiness. "The child is fainting," she heard her mother say. "None of you understands how sensitive Beatrice is." The baby was snatched from her arms; she was made to go lie down on a bed; long afterwards she was haunted with a sense that somehow she was "queer." Or there was the time her old nurse, Fanny, came back to Tulse Dale Lodge to visit. Since she had left the Tanner family, Stella had thought of her with longing, often crying herself to sleep at the memory of affection lost. Now she looked forward to Fanny's visit impatiently; she would throw her arms around her old nurse, who had grown even more loved in absence, and kiss her. The awaited day came, Fanny came, but did not recognize her, saying in respectful tones as she eyed the tall girl with long black braids, "Surely this big girl isn't Miss Beatrice." "She did not know me," said Stella, "and I knew her so well, and I loved her so much. The pain I suffered at the sudden baffling of my joy is indescribable."

When Stella was thirteen, her eldest sister, Nina, was married to Ernest Hill from Tulse Dale Lodge, and in November of that same year her father, with Edwin, Max, Aunt Dora, and her five children, sailed from Liverpool on the steamship *British Empire* for America, bound for Texas to make the family's fortune again. On the fifth day out the heaving of the ship subsided enough for John Tanner to address some lines to his "darling Lulo," recording his favorable impression of the *British Empire*: "We have 4 substantial meals a day . . . beautiful fresh fish, Lobsters, Butter, Milk, Bread etc. every day. Beef steaks and Mutton chops at each Meal besides apples, Pears, Grapes, Oranges, Figs etc. at lunch and dinner. . . . I feel very distressed at times when I think of the extravagant fare we are treated to and how little you have to be content with at home. It is indeed a shame that such differences should exist. . . ."

If Lulo and Stella were little entertained by the picture of their father and brothers gorging themselves on ship fare, Louisa Tanner might have been even less entertained by her husband's enthusiastic accounts of the

American ladies on board. "The American ladies appear, from the two specimens on board, at a considerable advantage in many respects as compared with the ladies in England. They are so well informed and seem to be at home everywhere and I think they are more earnest & sincere in all they say & do. They do not indulge in complimentary remarks—no sort of servile flattery—all that is meant is expressed." Thus entertained, the travellers were passing the evenings very pleasantly, although the voyage was taking longer than expected. "I am sure Beatrice would have enjoyed all this very much," concluded her father. "Tell dear Beatrice that I hope she is a good child. I shall write her next time."

On Tuesday, November 19, after almost thirteen days at sea, the pioneers finally docked at a Philadelphia wharf. John Tanner had virtually no money. With some misgiving but with far more confidence, the party set out by train for Rossville, Atascosa County, near San Antonio, where James Cumins, Aunt Dora's husband and Tanner's nephew, had already settled and where two other British families, the Suters and the Hearns, had established themselves on farms. Less than a month after his arrival in America, John Tanner, the British colonialist, reported to Lulo his shock and disbelief:

... We are in a perfect wilderness here and, excepting our own little circle, we have but few opportunities of coming in contact with what we regard as rational beings. The farmers in this district are principally Mexicans with whom we can have no intercourse, the men are a lying, thieving set and very crude and dirty in their habits. ... The American labourers and farmers are a strange set, their appearance is almost as objectionable as that of the Mexicans and they are equally lawless. A dispute about a dog, or the exchange of a few harsh words generally terminates in pistol shots. The worst feature in the country is its social condition. Every common vagabond regards himself as your equal. He obtrudes himself upon your society, talks and deports himself with all the freedom and familiarity of an old acquaintance. Cursing & swearing, spitting, drawing insects from the head and cracking them before your very face, and every conceivable species of filthiness are the sort of "entertainment" one *has to endure* here. I assure you that the old Irishman who brought apples & oranges for sale to Tulse Hill is a far more respectable animal and fitting companion than the generality of men to be met with here. ...

You will doubtless see my letter to Harry before you get this and you will know how bitterly we are disappointed in every thing here, the climate excepted, and even that is so variable that we cannot reckon with any certainty from hour to hour whether we shall require our great coats or go about coatless. ... We have no doors to our log cabins and the cold wind beats on us and over us just as much as if we were in the open fields, and of course I am full of aches and pains. We have a huge fire made of heavy logs of wood and just within a foot of it Hearn and Stanley [Cumins] take their position for the night. I lie in a couple of trunks close by and in a small compartment immediately adjoining, James & Dora & all the children with Edwin and Edmond [sic] are packed together like sardines in a tin case. . . . The discomfort and privation of farm life really cannot be imagined. . . . The dirt and unpalatable & scanty food with all the revolting surroundings and associations are sufficient to break down the stoutest heart.

On Christmas Day John Tanner turned forty-nine. One bright note of the season was the "heaps of letters & Xmas cards" from Nina, Lulo, and Beatrice back home. The brightest note on Christmas Day was the celebratory appearance of two turkeys, apples, and a birthday cake nicely frosted with the initials "J.T." in blue. Their ordinary fare consisted of black coffee, meal bread, and boiled beans faintly flavored with lard— hardly up to *British Empire* standards. In the first month of the new year, 1879, he and the Cuminses pooled their resources and rented a farm with fifty-five acres under fence and a two-room house for the ten of them. There was money to be made in farming, he told Lulo: he could see that— if only there was not the prospect of being starved out by a bad season before they got under way, and if only the money did not melt away so fast. Tools, ploughs, horses, harnesses, wagons, and horse feed all cost very dear, and they had yet to buy corn seed and "a heap of things" they'd no idea about when they decided to farm. By mid-January, Tanner reported, he was working a plough ten hours a day, had almost been killed breaking a horse into the work, and weighed ten stone instead of the fourteen he'd weighed when he left England. Edwin had become "a walking skeleton," so wan and ill-looking at times that his father felt thoroughly heartbroken and sometimes had to hide himself and cry over the deplorable state of affairs. The slow but willing Edwin was Tanner's chief comfort during these months of hard labor and disillusionment when, in the mornings, ice stood six inches deep in the buckets, and an evening meal provided nothing but a slab of bread and molasses washed down with coffee for which there was no milk, let alone cream. Max, on the other hand, was proving extremely troublesome—evading work, spoiling what he undertook, meeting reproof with excuses and quibbles, talking back. His father was seriously thinking of placing him with some strict disciplinarian under whom he would be forced to work and learn something. "I think it would have been a terrible thing if you and Beatrice had accompanied me," Tanner concluded to Lulo with justice. "Give dear Beatrice my love and tell her I shall write her next time."

The plain facts should have discouraged anyone. Edwin's only talent—
and it was not a large one—was for painting. Max was too "sensitive" to
stand hard work for long. Mr. Hearn had given up the hope of striking it
rich, and was vainly trying to find a few pupils for elocution lessons in the
small and poor town of San Antonio. James Cumins had energy and some
capital, but no experience of Texas farming and trading. Tanner himself
was a *déclassé* Anglo-Indian, hardly equipped to flourish on the frontier.
They were all, in short, genteel British, totally out of their element in the
Texas of 1879. Only Aunt Dora seemed to thrive on poor food, back-
breaking labor, and the dusty, barren, snake-infested land; but then Aunt
Dora was not bringing in any money.

Yet John Tanner possessed seemingly limitless optimism. Although his
schemes, one by one, came to nothing—his investments in the Pure Ice
Company, his stake in a Mexican silver mine, his shares in Texas copper—
he could always come up with new schemes to take their place. He intended, for example, to go into the typewriter business, since he felt sure
that the machine was a coming thing. More immediately, as he wrote Lulo
on February 22, "I have an idea that Tinned Fowl Curry would prove a
very lucrative business . . . if Mr. Gregory or any one else in England
would be disposed to go into the business. I would work it here, but to do
so the party in England would have to advance about £150 . . . I could
supply a novel kind of curry packed in large Tins—6 inches high and 4¼
inches in diameter—and containing Fowl, for 3 shillings. . . . This ought to
realise from 4*s.* to 4*s.*/6*d.* very readily in the English market. The coopera-
tive stores, Clubs, Restaurants and Hotels ought to be canvassed as well as
the large grocery Establishments. I reckon that some 400 to 600 Tins
would be absorbed daily in the above named Establishments and the business would therefore be an important one. I think Harry might begin to
move immediately in the matter."

If only someone would advance him £150 . . . Perhaps John Tanner
knew he was only spinning daydreams, since he plotted his great curry
scheme with his twenty-year-old daughter, Lulo, an unlikely accomplice.
He went ahead, getting a fancy label printed for his "Texas Caponaise,"
experimenting with beef and egg curries in addition to the fowl, and finally
perfecting a mild curry powder for British taste which, when mixed with a
cup of milk and a heaping tablespoon of lard, turned an impressive blood-
red.

By April, however, even John Tanner was not sanguine. Texas was in
the grip of a terrible drought: there was no chance now of any crop being
raised. A family of six nearby had existed on water for the last four days.
The Suters must perish of starvation if no help came from home. The

Hearns had given up and were on their way back to England. Max was so clearly of no use in Texas that he was sending him home (first class) because he might be fit for an office job. Max was bringing about fifty boxes of the curry powder with him. Could Harry canvass the stores? If someone could only send him £50, he knew he could sell the powder in the northern Texas towns. The "Caponaise," on the other hand, would require an advance of £200. . . . Frightfully warm . . . an effort to walk across the room. Snakes and all kinds of poisonous insects in their glory. Everyone afraid of rattlers coming into their beds at night. If only the boys could be got away from this infernal hole. Couldn't Harry find Max a place in some office? And finally, as he closed so many letters, his best love to the daughter he could never talk to as he did to Lulo: "I am sending a copy of 'Woodland Echoes' to Beatrice. Tell her with my fondest love that the girls in America are all capital musicians," or perhaps, "Tell Beatrice with my best love that I am looking out for her promised letter."

Shortly after the male Tanners had sailed, Miss Katherine Bailey returned to Tulse Dale Lodge, and Mrs. Tanner, Lulo, and Stella moved into a small house taken by Uncle Harry at 14 Acacia Grove in Dulwich. There Stella languished for two years without hope of any further education or social opportunity, while Max returned at the end of August 1879 bearing packets of the curry powder for Harry to peddle somehow, and Lulo went off to governess with a family named Gibson in Berwick. At fifteen, however, life even in Dulwich was a constant adventure, and in April 1880 Stella sent Lulo a budget of news written in her breezy, telegraphic style:

Many thanks dear for your jolly letter but I wish you hadn't ended in such a melancholy way. Surely you dont imagine if *I* was married I should let you be a governess. You would have to put your independent spirit in yr pocket & come & live with me. If we quarreled you could go & stay with Nina for a few days & then (I speak from experience) no sooner you were gone than I should want you back again. . . . Poor Miss Baily has been ill. They put her in a damp bed & she got irrecipelis in her leg (I dont know whether I have spelt it right but I suppose you'll understand). Spent Saturday evening at the Colemans. Heaps of people there. Enjoyed myself rather. Nina has left the High School & is going to join the English Literature Class at the [Crystal] Palace. She has not begun to learn the organ yet & is learning the piano there. I think she plays *vilely*. Nina's piano is simply a darling. The tone is lovely. Just fancy Max not liking it. . . . I only saw Mr. Reid for an hour & certainly *did not* fall in love with him. He has promised to take me to the theatre. Think we'll go next week. I look such a fool in my jersey. Everybody stares. Boys call out "Skinny be be" & "Oh, I say, look at my waist" & sometimes by way of variety "Lampost" [*sic*]. . . . Max is grow-

ing so horribly vulgar it is no use Mamma correcting him. She might as well
the wall. Poor Harry is in better spirits now his old friend is back again but
though his spirits are good a blind man can see his health is failing fast.
I've had no time to read Longfellow yet. . . . Good bye dear old Girl, love
from Beatrice—

Fortunately for Stella, Miss Bailey recovered from erysipelas and proposed a year in Paris for the restless girl whose fast-developing dark beauty
and artistic longings seemed to demand something more than Dulwich for
their shaping. Stella herself had always been attracted to "Aunt Kate," the
tallest and thinnest person she had ever seen, a seventy-two-year-old spin-
ster who in her youth had been a friend of Lord Byron and Tom Moore,
and now maintained an apartment in Paris at 34 Avenue de Villiers and a
circle of friends who to a young girl seemed the ultimate of sophistication.
There was no money at home, little chance of meeting people with good
connections, little chance of any suitors besides the dubious Mr. Reid and
boys who taunted the long-legged girl with "Skinny be be" and "Lampost."
A year in Paris seemed like a rescue.

Looking back at that year, Stella saw it as the time when her impres-
sionable nature developed a deep and lifelong love for social grace and
distinction, and for that slightly artificial atmosphere in which a sudden
truth or vulgarity would be a breach of taste and decorum—not that she
would ever be able to suppress a delight in shattering that atmosphere,
much as she admired it. In plainer terms, the year in Aunt Kate's Paris
drawing room made her something of a snob. She also remembered it as a
year that taught her another kind of male attention, even though Aunt Kate
indignantly cried *"Singe!"* at the gentleman who thrust a ticket for a box at
the opera into Stella's gloved hand, and immediately hailed a fiacre to
whisk her charge from the scene of threatened debauch. It was difficult to
know what to believe. When Aunt Kate told stories of her youth, her eyes
would sparkle. "Ah," she would sigh, recounting some love story, rolling
her eyes upward in a fashion to suggest all kinds of illicit pleasures to an
imaginative young mind. This was Stella's unofficial education. Officially
she had a governess to teach her French, another to teach her piano, and
was taken to every gallery and museum in Paris. At the end of the year,
when she was sixteen, she was sent back to her mother and Uncle Harry in
Dulwich.

The news from Texas that year was not cheering. Instead of sending
money to England, John Tanner was now reduced to begging it from his
family. Evidently not in communication with his wife, he wrote urgently to
Lulo. Why had not Harry sent him the £6 he owed him? He had got

someone to buy one hundred boxes of the curry powder for $6, but the £45 sent by Nina's husband, Ernest, was already gone. He and Edwin had got work during the cotton-pressing season, but the Cuminses were wiped out when a frost killed their entire cotton crop. His position was most harassing, and Lulo must get her mother to send him £7 or £10 out of the £20 left in the bank. The anxiety over money was killing him. He must have that £7.

At home the situation was not much more prosperous. Uncle Harry, with a clerk's job in the City, and Ernest Hill seemed to be the main sources of income, although, as Stella reported to Lulo in November, Ernest had not sent the £2 he promised Max, and Mamma, who had not gotten up for a week because her chilblains were much worse, was terribly worried. She herself had moved into the little bedroom, where it was much cosier and warmer, and had finished the socks for Nina's baby and sent them, and Nina was pleased. They'd heard that all the money they'd sent to Texas had gone for "backy" and sweets—was it not sickening! Harry's cough was just the same, his temper improved slightly. Yet she was able to close this rather dreary letter with the news that she herself was really quite well.

One frequenter of Dulwich drawing rooms during those years when Beatrice Stella Tanner was undergoing metamorphosis from a tall, thin girl with long black plaits to a young woman of haunting beauty remembered her as graceful and intensely restless, one moment reclining on a sofa smoking an Egyptian cigarette ("Quite a thing for a young girl to be doing in those days!"), the next moment jumping up to throw the half-smoked cigarette in the fire and cross the room to the piano to play Schumann or Schubert with great charm and finish, then suddenly abandoning the piano to return to the sofa, where she would lie back gracefully, talking and laughing—never seeming to know quite what to do with herself. The restlessness was constitutional, yet had also an immediate cause: she had glimpsed a life of charm, comfort, and excitement in Paris; she had no means to pursue it. She had great energies, possibly great talents; they had no outlets. She could not count on Papa or Harry to help her realize her dreams; by some means she must find a way to realize them herself.

# TWO

## *1881–1884*

*H*ER FIRST THOUGHT was of music. On her return from Paris her
father's cousin, Eliza Hogarth, heard her play and offered to pay for
training as well as contribute a quarterly allowance. It was arranged that
Stella go twice a week from Dulwich to the Guildhall School of Music in the
City, where she was assigned to piano master Thomas Ridley Prentice. With
nothing but occasional strumming on the instruments of her sister and
friends and the casual lessons in Paris, Stella found that she had a great
many bad habits to unlearn. Prentice discovered, on the other hand, that
his pupil had a sureness of touch, a muscular dexterity, and a feeling for
music that were above the ordinary. He began to take great interest in
Beatrice Stella Tanner; he believed that with application she could become
a real musician.

Stella took her gift less seriously than did her music teacher. She had
suddenly developed a passion for reading as strong as that for music, and
after persuading her mother to convert a small box room into a study, she
spent hours there poring over her uncle's books, writing out passages that
caught her imagination, making notes on what she did not understand. Her
taste was eclectic: J. W. Cross's *Life of George Eliot*, George Henry Lewes's
*Life of Goethe*, Thackeray's *English Humorists of the Eighteenth Century*,
Madame de Staël's *Corinne*, the works of Whitman, Longfellow, Milton,
Keats, Tennyson, Daudet, and Balzac. In the evenings she would take the dis-
coveries of the day to Harry, and they would talk over what she had read. He
had the ability to make difficult things easy, as well as to turn serious conversation into nonsensical fun. There were long, pleasant evenings: her mother
strumming the guitar, Stella and Harry bent over the chessboard, or perhaps
Harry reading aloud while Stella half-listened, half-dreamed, the dog or the
cat on her lap.

There were also more lively times: parties at the Giffords' and long talks with Maud Gifford, her first close friend. Maud was beautiful, Stella thought enviously, with an elegant figure and stylish clothes and heaps of admirers who took her to balls. There were expeditions with the Urquharts, cousins of the Giffords, and their daughter Owney, "a lovely gentle girl with a fascinating lisp." There were musical evenings with the charming Bowring Spence and his lovely Italian mother and sisters, and with neighbor Dr. Curling ("Curley") Bates, who was also a talented actor. Or perhaps Willie Strickland would get them tickets to the sports, and she and Max would go to cheer on the Red Stockings as they took sixteen prizes. Or there were concerts at the Crystal Palace and sometimes a matinee: she had enjoyed Sophie Eyre in *Plot and Passion.* And there were long country walks with Maud and George Gifford, Owney and Max, and Max's friend James Nasmyth. Watching his restless, flirtatious niece these months, Uncle Harry was moved to compose a poem of sorts to Beatrice: "Her Motto: Viva la Bagatelle":

> A nobler yearning never broke her rest
> Than but to dance and sing, be gaily drest,
> And win all eyes with all accomplishment;
> For ah, the slight coquette, she cannot love.
> And if you kissed her feet a thousand years
> She still would take the praise and care no more.

There were also card parties (Stella was sharp at cards) at the Giffords' in the evenings. It was at one of these gatherings, when she was seventeen, that she met a quiet, black-haired young man named Patrick Campbell. He was tall, slender though muscular, extremely reserved, very well-mannered, and had a vulnerable, almost childish gentleness about him. Seeing that she could fascinate and rule him, Stella was immediately attracted.

Pat Campbell had come up to London at the end of Michaelmas term 1880 from Wellington College, a public school in Berkshire established primarily for the sons of deceased officers. He was not one of these, but the son of Patrick Campbell of Stranraer, Scotland, currently a manager of the Oriental Bank Corporation in the City, and living not far from the Tanners in a house called Ellerslie on Sydenham Hill. He had arranged that his son be given a position as clerk with the Oriental Bank, though perhaps with little expectation, for Pat Campbell at Wellington had shown himself little disposed to studies, staying in the low forms from his entrance in 1876 at the age of twelve to his leaving. Nor was he a school leader, remaining simply one of the thirty boys in Blücher Dormitory throughout his career. He was, however, a solid if not outstanding athlete, playing three-quarter in the Blücher rugby fifteen, and bowling for the First Eleven cricket team. An 1880 school photograph of the First Eleven shows him standing next to D. J. Medley, also a keen cricketer but, unlike Campbell, a scholar who became Head of Blücher, then Head of the whole school. Pat Campbell looks very much the schoolboy: his cap at the back of his head, plenty of dark hair, good-looking in a rather uncouth way. But there was a gentle, tender side to his nature as well. He loved the out-of-doors, and at Belmont, the family home in Scotland, learned from an old gamekeeper the names of birds and flowers and their ways. He was ten months older than Stella, eighteen when she met him, still devoted to the memory of his dead mother, shy, rather backward with young ladies. The dark-eyed girl who flirted with him almost defiantly captured him. He fell deeply in love.

About Pat Campbell, Stella had mixed emotions. She had little thought of settling down. She wanted a great deal from life—luxury, adventure, society—that there seemed little chance of his providing. Above all, she wanted some outlet for the restless, only half-sensed need in her for self-expression, whether in music or some other form of art. Besides, she liked the attention of other men; she had gotten a reputation in the neighborhood of being rather fast, deserved or not. In fact, she wrote to Lulo, there had been a painful quarrel: Mrs. Gifford and Mrs. Nasmyth had each expressed the wish that Miss Beatrice Tanner not enter her home again. Mrs. Gifford, Stella explained, was jealous of her friendship with Maud and objected to her daughter forsaking domestic duties to run off and talk and walk with Stella. She had also been hearing with disapproval that Miss Tanner had considerable influence over her son George. But the immediate cause of banishment was the coupling of poor Stella's name with that of Mrs. Robinson ("an awfully fast woman, in fact, scarcely respectable," Stella reported to Lulo), who had remarked to a mutual friend, "There is only one man I could never make flirt with me, and that is Pat Campbell!" "*You* couldn't make Pat flirt," replied the friend, "but Stella has managed to." Mrs. Robinson lost no time in spreading the story of Stella's conquest to interested ears, "so I have no doubt," continued Stella, "that it is greatly owing to that woman's ridiculous jealousy that all this disagreeableness has come about. I oughtn't to bother you with such petty stuff."

"You ask me whether I love anyone," she concluded frankly. "I love Pat's love. Had he money I would marry him this moment. I respect him. I don't think the world holds a more honorable goodhearted man—but he has no artistic nature, very little love for music & less for the drama. When I am with him, what is simple & honest in my nature comes forth. He is afraid of me. We might be happy together if there were heaps of money, but as things are, it would be awful."

Whether there was any connection between Pat Campbell's lack of interest in music and Stella's decision to leave the Guildhall is uncertain; it is
more likely that she found herself too occupied by lovemaking to care
much about her studies. This, even though at the encouragement of Mr.
Prentice she had competed against 365 other girls and won a three-year
scholarship to study music in Leipzig. But Pat would not have liked hearing
that Stella might leave England for three years, and Stella at this point
lacked the commitment to devote the next years of her life to hard study.
As a result, Mrs. Tanner received in late September 1882 the following
letter of protest:

My dear Madam,
    I much regret to find from your daughter, Miss Beatrice Tanner, that
she will leave the Guildhall School of Music at the half term. Personally, I
shall be very sorry to lose her as a pupil, as she is much interested in her
work, has great talent, and makes rapid progress.
    But I feel that, quite apart from my personal feeling, it is my duty to let
you know what a very serious thing it seems to me that Miss Tanner should
not complete her musical education. . . .
    I have no hesitation in saying that she has a very great talent indeed, and
that if she works in a proper spirit, and is properly directed, she is sure of
attaining a very high position. It seems to me, therefore, that it would be a
*wrong* thing if such talent were not to be properly developed. . . .
    You will see that I look on the matter as a musician. . . . I trust that you
will pardon my writing strongly. It is not too often that one meets with real
talent, so that it is all the more sad when there seems to be a prospect of its
being wasted.
    Perhaps I may be allowed to add that the very great pains which I have
taken with Miss Tanner give me a right to speak.
    Believe me, Dear Madam,
                                        Yours sincerely,
                                            Ridley Prentice

Ridley Prentice was a musician of some reputation, and Mrs. Tanner felt
great disappointment. But her daughter was impatient and headstrong and,
as her mother had already learned, would do exactly as she pleased.
    To comfort herself for having left the Guildhall, Stella hired a piano at
10s./6d. a month, of which she paid half and Max half, and began giving
music lessons to earn a little money. In early 1884 she was making £2 10s. a
month. By the early spring of 1884 Pat Campbell was coming to see her
almost every day. To Lulo she confided her indecision and her growing

involvement with the young man she called "my boy." She wondered whether her sister would like him, for "he isn't a bit good looking. *Very quiet* & awfully cold to everybody—most unforgiving & most easily offended. Never argues or joins in a conversation for the sake of talking. Has a kind sympathetic way of listening if any one talks about themselves. He has straight black lanky hair—none on his face. A weak mouth *very*. A nose peculiar to himself (it was broken once I believe)—beautiful hands, not delicate but a good shape. Everyone here is rather frightened of him . . . no one ever attempts to chaff him about me. It is most strange the respect he inspires. He is dreadfully generous & rather extravagant . . . isn't a bit artistic, or well read & doesn't take the slightest interest in human nature."

Lulo followed the fluctuations of her sister's attachment faithfully, sometimes becoming positively ill with worry over Beatrice's troubles. Stella apologized in a letter of April 4, 1884, for inflicting her woes. She had told her, she confided, all that could be *written*. As for Pat Campbell: "Poor boy," she continued, "he is indeed to be pitied. Sometimes I love him madly—no sacrifice seems too great to be made for him. At other moments I feel almost indifference towards him. He is going away soon, I hope not before you have seen him. I have almost made up my mind to go with him & begin a new, better life. If I only had courage to give up my old aims. All my love for music is quite dead—"

That day Stella still might have weighed carefully whether she felt love or indifference for Pat Campbell, and perhaps have decided to reject him. Weeks later the decision had been made for her. Again she half-confided in Lulo: "Is it madness to marry Pat on £200 a year? Isn't it better than living this sort of life? I am feeling so wretched & ill & my boy wants me to marry him at once without saying a word to anyone. We were nearly married on the 17 of April. I telegraphed him on the 15th *not* to get the license, because somehow I couldn't take such a step without telling you, old girl. I don't know why I have told you now. Want you to have some idea of all I have gone through—then you will understand better why I feel so languid & ill."

In 1884 there was only one course for a young woman who was pregnant, ignorant of alternatives, and solicitous for her reputation. Besides, as she had told Lulo, sometimes she loved Patrick Campbell madly. By mid-June she was sure of her condition, and the lovers began to plot in earnest. The wedding must be secret, an elopement. She must get away from home under some plausible excuse: she could say she had got a position in Bournemouth as a daily governess and music teacher. In fact, she would really go to Bournemouth; Owney Urquhart and her mother lived there and Owney knew the city. Pat could try to get a promotion in London, Stella could seriously look for music pupils, and as soon as he could, he would send for her. They decided they would be married the first day of summer.

The decision made, Stella had only to wait out the days until the twenty-first of June, on the surface living the life of an obedient daughter, in secret preparing to become Patrick Campbell's wife. There were disappointments. In early May old Campbell's Oriental Bank announced failure, cancelling any notions of a rich and open-handed father-in-law. As a result, Pat did not get the appointment he expected for £150 a year and was forced to accept another for £100. There was uneasiness. She did not know what to do about Nina, who must not know until well after the fact; she thought Lulo might prepare her for the unpleasant surprise by inquiring in a letter whether it was true that Beatrice was engaged. She did not know what to do about Aunt Kate, who was sure to die of shock if Stella married without telling her. She wished she knew Pat's family a little: he had two older brothers, one in the Army and one in Ceylon, sisters who sounded pleasant, a stepmother and three little stepbrothers and -sisters to whom he was devoted. Everything seemed suspended, quite unreal. On June 16 she opened a package from Owney to find a splendid red satin parasol lined with red silk and Spanish lace and half a dozen white silk handkerchiefs, broad-hemstitched. "They are my wedding presents!" she exclaimed to Lulo in disbelief. "What a farce it all seems—"

The night before the flight from Dulwich, Stella gave music lessons until nine. It had been arranged that at six o'clock the next day Owney would send Mrs. Tanner a telegram from Bournemouth saying that Beatrice had arrived safely. Stella had already written her mother a letter to be posted Tuesday, the twenty-fourth, again by Owney from Bournemouth, saying that she felt much better and that everyone was being very kind to her. It now remained to write a last hasty note to Lulo:

Everything is arranged for to-morrow. Pat had the license & ring in his pocket yesterday. He has seen the clergyman about it. To-morrow at 11 a.m. —not a friend or relation in the church.

. . . The lies I have been obliged to tell Mother would make your hair stand on end. . . . How strange, they try to get rid of me, but never dream that I have in heart left them forever.

I am very weak & mother seems a little anxious at my taking the journey alone. I have grown so frightfully pale & thin [in] my face. However I eat & sleep so it's all right. Think of me darling, but don't worry. Pat is *so* good that I can't help loving him. He is not what I wanted. I feel like one who has prayed for a precious stone, & the angels bring a flower & I can't help loving its beauty, but oh, my darling, it is not a bit what I wished for.

The next morning Stella kissed her mother and Uncle Harry goodbye, promised to get plenty of rest at Bournemouth, and went off to meet Pat Campbell for the eleven-o'clock ceremony. He had chosen St. Helen's, Bishopsgate, in the City. And so they entered the narrow passageway of Great St. Helen's that expands into a plot of tree-lined green, walked toward the gray stone church sunken at the end and through the doorway and down the entrance steps into the large, cool, low-pitched nave dimly lit through Victorian stained glass, and said their vows flanked by the tombs of great and prosperous Lord Mayors, aldermen, and merchants of the City, the sort of men that Pat Campbell, junior clerk, could never hope to be. John Edmund Cox, Vicar, pronounced the ceremony; it was witnessed by James Balfour, a friend of Pat, and Mary McDonald, the old woman of the church. Pat had turned twenty on April 17; he gave his age as twenty-four. Stella was nineteen; she called herself twenty-one.

Their destination after the ceremony was Staines-on-Thames. At Waterloo Station Stella found time to scribble a brief note to the faithful Lulo, who would have been thinking of her intensely that day:

Dear little woman—
Don't worry yourself. It is all over. I did not feel ill a bit, quite calm. . . . The dear old clergyman kissed & all were so kind. I should have liked you to have been there, old girl, but perhaps it was just as well you were not for you would have made me cry. . . .
Pat says you are not to think him a brute. It is quite the best thing we could do under the circumstances. My ring looks so pretty.
Goodbye darling. I shall always love you best in the world.

During the next few days, spent at the Pack Horse Hotel on the river in the pleasant rural country above London, Stella tended to forget that she loved Lulo best. They had such a charming room with a balcony all around, and the hotel was "quite on the river." It was exciting to wear a wedding ring, and exciting to be called Mrs. Campbell. People stared at them—the slender, dark, attentive young husband and the tall, thin, pale bride with enormous black eyes and red satin parasol—and Pat looked so funny when they did. The stretch of Thames at Staines proved splendid for punting; they were on the river all day. Pat handled the boat like a magician—it seemed to glide without effort or sound, straight and swift, while he gazed into her eyes, speaking little, adoring her. They picked wildflowers; a bird flew into her hand. "Even the wild birds love you," said Pat. They indulged in little extras: biscuits, lemons, whiskey—it was, after all, their honeymoon. And there was time for the inevitable letter to Lulo,

a letter Pat begged to read to see if Lulo would think his Stella happy.
And Lulo might have, with reservations. "It is so grand here," wrote Stella.
". . . Pat is so good to me. I shall be happy with him I feel sure. It is difficult
to write darling, my heart is so full. . . . Ah my darling I *am* happy, but can
one be in a delirium all one's life? My boy says he longs to know you.
Goodbye my sweetest sis. All my love to you. . . . When I see you I will tell
you all about everything."

On Wednesday, June 25, after breakfast, they left Staines-on-Thames,
Pat for his new office job in the City, Stella to stay with Owney at Bournemouth until the news that she was married could be broken and she could
return. They would be happy together, she felt sure. Yet she had no faith at
all in Pat's ability to succeed, earn money, and rise in the world. "It makes
a lump come in my throat when I think all my dreams about society will
*never* be realized," she had written Lulo after her decision to marry. "A
poor man's wife is seldom fit for anything but a superior sort of servant. . . .
My life is sure to be a short one. I wish it to be. Why am I cursed with
poverty—I who hate it so?" She had even graver doubts about her own
feelings, despite the happy honeymoon. "When Pat first cared for me, I was
only flirting," she had concluded that same letter. "I dared not continue, so
I abandoned myself to his love, knowing that it would probably be my
curse."

# THREE

## 1884–1886

*I*N LATE SUMMER Stella returned to London, and the couple took rooms at 17 Milton Road, Herne Hill, just up the Croxted Road from Uncle Harry's house in Acacia Grove. She had predicted that a penniless marriage would be hell for one who had cherished ambitions of social status; she had predicted well. Although they loved each other, lack of money dominated their lives. Pat often worked until nine at the insurance office, then brought work home with him. His father grudgingly sent him an allowance, but relations between them were strained. Campbell had spotted the announcement of his son's marriage in the paper, thought him "an arrant fool" for having placed it, and warned him to expect no help beyond the monthly allowance. Their debts mounted steadily; there was never enough, it seemed, for even the bare necessities. The young husband lived in terror of being disgraced at the office by a summons from one of his creditors. Stella dealt with daily catastrophes her own way. "I don't think I worry," she wrote her sister the first day of September, "but I cannot live in the present. It is such weary work, Lulo, when ones heart is always dipping about in the past or building some impossible heights in the future."

She was forced to deal with the present by Lulo's visit two days later. Stella still had told no one about the baby, although she was now five months pregnant. On the morning of Lulo's arrival, wanting to tell her but realizing that Lulo might promptly inform Nina, she forestalled the revelation by telling Nina herself that the doctor thought she was in an interesting condition. At the same time she swore Nina to secrecy so that she herself would be able to break the dramatic news to Lulo. Lulo came and, as usual, although Stella meant to ask her about her painting and her unhappiness with the Gibsons, they spent the whole time talking about Stella. The great revelation was made, and Lulo properly distressed and impressed, although Stella was still cautious enough to add that she was sure the doctor was mistaken. To Lulo she poured out her troubles: no money for baby things if indeed a baby was on the way; Pat in delicate health, drudging away with little hope of promotion; old Campbell terribly cold. She had also been very hurt at Eliza Hogarth's neglect: no wedding present or acknowledgment of her new situation from her former benefactor. Lulo listened and sympathized and went away quite staggering under the burden of her sister's woes, while Stella herself felt agreeably lighter-hearted for the meeting.

The next day her mother paid a call with, surprisingly, Eliza Hogarth. Louisa Tanner had not forgiven her daughter, and Stella could not forget her mother's heartbroken cry when she had finally told her of her marriage. Today her mother hardly spoke to her, although she gushed over Pat, who flushed with embarrassment when she kissed him on both cheeks in front of Eliza. It was not a comfortable visit. Eliza was very kind to Stella, but stiff with Pat, and Pat was obviously terrified of the old woman. Before leaving, Eliza had time to take Stella aside and tell her that in marrying she had done quite the best thing she could do. So she approved, yet she did not slip a little gift into Stella's hand along with the blessing. As a result, Pat sat down to write his father begging for a promissory note for £100 within the next six months. Stella had no one to ask: Harry and Ernest Hill were sending money to Texas.

Autumn dragged on, money worries dragged on, fear of her confinement began to prey on Stella's mind. Lulo paid another visit on October 1 and found her sister definitely pregnant this time. "For God's sake don't worry about me," Stella wrote her at Nina's the next day. "If the little one is here before you come back, all the better—it will be pretty & not all red & nasty. If I am very ill you shall be telegraphed for & I'll let you know all our troubles. . . . How I wish I was coming with you. Read in the train & don't think." But it was difficult for Lulo not to fret herself sick over Stella's unhappy situation. She comforted herself with the thought of the flannels she would hem for the baby and the shawl she'd crochet for poor Beatrice during long, lonely evenings at the Gibsons'.

At the end of October an unexpected financial crisis occurred when the Giffords' daughter Edith died suddenly of galloping consumption. Although Stella had not seen the Giffords since she had been forbidden their house, she felt Pat must attend the funeral at Nunhead Cemetery out of common civility—only he had nothing to wear. She had already popped (pawned) every mortal thing she owned, including her cloak, to get them through October. Coal cost sixpence a scuttle, and they used two scuttles a day. There wasn't a penny for the baby, not a penny for food and washing, barely a few shillings to pay Pat's fare to the office—and now Pat needed a

top hat and gloves for the funeral. Or so Stella reported to Lulo, recounting her worries over "such heaps of things."

In fact their situation was difficult enough, made more difficult by the
constitutional impracticality of both. Pat did get outfitted for the funeral,
and quite sympathized with his beautiful wife's need for a new tea gown or
a black lace-and-satin party dress, even though Mrs. Marston, the dressmaker, could not be paid. He appealed again to his father for £100 so they
might find rooms more suitable for a couple with a baby; Campbell sent
him £10, which, he informed him, he had deducted from his grandmother's
legacy. "The letter was cruel," Stella wrote Lulo, "telling him to ask for no
more help, calling him a fool etc. etc. He is as hard as bricks that old man."
Far kinder were the Harrises, a barrister and his wife who were charmed
with the handsome young Patrick Campbells. Stella sought them out for
distraction, going one day for lunch and staying until nine in the evening.
Harris actually asked Pat to call on him with a list of his debts with an eye
to helping him out of his most pressing obligations. Unfortunately, this
also meant bringing a list of Stella's. She cringed at the thought, but Mrs.
Marston must have her money, so she reluctantly tallied them up. But a
loan from Mr. Harris could not stem their compulsion to spend more
money than Pat made.

Kinder even than the Harrises was their landlady, Mrs. Holden. Much as
Stella wanted to move, she knew they could not expect to find another like
her. She promised them the large bedroom upstairs for Stella's confinement
for the same rent they paid currently. When they could not pay that, she
not only did not ask for the money but lent them small sums. How often
they might have gone without dinner had not Mrs. Holden handed over a
shilling or two, Stella shuddered to think. So although she felt she would go
mad in the next two months worrying about the baby's arrival in unsuitable
surroundings, they could not leave Mrs. Holden. Besides, Campbell had
refused the £100.

All this she confided to Lulo, as well as her deeper dissatisfactions with
her situation. "Do you know Pat's real age?" she demanded. "21 [sic] last
April and he will soon be a father. I feel as though I [have] done him an
irreparable wrong, & sometimes as though even yet I [have] not reached
the turning point of my existence. It is so hard to realize that I have nothing
to look forward to but the monotony of daily cares that are so trivial, so
soul-shrivelling. Perhaps the little excitement in the thought that some day
when my boy is a man he may weary of my pale face & incomprehensible
nature will keep me alive. . . ." The subterfuge also bothered her: "For
Gods sake remember in writing to Nina & Mother not to breathe a word
about my little one coming before March."

By the end of December Stella had persuaded Pat of the necessity of a move, this time to 8 Geneva Road, East Brixton, still in the general vicinity of Acacia Grove. The Firths seemed as obliging as Mrs. Holden, promising them the large upstairs bedroom for Stella's confinement; but weeks went by and still it was unfurnished: no blinds up, no carpet, no bed. Owney Urquhart came to be with Stella during these anxious days and, not incidentally, to be near Max, for the two were falling in love.

On January 13 Pat came home very tired at ten o'clock to find Max and Owney there, and Stella complaining of "a toothache in her back." Max finally left, and the couple went to bed in their tiny downstairs bedroom, but by one o'clock Stella's "toothache" had gotten so much worse that they sent Owney to wake Mrs. Firth. This took a long time, since, after promising through the door to come immediately, Mrs. Firth promptly fell asleep again. By the time she was roused, Stella was in stiff labor. Mrs. Firth got her into the dining room and onto the couch while Owney and Pat frantically heaved the bed up the stairs into the large bedroom, lit a fire, and hooked up some red curtains Mrs. Tanner had sent in a desperate attempt to make the room look comfortable and cheerful. Pat helped his moaning wife upstairs, got her into bed, and left her to Owney and the sleepy Mrs. Firth while he rushed out for the doctor, falling down the ice-slicked front steps in his hurry.

The doctor promised to step round, and told Pat to go for the nurse. Unfortunately, the nurse lived at the far end of Tooting, and there was not a cab in sight. As Pat stood hesitating outside the doctor's door wondering what was to be done, a cab drove up to the house opposite and a gentleman alighted. Pat ran to stop it and, after some argument, persuaded the cabby to drive him to Tooting. But the man had no idea where in Tooting the address was, and the streets at three in the morning were empty even of policemen. They drove up and down aimlessly until the frantic Pat finally saw a light in a cottage and had the driver stop. After hammering at the door for minutes, he heard a woman on the other side, although she would not open the door. Poor Pat had to work the piece of paper with the address through the keyhole, and then the voice behind the door said she did not know, except that she thought the house might be somewhere about two miles nearer Clapham. There would be a policeman on the bridge a half mile farther on: they could ask directions of him. They found the policeman on the bridge, but he did not recognize the address—they must inquire at the police station farther along. At the station the distraught husband was finally given directions, but when the cabby finally found the neighborhood, they also found six identical terraces, none with a street sign. There was nothing to do but knock at every number six until the nurse was produced. Pat hammered at the first until a window was thrown up, a head appeared, and a woman directed him farther down the road. Another dive into an unmarked terrace roused a drunken man who could tell them nothing. Finally the number six in the fourth terrace yielded a pleasant-faced middle-aged woman who was the nurse and who agreed to come immediately.

At quarter to five they were back in Geneva Road, where they found the doctor very relieved to see the nurse. Pat was left to wrestle with the cabby, who wanted fifteen shillings for the three-hour adventure. Pat managed to talk him down to thirteen, a triumph diminished when, ransacking the house, he could only come up with five. Persuading the grumbling driver to call back in the morning for the rest, Pat rushed upstairs to find Stella assuring the doctor he need not be afraid to give her lots of chloroform since she'd had it last year for having a tooth pulled—a lie, as he knew. Against his principles, the doctor gave the struggling mother as much as he dared; still it was more than four hours longer before Stella was finally delivered of a boy. Dazed and elated, Pat telegraphed Mrs. Tanner, who arrived at two the next afternoon and promptly set about making the room more cheerful by ordering a carpet and hanging up blinds. Then he remembered Lulo: "Just a line to say that Stella was prematurely confined this morning at ten o'clock of a little boy. She was very ill but am happy to say is now better. The dear little mite is the smallest thing you have ever seen but the doctor gives us great hopes." So the pretense was to be maintained, even in the family.

Pat kept Lulo posted each day. There was no use her coming up. Stella was weak and in pain, but wonderfully bright and so mad over the wee thing. Baby, at the moment of writing, was contentedly sucking its thumb and quiet as a mouse. Poor little Stella had got through much better than he'd expected, though nurse had forbidden her to write letters for a week. Owney had sent over two lovely bibs and a white shetland shawl, scent, and ribbons for the new mother. Owney had wanted to stay until the ordeal was over, but had looked so sick and white that Pat had sent her home with the cat to keep for the duration; and now Stella was wickedly saying that the baby did not make up for the loss of puss. On Saturday Nina had come and thought the little kiddy so lovely that she nearly ate it up and wanted to take it home with her.

So Pat faithfully reported, writing another letter on Sunday, lying next to Stella on the bed, with the baby they had named Alan Urquhart (but would always call Beo for "beloved one") lying asleep on her arm, until Stella seized the pen to scrawl, "Nurse isn't looking so I must tell you baby is lovely, & I am *so glad* it's a boy for a big reason that I will tell you when I am well enough to write you a long letter. Thank you darling for all your love & anxiety I shall soon be well," and then relinquished the letter-writing task to Pat again.

Stella mended slowly that late winter when she turned twenty, bleeding for a month after the birth, nursing the baby with difficulty. Nights when Pat worked late and the baby slept in its bassinette, she would sit brooding in front of the fire over the course her life had taken. She, Pat, the baby, and the nurse were now living on £60 instead of £100 a year: Pat had been demoted again. Clearly she must do something to earn money. She could go back to giving piano lessons, although she would have to give them from morning to night to earn anything at all. Or—it was a thought that recurred more and more often—she might go on the stage. She had already been asked to give several little readings here and there; they had been well received. Dr. Curley Bates acted in amateur theatricals and was encouraging her to join them. Although Aunt Kate had taken her to the theatre only once in Paris to see Pailleron's *Le Monde où l'on s'ennuie*, it had been, she remembered, as though some unexpected door had opened; for months afterward she had gazed through that door and beyond. Before her marriage she had gone to the theatre as often as she'd been able to find ticket money. She felt she perhaps had some gift, some "secret" to tell the world. But she could imagine the future of an actress all too clearly: sleeping all day, at the theatre all night; obliged to act low parts in low companies for the sake of the money; Pat sad with sitting alone evening after evening; little Beo shrinking from her painted face—a future hardly less grim than the present.

Discouraged, she took up her pen to write to Lulo, whom she had neglected since the baby's birth. "My darling . . . I believe you have lost the thread of my life—& I meant you should. You cannot help me, so why sicken you with the reality. The ideal has vanished for me, but you can retain it a little longer. And your letters gladden far more than they would if sympathizing with what I try never to let my mind dwell unnecessarily upon—ghastly worries, that stand like so many grinning skeletons before me, blocking the path I would tread so gaily—I wave them back trying to hurry on. . . .

"I have to take from Mother now every week. That means *still living on Uncle's charity*. That is the most grim skeleton & one that needs all the strength of mind & body to keep from suffocating me. And my boy cannot understand these things—his life is love & love his life—his words 'Why worry darling—we have each other & that pet baby & things will get better soon.' . . .

"You seem to have many nice friends & time to read & to paint there. I envy you more than I can say—when days & weeks pass in washing & nursing a baby, putting two rooms straight & acting to those around me as though the happiness of my life were complete. I have love it is true, but love without comfort is a sorry sight—like some beautiful cripple."

Stella was suffering a not uncommon malady. She believed that if only there were enough money, she would be content, for at times, when her mother and Pat were both there, she was cheerful, even quite lively. She believed that if only Pat would take hold, she could stop worrying and leave the future to him. In fact her discontent lay with herself. She had great energies and gifts and no clear idea how they could be used, or even what they might be. Of course, it would have been unusual in the last decades of the nineteenth century for a young suburban mother to understand the nature of her discontent, and Stella did not.

She did realize that she was not domestic. Lulo often complained of dissatisfaction with her own life. Six years older than Stella, she found herself longing for a home and strong ties; she was ready to give the Gibsons notice and come back to Acacia Grove for want of a home of her own. She got no sympathy from Stella, who advised her in strong terms that if she gave notice, she would certainly regret it. There was nothing at home except Mamma sacrificing and sacrificing to keep Harry and Max happy, and Harry and Max getting more and more selfish every day. She thanked God she was out of it. Of course, they would all be delighted if Lulo came home—for the first few months. Then would come hints that she might go to Nina, or see about a teaching position and a room in Dulwich. And there were no teaching jobs in Dulwich, and the only home where Lulo was welcome—hers—was no home at all.

So Lulo did not give notice, but looked forward to her summer holidays. On June 21, their first anniversary, Pat sent a welcoming note to his sister-in-law: "How happy we both are at the thought of having you with us again, and won't you just love our baby, he is perfect & such a sweet disposition, I am sure he will be like my Stella. This blessed day makes us both so happy and our love has grown with the year. . . . Stella grows sweeter each day in face as well as in character, somehow I always think that only you & I in the world understand her." Puzzled at the contrast between Stella's misery and Pat's bliss, Lulo came, played aunt to Nina's Fred and Roy and Stella's Beo. Everybody they met exclaimed what a big, healthy fellow Beo was for a premature baby of seven months. "I don't think anyone believes!" sighed Stella.

Although she nursed Beo longer than she wished, to avoid another pregnancy, early in 1886 Stella found herself pregnant again. The couple moved again that year, this time to 6 Uxbridge Villas, Norwood; and there on Monday, September 27, Stella gave birth to a daughter. Avoiding the Italian complexities of Maria Luigia Giovanna and Beatrice Rose Stella, they named the baby simply Stella. "A little queen, with such beautiful hands," rejoiced Mrs. Tanner.

Stella's labor was easier, but a few weeks after it was born the baby fell sick. All one Sunday evening it was dreadfully ill, and Stella and the nurse sat up with it until, at two in the morning, the nurse took fright and sent Pat rushing for their old Dulwich neighbor Curley Bates. He came promptly, decided that Stella's milk was wrong, and stayed with the mother and child until Monday noon. Watching him solemnly feed her baby, looking at its little tongue and testing the warmth of bottles on his wrist, Stella felt overwhelmed at the kindness of this dear friend and sure that if the baby lived, he had saved it. Dr. Robertson, the delivering physician, came over too, and assured the parents that they had nothing to fear. Yet on Monday evening the baby was restless and seemed in pain. Hanging over the bassinette, Stella agonized—the baby seemed smaller than when it was born, its blue eyes were enormous, the hands thin and blue-veined, the small face so pinched it looked like a tiny old woman's. She must have it christened at once. She herself felt terribly weak and helpless; the worry had set her back. And there was the usual crisis: Pat had tried to borrow money everywhere and had failed.

Reading the familiar bulletin of disaster, Lulo might nevertheless have caught a new tone. Stella not only had been hanging over her sick child, she had also been thoroughly enjoying Eric Makay's book on Beethoven, marking all her favorite passages and coaxing Curley Bates, after the baby had fallen asleep, to come sit on the bed and listen to her read the choicest bits aloud. Although she had hardly touched the piano since her marriage, that very Monday afternoon she had managed a practice, and found it very sweet to get to the piano again. And when she had told Dr. Robertson that she still had milk and was willing to nurse, she had not been displeased to hear that under the circumstances she must not dream of it.

In fact, a change had come over Stella, one which in retrospect she recognized as significant. One hot night in late August, a few weeks before she expected her second child, as moonlight streamed through the open window, she had lain awake next to her sleeping husband trying to see into the future. Pat's "Why worry, darling? Things will get better soon" was not enough. Too restless to sleep, she finally slipped out of bed, taking care not to wake Pat or her sleeping son, threw on a dressing gown, and stole down the stairs and out the back door leading into the narrow garden. There she paced, looking up at the window of the room where her husband slept calmly, wondering what was to be done to support a family of four.

She could not count on Pat. She must help. Yet she still did not know with any certainty what she could do.

"With the daylight," she remembered, "something entered my soul, and has never since left me—it seemed to cover me like a fine veil of steel, giving me a strange sense of security. Slowly I became conscious that within *myself* lay the strength I needed, and that I must never be afraid."

Whether self-reliance was born that night or whether her "secret" had revealed itself at last, she could not say. She did know that in the gray light of morning she went quietly back up the stairs and lay down beside the husband who was only a boy, with a new determination.

## *1886–1889*

*Y*ET STELLA HUNG BACK when in November Curley Bates suddenly
asked her to take the leading part in a production of Mark Quinton's
*In His Power.* The Anomalies Dramatic Club of Norwood boasted 365 members, each contributing £3 3*s.* a year to stage three performances of two plays.
When the woman intended to play Marie Graham fell ill, Bates knew immediately who could fill her place, even though Stella Campbell had done
little performing beyond recitations of "A Social Conversation" and "The
Lifeboat" back in the days when she and Pat were courting. But Stella was
terrified of the idea: she had only recently recovered from little Stella's
birth; she was not at all certain that her secret was ready to be told. Friends
encouraged her, however, telling her that getting out of the house would
cheer her up, and finally Pat himself convinced her to make the attempt.

Two critics were present the evening of her debut on November 18 as
Marie Graham, a devoted wife who has to foil the machinations of an
Italian spy. The critic from the *Era* became thoroughly out of temper when
he found that no seat had been reserved for him at the Lower Norwood
Institute; he found the club members acting as stewards in claw-hammered
coats and white chokers supremely ridiculous; he found the Anomalies as
an acting group singularly unimpressive. Only one thing about the evening
pleased him: "Mrs. Campbell's acting as the wife had more than ordinary
intelligence, and her elocution showed cultivation. She possesses dramatic
instinct, and should do good service for the club." The *Stage* liked her even
better: "The Anomalies are fortunate in counting Mrs. Campbell as one of
their members. It was this lady's first appearance on any stage on Thursday,
and her performance was therefore the more extraordinary. Mrs. Campbell
possesses a natural depth of pathos and yet a power and earnestness, which,
joined to a graceful, easy manner and charming presence, render her a
most valuable acquisition."

Stella appeared three times as Marie Graham, clipped the notice from the *Stage*, and returned to Pat, her babies, and their debts. But the success of her performance at last decided her. If she had succeeded as an amateur, she could perhaps succeed as a professional. She must earn money. She knew what people thought of actresses; she knew how shocked her mother and the Victorian Nina would be. She got a part as a little French *modiste*, a lady by birth, a graceful, pathetic creature—not the main part but the most human, she thought—in a production of *Duty*, adapted from Victorien Sardou's *Les Bourgeois de Pontarcy*. The day of opening she wrote Lulo:

> I am just writing you one line my darling before going off to rehearsal. I feel the die is cast. I do hope I shall get on. I have always felt the stage would be the end & now I am almost certain.
>
> My darling do let your letters show me that you have faith in my talent & let them help me on. Uncle Reader told Pat plainly on Saturday that he could do *nothing* for him, & just you think of our debts. I must work & work *at once*—not look back & not look forward—just work work work. If I only felt stronger. I am so afraid I shall faint tonight.
>
> Love you darling. I do hope you are thinking of me.

After the *modiste* she played Marie de Fontanges in *Plot and Passion* and had "a flattering local success" as Alma Blake in *The Silver Shield*; then there were no more opportunities. "The hopelessness of things is frightful," she wrote in the new year, 1887; "I feel so reckless Lulo. Wish I could hang myself." Her world seemed to be falling apart. She'd had her photograph taken, but had gotten so thin and wan it was unrecognizable, she thought. She discovered a hole in one of her front teeth; the sight made her positively ill. Max had refused to pay his part of the piano rental this month; she would have to send the instrument back. Pat looked terribly worn and anxious, and was getting absolutely nowhere in the City. It became apparent that some drastic step must be taken: they decided that since he could make no money in England, he must go abroad. Their first thought was America, but continually desperate letters from John Tanner and Edwin lessened its attraction. As for his going, she did not know how she could live without his love. "Lulo, my life is proving literally intolerable to me," she wailed. "I have a strange fear that some sort of crisis is near. . . ."

Eventually Pat decided against America and for Brisbane in Australia, where a relative, William Ross, might find him a position. If England could not provide a living wage, perhaps her colonies could. They told themselves that when Pat should make some money, Stella and the children would come out and join him. They told themselves that parting was inevitable and the best way. They told themselves that there was a fortune to be made out there with just a little luck and enterprise. They told themselves that the joy of reunion would make separation bearable.

On October 5 Stella asked Lulo to accompany her to Victoria Station, where Pat would catch the boat train. He would meet them there. But they were late and they missed him. When she realized that Pat was lost among the crowds hurrying for trains, Stella fainted. She regained consciousness to find a woman in nurse's uniform lifting her head and giving her water, and Pat gone. At home there was a telegram: "GOOD-BYE, DARLING, DID MY BEST TO SEE YOU. DARE NOT MISS ANOTHER TRAIN. PERHAPS IT WAS BETTER."

The painful parting convinced Stella that she was at last on her own. As long as Pat had struggled on in the insurance office, she had hoped for promotion or a new job. Now she was free to pursue her own way. She wrote Pat often that autumn, asking him whether he minded that she intended to act again. Pat's reply was characteristically indulgent: "Act as much as you like. I know you love me; that is enough. . . ."

She returned to the Anomalies, acting in *Blow for Blow, The Money Spinner*, and *The Palace of Truth*. It was experience, but not money, and she was forced to ask Pat to beg his father to stand surety for the rent; surprisingly, old Campbell agreed. In December Pat wrote from Brisbane: he had got a berth in the B.I. Company office at £2 a week—not very much, but a start and he was sure the pay would increase soon. In January 1888 he sent a check for £29 15*s.*, all he had been able to scrape together. There were grand reports every day about gold. A fellow he knew was going prospecting in North Queensland—he'd promised to let Pat know at once if he found anything good. The next report in February, however, was hardly grand. He'd been laid up with fever for the last ten days and was still terribly weak. He had little news. By May he had given up Brisbane and gone on to Sydney, hoping to catch a boat for Kimberley, South Africa. Her "sweet letter" had reached him there. He was constantly haunted by the fear that she would learn to hate him; her goodness and patience couldn't last. By June he had gotten as far as Mauritius in the Indian Ocean. There he was stuck until the end of July without a penny until the *Dunbar Castle* put out for Africa on the twenty-eighth. "I feel utterly miserable," he wrote that day. ". . . My money has given out, and I am obliged to draw on my father for my passage from here. I can't help it. I am afraid he will be wild, but it is the only thing I could do. . . . Stella, darling, don't get disgusted with me. God knows I have done my best. . . . I do hope Kimberley will be the end of our troubles. I cannot write more. It is awful to be the means of so much misery to you, for I worship you, my darling. God bless you and the children."

That early autumn Stella fell wretchedly ill with the quinsy. One side of her throat closed completely, and for a week she could swallow nothing but liquids. But she was too restless to lie in bed, so she continued to give music lessons and receive visitors. One of these, a Mr. Mainwaring, came three times that week and sent letters. No, she did not *love* him, she reported to a worried Lulo—rest assured, she never would. But he had theatrical connections, and as soon as she was well, he was going to take her to Edgar Bruce's theatre and introduce her to Bruce, who was single and a great admirer of the ladies.

It was not Mainwaring who provided an entry, however, but F. W. Macklin, an occasional actor with the Anomalies, and now at the Haymarket. On September 13 Stella opened a note recommending she see Mr. Harrington Baily, a theatrical agent, and mention Macklin's name. Stella immediately set about having a new dress made for the interview. On the twentieth it was ready and, fixing some daisies in her hat, she set off to find Mr. Baily's offices in Buckingham Street. The fact that everyone stared in admiration as she walked up the Strand could only be reassuring; yet as she was searching for the office number, she caught the sound of piteous mewing and looked down to see in the gutter a poor cat vainly licking her drowned kittens. She hurried on, found the number in the Adelphi, mounted a flight of stone steps, and was shown into the office. Baily rose to greet her, holding out his hand. She opened her mouth to speak and burst into a flood of tears. As she wiped her eyes and explained haltingly about the dead kittens, Baily ushered her into an inner room, ordered his housekeeper to bring her a cup of tea, and discreetly withdrew. A quarter-hour later he returned. He could, he was sure, promise her an engagement very soon at three guineas a week to start and possibly more. So Stella paid the guinea fee, signed herself "Miss Stella Campbell" in his book of hopefuls, and went away feeling that her career had begun at last.

A major concern was her babies—Beo going on four, little Stella two that month. She and Lulo had already discussed the possibility of living together in Pat's absence, and Lulo now offered to come and stay at Uxbridge Villas if Stella got an engagement. But Stella was not enthusiastic: "You better not decide till all is quite settled, & if you don't care about it, Owney is willing. I can't help thinking the responsibility & anxiety would be too much for you." Another concern was She, a little pug who brought Stella's shoes, stockings, and boxes of matches to her pillow mornings, trying to wake her for play—"the sweetest dog in the world," said Stella, a passionate lover of animals. Meanwhile she went over to the Young Women's Christian Association at Gipsy Hill to hire a "religious servant." A touring mother could not be too careful.

Harrington Baily was almost as good as his word. "Dear Madam," Stella read on October 1: "Would you entertain an offer to play Mrs. Lynne Loseby in 'Bachelors'? She is a young and handsome widow. Terms must be low. It is an engagement I should advise you to take, it will be a start." The next day she called at his office and accepted the part in Robert Buchanan's and Hermann Vezin's play, then ran home to tell her mother and sit up all night making frocks from material donated by friends. Rehearsals were to begin on Sunday, October 14, at the Mona Hotel, Covent Garden, and Stella was handed her first contract:

Frank Green's Company
October 16th, 1888

Dear Madam,

    I hereby engage you for my tour of *Bachelors* to commence at the Alexandria [*sic*] Theatre, Liverpool, on October 22nd, 1888, at a salary of £2 10*s*. per week. Fares paid to join, and while on tour. You to give one week previous to opening for rehearsals. This engagement subject to a fortnight's notice on either side and to the usual playhouse rules and regulations.

Frank Green.

Meanwhile Pat had reached Kimberley. Of all places in the world, this diamond-mining area, an empire conceived and at that very moment being consolidated by Cecil Rhodes, seemed to hold out the most glittering promise of wealth. When Pat arrived, Kimberley had been chosen as the name of the town into which the Du Toits Pan, De Beers, and Kimberley mining camps had merged. Thanks to the influence of William Ross, Pat's dreams seemed on the way to being fulfilled in a modest way. That fall he was able to announce to Stella that he had a billet with the Kimberley Central Diamond Mining Company for £300 a year. His predecessor, fired for drunkenness, had got a £50 raise after three months; he hoped to get the same. Ross thought he should be able to get something even better soon. It seemed a splendid place for making money. He knew Ross would put him in the way of anything good. He hoped all this was a comfort to his darling.

Stella replied encouragingly, and told him her own good news, the tour of *Bachelors*. But she could not be comforted by the eternal "things will get better soon" optimism of her husband. Far from believing that Pat would make their fortune, she was priming herself for the fight to support her children and herself, and to make enough money to bring Pat home to them.

On Sunday, October 21, Frank Green's company started for Liverpool, where they would open the next day. On Monday morning Stella went out for a walk. Trembling with excitement, missing her babies, she paced the streets, aimlessly loitering at shop windows. As she stood staring at a draper's display without seeing it, she heard a kind voice murmur, "You look very pale, Miss; won't you come in and sit down?" Stella walked in, sank into a chair at the counter, and the draper listened sympathetically while she confessed that she was to act at the Alexandra that evening for the first time in her life in a real theatre. He could hardly help taking an interest in the thin, high-strung young woman whose large, dark eyes made the pallor of her face almost unworldly. He promised he would be at the performance that evening, and Stella went away slightly comforted to know that she would have one friend in the theatre at least.

She was cast as a young widow whose chief function in the plot was to receive the attentions of the hero, Charles Lovelace, played by Oswald Yorke. She had no training, a little amateur experience, no technique, and the voice, as she described it, "of a singing mouse." All she possessed were instinct and presence. Instinct came to her rescue that night. "When I came on to the stage," she recalled many years later, "my first feeling was that the audience was too far away for me to reach out to them, so I must, as it were, quickly gather them up to myself. . . ." The technique won from the Liverpool *Citizen* the observation that "The character of Mrs. Lynne Loseby found a most vivacious representation in Miss Stella Campbell"; but although Buchanan and Vezin were established playwrights, the *Bachelors* tour ended January 26, 1889, without reaching London, and Stella was out of a job.

She returned to Acacia Grove, where she had left Beo and little Stella with her uncle and mother, to find a letter from Pat that was far less enthusiastic than his last. He was trying to get a new billet at £500 a year, but meanwhile life in Kimberley was monotonous. Instead of discovering diamonds, he was making a collection of stones for the Paris Exhibition, an interesting enough job since some of the diamonds—palest fiery emerald, jet black, amber, purest water—were superb. Then realizing, perhaps, that a description of diamonds might not entertain a struggling wife, he changed his tone. "I feel so anxious about you," he told his "own blessed wife." "Promise me not to run risks. Send me all your criticisms. I am so anxious to hear. I know you will be a success. Think as well as you can of Daddy." By January 1889 Pat had begun to hate Kimberley. Instead, he wanted

Rhodes to send him north into the interior to Matabeleland. Everyone was saying that the first fellows sent up would make their fortunes. Flushed with new enthusiasm, he wrote his wife: "I believe this last scheme of Rhodes' will turn into a company every bit as large and powerful as the old East India Company. From all accounts the country to be opened up is magnificent, and full of minerals far superior to anything yet found in Africa. The only difficulty is transport, and Rhodes is going to run a railway to the Zambesi. There is a wonderful future for Africa, if Rhodes only lives." He himself, he told Stella, was going to do his level best to get sent north as an empire-maker.

The possibilities seemed dazzling. Meanwhile Stella waited for another engagement. It came that April with Millicent Bandmann-Palmer's Company, but this actress-manager drove a harder bargain than Frank Green. Only £2 for seven performances a week as Rachel Denison in *Tares*; understudy and act any other parts if needed; find her own dresses and rehearse for two clear weeks in London prior to touring; pay her own rail fare to the opening town and be there in time to rehearse on Monday morning, April 22, and perform that night. Without knowing exactly how she could support herself and send money home to Uncle Harry for the babies, Stella signed the contract.

Now that she was definitely launched on an acting career, she wrote to Aunt Kate in Paris, asking her blessing. Back came a horrified reply:

> . . . Poor, unfortunate child, may God help you, if, as you say, the die for evil is cast. I can only pray, as the only chance to save you, that you make too decided a failure ever to try again.
>
> Good God, how could you think I could write and wish you success? *How thankful I feel* that it was not whilst with *me* that you took the wrong turning. . . .
>
> How can a woman bid with pleasure farewell to her best and happiest heritage—name, reputation, affection—to allow her every look and movement to be criticised by all the common jeering mouths and minds of the public. . . . Texas would have been better than this. . . .
>
> Poor, dear child, good-bye. I cannot see for my tears. Oh, Beatrice, how could you?

Dublin, Birmingham, Glasgow, Edinburgh, Newcastle, Liverpool, Manchester, Hull, Camberwell, Cambridge, Bradford, Leeds, Islington. Bad rooming houses, freezing or sweltering trains, constant rehearsals, seven, eight, or even nine performances a week. Touring, Stella discovered, had little glamour. But she liked *Tares* better than *Bachelors*, and she had a line that never failed to draw frantic applause:

SHE: Leave my house!

STELLA: My house is truth and honor, and in leaving, I turn you out.

She liked the company, and one of them, a young actor named Lyall Swete, fell madly in love with her. She did not like Mrs. Bandmann-Palmer, an autocrat who believed in the old-fashioned declamatory school of acting and was so stout that she drew shouts of "Jumbo!" from passersby. Mrs. Bandmann-Palmer also took an immediate dislike to the fragile-looking young actress who compelled an audience to watch her not so much by acting but by being the character of Rachel Denison. Miss Campbell's voice was low, her gestures nervous, she moved about in a strangely unstagey, sometimes even off-hand way. "The school of squirmers," decided Mrs. Bandmann-Palmer contemptuously, baffled by the unusual beauty who did not act by the rules. Her insults became more frequent, and Stella was not one to stand for insult long. In May she gave the required fortnight's notice, announcing that she could no longer support the manager's "constant in-civilities."

She stayed with the company until they reached the Grand Theatre at Cardiff. There she was given a farewell supper party by the company, who had sided with her in the dispute. They were all to contribute a performance to the evening's entertainment. Stella trimmed a white dress with a border of real green ivy leaves, and draped it Greek fashion. She chose to recite Tennyson's "The Sisters," and because she felt so strongly the sympathy and support of her fellow actors, she poured out her "secret" to them that night unrestrainedly. The company responded with a letter above all their signatures, expressing the admiration they felt for her portrayal of Rachel Denison and their regret at losing so true a friend and excellent an artist. And then Stella went back to Dulwich, a little more experienced, but again without work, and again dependent on Uncle Harry and Pat.

In September word came from the husband who had now been gone almost two years. In the great shuffle going on in Rhodes's South Africa, Pat Campbell was finding himself lost. That year the De Beers group had purchased the Kimberley mine for £5,338,650, putting the whole diamond production of the Kimberley fields into the hands of De Beers Consolidated Mines. In the shift of personnel Pat lost his billet. He had tried to obtain another, but could get no word from the De Beers people; he had tried to see Rhodes, but Rhodes was "busy"; he had tried to learn the plans for Matabeleland, but failed. As a result, he could send no money that September. Yet she should not be utterly discouraged, he told her: he had a very good name in Kimberley; it was just that things were very dull there now and few billets going.

She was not utterly discouraged, for that autumn she got an engagement that was a decided advance over the Green and Bandmann-Palmer tours. Ben Greet had founded the Woodland Players in 1886, a touring group that played Shakespeare's pastoral comedies out of doors all over England. With Greet, Stella had the chance for solid acting experience in parts like Rosalind, Viola, Helena, and the Princess in *Love's Labour's Lost*. And so once more she kissed Beo and little Stella goodbye, and set out to learn Shakespeare. Always uncertain about her name—she was Beatrice to the family, Stella to Pat, and signed herself alternately or both—Stella now chose the stage name Mrs. Patrick Campbell. She had some precedent for doing so: Maria Theresa Kemble played as Mrs. C. Kemble and Constance Benson as Mrs. F. R. Benson, Maud Tree acted as Mrs. Beerbohm Tree and Madge Kendal as Mrs. Kendal. Yet actresses who used their husbands' names usually acted with them or came from a famous acting family like the Kembles; their married names provided instant identity. "Mrs. Patrick Campbell" had no built-in magic. But it sounded respectable, it provided some protection on tour from unwelcome male attention, and it was a pledge of loyalty to the husband who was trying his best for her in faraway Africa.

From that husband she now received word that he was at last leaving Kimberley for Matabeleland. There were fifteen men going, all connected with the De Beers Company and mostly friends of Cecil Rhodes. He did not really know what opportunities lay ahead, since they were not told anything, but he supposed they were all to get commissions in the new British South Africa Company. Since they were being sent up by Rhodes, who was a sort of king out there, everybody felt sure they were bound to make their fortunes.

At this news Stella went out and bought three silk handkerchiefs and a ring. She sent these to Uncle Harry with instructions that he must do them up in a small, neat parcel and send them to Pat in Kimberley. *"He leaves Thursday night* for goodness sake send it in time," she pleaded. Everybody, Pat had said, had encouraged him to go to Matabeleland; everybody seemed to think his future bright. Well, he could not want his success more than she. Meanwhile, she confided to Harry, she had recited "The Sisters" to her manager, Ben Greet. He had looked dumbfounded. She really thought she could get him to put on a play just for her.

# FIVE

# *1889–1890*

*T*HAT SUMMER OF 1889 Stella made her debut with Ben Greet's Woodland Players as Rosalind in *As You Like It* at Merton College, Oxford. It was a part to which she could bring her natural gifts of grace, liveliness, mockery, and wit; it was also a part that tested her, for nearly every great actress had made a success with Rosalind and comparisons were inevitable. She had no experience or training in acting Shakespeare— no training in acting at all. Yet: "Performance over and a BIG success," she wrote her mother. "Actually Greet & all the company came & congratulated me. I almost cried. I didn't feel a bit nervous. But such a fuss—we had to have tea at the college, & to-night we play The Midsummer Night's Dream at Merton Hall & the whole company have been asked to a big supper. I am simply dead. We have been introduced to dozens of people all paying compliments. The Epilogue went beautifully. . . . Too tired to write more. Hope your back is better, Love to my dear dear babies." And then it was on to Bury St. Edmunds, Huntingdon, Bradford.

She began to learn something about the stamina required of the actor on tour. Sturdy, blue-eyed Ben Greet had amazing vitality and expected the same of his actors. He could be severe at rehearsals, unnerving when he talked to actors onstage during a performance, kindly when he carried them up hotel breakfast the next morning. But for Stella the endless jolting in railway carriages, inadequate dressing rooms, and poor hotels were exhausting. Lulo would never believe how busy she was. Five towns a week and two performances a day. On top of it all, making all her own costumes. She had sewn every stitch of her Olivia dress for *Twelfth Night*: white satin, lace, and pearls, a Mary Stuart cap and collar—"such a fag." And then she'd had toothache, neuralgia, and the complaint days, and had been too tired to attend more than one rehearsal of *Twelfth Night*. Room and board cost eighteen shillings: she was living on a few shillings a week and trying to send home half her salary, but had had three rude letters about bills.

Pat's father had not sent the money she'd begged Pat to ask him for. She was often hungry; her stockings had runs. Pat wrote less and less often. He might be dead of fever, she often thought, or mauled to death by a lion. There were other worries. "I feel homesick for my babies," she told Lulo. "I feel they worry Mother & it does pain me so. If I could only think they were with someone who loved having them. Uncle does, I know, but it's Mother who dislikes it." Yet she knew Uncle was disappointed when, as it sometimes happened, she could only send thirty shillings a week. "If I could only send some more money," she despaired.

Summer turned to autumn, and Greet engaged her for his fall and winter tour with the Comedy Company. She played Adrienne Lecouvreur, Lady Teazle, Kitty Clive, and Millicent Boycott again in *The Money Spinner*, eight performances a week, often twice a day. "One night the management, to save expense, sent us on to our next town by the 'milk train,'" she remembered. "We arrived at 5 a.m. on a winter's morning, and I had no room to go to. I asked a kindly-looking old porter if he knew of any rooms, and he advised me to go home with him. His wife, he said, had a little room to let. He looked a most trustworthy individual. . . . So I went along with the kindly porter. I remember the small attic under the roof. It looked tidy and clean, so far as I could see by the light of the candle. I got into bed and fell into a deep sleep—I was worn out, I never could sleep in a train. I awoke with a start. The grey morning light came through the little window, which was almost on a level with the floor; the ceiling slanted to the top of the window. At first I could not remember where I was, or *where my children were!* I was lost in terror, and I instinctively screamed 'Mother!' The sound of my voice brought me to my senses. With the loss of memory my resistance had snapped, and I knew fear."

Although Stella liked to dramatize the hardships of touring, she knew very well that the experience was invaluable. Every day was a challenge. She kept no diary, but lived "in front of the moment, not criticising the hour." Every minute was occupied, each performance taught her something of her craft. Then in January 1890 an event occurred that forecast her future as an actress. Hermann Vezin, playwright and tragedian, had a pupil for whom great success was predicted. It was decided that Laura Johnson make her debut as Julia in a benefit performance for Greet of Sheridan Knowles's *The Hunchback* at Colchester. Greet asked Stella to quickly study the light-comedy part of Helen; from London a straw-colored wig and a high-waisted pink satin dress were rushed down. The high point of Stella's role came in the comedy scene in Act V, when she woos her clownish cousin, Modus. "Cousin Modus!" demands Helen. "Have you not got a tongue? Have you not eyes? Do you not see I'm very—very ill, and not a chair in all the corridor?" "I'll find one in the study," replies the obtuse Modus. "Hang the study!" cries Helen, who only wants him to take her in his arms.

On the night of the tenth, Clement Scott, doyen of London critics, actor-manager John Hare, one of the Messrs. Gatti, owners of the Adelphi Theatre, and Hugh Moss, who would found the famous Empire Palace Music Halls, were among the notables in the audience down from London to discover Laura Johnson. Stella made her own discovery that night. She found that she thoroughly enjoyed playing the comedy scene with Greet, and that when she was amused herself, the audience laughed. Contemplating this new power as she walked back to her lodgings after the performance, she became aware of footsteps coming after her. She quickened her step until she was almost running, but a man nevertheless overtook her. Introducing himself as Hugh Moss, he said he only wanted to assure her that she had made a great success that evening; that although Scott, Hare, and Gatti had come to see Laura Johnson, it had been Mrs. Patrick Campbell who had won their hearts. Stella thanked him in confusion and hurried to her room. That night on the train up to London, Laura Johnson was not the topic of discussion among press and theatre managers, and, although the local paper was forced to spend most of its paragraph on the star's performance, it was lukewarm at best. Stella got only a line, but it was glowing: " . . . a special word is due to the brilliant acting of Mrs. Pat Campbell, who as Helen displayed really high talent."

The successful performance was repeated the next night, and in London the Gattis arranged for a special matinee of *The Hunchback* on March 13 at their Adelphi—with Stella and Greet, without Laura Johnson. It did not result in an immediate London engagement, yet Stella felt more and more that London was her destination. Still, her acting was uneven. She could perform like an angel, or break up when she allowed her nerves to rule her, like the time when Greet asked her to play principal boy in the pantomime *Aladdin*. The velvet suit sent down from London was "a horror"—made for a very stout woman, so that the bust had to be stuffed with tissue paper; she went onstage already hating the part. At one point she was required to come down to the footlights and sing a song that began, "They say the years have swallow's wings, but mine have leaden feet," and deteriorated from there. Feeling a terrible fool, she faltered, stopped, and burst into tears. Greet laughed, but did not offer her another pantomime role.

Instead, she was offered another summer tour playing Rosalind, Olivia, Helena, the Princess, and, this time, the part of Queen Eglamour in a little play by Louis N. Parker called *Love-in-a-Mist*. Parker was rather an exotic figure, born on the Continent of American and English parents, speaking English as a fourth language after Italian, German, and French, looking strangely foreign with his dark hair and skin among the pale British. Like many men, he looked at Stella Campbell and fell in love. He listened to her recite "A Ray of Sunshine" and assured her rapturously that it would "ring in his ears forever." He decided to write a play especially for her about a composer, Maris, whose early opera (judged worthless by him) is stolen by his pupil Pietro, but is finally retrieved and performed by his wife, Stella, to Maris's renown. Though the one-hour play was comparatively slight, Stella Campbell as Stella Maris would have to convince the audience she was so gifted that at a moment's notice she could step on the stage and sing and act a new opera. Though it had been done in real life, Parker knew that this kind of Cinderella transformation was usually greeted with scepticism from the stalls and catcalls from the gallery. It would require a *tour de force*, yet Parker was confident Stella Campbell could manage one.

Greet's company first performed *A Buried Talent* in Glasgow in May 1890. Critics did not go wild: they said that Greet was fairly successful as the composer Maris; they said that Mrs. Campbell acted very gracefully as Stella Maris and rendered valuable aid. She had been plausible, therefore, and Greet thought well enough of the play to bring it to London for a single matinee at the Vaudeville Theatre on June 5. It was Parker's first London performance, just as it was Stella's first performance in a prestigious London theatre. That afternoon she dawned upon Parker as a revelation. She was pure joy, she radiated charm and grace, her voice was music. She convinced the audience that appearing in an opera without having sung a note of it before was child's play; she convinced him that as an actress she could do everything and anything in the future that she chose. Of the critics who noticed the play, Stella was particularly anxious about Clement Scott. While Scott might not be able to make or break a reputation, his column was always important. It did not displease her, then, to open the *Daily Telegraph* and find herself called "a graceful and accomplished artist, who, having gone through a valuable apprenticeship in the country, cannot be long before she is permanently settled in London at some house devoted to refined comedy."

Meanwhile there was the summer tour played out of doors at zoos, botanical gardens, pavilions, aquariums, piers—wherever Greet could find a suitable setting for pastoral drama. From Weston-super-Mare, a popular seaside resort on the Bristol Channel where the company had paused for two performances in a day at the Pavilion on the Grand Pier, Stella wrote Lulo with enthusiasm: "Read the new play 'Love-in-a-Mist' today. So lovely—a dream. We all sat around a little red table & read our parts.

Greet is my lover & has cut out the most passionate lines because he thinks the people will laugh." By the time the company reached Worcester, she was less light-hearted: "I feel the success of the play depends on me & I feel nearly mad with anxiety about it—it is such a sad dreamy part—& me open at Birmingham!"

After Birmingham July 2 to 5, the company went on to Cheltenham, a fashionable inland spa at the base of the Cotswolds, performing at the Montpellier Gardens in a marquee because of rain. As usual, Stella confided the terrors and triumphs to Lulo:

Darling—

. . . We produced "Love's Labour" on Tuesday & Love-in-a-Mist last night. I have had both dresses to make & the study. I was disgraceful last night: rehearsal all the morning, played "Twelfth Night" in the afternoon, & the new play in the evening. Had to sing 3 verses, dance a minuet, curse & scream & faint, besides play two strong love scenes. I hope to goodness I shall be better tonight. I was simply shaking from fatigue & my voice fell to almost a whisper. I wish you could come & criticise. You'd go mad over my Eglamour dress—white serge & green—palest, edged all over with silver lace.

Greet, she continued, had offered her a job in the fall touring with Sydney Grundy's *A Village Priest*, £6 a week for three months. She thought she'd accept; it would be a certainty until Christmas, and by then Pat might send money. Greet and the managers of every theatre where they had played were telling her that she was the best Rosalind of the day. She herself was better pleased with the character now: she'd got her so merry, and audiences enjoyed her performance so. One man had told her he had shut his eyes and thought Adelaide Neilson had come back to earth. But there were still difficulties—the terrible bills (she'd had to sell all her furniture except the lamp and rocking chair to give money to Mamma) and her voice, which could fail her suddenly. "There is such a lot for me to learn before I can ever please myself. My heart sinks at the prospect. . . . I feel so worn out & I look so ugly. Write to me." To make sure Lulo would, she included her itinerary: Cheltenham till July 13, then Salisbury, Southampton for two days, Winchester, Yeovil, and on the nineteenth Parker's own town, Sherborne. Despite the fellowship among Greet's thirty-two players and her particular friendship with the actress Violet Raye, she was lonely. "How is my blessed mite?" she would ask. "Do talk to her about me." She was very anxious for Lulo to come see her act; in fact, she wished the whole family could come. If she sent the fares, might they come and tell her how they liked her?

The company's engagement after Cheltenham was an event, for they were to act *As You Like It* and *A Midsummer Night's Dream* at Wilton House, the magnificent seat of the Earl of Pembroke. *As You Like It* had first been acted at Wilton House, the home of Shakespeare's friend William Herbert (it is said that Shakespeare himself acted the part of Adam in the Great Hall); Sidney wrote most of his *Arcadia* there; the names of Massinger, Jonson, and Spenser were also associated with the great house. There was thus considerable excitement among the company now about performing before the current lord of the manor and his guests, and about the social festivities, for they were invited to luncheon before the afternoon performance and supper after the evening's *Midsummer Night's Dream*. Stella felt some confidence: she was young and beautiful, she had a lovely new frock for the occasion of pale green pongee silk draped with black lace, and new gloves. Nervously excited, she thus met her first lord, "very tall, extraordinarily handsome, with a fine figure and hazel eyes—the colour of the water of a tarn—full of deep, gentle sympathy, beautiful features, and a short, curly beard." Among myriad impressions that day, Lord Pembroke made the strongest: his winning manner quite captivated her.

Not all guests showed Pembroke's tact toward Greet's players. Lady Horner had come over from Mells Park, bringing with her young Edith ("D.D.") Balfour; they were met at the Hall door by Lady Pembroke, who drew them quickly inside and whispered that they were not to be seen by the guests but were to dress up to impersonate two actresses from Greet's company—it would be such fun. So Frances Horner tucked her blond hair under a wig, rouged herself thickly, assumed a loud, brassy manner, and called herself "Mrs. Greet," while D.D. Balfour, also heavily rouged, disguised herself under a bonnet with a thick veil and a long red cloak. Not really expecting to fool anyone, they went out onto the lawn, where Lady Pembroke, choking back laughter, introduced "Mrs. Greet" to her husband and D.D. Balfour to Lady Brownlow, Lord Ribblesdale, and others. To their amazement, no one recognized them, although D.D. heard one guest murmur, "That one is rather like Miss Balfour, if Miss Balfour were pretty." Lady Horner threw herself into her impersonation, leering seductively, declaring loudly that her favorite part was Juliet, and actually extracting a promise from one young man that he would take a box at her benefit. The same young man had just persuaded Miss Balfour to walk in the woods with him after the matinee when the real actors arrived and were seated for luncheon on the lawn at a table near the impersonators. Conscience-stricken, Lady Pembroke rose hurriedly and whispered to her table, "It's no use going on; that's Frances Horner and D.D. Balfour, and you must be quiet about it because of the next table!"

Greet's company were happily oblivious to the insult, thinking only that there were some rather strange people at Lady Pembroke's table; but the hyper-sensitive Stella was very aware as the afternoon progressed of the patronizing attitude of some of the guests. She looked so uncomfortable, in fact, that the Hon. Mrs. Percy Wyndham took pity and encouragingly put her arm around the young actress's thin shoulders. From early child-hood Stella had worshipped grace and charm. Now she saw a white-haired woman whose face and bearing radiated distinction. Had she known she was the mother of the beautiful Lady Elcho, who was married to the future Earl of Wemyss, and "Aunt Madeline" to an aristocratic circle of friends, she would have been quite overwhelmed. As it was, Mrs. Wyndham's and Pembroke's kindness took away much of the sting of snobbery dealt by less generous guests.

The afternoon was cloudy, but the weather held, and the company per-formed *As You Like It* in a little open glade bordered by great, spreading trees and backed by undulating green grounds. The evening performance of *A Midsummer Night's Dream*, played by lantern and moonlight on the dewy grass, merged play and reality, casting for Stella a glamour over the night and the verse that was magical. She travelled back to Salisbury that night in a trance, feeling that she had been both an artistic and a personal success in the kind of world she had always dreamed of attaining. "They all believe in me now," she wrote to Lulo the next morning before the com-pany set out for Southampton, "—but it has been a struggle! And everyone thinks I am so lucky & that it has been no trouble or pain or anything. How little people know!"

Not to be outdone, Lord Brownlow, brother-in-law of the Earl of Pem-broke, invited Greet's company to play *As You Like It* at Ashridge Park, his mansion set in the midst of a vast deer park in Hertfordshire. Here in the place where Elizabeth was arrested in 1554 by order of her half-sister, Queen Mary, Stella played Rosalind to Frank Rodney's Orlando and Greet's Touchstone on a green slope under massive trees so old and gnarled that they had almost ceased to bear leaves. Besides a beautiful setting, the performance also featured a herd of some hundred deer driven with great effect across the woodland stage. Stella was made much of by Lord and Lady Brownlow, for Lady Brownlow had been much impressed with her at Wilton House and already saw herself as something of a patroness to the lovely young creature.

Many years later Louis Parker would still think Stella's Rosalind and Eglamour two of the most alluring performances he had ever witnessed. Now he was completely enchanted. They played *Love-in-a-Mist* in the grounds at Sherborne and "She wandered through glades like an exquisite queen of dryads," rhapsodized the playwright; "and she spoke a sonnet in a way which persuaded me I was a poet: and, oh, climax! she sang a song of my setting, and her golden voice fetched my heart out of my body and brought it rolling to her feet: and my one ambition was to be Ben Greet's baggage-man and follow the company around the world, ever making my poor heart Mrs. Campbell's footstool." Unaware that Stella had changed her mind about the play, finding it and the music very unequal, Parker followed the company as far as Torquay; but Stella Campbell was not in love with him, and he could find no excuse to stay on.

By the time they reached Torquay on July 20, Stella was actually feeling wretched. Illness had cancelled much of the confidence she had won at Wilton House and Ashridge Park. She caught chills playing out of doors night after night. Her throat was affected by the damp, heavy air; her voice suffered. At Torquay *Love-in-a-Mist* was played as love-in-the-rain to a paltry audience at the Recreation Ground, and Parker agonized, knowing that Stella had to change her dress four times in a bell-tent that drew rain rather than repelled it. "I have had cold compresses on always & a plaster on my chest & lots of flannels," she wrote Lulo from Abbey Mount, where she and Violet Raye had put up for the week. "I have been nearly mad with depression. I am quite sure I shall end in a lunatic asylum. Poor Pat—I don't suppose I will ever see him again. I am feeling so bewildered, I don't know what is the matter with me." Chiefly she worried about her acting. "I am very dissatisfied. I don't know what this out-of-door playing is doing for me—whether it is giving me breadth & strength or making me boisterous. . . . I don't think I ever thought I was a genius but now I'm almost convinced I'm not even talented, for now my voice has gone I can scarcely get through my parts. All my effects were purely vocal—my *poses* are so hard, gestures etc. & I feel sick at the thought of next week & how I am going to get through this." Her need for Lulo had become almost overwhelming. She believed the tour was going on to Folkestone; Lulo was not far away in Berwick: she *must* arrange to come. She would try to send the fare, though £3 10s. had gone to London this week to pay off debts.

During the week, however, letters from her mother and much-missed children and the balmy climate of Torquay cheered her considerably. She was also encouraged by the fact that Louis Parker had promised to write her another play—a bold, poetic tragedy in three acts and blank verse. She had also heard that actor-manager Herbert Beerbohm Tree wanted her for the Haymarket, but about this Stella was cool. She had no intention of appearing in London except as a leading lady, even at the prestigious Haymarket; she would rather stay with Greet until she could act Parker's new play in the West End. "It should break my heart if I had to play 3rd fiddle to Mrs. Tree & Julia Neilson," she told her mother. With Louisa Tanner she tried to keep a cheerful front, telling her she had no right to grumble over hardships: "This tour has taught me more than I could have learnt in 6 years playing small parts in town."

Yet she resigned from Greet's autumn *Village Priest* tour, and she and Greet quarrelled. Not explaining which came first, she defended herself to Lulo, enclosing a "rude letter" she had just received from Greet. "There is not a line of justice or truth in it. Parker said I was the only earnest member of the Company & that it's the praise I got at the Brownlows that has made him hate me. I really believe the man is mad. . . . Coffin said when Greet is angry he says & writes just anything that comes into his head whether it is true or not, & I must look upon it as nonsense. I thought the man so great. Now I am convinced he's a fool." Greet's behavior also convinced her that in the acting profession men were more jealous than women. But what really seemed at issue was Stella's growing conviction after a summer of praise that she was meant for London rather than the provinces. Yet on Sunday, August 3, from the Isle of Jersey:

My darling—
   I have smashed up—voice gone. Have seen two Doctors, they have been every day since Thursday. They say I must have rest. I have played for a week. I leave the Co on Wednesday at Weymouth & go to the Urquharts. We leave tomorrow morning at 8 a.m. for Guernsey. I am afraid you won't have time to write there, so write to Bournemouth. My heart is broken at my strength failing. I have taken great care of myself—what is to be done—
                                                            Your own B.


Too ill to stay with the Urquharts, Stella returned to Acacia Grove. For weeks she stayed in bed, writing on a slate when she wished to communicate. Not being able to speak to her children distressed her; when she did get up and tried to play with them, she was quickly exhausted. Still there was nothing vitally wrong with her, and finally she was able to accept Owney's hospitality at Cromarty, the house on West Cliff Road in Bournemouth named for the Urquharts' Scottish family seat. She took little Stella with her to be examined by a Dr. Geoffry Frost, famous for treating eyes, throats, and women: her daughter was having trouble with her sight. Frost examined them both. Little Stella had excessive far-sightedness in one eye, a problem easily cured by wearing Sample's glasses for a year—except that the mother could not afford to buy them. About her own condition he looked very serious and predicted it would take three months to heal; she must stay in Bournemouth. As far as Stella could make it out, she had strained a vocal cord so that it was now slack instead of taut, and had then caught a cold which produced inflammation. Frost promised to cure the inflammation and improve her general health, but only time, he said, might cure the voice.

Recognizing Stella's financial embarrassment, Dr. Frost donated Sample's glasses and offered to take in little Stella so her mother could rest. The invitation produced embarrassments of its own. The Frosts were wealthy: kept an enormous house with servants, ran up carriage expenditures of £500 a year, put great stress on appearances. The Frosts' little girl was "dressed like a fairy," while little Stella needed so many things—a sailor frock, new boots, hat, stockings, stays, a warm jacket. Her mother was ashamed to send her looking so shabby. Besides, the Frosts were very strict. They did not allow their little girl to speak at meals and were terribly severe when she broke things, whereas when little Stella dropped a toy, she merely said winningly, "Dear me, I have broken this. How silly I am. I suppose it had better be thrown away"—and Stella would laugh indulgently.

So she postponed her daughter's visit, spending the days playing the harmonium, talking with Owney, mending clothes, and getting to know her dark-eyed daughter. She was so odd, so full of moods—Stella did not know how to correct her, or whether she should. She spoke beautifully; could say tongue-twisters like "mixed biscuits" and "shop snuff, store snuff" much faster than her mother. When a letter came from Aunt Lulo, she wouldn't let her mother read it, but preferred to make it up herself: "So glad, my dear child, you go to the Doctor's, and I hope you are good, *very* good. You needn't have a glass eye—oh, dear no!" She was, in fact, a wonderfully good and sweet child, and sometimes quite wrung Stella's heart, waking up in the middle of the night, for example, and confiding in a most solemn tone, "I wonder if Daddy is thinking of me, because I am thinking of him, and when I was quite a wee baby he took me on his knee," or saying wistfully, "I think Auntie Lulo's present will come before my *next* birthday, do you, Mamma?" For little Stella had turned four that September and, as Stella had written Lulo significantly the day before: "I don't for a moment suppose she will get any presents unless Uncle sends her one."

Certainly a birthday present was not forthcoming from Texas, although John Tanner did write his "darling Beatrice" that September. Advice from a father dependent on his family for the last ten years loses credibility, however kindly meant; and Stella perhaps little appreciated her father's concern: "I would advise you to give up the Provincial tours, as they necessarily expose you to very trying climatic influences and severe hardships generally. I have often thought of your hard work and how you must be overtaxing your physical powers, which, I am sure, are not equal to the struggle you are making—and it pains me, more than I can tell, to find myself so utterly unable to do anything for you. . . . I am trying my best to make a bit, but, up to the present time, the fates have been working persistently against me."

America had indeed dealt the Tanner-Cumins contingent a short hand. Edwin had lost his job with the Arkansas Pass Railroad Company and was trying to sell his oil paintings for $20 apiece; but not only did he work slowly—his father feared he might be color-blind! Farming had been abandoned. Jim Cumins worked for a wagon company, Aunt Dora taught piano, daughters Theresa and Angi taught school, daughter Rosa and Mr. Tanner stayed at home in their joint menage at 704 Nolan Street in San Antonio and kept house. There were a few comforts: Edwin had won two first prizes at the San Antonio fair; the Cumins girls, perpetually jealous of Beatrice, were losing their good looks; friends in London reported that in all their travels they had never seen two more lovely children than Beo and little Stella. Yet that news also brought sadness. "I fear I shall be denied the happiness of ever seeing your dear little ones," Tanner concluded his letter of September 12. "I am now at almost the close of my sixtieth year and feel I cannot hold out much longer."

Stella had more pressing worries than her father, however. Enforced idleness gave her time to brood about her absent husband and her health. Letters from Pat had stopped altogether. Yet one day a lady just returned from Kimberley visited the Urquharts. She spoke very highly of the expedition for Rhodes, and seemed to think that Pat Campbell was very lucky to have anything to do with it. This cheered Stella a little, yet she was tired and discouraged. "I often wish him home," she told Lulo: " . . . I want to 'throw up the game' & let him play now & me only watch." At times, like John Tanner, she thought she simply could not hold out much longer. "I don't so much *wish* I were dead, as *feel certain* I haven't very much longer to live. Still it is no use thinking about it & I don't mind—only you might remember, if Pat comes back with money & I am not here I would rather *you* looked after the children than anyone else—make them refined & artistic & broad-minded."

Most discouraging of all were thoughts of her career. She very much regretted the ill-feeling toward herself she had left behind with her quarrel and resignation from Greet's company. She had also ended feeling very dissatisfied with the work she had done. Both Laura Johnson and Vezin had accused her of affectation. She appealed to Lulo, who had, after all, come to see her Rosalind. "Am I very *affected* in voice & delivery? Tell me, do you feel you would like me better if I were myself?" Laura's criticism might be professional jealousy, yet Stella went over the question again and again: if the voice and manner she affected *appeared* quite natural, then surely affectation was all right?

The immediate question was employment, however. F. W. Macklin had asked her to play the lead with him at the Lyric Hall, Ealing. Name her own terms—yet of course she had to refuse. She pined to be at work again, yet confessed to Lulo, "I am feeling thoroughly convinced that I shall never be of any use again—my voice is *done for*."

Too restless to stay the prescribed three months at Bournemouth, she returned to London again; too out of sympathy with Dulwich, she stayed with Laura Johnson in her "grubby little room in the Strand." The voice did not come back—she spoke hoarsely; the high notes were gone. Through connections of the Hills, she was taken to see two physicians. Dr. Butler Smyth found a patch on her lung; Sir Felix Semon, a famous throat specialist, went further: he diagnosed phthisical laryngitis, told her she must give up her profession and live abroad. "You must be a fool!" cried Stella angrily. Sir Felix was delighted; they became friends immediately. On his recommendation, she accepted a renewed invitation from the Frosts to stay at Clovelly, their luxurious home in Suffolk Road, Bournemouth. Penniless, she went down to enjoy weeks of dinners and carriage drives, thankful when Eliza Hogarth sent her enough money to reclaim her winter jacket, which had been refurbished in London for thirty-five shillings. She wished she could stay at Clovelly all winter; she was convinced that one London fog would finish her voice forever, yet there was no way she could afford a wardrobe or servants' tips. More than anything, she simply wanted to act again. "I am burning for an audience & some lovely words to say," she told her sister. "Lulo, if I set to work with all my might, shall I ever be great? Somehow it seems *so odd* to me that Greet never recognized in me the gift I thought would make any man patient & that would have made him risk all to bring me before the world. . . . Oh, if I could only know the value of myself."

Besides the frustration of not being able to work, there was persistent loneliness for Pat. "I am so tired of waiting for him," she sighed. "Sometimes I long for him so that I feel the same pain I felt at the station when he went away. Do you remember? Oh, the agony of it—ugh!" She continued to send letters to Africa, but September had gone by, and October, November, and December, and there was no word. Unconsciously, perhaps, she had already said goodbye to him, for the previous spring she had struggled with some lines that expressed her conviction that their ways must be separate. She called her poem "Affinity":

Tired with toil, this art toil that leaves
   The soul still hungry . . .
I laid me down—too weary to rest
   Too tired to weep—with a sad dread lest
Death should end all my hopes of fulfilment—

   And I dreamt
That I was alone on a dark long road
   No end it had, no curving—and I
Was alone in the darkness; and I knew the road led to Fame.
And I felt—oh, I knew—that to fall must to me mean to die,
But fall I must for weariness
   With nothing to lean on—to rest and take breath. . . .

When sudden the darkness in front of me thickened
   And shaped itself to thy dear strong form
And arms outstretched and dear eyes glistened
   And you smiled and whispered, "Come lean on me.
"I'm alone in this road not known to all men
   "And finding *thee* here, my soul finds rest."

And you folded me close and the stars shone then
   And the faintness left me; and the road was fair
And toil was easy and life was blest
   With thy heart for my love: for my head, thy breast.

And then I woke.

Oh, love: not together we wend our way
   Up the road to fame through art to God.

# SIX

# *1890–1893*

*I*N LATE FALL Stella returned to Dulwich. Her strength slowly revived, although it became evident that her singing voice would never come back. In January 1891 she heard again from Pat, who had been silent since August. He had been riding as emissary all over South Africa, he explained, from Manica to Matussa to Palapye to Kimberley again. At Palapye he had met Rhodes, who had been extremely pleased to see him as the first member of the Pioneer Expedition to come down from Mashonaland; at Kimberley he had been interviewed, feted, and lionized—quite sickening after the rough, free life he had been living so long: he was glad to be back at Fort Salisbury, Mashonaland, again. Splendid reports were coming in all around about gold; his own prospects were a thousand times better than before; in a year or two he would surely be back in London with some kind of fortune. Meanwhile he had received her letters, and

> They terrify me to think how nearly I have lost you, my own true blessed wife. What a brute I am to leave you all alone to fight so hard a battle at home. And now I am afraid that most, if not all, the money due to me for the last six months has been paid towards my share of the expenses of our prospecting party. . . . I only get £15 a month now and rations. The Company will not pay high salaries at first; they promise that in a few months they shall be increased materially. . . .
>
> Tell Beo that I have seen lots of lions and tigers, too near to be exactly pleasant, but have not had to fight one yet. Perhaps I may kill one some day and send him home the skin. . . .
>
> This is a wonderful country. Good-bye my own.
>
> Yours for ever,<br>Pat

A postscript promised he would try to send money by the next mail. So Stella was reassured that Pat was healthy and optimistic, and began to look about for a way to return to the stage. She had not been forgotten: she had made a strong impression at Wilton House and Ashridge Park, and she had made up the quarrel with Greet. She began to think of a London matinee, and on February 19 managed to appear as Lady Teazle to Hermann Vezin's Sir Peter at the Adelphi for a single performance. Although Sheridan was not much in their line, the Messrs. Gatti were impressed, and the performance was spoken of highly. But Rosalind had been her greatest success. If Greet would lend his company for three matinees of the forest scenes from *As You Like It* and Parker's *A Buried Talent*, she believed her success in London would be assured.

Madeline Wyndham had both literally and figuratively put her arm around Stella, promising that if a theatre and company could be found, she would guarantee the patronage of royalty. Stella herself appealed to the Countesses Pembroke and Brownlow for support. Lady Pembroke assured her that she and the Earl would gladly give their names as patrons; if she could have the matinee before Easter or in June, they would even attend, otherwise they would be abroad. "I should have thought an evening performance more popular," added Lady Pembroke, innocent of the difference in cost between an afternoon and an evening production, "but I am not a judge on these matters." Lady Brownlow was even more gracious: "I shall be delighted to give my name to your proposed matinée & so will Lord Brownlow. . . . I do hope much that your health is better & that you will prosper in your work. We often think & talk over the pleasant days you gave us at Wilton & at Ashridge. . . . Have you left Mr. Ben Greet's Company? or how is it all? I shd like to hear as I take a great interest in you." And finally Lord Pembroke himself wrote Greet, vowing that the freshness and spontaneity of Mrs. Campbell's Rosalind made her impersonation the best that he had ever seen, and adding that if Mrs. Campbell ever acted in London, might he be there to see.

But aristocratic patronage did not include money. Of course, Lulo shared her sister's plans, and now took her own steps to promote Stella's matinees, appealing to Eliza Hogarth's husband. "This is important business in strict confidence," she wrote on March 5. "In order to produce 'As You Like It' at a series of two or three matinées Stella requires the immediate loan of £200. If you could find me anyone who would advance her this sum for three months at 10 per cent—*on good security* (I do not think her father-in-law would refuse) she could produce (certainly within six weeks of advance) at the Adelphi or Vaudeville theatres the forest scenes from 'As You Like It' & 'A Buried Talent.' . . .

"The Countesses of Pembroke & Brownlow both assured Stella that her 'Rosalind' was unsurpassed by Mary Anderson, Ada Rehan, or *anyone.* . . .

"Stella would take London by storm if she could *dress, rehearse, & advertise* these matinées thoroughly. You can have no idea how exquisitely refined and charming her 'Rosalind' is. It held me entranced & spell-bound. Her Lady Teazle was—well—in comparison—almost a *fiasco!* The matinées would be under the patronage of the Earls & Countesses of Pembroke & Brownlow. To the 1st Stella would invite all the press, leading managers, professionals, etc. The 2nd would draw the public and repay all expenses & the 3rd we will hope will benefit *her!*

"However there is a remote contingency which must be faced. Should the profits not reach the sum of £220 we must have security. If this is forthcoming can you advance the sum? Please let me know & then I will write to old Mr. Campbell and ask him to stand security, but please do not mention this to Stella or anyone, as it might raise hopes that will never be gratified.

"I am sure Eliza will agree with me that the matinées given on the best scale, perfectly dressed, mounted & rehearsed & advertised is the only way to insure success—anything less will mean slipshod failure; a ruin of Stella's chances of success for two seasons or more—and she ought not to ruin her voice & health any more by ill-paid, over-worked performances—when in reality there is no actress in London to come up to her."

Stella finally decided to make a journey to Stranraer and appeal to her father-in-law in person to stand security. Old Campbell had been contemptuous when she went on the stage, but good notices and her successes at Wilton and Ashridge Park had softened him. Still she was apprehensive, and took along little Beo as ambassador. On the train she continued to plan, writing Lulo that she must immediately contact Mrs. Thornhill, a friend of the family, and ask her to try to get the Prince of Wales's Theatre in Coventry Street for her Rosalind. It was rather a long shot: the Prince of Wales's currently belonged to Horace Sedger; Uncle Harry had just discovered that Mrs. Thornhill and Mrs. Sedger were great friends; Mrs. Thornhill could persuade Mrs. Sedger to influence Mr. Sedger. Lulo must do her best and tell Mrs. Thornhill that Ben Greet was going to manage the production. Ben Greet's brother William was acting manager at the Prince of Wales's; they'd had a row, but that didn't matter. "I long for the matinee, & feel sure it will make me," urged Stella.

She eventually was able to raise enough money for one matinee at the Shaftesbury, the first theatre in the new Shaftesbury Avenue which would become the heart of London theatreland. Madeline Wyndham kept her promise, and the performance "under the distinguished patronage of H.R.H. Princess Christian of Schleswig-Holstein" boasted the only slightly less distinguished support of the Duchess of Abercorn, the Earls and Countesses Pembroke and Brownlow, Countesses Grosvenor, Spencer, and Yarborough,

Ladies Brassey, Fitzhardinge, and Gaisford, and, of course, the Hon. Mr. and Mrs. Percy Wyndham. After this list of luminaries the cast hardly seemed important; yet the program also noted that Nutcombe Gould played Jacques; Albert E. Drinkwater, Adam; Greet, Touchstone; and Violet Raye, Celia that Thursday afternoon of June 18, 1891, when Stella proved before a large and fashionable audience that she was destined—in the words of Clement Scott—to take a conspicuous place in her profession. In fact, the press was almost entirely enthusiastic.

But it was the approval of her audience that Stella craved equally. She had no intention of entering society by the only route hitherto open to the actress: through the back door as mistress to some lord. She had dressed with care that day at Wilton House not to attract sexual attention, but to impress Pembroke's guests socially. The fact that the stage and actors had only recently achieved respectability did not impress her. She had never for a moment considered herself anything but respectable. Now she wanted what no actress had ever before achieved—entry to the aristocratic world as friend to both duke and duchess, countess and earl. That afternoon at the Shaftesbury Stella realized her ambition. The Hon. Mrs. Percy Wyndham became "Aunt Madeline"; the front doors of the great opened. What she did not win was an engagement at a prestigious West End theatre; in fact, she could not have accepted one if she had, since on June 9 she had signed a contract with the Messrs. Gatti to play a leading role at the Adelphi beginning in July.

She was still Pat Campbell's wife, as letters from Fort Salisbury reminded her, although they came infrequently and, when they did, told of flood, fever, food supplies run low, fights with the Portuguese, death. Yet one of their company had discovered the legendary "Kaiser Wilhelm" goldfields and one of their prospectors pegged out fifteen claims, the start of his fortune. Pat was very hopeful, though hope had turned to prayer: "Sweetheart, I pray God I shall be able to make a lot of money to be able to come home and make you comfortable, and give you all the pleasures that I long to, to repay you for all the misery and discomfort I have put you to."

Besides painting a portrait of Stella that had hung in the Shaftesbury lobby, Lulo immediately reported her sister's success to John Tanner. He replied in July, pleased and proud and ready to affirm that any critic who objected to any part of her Rosalind must be discounted. "I am bewildered to think how Beatrice could have managed so well. She must be endowed with gifts that exceed everything I can possibly imagine, for, after all, she has had no training and very few opportunities of seeing good acting to enable her to adopt the most approved conception and representation of characters." He had been terribly pleased to get Beatrice's two beautiful photographs. He had heard that Beo was the loveliest child in Europe.

Could Beatrice send pictures of the children? He was sending Harry a couple of mining properties that he thought promised well. For once he wrote little about himself, except that he must have money . . . immediately.

Relying neither on gold mines nor Texas mining properties, Stella accepted £7 a week from the Gattis to play Astrea, the villainess of George R. Sims's and Robert Buchanan's *The Trumpet Call*. Although the Adelphi featured mere melodrama, the theatre was grander, more sophisticated, and more spacious than any other commercial theatre in London, including the Lyceum, where Henry Irving and Ellen Terry reigned. Set back from the Strand and approached through a dingy series of corridors and halls, the elegant "Theatre Royal, Adelphi" nevertheless boasted a grand-tier balcony made of openwork so that the dresses of the ladies could be seen, an ornate hung ceiling, superior viewing, and a proscenium opening thirty-eight by thirty-five, compared to the Lyceum's thirty-five by thirty-two. *The Trumpet Call* was not exactly a come-down from open-air Shakespeare, therefore; the pay was £2 more and it was a regular London engagement.

The plot of *The Trumpet Call*, as the *Globe* critic was to remark, proceeds from improbability to impossibility. It involves a hero, Cuthbert Cuthbertson, who enlists in the Royal Horse Artillery, leaving his wife, Constance, vulnerable to the persecutions of her villainous cousin and a *soi-disante* first wife who returns starving, mad, mocking, and vindictive. Both villain and villainess are of course vanquished, and in a spectacular finale Cuthbert, reunited with Constance, receives a medal for valor before picturesquely massed troops of Royal Horse Artillery. The audience was expected to groan when virtue was threatened, hiss when vice revealed its awful face, cheer when the heroine was rescued—and always did.

For the part of Constance the Gattis had engaged Elizabeth Robins, a beautiful chestnut-haired American actress who, for different reasons, had as little business at the Adelphi as Stella. For Elizabeth had read a new playwright, the Norwegian Henrik Ibsen, and found at last a dramatist who depicted women as human beings with minds and wills of their own. The revelation had led her to accept the small part of Martha Bernick in an 1889 production of *The Pillars of Society*; then, joining forces with another American actress, Marion Lea, she had pawned her jewelry as security, rented the Vaudeville, and in April 1891 played *Hedda Gabler* in a series of matinees that won acclaim from enlightened members of the audience and press. Just as T. W. Robertson's *Society* in 1865 had changed the course of English drama from crude melodrama to comparatively realistic social comedy, so Ibsen now challenged drawing-room convention with social realism. But Ibsen did not pay, and that summer Elizabeth exchanged art for a salary and found herself cast opposite a tall, thin, nervous actress whose low voice often faltered during rehearsals and whose subdued yet affecting acting hardly seemed Adelphi style. The two had little in common. Elizabeth Robins was a militant feminist and pioneer of the New Drama. Stella cared nothing for feminist causes, being too busy pursuing her own career, and knew little about either the violent controversy the New Drama was generating or its supporters—Charles Charrington and Janet Achurch, J. T. Grein, William Archer, Bernard Shaw.

Yet Elizabeth impressed Stella considerably. Her special gift, decided Stella, was the swiftness with which she succeeded in sending thought across the footlights. Emotion came second with her, personality third. Elizabeth's seriousness and cleverness delighted Stella, although in the part of Constance they found limited display. In fact, both Stella and Elizabeth were intelligent actresses, although Stella's great gift was the swiftness with which she succeeded in transmitting personality across the footlights. She had been praised in her debut with the Anomalies for acting Marie Graham with more than ordinary intelligence, and had been praised with Greet for giving the impression that the women she played were both feeling and thinking creatures. Yet it was not exactly intelligent acting that marked her debut at the Adelphi on the evening of August 1.

As the gypsy-blooded Astrea, Stella was required to brood darkly over her wrongs, burst into wild snatches of song, lapse into listless despair, start up in reckless abandon, laugh with hollow mockery—all the while exuding a motiveless malignity which had to appear probable. This was easy. The real challenge came in the midst of a tragic scene when her ragged black skirt, carelessly fastened together by the dresser, suddenly dropped to her ankles, leaving her standing in full view of the audience in nothing but scanty drawers. There was a shocked silence; then a few of the audience began to titter, but only began. Fixing them with a glare of indignation, Stella quickly gathered up her skirt and, holding it together with one hand, majestically mounted a narrow flight of stairs, turned, delivered her exit line, "Oh, God—may I never wake again," with perfect composure, and disappeared—only hoping that the line had not been spoilt.

The young Robert Hichens was in the audience that night. "I saw Mrs. Patrick Campbell on the stage of the Adelphi Theatre when she was almost unknown," he would remember. "It was on a first night and she was acting in a melodrama the part of an almost starving girl. At that time she was intensely thin, as Sarah Bernhardt was in her youth, and had a strange dark beauty. She was already completely self-possessed, as she showed when an unfortunate accident happened. She was playing in a scene on the big stage and was dressed almost in rags. In the middle of the scene something keeping her rags together gave way, and they fell down and revealed her in—well, let us say very little. There was a guffaw from the gallery, but Mrs. Campbell, with dominating aplomb, snatched up the rags, folded them quickly round her slim body, and held them together till the scene was finished. She was rewarded with what was probably her first ovation."

She was rewarded again next day by unanimously favorable reviews. The *Times* approved. The *Globe* announced that she had acted Astrea with "very genuine power." The *Daily Telegraph* decided that "Mrs. Campbell more than justified the confidence which had been placed in her." A few critics discreetly approved her poise during a certain crisis: "Her merit was at once recognised, and at a terribly awkward moment the lady showed that she had consummate nerve and rare presence of mind—rewarded, as they deserved to be rewarded, by the generous chivalry of a typical British audience." Yet the incident was not over. Anonymous letters began to arrive at the Adelphi, insinuating that the actress had arranged the skirt drop to score certain notoriety, and it soon became freely circulated that the "accident" was no accident at all. Stella received the accusation as she had the laughter, with contempt.

Scandalous or not, her success was startling and immediate. In a genre noted for excess, she had acted with subtlety and thoughtfulness, making villainy far more appealing than Elizabeth Robins could make virtue. She had that ineffable magnetism that compelled an audience to watch every movement she made; she had that magic which is finally personality. Outclassed, Elizabeth Robins left the cast to tackle Shakespeare and more Ibsen, and Evelyn Millard took her place until *The Trumpet Call* closed on April 21, 1892, after 220 performances.

Two days later Stella reappeared as Elizabeth Cromwell in *The White Rose*, a historical drama, again by Sims and Buchanan, with Leonard Boyne exchanging the role of Cuthbert Cuthbertson for that of Colonel Markham Everard and blond, sweet Evelyn Millard remaining with the company as Alice Lee. The Gattis raised Stella's salary to £12 a week, and again critics praised her acting, Clement Scott writing that diction more admirable had not been heard for many years on the popular stage and that her final scene with Cromwell "elevated the whole scheme from melodrama or romantic drama into a work of high and artistic ambition." But Adelphi audiences did not want works of high and artistic ambition, and *The White Rose* withered after fifty-two performances to make way for the prolific Sims's and Buchanan's *The Lights of Home* on July 30, featuring the wreck of the steamship *Northern Star* and Stella as the betrayed heroine, Tress Purvis. "The Adelphi is itself again," sighed the *Globe* in relief.

It was inevitable that Stella should attract the attention of George R. Sims, a successful playwright, journalist, and bachelor of forty-four—and perhaps just as inevitable that Stella should be attracted to Sims. He was everything that Pat was not: worldly, wealthy, influential. He had luxurious apartments in Clarence Terrace, kept ponies and a smart trap, bred bull-dogs as a hobby. He was handsome in a solid British way. He fell violently in love with the fascinating Stella Campbell, and Stella found herself quite swept off her feet at first by the romance. She visited him at Clarence Terrace and invited him home to Newcote to meet her family; they saw each other discreetly in public. "Darling, I love you really truly for ever & with all my soul—and I want to please you in all things," she told him; yet was forced to add, "and I hate myself for that part of my nature that is teasing & cruel"—for she knew that what she felt was not love in the sense that Sims meant it. Much of the time she felt simply gratitude: "Thank you dear . . . you are so good & kind . . . bless you." She signed herself always "Pickles," the pet name betraying the lighter nature of her attachment, had Sims cared to take the warning.

Meanwhile the strain of acting told increasingly upon Stella. Her throat threatened to become a chronic problem; she was often absent from the cast, once for an entire six weeks. Lulo conveyed her worries to John Tanner in Texas, who received the alternate reports of Beatrice's triumphs and setbacks with concern. He himself had almost died in the fall of 1891 of carbuncles and heart trouble. The joyous news of Beatrice's success in *The Trumpet Call* had acted like a charm for a few days; then extreme difficulty in breathing precipitated another crisis which no one thought he would survive. He firmly attributed his recovery to the Electro Belt that dear Beatrice had sent him; he devoutly wished she herself would consult Dr. Moffat the Electrician, for he knew the Electro Belt would be the best thing for her throat and general health. "You must convey my fond love to Beatrice," he urged, "and tell her no words could convey the pride and satisfaction I feel for all she has accomplished." Now that she had suc-ceeded, he was prepared to believe he had recognized her genius all along. "Nothing is now wanting, I think, to establish Beatrice's claim to the fore-most rank in the profession," he wrote after hearing of her success in *The White Rose*, "and she has not astonished *me* in the least, for I judged from the very beginning, that she would make as big a name as her loftiest ambition could desire. . . . I am waiting so *impatiently* to learn *everything* that concerns dear Beatrice." Thus the father who regretted the money spent on his illness "to save a life that was scarcely worth saving" gradually began to live for news of his daughter's success, having resigned hopes of his own.

On Michaelmas Day Stella was well enough to join the cast of *The Lights of Home* for a holiday on the Thames, but in October she collapsed.

"I remember how it began," she later wrote. "It was a Saturday; we had played two performances; during these performances I kept feeling a strange icy sensation on the top of my head, gradually creeping down my spine. I said to some of the company, 'Don't come near me, I am sure I am going to be very ill, and it may be something catching.'

"When I went back to my rooms after the performance, these shiverings became worse. I lay awake all night longing for the daylight. I felt, if the day did not come quickly, I would be too ill ever to get home to my children and to my mother.

"When the landlady came to my room in the morning, she helped me into my clothes. I could scarcely stand or see. She called a hansom cab, helped me into it, and told the man to drive to 'Newcote,' my uncle's house in Dulwich.

"The drive seemed interminable, and my eyes shut against my will. When the hansom cab arrived at the gate, I couldn't move my hands or body. The man got down from the box and rang the bell, and the servant and the man helped me out. My mother came into the hall with the children. I remember saying, 'Mother, I am ill,' and the feeling of not being able to stoop down and kiss the children."

Nine days of uncertainty followed. Shaded candles appeared at her bedside, faces hovered over her. Doctors came and went and diagnosed typhoid fever. Delirious, she was seized with wild urges to sing as loudly as she could just to hear her own voice and keep herself alive. The frightened faces clustering round oppressed and angered her: she felt she must suffocate and tried to wave them away.

At the Adelphi, blond and beautiful Dorothy Dorr took her place as Tress Purvis, but it was not the same Tress, as George Sims above all others knew. Lulo was now living in Ealing and with her sister constantly. Sims contacted her, recommending doctors; she wired that everything possible was being done. "Glad to get your wire," replied Sims. "Have been most anxious all day. I will send my man down tomorrow afternoon for the latest news about four. Send me a wire in the morning if there is anything your sister may have which he can bring as he will drive one of the ponies. When she is well enough to have a little message you will tell her that my every thought has been of her . . . and that we are all thinking of her & praying for her recovery. Everyone who has heard of her illness is deeply grieved for she has won all hearts by her gentle ways & her loyal persevering. The Adelphi Company are terribly distressed and feel her illness most deeply."

Sims also enclosed £20. If Lulo needed more, she had only to say, for he had £50 of Stella's, having put her money on two winners at Sandown Park and, on October 26, on La Flêche for the Cambridgeshire handicap at Newmarket, which the filly had won—as she had, incredibly, the Oaks, the One Thousand, and the St. Leger that year. In fact, Lulo had only to ask for any sum at all, said the infatuated Sims—anything Stella might need was hers.

After days of delirium Stella became very quiet until one day she heard someone saying quite close to her ear, "She is sinking." At the sound of those words something flared up in her. "I cannot die," she heard herself thinking, "there are the children." The doctor noticed a change, seized a bottle, and poured neat brandy down her throat. Gasping and choking, she struggled back to consciousness, and the long days of recovery began. She slept and slept, and when she opened her eyes, she soon lapsed back into sleep again.

From Sims came hothouse grapes, flowers, and assurances that he was Lulo's to command. He invited Lulo to Clarence Terrace, where he advised that Harry Tanner write a letter giving notice to Mrs. Groom, Stella's landlady in Weymouth Street. He did not like her at all; he was sure she would be as nasty as possible and charge Stella rent as long as her things remained in her room. The notice would protect Stella's interest and oblige Mrs. Groom to give up her possessions to Lulo. Day after day his messenger arrived at Newcote with basins of turtle soup accompanied by messages urging it as the most nourishing thing possible for the invalid. As Stella began to sit up in bed, Sims was seized with a new worry. "Don't let Stella smoke yet," he warned. "I'm sure it is bad for her. The nicotine from the cigar would be very bad internally just now." Stella also had a new worry now that she had begun to recover. "I overheard what my fever had cost you," she wrote Sims the day after she had tried to walk again. "It is a loan—every penny shall be returned—it's sickening—what must you think. George, come & hold my hand & say it was out of love not pity—say something to take away the shame of it."

In December she was well enough to visit Owney in Bournemouth, and in spirits enough to joke about her hair, thinned by fever and sheared: "So you think you can love me with a bald head & if I have to wear a wig will you hold it on for me? Fancy if my hat were to blow off and all my hair in it in Portman Place. . . . Oh, Lulo, my darling, I should go mad. How I am punished for my vanity. . . . My new part at the Adelphi is, I hear, a *boy*. I *won't* play it. I have written to Gattis—or at least *a* Gatti—to say I would sooner break my engagements than come on in trousers & my own hair as a boy. Norman writes me that the authors wrote me a boy to *suit my hair*. The BEASTS! Oh, Lulo darling, what shall I do! . . . I mixed some of

Mother's massuse for my hair & Owney thought it was jam and ate it in the night by mistake, & in the morning she had a beard & moustache. Oh, Lulo, isn't it awful!"

By January 4, 1893, Stella was back at the Adelphi playing Belle Hamilton in still another Sims-and-Buchanan melodrama called *The Black Domino*. The Gattis had cut her salary from £12 to £8 a week, and she was burdened with the debt to Sims that had to be paid. She was very fragile. Her dark hair was beginning to grow again, but she looked bloodless, unearthly. She played the discarded mistress of Lord Dashwood, according to the distinguished critic of the *World*, William Archer, "with an effectively undulant and Bernhardtesque languor." She could not manage anything more, and she was haunted by a terrible depression that she could not manage to shake off.

"My bodily strength returned," said Stella, assessing the aftermath of those months of helpless dependency, "but my nerves were never again the same: something snapped that never mended. The sweetness and the calm strong faith of youth, and the belief that I could depend upon Pat had gone for ever. The months and years of parting from him, the hard work, insufficient food, insufficient rest, and the strain of my long illness had killed it all."

Yet she stood just on the threshold of brilliant success.

# SEVEN

# 1893

*D*URING THE MONTHS that Stella lay ill with typhoid fever, George Alexander pondered the question of what actress to cast in a daring new play he had bought from Arthur Wing Pinero for the St. James's Theatre. Fed up with the tendency of New Critics to rave about Scandinavian drama at the expense of English, Pinero had written a serious piece with a modern setting in answer to the current vogue for Ibsenite realism. In *The Second Mrs. Tanqueray* he had attempted "a rational, observant, home-grown play" about a woman who tries to live down her sordid past by marrying a decent man, fails, and kills herself to rid her husband and his virtuous daughter of her influence. Pinero felt compelled to punish his heroine for daring the sexual freedom that males took for granted; yet Paula Tanqueray *was* a heroine, and Pinero did not sentimentalize her. She was neurotic, selfish, sensual, reckless—a complex woman and therefore real. She was a rebel, and the play was on her side. He had intended it for John Hare at the Garrick, but Hare declined to chance it. Alexander, who had also had the intelligence to produce Oscar Wilde's *Lady Windermere's Fan* with Marion Terry in 1892, decided to risk a series of matinees at the St. James's.

Unlike some actor-managers, Alexander respected and consulted his authors. The search for the ideal Paula Tanqueray, therefore, was a joint one, with the meticulous Pinero having very definite ideas of his own. He had first thought of Janet Achurch, the actress who had electrified London with her creation of Nora Helmer in Ibsen's *A Doll's House* in 1889; he went with a good deal of eagerness to a revival in April 1892 at the Avenue, but there came down with a crash. During her absence from London on tour Janet Achurch had become addicted to morphia and brandy. The genius was still there, but coarsened, uncontrolled; and Pinero rejected it.

His next thought was of Olga Nethersole, who had played in his *The Profligate* in 1889; although she too could be rough and melodramatic, she had power, and Pinero hoped that John Hare might sublet her from the Garrick to play Paula at the St. James's. Winifred Emery was another possibility; yet, as Pinero told Alexander in December 1892, one could not count on her to act the next season: she might be ill, she might be pregnant, "a dozen chances might intervene." At the end of January 1893 Pinero had lost his original enthusiasm for Olga Nethersole: "I do wish heartily I could bring myself to see her in the part, but I writhe when I think of it. There are so many elements in Paula which would direct attention, I fear, to the indisputable maturity." Lily Hanbury? A possible Paula. The best, the most attractive actress, Pinero believed in April, half a year after the serious search had begun, would be Julia Neilson, the darkly seductive, sometimes poetic actress under contract to Tree at the Haymarket. But now that Alexander had decided to risk everything and put *The Second Mrs. Tanqueray* into the evening bill, Pinero longed for some actress unknown to West End audiences: someone fresh, surprising, fascinating—as daringly new as his play. On April 7 he started to scout the playhouses, beginning at the Adelphi.

Alexander had his own suggestions. He could accept Olga Nethersole, but felt more disposed toward Elizabeth Robins, who in *Hedda Gabler* had created a nervous, neurotic, modern character not unlike Paula Tanqueray. He also believed that Lena Ashwell, a young actress noted for "thinking women" roles, might do. There was always Maude Millett, a member of his company currently playing with him in *Liberty Hall*; she was capable, proved. Meanwhile he sent his wife, Florence, and his friend Graham Robertson out to scout the town. Night after night, theatre after theatre, however, their search failed to yield an actress of real interest.

"One evening we set dutifully out for the Adelphi to inspect Miss Evelyn Millard, then playing the heroine in the usual Adelphi piece, at that moment called 'The Black Domino,' " said Robertson.

"Miss Millard was very beautiful, very gentle, very sweet, about as like Paula Tanqueray as a white mouse is like a wild cat; another evening was evidently to be spent in vain—when the scene changed and the wicked woman of the play came on.

"She did not look wicked—a startling innovation. She was almost painfully thin, with great eyes and slow haunting utterance; she was not exactly beautiful, but intensely interesting and arresting. She played weakly, walking listlessly through the part, but in one scene she had to leave the stage laughing: the laugh was wonderful, low and sweet, yet utterly mocking and heartless.

"Florence Alexander and I both realised that there before our eyes was the ideal Paula Tanqueray. If she would only move, speak, look, above all, laugh like that the part would play itself. Neither of us knew the lady, who, the programme stated, was a Mrs. Patrick Campbell."

Robertson and Mrs. Alexander rushed home from the theatre to tell Alexander that Paula Tanqueray had been found. "No name," said Alexander gloomily. Then Pinero reported his own search. He dismissed Lena Ashwell as "a profoundly uninteresting young person." He too had seen *The Black Domino*, but "Mrs. Patrick Campbell is playing in such a poor piece that it is difficult to form an estimate of her powers. She is however a very interesting actress, so much makes itself apparent. Whether in a theatre such as yours, and under such good influences as we should hope to bring to bear upon her, she could rid herself of a certain artificiality of style, engendered doubtless by her present situation and surroundings, is a riddle which I cannot pretend to solve. I should like you to see her; if you have another attack of influenza you might lay up in a box at the Adelphi!" Yet Pinero decided that Alexander's suggestion of Maude Millett still held the field.

Alexander had planned *The Second Mrs. Tanqueray* for the autumn bill; it now became apparent, however, that *Liberty Hall* could not last the season. The time was right for his *Tanqueray*, Pinero urged; but he had changed his mind again. "Miss Neilson would be the thing, could we get her. Failing this, Mrs. Campbell would be an interesting experiment. . . . Supposing Miss Neilson and Mrs. Campbell are absolutely unobtainable I suppose it would be impossible to restore Miss M.T. [Marion Terry] so reverently and artistically as to revive a sense of her original architectural proportions?"

Alexander wrote to Stella making an appointment for an interview at the St. James's. It came at the right moment. Disappointed with poor attendance and bad reviews, the Gattis had decided that it was Stella who was killing *The Black Domino*. Nothing she did got over the footlights, they complained; and gave her a fortnight's notice. It came as a shock when she needed money so badly and thought her position at the Adelphi secure. She dressed for the St. James's interview with calculation, therefore; she badly needed the part.

Alexander and Pinero saw a tall, thin young woman, dark hair curling under a yellow straw bonnet trimmed with cherries and tied under her chin with a narrow black velvet ribbon. Most women hid their necks in folds of écru net after the fashion of the Marchioness of Granby. This actress's throat was bare, its whiteness accentuated by the long streamers of black velvet. She had large, haunting, dark eyes and a bearing that was at once fragile, sensual, and defiant. Whether she could act or not, both Pinero and Alexander saw that she *was* Paula Tanqueray.

After questioning her briefly about her experience, Pinero began to read the play. Either by calculation or expedience, he began toward the end of the first act with Paula's entrance into Aubrey Tanqueray's chambers in the Albany—that is, after the conversation between Aubrey and Cayley Drummle which reveals that Paula is a high-class prostitute. Stella heard only, "Paula enters and throws her arms round his neck. She is a young woman of about twenty-seven: beautiful, fresh, innocent-looking. She is in superb evening dress." The fact that the innocent-looking woman has been waiting in Aubrey's bedroom at eleven o'clock at night for him to dismiss his friends might have made her suspicious; instead, she felt only the reality of Pinero's play after the falsity of Adelphi melodrama, and her heart began to pound with excitement. Alexander and Pinero were delighted with her intuitive understanding of the role, and offered her the engagement immediately.

But when Stella went back to the Adelphi to tell the Gattis about the wonderful new part offered her at the St. James's, A. and S. were strangely unenthusiastic. They shook their heads. Perhaps it had all been a mistake. "What's good enough for Mr. Pinero is good enough for us," they said, and withdrew notice, leaving Stella bound to the Adelphi and *The Black Domino*.

Finding themselves back where they started, Alexander and Pinero quickly decided upon Elizabeth Robins, who, with her beauty and intelligence, might be depended upon to make something more of Paula Tanqueray than a common adventuress, although she looked too wholesomely American for Pinero's taste. Her last role too had had nothing to do with the kind of woman wanted now for the St. James's, although her *tour de force* creation of Hilda Wangel in Ibsen's *The Master Builder* had made critics take notice. Alexander had gone to the Trafalgar Square Theatre and been impressed, and Stella would later call Elizabeth's Hilda Wangel the most intellectually comprehensive work she had ever seen on the English stage.

Elizabeth Robins it was to be, then, when the Gattis discovered that not even an actress in demand with Pinero could save *The Black Domino*. They sent for Stella. "If you are still wanted at the St. James's, you can go at the end of a fortnight," they told her. Stella hurried to the St. James's and found Elizabeth Robins engaged. It was a crushing disappointment. But Pinero did not intend to be cheated. Elizabeth Robins could act Paula Tanqueray, but Mrs. Patrick Campbell would *be* Paula Tanqueray. Pinero wanted being. He and Alexander decided to put the position frankly to Elizabeth, and Elizabeth, who could have fought and held them to her contract, surrendered the part instead. It was a great sacrifice, for she fully realized the importance of the play.

On May 1 Stella signed a contract engaging her at £10 a week for rehearsals from May 13 to 26 (she would play in *The Black Domino* at night), then £20 a week for the run of the play. The next day she opened a note from Elizabeth:

I suppose Mr. Alexander has told you of what occurred Sunday and yesterday. I congratulate you upon your splendid fortune in having *The Second Mrs. Tanqueray* to play.

From what I heard read of the part, it is the kind of thing that comes along once in an actress's lifetime, seldom oftener, and that it has come to *you* is my best consolation for having lost it myself. You will play it brilliantly, and your loyal service in less congenial *rôles* will find its reward in this glorious new opportunity. There is to my mind no woman in London so enviable at this moment, dear savage, as *you.*

The enviable woman, however, still faced many difficulties. Alexander had engaged her on approval. This hurt Stella's feelings: she knew Pinero had only chosen her for her looks. Then the fact that an engagement at the fashionable St. James's was the chance of a lifetime did not prevent the rebellious Stella from not taking at all to its handsome, impeccably groomed manager. She was perversely stubborn. When she knew she had to be grateful, she felt irresistibly compelled to be proud; when it was demanded that she take a situation seriously, her impulse was to laugh. Alexander was a sober man who expected gratitude. Remarks like "Don't forget you are not playing at the Adelphi now, but at the St. James's" set her teeth on edge and inspired irreverence. She recoiled from Alexander's official manner, and declined to take the St. James's hierarchy seriously. She felt a wild desire to laugh and play the fool, since they evidently thought her one. Instead, she contented herself with flicking innocent but barbed remarks at Alexander's urbane composure. They stung, and he became more official than ever.

Knowing very well that she had something to learn about acting, she also had a stubborn belief in her own instincts. But Pinero was a martinet who knew exactly what he wanted from each player. Tall, rather thickset, his black mats of eyebrows beetling below a completely bald, domelike head, he would pace along the stalls, hands clasped behind his back, delivering advice that was as measured and deliberate as his footsteps. He intimidated the excellent company: Cyril Maude as Aubrey's best friend, Cayley Drummle; Maude Millett as Aubrey's daughter, Ellean; the gentle, refined Nutcombe Gould as Frank Misquith; Amy Roselle as the superior Mrs. Cortelyon; Ben Webster playing the brief but important part of Captain Ardale. He did not intimidate Stella. Although she sat listening quietly as he explained in detail what he wanted from her, she resented being treated like a child who must be taught its ABC's. She privately received every suggestion as a snub. She had no inclination to listen, but always wanted to do, according to her feelings about the role, not Pinero's. She was often abstracted, nervous, near tears. Sometimes she was openly rebellious. At one point Pinero painstakingly demonstrated the way she must play a scene of passion: she must storm across the stage and sweep everything off the grand piano in a fit of rage. Stella listened, stormed, reached the piano, stopped. "Here," she said coldly, selecting a small piece of bric-a-brac, "I knock something over," and dropped it delicately onto the carpet. The company was horrified, though secretly amused. "I could not make her rough and ugly with her hands, no matter how angry she is," she later explained to Pinero. "All right, my child, do as you like," said Pinero, giving in.

But Alexander and Pinero grew gloomier day by day. They were both extremely apprehensive about the play's reception. Victorian audiences were not used to courtesans on their stage, particularly when the courtesan was unashamed. More than this, their leading lady who should have been so grateful for her big chance was proving a wilful savage. The frustrated Alexander turned on his wife and Graham Robertson. They had made, he told them, a great mistake. They had seen a second-rate actress in a third-rate production and, merely because she had not been bad, had thought her good. Florence and Robertson put on a brave front; privately they told each other they wished they'd never paid a visit to the Adelphi.

At last rehearsals reached the third act and the point in the play when Paula is required to sit at the piano and strum a valse. Stella took this bit of stage business seriously, begging to be excused until she had prepared something suitable. But Alexander had had enough of Mrs. Patrick Campbell's whims. "We would like to hear whether you can play," he said curtly from the stalls. Stella was offended and instantly on her mettle. Seating herself at the piano and holding up her blue-and-gold prompt book conspicuously in her right hand, she began to play with great skill and beauty a piece by Bach for the left hand alone. She was quite aware of the effect she was producing on the entire cast, and prolonged the surprise for about three minutes. At last an expressionless voice from the dark stalls said, "That will do, Mrs. Campbell. We will go on with the rehearsal, please!"

From that moment there was a difference. "Dear child!" exclaimed Pinero, coming onstage and catching hold of her arm; and Stella felt that at last she had won his confidence. Then Pinero's wife, Myra, came to a rehearsal and startled the still downcast Alexander by saying, "Well, I don't know what you're talking about. *I* think she's very good." The tide, Graham Robertson could report, had begun to turn. Pinero became more and more indulgent with the strange creature who after all might confirm his renown as a playwright. When he saw she was nearly fainting from exhaustion, he rushed for Brand's Essence of Beef and a spoon, and stood by while she swallowed it. There were other concessions. She loathed the stiff hairdo that the artistic advisor, Florence Alexander, had conceived for Paula, arguing that no woman could go through four acts of tumultuous passion and finally commit suicide looking like a hairdresser's dummy. She got permission to let her loosely piled black hair do what it liked as the play proceeded. She adored Paula's sumptuous clothes—a tan cloak banded and collared with beaver and lined with violet velvet, a sunset-colored satin gown glittering with gold fish-scale sequins, a magnificent gold-embroidered yellow satin cloak bordered with yellow ostrich feathers and lined in emerald velvet. But it was a theatre rule to wear a cotton wrap over one's costume until the entrance cue. Stella protested, complaining that the wrap made her feel like a snuffed-out candle, and was finally permitted to do without the offensive garment. Then at last came the final dress rehearsals.

Pinero had veered between hope and despair about his play. In early May he wrote to Edmund Gosse, George Meredith, Henry James, and the publisher William Heinemann that, although it was not his habit to invite people to his opening nights, he would appreciate their presence on this occasion since *The Second Mrs. Tanqueray* was a play for grown-ups and they were among the few grown-up people whose opinion he respected. On May 24 he was resigned, telling the writer Joseph Hatton, "I am grateful to you for your good wishes in respect of Saturday night. The play is a risky one and, at best, must offend many people. But it will be all right in the end—a long time hence, I mean—when we all settle down and review matters calmly and pleasantly." He arrived at the first dress rehearsal with a lantern, notebook, and pencil, prepared to sit in the dress circle and deliver his final criticisms. Instead, his leading lady came to him, imploring that he not interrupt because she wanted to play the part that day as she conceived it, for him alone. "I kept my word," said Stella, "and to that dark, silent house and that solitary man I poured out my 'secret' with the fire and feeling of my temperament and imagination. I wanted to plead for 'Paula,' I wanted her to be forgiven and remembered. Cyril Maude and Maude

Millett implied by a furtive squeeze of my hand, now and then, that I was doing well." Pinero watched and listened, and went away to the Garrick Club afterwards to say wonderful things of "the fragile creature of Italian origin" who had lifted his creation into the realm of greatness.

The last dress rehearsal took place on Friday before a handful of people scattered in the stalls. Stella again drew on her inspiration, but this time found nothing. With instinctive self-preservation, she did not try to force herself. But although the rest of the company seemed to understand, she could feel the depression of Alexander and the onlookers in the dark theatre as with every act she grew more dull, flat, and listless. Afterwards Pinero tactfully kept his distance. He knew his actress was worn out; he also knew that opening night would be a toss-up. If she could recover physically and psychologically, she would triumph. If she could not—well, second chances came seldom in the theatre.

Stella went back to her rooms in Duchess Street, where Beo and little Stella were keeping her company, and crawled into bed with her dog She, knowing that she had disappointed everyone and that she could not have helped disappointing. The radiance, charm, and swiftness had simply not been there. She understood for the first time how some actors had to resort to drink simply to drive their bodies to perform. She understood for the first time the terrible trap of acting, the heavy demands it made upon one's emotional and physical stamina. What would happen if that terrible physical flatness came over her tomorrow night she could not bear to imagine.

Toward morning she fell asleep and dreamed that there was a door opposite her bed and that it slowly opened and that up near the top a little black kitten put in its head. She woke up laughing like a child and, when Beo and Stella tumbled onto her bed, told them about her lucky dream. The black kitten reminded her of another favorable omen. Rehearsing in her room one day, she had tried to give shape to the weeping scene that accompanies Paula's plea for another chance. She tried moaning and snuffling and sobbing, but grew more and more dissatisfied with all the conventional noises of a woman's sorrow until she finally hit upon the idea of breaking the torrent of grief by pausing deliberately to blow her nose. The sudden realism so affected She that the pug put back its head and howled and howled. If she had been able to move a dog, Stella reasoned, might she not be able to move a human audience as well?

On that Saturday of May 27, 1893, London playgoers might have chosen Duse as Camille at the Lyric, Irving in *The Bells* at the Lyceum, Oscar Wilde's *A Woman of No Importance* at the Haymarket, Irene Vanbrugh in *Uncle Dick's Darling* at Toole's, the popular *Morocco Bound* at the Shaftesbury, or Nellie Melba and Fernando de Lucia in *I Pagliacci* at

Covent Garden. A good many crowded to the St. James's. That night the stalls were packed with the fashionable as well as a few ordinary first-nighters and the grown-up contingent invited by Pinero. Alexander had the luck to be acting; for him the agonizing was postponed until after the performance, when he could begin to worry about next day's notices. Pinero always found it torture to watch his plays, however, and tonight felt a double-edged anxiety: would the audience tolerate his play, and would Mrs. Patrick Campbell pull through?

Stella put Beo and little Stella to bed early and, taking up She in her arms, went down to the St. James's Theatre and through the stage door in Angel Court, nervously primed for the fight. She was not to make her entrance until two-thirds through the first act, when she would burst into Aubrey Tanqueray's room late at night in yellow satin and throw her arms around him, crying, "Dearest!" Pinero could not stand the strain of waiting. Ben Webster, whose entrance came late in the play, arrived at the theatre during the first act and found Pinero pacing up and down the alley outside the stage door. "How's she doing?" asked Ben. "Haven't heard a word," replied Pinero. "Alec says she'll be all right if she doesn't crumble." When the interval was called, Pinero went to his wife's box. Myra Pinero shook her head negatively and told him to go and encourage the actress. Pinero knocked on Alec's door. "How is she?" he asked. Alexander replied gloomily that he thought she was crumbling. Pinero hurried to Stella's dressing room. "My dear lady," he exclaimed, seizing her damp and trembling hands, "magnificent! If you play the second act the same way, our fortunes will be made." Stella only stared at him blankly. A few moments before the second curtain he caught her in the wings slipping something into her bosom. "What is it?" he asked kindly, and she showed him a photograph of a dark-haired little boy.

The second act ends with a powerful scene. Aubrey has sent his daughter away from the house, and Paula understands immediately that it is to remove Ellean from her influence. She has struggled to be a good wife and stepmother, she has done her best to win Ellean's love; this is her reward. In bitterness she threatens to return to her old life:

AUBREY (*facing her*): And could you, after all, go back to associates of that order? It's not possible!
PAULA (*mockingly*): What, not after the refining influence of these intensely respectable surroundings? (*Going to the door down L.*) We'll see!
AUBREY: Paula!
PAULA (*violently*): We'll see! (*She goes out. He stands still looking after her.*)

After Stella's exit there was a tremendous burst of applause. The curtain was raised again and again, an unheard-of event in the midst of a play at the St. James's. There were cries of "Author! Author!" Pinero did not appear. Stella heard the noise with bewilderment and irritation. Surely if the audience had been deeply moved and interested, it would have kept silent.

In the third act Paula invites the vulgar Orreyeds to Aubrey's house in retaliation, but can only feel contempt for her former friends. The revelation is devastating because it makes her realize that she belongs nowhere. The culmination of her misery comes in the last act, however, when a Captain Ardale appears, engaged to Ellean, whom he has met abroad. To her horror, he turns out to be one of the men she has consorted with in London. Ellean finally recognizes the truth about Paula, not because Paula tells her but because "From the first moment I saw you I knew you were altogether unlike the good women I'd left; directly I saw you I knew what my father had done. You've wondered why I've turned from you! There— that's the reason!"

Aubrey tries to comfort Paula with plans for the future, but Paula is now convinced that she cannot escape her fate. "I believe the future is only the past again," she tells him, "entered through another gate." She hurries from the room and Aubrey is left to mourn the unhappiness of his poor, wretched wife. Ellean discovers her stepmother's body. "I—I went to her room—to tell her I was sorry for something I had said to her. And I *was* sorry—I *was* sorry. I heard the fall. I—I've seen her. It's horrible." And as Stella played the part, it was horrible. A perceptible shudder ran through the crowd at Ellean's announcement. Stella had made the reckless, passionate, hopeless Paula Tanqueray a real, suffering, tragic being.

At the fall of the curtain a tremendous ovation swept the theatre. Pinero appeared before the curtain; the applause became deafening. The audience rose to its feet and waved handkerchiefs as they cheered. Crowds of people swarmed onto the stage. Stella stood stupefied as people seized her hands and poured out congratulations. Alexander tried to introduce her to a few, among them Graham Robertson, who had discovered her at the Adelphi. "She gazed at the people thronging round her as if they were figures in some strange fever dream from which she wished to wake," said Robertson. And then she was gone, escaping to her dressing room, where she stripped off her costume, got quickly into her street clothes, caught up her dog, and slipped out the stage door. Outside she met Cyril Maude and they exchanged a few words. She seemed to have no idea of her own personal triumph, thought Maude; she thought all the applause was for

Pinero and his brilliant play. At home she fell into bed exhausted, glad the play had been a success, glad the first night was over.

Madge Kendal was among the theatre people who awaited news of Alexander's first night. "By this time he will have made the success of his life," she said during the course of the evening, "or will have been torn in pieces." Some had known early in the evening. As soon as Stella uttered the first word, "Dearest," Sir John Poynter had leant back in his stall, knowing the actress would triumph. Henry James had responded to Pinero's invitation and had been held in the grip of a strong hand by the play; he began to think of Alexander as a manager for whom he himself might write a serious drama. Not only the famous had been dazzled that night. A young playgoer named J. M. Bulloch would remember Stella's performance 3,531 plays later as the most memorable piece of acting he had ever seen. Perhaps no one had been more affected than two young gentlemen who had shouted themselves hoarse at the fall of the curtain and then, too overcome to speak, walked through the quiet, gaslit streets in silence until they reached the first one's front door. "We shall remember this night when we are old," they told each other solemnly, and parted.

Alexander, with Florence, who never missed a first night at the St. James's and was always given an ovation in her box from the gallery, drove home in their brougham to Pont Street, where a servant always waited with his master's slippers and supper. Alexander hated to eat alone, so Florence sat down with him, since she did everything possible to keep her husband happy. First nights for Alexander were always difficult, responsible as he was not only for acting the lead but for seeing that everything about the production went smoothly. This one had been an incredible success. Of course, the personal triumphs had been Mrs. Campbell's and Pinero's, as he'd known they would be if the play went at all: in accepting a piece dominated by the heroine, he had done what few actor-managers would do. Still, he was more than satisfied, since the whole venture had proved a credit to his beloved St. James's.

The next morning Beo and little Stella climbed into bed with their mother and She, and Stella told them all about the applause and said she was sure the play would have a long run, and did they remember the dream about the black kitten? For a treat they asked the landlady to carry them up breakfast, and there in bed Florence Alexander eventually found them. Why, demanded Florence, had Stella left the theatre so abruptly last evening? She had taken the St. James's by storm. She had made a dazzling personal success. Overnight her name was famous.

# EIGHT

## *1893–1894*

ᴇVEN THEN Stella did not realize the meaning of Florence Alexander's words. Instead, she sat down to write on Monday to the man who, in her mind, had managed the success, taking more care with her penmanship than usual:

My dear Mr. Pinero,—

I must write and tell you how full my heart is of gratitude towards you— and how distinctly in all the excitement of Saturday stands the memory of your kind encouraging words to me. I was trembling with fear that through the excessive nervousness I felt I should entirely fail to do justice to the wonderful part you had entrusted to me. And when you came to my room and spoke so kindly to me it braced my heart up wonderfully.

I am glad to read how fully the greatness of your work is recognised, and words cannot express the pride I feel in having been trusted with "Paula."

Yours most sincerely,
Beatrice Stella Campbell

Her first letter of congratulation came from Bessie Hatton, whose engagement at the Adelphi had ended on the night of Stella's triumph, the Gattis finally having decided to take off *The Black Domino*. "You certainly have walked all over the swells," applauded Bessie. "Bravo, your fortune is made." She could not resist quoting for Stella a song she'd heard a dirty little boy singing in the street—it seemed so applicable:

> They knocks 'er down
> And they blacks 'er eye;
> But she gets there
> All the sime.

As for herself—well, she did not think the Adelphi would open again for some time.

Reading the endless notices, Stella could not help eventually absorbing the fact that, much as Pinero's play was admired, it was her performance that was considered the miracle. Alexander's solid acting as Aubrey Tanqueray was comparatively little noticed. Pinero's play—yes, it was wonderful, but many critics were beginning to see that it was a little thin, and that without Mrs. Patrick Campbell's delightful, terrible, and astoundingly truthful incarnation, *The Second Mrs. Tanqueray* was more a well-constructed framework than a full-fleshed drama. Perhaps nothing told her success more surely than the fact that her name that last week in May was heard far more than Eleonora Duse's. Duse had played Fedora and Camille at the Lyric before the opening of *Tanqueray*; her triumph had come first, but in many people's minds the triumph of Mrs. Campbell had eclipsed that of the great Italian actress.

Maurice Baring conveyed some of the impact of Stella on London that spring. He was in Florence during the first excitement of her Paula, and there received an imperative letter saying he must come home at once and see Mrs. Campbell act. He came, could not get tickets for the St. James's immediately, attended a few other performances while waiting impatiently for *Tanqueray*, finding British actors stiff, affected, and slow after the spontaneity of Italian acting. Then he got seats at the St. James's. During the expository first act he still felt the artificiality of the acting, "and then Mrs. Patrick Campbell came on to the stage, and her slowest gesture and most deliberate note were made and struck before one had time to know how it had been done. Instead of seeing nothing but mechanism, one could not believe in the existence of any mechanism at all. One was face to face with nature and truth; and as the play went on one forgot to think about it at all; one was merely conscious of 'infinite passion and the pain of finite hearts that yearn.'" "What a Hedda Gabler she will be," he exclaimed to his companion, "and why not Lady Macbeth!" In all that hot and radiant summer, said Baring, the excitement caused by Mrs. Campbell's acting was the most incandescent factor.

For Louisa Tanner, Uncle Harry, and Lulo, Stella's overnight success seemed a miracle. The abandoned music career, the runaway marriage, the temperament and selfishness, the long hours of nursing required during her illness, the still longer hours of caring for her children—all could now be forgiven and even cherished as the price paid for genius. No one revelled more in her success, however, than John Tanner, now sixty-four, his once black hair heavily salted with gray, his schemes for prosperity baffled, his estrangement from his wife complete, his only hope for health now centered on borrowing enough money to buy an Electropoise machine.

> ... It was really very good of you to save me a lot of anxious suspense by sending on, so quickly, the cuttings about Beatrice's new play [he wrote Lulo on June 13]. They reached me this morning, when a number of visitors were with us and, of course, everyone was delighted and the exclamation on all sides was, "O! that I had a little of the talent of Mrs. Patrick Campbell." I felt satisfied, all along, that Beatrice would not fail to add to her laurels on this occasion, but she seems to have done more, and raised herself to the very pinacle [sic] of histrionic fame, and, even, in doing this, she has verified what was a foregone conclusion with me, that, in fact, she would not be long in taking the lead. I had written Michael Hearn for his candid opinion of her powers. His reply, which I got only a week since, says, "Beatrice is a most admirable actress and quite equal to Ellen Terry and Ada Rehan. Rest assured she will be a star in her own time." ...
>
> All this is most gratifying and, at times, even bewildering to me, for it seems so strange that Beatrice should posses [sic] such marvellous powers, considering the little opportunity she had of acquiring them. . . .
>
> There is no doubt that Beatrice inherits most of her artistic proclivities from her mother, but it must not be forgotten that my Cousin, Madame Albertazzi, was the best Prima Donna of her day and a special favorite of the Queen's.

One thing did trouble him, however. The press was already trying to make out that Beatrice was in needy circumstances when she took to the stage. Since whatever she said now would become part of public record, he felt strongly that she must impress upon the public mind that she did not take to acting from necessity, but because she had a penchant for it. He had, in fact, written out a little "preamble" for her that she ought to have printed and ready to hand to all interviewers: it was most important to set the record straight.

Apart from this, he was simply overwhelmed by her success. He had copied out some thirty reviews of *The Second Mrs. Tanqueray* and sent them to Louisa Suter; he talked of her everywhere. People in San Antonio were saying they would travel hundreds of miles to see her if she visited America, although he agreed with Beatrice that she must wait until her fame had spread over the whole country before attempting an American tour. "I don't think I would have the nerve to witness one of her performances," admitted John Tanner. "It sends me into tears whenever I think of all she has accomplished under every possible disadvantage and difficulty. If she had failed as 'The Second Mrs. Tanqueray' I am sure it would have killed her." His own news was as usual. Edwin had lost his last job, was now working in the machine shop of a railway "amongst Mexicans and in the hot sun," was netting about $40 a month and not saving a cent. He himself had given up all medicines, although still afflicted with severe "spasms." He very much wanted an Electropoise, if only he had money to buy one. . . . From the other man who would have liked the public to know that Stella had not taken to acting from necessity—Pat Campbell—there had been no word for many months.

Interviewers, invitations, letters of congratulation and admiration poured in upon Stella. Still weak from typhoid and worn out from the nervous excitement of creating Paula eight or nine times a week, Stella nevertheless found acting far less exhausting than the curiosity and publicity that now tracked her everywhere. Some people were well-intentioned, like Myra Pinero, who invited her to her Monday at-homes in Hamilton Terrace, or the Earl of Wemyss, who insisted that he must meet her. Others struck her as mere thrill-seekers curious about the latest London sensation. They did not care what she really thought or felt, only that they could boast of having "Mrs. Tanqueray" at their tables. She came to dread the curiosity in the eyes of those who suddenly recognized her in the streets or shops; curiosity, she discovered, had no feelings. She was bombarded with questions. How old was she? What did she look like offstage? Was it true she had a husband off in Africa and was he really the father of her children? Did she have a lover? Did she make up before she went to the theatre? How could she remember all those words? Was she in love with Mr. Alexander? Was she in love with Mr. Pinero? Were they both in love with her?

Everything about her—her hair, bonnets, children, figure, voice, piano-playing—became public topics. One beautiful woman leaned across a dinner table, having caught a remark of Stella's. *"Have* you a mother?" she breathed incredulously. "How *interesting!"* Stella was told of a certain lady's scepticism when informed that "Mrs. Tanqueray" was an ordinary married woman with two children. The lady had assumed that Mrs. Patrick Campbell was a *demi-mondaine* and had gone so far as to quiz the tradespeople near Duchess Street about her reputation. This kind of slander bewildered Stella most. People were assuming that since she portrayed a fallen woman with such utter conviction and naturalness, she must be one. Men made love to her as a matter of course; then *she* was accused of being an abandoned woman. "Did anyone see me as I was, I wonder?" asked Stella. "A fragile, unsophisticated young woman, still almost a girl, whose heart and nerves had been torn by poverty, illness, and the cruel strain of a long separation from the husband she loved. Brought up in a little suburb of London by a religious Italian mother—almost a recluse—adoring her children with an anxiety that was an obsession; unable to brook patronage in any form whatever, with the tenacity of an English bulldog and the tender apprehensiveness of some wild creature: passionately living in a romantic dream-world of her own."

But the characterization was itself romantic. Stella was twenty-eight, hardly a girl. She was unsophisticated, true—a savage, as she liked to call herself; yet she had struggled to the top, accumulating a good many influential friends along the way. She adored her children, but was perfectly able to leave them to pursue a career. Her pride, tenacity, and romanticism were strengths, as were a strong vein of common sense, a daredevil humor, and a reckless indifference to consequences. Her tongue was already something to be feared. Thus she was not exactly a victim that summer of 1893 when she turned all heads and cries of "There's Mrs. Pat!" pursued her down the streets.

There were new contacts of a different order, however. The first were the artists and intellectuals who, she felt, were curious about her not so much as a person as an artist. J. W. Mackail, Oxford professor of poetry, called her performance "just the sort of acting one dreams of, but never expects to see"; he and his wife, Margaret, daughter of Sir Edward Burne-Jones, quickly became two of her closest friends. Philip Burne-Jones, Sir Edward's son and himself a painter, became an intimate. Max Beerbohm, Edmund Gosse, Edward Marsh, J. M. Barrie became part of her world. And one day a note came from Oscar Wilde, connoisseur of actresses and at the moment the greatest wit and playwright in London, begging to bring to her dressing room after the third act "a very brilliant and wonderful young artist and a great admirer of the wonder and charm of your art," Mr. Aubrey Beardsley. "He has just illustrated my play *Salome* for me, and has a copy of the *édition de luxe* which he wishes to lay at your feet." The twenty-one-year-old Beardsley came, saw, and decided he must translate with his own peculiar morbidity the image of the new actress on paper.

There was a second order of friends whom Stella found even more congenial. These were the old names, the good names, whose great country and town houses, carriages, and servants were now at her disposal. She had always liked luxury and the kind of easy manners that freedom from middle-class anxiety permits. She was an aristocrat by temper: high-spirited, demanding, graceful. She felt instinctively at home with the kind of people Madeline Wyndham's and Pembroke's patronage brought her: Lord and Lady Elcho, whose eldest son, "Ego," and daughter Cynthia were Beo's and little Stella's age; Lord Elcho's father, the Earl of Wemyss; the Manners family, headed by the Duke of Rutland; the Pembrokes, the Horners, the Brownlows. She had no intention of being merely a "player" when the doors of the best houses were opening to her.

These new friends made up for the loss of her sister. Ever since Pat Campbell had gone abroad, Stella and Lulo had been close with the intimacy of one who loves and commands and one who loves and obeys. Since Stella had gone on the stage, Lulo had faithfully advised about costumes, clipped her sister's reviews, written letters Stella was too busy to write, pacified creditors, watched after the children, and nursed her when she was ill. In return Stella had admitted Lulo into her glamorous life. One day during *Tanqueray* rehearsals, however, Lulo had come to Duchess Street bringing with her a young woman named Josephine Jones. At first Stella did not take it in. She was full of her new part, very anxious about her West End debut. She wanted Lulo's advice and sympathy; she'd always gotten it. And now Lulo sat by the fire with Joe and was absorbed, not in her sister's trials with Paula, Alexander, and the St. James's, but in conversation with a perfect stranger. Quite clearly it wasn't Stella and Lulo any more, but Lulo and Joe. Stella had two weapons against pain—laughter and sarcasm. She used them liberally that day. Nursing her hurt after their departure, she gradually began to see that her way lay apart from Lulo's. In her poem "Affinity" she had seen that Pat must be left behind if she were to succeed. Now she saw that Lulo must be left behind as well. The revelation comforted her for having already been left by Lulo.

Stella turned to her new friends. Little Phil Burne-Jones adored her, and she appreciated his talent for painting, his love of the theatre, his sense of the comic, and, above all, the exaggerated devotion he offered her. One of the most memorable days of that memorable *Tanqueray* season came when Phil took her to his father's house at North End Lane. The Grange was surrounded by a large garden; its interior was filled with Italian pieces, William Morris's furniture, and Burne-Jones's own paintings. There was a sense of remote other-worldiness achieved by beauty that was both rich and pure. Stella had no formal education in art, but she recognized at once that Burne-Jones's Pre-Raphaelite mode spoke in her own aesthetic language. Sir Edward was hardly less impressive with his spiritual face and playful charm. "I generally go and see Burne-Jones when there's a fog," said Ellen Terry, one of his admirers. "He looks angelic, painting away there by candlelight." "An unspeakable, enveloping tenderness emanated from him," said Stella, "as though he would shield one and all from the pain he knew life must surely bring."

She was asked back and became an intimate. She did not take to Lady Burne-Jones, however; her too correct manner made Stella feel self-conscious. One day when she was lunching at the Grange and looking uncomfortable under Lady Burne-Jones's attention, Burne-Jones threw her a mischievous look, left the table, and returned a few moments later cowled and robed like a monk, chanting some mumbo-jumbo from a medieval book. Everyone burst into laughter and the atmosphere relaxed. Burne-Jones, Stella decided, made her trust herself; Georgiana Burne-Jones made her doubt. But perhaps that was because Stella so obviously preferred "Dearest," as she always called him. Of all his paintings, she loved best the one called "Arthur in Avalon," an immense canvas he had worked on for years, trying to project his last vision of a world of beauty into which he longed to escape.

In Burne-Jones's studio Stella met the man who had discovered her at the Adelphi: she and Graham Robertson became good friends. The artist William Rothenstein also met her there. "I had the privilege of visiting two or three times, when his studio was full of graceful, aesthetic young women," said Rothenstein. "Mrs. Patrick Campbell, then at the height of her fame, was evidently a familiar; she had lately achieved sudden and dazzling recognition as Paula Tanqueray in Pinero's play. Very beautiful she was, with a rich beauty; her dark eyes, full lips, and heavy black hair, making her face look strangely pale."

Her beauty was one of the more debated questions of the day. Some considered her "divine," "exotic," "shatteringly beautiful." Others thought her morbidly pale, too thin and languorous, too foreign-looking to be a type of beauty. Her face was far from perfect. Despite Rothenstein's observation, her lips were rather thin and certainly uneven. Her nose was strong. She was over five feet nine inches—too tall, some thought, and rather overpowering, even rather masculine. Stella was perfectly aware of the controversy. It amused her to imagine the whispers behind her back: "She does not know how to do her hair—has positively no *savoir faire*"; "Her eyes are beautiful, she has wonderful hair, and her jaw line is Pre-Raphaelite"; "Her upper lip is too long"; "Her hands are lovely"; "She isn't my type." A strong sense of the absurd saved her from taking it all too seriously. "My eyes are really nothing in particular," she would remark of her most admired feature. "God gave me boot buttons, but I invented the dreamy eyelid, and that makes all the difference."

That summer she was painted as Mrs. Tanqueray, her little pug dog in her lap, by Solomon J. Solomon. It became one of the most talked-about pictures of the year. At the Academy, where she was escorted to see it by Phil Burne-Jones, she was mobbed, and Phil had to arrange for her escape by a side door. She sat often to Sir Edward, a compliment since he seldom used non-professional models. Aubrey Beardsley drew her pencil-thin in profile for a projected issue of a new periodical, the *Yellow Book*. She and Rothenstein crossed paths again at Stanway, the Elchos' home near Winchcombe in Gloucestershire, one of the loveliest houses in all England. There he drew her in pastel. "The drawing was quite unworthy," said Rothenstein; "but in her high-handed way, she insisted on keeping it, and carried it up to her room. It was only by threatening to make her pay a gigantic sum for the drawing that I got it back and destroyed it. She had a beautiful daughter, Stella; Stella and Cynthia, Lady Elcho's daughter, a lovely pair of children, ran wild together like hares on the mountains, when they were not making sticky toffee in the playroom barn."

Max Beerbohm reported to Rothenstein with amusement that Stella had told his sister Constance that she "was afraid Mr. Rothenstein did not succeed in his drawing, *but perhaps when he has got it in his studio he will be able to touch it up.*" Stella had already met Max's half-brother, the tall, eccentric, red-haired Herbert Beerbohm Tree, when she had asked at the Haymarket for an engagement in Adelphi days—without success. Constance was easier to know, a plain, excessively tender-hearted woman who let herself be victimized, yet who possessed a certain shrewdness. "I do love to talk to her," she said of Stella, "for she has a devil. I now know why she always interested me so much: as long as a person is nice-looking and clever, a devil is a tremendous advantage."

Her devil gave Stella a reputation for recklessness, however, which, coupled with constant male pursuit, made many believe she was a loose woman. In town in early August the Earl of Pembroke sought Stella out, and in that handsome, noble presence Stella found herself pouring out the terrible difficulties of life as London's most notorious actress. Pembroke was very moved, writing her the next day that her confidences had made him realize how desperately unprotected she was and how precarious her life must be in such a constant state of siege. If she "listened to men," he told her delicately, she would be cut off from much that was valuable in life and paid poor compensation. He supposed the best protection for a woman in her position lay in a passion for her art and career; then she could look upon men "as mere dummies or useful adjuncts in her busy life." He hoped she would not be angry with him for daring to say so much: "I shall not write or talk in this strain again; it's your fault for touching me so much." Looking back on this first season of her success, Stella found it had been "hideously difficult." For men a beautiful actress was natural prey. She hardly knew what had saved her from a hundred traps.

She continued to regard the still infatuated George Sims as one of these. "You inspired a wild passion in a woman, a passion that for the time being warped art, reason, health, pride—everything," she tried to explain. "But as the order of things is that the world goes round & round—in time art, reason, health—not pride—came back again." Sims felt the change. He accused her of playing with him; she did not know the meaning of love. "I think I know only too well what love means," replied Stella; "the aches & pains & miseries it brings, & what a small share of happiness." He disliked her lively concern for her reputation. Stella responded by sending him a newspaper paragraph written "by someone who knows evidently the age of my boy correct. You can't be surprised that I am not eager to be seen with my best friend." He protested that her indifference was killing him. "You want to be rid of the burden," replied Stella mournfully; " 'anything for peace & a good dinner.' Well, if I had a heart it would break. As it is—Oh George, give me another chance! I know I'm a horrid irritating silly vain woman—but you are very dear to me." He accused her of ingratitude. "My dear dear *dearest* friend," protested Stella, "—I forget nothing—*nothing.*" But she had her own dissatisfactions. "This silken thread business is damnable," she complained; "I like my love to be bound to me by *iron* chains." And gratitude could wear thin. "I am indebted to *no one* in the world but *you*—& my God don't you let me know it!"

At the end of July, Alexander closed the St. James's. *The Second Mrs. Tanqueray* had brought him handsome profits and he decided to increase them, announcing a ten-week autumn tour of *Lady Windermere's Fan*, *The Idler*, *Liberty Hall*, and *Tanqueray.* He allowed Stella half-salary during the break, so that she did not have to spend her holiday on Streatham Common, as she feared, but went away to Margate, a popular bathing spot on the Kentish coast. In London she frequently put Sims off with pleas of illness, fatigue, and the "C.D."; for appearances' sake, she did not allow him to accompany her now. "You talk about being alone!" she wrote the dissatisfied man. "Last night from 8 to 10 I walked about the cliffs with my Bayo & if it hadn't been for that child I think I should have gone mad & dashed myself to pieces. My state is absolutely unholy. I live in fear & trembling of the tour. *If* Pat would only come & bring some money with him—then I would plea illness & there would be some peace. . . . Why are you always doubting? You know after all that has been there can be no forgetting."

Margate became "unbearable," and she changed rooms to nearby Westgate-on-Sea, where she was immediately sought out by Ben Greet, Jack Oliphant, Haddon Chambers, Sydney Grundy, J. L. Toole, Clement Scott, Beerbohm Tree ("quite mad"), and dozens of others. "The sand of Egypt is the only place where one might have some quiet," sighed Stella. "I have come to the conclusion that being a celebrity is just about the most rotten thing on earth." She was worried about money, as usual. "My success seems such a sham to me," she told Sims, "—being penniless. I have enough money to settle for this week—that's all." One morning she woke up to find that the heart-shaped emerald Sims had given her was missing from its setting: "I'm afraid it's a very ill omen." Finally her "selfish holiday" was over. "Leave by ten eighteen meet or wire Newcote re this evening," she telegraphed Sims on August 25, and at eight that evening they were together again.

In September Stella finally received a letter from Pat written the previous June. His life had become quite monotonous: bossing Kaffirs, making culverts, marking out cuttings—the work of a construction-crew boss with very low pay and no pay at all when fever had laid him up for five weeks and the £20 he'd managed to save went for doctors and medicine. "I long to leave Africa," the hapless man continued, "where I have had nothing but bad luck. . . . I am coming home the first moment I have the money." He had heard nothing of her great success, had received none of her anxious letters begging him to return.

Pat's dreams were baffled; John Tanner's were finally put to rest. In late September Lulo heard from Edwin. Their father had been very ill that summer; then one day Edwin had come home to find him slumped on the bed, struggling against suffocation and gasping, "Edwin, I am *very very* sick." Edwin had stayed at his bedside for nine days, John Tanner indicating he knew him by pressures of his hand. "Papa was too much agitated by spasms and discomforts of disease to say much. He would sometimes say, raising his voice in despair, 'Edwin! Edwin!!' and sometimes addressing Uncle Jim, 'James, what shall I do?' or to Auntie, 'Dora, what's the use, what's the use of all this?' . . . Of those dear ones away Beatrice was the only one I heard him speak of and then when in a state of semi-insensibility. It was hurriedly said and amidst gasping respiration, but I could distinguish the name 'Mrs. Tanqueray.' Poor Papa, it was his dearest hope to behold Beatrice again in the flesh. . . ."

John Tanner died on August 8 and was buried at 5:30 the next afternoon. Aunt Dora confirmed his last words, telling Lulo she had heard her brother-in-law murmur "Lady Tanqueray" and that was all. Now that he was dead, all the unpleasantness and unkindness were forgotten, only the memory of his goodness remained. From all sides came praises of his generosity and kind heart. It would have been better for everyone, Dora told Lulo, if they had all written more openly to their poor father. "However he was too good & kind to resent or remember, and all ways ready to excuse everyone and judge them according to his own generous nature. He never would believe you *all were hard up* & this old story often occasioned unpleasant arguments amongst us, but his love for you all was allways the same. . . . your poor mother, Lulu—although she had plenty to forgive, the blow must be terrible." She had gone through his things, saving a little pincushion he used constantly, an old looking glass, his walking stick and glasses, and a pair of white gloves. He had bought them for the "Zingori Ball," and, poor John, how they had teased him for trying to be the "Giovanatto" of the ball, dancing so long and hard that in a great sweat he had pulled off his flannels and promptly caught the cold that had proved fatal. Beatrice's latest picture had arrived the day of the funeral. "I had it framed," said Dora, "for I knew *he* would have done it. How he did look forward to seeing her."

Stella heard of her father's death from Uncle Harry; then Edwin wrote her himself. The thought of her father's last words brought her strange comfort, she told Lulo, yet she was troubled about his sad end in that strange land. She felt guilty that she had not helped him more financially, yet surely Edwin would have mentioned it if Papa had been in need. She would send Edwin £2 or £3 next week, if Lulo thought he really needed it; she did not grudge it, only she had just begun to save a little money herself at last.

For months eager playgoers in the provinces had been longing to get a look at the new celebrity over whom the London journals raved so immoderately; and in October, as that eager playgoer James Agate recalled, the famous Mrs. Patrick Campbell "burst upon the provincial darkness" in all her glory. Stella and *Tanqueray* made exactly the sensation and profit that Alexander expected. "The interest of the performance centres, of course, in Mrs. Patrick Campbell's Paula," wrote the distinguished critic W. T. Arnold, as virtually every critic wrote that autumn. "It is a character-study of extraordinary fascination, and puts the actress in the front rank of her profession."

Her colleague Ben Webster saw a different side of the actress. "Heaven knows what she is!" he wrote his wife, May Whitty, after playing Lord Darlington to Stella's Lady Windermere. "I should say drunk; but as she fooled the entire evening and made remarks to me when her back was to the audience, she kept me completely self-conscious and nearly dried me up once—that she wasn't a genius, that she had no dramatic instinct I knew, but that she hadn't one throb of artistic feeling which might have led her to approach her task seriously or at least have a little consideration for the possible nervousness of others, I only learned last night. . . . I pray that I may never have to act another scene with her as long as I live." There was also friction between Stella and Marion Terry: Alexander had made the mistake of taking two leading ladies on tour. Marion, Ellen's younger sister, now forty, was "a terror," but behaved beautifully in the theatre, upstaging Stella, a terror who did not know how to behave. The tour ended with no love between them, especially since Stella's Paula utterly eclipsed Marion's Mrs. Erlynne.

Alexander's share of the receipts came to £7300 10s./13d. Of that amount £4392 9s./8d. was taken by *Tanqueray*. Stella's salary for the ten weeks amounted to £200, minus the nineteen shillings she was docked for missing a performance and a half. On November 11 the St. James's was lighted again, and to show his appreciation of her part in his success, Alexander raised her salary to £30 a week. Nerves, however, were beginning to fray. Stella still could not bring herself to appreciate the dandified actor whom Henry Irving had once chid during rehearsal, "Now, Alexander, not quite so much Piccadilly." The carefully waved brown locks, perfectly creased trousers, and handsome profile did not charm her. She considered him a competent performer at best, his super-efficiency in management a substitute for great acting. He struck her as humorless, a crime she could never forgive. "Playing to his Aubrey was like playing to a walking stick," she complained. But he had raised her salary and the crowds at the St. James's were as large and enthusiastic as ever, so they did not openly quarrel—until the Boxing Day matinee.

After the Wednesday matinee on December 20, the St. James's was dark through Christmas Day. Stella went home to Uncle Harry's on Saturday to find Beo seriously ill with what the doctor diagnosed as diphtheria. She hurried guiltily to his room and sat with him all night, all the next day, and all Sunday night. At half past eleven on Monday morning the doctor came, decided it was only tonsillitis, and told her she need not be alarmed.

Stella had the rest of Christmas Day to pull herself together for the matinee and evening performance the next day. Beo still needed nursing, trains were off-schedule; as a result, she arrived for the matinee just as the overture struck up. With the length of Aubrey's first scene with his friends to dress, she hurried into her gown and cloak, hastily did her hair, rushed onto the stage, and could not remember a single word of her part. She sank down on a sofa, quite bewildered, while Alexander himself went to get her the book. As he handed it to her, she heard him murmur, "The woman's drunk!"

Although she smoked cigars and Egyptian cigarettes, Stella drank little. She played the rest of the scene in a cold fury and, when the curtain fell, stormed upstairs to her room and began dressing to go home. Thinking she was ill, her understudy, Charlotte Granville, started preparing to go on for her. Then Maude Millett stuck her head in the door and Stella poured out her story. Maude was terse: "Beerbohm Tree's in front; think of your career." She disappeared and came back almost immediately with a bottle of champagne from Willis's Rooms next door, and made Stella down a tumblerful. Stella hurried into her second-act costume, went out, and played superbly.

Afterwards Tree came round to her dressing room. Although he had once dismissed her plea for an engagement at £4 a week ("It was dark and I did not see your face"), he now offered her £60 a week to act with him at the Haymarket. Stella promptly accepted; then went to Alexander, told him she had heard what he said onstage, that she had accepted an offer from Tree, and that although she was bound to honor her contract till the end of the season, she would never speak to him again.

Alexander was profoundly frustrated. His actress was magnificent, their personal relationship impossible. Earlier that month he had read Henry Arthur Jones's new play, *The Masqueraders*. He wanted Ellen Terry for Dulcie Larondie; he had an option on Stella Campbell for his next play; Ellen was not available. Could he bear another round with Stella? That became his chief concern as *Tanqueray* went into March of 1894 and his leading lady maintained a haughty reserve offstage. Because of her lapse of memory that day, the rumor was now circulating that she drank (any actor's slip invited that interpretation), and this, coupled with the widespread belief that she herself was a Paula Tanqueray, multiplied the damning speculation. That Alexander, who should have known better, had accused her of drunkenness deeply wounded her. She was determined not to forgive him.

For the past half-year Stella had struggled to reconcile George Sims to the fact that she could not love him, without losing him as a friend. Now she could not cry over "his brutal letter"; she could only tell him "a little story" that went, "Once upon a time there was a man who had lived his life & made a name when he was scarcely in his prime—& he loved seeing the fruits of his labor round him—his horse & his ass—his best beloved ones were dead. One day he met a woman—a weird woman—a story-woman. And the woman loved him because he had had the courage to live his life—& because he had made a good name—a human name. And he thought the woman would look well with his horse & his ass—a sort of fruit of his labor for his fellow men to envy of him. But the woman—the sad woman with the story-face—was ashamed of her love & only whispered it in the dark to God—& it nearly drove her mad, & God let her be mad for a little to test her heart. And then the man with his knowledge of life said the woman didn't love him because she wouldn't be shown with his horse & his ass to the envy of his fellow men—& then there were estrangements & misunderstandings & misjudgments, & the woman learnt her lesson—the bitterest lesson of all." It was clear to her that they must part; he, too, often longed to be free. "You are right," she agreed; "you must work & work *well*. We have each our lives to lead & the great thing is not to be *hindered* in any way."

Meanwhile she continued to write to Africa, begging Pat to come home, since she had cleared off a number of debts and was making enough money for both of them. Pat replied on the last day of 1893, thanking his "own Stella wife" for her immeasurably kind and loving letters. He was coming home as soon as he could get passage money. He was afraid she would find him greatly changed; he prayed God that she would not turn from him. On March 12 Stella finally received word that he was in England. She telegraphed immediately:

JUST RECEIVED YOUR LETTER, REPLY PAID WHETHER I SHALL POST MONEY TO YOU AT ONCE. BORROW ON MY NAME IF POSSIBLE, IT WILL SAVE TIME. LET ME KNOW, DEAR, WHERE TO MEET YOU. SO GLAD YOU HAVE COME.

---

# NINE

## 1894–1895

---

$\mathcal{T}$HE REUNION was a shock for Stella. "When Pat arrived I saw in his eyes that youth, with all the belief and faith in his own efforts and his luck, had gone: his health and his energies were undermined by fever, failure, and the most bitter disappointments. Nothing had come of his hard work, his hopes, and his sacrifice." The look of defeat in his eyes pained her. Only his gentleness and tenderness were the same: he still loved her.

The shock was far more severe for Pat Campbell. He had left a twenty-two-year-old wife with two small children in the suburbs giving piano lessons for pocket money. He returned to find that wife the toast of London. His children were strangers: Beo a beautiful and spoiled nine-year-old; little Stella a shy, exquisitely dressed child of seven who called her famous mother "Mam*ma.*" His health was very bad; every few days he suffered attacks of malaria. He had not a penny to show for the African adventure, but must live off his wife, whose money, however, could not accommodate the extravagant life she was living. He wanted his wife and children to himself, but soon learned that when Stella was not at the theatre she was besieged by friends, acquaintances, strangers, admirers, dressmakers, photographers, and interviewers, and constantly rushing off to luncheons, balls, country weekends, matinees, receptions, teas, benefits, at-homes, galleries. The curiosity he excited as the husband of "The Second Mrs. Tanqueray" was intolerable to him, a quiet, even taciturn, man. Even when he might have enjoyed the entertainment, he flinched under a sense of obligation to people whose champagne and carriage drives he could never return. And there were sneers. Lunching one day at a fashionable restaurant, he and Stella met Oscar Wilde, for whom the name "Mrs. Pat" conjured up just that mixture of middle-class prudery and upper-class rakishness he attributed to Stella. "Your *hus*band?" exclaimed Wilde, staring incredulously at her escort. "How su*burban!*"

Meanwhile one question dominated theatreland. What would—what could—follow *Mrs. Tanqueray?* Alexander wanted a realistic, modern play with romantic parts for himself and Stella Campbell that would add to the glamour they had achieved as Aubrey and Paula. After Pinero, Henry Arthur Jones seemed to be the British playwright of the moment. Back in December 1893 Alexander had read the script of *The Masqueraders* to Florence, who had been as delighted with it as he. "She feels there is only one Dulcie," he told Jones, "and that is Ellen Terry. Whether Mrs. P.C. will be able to show the requisite amount of fun, and still more the necessary refinement, is a moot point."

All London waited for the reappearance of Mrs. Patrick Campbell, most with unreserved enthusiasm, some more cautiously. William Archer, dramatic critic of the *World*, was among the latter. He had revisited *Tanqueray* after eight months. Declaring that Mrs. Campbell had even improved upon her earlier performance, Archer still hesitated. There was not the least doubt that her Paula was a very remarkable creation or incarnation, but he was inclined to await her appearance in some other character before he could commit himself to that much used word "genius." People were comparing her to Duse, Modjeska, Bernhardt. He would wait and see.

Stella was of course aware that her second appearance at the St. James's would be a test. The knowledge might have made her humble, co-operative, and anxious to play Dulcie Larondie to the best of her ability. But Stella had her perverse devil. She did not like the play, and entered into rehearsals in a spirit of smoldering rebellion. She and Alexander picked up their quarrel exactly where they had left it, neither speaking to the other except when their parts required it. She did not like the role of Dulcie Larondie, and she looked upon its cockney-speaking author coldly. "Mr. Jo-o-ones," she began to call him, drawling out the name to make it sound immeasurably long and immeasurably commonplace.

An uneven mixture of melodrama and social criticism, *The Masqueraders* opens in the tap-room of an inn where barmaid Dulcie Larondie attracts all eyes. Eventually the idea of an auction takes hold: a kiss from Dulcie to the highest bidder. Both the corrupt Sir Brice Skene and the idealistic astronomer David Remon want Dulcie; Sir Brice wins the kiss with a bid of three thousand guineas. Dulcie accepts the offer of marriage he throws in with his bid, and Remon has to be content with kissing the hem of her skirt as she goes off to join Sir Brice. Three years later Dulcie has a daughter and her gambling husband is penniless. It is now Remon's turn. Famous and rich, he offers her his checkbook to pay her husband's debts. Dulcie is naturally hesitant, but Remon tells her that they are all masqueraders, that there is no truth but in the stars, and that accepting his help is the greatest kindness she can do him. In Act III, Dulcie is again bid for. Remon, who has only six months to live, challenges her husband at cards: Dulcie and her child to the winner. This time the prize is Remon's, but when Dulcie reluctantly joins him, she destroys all his hopes by telling him that living with him unwed is more horrible to her than living with her detested husband. Defeated and dying, Remon releases Dulcie "sweeter unpossessed," knowing he will never see her again save "on some little star in Andromeda."

The auctioning of Dulcie's kiss and the game of cards were dramatically effective. Jones had also thrown in a "new woman," Lady Charley Wishanger, played by Irene Vanbrugh in a red wig and a monocle; a few Wildean para-doxes—"Marriage is the last insult one offers to a woman whom one re-spects"; a touch of evolutionism—"If we fail, we shall have sacrificed ourselves for the benefit of our species"; and a good deal of heavy criticism of the marriage market. Yet the play was already dated among more advanced "iron brows" by Jones's refusal to let his star-gazing hero and long-suffering heroine consummate their love. The message of the play turned out, after all, to be woman's duty—and that message was old.

The part of Dulcie Larondie, which she was to play in a reddish-gold wig, struck Stella as unreal, and much of the play too in bad taste. She did not like drawing beer and having her kiss sold to the highest bidder. She did not care for lines like "Nell, there ain't any good men left in the world," or Dulcie's sneering "Yah, yah, yah, yah, yah," which Jones during rehearsals mercifully reduced to "Yah, yah, yah!" The gorgeous pale pink brocade gown glittering with silver fern leaves, trailing a skirt looped up over a petticoat shimmering with silver embroidery, that she wore for a salon scene in the second act failed to comfort her. Perhaps she liked least the submissiveness of Dulcie, who allows herself to be bought by both villain and hero. She had tried to make Paula complex and tragic; she saw little in Dulcie to elevate. She approached the play unwillingly and fought all the way. "Put a bridle on my tongue & humble my spirit," she wrote in her brocade-covered play book. But the bridle often slipped and the spirit re-mained unhumbled. Despite Alexander's managerial skill, rehearsals at the St. James's became a battle.

On April 21 *The Second Mrs. Tanqueray* ended its run after 227 Lon-don performances, having brought Alexander £36,688 13s. in receipts, made Pinero's reputation, and put Stella at the head of her profession. Pinero sent his actress a brooch on the last day with his deepest gratitude. Lulo, Joe, and Uncle Harry attended the last performance, and Harry wrote his niece afterwards in a burst of pride:

You are really a wonderful woman that you are able to keep from losing your head under the intoxicating influence of all the applause, and praise, and presents, and letters, laurel wreaths, bouquets, and suppers, to which your enthusiastic admirers and friends love to treat you. I was indeed delighted to witness the spontaneous and splendid tribute of applause which the house paid you on Saturday night. I do believe some in the gallery could have gone on applauding you before the curtain "till it were morrow." And you received the hearty applause so gracefully and sweetly. It was all delightful.

I suppose you heard that one young fellow in the centre of the gallery, when all the other people had left their seats and were filing out, remained fixed in his place in a sort of reverie, and when told by the attendant that he must move, cried, "Oh, no, I am going to wait here for *The Masqueraders.*"

The young man had a week to wait for the reappearance of his heroine, however. During those days Stella and Pat went to stay at North End House in Rottingdean, at the foot of the Sussex Downs, lent to them for a second honeymoon by Sir Edward and Lady Burne-Jones. There Pat had his wife almost to himself at last, and they could try to knit their lives together again. It was not easy. Pat did not want to talk about the years in Africa. He did tell her about one big-game shooting expedition, and how his dear friend was mauled by a lion, and how he carried him miles until he died in his arms. He had buried Hannay as best he could. Only this horror to bring back, instead of the lion and tiger skins he'd promised Beo and the fortune in gold mines he'd promised his wife.

Yet with Stella and the fresh air of the downs and the quiet comfort of North End House, Pat revived. "This place is so beautiful," Stella wrote Lulo that week, "& the comfort & peace & the dear little dog car & pony, & drives into Brighton every day—& dinner at the Metropole with the Trees & Parker. . . . How did you & Jo enjoy the show on Saturday. The audience was horribly noisy & I was very tame, I thought. Pat is well & very happy." A letter from "Dearest" (Sir Edward) arrived, begging them to stay for months and months, telling Stella to throw any books, furniture, or pictures that annoyed her out the window, telling her to order a piano from Brighton. But Stella had to be back in London for the premiere of *The Masqueraders* on Saturday, April 28.

Alexander awaited opening night with dread. Except as David and Dulcie, he and his leading lady were still not in communication. There was no tactful Pinero to intercede for him. He had made the terrible mistake (he now realized) of letting Stella Campbell know she could upset him; this admission of vulnerability only inspired her to new caprices. She could (he now admitted) break or make a production: one moment she could be listless, derisive, bored; the next she could come to life and lift an audience to ecstacy. He had no idea which mood would have Mrs. Pat in its grip on opening night.

But he might have guessed. Stella did not like the part or the play, and was determined that the audience should know it. She accomplished this by removing herself emotionally from the action on the stage. Not even the presence of a glittering first-night audience that included the future King George and Queen Mary and Lord and Lady Randolph Churchill could inspire her to play Dulcie as she had played Paula. Recklessly she dared to lose all she had gained. It was as though she deliberately challenged the public: you loved me when I was good, she seemed to be saying; love me now even though I choose to be bad.

Clement Scott did not choose to do so. "Here we had a play brilliantly mounted, accurately presented, a marvel of production even in these days of astounding realism," he raged in the *Daily Telegraph*; "and behold the whole thing, actors' work, sumptuous decoration, gorgeous mounting, and the author's brilliant brain work, within an ace of being wasted because the most talked about actress of the day would not, or could not, understand one of the most beautiful, complex, and subtle studies of women that any dramatist has offered us in the whole range of the modern drama. . . . Was ever a finer dramatic opportunity given to an actress? But Mrs. Patrick Campbell passed it over as insignificant and beneath her notice. A Sarah Bernhardt would have leaped at it. . . ."

Not all critics agreed that Dulcie Larondie was a great dramatic opportunity, William Archer among them; many praised her performance, condemning Clement Scott for treating her brutally. Letters of sympathy poured in from friends and strangers. Pembroke had been too ill to attend her opening night, but had read *The Masqueraders* and found it "full of crudities, absurdities, and anachronisms," though it had some "cleverness and go." "Nor does your part seem to me altogether a bad one (except that I can't conceive how you get through the 'Yah, Yah, Yah' business without sending the audience into convulsions) if *Mrs. Tanqueray* had never been written. As it is, it is really cruel—Dulcie is only a weak edition of Paula under different circumstances. . . . This is really too bad, and I sympathise sincerely." Such letters lulled Stella's conscience. If the Earl of Pembroke thought Dulcie a poor part, then Alexander, Jones, and the critics didn't really matter. She might better have heeded Dearest's advice, however. He also sympathized and advised her not to waste time reading critics, but only because there was a better critic—"one's own savage, bitter self." Had Stella begun to cultivate this critic, she might have had more difficulty excusing her throw-away performance of Dulcie Larondie.

The result was predictable. It encouraged the suspicion that she was a one-part actress, a fluke. Writing to Elizabeth Robins from Rome, Henry James voiced a not uncommon doubt: "I . . . want to hear if Mrs. Campbell is only relatively, or quite positively, a failure in Jones's play—and if you've seen the latter? If she *is* a failure what was the meaning, or verity, of all the exaltation of her 'art' and talent and charm in the other thing? Such qualities, when an actress has them, don't pop in and out of holes (out of parts) like mice! But you will tell me all about this—over a glass of vermouth."

The play was not a failure, however; only a misery to its co-stars. The feud continued, and at least once erupted during a performance. There was a scene in which David Remon had to clasp Dulcie Larondie "with sudden abandonment" and proclaim his love. Alexander clasped, but proclaimed his passion with such a wild glare of hatred, as though he would like to have wrung her neck, that Stella burst out laughing. This was an unheard-of breach of decorum on the stage of the St. James's. As soon as the curtain fell, Alexander sent his stage manager to Stella's dressing room. "Mr. Alexander's compliments," announced Mr. Vincent, "and will you please not laugh at him on the stage?" Stella could never resist deflating pomposity. "My compliments to Mr. Alexander," she retorted, "and please tell him I never laugh at him until I get home."

*The Masqueraders* ended its first run on July 30, and again Alexander prepared to tour after the August holidays with both Jones's play and *The Second Mrs. Tanqueray* on the bill. This time, however, Stella Campbell was not in the company. Blond, blue-eyed Evelyn Millard took over the role of Dulcie, and Charlotte Granville was given Paula. Both Alexander and Stella had had enough.

About this time Stella moved from lodgings in Manchester Street to 53 Ashley Gardens, settling with Pat, Beo, little Stella, and She at an address that was almost Belgravia, almost St. James's. There she created an atmosphere of comfort and charm in the blue-and-white drawing room with its big bow window. There were cosy couches, silver curios, her piano. Handel's snuffbox and shoebuckles presented by Curley Bates, and an old spyglass in a velvet case, also believed to have been Handel's. Kelmscott Press volumes bound in gold-tooled white vellum and tied with narrow green gold-tasseled ribbons. A sketch of Ellen Terry as Ophelia by her first husband, George Frederick Watts. A water color of herself by Lulo. Shimmering brocades adorning the tables. Palms and heaps of fresh flowers, tributes from countless admirers. Stella herself, dressed like a duchess in her favorite sables, silks, and satins dripping with lace and passementerie. And Stella's friends, always Stella's friends.

One of these was Irene Vanbrugh, the young actress who had played Lady Charley Wishanger in *The Masqueraders*. Stella liked and encouraged her. "She was charming to me and we became friends," said Irene, "and I spent many amusing days in her flat in Ashley Gardens where she was the centre of an important and very distinguished circle of friends, among whom she numbered Sir Edward and Lady Burne-Jones and their charming daughter and son-in-law, Professor and Mrs. Mackail. Her own two children were a delight to me—Stella, a shy and very lovely girl rather harassed by her brilliant mother, and Beo, a spoilt attractive boy." Irene did not fail to notice Pat's plight. "Her husband, Patrick Campbell, was silent, quiet, and bewildered in the strange atmosphere in which he found it almost impossible to be anybody—certainly not himself."

With Pat home, Stella could find it easier to forgive Lulo's desertion. "From all I hear, dear Lulo, my objecting to your enterprise causes you unhappiness," she wrote from Ashley Gardens. "Please, I don't object *any more* to anything. Go your own way & for Gods sake be happy." Eventually, paying a visit to Nina, who was expecting another baby, and discussing Lulo with their older sister, she came to regard the situation even more favorably. "On the main point we all agree," she told Lulo afterwards, "that you are & look much happier than you ever have in your life before—& the secret of it is that with 'Jo' you can do as *you* like. With me you would have had to do mostly as I liked—& so with Nina & Uncle & Mother (if she had even a few pence of her own)—& any stranger, companion or child's governess that you were. So everything is for the best—indeed now I regret nothing, and I am sure even Nina will have to own someday that I have struggled hard to do the best for all of you, as well as myself. I am very glad you have 'Jo' & I hope you won't help her lose her money & that you love her as much as she loves you."

In these months Stella tried her best to establish some kind of regular life for the four of them without giving up the celebrity's life she was quite happy to lead. People who expected to find her in bohemian lodgings were always surprised at the orderly charm of her flat. Beo went to school at Ripley Court in Surrey, and Stella hired a Miss Rentry on a month's trial as governess to her daughter and companion-secretary-housekeeper to herself. "Little Stella seems to love being here," she told Lulo. And Pat, thank God, seemed to be recovering his health and was looking around for something in the City. And for Mrs. Patrick Campbell, Herbert Tree was looking around for a play.

Stella's contract stipulated that, should Tree go to America, he had the option of leaving her behind with half-salary; that, should she go to America, her salary would increase to £80 a week, with not more than three parts a week to play; that no one in the company was to be given greater prominence in the advertisements; and that Tree had the option of re-engaging her for the 1895–1896 season. This was favorable, yet her salary—£60—was what Alexander had paid for Dulcie at the St. James's. Eventually Tree decided upon C. Haddon Chambers's *John-a-Dreams*; he'd had a success with Chambers's *Captain Swift* in 1888. At a reading Stella noted that her role seemed oddly familiar. Kate Cloud, now a celebrated singer dripping with sables and lace, had a past, like Paula Tanqueray. And two men wanted her: one a poet and visionary (like David Remon), the other a wicked baronet (like Sir Brice Skene). The play began and ended on the baronet's yacht, *Moonbeam.* In between, poet and baronet contested for Kate, the poet with invocations to waves and moonlight, the baronet with opium. Finally the poet hero and his clergyman father boarded the yacht to save Kate from dishonor as the *Moonbeam* flew out to sea.

Stella got along better with the impulsive, romantic Tree, who ran his theatre through the force of personal magnetism and a competent stage manager, since he himself was notoriously careless and absent-minded. *John-a-Dreams* opened on November 8, 1894, and Stella played Kate Cloud with much of the enchantment she had shown as Paula; but if Tree had hoped that the actress would give him a hit, he had chosen the wrong play. Stella's forte was playing an intelligent, feeling woman in rebellion. Chambers had built no such scope into Kate Cloud. "It is entirely the fault of the author," sympathized the *National Observer*, "that we cannot quite believe in Kate Cloud. But . . . Mrs. Campbell brings to it all the subtle undefinable charm, the intensity of subdued emotion, the absolute spontaneity and avoidance of conscious effect, that promise to make her the Eleonora Duse of the English stage."

But a few critics were becoming bored with the "woman-with-a-past." Clement Scott, for one, sighed that he was weary of "these soiled doves of modern romance" and their perennial problem of how a lingering stigma is to be wiped out and leave no trace to mar the future. The more astute Archer saw that Chambers had given Kate Cloud a past for two reasons: first, because that kind of titillation was currently in fashion; second, because the plot demanded it. "The heroine has frayed the hem of her robe on the Piccadilly pavement to no other end than that she may insist on giving the hero half an hour for reflection, that half-hour being essential to the execution of the villain's plot." Kate's past had nothing to do with her character; the frayed hem was mended to perfection, she was all purity and refinement. It seemed the problem of so many modern plays—the dramatist dared to make his heroine sexually experienced, then lost courage and refused to show any reflection of that experience on her character.

Pinero's daring to show Paula as inexorably tainted had created the impact of *The Second Mrs. Tanqueray.* Of course, one could argue that Chambers was the more progressive in showing that sexual experience was no more contaminating for a woman than for a man. Yet *John-a-Dreams* lacked the excitement of *Tanqueray* or even *The Masqueraders*, and on December 27 Tree took off the play. Maud Tree presented Stella with a bunch of orchids in a silver holder. Tree went to America. Stella stayed home.

Although it was early in her career, Stella was clearly not going to enjoy playing leading lady to an actor-manager. Over at the Lyceum, Ellen Terry managed to maintain her sixteen-year reign as Henry Irving's queen by her policy of never interfering with the autocratic actor. Always his friend, perhaps his lover, she was nevertheless awed by him. She asked for nothing, smoothed his way, never contradicted. "Every little miss" at the Lyceum gave Irving more trouble than she, Ellen told Bernard Shaw ruefully. Her immense popularity and a salary of £200 a week made her situation tenable, of course. Yet she was aware that it was Irving who chose the plays, Irving who dictated policy, Irving who set the tempo of their acting. Sunny and good-tempered on the surface, Ellen often felt resentment, much as she revered her distinguished partner. But Stella had no such self-control. She could hold neither her temper nor her tongue; she was no actor-manager's foil.

After two disappointing plays the public waited for her to confirm the gifts she had shown as Paula Tanqueray, and Stella waited for another part to which she could bring her magic. She did not have long to wait: Pinero was writing her a new play to be produced by John Hare at the Garrick. It did not come easily. In the autumn of 1894 he was hoping to have it finished by Christmas, but found he had to refuse Henry James's invitation to the first night of the novelist's *Guy Domville* at the St. James's on January 5 because he couldn't take off even a Saturday evening. It should have been finished long ago, he apologized to James, but had turned out to be a more perplexing job than he had reckoned for. To increase the pressure, John Hare's production of Sydney Grundy's *Slaves of the Ring* at the Garrick was an obvious failure, and Hare needed Pinero's play immediately to replace it.

*Slaves of the Ring* came off on January 16. Though still under contract to Tree, Stella signed an agreement with Hare to play seven performances a week for £60, again no advance over her last two contracts. But the play written for her was an advance; and in February Hare called rehearsals for *The Notorious Mrs. Ebbsmith.*

# TEN

## *1895*

M RS. TANQUERAY had been "the second," Mrs. Ebbsmith was "the notorious"—an indication of how much more daring Pinero thought his new play. Paula Tanqueray was a kept woman; Agnes Ebbsmith is something worse: a new woman. She has ideas and a cause, and, as Pinero saw, a woman with ideas is more shocking than a woman with a past. Formerly a platform agitator, Agnes is now nurse and lover to Lucas Cleeve, a high-strung young man several years her junior who, because of a nervous breakdown abroad, has rejected both his career and his wife back in England, and now with Agnes devotes himself to urging their views about marriage.

Their views are radical. From a wretched home with ill-matched parents, Agnes had early stepped into an equally wretched marriage. "It lasted eight years," she tells the shocked but interested Gertrude Thorpe, sister of the Reverend Amos Winterfield. "For about twelve months he treated me like a woman in a harem, for the rest of the time like a beast of burden." Lucas Cleeve has also been disillusioned by his marriage of convenience, although he tolerated it for less than three years—"Men don't suffer as patiently as women," explains Agnes. As a result, both of them have renounced marriage and are living together in Venice. "You would go your different ways if ever you found that one of you was making the other unhappy?" asks Gertrude incredulously. Agnes affirms it. "We remain together only to help, to heal, to console. Why should men and women be so eager to grant to each other the power of wasting life? That is what Marriage gives—the right to destroy years and years of life. And the right once given, it *attracts, attracts!* . . . We are done with Marriage; we distrust it. We are not now among those who regard Marriage as indispensable to union. We have done with it!"

For 1895 this was radical thinking and practice. But Agnes is defeated: she retracts, repents, suffers. Her first defeat comes when she discovers that Lucas doesn't really care about the cause, but is eager for her to drop her "plain Agnes" role and become a sensual woman for his pleasure. She capitulates by putting on the daring dress he has bought her. The gown transforms her. She admits that to be desired by a man is a woman's greatest triumph. "Dear me, how amusin' you women are!" sneers the cynical Duke of St. Olpherts. "And in your dowdy days you had ambitions! They were of a queer, gunpowder-and-faggot sort—but they were ambitions." "Yes," replies Agnes, remembering that once her dream had been to lead the masses out of ignorance, "that is what I once hoped would be my hour. But this *is* my hour."

But she must be brought lower. The weak Lucas is persuaded to return to England and live with his wife for the sake of his political career. For Agnes there would be "the suburban villa, the little garden, a couple of discreet servants"—the usual trappings of the mistress. Informed by St. Olpherts of the plan, Agnes is incredulous: "His love may not last—it won't!—but at this moment he loves me better than that! He wouldn't make a mere light thing of me!" "Wouldn't he!" smiles St. Olpherts. "You try him!" She does; Lucas fails the test.

Had Pinero wanted truth, this should have been the climax of the play. Agnes is faced with the reality that the man she loves will put convenience before principle and, for his own happiness, urge her to do the same. She has the choice of returning to England as his mistress and renouncing her beliefs, or being true to herself and renouncing Lucas. The dilemma is severe, for there are two Agneses—the "lean witch of the Iron Hall at St. Luke's" and the sensual Agnes of the bare white arms and passionate heart. And, had Pinero remained true to the character he created, Lucas Cleeve would have returned to England alone. A wiser Agnes would have kept her faith, having learned, however, two hard lessons: that the time for her ideas had not come, and that she was far more vulnerable to the comforts of conventionality than she believed.

But Pinero chose to muddle truth with religion. Belatedly the audience is made to discover that Agnes only took to social reform because religion had failed her. "I'd trusted it, clung to it, and it failed me," she cries to Gertrude and the Reverend Winterfield, striking the Holy Bible with her fist. "Never once did it stop my ears to the sound of a curse; when I was beaten it didn't make the blows a whit the lighter; it never healed my bruised flesh, my bruised spirit!" Throughout the play the Reverend Winterfield and his sister have been circling Agnes, fascinated and repelled by her life of sin. (Lucas's life of sin is apparently irrelevant, though he is committing adultery and Agnes is not.) Now, as they leave the room, Agnes hurls the Bible into the fire. A loud cry hurries them back: Agnes has thrust her arm into the stove and pulled the book out of the flames.

They know now she can be saved, and Agnes goes back to England to live with them, humbled, converted, and convinced that she has irreparably wronged Lucas's wife.

"The *rôle* of Agnes Ebbsmith and the first three acts of the play filled me with ecstasy," said Stella. "There was a touch of nobility that fired and inspired me, but the last act broke my heart. I knew that such an Agnes in life could not have drifted into the Bible-reading inertia of the woman she became in the last act: for her earlier vitality, with its mental and emotional activity, gave the lie to it—I felt she would have arisen a phoenix from the ashes.

"That rounding off of plays to make the audience feel comfortable is a regrettable weakness.

"To me Agnes was a finer woman, and the part a greater one, than Mrs. Tanqueray . . . she was a new and daring type, the woman agitator, the pessimist, with original, independent ideas—in revolt against sham morals." But, as Stella saw in retrospect, in 1895 the suffragette with her hammer in her muff had not yet risen up in England; and again, as in *Tanqueray*, Pinero did not dare to let his revolutionary woman go unpunished.

Stella liked John Hare, manager of the Garrick since it had been built for him in 1889. He had, she thought, "a delicious way of looking at you on the stage with an absolutely sane eye." He was playing the Duke of St. Olpherts, the best part after Agnes Ebbsmith; lines like "I can't approach women—I never could—in the missionary spirit" could momentarily eclipse Agnes's tragedy, she knew. Exacting and courteous, Pinero manipulated his actress with tact, and Stella allowed herself to feed gently from his hand. He sent out copies of the play (published by Heinemann) to critics Scott and Archer to give them time to adjust to its provocative subject. Yet, although Pinero made a few cuts at rehearsals, the play remained untouched by the Censor, and the anxiety that had marked rehearsals of *Tanqueray* was absent now.

For the unsympathetic but important part of Lucas Cleeve, Hare had engaged Johnston Forbes-Robertson. It was a happy reunion, since Forbes-Robertson had made a great name for himself in Pinero's *The Profligate*, Hare's first play at the Garrick. Stella saw a slender man of forty-two with clear gray eyes and dark, curling hair. Although just her height, he moved with natural grace and distinction; his hands were fine and supple; his rich, melodious voice perhaps the finest on the stage. Like Stella, Forbes was a natural actor; unlike Stella's, his natural style had a pedigree, for the Shakespearian player Samuel Phelps had taken a fancy to Forbes and coached him in the technique he had inherited from Garrick through Mrs. Siddons and Macready. Forbes had acted with Mary Anderson in England

and America, and played Romeo to Modjeska's Juliet when Stella was only fifteen. His experience and presence thus intimidated her, while his patrician manner intrigued her. A quick attraction sprang up between them.

Before *The Notorious Mrs. Ebbsmith* opened on March 13, 1895, advance bookings beat the previous record at the Garrick. Stella wished Agnes might have risen like "a phoenix from the ashes" in the last act. Instead, she rose like a phoenix from the ashes of two mediocre performances as Dulcie and Kate, not only equaling her performance as Paula but, in the opinion of many, surpassing it. The cheers at curtain fall were deafening. The curtain rose again and again—the audience could not seem to get enough of the tall, unearthly figure of Mrs. Patrick Campbell. This time it was clear to many more that it was the actress rather than the play that was superb. "What I thought of the play?" said Edmund Gosse. "Well, I have a great difficulty in saying, for, to tell the truth, you swamped the play for me. The play was—you." Jack Mackail was there the first night, went again on Friday, and returned with Margaret the following Wednesday. "You are with the Immortals now," he wrote after the first performance. "I can't begin to talk about it; it seems like an insult to praise it; it was like the inner flower of fire. . . . The splendour of you!" "Sir John Hare and Mrs. Patrick Campbell both played magnificently, and Mrs. Campbell enjoyed a triumph," raved Maurice Baring. "She held the audience at the beginning of the play by her grace, and by her quiet magnetic intensity, and then swept everyone off their feet by her outbursts of vituperation. . . . After the third act the audience applauded deliriously, and the next day the critics declared unanimously that Mrs. Campbell had the ball at her feet."

Stella's Agnes dazzled even the most hardened. Bernard Shaw, currently dramatic critic for the *Saturday Review*, brought to his work a brilliant mind, a slashing style, and the determination to expose everyone in the theatre not going his way as hopelessly benighted. Pinero's way was not Shaw's way. Pinero might clutch a few of the seamy garments of the New Drama about him, but Shaw detected evening dress underneath. He had dismissed *Tanqueray* as a play "all about a poor lady who committed suicide because they wouldn't let her finish playing her piece at the piano"; he howled with rage at the ode to duty that ended *The Masqueraders*. He went to the Garrick ready to pounce on Pinero's pretensions to hard realism, and his notice announced, predictably, "I disliked the play so much that nothing would induce me to say anything good of it."

His opinion of the actress was something else, however. He had had his eye on her from the beginning. In 1893, for example, looking about for an actress who would dare to play his brothel-keeper in *Mrs. Warren's Profession*, he told J. T. Grein, "I should be content, myself, with Mrs. Patrick

Campbell. The part is a vulgar one; but unless the vulgarity is the artistic vulgarity of a refined actress . . . the part will be unendurable." He had been able to explain to Charles Charrington why his wife, Janet Achurch, did not get Pinero's bid for *Tanqueray*: "The fact is, Pinero has a very fine sense of the people he wants for his particular style of work; and Janet has not [*sic*] adequate idea of how completely she belongs to another epoch. Mrs. Pat is exactly the woman for him. He is in the position to have exactly what he likes; and naturally he is not content with mere acting . . . he wants *being*; and [Janet] *isn't.*" Now he approached Stella for the first time as a critic. There was only one good thing to be said about Pinero's play, he declared, and that was that its unreality left Mrs. Campbell free to do what she liked with Agnes Ebbsmith, "the result being an irresistible projection of that lady's personal genius, a projection which sweeps the play aside and imperiously becomes the play itself. Mrs. Patrick Campbell, in fact, pulls her author through by playing him clean off the stage. She creates all sorts of illusions, and gives one all sorts of searching sensations. It is impossible not to feel that those haunting eyes are brooding on a momentous past, and the parted lips anticipating a thrilling imminent future, whilst some enigmatic present must no less surely be working underneath all that subtle play of limb and stealthy intensity of tone. Clearly there must be a great tragedy somewhere in the immediate neighborhood; and most of my colleagues will no doubt tell us that this imaginary masterpiece is Mr. Pinero's Notorious Mrs. Ebbsmith. But Mr. Pinero has hardly anything to do with it. When the curtain comes down, you are compelled to admit that, after all, nothing has come of it except your conviction that Mrs. Patrick Campbell is a wonderful woman." It was not a conviction that Shaw would easily shed.

Stella was not allowed to glory as Agnes Ebbsmith long, however. Tree's American tour had brought him neither financial nor critical success, and he decided that his return must be spectacular. Stella's triumph at the Garrick tantalized him with dreams of an equal triumph for the Haymarket, especially in a crowd-pleaser like Victorien Sardou's *Fedora*, "a part to tear a cat in." Understandably, Stella did not share his enthusiasm. Despite objections, she loved Pinero's play, writing in her copy, "This play was produced at the Garrick Theatre on Wednesday, March 13 1895, and I had the happiness of being the first to play Agnes Ebbsmith." She was already exhausted with eight performances a week, inspiring from Myra Pinero a note of warning: "You are so gifted and have made such a gigantic hit. I don't want your voice to show wear. . . . It struck me last night you were *tired*. Am I right? Do give up late hours and rest all day if you can." Now she was expected to go on with *Ebbsmith* and at the same time rehearse *Fedora*, a part written for the vocal acrobatics of Sarah Bernhardt. She protested, but Tree would not release her. "It was an impossible feat," said Stella correctly. "I had only time to study the last act—the death scene—of this more than exacting *rôle*."

On May 11 she left the Garrick, having written Pinero of her disappointment. "Accept my thanks for your letter and for the very kind sentiments it contains," he replied. "You have my warm wishes for a continuation, under Mr. Tree's management, of the success which you have so worthily and so conspicuously won elsewhere." It was hard to be sporting when his play was being robbed of its life-blood. Olga Nethersole replaced Stella, "And this most brilliant and successful play," as Stella put it, "unfortunately did not survive the change of cast."

Thus far Stella had created all four of her West End roles. The part of Princess Fedora Romazoff was a great acting role that required a standard technique. "We know quite well what effects the author intended," explained critic William Archer, "and by what methods they are to be attained. No novelty of subject, no intellectual interest, distracts attention from what may be called the sheer mimetics of the performance—the realisation and expression of Fédora's states of feeling. . . ." Sarah Bernhardt had been exploiting *Fedora*'s pyrotechnics since the play's sensational opening night in Paris in 1882: sumptuous wardrobes, dazzling entrances, vocal tricks that ran the gamut from sibilant cooings to spine-tingling shrieks. Stella was already famous for her "wind-in-the-chimney" voice, but it did not have Bernhardt's range. Nor did she have time to develop it, or even to adequately absorb the part by the night of the play's opening on Saturday, May 25.

Such was Stella's dazzle at this time, however, that with audiences she could hardly do wrong. "With its first audience Mrs. Campbell's Fedora unquestionably triumphed," conceded the *Morning Post*. "The personal charm exercised by this actress is undeniable. Her expressive features, her graceful figure, the searching quality of her voice, the careful distinctness of her enunciation, the significance of her rare gestures, all count for much in all she undertakes." But not all critics were lulled by her extraordinary popular success. The *Daily Telegraph* declared that there *was* only one way to play Fedora—the Bernhardt way. Frustratingly, the actress had even risen beyond those heights, yet it had not been enough. "For three acts Mrs. Patrick Campbell was in a daze or a dream; for one act, that the last, she played Fedora with a pathetic beauty, a natural charm, and a passionate tenderness such as have never yet been applied to this most difficult part by Sarah Bernhardt or any of her successors. Had Mrs. Campbell played the first three acts as she did the last she would have stood without a rival. Unfortunately she did not."

In the spring of 1895, however, there was really only one critic whom actors, managers, and playwrights had learned to dread. Shaw disliked Sardou and all he stood for: in a review titled "Sardoodledom" he destroyed the play that next week. He scorned Sardou's elaborate plots, so bristling with postal, telegraphic, and police arrangements that the main business of the play was hopelessly entangled. He derided Sardou's characters: Tree's Loris Ipanoff, "a vulgar scoundrel as far as he is credibly human at all," and Fedora, who "sinks to his level when, on learning that her husband preferred another woman to her, she gloats over his murder." He scorned Mrs. Campbell's acting: bad as the play was, her acting was worse. But Shaw's chief objection to the current London stage was plays that made sex the most important motivation in the world, so that the hero never lifts a finger unless he is sexually attracted to the heroine, and the heroine exists only to arouse the sexual interest of the male. For the theatre to make sex, that "most capricious, most transient, most easily baffled of all instincts," the basis of its appeal was not only "an intolerable perversion of human conduct," but a terrible bore.

Stella Campbell possessed great sex appeal. Dismayed by its attraction, Shaw sought an outlet in ridicule. Tree had a terrible time playing the melodramatic villain in Polish make-up, said Shaw. "Besides, Mrs. Campbell ruined his clothes. Wherever her beautiful white arms touched him they left their mark. She knelt at his feet and made a perfect zebra of his left leg with bars across it. Then she flung her arms convulsively right round him; and the next time he turned his back to the footlights there was little to choose between his coatback and his shirtfront. Before the act was over a gallon of benzine would hardly have set him right again." Yet Tree had his revenge, Shaw observed, for when he fell across her body, he managed to transfer a large patch of his black dye to her cheek, which was in plain evidence when the lady took her curtain calls. Shaw could recommend soap and water to Mrs. Patrick Campbell; it was an excellent cosmetic and had the added merit that it did not leave her lovers marked for life. Archer had said "the sight of Mrs. Campbell charmed the masculine senses"; Shaw admitted that the moment she appeared reason collapsed and judgment fled. But he was determined not to be Ulysses to this Circe.

After two weeks of *Fedora* the fatigue that Myra Pinero had noticed in *Ebbsmith* won out, and Stella lost her voice. Maud Tree learned the part one night and played it the next—such are the hazards of being wife to the actor-manager. The play closed prematurely on July 19, unfortunately (as

Stella would have said) not surviving the change of cast. She did not grieve deeply over her defection. It rather served Tree right for taking her away from the Garrick.

She had the summer to recover. Beo came home for the holidays, and Stella continued to spoil him. "I was very good in church today, Mamma," boasted Beo one Sunday. "How did you manage that?" asked Stella. "First I saw how long I could keep one eye shut," confided the boy, "and then the other." Stella laughed indulgently. Her relationship with her daughter was different: there was already rivalry. "I was so frightened of mother, I would hide under the table when she came home from the theatre," the daughter would say years later. Irene Vanbrugh had noted that little Stella was "rather harassed" by her famous mother. Yet in letters to Lulo, little Stella was always "the baby," "the pet."

Stella now wrote to Lulo: "Pat & Bayo go to Stranraer on Monday. Would you care to come & stay for a bit? You can have Pat's room. . . . You need only see the people you care to—& there's no need for dress. I have pieces of white lace to work transformations with. Phil would take you to the galleries & Watts's & other studios & in fact I think you might be happy. . . . When you want to go & see Jo you can—& only one thing I ask you—don't bring her here. There—I shall not be hurt if you refuse & I shall be *very pleased* if you come. . . . It's only her voice & ways that get on my nerves. She is a dear girl, I know & very sweet to you." Stella had quite made it up with her sister, and had begun to encourage her to go on the stage. She even wanted her mother to take a part someday: she believed the whole family had acting in their blood.

After the failure of *Fedora*, Tree left for a holiday at Marienbad. From the spa he wrote to Maud, encouraging her not to think of her performance as a failure and, at the same time, girding himself for the fall season, when he hoped that *Trilby* would prove the success *Fedora* had not. "I feel this Marienbad cure will set me up for the entire year," he wrote hopefully, "and I know it is important that I should have all my powers for the coming campaign—especially as Robertson is now in the field."

In the autumn it was Henry Irving's custom to lease the Lyceum and take his company on either a provincial or an American tour. That fall he and Ellen Terry would make their fifth visit to the United States, his first as Sir Henry, for in May Queen Victoria had knighted him, an unprecedented honor for an actor. That summer Forbes-Robertson bid to take the Lyceum for the fall season. He had not forgotten Stella; he was perhaps already in love with her. Shortly after she left the cast of *Ebbsmith*, he approached her with an offer to play Juliet to his Romeo. His terms were generous and binding. He would pay her £30 a week until her contract with Tree expired, she not to play in any other theatre before acting Juliet. After the expiration she would receive £100 a week. Dresses provided. In addition to the £100, two per cent of the gross receipts whenever they should exceed £180 per performance, percentage to be paid weekly. Salary suspended if unable to perform, and Forbes-Robertson to have the option of her services for the next Lyceum play. On May 20 Stella had signed.

That summer, therefore, was not just country weekends at Stanway and Mells and Clouds and carriage drives through Richmond Park and dinner at Claridge's. There was her serious London debut as a Shakespearian actress to think of: the dread of living up to Lyceum standards, the knowledge that Irving had let Forbes have the Lyceum only if he could get Mrs. Patrick Campbell. There was also the knowledge that Forbes already thought of her as something more than a leading lady. Neither prospect made her very happy. Writing condolences to the Countess of Pembroke that August for the death of her husband, that handsome lord who had first encouraged her Rosalind, Stella could not help speaking of her own worries. "I wish I could help you," wrote the Countess sympathetically in reply. But only hard work and courage could help her with Juliet; and with the man who would play her Romeo, only the dictates of her conscience and her heart.

# ELEVEN

# 1895

*S*TELLA HAD ALREADY succeeded as a Shakespearian actress, of course. "Youth in my memory is Mrs. Patrick Campbell, playing in the open air for Ben Greet's Company at the Clifton Zoo," wrote the author Stephen Gwynn. ". . . I saw a Rosalind whose speech was running music, giving the verse all its inflections as easily as a bird sings; never denying you the rhythm, yet always moulding the rhythm to the meaning; and with this melody ran another speech of gesture, as fluent and as naturally varying, one movement passing without break into the next. . . . The gaiety, and the sparkle and the woodland music that are in Shakespeare's romantic comedies as nowhere else in the world . . . she . . . brought us walking and speaking and laughing and singing there before us. . . . Nobody, not even Miss Ellen Terry ever played one of these parts as Mrs. Campbell played Rosalind under the sunshine that summer afternoon."

But outdoor Shakespeare with a touring company was not Shakespeare at London's most prestigious theatre, where Irving and Terry held court with elaborately mounted productions of the Bard. Nor had she played opposite an actor trained in classic Shakespearian style. She knew she could not acquire this training in a few months; she decided, therefore, to make her Juliet simple and, above all, young. She began to go through her part with a coach, trying the balcony and "What's in a name?" speeches perched on her piano in place of a balcony, but had a hard time finding an artistic position that day, she told Lulo, because she was afraid of falling off. As opening night approached, she grew more and more apprehensive and clutched at Lulo for advice. "Does it look well when I fall on my knees after the scene with nurse & cards?" she demanded after a rehearsal. "Are the tears there when I weep real? Can our faces be seen enough at the window at the farewell? Did I look well on the tomb—is the veil close enough to my face—can you see my features through it—was the fall right &

the language delivered simply enough—or would tears in the voice be better there?"

Stella was not the only apprehensive one. This was Forbes-Robertson's first experience as manager. He would gladly have remained an actor on hire. He had little business sense and the speculative nature of theatrical management was distasteful to him. He also knew that the duties and anxieties of management would handicap his performance, already handicapped by the extreme nervousness he always felt on stage. But he wished to take his place in the front rank; other actors younger than he had taken up management, and he saw no other way to compete with them. He was lucky enough to engage his brother Ian Robertson as stage manager, since Ian had acted and managed in America with Modjeska, Julia Marlowe, Lawrence Barrett, and Edwin Booth. Ian was devoted to Forbes; it was he who finally assumed the heavier burdens of the production, not the least of which he discovered to be dealing with the moods of Mrs. Patrick Campbell.

On the morning of September 21 Forbes surveyed the situation and was not cheered. Nutcombe Gould, cast as Friar Laurence, had one arm in a sling. Charles Coghlan, summoned out of semi-retirement to play Mercutio, was paralyzed with nervousness at the thought of his reappearance in London after many years. And his leading lady had every appearance of cracking. "Mason's write that the way I do my hair with the pink dress spoils," Stella scribbled feverishly to Lulo. "Does it look very modern? I only have about 3 minutes. What can you suggest? Shall I have it down all the while? Does my head strike you as *modern?* Let me know at once. I am beginning to feel so nervous. I shall be thankful when its over. My cold is dreadful & my voice queer today. . . . Draw a suggestion for a head. Your B."

That evening Louisa Tanner, Uncle Harry, Nina, Lulo, and Pat Campbell joined the resplendent first-night audience to see their Beatrice triumph or fail as Juliet. (Max had refused to come because he did not like to be kept up so late.) The air was electric with expectation. The pittites and gallery had come early, armed with campstools, flasks, and packets of sandwiches; even the occupants of the private boxes and numbered seats were in their places well before curtain time. Diane Creyke, a friend of Stella's, shared the excitement. "It was very amusing watching the people arrive," she said, "only I didn't know who they were. One woman was tremendously applauded by the gallery, and got up from her stall and bowed. The curtain went up at eight, and when Mrs. Pat came on there were tremendous cheers. It was most exciting. She looked excessively young, with her hair down and a wreath of flowers. Her ball dress was lovely—a mixture of flame colour and cloth of gold with angels round it. She didn't seem a bit nervous, but her voice was not very strong. The audience was tremendously enthusiastic, but I was rather disappointed there were so many scenes, and it seemed disconnected. But Mrs. Pat, except for not speaking loud enough, was perfection."

Pat Campbell came round between the acts with a message from Stella that Diane must come back to Ashley Gardens for supper after the performance. She went, and found Nina and Lulo, little Beo and Stella, Mrs. Tanner, Uncle Harry, two ladies she didn't know, and Irene Vanbrugh. They began supper without Stella, who had been kept at the theatre, but in the midst of it she burst into the room in white muslin with her hair down and rushed at her mother, crying, "Oh, Mamma, your daughter has been making such a fool of herself!"

Not all critics thought so the next day. "Not the above-named pair, but love itself is the hero of this play," rhapsodized A. B. Walkley. "These words of Heine's came into my mind as I sat in the Lyceum on Saturday night, listening to the most exquisite of all love poems, feeling that love was not only there pictured on the stage, but in the air all around me, the central interest, the dear secret or else the sacred memory of all the men and women in that crowded house. The place seemed turned by the magic of the poet's and the actor's art into a very temple of love." Then he turned to the Juliet. "Here is Mrs. Patrick Campbell, with her child's face, her black eyes and raven locks, her mere slip of a body . . . with the child's simplicity of mien, with every index of a child's heart. Listen to her in the balcony scene, the soft words of love pour from her lips like the babble of a brook. . . . She leans forward, far forward, till her hair tumbles down so as almost to reach Romeo, and murmurs in tones so true, so heartfelt, that they send a thrill through the hushed house, 'Dost thou love me?' . . . Mrs. Patrick Campbell gives us—as no other actress to my knowledge has given us—the child in Juliet. There, for me, is the beginning and end of the matter; so that a more delicious embodiment of Juliet I do not hope to see." Stella could have smiled over that review: Walkley was not an easy critic to win over, nor had he ever particularly been her partisan.

But, as Walkley had interrupted his review to marvel, some critics did not agree. Clement Scott, for example, deplored the modernism of the production. "But they tell us to-day that moderation and suppressed passion, uniformity and unconventionality, are all that need be required for this lovely study. It is all to flow on evenly, smoothly, like a limpid stream or a babbling brook. There are to be no cataracts, no whirlpools, no roaring torrents, in the most passionate and powerful play ever written. It is bad taste in the present age to be enthusiastic—'Bad form, don't yer know'—so it is not the correct thing to play Juliet above your breath, or to 'let yourself go,' as the phrase has it, in one of the grandest characters for a great actress ever conceived. What on earth have monotony and a droning intonation to do with the passionate young lovers of Verona?"

Some critics were divided, finding both good and bad in her performance. During the next days she listened to these, trying to adjust her interpretation to suit them. One critic, for example, praised her in the scenes of tenderness, but decided she lacked the strength for the vehement passages, which she played roughly, changing suddenly from a sweet and gentle girl to a desperate woman. Stella pondered this eruption of Paula Tanqueray into her Juliet, and got Lulo to come again and criticize. "Where are the exact points when I seem too much the woman and to lose the girl's anger—was it with the Friar at 'Bid me leap'?

"I meant 'Here such a coil' to mean that," she continued, defending her interpretation, "but to keep up the rhythm I accentuated *such* & the meaning is clearer if I accentuate *Here*. I thought I took that about the stars much more poetically last night. Yes, it is the grandioso note that is wrong. I *must* keep it *all* simple. . . . You have said nothing about the tomb scene. I particularly want to hear about that. The critic didn't think it impressive. Did I look as pretty as *Fedora?* Was the potion scene *better* without the crash or orchestra? Didn't it seem to you the dance was played a little quicker last night? Did I get on the bed more gracefully & could you see I was swallowing the poison? . . . Did my feet look right on the tomb, would Veil look better all over body?" That flood of questions unleashed, she explained an omission. Juliet constantly calls Romeo "sweet"—"Sweet, good night!" "Sweet, so would I." She had left a lot of these "sweets" out, she told Lulo, because "I DREADED being a *sentimental* Juliet."

Her conception of the part reflected the strengths and weaknesses critics found in this *Romeo and Juliet*. Most thought it visually stunning. All agreed that the pair could hardly have *looked* a more ideal Romeo and Juliet. Most critics were enraptured with the love scenes. Criticism of Stella hit at her dread of being overly sentimental. By going to such lengths to avoid sentimentality, they charged, she failed to inject her creation with the girl's passion and earthiness. She had played her wistfully, poetically, elegantly, tragically, exquisitely, youthfully. But the Juliet of the "Gallop apace, you fiery-footed steeds" speech, the Juliet eager to give up her maidenhead, panting for the night and the consummation of their passion, was missing.

Eventually the speech itself was missing: Stella simply dropped it, a frequent practice in the prudish Victorian theatre, but inexcusable by 1895. This crime pinpointed for Archer all he believed wrong about the new

Lyceum *Romeo and Juliet*. It was intelligent, pretty, lyric, but no "ground-swell of passion" had seized and transported players or audience. He did not think the pair ideal: "Mr. Forbes Robertson and Mrs. Patrick Campbell . . . suffer from opposite defects: the one has skill without temperament, the other temperament without skill. Mr. Robertson can act Romeo, but cannot look or feel the part; Mrs. Campbell could *be* Juliet if she only knew how to act it." Archer shook his head over the success of the opening night, dismissing it as the audience's eagerness to applaud "a beautiful and very popular actress in a character of traditional renown," a pleasure that the playgoer will not easily be cheated of.

"Why, then, should I play spoil-sport at the feast?" he concluded his review of September 25 for the *World*. "Simply because if Mrs. Campbell's Juliet passes muster as a good, not to say a great, performance, there is an end of an art that I am old-fashioned enough to love—the art of Shakespearian acting. Its tradition will be lost more hopelessly than ever, and no one will believe that there are really great and vivid and poignant emotions to be got out of Shakespeare on the stage. I have very little doubt that Mrs. Campbell has other than the merely physical qualifications for the character, and might be a fine Juliet if she would be at the pains of mastering this noblest branch of her art. As it is, she does not even suspect its possibilities. She has somewhere said, if I am not mistaken, that she has never seen another Juliet and knows nothing of the traditions of the part. The more's the pity! It would need a genius comparable with Shakespeare's own to discern unaided all the delicate lights and shades of his conception, and to recognise (to say nothing of grappling with and solving) all the technical problems which he presents to his interpreter. Let it not be said that I am clamouring for a stagey, conventional Juliet. I do not erect tradition into a law, but simply assert its uses as a guide. If it does no more, it concentrates attention upon details, and reveals the existence of difficulties and opportunities which Mrs. Campbell passes gaily by, in total unconsciousness of their existence. If she will consent to regard Saturday's performance as a very slight first sketch for a portrait to be studiously retouched and elaborated, she may one day be the Juliet she looks—and I can wish her nothing better."

It was not Archer's last word. In October he returned to Stella. His article had been written, he said, before he had seen any other reviews and without any suspicion of the extraordinary divergence of opinion Mrs. Campbell's Juliet would excite. It had not crossed his mind that anyone who had ever seen a great Shakespearian performance would find hers adequate. What had been his astonishment, therefore, to find critic after critic going into raptures over an impersonation in which, after the balcony scene, he had been unable to discover a single thrilling moment. This disagreement could not be simply dismissed with "There's no accounting for taste." There were not only traditional standards for Shakespearian acting, but clear indications in the play itself of the kinds of effects Shakespeare intended. Mrs. Campbell had ignored these effects, yet had been praised. Her Juliet, therefore, brought to a head the question of whether the traditional art of Shakespearian acting was to survive. No one hated the old mouthing, ranting Shakespearian school more than he, but that did not mean that all method whatsoever should be abandoned. He could not believe audiences disliked lyric fervor and variety of expression: they had only forgotten all about them. To prefer Mrs. Campbell's Juliet was like preferring *Tristan and Isolde* on a pianoforte. Perhaps this was the coming thing. But in the meantime he could "only marvel to see lack of force, lack of skill, and lack of understanding, accepted as the revelation of a new art."

The analytical restraint of British journalism was lacking in an American report of Stella's Juliet. "A LONDON IDOL IN DANGER," Arthur Warren cabled to the New York *Herald Tribune* on September 25. *"Is She a Great Actress or a Fad of the Hour?"* He went on to urge the latter. Mrs. Campbell was "one of the phenomena of our time." She had won popularity at a single leap, and never, he believed, had there been such instant popularity with so little reason. "A weird, untrained personality," a depressing failure in *The Masqueraders*, ordinary in *John-a-Dreams*. The actress had much to learn about her art. And her performance as Juliet? Lamentable.

No one had been more dissatisfied with her performance on opening night than Stella herself. She continued to listen to critics and worry over her part, writing Lulo, "I have just heard from a critic of the Pall Mall Gazette. A most kind letter. He was in front last night—the only thing he didn't like was the *tomb scene*. He said I wasn't impressive—& I was *all in the dark* & the pause over the stabbing dropped the tragedy. I suppose he couldn't see my expression in my face to explain the pause. Don't you think it would be better if I fell directly I stabbed myself & then crept to his body & fell over it? I think it would. Let me hear." For Stella to turn to Lulo for help when she needed guidance "in all the delicate lights and shades" of Shakespeare's conception, according to Archer, was pathetic. For her to focus on visual stage effects was to run away from the real problem. What effort Forbes made to strengthen her understanding of the lights and shades is unclear; a manager who would let his Juliet drop the "Gallop apace" speech was either satisfied with her performance, intimidated by her temperament, or infatuatedly in love.

As for Bernard Shaw, no one would dream that he would let Stella's acting slip by unscathed, and, indeed, he dismissed it altogether. "As to Juliet, she danced like the daughter of Herodias," he wrote in the *Saturday Review*. "And she knew the measure of her lines to a hairsbreadth. Did I not say, long ago, that Mrs. Tanqueray's piano-playing was worth all the rest of her? And yet I was taken in by Mrs. Tanqueray—also by Mrs. Ebbsmith, as we all were. Woman's great art is to lie low, and let the imagination of the male endow her with depths. How Mrs. Patrick Campbell must have laughed at us whilst we were giving her all the credit—if credit it were—for our silly psychologizing over those Pinero parts! As Juliet she still fits herself into the hospitable manly heart without effort, simply because she is a wonderful person, not only in mere facial prettiness, in which respect she is perhaps not superior to the bevy of 'extra ladies' in the fashionable scenes in the new Drury Lane play, not even in her light, beautifully proportioned figure, but in the extraordinary swiftness and certainty of her physical self-command. I am convinced that Mrs. Patrick Campbell could thread a needle with her toes at the first attempt as rapidly, as smoothly, as prettily, and with as much attention to spare for doing anything else at the same time as she can play an arpeggio. . . . Her Juliet, nevertheless, is an immature performance at all the exceptional points. . . . All the conscious ideas gathered by her from the part and carried out in planned strokes of her own are commonplace. There is not a touch of tragedy, not a throb of love or fear, temper instead of passion: in short, a Juliet as unawakened as Richard III, one in whose death you dont believe, though you would not cry over it if you did believe. Nothing of it is memorable except the dance," concluded Shaw of Stella's brief *pas de seul* with Paris's sword, "—the irresistible dance."

Privately, Shaw began to use Stella Campbell as a thorn to prick Ellen Terry, whom he began to court on paper that autumn. He had finished *The Man of Destiny*; he intended it for the Lyceum, having modelled the "Strange Lady" directly on Ellen. Now he dangled the manuscript temptingly before her, and from America Ellen replied enthusiastically, "Just read your play. Delicious." Shaw fed on her praise for a while, then realized he had nothing more substantial to go on than her friendly note. She was only playing with him, he told her. "I will go to that beautiful Mrs. Patrick Campbell, who won my heart long ago by her pianoforte playing as Mrs. Tanqueray, and make her head twirl like a chimney cowl with my blarney. *She* shall play the Strange Lady—she and the passion-worn Forbes. Yes, it shall be so. Farewell, faithless Ellen!" Ellen pretended to take him seriously. "Your letter! Very well—Pat-Cat! . . . I am sure Mrs. Pat would look much nicer but I think I could play it better." Shaw agreed. *"Anybody* can play Shakspere: you are wanted for other things. Mrs. Pat

Campbell entrances all London as Juliet, with a skirt dance. At the end, to shew that she is not going to give herself more trouble than she can help, she takes the dagger, and with a superb laziness, props it against the tomb and leans against the point, plainly conveying that if it will not go in on that provocation, it can let it alone. Then she lies down beside Romeo and revolves herself right over him like the roller of a mangle, leaving his sensitively chiselled profile perceptibly snubbed. Nothing will persuade me that Shakspere ever carries a modern woman with him right through: even Duse could do nothing with Cleopatra. . . ." For all his jeering, the possibility of the new acting team at the Lyceum for his drama did not escape Shaw. Except for Florence Farr's production of his *Arms and the Man* in 1894, his plays had proved commercial failures. The mere presence of Mrs. Patrick Campbell in one of his plays could make his fortune.

*Romeo and Juliet* ran for seventy-nine performances until December 21. For comfort, Stella had Walkley's praise, which he repeated in *The Album* in October: "I look for an impression of sincerity and beauty from the character as a whole, and I can only say that Mrs. Campbell gives me this impression in a high degree. For me, her Juliet is from first to last an exquisitely truthful and moving performance." She had the comfort of Edmund Gosse's "Your Juliet is an incarnation of girlhood as a poet dreams of it." She had Jack Mackail's "The more I think of your Juliet the finer and more delicately beautiful it seems, and the more eager am I to see it again." She had her friend Barbara Webb's "Well, if it gives you any satisfaction to know that you made people cry and drive home with aching hearts and too excited to sleep, you may have it."

Looking back on her Juliet years later, Stella said, "I played Juliet simply, unpretentiously; I hope with the wonder and the rapture of a romantic, passionate child. In those days, as in these, a declamatory style, exaggerated gesture, rhodomontade in any form, were to me ridiculous. Pomposity, a sense of one's own importance—slow music, gradually getting louder as the artist appears—the unnatural lifting of the voice at exits, compelling the audience to clap their hands—any meretricious form of stage effects exasperated me. I wanted nothing to interfere with the fundamental atmosphere of beauty, simplicity, and truth. Whatever the gamut, it must be within reasonableness; and the 'bottom rock sane.'" Acting, with a capital A, she disdained. In that sense, she did not think of herself as an actress, or of the theatre. "The fag of stage life was not in my blood," she said; "an untidy dressing room; a dresser who called me 'my dear,' smelt of beer, and scratched with a hook down my back until she happened to come across the eye, wore me out." She was often tired; inexperience with fatigue, she felt, many times rendered her performances ineffectual. As the last night neared, she wrote across a photograph of the balcony scene, "Three months' run, and I so miserable at not having played better on the first night." She had no intention of tackling the role again: "What matter, Juliet was over for me, forever!"

Personally, too, these months were troubling. Forbes-Robertson's feeling for her could not be disguised. There was talk, and her fundamentally respectable nature recoiled. There was Pat, poor Pat. She still thought of herself as a wife and mother, a good girl brought up in Dulwich. She could not return Forbes's feelings openly, yet everyone knew that the lovers of *Romeo and Juliet* did not drop their roles offstage.

# TWELVE

# *1895–1896*

*T*HAT DECEMBER Stella collided again with Henry Arthur Jones and his latest play. *Michael and His Lost Angel* was to be H.A.J.'s favorite of all his plays. He wanted Irving and Terry to do it for the Lyceum, but Irving didn't like it; and instead Forbes took it for him and Stella, and H.A.J.'s hopes for a success with that romantic and popular pair soared. At the very mention of "Mr. Jo-o-ones" Stella frowned, but Forbes begged her to come to a reading at his home in Bedford Square, and so she came to hear H.A.J.'s story of an erotic clergyman or, in loftier language, a clergyman's struggle between his lust for a woman and his commitment to the Anglican Church, passions which cannot possibly co-exist.

Audrie Lesden, a wealthy woman separated from her husband, comes to find Michael Feversham, having been strangely moved by his book *The Hidden Life*. She is bantering and blasphemous, calling herself his "bad angel" and finally confessing she has made a pact with the devil: their two souls, if the devil will give her Michael as a lover. Despite his initial repugnance, Feversham is drawn to Audrie. When she pursues him to an island and he realizes they are alone, he gives in to passion and they spend the night together. The recoil is inevitable: Feversham dons a hair shirt, fasts, prays. The deserted Audrie despairs and sickens. "What's the matter with you?" asks a friend. "Life's the matter with me, I think," says Audrie. "I've got it badly, and I don't know how to cure myself." Death is the only cure, of course. Although her husband dies and she is free and Michael loves her, it is too late. She dies in his arms, and Michael gives himself up to the Roman Catholic Church, crying, as he throws himself across her body, "I'll believe all, do all, suffer all—only—only persuade me that I shall meet her again!"

Stella listened to H.A.J.'s slight cockney accent and curled her lip. "But it's so *long*, Mr. Jones," she protested, "even *without* the *h*'s!" She decided her role was uninteresting and the play vulgar. She disliked the mingling of passion and religion. She disliked Audrie's appearance in Michael's church in dazzling jewels and evening cloak, and disliked playing a whole scene on sanctified ground. Audrie's feelings for the clergyman did not inspire her: "Love is hardly the word," says Audrie. "It is more like—if a man could create a dog, and be her master, friend, father, and God, I think she would feel towards him something of what I feel towards you." That was not Stella's style, although in Audrie's "I shall hang about you, worry you, tease you, tempt you, and at last, destroy you" she might have recognized some of her impulse toward Forbes. The play almost seemed a parody of their relationship: the married woman estranged from her husband who sexually tempts the serious man of principle.

She came to rehearsal only for Forbes's sake (she said), and she played the bad angel there with a vengeance. "Oddly enough, I have never been known to weep at a rehearsal," said Stella, "however heartbroken and weary I have been." The same could not necessarily be said of those who rehearsed with her. Henry Arthur was a stubborn man and did not weep, but he raged. She wanted lines cut. She hated the church scene and said so. She objected to Audrie's "I must just titivate a cherub's nose, or hang a garland on an apostle's toe." "It's pro*fane*, Mr. Jo-o-ones," she carolled, bringing the action onstage to a halt. "It's not profanity at all," H.A.J. shouted angrily from the stalls, "it is in the part!"

"If Mrs. Campbell is to play the part," he wrote to Forbes after one gruelling session, "she must play it exactly as it is written and upon the lines that I have laid down. But I feel it will be impossible to go through rehearsals without such constant scenes that it will be far better to engage Marion Terry. I am sure you will be wise not to risk it. Please understand I will not have the text altered. I must ask you to at once send me notice of any rehearsal that may be called, as I shall insist upon the right of being present, and if I find the least attempt is being made to alter the text or to play the piece in any way prejudicial to its success, I shall take the utmost means to enforce my undoubted rights."

Stella was not H.A.J.'s only trouble. Nutcombe Gould, who had played a fine friar in *Romeo and Juliet*, threw over his part because he did not like the play. H.A.J. even managed to annoy the courteous Forbes, at one rehearsal interrupting him in the middle of his lines to object to his delivery. "Well, you just come up here and do it yourself, my boy," replied Forbes smoothly. It added little to Henry Arthur's comfort that when he did go up, he could not. Then too Forbes disliked the title, telling Jones that "lost angel" had been a term for a lady of pleasure for many years: why not the simple and dignified *Michael and Audrie?* But although several newspapers had also commented unfavorably on the title, H.A.J. was adamant. "I have never been so anxious about any part I have ever played as I am about 'Michael,' " Forbes wrote to Jones as opposition to the play grew on all sides. ". . . There are one or two small cuts that I hope you will allow me to make in the second act; and I still hope you will permit me to omit the 'image' speech in the fourth act. I cannot expect you to share my awful anxieties, I can only say that no money is being spared, and that we are doing all in our power to produce the play to your liking. . . . There is no unfriendly feeling on my part towards you. Pray put that out of your mind. . . ."

That December Stella arranged a gala family Christmas celebration, with sherry, a goose, puddings, sugar plums, and chocolates; and chose many little gifts, including twelve handkerchiefs for Pat, collars for the dogs (there was a new puppy, Humpadincka), and heliotrope handkerchiefs, a Scott and a Dickens, a gold pencil case, and her pictures to be distributed among the family. She also arranged to "tip" Lulo £2, Edwin £8, and Nina and the boys £1 apiece. Presumably she needed no reminding about presents for Beo, little Stella, and Forbes, since she did not bother to jot down notes for them in her pocket diary.

The season's goodwill did not alter her attitude toward *Michael and His Lost Angel*, however; and on the first day of 1896 she wrote to H.A.J., "I am most sorry that I could not enter right heartily into the part of Audrie, and that I felt obliged, in duty to my own feelings and to you as the author, to resign it. I thank you for your kindness in wishing me to play the part. With good wishes for success and all happiness in the New Year." Henry Arthur was hardly less polite. "If you did not feel at home in the part I am sure you have acted wisely both for yourself and for us, in giving it up. I have sometimes felt that you think there is still some bitterness remaining in my mind from the old misunderstanding in the Masqueraders. I wish you would be persuaded once for all that it is not so. I have tried during the last few weeks to work comfortably with you. Tell me how it is that I have not succeeded." Extremely reluctant for every reason to lose Stella, Forbes went to Jones's house at North Gate, Regent's Park, and suggested that he ask Mrs. Campbell "very nicely" to reconsider. With Forbes, Jones dropped the courtesy. "I'll see her damned first!" said H.A.J.

And so Marion Terry, who always behaved nicely and was anathema to Stella, came in to play Audrie Lesden, and Stella went into the country. "My darling," Pat wrote her there comfortingly, "Thank you so much for all your kind thoughts about me. I was obliged to go to the office to-day. I think it is a touch of influenza I have. Dear, I cannot tell you how pleased I am that you are not playing in Jones' play. . . . All my love to you, my own darling wife, Daddy." Again, Stella allowed the sympathy of family and friends to acquit her and lull her sense of responsibility to her profession.

*Michael and His Lost Angel* opened in London and New York simultaneously on Wednesday, January 15, 1896. The play raised a howl of
controversy: there was no middle ground—critics were either enthusiastic
or scathing, but the major critics disliked it. An exception seemed to be
Shaw, who called it "a genuinely sincere and moving play." But then Shaw
reversed himself, going to the heart of the play's weakness. Michael and
Audrie meet for the first time after sexual consummation. "You're sorry?"
asks Audrie. "No. And you?" "No." "Now, after this, what does the clergyman do?" asked Shaw. "Without giving another thought to that all-signifi-
cant fact that he is not sorry . . . he proceeds to act as if he really were
penitent, and not only puts on a hair shirt, but actually makes a confession
to his congregation in the false character of a contrite sinner, and goes out
from among them with bowed head to exile and disgrace. . . ." The result
was a play without a hero—and a heroine, for Shaw found Audrie as self-
defeating as Michael: she dies "of nothing but the need for making the
audience cry, and . . . she is a deplorable disappointment considering her
promise of force and originality in the first two acts."

Then, after calling Michael and Audrie weak and fatalistic, Shaw reversed again. "There never was a play more skilfully designed to fit the
chief actors than this was for Mr. Forbes Robertson and Mrs. Patrick
Campbell. But though Mr. Jones was able to write for Mrs. Campbell such
a part as she is not likely to get the refusal of soon again, he had to depend
on Mrs. Campbell's artistic judgment to enable her to perceive the value of
the chance. The judgment was apparently not forthcoming: at all events,
Mrs. Patrick Campbell vanished from the bills as the day of battle drew
nigh." Without her, the play quickly foundered, leaving Forbes-Robertson
and Jones quarrelling over why it was shut down so quickly.

"I did not like forsaking my manager, or offending Mr. Jones, or fore-
going my salary," Stella commented many years later, "but there was something in that play I could not stomach." By now it was clear that when Mrs.
Pat—or Mrs. Pattikins, the Pat, Mrs. P.C., or the Pat-Cat, as she was
variously called—could not stomach a role, the play, with or without her,
was doomed. Perhaps she and Forbes could have made a success of it. Had
they allowed the chemistry to work the magic it had in *Ebbsmith* or *Romeo
and Juliet*, they might have made a modern Heloise and Abelard out of
Audrie and Michael, if not a Tristan and Isolde. And then the critic of the
*Saturday Review* could have had the satisfaction of denouncing Jones's
play as decadent romantic humbug.

Fortunately, she liked the next play Forbes offered her, John Davidson's
blank-verse translation of François Coppée's fifteenth-century Balkan drama

*Pour la couronne.* She also liked John Davidson, perhaps because she had so conspicuously disliked H.A.J. Davidson, a small, bald, dark-bearded Scot with bright eyes and a birdlike manner, had a sense of fun under his grave exterior that endeared him to Stella. During one rehearsal, as they watched an actor wildly wave his arms and rave in the throes of a "big" speech, Davidson caught her eye. "Now, if he behaved like that in Piccadilly," he muttered in his Scots burr, "he would be arrested." Stella burst into laughter, stopping the rehearsal with merriment she was too helpless to explain. "John Davidson and I were very friendly," said Stella, "and I remember I talked much to him about Racine's *Phèdre* and what Sarah Bernhardt's performance of 'Phèdre' meant to me, and I commissioned him to translate it for me." Altogether, Stella considered *For the Crown* "fine," Winifred Emery's Bazilide "excellent," and Forbes's Constantin Brancomir "well played." She considered her part "little," but the Greek slave Militza appealed to her. For the part she wore a stunning divided skirt of red and gold with a green-and-gold sash swathed around her hips, a huge, heavy silver necklace, and a green-and-silver embroidered scarf tied turbanwise over her long black hair. She also had a little poem called "Butterflies" that Davidson allowed her to recite rather than sing, which promised to be a show-stopper:

> At sixteen years she knew no care,
> How could she, sweet and pure as light,
> And there pursued her everywhere
>    Butterflies all white.

> A lover looked, she dropped her eyes
> That glowed like pansies wet with dew.
> And lo! there came from out the skies
>    Butterflies all blue.

> Before she guessed her heart was gone
> The tale of love was swiftly told,
> And all about her wheeled and shone
>    Butterflies all gold.

> Then he forsook her one sad morn.
> She wept and sobbed, "Oh, Love, come back!"
> There only came to her forlorn
>    Butterflies all black.

At Ashley Gardens that February, however, her private life was chaotic. During an onslaught of domestic concerns her health broke down. "I'm a beast," she wrote apologetically to a theatre patron, Gabriella Enthoven, "but my drugs acted like an opiate & I just couldn't do anything but send telegrams to let people know I was alive. . . . I've been managing new servants & busted boilers, marking house linens etc. etc. My lady-companion-usefulhelp-amuensis [*sic*]—my little daughter's governess & my housekeeper arrives next Thursday—& then hurrah for art! . . . I have lots of new photos for you to choose from, but my face only looks happy when I am eating or kissing or drinking, as the picture I am sending you proves." Pat's health continued a problem, she told Lulo (enclosing in the letter, as usual, "what I can"): "Sir William Broadbent and Dr. Semon are coming to have a consultation so we shall know exactly how it is with Pat & what's to be done." There were also two new dogs in residence—Billie and Buttons—and, apart from work at the theatre, a social life so strenuous that she was often obliged to cancel a supper at the last moment by telegram, sending her disappointed hostess a photograph instead.

Before the new play opened, she escaped to Paris for a few days with Mrs. Ian Robertson, leaving the new helper, Alice, in charge of Pat and little Stella. On February 18 she saw Réjane, who had captivated London in 1893 with *Madame Sans-Gêne*, in a matinee of *Viveurs*. "She was so good—great at moments," she wrote Lulo. "She plays much better here than in England." She wanted to linger on in Paris awhile; would Lulo write the children and tell them she would be back in a few days. "I will try & bring you something nice," she promised, also advising Lulo to buy a nice short jacket since the weather was so suddenly warm and charge it to her. "I feel so sick about 'Pour la Couronne' & I dread returning to it," she added, her enthusiasm mysteriously evaporated.

*For the Crown* opened on Thursday, February 27, and proved a popular success. A few critics hesitated over her performance, Clement Scott calling her *a* Militza but not *the* Militza of the poem, and another wondering why she had chosen the part of the gentle slave girl instead of the splendid, imperial, passionate Bazilide. Most did not wonder. Said one: "Militza herself is played with magical beauty and sorcery by Mrs. Patrick Campbell, whose presentation of the slave maiden is unsurpassable in allurement. Nothing could be more natural and convincing than her love scenes, and the plaintive utterance of her exquisite voice goes straight to the heart." And Robert Hichens, who had been so impressed with Stella in *The Trumpet Call*, was overcome again. "I still remember her death. . . . At the end of the play she was stabbed and fell to the ground. Accustomed to the tricks of the theatre, I expected a rapt look to transform her face for a moment before life flickered out of her. But directly she was stabbed every bit of expression in her vanished, and she became, as it were, merely dead matter. The spirit had fled. What was left had no meaning. As she fell forward facing the audience one saw neither rapture nor horror—only darkness. Death! The temple deserted! All the poetry gone! Only flesh left to be shovelled into the grave!" But an even earlier admirer of Stella's was disappointed. Stephen Gwynn found everything changed from the spontaneous Rosalind who had enchanted his summers. "Somebody had been telling her that certain notes in her voice were marvellous," he concluded, "and on that limited range she spoke the whole part, or rather chanted it, monotonously."

Clement Scott called the play fine and bold, Forbes-Robertson's acting was universally admired; yet, as Stella was getting to know, the ginger-bearded critic of the *Saturday Review* could be relied upon to dissent. Bernard Shaw found Winifred Emery prosaic, Forbes as Constantin filling "a brainless void," though he filled it like an artist, and Davidson's translation rhetorical folly. "And Mrs. Patrick Campbell, what of her? Ah, the change from that mournful first night of the slain 'Michael and the Lost Angel,' when we were all singing, both on the stage and off:

> But what are vernal joys to me?
> Where thou art not, no Spring can be.

What a ballad could have been written then with the title 'Come back from Dorchester'; and what terrible heart twistings we suffered when we knew that she would not come unless we gave her Henry Arthur Jones's head on a charger! Well, we gave it to her; and on the first night of 'For the Crown' we agreed, before she had been three seconds on the stage, that her return was cheap at the price: nay, we would have given her Shakespear's head as a makeweight if she had given the faintest pout of dissatisfaction. You will tell me, no doubt, that Mrs. Patrick Campbell cannot act. Who said she could?— who wants her to act?—who cares twopence whether she possesses that or any other second-rate accomplishment? On the highest plane one does not act, one *is*. Go and see her move, stand, speak, look, kneel—go and breathe the magic atmosphere that is created by the grace of all these deeds; and then talk to me about acting, forsooth! No, Mrs. Campbell's Militza is an embodied poem; and if it is much more a lyric poem than a dramatic one, why, so much the worse for dramatic poetry! This time, too, the poetry was not without a little tenderness as well as much beauty of movement and tone. The old vituperative note was not heard; and there was an access of artistic earnestness and power. Possibly the vituperative mood had exhausted itself on the devoted author of 'Michael.' "

Half-needling, half-raving, Shaw thus let himself be beguiled. Far more than any other critic, he took the personal note with her: exposing her quarrel with Jones, hinting at her love affair with Forbes, ignoring the actress for the woman. Yet the note of admiration was unmistakable and might have interested Stella had not Shaw's socialist, Ibsenite, committee-man world been so remote from hers.

*For the Crown* achieved ninety-four performances, closing May 30. If Stella had felt sick about that play, it was nothing compared to what she would feel about the next play chosen by Forbes as a showpiece for her talents. A translation of Hermann Sudermann's *Heimat* (1893) by Louis N. Parker, *Magda* told the story of a famous singer's return to the small German town where she was born. Magda blazes upon the *Bauernvolk* in her rich clothes, scent, and flowers, making the provincial home she left seem by contrast tragically bare and mean. Her father, the Colonel, is unimpressed with her success, however, looking upon her only as an erring daughter to be rescued; he expects her now to stay at home, but Magda shudders: "I felt it the first minute I came. The paternal authority already stretches its net over me again, and the yoke stands ready beneath which I must bow." The conflict is intensified when Councillor von Keller arrives with a bouquet. Magda hurls it away. He was her first lover; he deserted her; he does not know she had a child by him. Magda tells him now, then scorns his offer of marriage as reparation. When she was young, marriage would have saved her from shame and struggle; now it can only enslave her. But her father is pathetically grateful for the Councillor's offer, inno-cent of any suspicion that the father of an illegitimate child may have some obligation to mother and offspring, and he insists that Magda marry him. Magda begins to yield, not to her father's commands but to the realization that the shame she has brought on the household has broken him. Ne-gotiations began, and Magda discovers that as von Keller's wife she will have to renounce her brilliant career for the drawing room. This is a blow, but it is nothing to the blow that follows: von Keller tells her she will have to give up her child, since acknowledging it would ruin his own career. Magda appeals to her father, but finds him adamant. His military sense of honor must be appeased: if she does not marry the father of her child, neither he nor his daughter will leave the room alive. Magda has one last card to play. "Well, then," she flings at the old man, "are you sure that you ought to force me upon this man—that according to your standards, I am altogether worthy of him? I mean—that he was the only one in my life?" "You jade!" cries her father, reaching for his pistol as he realizes his daugh-ter's meaning, but before he can fire he collapses and dies of a stroke. Magda is both beaten and liberated. "Would to God I had never come home," she weeps to Pastor Heffterdingt, a man who once loved her and who has counseled her in submission since her return. "None shall forbid you to pray beside his grave," replies Heffterdingt simply.

Like Paula and Agnes, Magda (Magdalene) is a woman who challenges convention to live life on her own terms, and pays for her rebellion with defeat or death. Unlike Paula and Agnes, Magda is an artist: she is punished not only for her sexual freedom, therefore, but for aspiring to a career in the male realm of art. Magda was a great role—both Duse and Bernhardt had played it in London in 1895—and one that seemed made for Stella, a wilful and passionate Magda herself, who had run away from and triumphed over suburban Dulwich.

*Magda* opened at the Lyceum on Wednesday, June 3, and was a failure. English critics found the play "hopelessly dull, verbose, commonplace, all noise, noise, noise, a dull German sermon!"—as they had when Duse and Bernhardt had acted it a year before. Shaw did not blame the play, however. Having asked of her Militza, "Who wants her to act?" he now found his question answered. He did; and she had not. "Mrs. Campbell has not lived long enough to get as much work crammed into her entire repertory as Duse gets into every ten minutes of her Magda. . . . If Mrs. Campbell's irresistible physical gifts and her cunning eye for surface effects had only allowed her to look as silly as she really was in the part . . . her failure would have been as obvious to the greenest novice in the house as it was to me." Go soon, he advised his readers; the play would not last long.

Her failure had not been obvious to first-nighters. "Never was such cheering heard in a theatre," the *Daily Telegraph* was forced to concede. "Mrs. Campbell was called half a dozen times." More important than that barometer was the judgment of the distinguished critic A. B. Walkley, who found her Magda better than either her Paula or her Agnes: "She gives us the woman's firm unyielding will. . . . No other English actress could, I am sure, approach her in the part." Undeniably, something more than Stella's irresistible physical gifts was present in her performance; yet the play failed and was taken off after fifteen performances. Nursing letters from Jack Mackail ("Your 'Magda' last night was the ablest and finest thing I have ever seen you do") and Winifred Emery ("I admire your performance only second to your Paula Tanqueray"), Stella brooded over her profound disappointment. She had failed as Dulcie Larondie, but that had been a deliberate failure. *Magda* she had cared about, and it had failed. Half a dozen plausible excuses occurred to her. Lyceum audiences wanted pageantry and spectacle, not three long acts with only a stove, armchair, horsehair sofa, and bowl of goldfish to look at. The play should never have opened on Derby Day when all fashionable London was out of town.

Forbes should have not cast himself as Pastor Heffterdingt—audiences did not like their favorites in minor roles. *Magda* was an intimate drama, and the Lyceum was simply too big. . . . But there was no time to look back. Desperate to save his season, Forbes called rehearsals for *The School for Scandal*, and the day after he and Stella left the stage as Heffterdingt and Magda, they stepped back on as Joseph Surface and Lady Teazle.

# THIRTEEN

## 1896–1897

*S*TELLA HAD PLAYED Lady Teazle in a single Adelphi matinee five years before. This time she was supported by an excellent cast that included William Farren, Sr., as Sir Peter, Fred Terry as Charles Surface, Rose Leclerq as Mrs. Candour, Cyril Maude as Sir Benjamin, and Forbes himself. But Stella was tired, nervous, unhappy. Surrounded by actors of the "fine old school," she rebelled; "their traditional method 'sat on my head,' " she complained, "—a green baize over the singing bird's cage." She was particularly out of tune with old William Farren, a classical actor steeped in the traditions of his father and grandfather. "Never once did Sir Peter address himself to *me*," she discovered. "The audience was his friend, his companion, and to them he confided his emotions."

"Of the play . . . I prefer to say nothing," yawned Walkley the next morning, "—especially as I am writing in one of those abominably shaky carriages which the L.C.D.R. Company is not ashamed to use for its Sunday sea-coast service. Mrs. Patrick Campbell looked very charming in pale green and silver last night, and the Kentish hops are looking very healthy this morning. They have at last removed the scaffolding from Rochester Castle, I see, and Mr. Farren's Sir Peter is as mellow and classical a performance as ever. And what a contrast in style and inspiration is that performance to Mrs. Campbell's wholly modern, neurotic, Pinero-ish Lady Teazle! . . . Yet the audience in general seemed to be delighted with the whole affair. Hullo—Faversham—all change!"

Archer reviewed the production unfavorably; but, unpredictably, Shaw liked it and even liked Stella. Little wonder that Max Eliot cabled his American paper, "THE QUESTION OF THE HOUR IN LONDON IS, 'CAN SHE ACT?' " There were bitterly opposed factions, he reported. "Mrs. Patrick Campbell is a genius," said some. "The lady has not the slightest idea of the art of acting," said others. Many critics believed her the Bernhardt of London and he, for one, was inclined to agree. Certainly she was unconventional, following in no one's footsteps. She was human to an extraordinary degree: had been a living, breathing Magda. Personally, Eliot believed the theatre had gained "a great and shining light."

As critics debated, the *School* went into July, Stella becoming more and more demoralized. Sometimes she did not bother to conceal her impatience. Acting the screen scene one night, she became exasperated with the slowness of William Farren and Fred Terry. "Oh, do get on, you old pongers!" she cried from behind the screen. "I let things go," she later admitted. Then on July 24 the famous Forbes-Robertson and Mrs. Pat season was over. Forbes the professional had scored in every role with the exception of the ill-fated Michael Feversham. Stella had divided the critics with Juliet, entranced them with Militza, alienated them with Magda, divided them with Lady Teazle, and set them buzzing by not playing Audrie Lesden. With audiences, however, she was unfailingly popular, the fascination of her person disarming criticism. And together she and Forbes had generated a new kind of theatrical magic. In place of the great groundswells of passion and rhetoric, they projected a fineness of spirit, intelligence, natural grace, and a strange androgynous beauty.

But Stella was tired. On August 1 the *Illustrated London News* announced that Forbes-Robertson would tour with *For the Crown* and *The School for Scandal,* "but it will be a disappointment to many in the country to hear that Mrs. Patrick Campbell does not travel with the Lyceum Company." Friends close to Stella were not surprised, however; nor was Uncle Harry, who tried to encourage his "dear demoralised thing":

No, *not* demoralised—never be that. Be different from all others, be *the one.* If Art has pushed too many over the precipice as being creatures of wretched, lumpish clay, spite of all their pretended aspirations, still *you,* walk you safely, securely along the edge. . . . Of one of his great knights, Ariosto says, "Natura el fare, e poi ruppe la stampa"—"Him Nature fashioned, then broke the mould." . . . Why not *you as peerless* in your own sphere? You can be. Art has placed in your hair the undying laurel. What will you do for the honour of Art? Lay upon her shoulders the golden robe? Or cast over her incomparable form the rumpled drapery, the chiffonage of demoralisation. . . .

But Stella found herself unable to accept her uncle's challenge that summer, and retreated instead to her other world: Frampton Court, Gosford, Dalby Hall, Mells, Clouds, Stanway—the world of earls, dukes, and baronets who were flattered to receive her, entertain her, and let the current little dog feed off silver dishes at their tables. There were also weeks at

Uxbridge with the Mackails. Margaret was her closest friend, and Margaret in turn loved Stella's wit, vivacity, and "wonderful realising sympathy." "My own Girl," she wrote back in London at the end of summer, "I wonder so much how all is going with you, and how Beo is, and how plans are, and when you will be in London and we can see you. . . . Now that we are settled, the summer with its long hot days, and you rushing in, and me in your nightgowns seems all a dream. . . . My love and thoughts are all round and about you, and will be with you in that awful country, darling."

But Stella did not tour America ("that awful country") that fall. She did not manage to act at all. Irving and Terry were back at the Lyceum, Ellen studying Imogen, and Shaw giving her advice. Although he was courting Charlotte Payne-Townshend, an Irishwoman with green eyes and a great deal of money, he and Ellen were catching fire as well, and letters shot back and forth between them. Shaw had not given up hope for *The Man of Destiny*, and he still teased Ellen with the name of her rival. Ellen played along. "Goodbye dear George!!! Give my love to—The Cat!" she wrote from the Savoy, where she was holed up, trying to impress Imogen's lines upon her increasingly bad memory. "Bless you!" she replied to Shaw's pages of instructions on playing Imogen. "If I were dark, and 30, I'd send you a kiss for it." When Ellen pretended to be terrified of a first night under the pitiless gaze of G.B.S., Shaw insisted she could annihilate nasty critics like himself more easily than nice ones, "who will believe anything you do beautiful, even if you introduce a skirt-dance out of jealousy of Mrs. Pat's Juliet." And after that first night: "I was greatly shocked by your entrance last night. You must have spent hours before the glass, getting up that success of personal beauty, merely to écraser Mrs. Pat. Do you think, at your age, it is right?" Shaw thus tried to encourage rivalry between the leading lady of the Lyceum and the actress who had usurped her place the past season. Ellen resisted and, as for Stella, she admired Ellen and had never met the critic who spoke of her so familiarly.

In November, however, she made a brief appearance in his world. Since leaving the Adelphi, Elizabeth Robins had cornered the Ibsen market in London, producing and acting *Hedda Gabler*, *Rosmersholm*, and *The Master Builder*. Now plans to produce a series of matinees of *Little Eyolf* at the Avenue were finally taking shape. Janet Achurch would play Rita Allmers, the mate-devouring wife; Elizabeth herself would undertake Asta, the sympathetic sister. There was another woman's part in *Little Eyolf*: the Ratwife is Ibsen's messenger of death who knocks at the Allmerses' door and asks if there are any little gnawing things they might like her to rid them of. Neither Allmers nor Rita understands, but their lame child, Little Eyolf, doted on by the husband and hated by the possessive wife, follows the Ratwife out of the house and is drowned. For this role Elizabeth approached her old friend and Adelphi colleague. A few matinees at the unfashionable Avenue Theatre for little money was not much of an offer for London's brightest star, but Stella accepted, perhaps agreeing with Uncle Harry that it was time to do something for the honor of art. She was also interested in Ibsen; she had applauded Elizabeth's Hilda Wangel and was eyeing Hedda Gabler for herself. Above all, she was conscious that she owed a great deal to the actress who had forfeited *The Second Mrs. Tanqueray.*

So Stella joined the Ibsenites. "IBSEN AHEAD!" Shaw proclaimed, stimulated by her presence. Theatrical London had put off the torture of *Little Eyolf,* said Shaw, "as one puts off a visit to the dentist. But the torture tempts us in spite of ourselves; we feel that it must be gone through with; and now, accordingly, comes Miss Hedda Hilda Gabler Wangel Robins, christened Elizabeth, and bids us not only prepare to be tortured, but subscribe to enable her to buy the rack. A monstrous proposition, but one that has been instantly embraced. No sooner was it made than Mrs. Patrick Campbell volunteered for the Ratwife, the smallest part in Little Eyolf, consisting of a couple of dozen speeches in the first act only. (Clever Mrs. Pat! it is, between ourselves, the most fascinating page of the play.) Miss Janet Achurch, the original and only Nora Helmer, jumped at the appalling part of Rita, whom nobody else on the stage dare tackle. . . . The subscriptions poured in so fast that the rack is now ready, and the executioners are practising so that no pang may miss a moan of its utmost excruciation."

"Who does not know the forlorn and furtive enterprises undertaken at 'unlucky' theatres, with afternoon sunlight coming through the side windows, at which Ibsen's masterpieces have been exposed to the adoration of the few and the laughter of the many?" remembered the critic of the *Academy.* The Avenue in Northumberland Avenue, built cheap and simple by speculator Sefton Parry (with, it was said, the express intention of getting it requisitioned by the South-Eastern Railway), was distinctly unfashionable, though theatre history of a kind had been made there in 1894 with Shaw's *Arms and the Man.* Yet these Ibsen enterprises always generated the kind of excitement and fellowship felt among a small group who know they are pioneers: J. T. Grein, founder of the Independent Theatre; William Archer, Ibsen translator and critic; Charles Charrington and Janet Achurch, Ibsen actors and producers; Florence Farr, sometime Ibsen actress; Shaw, Ibsen critic and apologist; William Heinemann, Ibsen publisher; and Henry James, Oscar Wilde, Arthur Symons, Edmund Gosse, H. W. Massingham, and many others who talked, read, and patronized Ibsen.

Although Stella considered the Ibsen contingent exclusive and patronizing, as if they had a monopoly on intellectual drama in London, she could not help catching some of the enthusiasm. But there were difficulties. Florence Farr was present at rehearsals because she was being paid £10 to understudy Janet Achurch. An alcoholic and morphia addict, Janet was now also pregnant. The role of Rita Allmers was strenuous and Shaw, for one, was afraid she would "help herself out pharmaceutically" simply to get through the performances. "It is useless to blink the fact that the risk is greater than usual in her case," he warned Elizabeth Robins, and suggested that in case Janet should break down, Florence Farr take the Ratwife and Mrs. Pat be got to take the part of Rita Allmers; the audience would consider it an event.

It considered even Stella as the Ratwife an event. Thanks to her presence in the cast, the crowd at the opening matinee on Monday, November 23, included others than the usual bearded and sandaled assortment of anarchists, bohemians, and Fabians. Pinero came to see his actress. The Mackails were there. Lady Burne-Jones shared a box with Forbes-Robertson. They did not, of course, outnumber the Ibsenites: Massingham, Archer, Mrs. Woods, Mrs. Green, Mrs. Poynter, Charrington, Heinemann, Shaw, and Charlotte Payne-Townshend, who had subscribed handsomely to stalls. William Rothenstein was also there, and amused himself "as much with the audience as with the play." Everybody was waiting to see what Mrs. Pat would do with a part that called for rags, a bent back, and a lot of aging charcoal about the mouth and eyes. "She played supernaturally, beautifully," said the captivated Shaw: "the first notes of her voice came as from the spheres into all that suburban prose: she played to the child with a witchery that might have drawn him not only into the sea, but into her very bosom." The first act and her part over, Stella then appeared in the audience gorgeously gowned, settled herself among friends, and commented on the rest of the play in sibilant whispers. "I have done my bit for charity," she seemed to say.

Although little Stella had shrieked in terror when she saw her mother got up as an old woman, the critics universally praised Stella's Ratwife. "She lived up to one's high expectations"; "she gives to this strange and difficult personage all the weirdness, all the eerie fascination, which she must have"; she "makes the most admirable and artistic use of her extraordinary personal advantages, and proves once for all the folly of measuring the importance and effectiveness of a part by its length." Then the enthusiastic Shaw visited the Avenue again and came away disillusioned. The first time, he explained, Mrs. Campbell had understood she was "no village harridan, but the messenger of heaven"; the second time, to his unspeakable fury, she had amused herself by playing like a melodramatic old woman, a profanation for which he would never forgive her. (It was perhaps the performance witnessed by Charles Ricketts, who wished devoutly that "shoes could be withdrawn from the feet in the Turkish manner and thrown.") Still, Shaw admitted, he liked being enchanted by Mrs. Patrick Campbell better than being "frightened, harrowed, astonished, conscience-stricken, devastated, and dreadfully delighted in general by Miss Achurch's untamed genius." More than a tribute to Stella it was a rebuke to Janet and the drugs that had ruined her control.

But it was not morphia, brandy, or pregnancy that drove Janet Achurch prematurely from the cast of *Little Eyolf*. The unusually good business conducted at the Avenue because of Stella's presence brought the production to the attention of a theatrical syndicate, which proposed taking the play financially off Elizabeth Robins's hands. Hearing of the offer, Janet went to the syndicate privately and negotiated her own terms. Outraged that Janet had acted independently and always her rival in Ibsen, Elizabeth encouraged Stella to underbid Janet's £25 a week for the lead. Of course Stella was successful, since the syndicate got a star for less salary than Janet; and, on December 4, having played Rita Allmers for less than two weeks, Janet learned just before curtain time that the part of Rita was no longer hers. The angry actress was allowed to play out the full two weeks until December 6, Shaw bullying her into accepting the situation gracefully for her "health's sake," which would be the official reason for her leaving.

"Mr. Heinemann gives me to understand that you wanted to hear my view as to your playing Rita," Archer wrote Stella, who, after all, was conscious of her position as newcomer among the Ibsenites and wished to placate their critic. "They are entirely favourable to your doing so. Of course, I cannot pretend that I don't regret the circumstances which have thrown the part open; but since they have occurred, I, for my part, can only rejoice in the prospect of seeing you in the character. . . . Let me once more congratulate you upon The Rat Wife. My own feeling about it you already know, but I don't think I have ever heard any performance talked of with such unanimity of admiration. Wherever I go I hear no dissentient voice."

Stella had a few days to learn the very difficult part; they were not enough. She got through two acts, but in the third entered with the play-book hanging from a ribbon tied around her waist, and referred to it. Warm congratulations, however, came from Herbert Asquith, thanks from Avenue manager F. J. Harris for her "true blue" good nature and courage, and felicitations from William Heinemann to his "dear friend": "You were divine and the book was scarcely noticed. . . . You have scored a triumph, and I know you deserved it."

Stella's Rita could not get past Shaw, however. In a devastating critique called "Ibsen Without Tears," he raged over the star's turning *Little Eyolf* into "a full-blown fashionable theatrical spectacle" and one of Ibsen's most anguishing heroines into a well-bred housewife. "She has seen how unlady-like, how disturbing, how full of horror even, the part of Rita Allmers is, acted as Miss Achurch acted it. And she has remedied this with a complete-ness that leaves nothing to be desired. . . . She looked charming; and her dresses were beyond reproach. . . . Her performance was infinitely reassur-ing and pretty: its note was, 'You silly people: what are you making all this fuss about? The secret of life is charm and self-possession, and not tantrums about drowned children.' . . . Goodness gracious, I thought, what things that evil-minded Miss Achurch did read into this harmless play!"

But it was Shaw's mission to pit all popular plays against the New Drama and all actresses against the Ibsen pioneers, to the inevitable detriment of the first. "Miss Elizabeth Robins would certainly not play Militza half as effectively as Mrs. Campbell," he had charged in his *Magda* review; "but can it be doubted by any one who has seen her play Hilda Wangel that she would play Magda, especially in the self-assertive scenes, twenty times bet-ter than Mrs. Campbell? . . . Miss Achurch, with no copyright monopoly of A Doll's House, has never been approached as Nora Helmer: Mrs. Camp-bell's attempt at Magda is the merest baby-play in comparison with that performance." Yet, said Shaw, these able actresses had had little satisfac-tion excepting watching prettily placid actresses in fashionable dramas win immense popularity by going through half a dozen tricks which they prob-ably taught their poodles when they had nothing better to do. It was a hit at Stella, although she had griffons and was hardly placid. She did not bring to the part of Rita Allmers Janet Achurch's histrionics (which Shaw had actually deplored), nor the sense of "death, disease, downfall, and disaster" beloved by Ibsenites. She did bring to it her fascination, and Shaw had a hard time forgiving the fact that Mrs. Pat's charisma weighed so heavily in the balance against the ability of Elizabeth and Janet. However, it was notices like "Ibsen Without Tears" that permitted him to boast to Ellen Terry that this time he had "smashed up Mrs. P.C." Ellen only smiled.

For Stella, playing Rita Allmers was less than an adventure. "Miss Janet Achurch, who played the leading character, fell ill, and I was asked at a moment's notice to play her part of Rita in this play," she wrote years later, maintaining the fiction of Janet's illness. "It was an alarming ordeal, for I was unable in the time given me to learn the words—I believe it was only a day. I tied the book by a ribbon to my waist and practically read it." The play closed on December 19 after twenty-five performances, successful for an Ibsen production. For her part in encouraging Stella to underbid Janet, Elizabeth Robins had the satisfaction of seeing her Asta Allmers overshadowed in the blaze of publicity surrounding Mrs. Pat. For Stella there was the reward of having her nerves further unstrung by the stress of playing Rita at short notice.

Ellen Terry had wanted to see "Little Eye-opener," as she called it, but was too fatigued with *Cymbeline* to go out in the afternoon. But Stella had gone that autumn three times to see Ellen play Imogen, the first to criticize, the last "only to look for beauties," she told Lulo, "and I returned with my heart full." "When she entered I felt she had come from the moon: when she left the stage I was sure the stars were greeting her. No one has ever had her magical step—that extraordinary happy haste, that made you feel she must presently arrive at the gates of Paradise. The evening I saw her as 'Imogen,' she forgot her words, and—giving a delicious look at the audience and then towards heaven—spoke three times in a voice that melted your bosom, this word: 'Beyond—beyond—beyond—' There was no 'Beyond' in the text, but it was the loveliest word I ever heard, and described her 'Imogen.'" She wrote to tell Ellen so, and received a polite reply: "I thank you for the kind message you sent me on Tuesday—At the same time let me congratulate you upon the several brilliant successes you made whilst I was in America. I sh$^d$ like to see the 'Juliet' (which my son tells me I sh$^d$ like immensely) & the 'Magda.' . . ."

Stella was still under contract to Forbes, who wanted to act again with her that winter in London, but they seemed to be floundering for a play that would satisfy them both, more particularly Stella. Perhaps it was for her sake that he finally decided upon *Nelson's Enchantress*, Risden Home's drama of Emma Hart's triumphant progress through ranks of men into the arms of Lord Nelson. Oddly enough, Pat Campbell helped finance the production when he introduced his unacknowledged rival to the wealthy financier Horatio Bottomley and Bottomley took an interest in the enterprise. The theatre Forbes chose turned out to be the Avenue, scene of *Little Eyolf*.

Calling on Stella just before the opening of *Nelson's Enchantress*, the reporter from the *New Illustrated Magazine* found herself ushered in by a maid and seated in the charming blue-and-white drawing room at Ashley Gardens. She was immediately pounced upon by two of the hairy, ratlike little dogs it had become so stylish for ladies to carry about with them since Alexandra had set the fashion. Mrs. Campbell shortly appeared, stunning in chiffon and lace, and introduced her to Buttons and Humpadincka (poor She was dead, and Billie was with Lulo). What part had she liked best? began the reporter brightly and inevitably. Stella had various replies. "Any part that is human," she was fond of saying. This time she startled the interviewer with, "I delight in them all—but Juliet, Rosalind, and then

Lady Teazle have been my favorites." There were more questions, and her new Lady Hamilton was discussed at length before the reporter was ushered out by the maid, convinced that the wonderful Mrs. Campbell was a "thoroughly conscientious artist." That there had been no sign of the "nerves" that had plagued Stella all that season was due in part to the new servant, Wrighton, "a delightful maid & devoted to dogs," Stella told Lulo.

The same letter referred to two new projects. "I have spoken to Greet about you & when this play is over he will probably arrange an appointment unless you have changed your mind." Stella was doing her best to launch Lulo on a stage career, negotiating with Wilson Barrett, Tree, and now Greet (currently cast as the painter Romney in *Nelson's Enchantress*) for a place for Lulo, even as a walk-on. The second project was a move from Ashley Gardens to 10 Mandeville Place. There was no indication that Pat would also transfer to 10 Mandeville Place; and, in fact, Stella undoubtedly took the rooms because she and Forbes, who lived very much in the heart of his family at 22 Bedford Square, needed a place to be together.

*Nelson's Enchantress* opened on Thursday, February 11, 1897. Stella's acting of the philandering Emma Hart in red curls and costumes that ranged from a mob cap and chintz to satin ablaze with diamonds drew praise; but the play did not, chiefly because England's beloved Lord Nelson did not emerge from the play a hero. "Of the popularity of Mrs. Patrick Campbell there can be no possible doubt," said one critic. "They admire her beauty, they love her frocks, and they encourage that staccato delivery of every sentence which they adore in a manner most gratifying to them all. The more pizzicato is her utterance the more they love it. Flowers, cheers, calls, again and again repeated, testified to the joy given to many by her mere appearance on the stage." Concerned more with her acting than popularity, Archer called her "beautiful and touching throughout," concluding, "The scene of the rupture with Greville is, in my view, the best piece of real acting Mrs. Campbell has ever done. It enlarges my conception of her powers." Unfortunately, it was generally agreed that Lord Nelson was not a good acting part for Forbes.

Shaw complimented Stella in print for even acting "occasionally, and that by no means badly"; then called upon her at 10 Mandeville Place on the afternoon of February 18. He had had Stella in mind for his plays for several years, dreaming of her for his dark, tempestuous Julia in *The Philanderer* and for his brothel-keeper, Mrs. Warren; he had had Forbes and Stella in mind ever since *The Man of Destiny*. Forbes was with Stella this afternoon, and he read them his new "puritan" play, *The Devil's Disciple*, a drama with a splendid part for Forbes as Dick Dudgeon, but nothing for Stella in the role of the minister's wife, Judith Anderson. It was his first meeting with the dangerous Mrs. Campbell, and he immediately forwarded the news to Ellen Terry that he loved Mrs. P.C. Not understanding his playful philandering at the beginning of their correspondence, Ellen knew better how to take such news now. "Well she's a very lovely lady," she replied, "and clever and amusing. I've always liked her, tho' I scarcely know her." On the other hand, said Ellen, "If Mrs. Pat were less vain, she'd do much more on the stage."

"I don't know what is going to happen to our play," Stella wrote Lulo on March 13; "Johnston leaves Monday." With or without her, Forbes had decided to tour: he was due at the Gaiety Theatre, Dublin, on March 22. She herself was not getting the rest she needed. Wrighton had been severely ill with influenza, and little Stella not able to go back to school at Mrs. Newton's, so that she had had her at Mandeville Place the whole week. As it turned out, *Nelson's Enchantress* closed suddenly on March 20 with a disastrous loss of money, critics and public both deciding that they wanted more from Mrs. Patrick Campbell and Forbes-Robertson than prettied-up historical romance.

"I am sorry if you didn't know about last night in time to come," Stella wrote to Lulo, who had missed the final performance. "The last ten days at the theatre have been such a pandemonium—& I have been feeling so ill & my nerves shattered. I believe I am simply physically unable to bear the strain of playing every night—& I am thankful it is over for the present." And then, said Stella, "The fatigue that had been gradually threatening me for many months reached the climax. *I could not work any more.*"

# FOURTEEN

# *1897*

STELLA DID NOT break down completely at first, but went with her ten-year-old daughter to Herne Bay on the Kentish coast to rest, taking rooms at 14 Ventnor Villas. There Lulo wrote her the good news that under the name Eleanor Tanner she had got a small part in *Hamlet* with Ben Greet's company. "My dear," replied Stella, "It's delightful to think of you so happy & excited. . . . Oh I do thank God you have got a line—& even if things are not all bright, they will never be the awful, dull dreary empty hideous nightmare they were—when the only happiness you could get had to come from me—& I was too bewildered & busy to give you the love you wanted. God bless you. I do hope you'll do beautifully. I'm sure you will & if Minnie dresses you—you'll be all right."

On Good Friday Stella wrote again, wanting to know more about *Hamlet*, what she was doing in *As You Like It*, and how Nutcombe Gould, threatened with blindness, was getting on. "Your enthusiasm brought back the old days so vividly to me," she said, remembering lonely months on tour with Greet, "& how I longed for you to be with me—& wouldn't press you because I was so possessed with the idea that it was wrong & selfish towards you—well, well—don't let me discourage you. I am sure if you speak up & aim at *ears* all the time—intelligence, refinement, & sweetness of voice . . . & reasonableness—you have them all. I hope Greet is nice. He needs a lot of *attention* as do *all* artists big or small." Her own situation, she added, was not as cheerful. Little Stella's cough was bad at night; the rooms were uncomfortable; she had sent for a doctor recommended by Dr. Semon.

That April, however, Stella was still well enough to think of joining Forbes on tour at Newcastle or Manchester, and when Lulo wrote to say she was out of work for a few days, Stella thought of asking her to come along to understudy a part in *Magda*, although "I feel very shy about asking you because it seems so cruel to take you from 'Jo.' If I join

Johnston we share—so we both pay everybody. I doubt I shall be well enough to go." For Lulo's acting there was sisterly advice: "I wish I could have seen your gentlewoman—do remember dear, you haven't only to speak loud enough to be *heard* but to *attract the attention* of the audience (especially in a small part). Mamma & Jo & your friends *are attending* & so would hear. However it will all come in time—but I know with myself that my friends hear me—& my enemies don't—& so it is with the best of voices if the speech is not emphatic enough."

As for her own condition: "I don't want it to get about I am ill—& it's only nerves. When you think of the bother I had moving into those rooms & the long rehearsals & the dancing & the fuss over Lady Hamilton besides all the other worries, & the illness of Wrighton & Stella & then my own, it's not to be wondered at. The doctor won't let me get up this week at all & he says I am not to read or write & has forbidden me to read my letters. I obey him as far as I can. If people ask you what's the matter—say I am a little run down after influenza!"

April wore on and Stella longed for London news in that Jubilee season. "Send me any beautiful bits about Dearest's picture—& about the opening of Her Majesty's & Mother's supper the next night. I shall have to refuse everything. It's a pity just this week I am not stronger." Tree opened London's most beautiful theatre across from his old Haymarket on April 28. Burne-Jones's "The Pilgrim of Love" was on exhibition for the opening of the New Gallery, directed by Comyns Carr and C. H. Hallé. But it was not Sir Edward's painting that created a stir at the opening, but a picture by his son, Philip. Slickly painted in dark greens, whites, and crimson, it showed a beautiful woman with cascading black hair in a clinging nightdress, astride a man collapsed across a bed. The woman's face is intent and joyful; her teeth are long and sharp. The picture was titled "The Vampire" and the woman looked like Beatrice Stella Campbell.

The painting had inspired a set of verses by Rudyard Kipling, Philip's cousin; printed in the catalogue, they offered the only explanation:

> A fool there was and he made his prayer
> (Even as you and I!)
> To a rag and a bone and a hank of hair
> (We called her the woman who did not care)
> But the fool he called her his lady fair—
> (Even as you and I!) . . .

"Treated with no little passion," remarked the *Illustrated London News*, "but leaves an unpleasant impression." "The Vampire" created a hum of speculation. Philip was madly in love with Mrs. Pat, bought her diamonds, furs, and carriages, but she heartlessly threw him over for Forbes-Robertson, just as she had thrown over her poor husband. She had ruined young Burne-Jones, and was now torturing Forbes with the same careless indifference—or so the story flew around.

Out of the commotion in Brighton, where she had gone with her faithful maid, Wrighton, because Herne was doing her no good, Stella wrote to Lulo at the end of April, sounding remarkably un-vampirish: "I don't know how Pat is, by the end of the week you must write and tell me. . . . I am so glad he has paid you. I felt sure he would, & that nice Edith Craig. She is a dear girl. Did Ellen come round? . . . Beo goes to Nina tomorrow. . . . I have sent her a cheque for £7, he wants so much. . . . don't worry in the least about me." She was getting worse, however. More doctors came and examined, but they could not calm her. She gave up talking about joining Forbes, although she hated the idea of giving in. She could not sleep, she could not rest, she could not hold back hysteria—and finally Pat, Uncle, and Lulo persuaded her to go to a nursing home, while Margaret Mackail tried to comfort away her tears of despair at her nervous breakdown.

On May 8 Lulo took her in the train to Rasta, a nursing home overlooking the sea on Chine Road, Bournemouth. There, as doctors felt her pulse, she laughed with tears streaming down her cheeks, insisting again and again, "I am all right, I am all right." "All the acting has done this," said Dr. Embleton. She was put in a little room with a high window out of which she could see only the sky. The door was always left open, and through it Nurse Ivens and Dr. Embleton came alternately to sit at her bed, where she tossed feverishly, unable to rest. She was given no medicine, only massage, which she hated. Days passed; no letters came, no names of family or friends were spoken, no visitors were allowed to see her, only Dr. Embleton, who held her hand and told her that she worked too hard and felt too much.

On tour Forbes anguished. "Wrighton wires me you want my address so I have just wired it to you," he wrote Lulo from Hull the day Stella entered Rasta. "What is it I can do? . . . Is it not dreadful that she does not get better? I do hope Bournemouth & a complete retreat from the world for a few weeks will do her good. I shall go & see Semon on Monday morning. I expect you have been very unhappy about her & I have been terribly anxious, & being so far away makes it worse." On May 10 he made a flying visit to London to play at the Metropole, Camberwell, and Lulo went to 22 Bedford Square to report on Stella in person; but she had no good news for him, and Forbes was obliged to leave immediately for Oxford. From there on May 17 he wrote to Lulo again: "Here we are in this beautiful place, the

Clarendon Hotel, but I can't enjoy it, because of my anxiety. . . . If you hear how she is getting on please let me know. It is a continual nightmare. I wish you would send me her address, I would like to send her some flowers. I came out badly last week, but I hope for better things. These have been stormy times, surely the sun will come out for us all soon. Pinero asked me last night about her. . . ."

Margaret Mackail also kept in faithful touch with Lulo, who was being run off her feet in Stella's absence since she was back with Greet again in a series of Shakespeare revivals at the Olympic Theatre in the Strand. Margaret was all practical advice. Stella had ordered an expensive dress from the Paris dressmaker Jeanne, who was to make a personal delivery in London. It must be stopped, said Margaret. "I will take the responsibility & brave Stella about it afterwards. It makes me sick to think of an expensive french dress being added to all the other debts when she starts life again, strong, I pray, but penniless. Don't you agree? & she ought to be protected from herself & this is a chance to do it. She can easily order another when she is earning money again. I long for Saturday to be over"—writing the day Stella entered Rasta—"& to hear she is safely in the hands of her good doctor & breathing the soothing air of Bournemouth. God bless her."

A week later Margaret wrote again. "I have sent the cheque. And cheer up—she has been there a week, & according to the doctor the first week is the most irksome of all; I should think in a fortnight we shall hear of real improvement, & when once that steadily begins we may be happy—for cases of that kind don't slip back. I have confident hope now of having her back stronger in body & mind than she has been for long. . . ." Besides sending money, Margaret also took it upon herself to visit young Stella at Mrs. Newton's (who had mercifully reduced her terms), and to come and applaud Lulo at the Olympic in her walk-on part in *Hamlet*.

From Bournemouth came signs, however, that Stella was not getting the complete rest she needed. On May 10, for example, she had written Lulo a check for £23, a sure sign that she was still worrying over bills. Margaret worried over evidence that the invalid was in communication with the outside: " . . . it doesn't seem to me to be the complete treatment for Stella to be receiving & sending messages. . . . I wonder if the Doctor knows of the proposal to have a heap of emotional letters ready for Stella the minute she is pronounced fit to receive notes. It sounds very unwise, & I shant contribute." She particularly wanted to know whether the head matron, Miss Stewart, was in touch with Forbes and whether he sent messages. When Lulo replied that he did, Margaret objected. "Please let J.F.R. know when you next write that Stella is not allowed to receive flowers from *anyone* except you and Pat." But Pat was remiss, so Margaret sent him a line:

"Miss Stewart writes to me that Stella has had no flowers for the last fort-night & seems to miss them a great deal." She wondered what had become of him—she wanted to talk with him about the arrears at Beo's school, since that debt seemed the most urgent. She was sending £15; would he please pay it to the headmaster, Mr. Pearce. As for little Stella, Margaret believed her situation most fortunate—such nice little girls, and Mrs. Newton a delightful, sensible mother: "I really hope she may be able to stay there till Stella is regularly back at work & able to make some permanent arrangement for her."

Besides Stella, Forbes also had to think about a theatre for the fall and—that perpetual problem—plays that would suit both him and his partner. He had had an interview with Shaw that day in London, which Shaw duly reported to Ellen Terry: "I have had a talk with Forbes. Mrs. Pat. is ill—nerves, disappointment, alarm at engagements not coming and money going (this as I *guess*: the chivalrous Forbes gives not his lady away). But even there, with Mrs. Pat. to right of us, Mrs. Pat. to left of us, Mrs. Pat. on easel and mantelshelf and wall, *you* were in the middle; and for that I forgave him his Mrs. Pat. and let him read 'The Man of Destiny.'" Forbes also asked for *You Never Can Tell*, which Cyril Maude had almost produced at the Haymarket, and Shaw had hopes. But, writing to Lulo on May 23, Forbes expressed disappointment: "I think to run over to Paris after the tour & see if I can't get a play. Shaw's play that was refused at the Haymarket is hopeless—the old story. I told him frankly what I thought." But he really had only one topic these days:

Have you any more news? I live in hourly fear that dear Beatrice has broken through the ordeal. I sent some flowers, & shall send more tomorrow morning. I wish you & she could have seen Cambridge with me. It is quite beautiful. I did nothing but think how she would have enjoyed it all, & the house full of bright joyous youth, at least so it was last night. The other nights were not good, as there was great excitement in the town about the women wanting to vote for the government of Cambridge, etc. etc. No advance yet with regard to theatre, which makes me very anxious. I do so want to have it all in hand against her coming out of her retreat. . . .

Bradford was not Cambridge, and Forbes found himself depressed with the ugliness of the town and frustrated because they would not deliver his flowers. He comforted himself with the thought that by the time his tour ended in mid-June her ordeal would be over. "I have not seen her for ten weeks," he wrote Lulo on June 1, "it is becoming unendurable." In June came the hopeful news that Stella was getting better, and he and Lulo found they could discuss something else, specifically her dismay that she had been inaudible onstage one night, although Uncle Harry had assured her he had heard. "If the Uncle heard you," replied Forbes, "it is all right, he would not say so if he did not. Vezin must be deaf." But he could not drop his favorite topic long. He was very anxious to hear what Owney, who had visited Stella, thought. He would be in town on the eighth and would call. "She has only two weeks more now," he rejoiced. "I pray Heaven she will come out well and strong."

Dear [Stella scrawled to Lulo in pencil on Sunday, June 20],

I have longed for a letter from you. The doctor has given me permission to write to-day. So I will ask you all the questions I want so much answered. When do Beo's holidays begin? Have any arrangements been made? Does Stella go to a day school at the Newtons? Tell me about them both. What has Pat arranged about money—bills, income tax, etc. It's dreadful to me to think Margaret is paying the money to these people, & I can't hear how much longer I must stay. Tell me about yourself, Greet's season. What parts you played & how you felt about them, how you were dressed—how you were noticed—& how you are, dear, & what further arrangements you have made. I want to hear all about your work—& about everyone & dear Mother & Uncle—

And Johnston. I have longed to hear from him & write to him, but have felt so helpless & weak & imprisoned. Have you seen him, how has he got through the tour. Has he been told not to write to me? I missed his flowers so much.

I ask you all these questions & dread your thinking it unwise to answer them. Lying here imagining all sorts of things is killing. The nurse I had for six weeks left on Saturday. Now I have another—the change is a relief. I wrote a cheque for £3–8/– on Saturday & paid it to Nurse Ivens, 1 Fairleigh Villas, Belgrave Rd, Slough—

If there is no balance will you ask Pat to see to it for me. Is he still at the Mandeville [Hotel]? Are my things there? And my little Billy—does Jo love him very much? Where is Wrighton?

I believe I may have one letter a day. I will write to Johnston when I hear from you. I don't know what has been said. Tell him what I say. I seemed to get better up to 3 weeks ago & then I stopped. The flowers Pat sent are very beautiful, but I fear expensive. Thank him for me. I was glad to see yesterday's wire from the children too—

Can you imagine what it is like here?—& no letters—only my thoughts that clear up nothing. Help me to bear it, dear. My fond love to my children & you all

Beatrice

And Nina—is she settled in her new house? I wanted to write you cheerfully
& my letter reads wretched—

By Wednesday Stella had heard nothing, and found the silence in her
weakened and isolated condition almost intolerable. "I am so bitterly disappointed there is no letter from you to-day," she wrote that afternoon.
"You must have forgotten I have heard nothing for 6 weeks—& how
wretched I am. I have no money & I don't know whether I can write a
cheque, as I don't know what the balance in the bank is. The doctor gets
furious if I speak of going—or writing more than one letter a day—the
position is both miserable & absurd. I am quite sick of everyone here & the
more I try to be hopeful the worse are the moments of depression. Has Pat
any money—how am I to pay for the change the doctor orders to follow
this? & after that what is to happen? I wish you had written. The last 12
hours waiting have been very hard. Tell me everything & what you feel &
think yourself. Sometimes I think I am forgotten quite—but this is silly of
me. . . ."

In her solitude, it was inevitable that reflections and dreams troubled
her. She often thought about Lulo—about the rift that had driven her into
the arms of Joe, about Lulo's accusations that she did not love her enough.
She thought of facing both Pat and Forbes when she was well enough; the
dilemma of satisfying two men who both loved her had, in fact, done
much to bring on the nervous breakdown. She thought about her reclusive
mother and the inevitable gulf created between them by the public life she
led. "Mother used literally to haunt me," she would later confess to Lulo,
"& one night I had a most awful terror that I had never slept with her—it
seemed to me the most awful thing in the world never to have slept with
one's Mother!"

On Thursday, June 25, Stella was comforted by three letters from Lulo
and a little Jubilee charm that she immediately attached to her bangle
bracelet. She was feeling better since Sunday. She was only allowed out of
bed an hour a day, and was sure it was the dullness more than anything else
that made her feel so sick and weary at times. That, and constant money
worries. "It isn't that I mind taking from dear Margaret," she explained,
"but I know she *cannot afford* it. You don't know how she stints herself
to help her friends. As for me I shall never touch money again—I hate it. I
can't keep it—and I can't spend it with any sort of discretion. . . . I am
afraid there is no money in the bank. There is a carriage bill here over
£10." It was so terribly hot that she needed summer clothing. Would Lulo
get out four chemises, four pairs of fine silk stockings, one fine muslin

petticoat, and a summer blouse from among her things and send them. Life was straggling back. Dr. Embleton would let her go tomorrow-week to Malvern for two or three weeks. "Do tell me what Pat arranged with the most pressing bills," she concluded her letter. "I am really strong enough to bear a little burden now."

And so Stella very slowly began to recover. She read William Morris's *Sigurd the Volsung* and found it beautiful beyond belief. She listened to the blackbird's song outside her window, delighted at the way it stopped short in amazement whenever it unexpectedly made a new note. Sunsets through the high window were lovely. She discovered she had a little money in the bank (though she had no idea how it got there), so the carriage bill could be paid. Whenever it was fine, she was allowed to get up and go out to walk ten minutes on the sands. On June 26 she met Henry James, also strolling there, over from Rye. "No doubt this treatment will do your character good!" said James. Stella reported the remark to Lulo appreciatively. "You must not mind pencil," she concluded a note of June 27. "I have just humbly asked for ink & Miss Stewart has sent up a message that the doctor doesn't allow ink to be used in the bedroom!! & I feel quite insulted—which is a sign that my nerves are not right yet! Tell me a little about your talks with Johnston. Do you speak frankly with each other. . . . How did you like the 'Profligate.' . . . Did you see Admiral Guinea? What did Miss Robins do? . . ."

On Thursday, July 1, Stella posted her last letter to Lulo from Rasta. Dr. Embleton had rejected the sea voyage proposed by Forbes as too monotonous. Instead, he had recommended Malvern and after that a trip to Scotland. Arrangements were under way for a nurse at Malvern: two guineas a week, groaned Stella—not cheap. She longed to have Wrighton, but Embleton vetoed the idea of two attendants at once. Dr. Embleton seemed to think it would take another month before her nerves got right again, but one nurse had told her she shouldn't do anything for a whole year. Just the last two days she'd had the complaint and felt horrid. ". . . I daresay when I am well I shall look back on these weary weeks with gratitude," she sighed. "Miss Stewart has just told me I am to have another nurse to go with me on Saturday. Oh, these nurses . . ."

Writing to Lulo, Margaret wondered whether the weeks had seemed very long to Stella, or whether she now really felt the benefit of the rest. "I am sure she must," she decided, "or she would not have stood it."

# FIFTEEN

# *1897*

AFTER EIGHT WEEKS at Rasta, Stella was escorted by Nurse Drury to the Malvern Hills and settled in Kensington Cottage, Great Malvern, a popular and fashionable spa. She was to remain there for two weeks and then go up to Scotland, but plans changed suddenly when the Marchioness of Queensberry wrote Lulo from Hatch House, Tisbury, Wiltshire, "I was so very sorry to hear how ill Beatrice has been, poor dear. . . . I am going abroad for the month of August & could lend Beatrice this place if she likes to come here with you & her children or any one she likes. I would have my servants & carriage for her."

The news, transmitted immediately by Lulo, cheered Stella very much, particularly as she had no idea how her recuperation for the rest of the summer was to be paid for. Meanwhile she settled down to the task of getting a little stronger every day. Her hair stopped falling out and she began to put on weight at last. She read *On the Face of the Waters* and *The Earthly Paradise*, although she could manage only a few pages of the latter a day. She went on donkey rides into the hills, found the donkeys sweet but the hills tiring. One day she and Nurse Drury went on a walk to a place called the British Cave, and there she borrowed a hammock from a hotel and got a boy to string it up in a little wood, and lay there swinging indolently in the trees from 11:30 in the morning till 6:30 that evening, except for a half-hour for lunch. Nurse Drury had an enormous appetite, she told Lulo, and dropped her *h*'s, and was very kind.

But Stella was not really very happy. She missed everyone, and Billie and Humpadincka very much. Her lethargy frustrated her: "I cannot read or write or walk or talk *much*—everything I am obliged to do a *little*—I feel suffocated & giddy *if* I do anything for long," yet (to Lulo) "this place is doing me a lot of good & when I feel a little stronger I shall get about more and it will work wonders." She was particularly anxious for Lulo to wrap up all the letters waiting for her and send them in little bundles so she could read a few a day for amusement. Lulo obliged and the packets began arriving: kind, anxious notes from Owney, Madeline Wyndham, Mary Sheridan, Uncle Harry, Lady Elcho, the Mackails, George Wyndham, Dearest, the Horners, Loulou Harcourt. Viscount Harcourt, unmarried and eligible, seemed particularly anxious about "dear Stella," keeping in touch with Lulo during the early weeks of her illness, and never giving up hope that Stella would be back in London for Jubilee Day to watch the procession from his place at 7 Richmond Terrace in Whitehall—until the thirtieth of June came and went.

Uncle Harry sent his usual sympathetic wisdom, though, Tanner-like, with more heart to offer than practical help:

It was really comforting news, dear, to hear that you are well enough to write and receive letters. Your deep seclusion created a cruel blank in the world, that was becoming absolutely painful. If, however, it has helped to give you back to certain health and to calmer and happier views of life, it deserves and it will receive our sincere and heartfelt commendations. The wish in our hearts, however, was that your eight weeks' retirement might be succeeded by the invigorating sweets of a sea voyage. Think what store of health and strength the sea change would endow you with, and you would return from it to your profession and to the stage really and truly a "new woman" indeed, in the worthy sense, of course, not in the "fin de *sickly*" signification of the phrase. . . .

. . . Of course I understand about your struggle; it could not be otherwise, but I felt sure of you, and that whatsoever fight you might have to fight, you would come out of the struggle, conquering and not conquered. . . .
Only be brave. . . .

"Dearest Uncle," Stella replied, "You have been right, you always said I never saw people and things as they were, that I lived in dreams—now I see, now I know, and I think the knowledge has nearly finished me. Where did you get all your philosophy and unselfishness? I am quite strong again physically—nervously, perhaps, not quite right yet. There are so many things I cannot bear to think of. . . ." One of them was Pat. Everybody had written except her husband; and it was only through Lulo and her own unanswered letters that Stella learned that Pat was "away."

Lulo herself was going on holiday with Mamma, who was ill and restless, to St. Leonards, and was taking bicycle lessons in preparation for the long, flat sea-front roads at that Sussex resort. "Can you mount yet?" Stella wanted to know. Muscularly co-ordinated herself, though she hated exercise, Stella took up cycling and soon was going for two-hour spins alone if

One of the earliest photographs of Stella

Henry Tanner                    Louisa Giovanna Tanner

Patrick Campbell

Stella and Beo, from her private collection

As a young actress

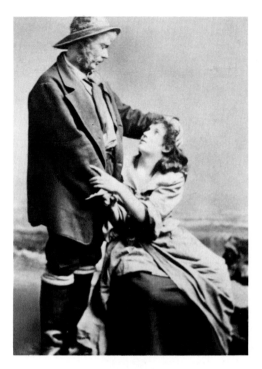

As Tress Purvis in
*The Lights of Home*, 1892

Stella with young Stella and Beo

As Paula Tanqueray

With George Alexander in the first production of
*The Second Mrs. Tanqueray,* 1893

With Herbert Beerbohm Tree in *John-a-Dreams,* 1894

With Forbes-Robertson in *Nelson's Enchantress*    With Forbes-Robertson in *For the Crown*

As Militza in *For the Crown*, 1896

In *The Notorious Mrs. Ebbsmith*

Portrait of Johnston Forbes-Robertson

Stella as Juliet

Stella and Forbes-Robertson in *Romeo and Juliet*, 1895

As Lady Macbeth

Stella as Ophelia

Martin Harvey as Pelléas, 1898

Gerald du Maurier,
from Stella's private collection

Ellen Terry

Elizabeth Robins

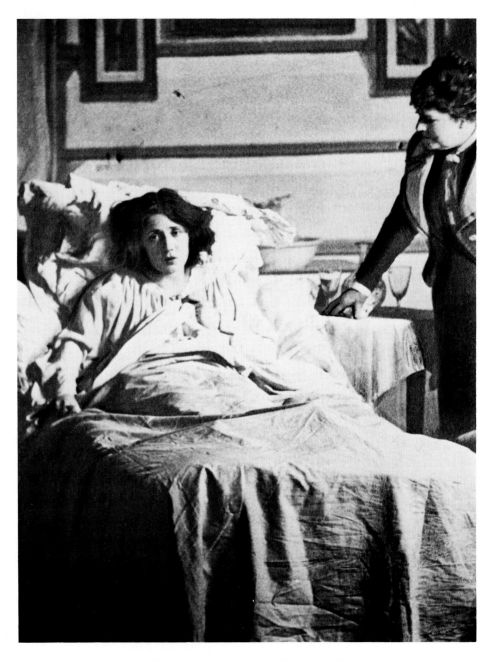

In *Beyond Human Power* with Mrs. Theodore Wright, 1901

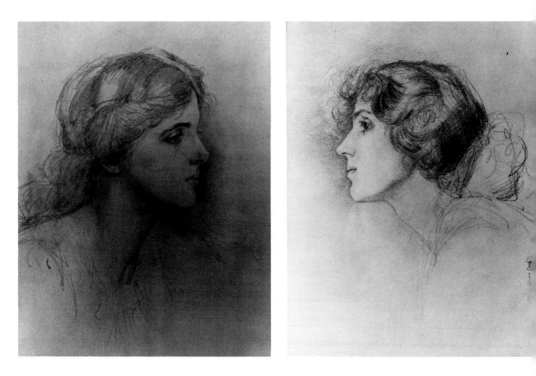

Young Stella (*left*) and her mother (*right*) in drawings by Violet, Duchess of Rutland

Stella and Gabriel Fauré,
by John Singer Sargent

Stella, Beo, and young Stella

Studio portrait of Mrs. Pat

Stella as Mrs. Jordan

Drawing of Mrs. Pat by Sir Philip Burne-Jones

Stella with Pinkie Panky Poo, 1901

only to get away from Nurse Drury, who could not ride. "I am so tired of her," said Stella. "She's a good soul but the *h*'s bother me so—with no one else to speak to." On one of her escapes through lovely, narrow lanes she found a pretty church and, hot with exertion, went in to rest in the cool, dark sanctuary. Presently the clergyman came and five people, and there was evensong. All the church doors stood open in the warm summer evening, the stained-glass windows glowed, the clergyman's voice droned, birds twittered in the hedges, and Stella felt at peace. But solitude continued to depress her. Loulou Harcourt wrote, asking her to call on an aunt who lived nearby, "but I feel shy," Stella told Lulo, "—it's nearly 12 weeks since I have spoken to anyone excepting the one meeting with Henry James." She did speak to at least one person besides Nurse Drury those Malvern weeks, however: a pretty young woman who drove out in a pony and trap, and was soon taking Stella with her. Ginny Moore was refined, lively, pretty, and socially ambitious. The combination appealed to Stella, and they struck up a solid friendship.

Back in London meanwhile, Forbes faced the problem of a theatre, a play, and, of course, a leading lady, since there was no certainty that Stella could join him in the fall. In July there was again an opportunity of taking the Lyceum, since Irving planned to tour; but he had no money this time, and was about to give up the idea when financier Horatio Bottomley again came to his rescue with an offer to back him. Irving himself answered the question of what to perform. "Play Hamlet," said Irving. "Do you really mean that?" asked Forbes, for Irving was not too old to revive his great success. "Yes," said the great actor-manager, "and I will lend you the scenery and the properties."

Forbes was deeply flattered and touched that Irving would hand over to him what could have been a profitable revival for himself. But he still hesitated. "Everybody plays Hamlet," he told Ellen, with whom he had once been very much in love; "it has been played to death; people are sick of Hamlet." Ellen replied promptly: "You would not have, say, a violinist refrain from playing some work of Beethoven's before an audience because that particular piece had been played by many other violinists?" Encouraged by Irving and Terry, Forbes decided to risk giving the world still another version of the Prince of Denmark. He wrote to tell Stella that he would open with *Hamlet* and probably follow it with *Othello*.

"Johnston writes he has taken that huge Lyceum for Sept, Oct, Nov," Stella wrote to Lulo in something of a panic. "He wants to begin early September. He writes happily about it. I don't know what to say. This is for your ears alone." She was not pleased herself. She was not a Shakespearian actress, Ophelia was a small part, and, besides, she was reading Maurice

Maeterlinck's *Pelléas and Mélisande* and had fallen in love with it. Still, she wanted to act, she needed money desperately, and she felt loyal to Forbes. "Have you a Shakespeare you could lend me?" she asked Lulo. "I am not sure where mine is. . . . I would take great care of it." Gradually she tried to forget her lingering weakness and depression and think herself back on the stage again. "Perhaps if I can only pluck up courage I can do it. Nurse heard me a little the other day & I trembled & shook & my heart beat so I had to go away & lie down. How can I rehearse & face Pat—& Johnston— but I'll try. It's better to die trying than going on like this."

The thought of playing with Forbes in September soon began to cheer her: she wanted to work, she wanted to help Forbes any way she could. Nurse Drury was leaving and Stella was glad about that too. She had often been rude, scolding, "There's no doing h'anything with you, you are so h'erratic!" until Stella shook like an old woman with palsy and felt she was going to be sick. Now she wanted Wrighton and, as usual, it devolved upon Lulo to make all the intricate arrangements with Wrighton, the children, and Pat, although Stella begged her to make no alterations in her holiday upon her account. The good news about Pat was that he had gotten a secretaryship to Archibald Ross Colquhoun. "I pray he will take a fresh interest in life," Stella wrote Lulo when she heard the news, for all that spring before her breakdown Pat had been looking so wretched it was dreadful; "I think he will." Bad news was that of the £15 he'd promised her for July he'd sent only £5. He had talked of coming partway to Wiltshire with her and the children. "I hope he won't," said Stella to Lulo. "I would rather not see him yet."

Stella was counting on Wrighton just as she counted on Lulo for everything including directions for getting from Malvern to Wiltshire; then Lulo wrote that Wrighton had given notice. Stella responded, as Nurse Drury would have said, "h'erratically." "I feel I can't stay here any longer so I go to-morrow by the 3.10 to Bath. . . . My nerves are all to bits again—& the complaint is late, & the loneliness here has worried me. . . . If I can work. Ophelia and Desdemona disappoint me so. I know Johnston wishes to play Hamlet & naturally Othello in London after the pains he has had, but there will be no time in 3 months to do any of the work . . . & then Johnston will want me to take less salary—& my bills & the money to go on living! Well, well, things don't seem easier, perhaps my courage will come back again when I get out into the world. . . ."

She found a nice girl to accompany her to Bath—literally picked her up in the street at a very reasonable price, a sweet girl who'd only been in London one day in her life. She hired her to keep her company a few hours a day and to pack for her. On July 28 she left Malvern with the nice Miss Walwyn and, arriving in Bath, took rooms in 27 Brock Street.

Dear [she wrote Lulo the next day],

I nearly wired for you to come this morning. I am glad I didn't—it would have been so selfish of me & I am better this afternoon. The girl is very kind but I am afraid she is frightened. I like her—

Johnston has arranged to open on the 4th & has only got the Theatre & the backer through the *combination*—I & he. . . .

I don't want to make you sad—but in the face of Johnston's letter there is one from the doctor saying if I attempt to work before the end of September I will break down again. Johnston says it will be his ruin if I don't open with him. Keep all this *private*, but write to me, dear, your wisdom.

Stella sent Forbes the doctor's letter. As a result, he came to see her at Bath on the first of August, their first reunion after sixteen weeks. He told her they had no choice. He had taken the theatre, he must open, but he thought he could postpone the opening a few days to give her a little more time. ". . . I think excepting he found me nervous & hysterical he thought I looked well," Stella told Lulo. She had quite changed her mind about her parts: "I have always loved Desdemona & Ophelia. It's only my weak head I am afraid of—& these extraordinary paroxysms that come over me. . . . The complaint has come on, but I have been ill nine days. Could not write or read for more than a quarter of an hour at a time—or talk at all or think of anything without crying—isn't it horrible. . . . The darling children tomorrow." Little wonder Miss Walwyn was frightened. Stella had broken down again, and visitors at Bath turned to stare at the famous actress being wheeled in a bath chair, her black eyes enormous in her pale, haunted face.

Then the children came at last—she had not seen them since early June; and they went to Hatch House, near Tisbury, and Stella had the beautiful little house with its walled garden and postern gate and Lady Queensberry's servants and carriage, and, most of all, the children to help her recuperate for the September opening. Although Hatch House was quite twelve miles from any town, Stella estimated, Clouds was nearby so that the Wyndhams could come over and see her. But when visitors did come—Lady Grosvenor and a party arrived in a carriage—she trembled so that she could hardly speak to them, and felt terribly foolish after they left. "I wonder when you can come," she wrote Lulo. ". . . Some moments I feel so bad & so terrified & often wish you were here with me."

Money constantly worried her. She had arrived at Hatch House with £1 in the world, and there were bills to be met there every Saturday. She wanted Pat to borrow £50 for her, which, if she acted, she would pay in September and October with interest. If she did not act—then Pat must call the Jew, Harry Shain. "I don't see what else can be done at the moment, do you?" she asked Lulo. Pat did borrow £100 for her with £14 interest to be paid in November, but paid only £50 of it into her bank. "You might find out why," she hinted. "Fancy you taking the trouble to make out accounts," she sighed at Lulo's suggestion that Stella might try a little budgeting instead of borrowing. "It's not laziness or cowardice on my part, but I simply *cannot* think of them." Despite his new secretaryship, Pat could not send money, although he finally did write to tell her that it would be best for her to join Forbes that fall; London would be very glad to have her back. But not Shakespeare: couldn't Forbes get her a really good French play?

The question of Lulo's career still occupied Stella. After Greet's Shakespeare season Lulo found herself unemployed. Genuinely glad that her sister had gotten through the "bewildering, wretched, suffering, inactive years" and found herself happy in the theatre, Stella kept offering suggestions. She thought a tour with Greet, if he would take her on, preferable to anything she could get in London. On the other hand, Constance Beerbohm had written daily letters to Malvern, every other one, Stella told Lulo, "wishing you could go to Her Majesty's. If you don't arrange with Greet now, I should write to Tree if I were you. Of course you wouldn't care to come to the Lyceum. I should make you nervous, I suppose. . . ." But the Lyceum was just the place that Lulo, who had little to recommend her but her sister's fame, seemed destined to go; and eventually Forbes offered her a place as understudy for the fall season. Joe Jones was relieved that Lulo had work. "My own little love," she wrote from Wrotham, where she had taken a cottage for a brief holiday, "I *am* glad about Robertson, my weasel—never mind about the 'screw'—even if you only get £1 we'll manage right enough."

Lulo came to Hatch House on Saturday, August 8, bearing Maltine for Stella and trinkets for the children. The conflict of loyalties to her sister and to Joe still troubled her, and Stella often felt obliged to reassure her. "No, my dear," she had written from Malvern, "I didn't run away with any idea that your Joe has made you love me less—in fact, I sometimes feel you *really* love me more now than you did. . . . I was often cruel to you to try & help to make you love me less & yourself more." Most often she simply said, "Don't ever think I don't love you." Tensions remained, however. Now that Lulo was engaged for the fall at the Lyceum, the old question of their living together came up, Stella urging that this time they could live in the same hotel, perhaps the Mandeville, together. Her reasons were not wholly unselfish: she and Forbes would be together a great deal, and a sister in the same hotel would quiet talk. But for Lulo there was Joe, and Joe wanted her to herself, so Lulo left Hatch House with the problem unresolved.

> . . . I will be quite frank with you & then I daresay you will be with me [wrote Stella, marking the letter "*Private*"].
>
> If we could be happy together & not fret each other I should *prefer* that we lived in the same hotel. . . . I think to people who consider such things— & there are many—it would *look much better.* You could spend the day with your friends & go sight seeing & all that sort of thing—only I don't want you to come live with me as a *return* for my getting Johnston to engage you. Do it because you love me & wish to—or not at all.
>
> You told me frankly enough, dear, that you couldn't understand "complex lives." I thank God the mysteries & complexities of life have not overtaken & overshadowed you. They have me—& if you are with me I know you will admit & respect them.
>
> If you would rather live with one of the girls—& indeed I could under- stand only too well your preferring it, say so frankly. Money has nothing to do with it. I particularly want you to enjoy the time. Of course you understand if we live together all business talks etc. must be *private* & you musn't [*sic*] let members of the company try & make you a go-between, or out of your own kind heart take up such a position. There—I have tried to write simply & truly. It isn't easy. I am sorry Joe is not well. My love to you both. Don't worry just say frankly. The time was over long ago for you to take your little sister as a responsibility. I had two reasons for wanting you to come—one because I thought it would help you—the other because I thought you might help me. . . .

Forbes had wanted to open at the Lyceum on September 4; then post- poned the opening night one week for Stella's sake. "I cannot believe I am going back," said Stella. "It seems impossible that I will get my nerves strong enough." But during August she slowly got better. The children were happier at Hatch House than she'd ever seen them. Long carriage drives in the Wiltshire countryside soothed her. Ophelia began to take shape in her mind, and the words came. News arrived that Sir Felix Semon had paid her Brighton doctor bills. She began to feel she might be able to rejoin the world again.

"All the acting has done this," Dr. Embleton had told her; but the cause of her breakdown had not been that simple. Her guilt at leaving Pat to become Forbes's lover had proved unendurable; the conflict of trying to be all to both men unresolvable. Lulo had repudiated "complex lives"; Stella had broken down under the pressures of hers. Yet to Lulo she had written from Malvern, "Hearts don't go on breaking over & over again." It was perhaps with this knowledge that she went back to London to face Pat, Forbes, *Hamlet*, and, as several doctors and nurses had warned her, the strong possibility of another nervous collapse.

# SIXTEEN

# *1897–1898*

*S*TELLA HAD FINALLY little more than two weeks at Hatch House before returning to London for rehearsals. Unable to control her nerves or her tongue, she immediately made difficulties. Ian Robertson acted as buffer between her temperament and the sensibilities of Forbes. Unfortunately, he could be dogmatic and sententious, qualities that brought out the very worst in Stella. She suffered and Forbes suffered far more. "Mrs. Campbell, *you are killing my brother!*" cried Ian during one rehearsal, catching sight of Forbes's haggard face. Certainly he was showing strain. Passing his house in Bedford Square early one morning, Ellen Terry on impulse went in and "pulled the new Hamlet out of bed." "Poor fellow," she told Shaw. "Hamlet's mother and young sisters and I cheered him up a bit. He looks sadly old for a young man. His poor long face!"

It was not only Stella, but the pressures of management and of reviving Irving's well-remembered role that weighed on Forbes. He was forty-four: perhaps he should not have waited so long to create his Hamlet. Many, too, were taking an extraordinary interest in the new production; everyone had an ideal of Hamlet that Forbes believed he was bound to disappoint. One of the most interested was Bernard Shaw. "Johnstone F.R. is in tribulation over his 'Hamlet,' " he had written Ellen at the end of July. "He turned up here the other day beating his breast, and wanting to know whether I couldn't write a nicer third act for 'The Devil's Disciple,' since Cleopatra was not ready for Campbell-patra. . . . I am certain I could make 'Hamlet' a success by having it played as Shakspere meant it. H.I. makes it a sentimental affair of his own; and this generation has consequently never seen the real thing. However, I am afraid F.R. will do the usual dreary business in the old way, & play the bass clarinet for four hours on end, with disastrous results. Lord! how I would make that play jump along at the Lyceum if I were manager." In place of managing, Shaw fired off a long letter of advice to Forbes which the actor received in kindly spirit, even carrying out some of the critic's suggestions. Although he had found his plays impossible so far, Forbes was listening more carefully to the theatrical plans of Shaw, who had promised a Caesar-and-Cleopatra play for himself and Stella. And Shaw himself was finding the pair inspirational. *Caesar and Cleopatra*, which he had been working on at Monmouth that September, had been driven clean out of his head by an idea for another play, in which Forbes should be "a west end gentleman" and Stella "an east end dona in an apron and three orange and red ostrich feathers." But while *Pygmalion* and the Caesar play were germinating, Shaw returned as critic to London for the opening night of *Hamlet* on Saturday, September 11, 1897, quite prepared for "the usual dreary business in the old way."

There were three types of applause, William Archer noted, having sat through two of the three hundreds of times. There was the thoughtless applause of good-natured first-nighters who clapped because clapping was expected of them and they would rather oblige than disoblige. There was the applause of personal fanatics who thought this or that actor the greatest who ever lived, and bellowed themselves hoarse no matter what he played or how he played it. Then there was the third and rarest kind of applause, easily distinguished from the others—when intelligent appreciation chimed in with good nature and fanaticism so that the spontaneous delight of the whole audience found expression. Then an actor with a sensitive ear could tell that he had won over not only the enthusiasts but the discriminating as well. It was the third kind of applause that greeted Forbes-Robertson as he took his triumphant curtain calls that night.

The day after the brilliant success Forbes went back to the theatre and found Sir Henry in his office, newspapers piled high on his desk. Irving's eyes gleamed under his shaggy brows. "You've done it, m'boy," he cried, striking the papers with his long, aristocratic hand, "you've done it!" Forbes had: his Hamlet was immediately acclaimed the greatest in living memory, perhaps one of the greatest in all theatre history.

Stella did not succeed so well. "The first actress who has made a failure in Ophelia"; "Mrs. Patrick Campbell's Ophelia cannot rank among her successes"; "uninspired, ordinary, and uninteresting"; "mannered and self-conscious, though beautiful to the eye." Several of these critics were to change their minds, put off at first by her very unconventional playing of a classic part. Shaw had no need to. "Mrs. Patrick Campbell's Ophelia is a surprise. The part is one which has hitherto seemed incapable of progress. From generation to generation actresses have, in the mad scene, exhausted their musical skill, their ingenuity in devising fantasias in the language of flowers, and their intensest powers of portraying anxiously earnest sanity. Mrs. Patrick Campbell, with that complacent audacity of hers which is so exasperating when she is doing the wrong thing, this time does the right thing by making Ophelia really mad. The resentment of the audience at this outrage is hardly to be described. They long for the strenuous mental grasp and attentive coherence of Miss Lily Hanbury's conception of maiden lunacy; and this wandering, silly, vague Ophelia, who no sooner catches an emotional impulse than it drifts away from her again, emptying her voice of its tone in a way that makes one shiver, makes them horribly uncomfortable. . . . Playgoers naturally murmur when something that has always been pretty becomes painful; but the pain is good for them, good for the theatre, and good for the play. I doubt whether Mrs. Patrick Campbell fully appreciates the dramatic value of her quite simple and original sketch—it is only a sketch—of the part; but in spite of the occasional triviality of its execution and the petulance with which it has been received, it seems to me to settle finally in her favor the question of her right to the very important place which Mr. Forbes Robertson has assigned to her in his enterprises."

Stella had some appreciation of the dramatic value of her Ophelia, however. Her sense of humor, which she did not mind turning against herself, had decided her, after her nervous breakdown, to make Ophelia genuinely mad. She had calculated the visual effects carefully, playing in her own long, dark hair, which she wound with anemones and purple woodbine and, in the mad scene, cradling bunches of river grasses, wild white roses, pink stocks, and daffodils in a black gauze scarf flung round her white dress. In the "Get thee to a nunnery" scene she sat with her head buried in her hands so that she heard only Hamlet's harsh words and could not see the arm outstretched and quickly withdrawn, the longing and pain of renunciation in his face—an effective touch. Yet, as usual, she treasured the comments of friends rather than critics: the Rt. Hon. George Wyndham said she was the best Ophelia he had ever seen; John Singer Sargent complimented her; and Mrs. Nettleship, costumer at the Lyceum, told her secretly that she "didn't care to see anyone act but Mrs. Tanq."

"I *am* so sorry we dont like the same things," Ellen replied from the provinces to Shaw, who had praised Stella's performance to the actress who had played a memorable Ophelia to Irving's Hamlet. "Quite honestly I'd love to like all you like, but Mrs. Campbell as Ophelia I know I could not like. Dont be that kind of donkey to say, 'Ah, yes, jealousy!' I admire Mrs. P.C. as much as most people but I cannot like her Ophelia. If she plays that rightly then she played Mrs. Ebbsmith wrongly, and Mrs. E was just splendid. The Saturday Review of to-morrow will, I expect, explain you."

It did, and at length. Forbes read Shaw's review and, despite the praise of his classic Hamlet, could not help cringing, since in addition to reviling Ian Robertson's Ghost and Miss Granville's Queen, Shaw attacked Irving's memorable version of the part with all his formidable skill; and Forbes idolized Irving. Forbes wrote the reviewer, good-naturedly deploring the censure. "On the other hand," said Forbes, "I rejoice that you have pointed out the beauties of the Campbell's 'Ophelia'—But the Lord bless your sweet life, I wish you were not a critic, as I said before."

Whatever Stella's contribution to Forbes's great performance, *Hamlet* was in for a long run. Stella and Lulo did not take rooms at the same hotel; instead, Uncle Harry about this time took a house at 8 Glebe Place, Chelsea, and Lulo and Joe lived there with him and Louisa Tanner. Pat Campbell left the Mandeville Hotel for 96 Queen Street. Beo travelled the twenty-five miles back to Ripley Court and Mr. Pearce. Little Stella stayed on with Mrs. Newton. Stella rented a quiet country place, Rake Mill, in Milford, Surrey, and went there as often as possible to rest. Lulo continued to juggle dogs, Stella's maid-of-all-work Alice, and the comings and goings of Beo and little Stella. "Dear Auntie," wrote Beo from Ripley Court, "Will you please go to the Mandeville & get a cannon of mine . . . and send it to me as quickly as possible." "My dear Lulo," wrote Stella, "If you can will you write to Alice, 39 Richmond Rd, Bayswater, find out what day she has arranged to meet Stella & meet her with Alice & see if the child has everything she wants . . . & let me know how she looks, etc. etc. I am afraid Pat will be busy & unable to see her off. Do do all you can. I am resting down here, my voice is better, but I will come up if you think it necessary. . . ." At least once Stella and Pat tried to discuss Stella's unhappy division of heart. "Pat came here yesterday and left at 6.00. We had a long talk. I tried to speak simply & truthfully, but he loves me in such a dumb, helpless way—it beggars me."

In December Irving and Terry returned from their tour of the provinces and paid a visit to the Lyceum. That night Stella was, in her words, "very naughty." Knowing that Ellen was in the audience, and egged on by the continual criticism of her playing Ophelia in her own dark hair, as well as by her personal devil, she played half her scenes with her black hair down and half in a blond Ellen wig. "I wanted to know which she liked best," said Stella innocently. Cleverly, Ellen never told her. She was not amused at this Mrs. Pattikins escapade, perhaps because it reminded her of her own little show-stopping ways such as giggling, sighing loudly, and not paying attention onstage. Irving made up for Ellen's indifference when he came to put his arm around Stella's waist after the performance and murmur, "Beautiful, my child, beautiful." But Forbes, a thorough professional, suffered greatly at these breaches of stage decorum, the more because they came from the woman he loved.

On December 13 Shaw reappeared to note the hundredth performance of the play's record-breaking run. He found that while the minor players were just beginning to enjoy themselves, the stars were sleep-walking through a blank-verse dream. "Mr. Barnes [Polonius] raved of some New England maiden named Affection Poo; the subtle distinctions made by Mrs. Patrick Campbell between madness and sanity had blurred off into a placid idiocy turned to favor and to prettiness; Mr. Forbes Robertson, his lightness of heart all gone, wandered into another play at the words 'Sleep? No more!' which he delivered as, 'Sleep no more.' Fortunately, before he could add 'Macbeth does murder sleep,' he relapsed into Hamlet and saved the situation." Forbes might well have mixed plays for a moment—he was studying *Macbeth* for a tour of Germany and Holland planned for February.

The acclaimed and profitable *Hamlet* finally closed on December 18 with Forbes exhausted. Stella had agreed to the tour on condition that when they returned he would produce Maeterlinck's *Pelléas and Mélisande*. Taking the children, she went off on holiday to Great Malvern, where on Christmas Eve she sent dearest Lulo "Just my love & kiss for Xmas day. I have nothing else to send you. It is quite beautiful here & I should love you to come for a day or two towards the end of my visit. Pat & Owney come this evening. I wish you great happiness & success in your work—& that I shall be of help to you. The children both send their love—my love please to Joe." But that Christmas Eve only Owney Urquhart Tanner got off the train; Pat did not come.

Stella spent the holiday going over her parts, finding Lady Macbeth "a stiff study" which, she feared, might take away her high notes for Ophelia, and worrying about Lady Macbeth's walk and arm and hand movements. Forbes wrote they would have thirty days in Berlin with *Macbeth*, *Hamlet*, and, on the advice of Ian and the agent, *Magda*. *Magda* instead of *Tanqueray* she thought a great mistake—like putting the weapons into the German critics' hands to damn them all. She thought Forbes flat and stupid as the father (he had switched from Pastor Heffterdingt) and the keynote to the whole play the original German, whose subtleties English actors did not begin to understand. "Of course you are coming," she scolded Lulo, who had written doubtfully. "Why don't you write to Johnston? He will tell you so. It's *such mock humility* that sort of thing—though I know how nicely you mean it. It can so easily be mistaken for dullness & stupidity. It's very dear of you—but other girls are writing in all the time—& to me too." Eventually Forbes sent her the cast lists and she found Lulo's name, so it was quite settled that Lulo was coming along for £3 or £4 a week to share a room with her unless, of course, Lulo preferred sharing with someone else. She had rethought *Magda*, and confessed herself "in the net" between that and *Tanqueray*. One was a sure success, but the other would be more interesting to work with. "I feel it was my best part," said Stella. But when it was decided for *Tanqueray*, she worried over the revival. Duse had played Paula's suicide in front of the audience, and Stella felt now it would be worthless to play it any other way.

She found Owney restless and unhappy that Christmas season. The Urquharts had strongly objected to her marriage to Max Tanner: Max was unemployable, occupied with his music and chess, nervously unstable— "queer." Despite the birth of a daughter, Marion, the marriage was disintegrating rapidly. When Owney left, Stella's nephew Roy Hill came. Stella found him terribly shy, and only got him to go out to tea once by pulling a tragic face and ranting about the tragic curse of shyness. Beo was cycling and taking photographs, and both children were wonderfully good, although, unfortunately, both had discovered the fascination of the cesspool. Between studying and playing with the children, their mother found time to compare nerves with Forbes's old love Mary Anderson de Navarro, learning that she was tormented with pains in the top of her head and back and was leaving with her husband for a cure at St. Leonards. She also found time to sit for publicity photographs to Mr. Downey, who came from London; but, as she told Lulo, "Directly I got into a position & expression I fancied, he said 'Look 'appy, think of 'im, and don't spit!' "—which inevitably spoiled the pose. Despite occasional attacks of nerves, it was a pleasant holiday, and she dreaded returning for five weeks of rehearsals twice a day. Just at the last moment, as she often seemed to do these days, she pulled back from Lulo's visit. Forbes was calling rehearsals for Thursday, January 13. If Lulo would like some bracing air, she should come Wednesday, although Stella did not feel the trip worthwhile for such a short time. She herself had no place to stay when she got back to London. Perhaps Uncle Harry would let her have his room.

Toward the end of February Forbes's company packed its baggage and set out for Berlin, Hanover, Hamburg, and Amsterdam. Things went smoothly enough until their train reached the German frontier and they began to feel the petty tyrannies of imperial Germany. But the *verboten* atmosphere could not repress Stella. Led by her, they improvised tactics to foil German officialdom. They discovered, for example, that pretending total ignorance of German worked wonders. When a braided official flung open the door of the compartment in which Stella, Forbes, and Lulo were travelling and ordered them to divide up their party and crowd into other quarters, all faces instantly became blank. Then, very solemnly, Stella would introduce Forbes in perfect cockney to the official as " 'Amlet the Dine." This always made a great impact; perhaps, suggested Forbes, they thought it was some sort of high title. On one occasion when a subordinate had failed to impress upon them the necessity of changing compartments, a more gorgeous official took his place. Straddling the middle of the carriage, with much spreading and folding of arms, shaking of head, and other indications of deep emotion, he delivered a tirade that grew more and more threatening and finally rose to a thundering military climax. To his utter consternation, the foreigners received the harangue with beaming faces, clapping of hands, and exclamations of "Wonderful elocution!" "What fire!" "What pathos!" "A born actor!" The official's jaw dropped, he stared speechlessly, then, throwing up his hands, he stormed from the carriage, nearly missing his footing as the train pulled away from the platform.

Forbes found Berlin a showy, tawdry town with florid public buildings and quite hopeless statues. Insolent Prussian officers strutted the boulevards, and the English company were appalled at the humble, even servile, way German citizens tolerated their ridiculous airs. Forbes ran into immediate problems when he found he could not get the stage of the Neues Opern-Theater for rehearsals, although they had come a week early specifically to rehearse. Negotiations with a *Schauspieldirektor* who lied about rehearsals, advertisements, scenery, and everything else drove his own manager to such distraction that Forbes had to send him back to London. Once the company was installed, however, proceedings went smoothly, even to rehearsing the supers, who, since the theatre belonged to the Emperor, turned out to be soldiers. And since it was the Emperor's theatre, the curtain must be raised the moment he and his suite were seated in his box in the center of the dress circle. Unprepared for this ceremony on opening night, March 3, Forbes found himself scattering with the rest of the stagehands to prevent his untimely introduction as Hamlet.

Kaiser William II patronized *Hamlet* and *Macbeth*, but avoided *The Second Mrs. Tanqueray*; it was rumored that Queen Victoria had requested that her grandson boycott the play. Stella and Forbes were astonished to find it a German custom to allow an hour break, usually after the third act, for the audience to take supper while promenading about the grand foyer —a hopeless disruption of the unity of the performance, said Stella. It was during this interval that Forbes, changing after the dagger scene in *Macbeth*, was summoned to the Emperor's presence. Half-naked, he hastily threw Macbeth's royal robe around him, found Stella, and the two of them followed a splendid pair of epaulets up a stairway to a receiving chamber crowded with tall, handsome, burly men in magnificent uniforms, from whose midst the Emperor came, holding out his hand, which Forbes took. "He stood about five feet nine, and was buttoned up to the chin in a uniform," said Forbes. "I noticed that the left wrist, which rested on his sword hilt, was very small indeed, shrunken, and there was a plain gold bangle on it. He spoke English well and fluently, with wonderfully little foreign accent." Stella had her own impression. "I was struck by the Emperor's personality: the impression of intellectual force, the powerful voice —the heavy moustache turned up at the ends—piercing steel blue eyes— and the little withered hand—a gold bangle on the wrist." The Emperor presented gifts: to Stella a diamond collarette designed as a series of inter-locking *W*'s, to Forbes a scarf pin. He spoke readily and intelligently about acting, the drama, *Macbeth*. "What a gentle voice yours is!" he exclaimed to Stella, who was suffering from a cold and could scarcely speak above a whisper. As they were leaving, he spoke to her again: "You must come again, if only to teach my actors not to bellow." "I wish, sir, that I *could* bellow," retorted Stella quickly.

Outside the door they were besieged by reporters whose previously patronizing tone was now replaced by much bowing and scraping. What had the Emperor said to them, *bitte?* Again pretending ignorance of German, Stella and Forbes took pleasure in not saying a word. "I did not see the Emperor again," Forbes recalled. "I had found this man to all appearances a courteous gentleman. Time proved him to be a poor, degraded wretch, with not a shred of honour, steeped in lies and infamy, and directly responsible for ten times more bloodshed than any aggressor mankind has ever suffered under through all history." In 1898 the infamy was not apparent and, as Lady Emma Cavendish, sister of the British Ambassador in Berlin, reported to Stella, "The Emperor has just been with my brother. He is loud in the praises of you and Mr. Forbes Robertson. . . . He thinks the rendering of *Hamlet* and *Macbeth* were the most perfect he had ever seen, and he was full of admiration." The German press generally agreed with the Emperor, even though the subdued, subtle, intellectual style of English acting differed radically from the German. " 'Nerve aristocrats,' they called us," said Stella.

From Berlin they travelled on to Hanover to play at the magnificent Königliche Schauspiele. It was controlled by "a Count Somebody" (as Forbes said) who took much interest in their visit and spoke with them in perfect, cultured English. He was particularly struck by *The Second Mrs. Tanqueray* and by the actress who played her. The ordinary people of his country, he told Stella and Forbes, could not understand a woman like Pinero's heroine: in Germany that class of woman was always underbred and vulgar; only in England and France was a Mrs. Tanqueray possible. By March 22 the company was playing in Hamburg in a third-rate theatre to scant and unappreciative audiences, and everyone was anxious to leave for Amsterdam, where they played in such a perfectly appointed and well-run municipal theatre that Forbes was ashamed to think that England with all her wealth and power did not have a single municipal playhouse in the land. Amsterdam audiences were incredibly enthusiastic, the house was packed for all performances, and when the curtain went down on the last production, *Hamlet*, the vast audience rose and waved their hats and handkerchiefs in a long and heartfelt demonstration.

The Amsterdam triumph behind them, the question of what to play back in England immediately arose again. Forbes had asked Stella to tour the provinces with him late that spring; she had held back, and without her he gave up the idea. But he did not like the proposed *Pelléas and Mélisande*, considering it a weak and morbid play. Ian Robertson was even more opposed to Maeterlinck. "Why do you want to make such a damned fool of Forbes?" he asked resentfully. But Stella had immediately fallen in love with the play. Jack Mackail had brought her his translation one day, written out in his own fine hand—an offering to the woman whose "queer beautiful radiance" captivated him. "This archaic poem of beauty, passion and loveliness, un-thumb-marked and un-dog-eared by 'tradition,' gave me peace and certainty," said Stella, the Pre-Raphaelite aesthete; "I had come into my own. I *knew* Mélisande as though she had been part of me before my eyes were open. I *knew* I could put the beauty of the written word into colour, shape, and sound." Then on February 9, before the German tour, Mackail had sent a little parcel to "dearest Stella." "My love & a thousand happinesses to you on your birthday: and I have nothing to give you but this: inside you will find a setting forth of the scenes for Pelleas which amaze me by the fewness of their number." So now she insisted. Forbes had promised to produce *Pelléas*; she held him to his promise.

This disagreement over repertoire marked the growing tension between Forbes and Stella as an acting team. Forbes wanted to play classical drama in the classical style that he practised so finely—the Hamlets, Macbeths, Othellos, and Romeos. Stella did not have a classic style and felt oppressed by the tradition overshadowing the roles of Ophelia, Lady Macbeth, Desdemona, and Juliet. She had ignored it, and had been harshly criticized for her rebellion. Nor could she accept the secondary nature of parts like Desdemona and Ophelia. After dominating as Paula, Magda, and Agnes, she did not at all like giving up center stage. She was also more eager than Forbes to experiment with untried plays and playwrights. Finally, even though they shared profits and Forbes often gave in to her demands, he was officially her manager—and Stella could not be managed.

Forbes kept his promise and booked the Prince of Wales's for Maeterlinck's play in June; yet they were conscious of a rift which had been sealed over for the moment, but which, each feared, could easily break open and widen in the future.

# SEVENTEEN

# 1898–1899

STELLA THREW HERSELF energetically into making her play the dream of beauty she imagined. Jack Mackail counseled with letters and sketches. Dearest suggested a long-wristed medieval tunic of gold that turned Mélisande into one of his own mystical maidens, wrapped in dreams, gossamer, and her own long hair. She believed the right incidental music was crucial, and decided that Gabriel Fauré's intimate, elegant style could best capture the play's atmosphere. She got her friend Frank Schuster to arrange a meeting with Fauré at Schuster's house in Queen Anne's Gate. He came, and Stella stumbled through a reading of Maeterlinck in her schoolgirl French. Fauré listened sympathetically, and humbly promised the actress he would do his best. The two of them posed for John Singer Sargent: Fauré in the foreground, white hair and white moustaches; Stella, graceful and delicate, looking over his shoulder. Fauré returned to Paris. The music at length arrived, and Stella was delighted: "He had grasped with most tender inspiration the poetic purity that pervades and envelops M. Maeterlinck's lovely play."

Resolved not to make a damned fool of himself, Forbes cast himself as the jealous husband rather than Mélisande's young lover, Pelléas, a part for which in any case he was too old. The subsequent search for the ideal Pelléas ended at last when Maeterlinck's translator, Alfred Sutro, saw Martin Harvey in *The Children of the King*, wrote him immediately, "You are Pelléas," and recommended him to Forbes. There was something exactly right about "Little Jack Harvey," as Ellen Terry affectionately called him: his youth, the delicate face and melancholy eyes, the curious timbre of his voice. Moreover, Harvey worshipped Maeterlinck and had long dreamed of playing Pelléas. Maeterlinck himself crossed to London to watch rehearsals —a tall, striking man affecting the high black satin stock sported by young Paris literati. He had never been quite able to visualize his boy-lover; at the first dress rehearsal he saw him incarnated in Martin Harvey. Maeterlinck's eyes filled with tears. *"Il a volé mon âme, ce M. Harvey,"* he declared. (A more eloquent compliment than that paid by Stella when, coming upon Harvey backstage in his winged Pelléas headgear, she exclaimed, "My dear, you look like a great *mawth!"*) Still, rehearsals were difficult, with Stella arguing with Forbes and Ian on points of interpretation and stage business. "I battled through at the theatre," she said; and this time she had Martin Harvey on her side.

One event spoiled Stella's happiness in her play. Coming out of the theatre on June 17, the last day of rehearsal, she saw placards announcing the sudden death of Sir Edward Burne-Jones that morning. It was a sorrowful shock. She was an intimate of the Burne-Jones household and had been looking forward to acting for Dearest the Mélisande he had inspired in so many ways. "I must write to you although I can say nothing," Madeline Wyndham sympathized on the day of the funeral. "Your heart is with Margaret to-day, this bitterest of days for Margaret and all his. . . . And I really grieve for you to have to act to-morrow with this on your heart, but so life goes on. He was to have dined (they were all coming to-night) with me for my birthday, but now he dines in the Courts of Heaven."

Forbes would not risk an evening performance of Stella's play. The first matinee took place on Tuesday, June 21, 1898, at the Prince of Wales's Theatre, a day that also marked Stella's and Pat's fourteenth wedding anniversary. Maeterlinck's play tells the tale of the beautiful Mélisande living in a castle by the sea, and of her first encounter with physical passion in the love of Golaud, whose desire awakens in her only fear; of Golaud's younger brother, Pelléas, and the gradual dawning of love between them; of Pelléas's heavy conscience and their farewell meeting in the wood; of Golaud's stabbing Pelléas to death in a fit of jealous passion; of Mélisande bearing Golaud's child, forgiving him, and dying. The gloomy beauty of the setting, Harvey's seraphic Pelléas, Forbes's passion-worn violence, and Stella's childlike, other-worldly beauty—all beguiled the audience's senses into that "willing suspension of disbelief" so necessary to Maeterlinck's precious symbolic dream.

"The play had an overwhelming success," said Stella, "M. Maeterlinck being still more warmly hailed as the Belgian Shakespeare." Critics who found the play faintly silly still praised Stella, several declaring that in Mélisande she reached the pinnacle of her art. "Her beautiful delivery of the words, the vague dreamy manner in which she moves through the scenes, and her exquisitely picturesque appearance—all make up an impersonation of rare physical grace, distinction and poetic charm," sang the *Times*. Said Walkley, enchanted, ". . . we view a Mélisande more beautiful to the eye and ear than the Mélisande of our dreams. . . . The sheer physical pleasure of the thing is not to be described." "It is not given to many women in a generation to be so beautiful as was Mrs. Campbell, when she leant out from the window, her whole body yearning towards her boy lover, yet with unconscious innocence suggested in some indescribable way: playing it was, play you felt it to be, yet behind every word and gesture of the girl at play, there was the woman latent," rhapsodized the Manchester *Guardian.*

Max Beerbohm rejoiced in the sight of Mrs. Campbell and Mr. Harvey treading "that dim and delicate path of beauty." "Mrs. Campbell is beyond comparison," said J. M. Barrie; "better than she has ever been in anything else." "Her Mélisande is pure delight," said Graham Robertson. Even the balanced Archer succumbed. Publicly and privately, in short, Stella heard nothing but praise; her belief in the play as a personal vehicle was justified. *"Je n'ai pas besoin de vous dire avec quelle joie j'ai vu votre beau triomphe,"* wrote the author. "You have taught me that one need never be afraid of dreaming dreams of too great beauty, since it is our good fortune now and then to meet a privileged being who can render them visible and real." If Stella felt any dissatisfaction after such wide acclaim, it was that Forbes-Robertson was receiving all the credit for the experimental triumph.

There was indeed one London critic who might have blown away the whole misty Pre-Raphaelite dream with a shout of laughter, but a month earlier his readers had opened the *Saturday Review* to find Bernard Shaw's farewell to dramatic criticism as he turned over the post to Max Beerbohm. A profound sigh of relief passed through theatreland. Never had a critic been able to thrust so confidently right at the heart of a performer's failure. "I should be delighted to pay his funeral expenses at any time," said Sir Henry Irving, Shaw's chief target in his three and a half years as critic. "First night nervousness was bad enough, but the night before his criticism appeared was worse," groaned Beerbohm Tree. "Now the playwrights may sleep in peace, and the actor may take his forty winks without anxiety," said Charles Wyndham, actor-manager of the Criterion. "We pretended he was not serious, but our fingers trembled as we turned to his articles. A good riddance, but how we shall miss what he might have said about the others!" sighed Stella.

*Pelléas and Mélisande* was given nine matinee performances until July 7. One afternoon Sarah Bernhardt, playing in *La Dame aux Camélias* and *Phèdre* at the Lyric, was brought to see the play by the famous wigmaker W. Clarkson. The wraithlike actress with the frizz of red hair was captivated by its beauty, and by the beauty of Mélisande. There were several meetings, and Sarah declared that she would like to play Pelléas to her new friend's Mélisande. "I thought it only a pretty compliment she was paying me," said Stella. She had been overwhelmed with Sarah's Phèdre, but had seen her in nothing else. Duse she had seen more often, but had not been overwhelmed, finding her too sad and too slow, though possessing great dignity. Mary Anderson she thought harsh and graceless. Ada Rehan disappointed—"very original & splendid when she is shrewish, but there is nothing poetical or aesthetic about her." She admired Réjane; she very much admired Ellen Terry. But Sarah was the first great actress she took to immediately as a person. "My *dear* Sarah!" said Stella.

After *Pelléas* closed, Stella and Forbes set out for the provinces, playing Maeterlinck and *Macbeth*, since Forbes planned to open at the Lyceum with the production that had been praised in Germany and Amsterdam. No letters to Lulo survive from this tour; probably few, if any, were written, for the growing estrangement that had seen Stella's "My dear darling" salutation cool over the years to "Dear Lulo, I send what I can" had at last erupted into an open quarrel. Lulo, who shied away from "complex lives," had found herself uncomfortably close to them on the tour with Stella and Forbes. The tour had also made it clear to her that she would never be more than a walk-on in the theatre—and this by courtesy of Stella. She had tried to imitate her younger sister and had failed; and discovered she did not love Stella better for the failure. Understandably, too, she was tired of playing Stella's errand girl. Certainly Stella was generous, buying her hats and gowns, often sending money, but the life of a paid servant no longer appealed to her.

For her part, Stella had her own objections to Lulo. She had gotten over the initial shock of Joe Jones and sincerely wished her sister happiness, but Lulo's affair with another woman did not make them closer. Lulo's growing religiosity was even more alienating. The previous Christmas Stella had merely acknowledged receipt of a religious bookmark from Lulo and Joe without thanks; now Lulo's Catholic enthusiasms were growing tedious. The sisters broke abruptly—"with vileness"—and the loving relationship of thirty years was over. Lulo gave up hopes of acting, took to painting miniatures, and dreamed with Joe of the day they might afford a little cottage together in the country.

In September Stella and Forbes were back in London to rehearse for opening on the seventeenth. Having triumphed with Hamlet, Forbes cautiously looked forward to another success with Macbeth. But there was trouble from the start. The scene designer—there were no less than sixteen different scenes—fell ill in the middle of his work and much of it had to be completed inadequately by assistants. The composer Forbes had commissioned months before to write an overture and incidental music failed to deliver at the last moment, leaving sixteen scenes to be changed without a note of accompaniment. Rehearsals under Ian's painstaking direction with endless shifting of heavy properties were nerve-wracking. Since Forbes allowed her Lady Macbeth prominence, Stella had no complaints about a minor role. Yet, despite the barbaric splendor of her costumes—one sequined all over like a coat of mail in gold, green, and blue; another a gorgeous robe of gold tissue emblazoned with strange birds and jewelled embroideries—she could not get the same barbarity into the part, finding herself after Mélisande out of tune with the atmosphere of terror and violence. Forbes found himself doubting whether the ideal Hamlet could after all be the ideal Macbeth. The fact that Irving and Terry's 1895 revival had misfired did not add to their confidence.

The first-night Lyceum audience was as indulgent as ever, but when the papers came in on Sunday, Stella and Forbes found the critics accusing them of the same flaws they had felt themselves during rehearsals. The horror and brutality were missing, said the critics: they played with too much intelligence, discrimination, and lyricism in a modern *fin de siècle*, rather than Shakespearian, mood. Walkley and Beerbohm were among the few dissenters. "Mrs. Campbell's Lady Macbeth is . . . novel and interesting," said Walkley, "but it is also something more, and something very important—it is a perfectly possible and plausible interpretation of the character. . . . Where her modernity comes in is in the substitution of a mysterious sensuous charm for the conventional domineering of a virago. I have tried to sum up this type in the word 'Baudelairean.' I see that my friend, the theatrical critic of *The Leader*, calls it an Aubrey Beardsley type, which is another way of putting exactly the same thing. The woman clings and kisses and casts a spell, she magnetises her Thane. When words fail she rests her two hands on his shoulders, almost winds herself round him, looks him straight in the eyes with a strange smile, and the poor man melts like wax. It is the 'Baudelaire' enchantress, the 'femme serpent,' and, as I have already said, it delights me . . . partly because it appeals to me as true, for Macbeth was moulded by his wife, not merely by the influence of a strong will over a faltering will, but by the witchery of woman over man."

In place of Shaw's method of systematic attack on all theatre not coming his way, Max Beerbohm offered an urbane, witty common sense. He did not have the puritan distaste for eroticism on the stage which had often caused Shaw to condemn Stella because she had captivated his senses. Max had no particular struggle. He liked women; his favorite possessed what he called "the charm of windowhood"—Stella's Mélisande windowed in her tower epitomized for Max feminine beauty. In society (as the socialist "downstart" Shaw was not), Max also approached Stella with more tacit sympathy. Not that he could not laugh at her pretensions. At his home in Upper Berkeley Street, where his small, bright-eyed mother in black silk and lace cap presided over delightful luncheons assisted by sisters Constance and Agnes, they had a catch phrase, "It's a first-class thing." "It came from Johnston Forbes-Robertson," explained Max. "He was somewhere, in some drawing-room, and he noticed a mezzotint of some eighteenth-century admiral that hung on the wall. He reflected how dreary it was. Mrs. Patrick Campbell sailed in. Her eye went at once to the admiral. She began rhapsodizing about him; she became aerated about that admiral—to the delight of the host, of course, who was a bigwig and hadn't realized he had such a masterpiece on his wall. Mrs. Campbell couldn't say enough about the mezzotint—it made the room, it transported you. When she had done, she swept down on Johnston. 'Don't you agree?' she demanded. Johnston was determined to puncture the tyre of Mrs. Campbell's ecstasy. 'Yes,' he said calmly, 'it's a first-class thing.' We never stopped using it," laughed Max. "When I was drama critic on the *Saturday* and came back to Upper Berkeley Street after a play and my mother asked me about it, that phrase would save me more ample criticism. It was a wonderful short cut for settling so many questions."

Although Max might have passed off *Macbeth* as "a first-class thing" at home, he gave it sympathetic praise in his column. He dismissed all talk about the Forbes-Robertson/Campbell modern *Zeitgeist* and neurotic subtlety and Pre-Raphaelitism as nonsense. The idea that *Macbeth* had only been acted in the blood-and-thunder convention of Mrs. Siddons was mere fallacy. If Mrs. Campbell and Mr. Robertson had made their appeal to intellect and beauty rather than to the sense of terror, intellect and beauty were universals, not something peculiar to the age. "Both took the line laid down for them by their natural method. I thought that both performances were very beautiful. It does not matter in what method Macbeth and Lady Macbeth be played, so long as they be both played well in the same method. A violent Lady Macbeth and a gentle Macbeth, or *vice versa*, would be a nuisance. Mrs. Campbell and Mr. Forbes Robertson act in perfect harmony. . . . Indeed, the whole production is a great success." But, added the puckish Max, he trusted it would be the last production of *Macbeth* for many years to come.

Most critics, however, called her Lady Macbeth a failure, and Stella did not disagree. One night after the curtain had fallen, Graham Robertson went backstage, profoundly depressed. He found Stella in white sleep-walking robes sitting in a gloomy little heap.

"Well?" she asked.

Robertson failed to conceal his feelings.

"Damn," said Stella simply. A melancholy pause. "But look here—that speech in my first scene—the Spirits of Evil—didn't that go? I worked and *worked* at that."

Robertson could not say it had.

"Oh, damn!" wailed Stella. "I can't do it. I feel all the time that the woman would not speak like that—she couldn't say such things—*I* shouldn't say such things."

"But Lady Macbeth isn't speaking," ventured Robertson. "She's thinking, and her thoughts are put into words by the poet."

"But you can't say such words *naturally*. Ellen Terry tried and what did she do? She chopped the lines into little bits and pumped them out in staccato jerks."

Yes, reflected Robertson; but Terry's hard, staccato jerks had "got there," whereas, although Stella spoke the Shakespearian periods with feeling for rhythm and melody, her delivery lacked grandeur and import. The modern school, he concluded, would have to learn declamation from the old before it could give Shakespeare rhetorical effect. Stella was a lyric artist; the epic still evaded her.

Their run at the Lyceum closed on December 10 after fifty-eight performances of *Macbeth* and five matinees of *Pelléas and Mélisande*. Discouraged, Stella and Forbes decided to part company temporarily. Disagreement about plays was becoming serious. Forbes was still eager for Shaw's *Caesar and Cleopatra*; Stella waited coolly, unimpressed thus far with Shavian drama. On January 13, 1899, Shaw went with his new wife, Charlotte, to tea at 22 Bedford Square to talk about the Caesar play, and Forbes was encouraging enough for Shaw to write to Max Hecht, principal investor in the new Lyceum Limited Company, "I have written a play—a magnificent, recklessly expensive play—for Forbes Robertson and Mrs. Patrick Campbell. . . . But Forbes has no theatre and no money, Macbeth having cleaned him out. He is at present rallying his backers so as to astonish London as Julius Caesar next winter. Now I think it extremely likely that Forbes isn't a good man of business, and that he will raise the money on unnecessarily hard terms unless he can persuade some able management to go into the affair with him. Why shouldn't the Lyceum Limited do this? On the whole, Forbes Robertson & Mrs. Pat look more like the heir & heiress apparent to Irving & Ellen Terry than any other pair."

Hecht did not take Shaw's suggestion, Forbes was indeed cleaned out, and Shaw found himself appealing directly to Stella, for that late winter she had left for the provinces with her own company on "Mrs. Patrick Campbell's Tour." She had hired Arthur Bertram, business manager for *Pelléas* at the Prince of Wales's; he had booked her from February 20, 1899, into the first week of April for Kennington, Birmingham, Dublin, Newcastle-on-Tyne, Glasgow, Liverpool, and Southport. Her company included the exotic and eccentric Courtenay Thorpe as leading man; her favorite, Nutcombe Gould; and a promising, young, aristocratic-looking actor named Harley Granville-Barker. Her repertoire—Tanqueray, Ebbsmith, and the part she wanted to conquer more than any other, Magda. With two popular plays, she did not need Shaw's *Caesar and Cleopatra*, although she consented to give a single copyright performance on March 15 at the Theatre Royal, Newcastle-on-Tyne, turning Shaw's mere kitten of a Cleopatra into an experienced pantheress. If Shaw expected her to add his play to her repertoire, he was disappointed. He did not give up, coaxing her to come to Hindhead (where he was recuperating from a foot infection) to discuss the play, telling her to bring "Caesar" along with her, and offering her the first act as a curtain-raiser. But Stella did not come. She did not appreciate Shaw's anti-romantic drama with its wise and urbane Caesar spurning the petty wiles of a very young Cleopatra and gladly turning her over to Antony. The great part was Caesar, and Stella did not intend to walk back into another Hamlet-Ophelia situation just when she had become star and manager herself.

Other changes were taking place in Stella's life. After her breakdown she had given up housekeeping, stored the furniture, sent the children to school, and moved into furnished apartments. But she had always wanted a home of her own. She finally chose number 33 in old Kensington Square, a white Queen Anne house of five floors with a white-panelled drawing room on the first floor, dining room on the ground, bedrooms on the second and under the mansard roof, and kitchen and servants' quarters in the basement. There was a garden in back, pathways of Dutch tiles bordered by beds of geranium and heliotrope and shaded with elms. Margaret and Jack Mackail were right around the corner in Young Street; the address was good and almost within her means. Her tour ended, she moved in with her Bluchner piano, her many fine books, her Murillo, Sargent, Burne-Jones, and Clifford, Handel's snuffbox and shoebuckle, and, of course, the little dogs. The children came regularly on holidays. Pat and Forbes came, but not together.

From the time of her first great success Stella had had plays thrust upon her personally by both established and unknown playwrights; but, with the exception of *Pelléas*, she had found no reason to take them, since her managers—Alexander, Hare, Tree, and Forbes—always decided what would be played in their theatres. She had broken away from Forbes to play the roles she liked; now, as her own manager, she could look about for plays. One of the first to come to her notice was professor Gilbert Murray's *Carlyon Sahib*, a drama about the tyrannies of an Anglo-Indian imperialist in India. The part of the Rt. Hon. Sir David Carlyon's daughter Vera, torn between loyalty to her father and horror at his crimes, appealed to her, particularly since Vera is a complex and intelligent woman whose struggle against her father involves the question of sacrificing her career as a doctor. "I am delighted with 'Carlyon Sahib,' " Stella wrote Murray, a young, able, and progressive scholar, currently Professor of Greek at Glasgow University. She had given a copyright performance at Southport on tour, and now decided to produce the play in London. She chose the suburban Prince of Wales Theatre in Kennington, where she was currently playing, and planned to open on Monday, July 19, 1899.

The combination of rehearsing *Carlyon Sahib* during the day and acting every evening proved exhausting; as she told Murray on June 15, "I am too tired with rehearsals to do myself justice at night." She was not really satisfied with anyone at rehearsals and most dissatisfied with herself. Lady Mary, Murray's wife, asked to come to the theatre; Stella put her off, "But do you come please, & sit in the stalls & just say ANYTHING you like to all of us," she invited Murray. She regarded the play as purely experimental and felt cautious about advertising it for more than a week; then allowed Arthur Bertram and the manager of the Prince of Wales to talk her into announcing a fortnight's run. She knew Murray was a scholar, not a popular playwright; but she had liked his play, and the challenge of doing what she liked was irresistible.

The British establishment could hardly be expected to applaud anti-imperialistic sentiment at any time. In 1899, two years after the enthusiasm of Queen Victoria's Diamond Jubilee and with hostilities mounting in South Africa, Stella might have foreseen that the conservative press would dislike a drama portraying a British colonial as a man who murders the child born to him by his housekeeper, deliberately spreads cholera among the natives by poisoning the wells, and cuts out the tongue of the native leader who could have testified to these crimes. And so, although Professor Murray "was twice drawn by the slim hand of Mrs. Patrick Campbell through the crimson curtains at Kennington's new theatre" to take his bows, the press the next day wiped that brief triumph from the record. "A more unfair and un-English attempt to misrepresent the great service which governs India could not have been made," declared the *Times*, adding, "The piece is to run at Kennington for a fortnight. But it can hardly be expected that so unreal a story, based on a motive which is so repugnant to the mind of Englishmen, will enjoy a long life." The *Times* did not err. Stella's only comfort was that the intellectual critics Walkley, Archer, and Max Beerbohm defended the venture and praised the acting ("Patricia did not know her lines & refrained from acting most of the times," was Murray's comment, however), and that the intellectual set who patronized the performances admired her for the experiment. They were, of course, too few. "Now that I have had time to think," Stella wrote Murray on July 4, "I see what a gross error I made in advertising the play for more than a week if I was *not prepared to lose money.*" Five per cent of the gross receipts did not make Murray's fortune either. But the venture stimulated them both—Stella, who had until now felt snubbed by the New Drama highbrows, and Murray, who had more plays in mind.

In fact, the adventure whetted Stella's appetite for management. Money was a problem, but with her genius for attracting the right kinds of friends, finding backers did not prove difficult. Curiously, of the group who put £12,000 into her hands that summer of 1899, two were friends who had come to her through Pat, so that once again the connections of that shadowy husband helped finance her career. They were Dr. (later Sir Starr) Jameson and Lord Grey, the fourth Earl. Both were Rhodesian administrators, both were close to Cecil Rhodes, both promoted the fortunes of the British South Africa Company. "Doctor Jim," as Jameson was called, had ridden north with the pioneer expedition to Mashonaland, and Pat had ridden with him. With Archibald Ross Colquhoun, Jameson had secured Manicaland for the Chartered Company; Pat was now secretary to Colquhoun. Compared to these empire-builders, Pat was a cipher, and Stella with some justification counted Doctor Jim and Lord Grey more her friends than Pat's; yet it was Pat's African ambitions that steered them to her.

Having found backing, Stella thought of Forbes, and the good parts (after all) she had played under his management, and his current financial difficulties, and his (continued) adoration and suffering, and all the (considerable) glamour of their partnership. "I begged that he should be included in the venture," said Stella. "This at first met with some objection, but finally I won my way." They agreed upon a joint season that autumn at the Prince of Wales's, where they had played *Pelléas*, although Forbes would actually be under Stella's management, since the money was hers. They could not agree so well about a play. As Stella remembered it later, Forbes was under contract to produce *The Moonlight Blossom*, a Japanese play by Chester Bailey Fernald, and agreed to join her only if this play was their first production. She was not enthusiastic about the play, but accepted the condition, taking some comfort in the fact that as Inamura Nanoya she could mince about in gorgeous kimonos, though at her height of more than five feet nine she was hardly a credible Japanese woman.

A September opening having been set, they separated for the holidays, Stella going to Stanway, where she had begun to look upon Lord and Lady

Elcho's eldest son, Ego, as an eligible match for her Stella, at thirteen developing into a dark beauty, though quiet and repressed under her mother's flamboyance. And subsequently to Mells, where golden-haired Frances Horner sat with her by the bedroom fire at night, running her hands through her hair, exchanging confidences about men, love, and life. At Mells they spent long days in the garden, where the family's greatest amusement was to swim in the lake, generally at a spot where it was forty feet deep. Apart from her brief experiment with a cycle at Malvern, Stella loathed exercise, but, given a bathing dress and told by Sir John Horner, "It's quite easy, jump in!" she jumped and locked her arms around his neck. "We both nearly drowned," said Stella. "Frances pulled me out amidst peals of laughter from the children. How young we were!"

She admired all the Horner children for their aristocratic beauty, but particularly liked little Mark, smothering her laughter one day when she heard him say to the coachman with inimitable dignity, "And are you a married man?" They had become friends one day at a luncheon party when the door opened and he stole in with a tiny cap pistol which, as he marched solemnly around the table, he fired deliberately at each guest. He was pointedly ignored until he came to Stella. He aimed, fired, and to his delight she slipped quietly off her chair onto the carpet—dead. But then she was very much a child herself—a fool, as she so often said—and could romp and clown with children happily.

By now, however, Stella was not only patronized by the aristocracy, but had become something of a patron herself. Her house in Kensington Square was becoming a rendezvous for artists, poets, aesthetes, playwrights, and the social set that wanted to know them. That year she adopted a young American whom she had seen dancing for her own amusement in Kensington Gardens. Stella entertained Isadora Duncan and her brother Raymond by playing the piano, singing old English ballads, and reciting poetry—but soon gave them hope that London might like to be entertained by them. She gave them an introduction to George and Sibell Wyndham, since all the currently important literary and artistic people converged at 35 Park Lane. The connection in fact proved a major advance in Isadora's career; for everyone came to see her dance there, and there she met Charles Hallé, who was to have a crucial impact on the development of her art.

It was as artist, patron, and manager that Stella called rehearsals that September, feeling that at last she had come into her own. Rosina Filippi ("a clever actress," said Stella), Frank Mills, and the fine comedian James Welch were engaged for Mitsu, Sakata, and Bummawashi. Perhaps the elaborate temple and garden sets, the exotic duel on stilts, the costumes— Stella in cream brocade patterned with dragonflies, a flame silk sash around her slender waist, and crimson chrysanthemums in her black hair—and the esoteric symbolism of the sacred flower which blossoms only once every thirty years by moonlight helped disguise from the players the fact that they were dealing with a stupid play. Yet a pair noted for their subtle, intellectual acting could not really have deluded themselves: not Stella, adopting the bent back, shuffle, and sing-song of Nanoya; not Forbes as the outcast nobleman Ita Arumo, yellowing his classic features and screwing his wavy brown locks into an Oriental topknot.

On opening night, Thursday, September 21, the curtain fell to hearty applause and cries of "Author! Author!" proving again the notorious unreliability of first-night audiences. Critics were not fooled. A play so lacking in vivacity and truth could not, said the *Globe*, hope for a very enduring success. The *Star* found the story irritating, the piece a mere curiosity which, with all the goodwill in the world, the critic could not accept as a substitute for a play. Max Beerbohm said that Stella as the coquetting, tea-pouring Nanoya was like a child playing the piano with one finger. J. T. Grein was blunt: "It is all vapour, and although I can understand how the Actress-Manageress, Mrs. Campbell, would see something in a play wherein she could wed her personal attractions to the silks and sashes and the capricious designs of Japanese fashions, I cannot for the life of me understand how a sober-minded man and a thorough artist like Forbes-Robertson could be induced to venture a small fortune and tremendous labour on such vapid stuff." "The production was a most expensive one; the piece a disastrous failure," said Stella herself. "The papers said that Mr. Robertson looked like 'Widow Twankey' . . . ; our attempt at impersonating Japanese met with no success."

Attempting to save the season, they added to the bill a short but powerful play called *The Sacrament of Judas* that Forbes had picked up from a Paris bookstall. Admirably translated from the French of Louis Tiercelin by Louis N. Parker, it contained a fine part for Forbes as Jacques Bernez, an apostate priest who is forced to give absolution—the sacrament of Judas —to the nobleman who has seduced and betrayed the woman he loves. "Instant and deserved success attended the production," said the *Daily Telegraph*; and the one-act play drew the town for several weeks. The Prince of Wales himself attended and sent for Forbes to congratulate him. He was very much impressed with the piece, but wondered whether Forbes had received any complaints from Roman Catholics about putting a confession scene on the stage. He had not, said Forbes, although he had had plenty of objecting letters from Protestants. Unfortunately, said Stella, who played the part of the seduced peasant girl, the play did not help matters financially. The disastrous *Moonlight Blossom* came off on November 11;

four days later *The Canary* by "George Fleming" (Constance Fletcher) took its place.

Stella thought Constance Fletcher, a large, pale young woman who had written the best-seller *Kismet* at eighteen, very clever; and audiences found her little play clever as well. In it Stella got to do something she had longed to try since seeing Réjane: comedy. She played the part of the "canary"—a silly, red-haired suburban wife named Sybil Temple-Martin who always dresses in yellow and is bored with her tedious, paunchy, and insensitive stockbroker husband. The play mocked the current "artistic" and "sensitive" woman seeking an "affinity" elsewhere, preferably with a pale, slender, aesthetic young man. Sybil finds one and, enchanting in bright yellow with crimson roses tucked in a low bodice and a huge hat of white chiffon dripping with ostrich plumes, keeps a rendezvous. But the "affinity" which had seemed so piquant in West Kensington pales in a dingy flat when her aesthetic young man wakes up with a hangover and snarls at her over breakfast. "Mrs. Patrick Campbell in particular revealed a probably unsuspected side to her considerable talent," approved the *Pall Mall Gazette*. "*The Canary* is little more than a comic *Frou-Frou* of the suburbs. But the enchanting sense of fun, the wilful prettiness and roguish charm, with which the actress dowers it, lend her picture of the rebellious simpleton a value far beyond its author's ken. It opens up, indeed, a world of possibilities for an actress who is even now something of an unknown quantity."

In *The Canary* Stella was supported by an engaging young actor named Gerald du Maurier; Forbes had left the company. "Private rumor and outward signs equal the end of the Mrs. Patrick Campbell–Forbes-Robertson partnership," a London correspondent cabled his Boston paper on December 4. "It has been hard for them to find plays equally suited to their capacities and their desires." They had hoped to form a stock company which they could manage together, the report continued, but that hope had not materialized. Association had widened, not narrowed, the conflict of temperaments and aims. Forbes-Robertson pursued a quiet and gradual approach to the ideal of perfection. Mrs. Campbell aimed at quicker and showier achievements. "Less substantial results and less arduous preparations satisfy her," believed the correspondent. "As Mr. Robertson craves quiet, so she craves nervous and brilliant bustle. He prefers romantic, poetic drama, she acutely contemporary life."

Certainly Forbes now craved quiet. He was, in fact, advised by doctors to take a long rest from the beautiful and tormenting Stella Campbell, and left for Sicily with his brother Norman, his nerves and health shattered, his love and partnership in ruins. The numerous Robertson family at 22 Bedford Square rallied round their stricken hero and hardened their hearts against the woman who had destroyed him. "Johnston had had the misfortune to love Stella, Mrs. Patrick Campbell," his daughter Diana wrote many years later. "With her destructive temperament, she needed only to know that a man was in love with her to begin her games and wiles and subtle art of torture. She mocked him, she played with him, she committed sins of such professional enormity as to make him shrivel in shame. . . . He reacted to her flippancies with violence and suffering. He did indeed become physically ill and could stand it no more. Stella, all injured innocence, claimed she could not understand what was the matter with him, and wailed, 'Betrayal, betrayal!' She took the script of a play they were going to do called *The Sacrament of Judas* and sent it back to him with the word 'Judas' underlined."

"Mr. Robertson's personality was not suited to any character in this comedy [*The Canary*], and he decided to break our partnership," Stella herself reported years later. "This seemed to me unfair to the enterprise, so much money having been dropped on *The Moonlight Blossom*, and the expense of launching the dual management. However, I returned to him his plays, and Mr. Gerald du Maurier acted the leading part in *The Canary*. My losses, I was told, were over £5,000." She had also lost the devotion of a passionate and sensitive man.

By tacit agreement they said little publicly about a liaison that was, after all, illicit. Once at least, however, Forbes broke silence at the mention of Stella's name. "Oh, yes," he remarked, "that little woman I was living with—that Ophelia."

# EIGHTEEN

# *1899–1900*

STELLA HAD LITTLE time for regret: she had, as usual, to make a living. "There was nothing to do," she said, "but to get into a smaller theatre and try and pull things through." She chose the Royalty, an intimate little playhouse in Dean Street, the heart of Soho. On December 27, 1899, she signed an agreement with Kate Santley to lease the Royalty from January 8 to July 7 for £90 a week, Miss Santley to allow Mrs. Campbell free use of scenery, fixtures, and properties, Mrs. Campbell to pay for orchestra, stage carpenters, property man, firemen, stage-door keeper, housekeeper, gasmen, cleaners, dressers, gas and electric light in, under, and outside the theatre, including the lamp at the end of Dean Street in Oxford Street, and all other expenses. The Royalty had seen such diverse attractions as *Trial by Jury*, *Charley's Aunt*, Forbes-Robertson in *The Scarlet Letter*, the Independent Stage Society's epoch-making production of *Ghosts*, Janet Achurch as the first Nora Helmer, Arthur Bourchier and Violet Vanbrugh in *The Chili Widow*, and 195 performances of *A Little Ray of Sunshine*, followed by a single performance of Shaw's *You Never Can Tell*. Stella was not the first actress to manage a theatre—Madame Vestris claimed that honor in 1830—but she was among the few.

For her season she assembled some good actors—Gerald du Maurier, Frank Mills, Yorke Stephens, George S. Titheradge, Albert Gran, Berte Thomas, and Courtenay Thorpe; and a competent group of actresses who would not compete with the star—Winifred Fraser, Beryl Faber, Elinor Molyneux, and Helen Boucher. The managerial staff of the Prince of Wales's stayed with her: Arthur Bertram, business manager; Pat's friend Frank Shackle, acting manager; Ian Robertson, stage manager.

Meanwhile the war increasingly occupied public attention. Between acts in theatre lobbies all over London, audiences gathered at the boards to read the latest news from South Africa—and the news was not good. British troops at Ladysmith were under siege; serious concern had become bloody reality. A loyal subject with little to detain him at home, Pat Campbell joined Lord Chesham's 10th Imperial Bucks Yeomanry and was sent for maneuvers to Salisbury Plain. The Yeomanry was a natural choice, for the rejuvenation of that outmoded service had been the brainstorm of Stella's friend George Wyndham, junior minister and leader of the Milnerites in the House of Commons. For Pat, enlistment offered a chance to revisit the scene of his defeat and this time to conquer. It also offered a gentleman's way out of an impossible domestic situation.

United with six other Wellingtonians and given a job he could do at last, Pat came back to life. "I am hard at work down here," he wrote his dearest Stella from the White Hart Hotel, "and everything looks very bright to me. I messed up with Lord Chesham and all his officers last night; they were all very nice to me, and I think I shall be of great service to him. I easily passed my riding and shooting test, and see the doctor to-morrow. I understand I shall have no difficulty in passing my medical. Chesham has asked me to stay down to-morrow and help inspect some recruits and horses. They have a splendid lot of men here, and he hopes to get us off by the 20th at latest. . . . I really think I have a good chance."

A review of the Imperial Yeomanry took place on January 26 at the Cavalry Barracks across from Regent's Park in Albany Street. The inspection performed, the Prince of Wales's last act was to summon Patrick Campbell out of the ranks and, in recognition of his wife's fame and beauty, confer upon him the honor of a handshake and a few benevolent words of farewell. His Highness was unfailingly courteous to the husbands of women he admired. Although Stella may not have shared the place of the Jersey Lily and Sarah Bernhardt in his stable, she was the kind of spirited beauty who did not remind him of his gentle Alexandra, and was therefore in his good graces.

That Friday night Stella launched her own season at the Royalty with the double bill of *The Canary* and *The Sacrament of Judas*. After the performance she gave a large supper on the stage in honor of Pat, who was supposed to leave on Sunday. But Sunday passed, and although one thousand troops of Imperial Yeomanry sailed, Pat was not among them. On February 2 the papers announced that for the 10th Imperial Bucks Yeomanry there was no fixed date of departure. So Pat was forced to idle in London while Stella threw herself into the business of making her season a success.

She intended after the current run to revive *Magda*. It was not her nature to return to failures. Although William Archer had confidence that she could develop her sketch of Juliet into a portrait, for example, she had had no intention of ever taking up Juliet again. Magda was different. She had worked hard on the part both before and during her 1899 tour, and performed a miracle. Louis Parker saw her new Magda, tried to tell her after the performance how wonderful she was, failed, and wrote instead: "I feel I didn't say half I wanted to nor the way I wanted to. I don't know why, but when I talk to you I always seem to be insincere or frivolous. Let me say quite simply, then, that your performance of Magda is superb. I have seen everybody play it—Germans, Duse and Sarah, and not one of them can pretend to come anywhere near you, and that is Gospel-truth. . . . I haven't had such a treat at the theatre since—I don't know when." She also had for fun a one-act play by Constance Smedley called *Mrs. Jordan; or on the Road to Inglefield* in which she intended to sport as the famous actress and mistress to William IV in a blond curly wig, plumed hat, and ermine-trimmed cloak before reappearing as Magda. Yet she viewed both plays as only stop-gaps while Constance Fletcher's translation of Rostand's *The Fantasticks* was in preparation. For this play, at Gerald du Maurier's suggestion, Ian Robertson interviewed a thirty-two-year-old actor with a long, comically wry face named George Arliss.

Arliss remembered the interview as casual in the extreme. All the Robertsons felt for names, and Mr.—er—Arliss was told that "somebody" had said he was doing quite good work at the—er—Vaudeville, and Mrs. Campbell was going to produce some play by that young feller who wrote —er—Pelléas and Mélisande—no, that was the other feller—this was—er —Rostand. Well, somebody thought he might do one of the old—er— fathers who have scenes together about their son and daughter and all that stuff, he didn't—er—really know much about the damn thing and it wasn't finished yet—Miss Fechter's—er—Miss Fletcher's version, that is, and as far as he knew, he would have to play some perfectly ridiculous old fogy, but the point was—did he think he could do it? Arliss cautiously suggested that Robertson make further inquiries from the "somebody" who had recommended him, and went away, rather doubting he would get the part. But Ian recommended him to Stella, "and there followed," said Arliss, "the most interesting engagement I had yet had."

Everyone knew about the famous temperament, and Arliss approached carefully. He found Mrs. Patrick Campbell an ardent worker who liked to have her own way and never gave up without a struggle, but who never, in his observation, assumed majestic or managerial airs. He found it difficult to reconcile her reputation as a socialite with her passion for work; as far as he could tell, she seemed to have no real interest outside the theatre. She was always concocting great schemes for new productions and special matinees; she was an indefatigable searcher for new plays. He waited to be lashed by the cruel tongue, but decided that she never said anything with *malice prépense.* "She had a quick brain and perhaps a too keen sense of humour. If a neat repartee came to her mind she could not prevent it from tripping on to her tongue, even if it carried with it an undesirable sting. She was always sorry, however, the moment she knew she had given pain and was the first to apologize—or to make extravagant presents to her victim. But she would do it all over again the next day."

*Magda* replaced *The Canary* and *The Sacrament* on February 19. Mrs. Tanner had a box and young Stella, thirteen, dark, and very pretty, sold programs. That night Stella gave perhaps the finest performance of her life. "Mrs. Campbell *was* Magda," said Graham Robertson, with no need to console backstage this time. "She played the part beautifully, showing the woman uplifted and transfigured by her art, but recognisably a development of the good-natured, hasty-tempered scamp of a girl who had run away from that respectable house many years before. It was a beautiful performance, full of the highest artistry and well meriting its great success." After the performance a large crowd that included the poet and critic Arthur Symons surged onstage. "You were splendid!" he exclaimed. "I never knew you could do anything so good!" Stella clutched him. "Do you mean that?" she demanded. "I thought nothing ever satisfied you." She then introduced him to her mother, "a dear old Italian lady, 78, and still almost pretty," said Symons. They had a long talk in Italian before Stella returned, flung her arm around her mother's neck, asked her how she thought she had acted, then (turning to Symons): "Well, what about the play?" "The play?" asked Symons wonderingly. "Yes, *Mariana*—the man is an idiot— won't you do it?—he insists about his name, but I'll do anything you like— have you interviewed in the papers, etc. etc." Then, as the crowd pressed in, "I'll write you in a few days and ask you to come and have a talk with me about it."

The next day critics confirmed the sentiment of the audience the previous evening: Mrs. Campbell *was* Magda. The contrast between the miserable failure of 1896 and the triumph of 1900 was almost unbelievable. Writing privately, the actress Rosina Filippi spoke for both critics and audience: "Please let me add my cry of enthusiasm to the many hundreds which have reached you to-day. You are great—grand—in *Magda*. The higher the emotions, the higher you rise to them. It is glorious, and I am very grateful to you for having given us all such a triumphant performance. I hope all London will see you and that it may be many and many a day before you piffle again in such horrors as *Moonlight Blossom*, or even *The Canary*. Lord! to think that you have *Magda* in your soul, and that you give us 'Mrs. Temple Martin'! Never, never, never do it again." And yet the slight *Fantasticks* was in preparation.

Disliking James Graham's translation of José Echegaray's *Mariana* as she did, Stella invited Symons to Kensington Square on March 11. He had met her a few days before at an ambassadorial function, got up in her "most stylish style." This Sunday Stella greeted him looking negligently artistic. "She curled up in chairs, knelt on them," Symons told his fiancée, Rhoda Bouser, "shook her head with such fury at some of the things I said that the hair on one side of her head all came down, got out books to prove to me that I was quite wrong in everything I said, talked contemptuously about 'young men like you,' and then asked my advice on everything she was doing! It was distinctly amusing, and we discussed various matters that *may* lead to something. But nothing with her gets settled. Now she wants *Mariana* adapted, not translated." As one of the first Englishmen to appreciate Baudelaire, Symons could also appreciate Stella's dangerous charm. " 'I am the torch,' she saith," he had written in his poem "Modern Beauty" and could have written of Stella, " 'and what to me/ If the moths die of me?' " And Stella the aesthete could appreciate Symons's delicate perversity and discriminating taste. Actually, Symons did not think *Mariana* a great work of art, though he considered it "a telling play." But Mrs. Tanner had seen Elizabeth Robins act Mariana, and thought it would exactly suit her daughter; and now Stella wanted someone like Symons to reshape the play even more exactly to her mould.

On March 16 Pat's company was finally ready to sail. That day the Royal Mail Company's steamer *Tagus* docked at Southampton while a "tremendous assemblage of spectators" watched five companies of Imperial Yeomanry board "amid excitement such as has hardly been paralleled since the work of sending troops away to war began." Within two weeks Pat was riding rifle in South Africa. He dug in with enthusiasm and was quickly promoted to sergeant. Stella and England seemed far away, his chance of proving himself very near. Few of his comrades knew he was the husband of Mrs. Patrick Campbell. One night at camp, however, as the soldiers were devouring letters from home around the campfire, one held up an illustrated paper with a photograph of Mrs. Pat. "I suppose this actress isn't any relation of yours, is she?" he asked Pat. "She's my wife," said Pat without looking up, and the mess grew silent.

Back in London, Stella continued a life that would have exhausted any ordinary person, accepting Symons's version of *Mariana* at two o'clock the morning of March 29. Then she changed her mind, declaring that *no* translation of the play would do; that it must be entirely rewritten and all the characters made English; that, in fact, a new English play must be made out of the Spanish one. Symons hurried to Rudolph Dircks, a playwright friend, and asked him to help with the padding, although he wrote all the important scenes with Mariana and her lover. He sent it to Stella; back came a wire asking him to come to supper after the theatre the next evening. When he got there, Stella said, "It's absolutely perfect, except"—then pointed out every word Symons had not written himself. He had to confess and admit further that he couldn't have done the whole play because it didn't interest him. "My dear child," said Stella, who was just his age, "you'll have to find out that one has to do things that don't interest one. *I* began like that; I don't feel like it now."

All this Symons confided to Rhoda Bouser in a letter of April 5. That day, near Boshof, Pat Campbell in the front ranks of a charge against Boer rifles with fixed bayonets was shot dead. Belief in the bullet had not yet overcome the superstition of the bayonet charge. With a combination of obsolete honor, romance, and stupidity, the British continued to send wave after wave of men charging into withering rifle fire, long after the slaughter should have taught them better. The next evening Pat and the other slain were buried by moonlight as the bugles sounded "The Last Post."

On Saturday night, April 7, after grueling matinee and evening performances, Stella found Uncle Harry waiting for her at the theatre door with a hansom. "Let us drive to the War Office and see if there is any news," he suggested. They drove down Charing Cross Road and into Whitehall. "Wait in the hansom," he said. He returned in a few minutes and shook his head: "There is no news." He was silent as they drove to Kensington Square. There Stella took off her wrap and they sat in the dining room. She noticed how white and drawn his face was, and how his eyes seemed to question her. Unsuspecting, she talked of her plans at the theatre. Suddenly there was a knock at the front door. She went to open it and found Pat's friend and her acting manager, Frank Shackle. "It's true," he blurted out. "What is true?" asked Stella. "Pat's killed." Stella realized that her uncle had known all along. The three of them sat in the dining room in silence. Finally Harry said, "I don't like leaving you alone, dear." "Stella is sleeping with me tonight," she replied.

After they let themselves out, she found she could not move from her chair. She did not know how many hours passed before she finally pulled herself up, crept to the stairs, and began to crawl slowly up, clinging to the banister with both hands. In her daughter's room she took Stella in her arms. "Poor Daddy has been killed," she whispered. Her daughter trembled, clung tightly. "Oh, Mother," she whimpered. Stella sat very still until her daughter fell asleep again. She thought of Beo, a cadet on the training ship H.M.S. *Britannia*, studying for his entrance exams into the Navy. Should he be told? She thought of her own life, emptied now of love. Gradually she too fell into a deep sleep.

The next day the doorbell began to ring and continued ringing. Letters and cards were dropped into the letterbox. Hundreds more poured in on Monday. She saw one or two friends; they seemed like strangers. She opened the letters and tried to read them. Lord Wemyss had written two, the first explaining that he had not come backstage Saturday night because his daughter Hilda was too tear-stained after seeing her Magda, the second commiserating after he heard the news of Pat. "Oh, my poor friend, is there anything it is possible for me to do? You know how gladly would I help you, body, soul, and spirit, if I could. Send for me if you would like to see me, or if I can be of any use to you or your child. And to think of you *last night* and *this morning!*"

Flo Shackle, whose husband, Frank, had unintentionally broken the news, comforted herself with the memory of how happy Pat had been the last months before leaving for Africa. "I will, if you like, talk to you more of the days at Enfield when he used to talk to me of you," she wrote. "He always said, 'If you knew her you would love her.' I do love you, and I would give anything to be able to help you bear this pain."

Arthur Symons told Frank Shackle immediately that he would agree to anything Mrs. Campbell wanted in the way of translation or credits, then wrote Stella: "I cannot help (though at the risk of seeming intrusive) writing to say how deeply sorry I am at the news I have just heard, coming at the very moment when you have proved to the whole world that you are the only actress on the English stage worth listening to. It is as though you have thus to suffer to counterbalance that triumph of your art, but do remember, even while you suffer, that only suffering greatens one when one is an artist. . . . There is no other consolation for unhappiness, but may one not accept so much consolation? It is what I wish for you with all my heart."

"I saw the report of your husband's death, and am writing to you to express my sincere condolence," wrote Beerbohm Tree from Her Majesty's. "You will, I know, be very sad at his loss, but he could not have wished for a better death. I always found him good and kind and full of charm and love of you."

Then, finally, the official cable from Lord Chesham: "PATRICK CAMPBELL WAS KILLED INSTANTANEOUSLY IN FINAL ATTACK, AND WAS BURIED WITH MILITARY HONOURS IN BOSHOF CEMETERY. I HAVE WRITTEN YOU FULL DETAILS." The full details contained the comfort of honorable praise: "fine soldier . . . no one doing better in the regiment . . . a good friend . . . loss will be much felt . . . ended short career with greatest honour that can come to a man."

Beo had to be told, and Stella wrote to her son on the *Britannia* anchored at Dartmouth; but it was not her letter that broke the news. "... I am so miserable about poor, dear daddy. The chaplain has just told me about him," Beo replied immediately. "I want to be at home so much now to be able to comfort you. I was confirmed to-day by the Bishop of Exeter. Only one week and four days now to the holidays. All next week is exams. Poor, dear daddy! It was rather hard the news coming on my confirmation day. Don't worry, mummy, dear. I wish I was home to comfort you. With all the world and the stars and seas and sun full of love and kisses and comfort from your loving son."

Stella closed the Royalty—it was Holy Week—and with young Stella went to Sevenoaks in Kent, a quiet, pleasant town set in beautiful country. She began to answer letters on black-bordered stationery quickly substituted for her usual notepaper bearing the Campbell boar's-head crest and motto *"Ne obliviscaris"*—"Forget not." "Don't you, dear uncle, feel torn and worried?" she asked. "Remember all you have done for him and for his children and for me . . . and if you didn't discourage him from going, remember that his going has brought him glory and peace and the everlasting respect and honour of those he loved. . . . Don't worry about me, dear uncle. When I see you again I shall be quite brave and strong and ready for work. You have helped me bear so much." Beo wrote again to say he was glad now that his daddy had died fighting and doing his duty, for everyone had to die sometime, and it was better to die fighting than home in bed. Yes, Stella reflected: in death Pat had won the success that eluded him in life.

Her return to the Royalty was charged with emotion. She was an actress who attracted enthusiastic admirers under normal circumstances. On Monday night the house was crowded with admirers mourning for her. She could feel the sympathy of the audience breaking in waves over the footlights; she could feel the pity and love in the warm applause. Some of the audience wept, and some of her company. She had to struggle against the emotion, or she would have broken down. "At the end," said Stella, "I was exhausted." Back in her dressing room, she quickly slipped into her dress of black mourning with its deep hem of crape, but did not remember to change her pale pink stockings. At the stage door in Richmond Mews the narrow, dark passage leading to the pavement was crowded with people, chiefly elderly women dressed in black, she noted in confusion. "Poor thing!" they murmured as she went swiftly past them. A hansom stood waiting. As she lifted her skirt to mount, she heard a horrified chorus of *"Oh*'s!" Her pale pink stockings looked like bare legs. "I felt a clown," said Stella.

Her passion for work made recovery easier and, in fact, inevitable. Yet sadness remained, all the heavier for the guilt that accompanied it. Lulo

wrote, and in her answer Stella expressed simply to the once-dear sister
what the dead man meant to her:

> I thank you & Joe very much for your dear kind letters. There is nothing
> you can do for me.
> My dear brave gentle Pat.
> The blessed honour & glory he has won—what it is & will be always to
> Beo!
> The old tender love has come back to me—& it will help me always
> always. I needed it so much. . . .
> I am afraid the shock must have been very great to you. He loved you.

There is a story in Forbes-Robertson's family that after Pat Campbell
was killed, Stella's Uncle Harry arrived at 22 Bedford Square to claim that
his niece's name had been much damaged by being coupled with Forbes's,
and to demand that he now do the right thing by her. If the story is true,
and if Forbes had been home, his sense of honor and his old love might
have persuaded him to marry Stella after all. But Forbes was not at home,
and Harry Tanner had to face his mother, "cool, contemptuous, and adamant." She sent him packing.

And then there are Stella's own words. "Men made love to me, and I was
accused of being a wicked flirt. I deny that. In more than one case I cared:
but my first love had taught me love's true face."

# NINETEEN

## *1900*

$\mathcal{S}$TELLA HAD THOUGHT that *Magda* would run for two months at best, but crowds kept coming to the Royalty to see a performance that many said surpassed those of Bernhardt, Modjeska, and Duse. "A supreme moment for me occurred at the beginning of the second act, one fearfully hot summer night in the uncomfortable little Royalty Theatre in Soho," said William Lyon Phelps. "Mrs. Campbell's acting was so magnificent that we forgot the heat. She was the prima donna who had left Main Street a long time before, and fresh from her triumphs, revisits her humble home. It is a stuffy little parlour, where it is clear nothing interesting has ever happened or can happen. Magda's mousey sister, a commonplace 'home-body,' dressed in unbecoming and cheap attire, is waiting alone in this depressing environment. Suddenly the opulent, voluptuous Magda foams into the room. She stops. She looks at the dreadful changeless furniture. Then she looks at her sister. Then she kisses her. Not a word was spoken, but I found that I was crying."

George Arliss, hired for *The Fantasticks* and on full salary with nothing to do, began to understudy the role of Schwartz in *Magda*. Albert Gran, contributing a very remarkable performance in the minor role of Lieutenant Max von Wendelowski, announced that he was forced to leave the cast to fill a prior engagement, but intended to return to the Royalty and his success after a fortnight. Stella got Ian Robertson to engage Harley Granville-Barker, the striking young actor who had toured with her in 1899, to play von Wendelowski in Gran's absence. Barker had remarkable qualities as an actor, Stella thought; yet her attention was more taken up with another young actor in her company, the irresponsible and charming Gerald du Maurier.

Gerald himself had fallen under the Campbell spell. He knew its terrors: the exacting perfectionism, the terrible sarcasms, the bursts of fury, the will that dominated and dwarfed everyone around her. He knew its joys: the wit, the witchery of the low, rather sullen voice, the sudden confidences, the amazing bursts of generosity, the sensual beauty of this woman eight years older than he. There was no peace, he learned: it was heaven, it was hell. Yet when he was away from her, exhausted, cursing her, nursing his wounds, he longed to be with her again. Besides, Stella was easy on him— she had taken a fancy to him. She had decided to teach him how to act.

Gerald reported the new friendship to his mother, who, with the rest of the family, had deplored his going on the stage; she was flattered that so famous an actress should take an interest in her boy. At first in letters to "Mummy" it was "Mrs. Campbell." Mrs. Campbell had asked Gerald to dine at Kensington Square, and Gerald had found her very kind. Mrs. Campbell spoke spontaneously and unaffectedly about everything, and encouraged him in his own work. Then when Mrs. du Maurier had a carriage accident, Mrs. Campbell inquired after her with such solicitude and was "so very sympathetic and nice" that Mrs. du Maurier was quite charmed. Rehearsals for *The Fantasticks* began, with the formidable Mrs. Pat dwindling into a love-sick youth, Percinet, and little Gerald expanding into a bravo, Straforel. There was not only work, however. Gerald wrote to say that he and Mrs. Campbell had driven to Hampstead in a victoria and had strolled about on the Heath, and Mrs. Campbell had been "very jolly" and they had enjoyed themselves "hugely." "And I am being very good," added Gerald, "not sitting up late or drinking too much, so don't alarm yourself."

Not all actors that season were as amiable as Gerald. Albert Gran returned to reclaim the role of von Wendelowski, and Granville-Barker immediately sent a letter claiming that Stella owed him his salary for the rest of the run. Surprised and indignant, Stella took the case to her lawyer, Bouchier Hawksley, who, after finding Barker inflexible, advised her to take him to court since he had neither letter nor contract to support his claim. "I was interested in the idea of being in a court," said Stella, "and dressed myself in my best." Arriving to find Barker in shabby clothes and frayed straw hat, she realized her mistake. Nevertheless, she went into the witness box and testified that she had made it clear to Mr. Robertson, her stage manager, that Mr. Barker's services were required only during Mr. Gran's absence. Mr. Barker in his turn admitted that he could produce neither letter nor contract, but said that he had certainly understood that he was hired for the run of the play, otherwise he never would have accepted the engagement. On being called into the box, Ian Robertson groped as usual for names and facts, and concluded that he did not at all remember what he had said in the interview with Mr.—er—Barker. This drew a frown from the judge, who asked him whether it was not his business to remember such conversations. The jury listened, retired, returned, and gave the verdict to the shabby plaintiff for £60. "What do I do now?" Stella asked Hawksley. "Go shake his hand and congratulate him," replied her lawyer. They shook. "Mr. Granville Barker did not look as triumphant as I thought he ought to," said Stella, "and I will go to my grave believing that he owes me £60."

But in view of her success with audiences and critics, it seemed a small loss. On May 29 *The Fantasticks* went into the bill as a matinee. Translated freely into rhymed verse by Constance Fletcher, it told the delightful story of a pair of star-crossed lovers who do not take their feuding fathers seriously, but eventually bring them to their senses in a frothy, charming, midsummer-night comedy of errors. As Bergamin, one of the feuding fathers, Arliss at last got an opportunity to play the role he'd been hired for. Nervously poised in the wings, he was absolutely staggered to hear Stella telling him that she loved an opening. Personally, he could pick out several tortures designed by the Spanish Inquisition in preference to this agony. But there was Mrs. Campbell, slim, clad in britches, "looking a picture," and actually pleasurably excited. The stamina, dedication, and enthusiasm of the actress impressed him again.

To be an artistic success, *The Fantasticks* had to be played fantastically. "No one was light enough, quick enough, extravagant enough," complained one critic, "—with one exception, Mr. Gerald du Maurier. He alone seemed to catch the spirit of the piece, and to understand what was wanted. He acted with infinite humour, dash, and grace. How much there is in heredity and parentage! Mr. du Maurier is French in family, and had a delightful humorist as his father." He also had a great actress as his mentor, although in this case Stella might have learned something from her protégé. Rejoicing in rhymed verse upon the English stage at last, Archer went on to observe that although Stella had played the youth with a great deal of charm, she had really only one device for imitating masculinity—plunging her hands into her pockets. Yet, again she delighted the public.

Playing Rostand in the afternoon and both *Mrs. Jordan* and *Magda* at night, rehearsing, continually searching for and reading new plays, keeping in touch with Beo, who had passed his exams and was preparing for a tour in the Royal Navy aboard the H.M.S. *Endymion*, pondering young Stella's future (she did not want her daughter to be an actress and was looking about for a good finishing school), giving little suppers and teas, appearing gorgeously attired at every fashionable event—Stella seemed these days to be driven by a demon. She often looked exhausted onstage, inspiring a letter from one playgoer begging her to spare herself at least one of the two weekly matinees for the sake of her health and a public who did not want to lose her. But Stella did not listen, contracting with Martin Harvey, who had since made a tremendous success as Sydney Carton in *The Only Way*, to end her season in July with matinees of *Pelléas and Mélisande*. Together they re-created their magic, her season ending on July 14 with a matinee of *Pelléas* and *Magda* at night.

*The Canary, The Sacrament of Judas, Mrs. Jordan, The Fantasticks, Pelléas and Mélisande*, and 154 performances of *Magda* in six months—an impressive season. Not one of the plays was what any manager would call a crowd-pleaser, but public and critics had been enthusiastic, and Stella engaged the Royalty again for the fall. Yet (and she could not quite explain it) she had not made much money; the £5000 debt remained; and so, instead of a holiday, she gathered her company together for a tour of Dublin and the big English towns.

On tour she redoubled her efforts with du Maurier. "Much of his charm, his delicacy, his ease of manner, and his assurance he owed to her," wrote his daughter Daphne in retrospect. "She worked tirelessly, taking infinite pains with him, and, being every inch of her an actress, she realised that this spoilt, restless young man might do almost anything if he chose to take a genuine interest in his trade and his own talent. There were scenes, of course, blistering rows and fierce reconciliations, days of sulky silences and days of riotous successes. And in this weird mixture of excitement, anger, and frequent disillusion Gerald developed his mind, his intuition, and his little grain of genius." In Dublin, where they had a brilliant fortnight, Gerald played opposite her Mélisande. "I have taught a clown to play Pelléas," said Stella, often irritated with Gerald's insouciance. But he was dazzled by her praise and encouragement, and believed he'd made the success of his career in a part that was totally out of his line.

She also taught him how to live. She herself lived largely—working hard both for love of work and because in her idealistic moods she felt her work a form of worship and thanksgiving. She laughed largely and fought fiercely. She hated or loved. She was honest, spontaneous. She had a huge appetite for beauty in all forms, even those she did not understand. She was a child and at the same time possessed of a certain inchoate wisdom. She was an invaluable lesson, and Gerald was grateful for her teaching. "Under her tuition," said Daphne, "he became a man of certain depth, understanding, and subtlety, instead of a spoilt, irresponsible boy. He learnt how to talk, how to be silent, and how not to be consistently selfish."

Because his mother was still recovering from her accident, Gerald wrote frequently that August and September. "I have just been out shopping with Mrs. Campbell," he reported from Leeds. "I've never seen such a person for buying old furniture, and things. My knowledge is getting vast on such subjects as Dutch and French antiques. Afterwards I played golf, and she walked round and sat about, it did her tons of good, and she's never been so well. Her son Beo is with us too, and is a fine fellow, May would adore him; he is a midshipman, all muscle and a profile like Pharaoh, and captain of everything. There is to be a supper-party to the company this week, and Mrs. Campbell says I am to do all my tricks!" But with Stella (or Gerald) no mood was lasting. "This is an awful place," he groaned as the tour went on, "rain all the time, and dirty lodgings without baths, and stale grease paint on the pillows. Mrs. Campbell isn't very fit, I don't think the air suits her, and she is all down and depressed. I am well, and oh, dear, I suppose I'm happy, as there is a lot of work and the parts are good, but I sometimes wonder if everything is worth while."

Stella also sometimes wondered. Leeds to Liverpool to Southport, where, unlike her company, she put up at the Hotel Royal, where the pillowcases were fresh and the service good. Yet she found the hot September days and stifling theatres almost unbearable. "The heat is slowly killing us all," she wrote Gilbert Murray. "I was at the Bush Farnham trying to rest for two days last week. I felt so weary, as though the weight of the weariness of every weary soul on this earth was upon me." She'd been too unhappy at Farnham to remember that he was nearby, much as she wanted to talk to him about the play he was writing for her. She was "wildly interested" in it, yet when she read the first acts, she did not spare criticism. The play was "a little shadowy," "boneless." Her part, Muthie: "I can't quite take hold of her." Was Murray trying to imitate Henry James? He should not bother: "James is an ass, & his assishness isn't in the least dramatic." She was particularly anxious for a play from Murray because Frank Harris's new piece might not do all she expected. Harris had come to Leeds to read *Mr. and Mrs. Daventry* to Stella and her company, and she was almost ready to accept the smart modern comedy. But she wished Murray would get on with her role: "Do let me die at the end," she urged; "let her kill herself. . . . I wish I lived near you & could jerk your elbow."

*Mr. and Mrs. Daventry* had a curious history. Back in 1894, while working on *The Importance of Being Earnest*, Oscar Wilde had been seized with an idea for another play, and sent off a brief scenario in four acts to George Alexander. As he sketched it, a fashionable man of rank was to marry a simple country girl, become bored, invite down to his country place a lot of fashionable *fin de siècle* people, and encourage his wife to flirt with a former admirer to distract her from his affair with Lady X. As it happens, the wife falls asleep on a sofa behind a screen, overhears her husband making love to Lady X, then, when Lady X's husband pounds for admittance, saves the whole situation by going to the locked door herself and apologizing for keeping his wife up so late. When her grateful husband approaches her, however, she recoils and later pours out her misery to Gerald, the young admirer who is rapidly falling in love with her. She reciprocates his love; yet when the mildly repentant husband asks Gerald to persuade his wife to forgive him, Gerald reluctantly consents. The wife will not hear of such sacrifice, however, and, by the power of her beauty, love, and conviction, forces Gerald to take her away with him. Pursuing, the husband challenges Gerald to a duel. Before it takes place, he again sees his wife. She declares her love for Gerald and states frankly that of the two she wishes her husband to die "because the father of my child must live." The husband goes out and a shot is heard. He has killed himself, and the curtain falls with the wife and Gerald clinging to each other in recognition of both happiness and tragedy. *"I think it extremely strong,"* concluded Oscar. "I want the sheer passion of love to dominate everything. *No morbid self-sacrifice. No renunciation—a sheer flame of love between a man and a woman."*

But before Wilde found time to work further on the idea, his own catastrophe of passion overwhelmed him. Exiled and short of money after his release from prison in May 1897, he began to negotiate with a number of people with a view to selling the scenario. Frank Harris—author, adventurer, and editor of the *Saturday Review* until he sold it in 1898 to buy a hotel in Monte Carlo—was in France frequently during this time and, hearing of Oscar's play, urged him to finish it. Wilde protested that he would never write again, then added: "Why don't you buy the scenario and write the play yourself?" Harris finally agreed, if Wilde would write the first act in his witty, epigrammatic way. Wilde reluctantly promised; Harris gave him £50 down with the promise of £50 more when the first act was finished, and returned to London under the impression that he had secured all rights to the scenario of *Mr. and Mrs. Daventry.*

Harris rapidly wrote the second, third, and fourth acts, then called one afternoon on the actress whose Ophelia had strongly impressed him: he would like to read her a play. Stella said at once she would take it for the Royalty, but made a condition. She would not hear of a first act written by Wilde. "Quite impossible!" she declared. "A play's not a patchwork quilt. You must write the first act yourself." Harris explained that he must consult Oscar.

Harris sent off his script to Wilde, told him Mrs. Campbell had accepted it, and said that if Wilde had not already written the first act, would he send him a detailed outline; he would attempt it himself. To his astonishment, Wilde replied coldly that he could write neither act nor outline, that Harris owed him money for Wilde's contribution to his debut as a dramatist, and, finally, that he had not only stolen his play, but spoilt it. Harris reported

Wilde's reaction to Stella. There, she said: now he *must* write the first act himself and, for the sake of contrast, provide Hilda Daventry with a mother. Harris agreed. "Some impish spirit" inspired him to make the mother appear much younger than the daughter—and Stella had not liked it much when she read it. Nevertheless, she had come around, and now when Harris arrived in Leeds they struck the bargain and talked casting. Harris considered Frederick Kerr one of the finest character actors on the English stage and proposed him for Daventry. For the part of Gerald, Mrs. Daventry's lover, Stella chose *her* Gerald. She had warned Arliss that there was no part for him in *Daventry*, but after his striking work on tour she wanted to use him and suggested the small part of an Irish servant, which he accepted.

Harris transmitted the good news to Wilde, who replied in a still viler temper that Harris had no right to the play but, as long as he had stolen it, he really must pay something substantial. Harris assured him that if he made anything off the play, Wilde would get money. Wilde replied that he was sure it would fail, and that Harris ought to get a good sum down immediately from Mrs. Campbell and turn over half of it to him. Finding the exiled playwright childishly impossible, Harris went over at the end of September to confront him. What, he demanded, had Wilde pretended to sell for the £50, if not the rights to the scenario? Wilde remained aloof. "Plays cannot be written by amateurs; plays require a knowledge of the stage. It's quite absurd of you, Frank, who hardly ever go to the theatre, to think you can write a successful play straight off. I have always loved the theatre, always went to every first night in London, have the stage in my blood...." But he finally settled for £175, £25 down.

Harris's troubles were not over. As notices of the forthcoming production began to appear, Harris suddenly found himself besieged with claims upon the scenario of *Mr. and Mrs. Daventry*. To his astonishment, he found that Wilde had also sold the plot to Mrs. Brown Potter, Horace Sedger, Leonard Smithers, Louise Nethersole, Ada Rehan, George Alexander, and Beerbohm Tree. Stella was due back in London on October 7; rehearsals were scheduled immediately after her return. Somehow Harris had to buy off or otherwise satisfy all claimants before production could begin. "Oscar, of course, had deceived Harris about the whole matter," said Wilde's close friend Robert Ross. But Oscar was unrepentant. "You have deprived me of a certain income," he charged Harris with the unreasonableness of a beaten man.

Amid a flurry of rumors that the next Royalty production was really a play by the infamous Oscar Wilde, and a continuous stream of angry, whining letters from Wilde to Harris, Stella and her company prepared for the opening of "A New and Original Play in 4 Acts by Frank Harris."

Stella remained cool. Daring as Harris's play might be, it could not unnerve the original Paula Tanqueray. The fact that *Daventry* was unlicensed by the Censor did not seem to worry her either. Harris himself, flamboyant at rehearsals in a massive, fur-lined coat, could not disconcert her, although he did his best to make her his sleeping partner during the *Daventry* collaboration. Making up before the first performance in her Liberty's print silk Japanese dressing gown, she could still say that she loved an opening night.

Many first-nighters who assembled at the Royalty on October 25 believed that Frank Harris had simply lent his name to a play by the convicted sodomite Oscar Wilde. Whispers ran along the rows, poisoning the atmosphere. The epigrams and pyrotechnics of the first act did nothing to dispel that belief. "Is there such a thing, Lady Hallingdon, as an English vice? What is the peculiarly English vice?" asks Mr. Daventry. "Oh, I thought everyone knew that, Mr. Daventry," replies the lady. "The English vice is adultery with home comforts." Equally Wildean seemed Lady Hallingdon's "There's nothing to match the first passion of a young man, except the last passion of an old woman!" (though it was no more than Harris's paraphrase of Balzac) or her "We don't dress for men; for them we—" "Wilde!" muttered the audience until the animosity threatened to break out openly.

But once the showy exposition that Stella herself had not liked had run its course, Harris's own voice began to be heard—and it was not Wilde's. The audience began to settle down and become absorbed in the story, and when the final curtain fell, many eyes were wet with tears. Many remained unconvinced, however, and the calls for "Author!" were by no means all friendly. Frank Harris was spared them; he was laid up at home with bronchitis, leaving Stella to brave it alone. She appeared before the curtain, ravishing in a fur-trimmed tea gown of white and palest pink. Mr. Harris, she announced, was not in the theatre. "I will, however, convey to him the favorable reception you have given—" she continued, but was interrupted at that moment by a tremendous uproar at the back of the theatre. Stella did not flinch. "—to Mr. Harris's clever play," she concluded loudly, with a defiant toss of the head.

Critics the next day proved almost unanimously hostile. Hysterical at the mere rumor of a Wilde play in London, Clement Scott did not relent because Harris's name was on the program, calling it "a drama of the dustbin" and the most immoral play of the century, bearing every earmark of its disgraced author. Walkley in the *Times* strongly objected to the "screen scene" in Act II: "If the scene is not absolutely indecent, it goes as near to indecency as anything we remember on the contemporary stage. So also does the dialogue. There is a certain joke about the object of ladies dressing which is quite unprintable." W. L. Courtney in the *Daily Telegraph* objected to the whole play: "Relieved of its talkiness and boiled down to its actual elements, 'Mr. and Mrs. Daventry' is always thin, never forcible, and frequently vulgar. To emphasize the latter quality is needless, for what Mr. Harris has to tell us is vulgar in its very essence. . . . Why not call his play 'The Adulterers' and hang the convention?"

The next day Harris recovered enough to see Stella. Brave before the curtain, she was shaken now with the newspapers in her hands, and talked of withdrawing the play immediately and cutting her losses. Harris shook his head. He was willing, he told her, to pay all the expenses of production in return for a half-share in it. Stella considered. "If you are willing to do that," she said, "I can afford to risk it." Harris promised more. "The bad press will make the play," he assured her.

He was right. Having learned nothing from actually making Ibsen a *cause célèbre* by his vituperations, Clement Scott now conscientiously provided the same service for *Mr. and Mrs. Daventry*, drawing flocks of fashionable people to the Royalty simply to see what was so shocking. The play's notoriety changed critical minds: the *Athenaeum* discovered that *Daventry* was "the most daring and naturalistic production of the modern English stage." Rumors that the play was Oscar's persisted, luring admirers and detractors alike. And then, as everyone had to admit, the acting was excellent. J. T. Grein found new hyperbole, calling Hilda Daventry the truest woman in Stella's gallery, truer than Magda, greater than Paula. He also congratulated Fred Kerr for playing the brute Daventry to the life. Du Maurier was praised for acting the young lover with tact and discretion, and Arliss made such a hit in the small part of Keane, the Irish servant, that Stella and du Maurier began to do everything they could to help his part along, even if it meant not keeping strictly to Harris's lines. And finally the Prince of Wales set his seal of approval on *Mr. and Mrs. Daventry*. The Royalty was a small theatre, so intimate that an audience could see every blink of an actor's eye, and the royal box was practically on top of the stage. His Royal Highness was so amused and leaned so far out of the box as he applauded one of Harris's ripostes that the startled actors felt sure he was going to topple out onto their heads.

Stella did not, therefore, have to withdraw *Daventry* and cut her losses. Yet, although she had seen the play's possibilities at once, she did not rank the role of Hilda Daventry high. "Do come & see the play," she wrote Murray the last week in October. "It is a little clever & where it's weak my part isn't strong enough for me to help. The public have had my guts & they are dissatisfied with anything less." She was still dissatisfied with the first act and, one day, even dissatisfied with her actors' make-up. Swooping down on a morning rehearsal, she made the startling announcement that she had observed that in real life all healthy men had blue chins. From now on she wanted all the men in her company to make up healthy. Taken aback, Arliss, Thomas, Kerr, and du Maurier protested that they were playing men in ultra-smart society, and that if they colored themselves blue, they would not look healthy but only like dirty shaves. "That's nonsense!" boomed Stella. "It would just look manly. All you men coming on every night with pink chins look like little girls! It throws the whole play out of perspective. Makes me feel as though I were placed amongst you as a chaperone." That night all the actors onstage sported blue chins. "I never heard exactly what happened," said Arliss, "but I believe her manager came round from the front of the house and told her she appeared to be surrounded by burglars and that she had turned a drawing-room comedy into a crook play. Anyhow, we were told we needn't do it any more."

Meanwhile, in Paris, Oscar Wilde, in pain and spending any stray francs on chloral, opium, and absinthe, sent a final letter accusing Harris of cheating him into an agreement so he could deal with Mrs. Campbell and demanding the remaining £150. Harris was drawing some hundreds of pounds a week for his share in *Daventry*, but still hesitated, thinking that Oscar might be faking illness to get money. Finally he sent his secretary, Tom Bell, over with cash and instructions not to give Wilde the money if he found him drunk, and not to give it to any "parasite" of Wilde's but only to the playwright personally. Bell arrived at the Hotel d'Alsace on November 30, and met a chambermaid carrying an armful of washing, who directed him upstairs. The door stood open. "Harris is right," thought Bell; "Wilde is all right and is gone out to the cafés." In the room, however, wax tapers burned and a white-coiffed nun sat by a corpse. Oscar had died a few hours earlier.

That late autumn and early winter of 1900, Gerald du Maurier in letters to his mother talked more and more about the woman he loved. No one could really say when the change had occurred, but now it was "Stella" rather than "Mrs. Campbell." "Stella and I are dining with the Trees tonight, darling," Gerald would write, or, "Stella isn't looking too well, spraining her ankle seems to have upset her," or, again, "Stella and I drove to Bath in a double horse shay, and she is looking marvellous, and the play is doing excellent business." His adoration was public knowledge by now: "Real Love of Her Makes Du Maurier's Acting Real," announced one sensational headline, but went on to claim that his love was unrequited; "She is much older." Stella herself was as silent about Gerald as she had been about Forbes; whatever people might guess, she would not confirm it.

Certainly du Maurier's affection had comforted her in the wake of Pat's death, and now, this fall, in the wake of a different loss.

The previous spring, while Forbes was recovering abroad, Ian Robertson had begun a tour of London theatres to find a new leading lady for his brother, who was beginning to show signs of interest in a fall season. The actress must suit the plays Forbes had in his repertoire (*Hamlet, The Devil's Disciple, The Sacrament of Judas*), but, more important, must be as unlike Stella Campbell as possible. Ian finally sent Forbes a list of actresses with comments. On it appeared the name of Gertrude Elliott, a young, dainty, gentle, dark-haired actress with no hips and less bosom. Ian praised her, but queried, "Can she play Shakespeare?" In Palermo, Forbes studied the list, wrote the name of another actress at the top, and mailed it back. A day or two later, as he was taking his customary stroll, a sudden impulse sent him dashing into a telegraph office, where he wired frantically, "IF NOT TOO LATE ENGAGE MISS ELLIOTT." As hours and days passed, he found himself wondering with less than philosophic calm whether the list or the telegram would win. His strange sense of urgency disturbed him. He was barely acquainted with the young woman—what could be the meaning of it? At last he tore open a telegram: "HAVE ENGAGED MISS ELLIOTT."

Forbes returned to England ready to tour that autumn with Ian as his stage manager again and Gertrude Elliott as his leading lady. By September they were engaged. Calling on Forbes in October, Shaw noted that "a certain laurel-crowned portrait" once occupying the place of honor had been replaced by a portrait of Ellen Terry. Three days before Christmas, in Streatham, where the tour ended, Forbes made Gertrude Elliott his wife.

# TWENTY

## *1900–1901*

*W*ITH APPETITE for experimentation, Stella continued to negotiate with Gilbert Murray that autumn, although she was becoming increasingly aware of the conflict between producing plays she liked and plays that would draw. She particularly wanted to see Murray's version of the *Hippolytus*, but was also thinking a great deal about his *Andromache*, which she had read. "I would be so proud to do it," she wrote, "but at the moment I do not see my way—I cannot approach my business people about it feeling as I do that commercially it is of no value—at present—we are fighting hard to clear up the heavy losses of last year. Let me have 'Muthie' as soon as you can. If 'Muthie' is the success it should be—then 'Andromache'!!! Don't work too hard at that other work of yours. The world is waiting for good plays!"

Meanwhile Stella had persuaded Max Beerbohm to dramatize a little thing of his own, an allegory of good and evil, for a curtain-raiser. *The Happy Hypocrite* went into rehearsal that autumn of 1900, with Max— small, very clean-shaven, his retreating hair immaculately groomed, his narrow shoulders sheltered under impeccable tailoring—appearing occasionally at rehearsals, but never saying a word. He did write out, however, a few "Vague Hints from the Author to the Company," hoping at the same time that they would not accuse him of trying to tell them their business. *The Happy Hypocrite*, said Max, was a fable, and thus should be acted as prettily as possible. The style, too, should be utterly fantastic. Over-acting was the order of the day. Lord George Hell must be a monster; Jenny Mere such a paragon of innocence as never before seen.

Profiting from the "Vague Hints," Stella's company made a success with *The Happy Hypocrite*, which was added to the bill on December 11 along with *Daventry*, its first act, at Stella's insistence, revised. After the performance Stella wired Max, who had taken refuge at the Hotel Metropole in Brighton. Max immediately opened a bottle of "the boy" and, having polished off the champagne, explained to Reggie Turner (who had recently had such a bad time in Paris with poor Oscar), "If I had been in London, I should have been horribly frightened, and could not have kept away from the theatre, and I should have been dragged on, pallid and deprecating, by Mrs. P.C. This lady, by the way, really is a rather wonderful creature. As stage-manageress she has been absolutely intelligent and sweet and charming all through." He did not give a damn if the papers slated it, Max the critic added: "The public, after all, is *the final court of appeal.*"

Feeling that the year had been successful enough to warrant a celebration, Stella planned a supper party for New Year's Eve after the performance. It did not materialize, however. "I was sorry your supper fell through," wrote Max, one of the invited, "but perhaps you will ask me next New Year's Eve. I suppose noone will ask me to see the next century in. If I am alive I shall be such a bore that noone will want to see me," adding gallantly, "But I am sure that if *you* are alive you will still be charming." The new year also brought a message from Lulo. Stella replied on the first day of 1901 graciously but briefly: "My dear Lulo, thank you for your good wishes it is very kind of you to have thought of me—I hope you will both be happy in the New Year & keep well & busy. Yours affectionately, Beatrice." She still wrote on black-bordered notepaper, but memories were not enough to reunite her with her sister.

*Daventry* continued to play to crowded houses, and Stella and her business manager were beginning to look for solid profits with the one-hundredth performance, when the death of Queen Victoria on January 22 promptly closed all theatres for a fortnight. Lewis Waller's reaction over at the Lyceum, where he was playing *Henry V*, was not atypical. Staggering into another actor's dressing room with grief-stricken face, Waller burst into tears, crying, "She's dead, Bill, she's dead!" The actor tried to comfort him, begging him not to take it so much to heart, but Waller was inconsolable. "It's the receipts, Bill," he sobbed; "the receipts are bound to drop." Stella waited out the fortnight while the nation mourned; then *Daventry* reopened on February 5 for the gala one-hundredth performance, and the elaborate souvenir programs could finally be used. Stella handed hers round to be autographed by the company along with everyone else's, jotting on the olive-green cover, "This doth unto Stella Campbell belong." Frank Harris's desperado face led the souvenir portraits. "Rosemary—that's for remembrance," wrote Elizabeth Kirby under her photograph as Lady Solway. "Bless the dear ladies," wrote Arliss, quoting Keane. Gerald contributed only his autograph.

But the spell of *Daventry* was broken. Harris did not blame the Queen, but did blame Stella for reshuffling the cast. Berte Thomas had taken over du Maurier's part as the young lover, du Maurier himself now played Mr. Daventry, and Frederick Kerr had left the company. It was perhaps foolish to substitute her beloved Gerald for Kerr, who had played to great critical praise, yet it was not only a cast change or the fortnight's hiatus that killed the play. Apart from its smart talk and shocking theme, *Mr. and Mrs. Daventry* was not really a very good play. As Shaw, who had never believed it Oscar's, was to remark: "If Oscar had written it, it would now be a classic." Nor did it give Stella the kind of role her audiences wanted for her. Max Beerbohm had seen immediately that the character of Daventry threw all others into the shade; "*Mr. Daventry* the play should have been called, simply," said Max.

Stella always had two reliables to fall back upon. Seeing the death of *Daventry* near, she decided upon a revival of *The Notorious Mrs. Ebbsmith*. This meant consulting the meticulous Pinero about casting. Arliss had seen, admired, and studied John Hare's performance as the Duke of St. Olpherts; he had played St. Olpherts on a provincial tour in 1895; he was extremely eager to play the part in this revival. Stella had never seen him as St. Olpherts, but had enough faith in him now to arrange an interview with Pinero. Stella wanted him, and Arliss suspected that she usually got her own way when she wanted something badly enough. On the other hand, he suspected that Pinero *always* got his. On the strength of one interview, however, Pinero decided for Arliss; and with Courtenay Thorpe playing Lucas Cleeve and young Gerald playing his father, *Ebbsmith* opened on February 27, 1901, four days after *Daventry* concluded its final and 116th performance.

Max Beerbohm was there, and summed up in his amused way both the failings and strengths of Pinero's play. Of the Bible-burning: "It is an exciting incident, I admit readily. And, of course, it makes an effective appeal to the religious consciences of such playgoers as don't think. But any meaning that it has is nonsense, and I suggest to Mr. Pinero that he might have been as exciting and as 'edifying' . . . if he had made Mrs. Ebbsmith throw the Bible (as she has previously thrown a bouquet) into the canal, from which it might have been retrieved by a pet spaniel. The dog, wagging its tail and shaking the water off its back, would have brought down the curtain quite as effectively, and not painfully, as does the lady, quivering over her scorched hand." Max was also put off rather than impressed with the play's "pretentious air of being somehow philosophic and Ibsenish." However, "Despite its inconsistencies, the part of Mrs. Ebbsmith is a fine one, and Mrs. Campbell invests it with all that quiet and haunting realism of which the secret is hers. Her glamour is as it has always been. Her art has become subtler, more potent." Stella notified Pinero of the successful revival and he, in his formal way, congratulated her: "That you should, after a lapse of some years, have repeated your former triumph is a feat of which you may well feel proud. For the rest, I heartily hope that the revival will serve the commercial interests of your theatre."

No one hoped it more than Stella, yet her bias was still toward plays that pleased her first. She and Forbes had wanted to try repertory; she had pursued that ideal alone, with the *Times* congratulating her that May for "giving us the nearest thing we have in London to that 'repertory theatre' which is being so much talked about; she is more ready to make experiments than other managers; she is willing to put on plays (such as *The Fantasticks* last season) for a few trial performances; she will revive year after year a play like *Pelléas and Mélisande* that has a rare attraction for the minority who delight in the subtly precious and poetic qualities of M. Maeterlinck's dramatic fantasy." Now she had two more questionably popular plays in her pocket: *Beyond Human Power* by the Norwegian Björnstjerne Björnson, considered second only to Ibsen as a playwright, and *Mariana*.

In José Echegaray's *Mariana* Stella would play an extremist of the Spanish type—on the surface cold and embittered; beneath her mask of indifference, passionate, idealistic, and ready to sacrifice her life for the sake of her mother's honor. As Paula and Fedora she had died by poison. She had died by the dagger as Militza and Juliet, and drowned as Ophelia; had expired in the wings as Lady Macbeth and in childbed as Mélisande. As Mariana she would be shot down at close range in her lover's arms by the husband whom she had made promise to kill her if she should dishonor him. But there were other qualities besides Mariana's beauty, violence, and idealism that made the part Stella's. Mariana has a reputation for heartless coquetry. "You call that flirtation?" asks a friend who has watched her captivate Daniel Montoya. "Say that she roasts him in a slow fire, that she torments him without pity, that she plays with him as a cat with a mouse: strokes him, sticks her claws in him; lets him go, springs on to him: makes fond grimaces at him and covers him with blood." Add to the character of Mariana a passionate partiality for her mother and disillusionment with men, particularly her father; a will that can break but not bend; wit, intelligence, and a taste for self-destruction—and it was understandable that Louisa Tanner, seeing Elizabeth Robins play the role at the Court Theatre in 1897, felt that her daughter must create Mariana herself.

*Ebbsmith* came off after seventy-nine performances, replaced on May 23 by *Mariana*. By now it had become clear to most critics that a typical Mrs. Campbell play was a star vehicle. When she had to share the spotlight— *Romeo and Juliet, Hamlet, Macbeth, Mr. and Mrs. Daventry*—her magic could not work full strength. Thus the *Graphic* could call Echegaray's play melodramatic and artificial, and Max Beerbohm label it mere foolish melodrama by "a distinguished and much-lauded foreigner, whose very name we are afraid to pronounce"—but when it came to Stella's performance, the praise was great. She played Mariana with a reckless spiritual abandon, a nervous intensity, and a direct and forceful tragedy that turned a heroine of melodrama into a living woman. She had been right to break with Forbes, who needed an actress like Gertrude Elliott to complement his own acting. Stella needed to dominate.

*Mariana* was too forced and violent for British taste, however. When Stella sat down with Arthur Bertram and Bouchier Hawksley to go over finances, she found herself more deeply in debt than before. She was terribly discouraged. On the one hand, she had achieved critical acclaim and established herself as the important English actress of the day. Yet there was no profit to show for it. Oscar had been right: he had advised Harris to get Stella to take a bigger theatre, since that little box could never make money. Harris had done well, however, taking in £4000 on *Daventry*; only Stella and her backers were losing. Despite the cautions of Arthur Bertram, Stella insisted on having her own way—and her way meant generous, even prodigal, management. She could argue that halving profits with Harris had put her management into the red, but having them all to herself would have been as disastrous.

There was nothing to do but revive *Tanqueray* on September 7, 1901, with George Titheradge as Aubrey, Winifred Fraser as Ellean, du Maurier as Captain Hugh Ardale, and Arliss (who had made a striking success of the Duke of St. Olpherts) as Cayley Drummle. If possible, Stella acted better than ever. "Nothing could possibly have been more successful," wrote William Archer, so long in coming over to Stella's camp. "Mrs. Campbell's strong and subtle portraiture of the hapless Paula came straight home to the audience with all the force and poignancy of truth." "I had not seen 'Mrs. Tanqueray' before," agreed John Davidson, her friend from *For the Crown* days. "It was exceedingly beautiful and powerful, sometimes terrible, and of extraordinary sweetness wherever a tender note was struck. Paula is like an opal of many hues and lustres, with stains of life, and wounds of passion through which the disastrous fires glow that shatter it in the end. There are no words in which to thank so incomparable an artist." Stella's Paula had become a household word, a legend—and she still played her with all the magic of what Shaw called "the heyday of her Tanqueradiance."

"All this work was done in a little over eighteen months against tragic odds," said Stella, "in the vain hope of saving the remaining £6,000 of the backers' money." But the day came when she was told that all of it—and more—had gone. "Mr. Bouchier Hawksley explained the calamitous position, and then he and I with a dear friend of mine—Miss Melicent Stone—had a long talk. I would not hear of bankruptcy. I felt I must be allowed to make one more effort." This effort, finally agreed upon at three in the morning, was an American tour. In October Al Canby, representing George C. Tyler of Liebler and Company, came to London and negotiations began. On the twentieth Canby handed her a contract. She was booked for a twenty-two-week tour of the major American cities. She would return between one-third and one-half of her weekly earnings to her creditors. She would open in New York.

America meant giving up for the present all the new plays she was longing to try. She still wanted something from Murray, although two performances of his *Andromache* had borne out her prediction that there was not a penny in it. Anthony Hope, whose novel *The Prisoner of Zenda* had created a splash in 1894, wanted her to reconsider a dramatized version of his book *The God in the Car*. She wanted very much to do Rostand's *La Princesse lointaine*, approaching Shaw for help, although he immediately declined to meddle with the fairytale scheme. At the same time he approached her: his *Three Plays for Puritans* had recently been published. "I will go through the book carefully," Stella replied, "—putting myself in entire sympathy with your idea."

This would be difficult, at least according to Shaw. In his preface to that volume Shaw deplored plays in which voluptuous love was the sole motive for human action. In fact, he told Archer, he could think of few plays to exclude from that category other than Wilde's, Shakespeare's, and his own. Now, one of the chief purveyors of voluptuousness on the contemporary stage, said Shaw, was Mrs. Patrick Campbell. "On the grosser plane you have The Conquerors," he explained, "with the rape on the stage, and the woman, when she recovers from the faint which saves public decency at the last moment, falling in love with the hero because she believes that the rape was consummated during her swoon. Then you have Carton's Tree of Knowledge, with the strangling match (same two performers) substituted for the rape. Leading up to this you have Mrs. Ebbsmith, with the (to A.W.P.) unreal, imaginary Trafalgar Square life suddenly changed into a glorious reality when the woman puts on a fashionable dress, & the man, at sight of her naked shoulders, knows what life & love are at last, & so does she. Then came Michael & His Lost Angel, still under the influence of the overpowering *odor di femmina* from Mrs. P.C. The same moral: the parson's social & religious work an unreal thing: love sweeping it away as the only real thing in the world. . . ." Notwithstanding these views, other critics had found that Stella's great contribution had been creating the intellectual, psychologically complex woman instead of submitting to the role of sex object.

Before leaving for America, she set out with her company on a short tour of the English towns. This time Gerald's letters to "Mummy" were not particularly cheerful. Once he wrote to say that he "longed to be home with her, and that this was a stinking tour in every respect"; again that he was "vague about his plans for the future, and that everything was in the air." The bleak mood coincided with the fact that he was not going along to America. Stella was not playing cat and mouse. She did not love him and, although he brought flair and distinction to every part he played, she still did not think him serious enough. Gerald himself would have been the first to admit that he had chosen acting because he was too lazy to work in an office and was unfit for anything else. He seemed unable, finally, to take himself seriously; it was part of his charm. Now he was being rejected by the woman he adored, and he was miserable. Yet Stella was terribly fond of Gerald du Maurier. "Our friendship was full of fun & kindness," she would write to Daphne du Maurier years later, "real respect & deep affection. Gerald's kindness & courtesy belonged to another age. He just didn't know how to be rude & his loyalty was an iron clamp. . . . Oh, the fun & gaiety of Gerald in those days—& he used to say I came next after Dan Leno for making him laugh! This offended me for in those days I thought myself a great tragic actress."

Back in London they played *Tanqueray* at night and, for seven matinees, Björnson's *Beyond Human Power* because Stella wanted to take it to America. The play tells the story of the bedridden wife of Pastor Sang, a faith healer. Clara cannot move and for weeks has not slept. Why, asks her sister, does her husband not heal *her?* But Clara cannot share her husband's faith; although she loves him, she feels he is "always going beyond his power." Undaunted, Sang announces that he will go to the church and pray. The church bell will toll continuously to let her know he is praying; he will not leave the church until he has received sleep and health for her, so that she may rise up and walk among them again. The bell begins to toll, the husband prays—and Clara's eyes close in healing sleep. Suddenly, however, a terrible, unearthly sound is heard, and a great avalanche roars down the mountainside, destroying everything in its path except the church. When the screaming and shouting subside, Clara is discovered sleeping as peacefully as before. God has answered Sang's prayers with a miracle.

The next act is almost entirely devoted to a great debate in the Sang house among various pastors gathered there to view the miracle of the sleeping wife and discuss its meaning. In the church Sang still prays for

Clara's health, the bell still tolls. But neighbors clamor to see the miracle, and Sang finally leads them into the house, the singing choir following. Suddenly the bedroom door opens, his wife walks into the room and toward him, her arms outstretched. Radiant with joy, Sang goes to meet her, but as he reaches her, she drops down at his feet. Sang falls to his knees, lifts her head, and gives an agonized cry. "But that was not the intention—?" he begins, then rises and looks heavenward. "Or—? Or—?" Clutching his heart, he falls.

Björnson's play was difficult to produce. It was, first of all, Norwegian, with all the bleak mysticism that English audiences found so uncongenial. Then the long debate in the second act about the impact of faith healing upon the doctrines of the Norwegian Church was not exactly a compelling topic among London playgoers. The miracle itself could just as easily provoke laughter as awe. And, finally, the part of Clara Sang was extraordinarily difficult. Not only would Stella have to play the first act immobile in bed, but the play would have to retain its interest even though the central character does not appear again until its very end.

The company played the first matinee of *Beyond Human Power* on November 7, with George Titheradge as Pastor Sang, du Maurier as their son, and Mrs. Theodore Wright, that fine actress who had dared Mrs. Alving in the first London production of *Ghosts*, as the sister. Stella made an overwhelming success.

"I went to the opening performance not altogether blithely," said Graham Robertson, "and beside me were seated two pressmen—pressmen of the wrong type. They were profoundly bored by their job—couldn't stand that kind of thing—supposed they must see a bit of it, but would slip out as soon as possible.

"The curtain rose upon a log-built room plain to bareness, a dreary glimpse of white mountains through a small window, a narrow bed, and on the white pillow a white face among masses of black hair, dark, haunted, sleepless eyes—the spell began to work. The whole house became as still as the still figure in the bed. Never throughout the Act did the almost painful strain relax until the dark eyes closed in a healing, miraculous sleep and the curtain fell in complete silence.

"One of the pressmen said, 'My God!' The other obviously could say nothing.

"The second Act was almost entirely taken up by an endless discussion between pastors of various denominations on the nature and possibility of miracles, but so overwhelming was the effect, so tense the atmosphere created by Mrs. Campbell in the first Act, that the disputing clerics were neither seen nor heard; all attention was fixed upon the unseen woman in the next room. She was waited for breathlessly, and when at last she stood for a moment upon the threshold, radiant, ecstatic, transfigured, then tottered forward to fall dead at the feet of the miracle-workers, we had all had about as much emotion as was good for us.

"This was great acting, great among the greatest. . . ."

Critics lauded her performance; colleagues wrote letters of praise. From Gilbert Murray: "That was simply glorious this afternoon. It has left me exulting . . . taken by storm. . . . I thought your acting, if I may say so, even better than I have seen it before—so firm and full of nobility as well as very subtle." From Edmund Gosse: "Permit me to congratulate you very warmly on your wonderfully delicate and spiritual performance this afternoon. We have come back dazed like people who have seen a vision. . . . Quite apart from the transcendent beauty of your personal part in the piece, you claim the highest applause from every serious-minded person for your courage in presenting a poem the interest of which is so unusual and so intellectual." From W. B. Yeats: ". . . Your acting seemed to me to have the perfect precision and delicacy and simplicity of every art at its best. It made me feel the unity of the arts in a new way. I said to myself, that is exactly what I am trying to do in writing, to express myself without waste, without emphasis. To be impassioned and yet to have a perfect self-possession, to have a precision so absolute that the slightest inflection of voice, the slightest rhythm of sound or emotion plucks the heart-strings. . . ."

But Björnson's play also raised controversy. While Max Beerbohm simply found the pastors "ineffably tedious," others in the audience took the spiritual problem seriously. Still others argued with Björnson's conception of Pastor Sang. Björnson's hero could only have performed those seeming or real miracles by possessing a religious genius, said Yeats. But Sang was "a mere zealous man with a vague sentimental mind—the kind of man who is anxious about the Housing of the Working Classes, but not the kind of man who sees what Blake called 'The Divine Vision and Fruition.'" The contrast between Pastor Sang's mediocrity and Clara Sang's delicacy and distinction pained Yeats, who was miserable until the Pastor was off the stage. "He was an unbeliever's dream of a believer, an atheist's Christian."

Yeats believed the fault lay in Björnson; Louis N. Parker, however, put the blame on Titheradge's conception of the Pastor. "I think (humbly) Mr. Titheradge makes Sang's death less spiritual and more tragic than it should be," he wrote Stella. "I think (humbly) Sang's mental attitude is never more than one of puzzled amazement. When he begins to realize you are dead he looks upward and says 'in a childlike tone'

'But that was not the intention—? . . .'

And I see him saying Or——? Or——? transfigured, with joy, as if he were receiving a message direct from God. And he clutches his heart and falls. Forgive me. Tell me to mind my own business." Shaw objected to Titheradge's death scene less humbly: ". . . he is wrong to gurgle like Othello cutting his throat. That scene gets far beyond the screaming & gurgling kind of realism. These physical obstructions and inconveniences have no business among the spiritual agonies." But, added Shaw, the general impression was overwhelming, and he congratulated her on "a really great managerial achievement. In future, when people ask me whether I go to the theatre I shall say, 'To the Royalty, not to any other.' "

"Thank you for your kind letter," Stella replied, enclosing a photograph of herself as Clara Sang in the walking scene. "I am so glad you were able to come. I took your advice. . . . There are no gurglings & bumpings. The chorus will always be hopeless." Shaw thanked her for the photograph, although *he* would have photographed her in bed, saying, "It's tempting Providence." But at last he agreed that there might be more to her acting than the powerful *odor di femmina*: "After all, there are lots of beautiful people about; and some of them can perhaps even thread needles with their toes; but they cant take a filament of grey matter from their brains and thread it infallibly through that most elusive of eyelet holes in the top of a dramatist's needle. Besides, that produces a new sort of beauty, compared to which natural beauty is a mere reach-me-down from Nature's patterns. Long ago, when everybody was maudlin about your loveliness, I snapped my fingers—admired nothing but your deft fingers and toes. Now I admire you ENORMOUSLY. You have picked the work of nature to pieces and remade it whole heavens finer. It is the power to do that that is the real gift."

With highest praise from artists like Yeats and Shaw, Stella could look upon *Beyond Human Power* as both an acting and a managerial triumph. The *Critic* proclaimed that she had "unquestionably placed herself in the front rank" and that as a manager she had few peers. Max Beerbohm summed up her accomplishments: "The Royalty . . . has prospered in Mrs. Campbell's hands. It was, before she came to it, one of the 'unlucky' theatres . . . and thus what Mrs. Campbell has in a small way achieved for it is commercially not less striking than what Messrs. Harrison and Maude have achieved in a large way for the [lucky] Haymarket. Yet Mrs. Campbell makes no effort to give the public what it wants. Her policy is simply to give the public what she herself likes. As she has no passion for sentimental comedy, or melodrama, or farce, or musical comedy, a thoughtless person might wonder how it is that such a policy has not spelt ruin. For most managers it undoubtedly would spell that so easily spelt word. For her it has spelt the more difficult word success, not so much because she is a great actress, but because the gods have endowed her with the added grace of a personality—magnetism, call it what you will—which the public is quite unable to resist."

Max was evidently innocent of the Royalty's finances or Stella's reason for an American tour. Björnson had not helped: she had again chosen a play too intellectual for the general public. Just behind Edmund Gosse at the first matinee had sat a critic from one of the big papers, muttering—unlike Robertson's overcome pressmen—"Fancy coming to a thing like this! It's about as amusing as a funeral!" His incomprehension was shared, and Stella found herself writing on November 16 to Murray, "There are 3 performances this week—*Tues., Wed. & Thurs*—& if you know anyone who would like to come & can't afford it, if you will send me names & addresses to box office I will gladly forward seats." She answered Yeats's letter, defending Björnson's play, but sighing over the limited taste of the public. Yeats replied sympathetically: "In London the subjects which people think suitable for drama get fewer every day. Shelley said that when a social order was in decay, the arts attached themselves to the last things people were interested in—imaginatively interested in. Here people look on the world with more and more prosaic eyes, as Shelley said they did in dying Greece. There, as here, nothing kept its beauty but irregular love-making. He called the poetry that had irregular love for subject and was called immoral, 'The Footsteps of Astrea departing from the world.' "

And so Stella reluctantly prepared to go to America, where—as Irving, who paid for the Lyceum with American tours, knew—there was money to be made. She would be sold by George C. Tyler and a publicity agent with the unlikely name of A. Toxen Worm, not only as a great actress but as a star. She had dozens of headline-making characteristics to exploit. There was her obsession with little dogs: Pinkie Panky Poo, the latest ratlike beast, a monkey griffon, would of course tour America with her mistress, dining off good china and sleeping in her bosom. There was her taste for a good Havana cigar after supper. There was her notorious wit. One remark alone had made it famous. Told of a homosexual affair between two actors, Stella had retorted, "I don't care what people do, as long as they don't do it in the street and frighten the horses!" There was the famous temperament. There was her reputation as a *femme fatale*. There was her reputation as a darling of the British aristocracy. There was the fabulous wardrobe—velvets, sables, satins, silks, tissues of flame, gold, and orange all trimmed with jet, jewels, feathers, gold and silver embroideries, sequins, ribbons, and lace. There was the image of the adoring mother of two beautiful children.

There was the famous wind-in-the-chimney voice. There was the legend of her overnight fame. There was the still unresolved dispute over whether she was a great actress or merely an irresistible enchantress.

All this Liebler and Company prepared to exploit as negotiations that late fall struggled toward conclusion. Finally it was only left to choose her company and buy the steamship tickets. Liebler wanted some well-known leading man and, as Herbert Waring was then popular and available, he was chosen. Titheradge was already included since he was needed for *Pelléas* and *Beyond Human Power*, both in Stella's repertoire along with *Tanqueray*, *Ebbsmith*, *Mariana*, and *Magda*. Waring and Titheradge were to be featured and well paid, with resulting cuts among the rest of the company. Stella very much wanted Arliss, whom she regarded as the cleverest member of her company; but Arliss had a wife and home in London, good prospects, and no reason to leave them behind for a comparatively low salary. At the last minute, through Stella's persistent arguing, Liebler met Arliss's terms, though obviously, thought Arliss, considering him of little importance.

Stella and company were booked for four months, to sail in December and return in April. She had never left her children so long before. Beo, on board his training ship, was no problem; but young Stella, now a lovely fifteen, was. She had been in four different schools, restless in all of them and much more interested in the excitement of the theatre. But Stella had definite plans for her daughter. She must be well educated, with every chance to make a happy and brilliant marriage and to bring up her children normally without the "nerve-shattering toil" Stella herself had suffered. Remembering her own year in Paris when she was fifteen, she decided to send her daughter to a finishing school in Dresden. That would take all notions of a stage career out of young Stella's head, she hoped, and send her back in a few years ready for a London debut and entrance into society. Whatever young Stella thought about Dresden, she could not withstand her mother: that October she went.

Stella and fifteen members of her company were to sail December 14 on *La Campania*, a fast ship known as the "Ocean Greyhound." Gerald du Maurier accompanied them to Liverpool. Stella, with her faithful dresser, Julia, her maid, mountains of luggage, and of course Pinkie Panky Poo, swept up the gangway. For Arliss, the most vivid memory of the entire voyage would be the figure of Gerald du Maurier waving farewell as the boat left the harbor.

# TWENTY-ONE

## *1901–1902*

O N THE EVENING of December 21, *La Campania* docked in New York harbor, and Stella descended the gangplank in a dark travelling suit, black crushed-velvet hat, black velvet cloak, and dark Russian sables. She was met by Al Canby and Bill Connor of Liebler and a group of jostling men with pencils and notebooks. Although she had been warned of the existence of American reporters, they still came as a shock. In England reporters were people one *sent* for on the rare occasion that one had something to say. Still, she was here to make money, and publicity was inevitable. "Tell them anything you like," she told Arthur Bertram, who had made the voyage with her, "as long as you don't tell them my age." They were already busily jotting notes about her startlingly white teeth and the heavy, ancient rings that studded her fingers. Had she been seasick? Yes, the first part of the voyage had been dreadful. What was the little dog's name? "Pinkie Panky Poo." Was he valuable? "Valuable!"—the low laugh. "She was a griffon bred at the Imperial Kennels and presented to me by the King of the Belgians." They'd heard she was an "intimate" actress: did she realize how big the theatres were in the United States? "I try to appeal to the understanding," said Stella, defending her quiet method. Her famous wardrobe? Stella was even ready to get personal. "Yes, I always wear stays, even when I act—people always want to know that!"

Breaking away, she went by cab with Julia and Wrighton to the Holland House. There a further obstruction arose when the desk manager noted bulging eyes and a wet black nose peeking out of Mrs. Campbell's sable muff. The Holland House, she was informed, did not accept dogs. Stella drew herself up to regal heights. "Then you may rent my lodgings to someone who cares more for her comfort than for her best friend," she announced, and swept magnificently out of the lobby. Eventually she found sanctuary at the Imperial, where, however, she also found more reporters.

She received them in the White Parlor, lounging against sofa pillows in black velvet. Lace trailed from her sleeves, noted one reporter, tangling in her rings; jewelled buttons studding her dress winked and gleamed. The famous white swelling throat was bare. As she talked, she constantly brushed back escaping strands of black hair with her shapely white hand. And she talked readily enough.

Was she really a "bad woman," the type she portrayed in so many roles?

"Just because I have black hair, it doesn't follow I must be a sinner!" laughed Stella. No, she did not play only wicked parts. "A woman with a future may be just as interesting as a woman with a past."

Did she classify herself as an actress of the "modern school"?

"Whatever I do," replied Stella, dismissing classification, "I must do to the life."

New York?

She had only arrived, but the noise was "simply harrowing."

Her fabulous gowns?

They were, rather. In fact, some of the lace on a *Magda* dress came from a gown worn by Madame du Barry in 1775 at her court presentation. "You may say it is worth a guinea an inch," confided Stella, solicitously untangling Pinkie from her long diamond pendant. Passersby paused to stare at the actress and her court. "How very American!" smiled Stella.

Eventually the reporters went away. Arliss and his wife, Flo, meanwhile had gone out to see the Fifth Avenue they had heard so much about and found themselves quite disappointed, unaware they were wandering up and down Sixth Avenue instead of Fifth. All in all, it was a predictably dizzying introduction to the new country, scarcely made easier by the fact that the very next morning the company had to leave by train for Chicago, where, due to a scheduling conflict in New York, they were to make their American debut at the richly elegant Grand Opera House on December 30.

In Chicago, where winter winds swept down Michigan Boulevard and out over the frigid lake, Christmas away from home in overheated boarding houses was forlorn enough, particularly for Arliss, who, on the Sunday before opening, had to run a frantic search for a dentist to pull a throbbing tooth. Eventually he and Canby found a man just closing his office door—a huge man, six feet six, broad and burly, sporting a gigantic cowboy hat. Just the kind of man, thought Arliss miserably, who probably slew buffalo on Sunday for relaxation. But the fellow was agreeable after all and, after the operation, dispelled their first impression entirely by remarking mildly, "Well, I guess I'll just slip back to the wife and kiddies." Stella fared better in her hotel, the suite crowded with American Beauty roses and scarlet poinsettias. Everyone was very kind. She and Pinkie had discovered cornmeal mush. She was rather adjusting to the reporters. She was quite looking forward to opening in *Magda*.

The night of December 30 the "elite of Chicago's swell-set" (as one reporter so elegantly put it) gathered at the Grand Opera House, ash-blond Mrs. Potter Palmer conspicuous in one box, white-haired Marshall Field austerely imposing in another. When the curtain rose on the prosaic Schwartze home and Stella burst into the dreary parlor with all Magda's glory and splendor, the audience interrupted the play for several minutes with an enthusiastic welcome. During those moments Stella had time to register the size of the stage itself: the great expanse emphasized by the few sticks of furniture, the gaping proscenium, the audience out there somewhere a hundred miles away. As on the first night of *Bachelors* thirteen years before, she felt she could not go out to that mass of people, but must again "gather them up to herself" through her own intuitive law of unities: a shaping of pauses, an alternating tentativeness and sudden precision interwoven with rhythmic movements, and, finally, a simple urgency which called the onlooker to listen to and love what she believed true and beautiful.

"I remember the applause at the end of the first act had an extraordinary quality," said Stella; "it was a roar that seemed to say: 'Ah! this is true, we are not going to be bluffed'—and I felt I had won." At the end of the first act she took five curtain calls. At the end of the second, the curtain rose and fell for ten minutes. "Before the curtain was down on the last act, I knew I was wonderfully rich in *friends*," said Stella. "All that applause could not be for my talent: I felt they had taken a fancy to me!" At the final curtain Mrs. Potter Palmer led the deafening ovation from her box, Marshall Field following from his. There were calls for a speech. As Stella appeared before the curtain, a voice from the gallery yelled out, "You're *it*, Mrs. Pat!" convulsing her with laughter. The next day the papers reported the triumph: "CHICAGO AUDIENCE GOES WILD OVER THE ENGLISH ACTRESS."

Conscious that it was not New York, much less London, Chicago welcomed celebrities all the more expansively. "Nowhere in the world are artists received with more warmth and enthusiasm than in Chicago," concluded Stella, "—that city where men fight against heat that stifles, and snows that kill: the miles of great, bare, flat front between you and beautiful Lake Michigan: not sand or stone, but black mud. . . . Further along . . . the great palaces, the 'homes' of the millionaires, looking on to that gorgeous lake that seems to reach to the end of the world—sometimes calm, sometimes with gigantic opalesque waves." The millionaires—Potter Palmer, George Pullman, Philip Armour, Cyrus McCormick, Marshall Field—and the chatelaine of Lake Shore Drive, Bertha Honoré Palmer, put their stamp of approval on Mrs. Patrick Campbell. As usual, she appealed to the women as much as to the men. They took her up eagerly—Mrs. Franklin MacVeagh, wife of the wholesale grocer and regular of the millionaires' table at the Chicago Club; Delia Caton, wife of the prominent lawyer Arthur Caton and mistress of Marshall Field, whose own wife was a semi-invalid; Mrs. Spencer Eddie, patron of the arts. Before Stella knew it, there were balls, dinners, suppers, luncheons, musical parties—and in her hotel suite a constant flood of nosegays, books, sweets, and roses "tall as girls."

With all this adulation, it did not really matter that as she reappeared as Paula, Agnes, Mélisande, and Clara Sang there were dissenters. There always had been in London; she had been simultaneously loved and hated—there was never indifference. The critic of the *Chronicle* criticized her lack of distinctness, the intimate method that appealed so much to others. The *Record Herald* deplored the Maeterlinck as a destructive play and claimed that the morbid and decadent *Beyond Human Power* should be called *Beyond Human Endurance*. In fact, Björnson proved too much for Chicago, Mrs. Potter Palmer announcing that she could not approve of the play. But no one objected to Stella more than Winifred Black of the *Chicago American*. Even before Stella set foot in America, the columnist had attacked her for a press release stating that she did not wish to open in Chicago, despite scheduling problems in New York. "Buffalo and Indians *are* a problem," sneered Miss Black; "but Mrs. Campbell did not have to worry: only the poorer classes of Chicago lived in trees." Now that Stella had arrived, all Miss Black's prejudices were confirmed. Coldly noting the banks of flowers and Pinkie ("a little butter-colored wisp"), she then turned hostile eyes upon Mrs. Campbell. The actress was not at all beautiful, she decided. Masses of dead black hair, long "saint-in-the-window" arms—a sorceress, a Botticelli angel, the Witch of Endor. She noted the high-heeled French slippers protruding from under the black skirt-coat; she also noted that whenever the actress did not like the conversation, the foot swung impatiently and the gilt buckle glittered. "Do you think or feel?"—the buckle blazes. No foot-swinging when Mrs. Campbell informs Miss Black that her daughter is in Dresden and her son a midshipman on the flagship *Glory*, China Station. But then, in reference to the Loop, "How is it possible for you to appreciate my spiritual plays with railways between you and the sun?" demands the actress, with much glitter of shoebuckle. Miss Black answered the question in her column: "They weren't expecting *you* when they made them." She tore apart *Magda*, admitting, however, that the actress had been received with tempests of applause. Her company, said Miss Black, was "beyond belief": *where* did Mrs. Campbell get such extraordinary-looking men! Still, no one was more extraordinary than the actress herself—this "High Priestess of the Decadent," this "Saint of the Order of Degenerates."

Audiences remained ecstatic. There were so many curtain calls and so many bouquets handed up that Stella was forced to announce in the press that she disliked flower presentations. She was not quite spared, however. One night during the first act of *Beyond Human Power* a group of young girls in a transport of adolescent heroine-worship suddenly sprang to their feet and began to pelt her with white roses. One hit Stella where she lay in bed as the immobile invalid, causing her to start and murmur a line not in the script. The papers loved it. They added it to the legend along with her jewels (she had dozens of hearts in gold and silver and precious stones; she always asked people who truly liked her to give her a heart), her dogs, and her reputation as the darling of society.

Stella furthered that reputation, appearing at a meeting of the elite Fortnightly Club of Chicago as guest of its president, Mrs. Potter Palmer. As usual, she was asked to speak. "My experience in Chicago convinces me that American women are the happiest in the world," said Stella, her eyes travelling over the assembly of wealthy and influential women. "Had Mrs. Tanqueray been of this new world the play must have had a different ending. Somehow I feel that problem plays will never be written about American women. For you women seem to me as free and happy as birds." She was constantly asked (she told them) to advise young women about adopting the stage as a profession. In England, where women had less equality and freedom, her answer might well be yes. Certainly the stage had been her own salvation. But, "Whatever advice I may give to others, I won't advise an American woman to forsake her happiness for the hardship and struggles of the stage. And yet," she concluded gracefully, "I can say heartily and sincerely that all my labor has been more than repaid by the gracious welcome you have given me in this new world."

Stella felt she must somehow repay the city's extraordinary hospitality. She was to open in New York at the Republic Theatre on January 13, which meant leaving Chicago on the eleventh. She appealed to Mrs. MacVeagh, who agreed to help her give a dinner on the tenth. Mrs. MacVeagh recommended the Auditorium, the vast structure designed by Adler and Sullivan that dominated the expensive row houses around Congress Street and Michigan Avenue, and helped with a guest list. On her last evening Stella entertained six tables of guests in the Palm Garden, among them a young American actress who had charmed London at the Lyceum a few seasons before, Ethel Barrymore. Stella shone that night with the "irresistible gaiety" one interviewer had noted in her. Which of the "perfect cargo of most sumptuous dresses, coats, and hats" made by Viola of Albemarle

Street she chose to wear is unrecorded. Perhaps the black tulle over gold, the skirt spangled with dull gold disks and covered with black roses and foliage sprays, each raised *panne* rose pinned with a diamond cluster at its heart and tipped with gold, the bodice repeating the rose motif and strands of diamonds drooping over the chemisette sleeves of soft white chiffon. Over this, to brave the wintry Chicago night, perhaps the evening coat of trained black velvet with broad ermine collar and green-and-gold-embroidered white satin tabs fixed with green malachite slab buttons, the whole topped with a lace scarf which she knotted on the left beneath great jewelled bosses.

"Chicago was like a wonderful nightmare," she wrote Uncle Harry, still feeling sick and jumpy after two nights on a train that pulled into New York three hours late on opening day. "Five plays in a fortnight, and nine performances a week, and speeches, and all the parties . . ." She was further discouraged by the fact that so much of the money she was making had to go to her creditors. She had beaten all records in Chicago, holding the record house, the record matinee, the record week, and the record fortnight with gross receipts of nearly £7000. The house had been sold out at every performance, scalpers getting $5 at the door for tickets that originally cost $3. But it would be many more hard weeks before she could hope to clear off the debt she owed her Royalty backers.

It was New York that Stella had to conquer, and Liebler was determined she should do so with all the publicity they could manufacture. It is perhaps cynical to imagine that A. Toxen Worm sent Stella to hotels he knew would not accept dogs so that she could promptly leave them in a whirlwind of indignation and press notices; but the scene did recur, and two or three hotels rejected Pinkie before Stella found the Park Avenue. Reporters had found it before she did: a dozen were waiting in the reception room. She had not slept for forty-eight hours and did not attempt tact. "How perfectly dreadful!" she exclaimed, eyeing the jostling group. "Why do you do it? Is it for your living? It seems to me so insulting!" Her suite was chaotic. Julia and Wrighton were trying to unpack, constantly bumping into trunks that spilled out into the hall and into each other. There was not a cup of English tea to be had for Wrighton, who had suffered constant bilious attacks since leaving England. But worse than reporters, cramped quarters, and no English tea were the rush and noise of New York City. It was a hellish din: grinding elevators, nasal bell-hops, shrilling newsboys, clanging streetcars, ruthless steam drills, and—since the subway was under construction—constant subterranean explosions as the tunnel was blasted inch by inch. And she was to play *Magda* that very night.

That evening New Yorkers with tickets to the Republic looked forward to what one newspaper called "the great event in New York theatrical circles this week." For her opening Oscar Hammerstein's theatre assumed the ceremony appropriate to a London star and socialite. A wide awning stretched from curb to entrance and liveried attendants were on duty to hand down elaborately gowned ladies out of carriages. Society turned out to welcome Stella: Mr. and Mrs. George Gould and party, Mrs. Dana Gibson, Mr. and Mrs. J. E. Schermerhorn, Mr. and Mrs. J. D. Archbold, and, in one box, Mark Twain and friends. The reception was gratifying, thought Stella, as she appeared for her calls—and yet it was not quite Chicago. She did not quite feel, as she had after that *Magda*, that she was so rich in friends.

No one in America, Arthur Bertram wrote to Henry Tanner, took any notice of press reviews. Certainly there was no body of critics in New York comparable to Archer, Walkley, Shaw, and Beerbohm in London; yet Stella paid attention to the press. She found, as she had in Chicago, that she did not universally please. Dorothy Dix called her Paula "vinegary" and "an unrelieved misery." Alan Dale found Stella appealing to the eye and ear, but "never provocative of enthusiasm." But it was her plays themselves that New York critics chiefly condemned: they found *Mariana* a horror, Sudermann dull, Björnson ridiculous, and *Ebbsmith* immoral. Yet her magic worked as usual. Theatregoers began to understand that something important was going on at the Republic, something different, something not to be missed.

Tyler, Canby, and Worm were not content to let Stella's genius speak for itself. They turned her New York stay into a circus—and Stella allowed or could not prevent the stunts. Tyler, not unnaturally, credited her for much of the publicity. Mrs. Pat, said Tyler, was the first really temperamental actress he'd ever run into; she quite knocked him over at first meeting. "Hers was one-hundred-proof temperament, but it was so interwoven with a grand sense of humor and an astounding charm that you laughed at and with her instead of trying to strangle her. Sometimes temperament is just a politer word for a bad disposition, and I have known actors whose temperament came in a pint bottle with a revenue stamp across the top. In Mrs. Pat's case it was beyond question the real thing, all wool and a yard wide. By the same token, she was one of the best natural press-agents in the business. It was almost impossible for her to do or say anything that didn't catch the public eye, although you could never say she was posing on purpose. It was just a matter of magnetic personality, or whatever big word you choose."

Some interviews had vestiges of dignity. One common question was "What do you think of America?" and Stella had ready answers. She found the liberty of American women amazing: they actually went to the theatre without escorts, and had such frank, free manners. She found American men more kindly though less sincere than Englishmen. Sometimes she enjoyed the tempo: "I like the rush of life that pervades everything. Everything's keen. In England there's conservatism and poise. In America there's impulse and life." But, as a whole, she did not find Americans serious. "They're not reflective, nor retrospective, you know," she told one interviewer, "just prospective."

A few reporters asked her about the stage. She replied that she found theatre accommodations on both sides of the Atlantic execrable. She found New York audiences less responsive than Chicago audiences. She found publicity interviews incompatible with being an artist and was granting them only because she discovered reporters got paid for them and she did not want to take the bread from their mouths. But she did not intend to coarsen her art to please either the American public or press. One interviewer followed her to the theatre to report her rehearsal technique. A member of the cast approached her. "Now, when I say the words, 'This will be my death,'" he asked, "do I turn to the audience or stand facing the wings?" "I should not recommend you to do either," replied Stella crisply. "You see, the words are 'This fatal grief will cause my death.'" Always word-perfect herself, the reporter noted, Mrs. Pat was intolerant of actors who were less.

But most questions were inane—"Why are you called Mrs. Pat?" or "What are your first impressions of New York?"—and Stella let the questioners know it. "Oh, do please talk to Pinkie here!" she cried, holding up the wisp of dog. "She's a bright little girl." The next morning she and Pinkie made headlines all over the country. Her photograph with Pinkie cuddled against her cheek appeared everywhere. The *Evening World* initiated a column called "Pinky Panky Poo—His Impressions," headed by a photograph of Pinkie looking rather aggrieved at both the constant misspelling of her name and misplacement of her sex. The two of them made the editorial pages when a disgusted reader wrote to the *Evening Journal* complaining that a woman's face was meant to be pressed against a child's, not the wild, crazy, snub-nosed muzzle of a beast. Back in her hotel suite Stella continued to murmur sweet nothings to Pinkie in her special language, a practice which led to another sensational distortion. "Those who have listened outside the great actress's bedroom door will have heard the words spoken to her by her deceased husband on the phonograph she carries with her always," confided one imaginative reporter. "She turns on the phonograph every night before she goes to sleep."

Nothing brought Stella as much notoriety, however, as the tanbark. "For a wonder, that was mostly accident," said George Tyler. "In New York

Mrs. Pat played Hammerstein's Republic Theatre. As was his custom, Oscar had built the thing on such a tiny piece of ground that the whole back of the house was right on the sidewalk—the patrons inside could hear a man cough across Forty-second Street—and every time one of the old-fashioned cable-cars went crashing over the frogs in the complicated switches outside, you couldn't hear yourself think in the auditorium. A good noisy play might stand some chance of surviving this competition, but a quiet piece was completely out of luck.

"Well, at Mrs. Pat's first Saturday matinée, of course, all the girls in town turned out to have a look at her magnificent wardrobe straight from Paris. She knew they'd be there—so, out of sheer perversity, she elected to do *Beyond Human Power*, a very quiet tense play in which she stayed in bed from beginning to end, so there was no wardrobe to see at all. Throughout the first act you couldn't hear a thing back of the first six rows but the clank and crash of the rapid transit system. I spent the whole entr'acte out in the box-office snorting my disgust to Bill Connor: 'Something's got to be done about this—we ought to get permission to bed the street down with tanbark.' A. Toxen Worm, our press-man . . . jumped at the idea. But he didn't bother about getting permission. He just procured and dumped the tanbark, forty wagon-loads of it, and explained to all and sundry, including the representatives of the law, that Mrs. Campbell was extremely sensitive to noise and had insisted on our doing it."

Stella herself had been completely mystified when Worm stuck his head in her dressing room and said, "If anyone says 'tanbark,' you know nothing." She did know that that night the din outside the theatre ceased. The next morning she had several more miles of headline: the tanbark caught the public's imagination like Anna Held's milk bath and Steve Brodie's leap. One press wit invented outraged letters from Broadway stars to the street-cleaning department, requesting similar favors. "I know you are a real nice man, and are always willing to help on a poor girl," May Irwin supposedly wrote. "The push-cart man makes so much noise in front of the Bijou Theatre that I cannot hear my own jokes, and am apt to spring a chestnut on the public. Please send seven cars of tanbark to me by return mail." From Anna Held: "I think it awful mean that Mrs. Campbell is getting all the tanbark. Won't you please send me 10 or 15 cents worth? I am very fond of rest myself." Lillian Russell: "I always did like tanbark, except I hear it makes the skin tough. If you can send me four or five carloads c.o.d. I shall be so grateful." And from "a bunch of Florida girls": "We do want a lot of tanbark so that we cannot hear the loud suits of clothes of the wicked bald-headed men who sit in the front row at the 'New York.'"

Not everyone appreciated Stella's notoriety. "She didn't need the tan-bark," said Oscar Hammerstein; "George Tyler barks all the time." Another British actress currently in New York laughed scornfully at the way Stella kept in the spotlight. Imagine—she turned up her nose at the handsome Republic after years spent at the Royalty, "one of the dingiest and dirtiest little bandboxes in all London." "She is fast turning herself into a laughing stock," sneered the actress, who preferred to remain anonymous. "Her tactics are only practised nowadays by comic opera stars or members of the Florodora Sextette." The tanbark was finally removed on January 22 by order of a borough president offended that permission had been granted over his head, but, whether she liked it or not, Stella was now known as the "Lady of the Tanbark." She found herself the most talked-about person in New York.

A. Toxen Worm's imagination continued to prove fertile. On January 25 Richard Mansfield, the great American actor who had given Shaw his first success in New York when he played *The Devil's Disciple*, gave Stella a dinner at Delmonico's. In a graceful speech he called her a "twin star" and suggested that she should play Lucretia Borgia to his Lorenzo di Medici. Worm took this up immediately, issuing a press notice that objected to the "twin star" label and assuring Mansfield that Mrs. Patrick Campbell was quite able to star by herself—not the most tactful way to encourage British and American theatrical friendship.

A brief lull followed the Mansfield dinner before events surrounding a matinee of *Pelléas and Mélisande* retrained the spotlight on Stella. In the first place, the production had to be moved to the Victoria Theatre next door since the orchestra pit at the Republic held only seven musicians and Stella insisted on a full orchestra for Fauré's score. Then, Stella was acutely conscious of the possibility that Americans might misunderstand Maeter-linck's rarefied dream-world. There had been occasional titters in London; how Americans ignorant of the Pre-Raphaelite aesthetic might react she dreaded to think. Stella therefore instructed the public in good manners: the audience must not come in late; they must not leave their seats until the very end; there was to be no chit-chat, please, and no standing or walking about during the performance. Next to make news was the price of tickets —$3 a seat. That price in the past had been reserved to Duse, Bernhardt, and Irving and Terry, said the papers. Mrs. Campbell, although she enjoyed "a certain weird popularity," did not deserve it. Much of the audience, therefore, took their seats at the Victoria on the afternoon of January 29 ready to criticize.

The most difficult scene in *Pelléas* for audiences to accept with a straight face was just the scene that believers found the most beautiful—the second scene in Act III, when, as Mélisande leans forward out of her window to take Pelléas's hand and her long hair tumbles over his face, Pelléas seizes and kisses it and, trying to hold her, ties it to the branch of a willow tree. New Yorkers did not let this pass unscathed. There were giggles when Herbert Waring kissed Stella's hair, murmuring, "Ah, see, it seems all alive" that turned into roars when he then tied her hair to a "willow" which was in fact a scraggly fir tree. All Stella's efforts to set the right mood had gone for nothing.

Afterwards, however, she invited New York society to Oolong tea on-stage. Assisted by socialites Mrs. Dana Gibson and Mrs. Clarence Mackay and waiters from Sherry's, Stella received the elite and charmed them as usual. Many of the guests lingered until 6:30, joining in the singing that often marked Stella's parties. Then a few guests went along with her to her hotel for a game of bridge whist. Stella was no longer at the Park Avenue. Bothered by the noise, crowding, and an intuitive voice that whispered more and more insistently, "Get out of this hotel," she had said to Julia after a week, "Pack up: I must go." Julia thought her mad, and only very reluctantly repacked the endless trunks, but twenty-four hours later the Park Avenue had been "blown to smithereens." Now, at the Hotel Majestic, Stella sat down to a game that, like everything else she did, made headlines the next day:

MRS. CAMPBELL WINS $22,000

"Wonderful are the resources of Mrs. Patrick Campbell. No sooner does her light begin to dim as the heroine of Pinky-Panky-Pooh and the tanbark, than she turns on the current and, lo, her stellar luminosity flares up anew." "I may say, without a bit of conceit," she was quoted as remarking, "that I am one of the best players in England." A denial of both quotation and winnings and another report placing the sum at $2000 did nothing to erase the impression that she had won enormously. "She has had more free advertising," concluded one paper, "than any actress since Lily Langtry."

Living with Flo in a boarding house on 25th Street just off Broadway, George Arliss watched the antics sadly. "Personally," said Arliss in retrospect, "I consider that her reputation in America was permanently injured by the efforts of a too-zealous Press department. Publicity at any price seemed to be their slogan. Some reports that were widely circulated would lead one to suppose that she sat up all night playing poker and drinking cocktails. While in reality she was a most moderate drinker—if, indeed, she drank at all—and she did not know one card from another. Her pet dog, 'Pinky Panky Poo,' was exploited *ad nauseam*. As though she were the only woman in the world who behaved foolishly about her animals! It was the kind of publicity that might have been resorted to in an effort to foist upon the public an inferior musical-comedy star."

Arliss was having his own kind of success in New York. Coming down to breakfast after his debut in *Tanqueray*, he had found himself shaken warmly by the hand and congratulated on his press notices. As the days went by, he began to realize that the press of New York had quickly developed a solid friendship for him, a friendship that leading men Herbert Waring and George Titheradge might well have resented, but did not. Soon after his appearance as the Duke of St. Olpherts ("easily the triumph of this presentation"), Arliss received an offer from impresario Charles Frohman, followed almost immediately by another from David Belasco. He had worked for years to get to London and was reluctant to sacrifice his dream of becoming a West End star, but Belasco proved convincing. He was also reluctant to leave Stella. Had there been any chance of her running her own theatre again back in London, he probably would have stayed with her; but there seemed little ahead for her but slavery until her debts were paid. Arliss regretfully arranged to leave at the end of the tour, not forgetting how she had believed in him and fought for him. "If you are with a good manager who believes in you, stick to him," he would advise young actors.

Stella continued to draw mixed reactions. *Pelléas* had stuck in many throats. "She acted with all the intensity of a stained-glass window," claimed the *Evening Sun*. Alan Dale was frankly rude. Calling the play "Silly-ass and Smelisande," he dismissed Maeterlinck as produced by Mrs. Campbell as "both nauseating and inane." He was also at work on an article about the star for *Frank Leslie's Popular Monthly*. With relentless sarcasm he exploded the notion of Stella as a first-rate artist. Mrs. Campbell had claimed she was well received in *Bachelors* and *Tares*. "I don't believe it," said Dale. She had misguidedly tried to update Lady Teazle. She always hunted out eccentric roles—Gilbert Murray's *Carlyon Sahib*, for example, was a nightmare with the atmosphere of the dissecting room. She obviously tried to model her diction on Ellen Terry's: there was the same peculiar staccato utterance, although not as pronounced now as it had been earlier in her career. Of one thing Dale announced himself certain: "She is not a great actress."

The most intelligent criticism, however, focused on her choice of roles. "Surely those fine eyes can be lit by the light of happiness, and that expressive mouth is not incapable of the smile which is not a sneer, but a gracious invitation to come and be merry, if only for a moment," complained *Harper's Weekly* of her uniformly morbid repertoire. "Her tall and slender form is ever stiff with the starch of misery; the fine sweep of limb has never a suggestion of the dance. . . . If the gloomy thing, and the gruesome thing, and the impossible feminine thing, are all that Mrs. Campbell can do, then she is lacking in the attributes which are the stamp of genius." "She belongs to tragedy," agreed *The Theatre Magazine*, "and should have a death scene in every play . . . but she is not yet a great tragedienne. . . . The truest statement of her art and the briefest is that she attains glimpses of the heights but lingers in the valley: she is a very gifted amateur. Having said this, one may proceed to contradict it. Mrs. Campbell bears herself as naturally on the stage as Duse. . . ." *Harper's Weekly* had to bow to the remarkable power of the actress's personality: "Frankly, we should sum Mrs. Campbell up as the most interesting feminine mentality that has come to us as yet from Great Britain; the most piquante as a personality; the most baffling as an artist. . . ."

There was only one critic in New York that mattered to actors, Stella was told, and that was Norman Hapgood. "For a long time nothing in the theatrical world has done so much good in New York as the visit of Mrs. Patrick Campbell," wrote that observer. Her plays had been much censured; "Nevertheless, it took but a few days for the idea to spread among people who care that Mrs. Campbell was something that must not be missed, and there were many who were turned away from the theatre every night. . . . Some of them liked Björnson best, some Maeterlinck, some Pinero, but all cared. They were in the presence of an art which would make a difference in their feelings and in their ideas. . . . My own opinions have been changed in several ways and always in favor of the author, a characteristic result of Mrs. Campbell's thoroughness of interpretation."

"Darling Uncle . . . I work, work, work, all the time," confided Stella to Henry Tanner back in London. ". . . Expenses are so heavy here it means my coming home without a farthing, however hard I work. . . . The audiences are not so large now; it is so warm, and I believe I am in the wrong theatre. . . . Perhaps you will see Mr. Hawksley and suggest that if I pay £8,000 now it will be sufficient, and others must wait. . . . I am writing in the night, after two performances and a rehearsal. . . . Nine performances last week. . . . I have been ill, my voice and appetite and my sleep went for four days, and have left me rather weak. Mrs. Clarence Mackay sent round all sorts of nice things; I am better, really quite well, only rather hoarse. I have played every performance; I was so afraid I would have to give up." Cheerful letters from her daughter comforted her. Stella loved Dresden and her lessons and couldn't believe she'd been there nearly four months, but she wished she could just run over to America and give her mother a hug—it would be so lovely to spend a few hours with her. Other letters were disturbing. Gerald wrote. He missed her and he wanted to marry her. But Stella was not in love with Gerald du Maurier.

For her last performance at the Republic on February 1, 1902, Stella presented the third act of *Ebbsmith* followed by *Beyond Human Power*. After the final curtain she appeared onstage in Clara Sang's white night-dress, her hair hanging loose down her back, and addressed the audience, who had greeted her performance with great enthusiasm. Thanking them for their warmth, she went on to say, "I see no reason why the drama should not be selected for its beauty and truth, its possession of those qualities which give worth to other aspects of life." Norman Hapgood agreed. "It is not only for excitement that we all go to the theatre, not to be carried off our feet by sheer power. It is to have three hours in which the mind and taste are encouraged, pleased, and corrected." Hapgood had found her most distinguished work to be "deep, clear, pure, and in the minor key." It was these qualities she now asked to be accepted as good acting and good drama.

From the Republic she went to the Montauk Theatre in Brooklyn, where Liebler had booked her through February 8, then prepared to leave for Montreal to play *Tanqueray* on the eleventh and twelfth. She was due back for the week beginning February 24 at the Harlem Opera House. On Monday the twenty-fourth she made headlines again: "MRS. PATRICK CAMPBELL LOST THREE HOURS." Someone, it seemed, had sent her on the wrong ferry; not a few suspected Messrs. Tyler, Canby, and Worm. Stella meanwhile had skirmished with Mrs. Cornelius Vanderbilt and got it into the papers. Mrs. Vanderbilt, it seemed, had sent a note asking her to recite at one of her parties as an entertainer. Stella did not answer. A week later Mrs. Vanderbilt called in a carriage with coachman and footman. Mrs. Patrick Campbell, however, was not at home. Finally the *grande dame* appealed to a mutual friend to persuade the actress to recite; Mrs. Campbell could even bring her little dog. At last Stella spoke. "It's this," she declared. "I must appear, don't you know, in society as a lady, or not at all." The mutual friend consulted Mrs. Vanderbilt. Could not Mrs. Campbell be invited as a guest? Mrs. Vanderbilt considered, shook her head. "No, the Prince of Wales may be democratic, but . . . !"

After Harlem, Stella's company again took to the road. For the tour she demanded and got a private Pullman, the front half for herself, the rear for her company. Liebler did not object to that, but when they discovered that she had sent her enormous caravan of luggage ahead, completely filled the company's half with it, and flatly refused to have it removed, they were not terribly amused. Another car was provided, however, and Stella and company left for Philadelphia, where they played to enthusiastic crowds at the Garrick the week of March 10. Next Baltimore, where they won good notices, and where Stella made news by reviving a fainting woman in the lobby with smelling salts, still in her *Tanqueray* dress. "I was always a good nurse," she was quoted as saying. On the last day of the Baltimore engagement the company missed the train to Washington and were left to hang about the station until the next at 2:30 a.m. Reporters hung about also, and were able to tell readers next day that Mrs. Campbell had sent a boy to a German restaurant nearby, with the result that the company feasted until train time on cheese, bologna, and beer. On March 24 she played Magda at the Columbia Theatre before an audience that did not include President and Mrs. Theodore Roosevelt (they never attended opening nights), but was heavily salted with Washington dignitaries, socialites, and members of the British Embassy. "BEFORE THE EYES OF A NATION: GREAT OVATION ACCORDED MRS. PATRICK CAMPBELL: WASHINGTON SOCIETY CHEERS HER TO THE ECHO," raved the papers the next morning. A Washington audience, one critic reminded his readers, might be considered the test of the whole country because of the variety of the capital's residents.

Boston prepared to welcome the British actress on April 7 for a week of theatre that would see Mrs. Fiske at the Tremont, Miss Ethel Barrymore at the Museum, and Mrs. Patrick Campbell at the Boston Theatre. Stella decided to open with *Tanqueray*, with Arliss playing his tremendously successful Cayley Drummle, Waring as Aubrey, Lucy Milner as Ellean, and Mrs. Theodore Wright as Mrs. Cortelyon. Advance notices had hoped that Boston would not be shocked by the actress's "problem play" repertoire and, although a few critics inevitably found the play "reeking with nastiness," the praise was generous. "Indisputable success" was the general consensus, and matinees of *Pelléas* and *Beyond Human Power* alternating with evening performances of *Ebbsmith* and *Magda* continued to generate enthusiasm. "It is because Mrs. Campbell adds to a fine personal beauty a rare intelligence, some 'temperament,' and aspiring artistic power, that she is irresistible," said the captivated Boston *Transcript*. Such beauty and such art were seldom found in one woman. Boston did not want to let her go.

The tour was originally to have ended in April, but Stella was such a success that Liebler decided to prolong it through May. The week of May 8 Stella played Detroit and then, as New York papers announced her imminent departure for England on the *Teutonic* (her company would sail on the humbler *Cymric*) and her decision not to spend the summer at Bar Harbor with friends, the troupe set off for St. Louis, where they found the temperature over 100° in the shade and not a breath of air inside the theatre or out.

St. Louis produced another news event. "CELEBRATED ACTRESS REUNITES POOR RELATIVES AND GIVES THEM $1000 IN GOLD," blazed a headline, followed by an account of how Mrs. Pat had discovered her poor old sick uncle, Mr. J. V. Cumins, living at 3538 Eastern Avenue in St. Louis. They had had an ecstatic reunion, Mrs. Campbell calling on the unusually handsome, blue-eyed old man in her stylish victoria to bring him big bunches of American Beauty roses, wines, and other delicacies, and taking him driving along the boulevards and through Forest Park. Then, on the last day of her visit, the celebrity miraculously produced her Aunt Dora, whom she had spirited from San Antonio to reunite with her husband. Mr. Cumins had lost his "gigantic fortune" in Texas, and he, his wife, and grown daughter had come to St. Louis to open a little shop; but the two women had grown discontented and returned to San Antonio. Now Mrs. Campbell brought them together in her hotel suite, blessed them, gave them $1000 in gold, and sent them back to Texas happy. Or so said the press. But of course it was exactly like Stella to give away money lavishly and then have to work twice as hard to earn it all over again.

"She made money for us hand over fist, something like five thousand a week clear profit both in New York and on the road," said Tyler, "but it finally wore us down wondering what she was going to spring on us next." Back in New York, Stella sent for Tyler and started proposing where and what she would play next season.

"But why tell me?" asked Tyler.

Stella explained that, exasperated as she was over all the errors made in handling her affairs, she knew she was legally bound to honor Liebler's option on her further services.

"True," said Tyler, "but you see, I'm not taking it up."

"What!" said Stella. "But think of all the money you've made!"

"It's an awful lot of money," said Tyler, worn down by innumerable bouts with the temperament, "but then I've got my health to consider too."

Stella stared, and then, said Tyler, "like herself and nobody else, she threw back her head and shrieked with laughter. It was utterly impossible to continue a quarrel with a woman like that for any length of time." But he had not relented by the time Stella boarded the *Teutonic* on May 22.

Stella had Pinkie in a satchel and, as reporters crowded round, she announced she would *not* surrender her darling to the care of the "ship's butcher." "I'll be back in mid-September," she promised, "to open at the Garden Theatre in two new plays. I'll be my own manager, but partially under the direction of Charles Frohman, since he owns the Garden Theatre."

"MRS. PATRICK CAMPBELL SAILS FOR ENGLAND AFTER SAYING AMERI-

CANS MAKE THE WORLD'S BEST AUDIENCE," a farewell headline announced that day, but it was not quite the last word for this tour. Murmurs of discontent still flew about the $3 she had dared to charge for seats, and disputes over her acting were still alive. Yet the tour had been a brilliant success; she had made, said one source, over $100,000. The New York *Sun* had, after all, spoken for the majority. "She didn't need the tanbark," said that paper. "She's first rate."

# TWENTY-TWO

## *1902–1903*

$\mathcal{S}$TELLA HAD REFUSED to turn Pinkie over to the ship officials, but a worse fate waited: in her absence England had introduced a six-month quarantine for incoming animals. The thought of confining her dog to a cage for half a year was unendurable; but then a message came from Uncle Harry saying Pinkie was safe. She could thank Nina, who had pleaded so eloquently that Pinkie would die separated from her mistress that the Board of Agriculture had relented.

Both Harry and Nina took the midnight train to Liverpool to meet her ship on May 27. Stella returned to find changes in her uncle's Chelsea household. Joe Jones had always longed to live in the country; coming upon an advertisement one day for The Long Plat, Nutbourne, near Pullborough in Sussex, she went to inspect and promptly bought the property. She added a new wing to the thatched cottage, and she and Lulo moved in to enjoy the flower and kitchen gardens, orchard, and large meadow. With Lulo and Joe gone and Harry in the City all day, Louisa Tanner was left too much alone. Beatrice could not take her, Nina either could or would not; and so it was decided that Stella's mother go to Gensing Lodge, a private *pension* kept by French Augustinian nuns at St. Leonards on the Sussex coast. Mrs. Tanner would not be far from Lulo, the nuns would be kind, the religious atmosphere congenial, the climate mild, and glimpses of the sea from her hilltop location refreshing. Now much alone, Harry began to spend a good deal of time at Nina's and more at Kensington Square.

Coldness between Stella and Lulo remained. Stella blamed her for breaking up the household in Glebe Place and forcing their sixty-six-year-old mother, to whom family was everything, into the arms of strangers. "No, indeed, I have not changed my mind," she wrote her sister. "It holds the same disgust & disappointment at the life you have chosen & the same belief that your criticism of me—& mine of you—would always have been a misery to us both & that vileness was better under the circumstances than endless argument—or what was worse—pretense. And so my dear God bless you & keep you well & contented until the end." Lulo was encouraged enough by this reply to visit Stella and follow the meeting with another letter. This time Stella had no blessings. "My dear Lulo, you are laboring under a mistake. It was no pleasure to me to see you—& still less is it to hear from you. Mother and Uncle will tell me whatever I ought to hear about Edwin. I shall not write again." Accustomed to being surrounded by family, Stella now had only her uncle, and they drew closer together than ever.

Stella did not act in London that summer. She had no money for a theatre. She had made money "hand over fist" for Liebler, money for Oscar Hammerstein, and had managed to wipe out more than half of the debt owed her creditors. The fraction earned for herself she had managed to spend on hotels, luxurious food, entertainments for friends, carriages and cabs, velvets and furs, young Stella's school, her mother's *pension*, Max's and Beo's allowances, Wrighton's and Julia's wages, long-stem American Beauty roses for James Cumins, and, back in England, a beautiful gift for Pinero, who thanked her for remembering him in "her triumphant course." The only solution was a quick return to America, and she arranged to sail in mid-August on the new *Oceanic*. She had been frustrated on the last tour by the lack of new plays to produce: as long as *Tanqueray* and *Ebbsmith* kept drawing, Liebler made her stick to them. Now, however, she had *Aunt Jeannie* by E. F. ("Dodo") Benson and Sudermann's *Es lebe das Leben* in a translation by Edith Wharton. The author had admired Stella's acting greatly in New York, but had been less enthusiastic about translating the play since she could not see how a tragedy based upon the German "point of honor" in duelling could be either intelligible or interesting to American audiences. She also objected to the title Stella liked, *The Joy of Living*. The ironic German title, "long live life," was virtually untranslatable, but by no stretch of the imagination did it mean "the joy of living," and she did not want to be accused of ignorance. But Stella overruled all her protests, and Wharton made and delivered the translation under the title Stella preferred.

With two new plays in her pocket and Pinkie in a Gladstone bag, Stella arrived in New York on August 20, 1902, and, fending off reporters, had herself driven to the Oriental Hotel on Manhattan Beach, where she intended to relax for a few days before beginning rehearsals at the Garden Theatre for a mid-September opening. "SHE'S BACK," a headline announced the next day, "with a one pound dog, thirty-seven trunks, and six hat boxes." Mrs. Osborne of New York would be doing her dresses, Edith Wharton was translating, and she'd engaged a new American leading man, Mr. John Blair.

Establishing her headquarters at the Fifth Avenue Hotel, Stella dove into rehearsals with an energy that raised whirlwinds about her. She directed all rehearsals, ruled on everything, and began to clash with John Blair. On September 4 Benson himself arrived from England and attended a rehearsal that same afternoon. Stella found his play "full of charm and elegance," an antidote to the heavy, morbid drama that critics had accused her of favoring last season. She was playing Jeannie Halston, a pretty young widow who, discovering that the man her niece has engaged herself to is a vile seducer, flirts with the bad lot herself to save her niece. That, essentially, was the plot of *Aunt Jeannie*, just as frivolous as Benson's popular novel *Dodo* and promising enough to have lured its author across the Atlantic for its premiere.

Unfortunately, Benson was not popular with critics the day after the September 16 opening. Although a solitary review called "AUNT JEANNIE A SUCCESS," it was buried under damnations like "Aunt Jeannie proves tiresome," "Aunt Jeannie is weak tea and talk," "Aunt Jeannie excells in the lost art of saying nothing." Alan Dale paid it the compliment of an extended attack, labelling it "an avalanche of words mis-called a play." "Could we," asked Dale, "be supposed to sympathize with an auntie, who, to save her niece, tempts that niece's lover, Lord Lindfield, into her arms, and then—likes him? . . . Mr. John Blair's dynamic kiss will not be interesting, even to the weak-minded." That kiss, however, attracted a good deal of attention. "She fastens her lips to his with a leech-like intensity," marvelled one reviewer, ". . . longer and longer . . . she throws her arms around him . . . her fingers drum his back." But Dale said it all as far as New York was concerned: "AN ENTIRELY HOPELESS EFFORT IS BENSON'S NEW PLAY."

There was nothing for Stella to do but console Benson on the execrable taste of Americans and immediately call rehearsals for *The Joy of Living*. During the last days of *Aunt Jeannie* an interviewer from *The Theatre Magazine* found her backstage and willing to talk about the failure. It had been a harrowing experience both inside the theatre and out, Stella admitted. Just before opening, Pinkie had licked off a generous application of flea powder and become deathly ill. While headlines described her weeping over her dying pet and unable to receive callers, Stella had somehow nursed Pinkie back to life—but it had been a nasty scare. Then there had been the night that performers and performance had been utterly distracted by "riotous ragtime jingles" from Madison Square Garden next door. They emanated, it turned out, from the African Section of William Brady's Congress of All Nations performing "Won't You Come Home, Bill Bailey?" How could actors take tea properly in Benson's drawing room with that infernal racket! An assistant had been despatched to ask if the African

Section could not be moved to another part of the Garden. No, was the reply: not even for Mrs. Patrick Campbell.

Now she turned mournful attention to the critics.

"What do they want? What do they want?" asked Stella plaintively.

"Who knows?" murmured the interviewer, a Mr. de Wagstaffe.

"Wait till they see Sudermann's Es lebe," she said, after a pause.

"Another 'problem'?"

"What drama in life is not?"

"Yet life has moments of blind cheeriness."

"Of course"—a caustic smile—"but I never studied for comic opera. Besides," she added quickly, "I can only play parts I feel to be the highest art, the best drama I can find."

"But why the problem play?"

"I could not make any impression as an ingénue, could I? Do you think I am suited to make people laugh—for their money? After all, some of us do think in this world, some of us do cry and suffer, and do heroic things in our souls. People do measure the height and breadth of their own lives—some people—and necessarily encounter problems.

"You know," pursued Stella, "I do not produce a play because it is by a great author, or because it is founded on a famous book. I have produced many of the first plays written by young authors, because I believed in their plays, and saw a way of making their problem of getting a production at least practicable to them." And she mentioned *Mrs. Jordan, Carlyon Sahib, Mr. and Mrs. Daventry, The Happy Hypocrite, Beyond Human Power,* and the ill-fated *Aunt Jeannie.*

During the next days de Wagstaffe saw Stella often. He noted that in conversation she was never still, but moved restlessly in her chair with the quivering energy of an angry tigress, her voice alternately mocking, vibrant, bitter, or sad. She would make a good general, he decided, although something of a martinet. She had no time for mediocrity, and stupidity put murder in her eye. She was not a happy woman in her nature, he thought: her happiest moments were on the stage. "She's a great deal of a man," complimented de Wagstaffe, "as any woman with brains must appear to be; it's only the women with emotions unattached to mentality who are exclusively feminine." Were she independently rich, she would have been a stateswoman, an organizer for public causes, a Madame de Staël. Instead, "she invites intellectual support in her plays, unconsciously developing the motive of her own being—the joy of temperament."

"I became an actress because I was bored," remarked Stella one day, pushing back strands of black hair.

"That is, after you were married," suggested de Wagstaffe.

Stella smiled faintly, then, balancing on the edge of her chair, leaned her elbows on the table. "It became necessary for my husband to go out to Australia for his health," she said, "and I was bundled off with the two children into the country to await his return. Waiting is a great talent; I never had it. One day I went to town, called on a dramatic agent, and had just paid my guinea to enroll my name for an engagement, when a traveling repertoire manager saw me, offered me a part at two guineas a week, and I took it." She dismissed the intervening years with a sweep of her hand and seized a bundle of costume sketches. "What do you think of these?" she demanded.

The subject was changed. "She likes to muster your forces for you," concluded the outmaneuvered interviewer, "she likes to take command of your purpose and lead it her own way, with executive speed, too."

It was that quality that collided with Charles Frohman during rehearsals of *The Joy of Living*. Stella believed in the play, and in her own interpretation of it as a tragedy built on the theme that the social sin reveals itself and cannot go unpunished. Fifteen years before the play begins, Countess Beata has been the lover of her husband's friend Richard. Although consideration for family ended the liaison, Beata has continued to love Richard with such intensity that she has developed heart disease. Meanwhile Richard has advanced politically through both Beata's and her husband Michael's influence, Michael even resigning his seat in the Reichstag for Richard. But old love letters of Beata's and Richard's fall into the hands of the political opposition and, threatened by public and family dishonor, Michael calls Beata and Richard to account. "Sin?" says Beata in one of those speeches that had become Stella's trademark. "I am not conscious of sinning. I did the best that it was in me to do. I simply refused to be crushed by your social laws. I asserted my right to live, my right to self-preservation; perhaps it was another way of suicide—that's no matter."

In a long discussion of honor after her exit, Richard is made to understand that although the scandal of a duel with Michael is out of the question, as a man of honor he should be eager to take his life to salvage the reputation of his party and his wronged friend. Richard asks for two days to consider, during which Beata sees how much he wants to live. There is no choice, then, but for her to take her own life. At an official dinner she rises to give a speech, ironically proposes a toast to "the joy of living," drains her glass, which contains a fatal dose of heart medicine, and leaves the room to die.

Edith Wharton had objected that "the joy of living" did not convey the irony of Beata's "long live life" toast, made when she knew her own glass was poisoned. Frohman had different objections. He and Stella were sharing the cost of the production, and it was a lavish one. "I am ashamed to say I remember candlesticks costing £12!" admitted Stella. They had also deadlocked over direction. "Mr. Frohman quarrelled with me over rehearsals," said Stella. "It was an intensely difficult play to rehearse. Beata was the emotional woman who does not weep: and I fancy he thought my reserve, and constraint, would be dull and ineffective." Frohman was a shrewd man with a sure sense of what would "go" on both sides of the Atlantic; Stella only cared that she was satisfied. Now Frohman insisted, according to her, on dropping the curtain at the end of the confrontation between Michael and Beata and Richard—cutting the debate about honor that followed. "I would not hear of it," said Stella; "so Frohman would have nothing more to do with the production, and I became solely responsible." Before the partnership was dissolved, there was a crisp exchange. Frohman had the temerity to call up a suggestion from the stalls. Indignant, Stella came down to the footlights. "Always remember, Mr. Frohman," she said haughtily, "that I am an artist." "Madam, I will keep your secret," retorted Frohman.

Had her friend Prince Hugo von Hohenlohe not been in New York to volunteer his knowledge of German court etiquette, or Heinrich Conried, manager of the Irving Place Theatre, not come over to the Garden to assist with rehearsals, Stella felt she never could have gotten through the production of the five-act play in two weeks while playing eight performances of *Aunt Jeannie* a week. But her troubles were not over. On October 16 John Blair announced his resignation. "She is impossible," the actor claimed. "I cannot play with her and keep my self-respect." From the beginning he and Mrs. Campbell had not gotten along. Rehearsals were amateurish: she could not direct and play her part too. Utterly intolerable, however, was the fact that she constantly said things about his acting under her breath. "I am so nervous I cannot possibly do good work," he complained. Asked about the difficulty, Stella expressed surprise: "I have had no trouble with him and I cannot understand why he should talk so." As a result of Blair's leaving, *The Joy of Living* had to be postponed until October 21 while Stella found a new leading man. She therefore quickly substituted *Tanqueray* after twenty-one performances of *Aunt Jeannie*, with Blair agreeing to stay to the end of its brief run. And then *The Joy of Living* had to be postponed two more days when Stella collapsed and had to be put to bed in the dark for forty-eight hours. Such was the price of temperament.

Edith Wharton claimed that, in spite of Mrs. Campbell's brilliant acting, *The Joy of Living* promptly failed. Stella called it a great success. One critic at least called it the most notable play of the year and her Beata remarkable. Others branded the play "nasty," "the climax of modern morbid licentiousness," "powerful but grewsome." Always negative about Stella, Alan Dale called it "a ghoulish display" and declared that nothing so distressing had ever been seen at the Garden Theatre before. The aging and puritanical William Winter, whose feeling for Stella amounted to detestation, branded most of the incidents in the play either "trivial, absurd, preposterous, or unclean. . . . Seldom or never has such a farrago of rotten nonsense been uttered from the stage as Mrs. Campbell enunciated in that scene of hysterical blather," charged Winter of the scene in which Beata declares that her lover has been her "discoverer" and "deliverer." "The drift of the preachment is a sentimental extenuation of conduct that everybody knows to be wrong." Winter ranked Sudermann with Ibsen, and Ibsenism "is rank, deadly pessimism . . . a disease injurious alike to the Stage and to the Public. . . ." Thinking of "the insufferable proceedings" of Mrs. Campbell, as well as of the "vapid personality and crude, affected, tedious, pretentious performances of her principal American associate, Mr. John Blair," Winter was moved to rhyme:

> And, further to relieve our care,
> Be pleased to capture Mr. Blair,—
> Conveying him across the main,—
> And never visit us again!
> For we are weary of the mess
> Of tainted females in distress,—
> The coarse, unlovely, long parades
> Of Arthur Wing Pinero's jades,—
> And there is nothing we could spare
> So well as you *and* Mr. Blair.

But *Life Magazine* had the last word: " 'The Joy of Living' is, as a play, soon to have the unpleasantness of dying"—and in fact it ran only nineteen performances, Stella losing heavily.

Before it died, the persistent de Wagstaffe encountered Stella two more times. On one occasion, after she had been rehearsing a difficult scene, he found her stretched out on a prop lounge in the wings, so oblivious to the commotion of carpenters, stagehands, and electricians around her that he tiptoed away. A last encounter took place one night backstage as she hurried to her dressing room. "She had unfastened a bunch of violets she had been wearing, and was crushing them to her face. Under the spell of the scene she had just played, everything was forgotten but the joy of temperament. She was radiant, beautiful, tender. 'You are better?' I asked. She had been ill the day before. 'Did you see me? did you see me?' she asked buoyantly. Then, anxious to share her delight with some one, she said: 'Violets; smell them. Aren't they exquisite?' and then she drew a deep breath again in their midst, and let them fall from her hand to the ground, as if her moment's joy were over."

From New York Stella travelled to the Colonial Theatre in Boston, where theatregoers had been so reluctant to let her go the previous spring. Although her own reception was enthusiastic, she substituted *Tanqueray* and *Aunt Jeannie* after a week of *The Joy of Living*, which Boston thought just as morbid as had New York. She spent Christmas in Philadelphia, giving a Christmas Day matinee of *Aunt Jeannie* and being royally entertained. At a supper one night at the Bellevue she was reported as having been shocked at the conversation of a certain gentleman who asked her, "What does a cow have four of and a woman only two?" *"Really!"* boomed Stella: "I am not accustomed—" "Feet," cried the gentleman hastily, "the answer's f-e-e-t!" An American had disconcerted her on another occasion, an inoffensive little man assigned to lead her in to dinner. Stella had suddenly turned lustrous eyes upon him. *"Tell* me: which would you sooner—love passionately or be loved passionately?" The little man took a deep breath. "I'd rather be a canary," he ventured.

It was usually Stella who disconcerted her dinner partners. One evening a solicitous gentleman leaned toward her. "Some man has made you unhappy," he murmured; "it is an insult to your sex to allow it, and it shows a lack of sense of humor." Stella considered the intrusion; then: "Do you know why God withheld the sense of humor from women?" she asked winningly. The gentleman replied that he could not guess. "That we may love you instead of laughing at you," she replied sweetly. Another evening she was listening to an elderly scientist drone on endlessly about ants— "They are wonderful little creatures; they have their own police force and their own army . . ."—until she could endure it no longer. Leaning forward with an expression of the most absorbed interest, she breathed in her claret-velvet voice, "No *navy*, I suppose?"

In January 1903 she announced her intention of making a two months' tour of the West. Before embarking, she played in Montreal, Toledo, and, in early February, in Chicago, where there were reunions with society friends and, unexpectedly, with her von Jasmund cousins, children of John Tanner's sister Emily and the Baron who had partnered Tanner's ordnance works for a time in Bombay. Hildegarde, married and living in Minnesota, came to Chicago alone to see Cousin Beatrice, and wrote ecstatically to Uncle Harry about the "sweet unaffectedness" and "the air of exquisite refinement" she displayed as Magda. Beatrice reminded her so strongly of her mother that she wept through the entire performance and stayed to see her in all her other plays. They talked of the family, and Stella spoke so warmly of Uncle Harry that Hildegarde longed to see all the English relations that she had never really known.

Then Stella plunged westward, experiencing the real vastness of America for the first time. Uncle Harry wrote to sympathize: how abominable for one who hated travel like Beatrice "to scour the country, and to bounce in and out of new places day after day in this fashion, like a pea in a frying pan." Until they reached the coast in April, there were five performances in five different cities a week; then in San Francisco the company finally settled down for two weeks of repertoire at the Columbia Theatre with *Tanqueray*, *Magda*, *Aunt Jeannie*, and *The Joy of Living*. They were a long way from home, and a long way from the cast that had played in New York. Two actors from her first tour remained—Adeline Bourne and Charles Bryant; Fred Kerr had taken over temporarily when John Blair left, but Emmett C. King had since replaced him as lead. And it was in San Francisco that Stella first encountered "Lord" Lowndes.

Lloyd Lowndes was not a lord at all, but had earned the title by virtue of tall, slender good looks, charming manners, a rimless monocle, and a knack of always inheriting little legacies just in time to save him from working. He had dabbled a bit in the theatre, appearing as "walking gentleman" with both Irving and Ada Rehan, and it was as "walking gentleman" that he now applied to Stella's manager, who took him on. He immediately decided that the only living genius on the stage was Mrs. Patrick Campbell; just as immediately—like most men in her company—he fell violently in love with her. She was gracious, but did not encourage him either as a lover or as an actor. Quite the contrary. One night a crusading clergyman pressed his way backstage in a gallant attempt, after the depraved play he had just witnessed, to save the temptress's soul. Stella reassured him. "Oh, don't bother about me. I really haven't time to be a bad woman. But here is Mr. Lowndes, who is not only a bad man, but a bad actor." The remark hastened Lord Lowndes's retirement from the stage, but did not discourage his passion for Stella Campbell.

San Francisco gave *The Joy of Living* "an extraordinary reception," *Tanqueray* and *Magda* were both great successes, *Aunt Jeannie* was as usual, and in May Stella was back in New York preparing to sail.

Though she would never live down her reputation as a "personality," she had not been at the center of a circus ring this time. She had rather quietly proved that she could win acclaim from audiences and critics, even if she could not choose popular plays. "*Life* believes Mrs. Patrick Campbell is the best actress to-day appearing on the English-speaking stage," wrote that magazine's critic. Certainly her method differed from the old school's—

there were no screams, few tears, no shredding a passion to tatters. Instead, there was an appeal to intelligence and experience, and such poise and naturalness as she moved about the stage that one did not think of acting at all, but only of a flesh-and-blood creature in her natural surroundings. Audiences looking for histrionics would, of course, be disappointed. But *Life* thought Mrs. Campbell's method a distinct improvement on the old school of rant.

On May 27 she made a last headline: "SHIP HELD AS ACTRESS CHATS." Pausing at dockside for a word with a friend, Stella, it seemed, had casually planted herself on a coil of rope, quite oblivious to the fact that the crew wished to cast off and that she was delaying the *Majestic*'s departure for Liverpool.

Pinkie was again a problem. Stella had written personally to Prime Minister Arthur Balfour, begging that the griffon be spared quarantine; Balfour had regretted in reply that the unscrupulous actions indulged in by *some* dog-owners made strict regulation necessary, regardless of petitioner. There was clearly no choice, then, but to resort to unscrupulousness herself: she contemplated a rather larger bosom, or perhaps a hip disease.

Stella returned to London looking, thought Uncle Harry, extremely well. This time she had enough money to take a theatre, and with characteristic energy she immediately set about mounting a production. Although *The Joy of Living* had won a mixed reception in America and failed summarily when played in German in a recent West End production, she stubbornly determined to test her version on London. The elegant, intimate New Theatre would be available later in June, and Stella hastily rounded up a cast headed by Martin Harvey and including Amy Lamborn and Charles Bryant from the American production. In the midst of rehearsals she had the dubious pleasure of going to the Coronet Theatre to watch the French actress Madame Jane Hading act Paula Tanqueray. Although in previous performances Hading had merely portrayed a typically sorrowful woman racked by inward remorse, "Thanks, perhaps, to the coaching of Mr. Pinero, who, together with Mrs. Campbell, sat watching the new Paula," observed the *Illustrated London News*, "Jane Hading makes an elaborate effort at detailing the woman, and so indulges in more whims and violences than usually mark her undemonstrative methods." Madame Hading was not the last actress Stella would have to applaud in a role she had made famous.

In the end there was less than a week to rehearse her own complex five-act drama. It was not enough. There were, observed J. T. Grein on the evening of June 24, only five members of the cast who were really in the picture, and of those five only three had important parts. The rest frankly needed prompting and seemed either uneasy or miscast, particularly Martin Harvey, who played the outwardly virile, inwardly weak Richard as both outwardly and inwardly weak. The shakiness of the cast put even greater pressure on Stella to pull the drama through, a difficult task since she had little to do in the first two acts. Her voice seemed to slip out of control at times as she played with unaccustomed vehemence to compensate for the hesitancy of the others. Often restless with the incomprehensibility of German politics and codes of honor, the audience still gave Stella an enthusiastic welcome back with call after call, and the applause for the popular Martin Harvey was affectionate.

After a curtain speech praising America and American audiences, Stella the spendthrift gave a supper onstage to sixty guests, including Vice Admiral Lord Charles Beresford, the Duchess of Manchester, Anthony Hope, and her good friend Lady Elcho. Sarah Bernhardt, who had played a matinee of *La Dame aux Camélias* that afternoon at the Adelphi, was also there, and still enthusiastic about playing Pelléas to Stella's Mélisande. Only the outstanding success of Debussy's operatic version of the play in 1902 had prevented her from doing a Paris production with Stella. They were still immense friends. "*Je suis très très heureuse d'avoir vu l'intérieure de cet être exquis, dont l'âme aussi jolie que le visage, et qui porte le nom de Beatrice Stella Campbell*," Sarah had written in Stella's birthday book the previous year; and this season, short of cash after the failure of her Napoleon play *Plus que reine*, she sent her secretary, M. Pitou, to ask Stella's help. Wonderful to tell, Stella actually had £100 in the bank, which she promptly lent her darling Sarah.

But *The Joy of Living* found no more success than Sarah's play. London audiences liked it no better than those across the Atlantic; critics almost unanimously condemned it, not least for Sudermann's indefensibly giving Countess Beata a fatal heart disease which robbed her suicide of all its tragedy. Stella's acting was generally praised, the *Westminster Gazette* testifying also to her great popularity: "Playgoers would be grieved if a season were to pass without the appearance of the brilliant actress called by the somewhat endearing term of 'Mrs. Pat Campbell' or even 'Mrs. Pat,' who at present occupies a unique position on our stage." But the only joy of living, J. T. Grein observed, was to be found outside the theatre after the gloomy performance was over. Again Stella's experiment had failed; again she quickly substituted *Tanqueray* after only twenty performances of Sudermann. This time Aubrey Tanqueray was played by C. Aubrey Smith, a rising actor, and brother of Beryl Faber, who had played with Stella at the Royalty; his first appearance in London had been as the Reverend Amos Winterfield in the original *Ebbsmith* at the Garrick. George Arliss, temporarily back in London, played his brilliant Cayley Drummle again, and again *Tanqueray* drew until she closed her brief run on July 30. The next day Stella gave a flying matinee at Eastbourne, sixty miles from London, and then went on to St. Leonards to see her mother.

Because of the expense of the Augustinian *pension*, Mrs. Tanner had been moved to rooms in a house close by. Stella found her mother lonely, surrounded by photographs of the family she had lost. She stayed with her a week, and in the end, persuaded that the unhappy woman could not bear the solitude, she arranged for her to go back to Gensing Lodge for at least six months. By that time, reasoned Stella, perhaps her mother would have made friends and would want rooms of her own in the town.

That autumn again there was no theatre for Stella in London. She had proved incapable of making money for her backers as her own manager, even while she scored as an actress. The actor-managers, their days numbered, were still firmly entrenched: Alexander at the St. James's, Tree at His (since the coronation of Edward VII) Majesty's, Charles Wyndham at the Criterion. Lewis Waller was secure in the popular *Monsieur Beaucaire* at the Comedy. Forbes-Robertson with Gertrude Elliott had had a run of nearly twelve months with *Mice and Men* in 1902 and was currently enjoying an even greater success with *The Light That Failed*. And at the Duke of York's, Henry Irving's son H.B. was giving one of his best performances in the title role of Barrie's *The Admirable Crichton*. Also in that play was the young actor Stella had left behind. After she had sailed on her first tour, Gerald du Maurier had been very down, adrift himself. He'd spent a lot of time in the Green Room Club, drinking too much, playing cards too much, not getting much sleep, and acting a part in the successful *Country Mouse* that called for little more than the grace that was his second nature. There'd been no more Stella to remind him that there was more to acting than lighting cigarettes and lounging, and that if he'd just pull his hands out of his pockets and get down to it, he could do great things. But then he'd met Muriel Beaumont and after a six weeks' engagement married her in April 1903, when Stella was playing in San Francisco. And now they were happily moving into their own home, and people were saying they hadn't seen Gerald looking so well in years, and he was quickly becoming one of London's most popular actors.

Stella continued to act where she could outside of London and to look for new plays. "May I see the altered version of Hippolytus?" she wrote Gilbert Murray. "I am still keen to do new & beautiful things, but it has taken me two years in America to pay my debts & I am very tired. If only we could all join & work faithfully together! In the end the public might come. . . ." Yeats's plays—*The Land of Heart's Desire, The Shadowy Waters,*

*Cathleen ni Houlihan*, *The Pot of Broth*, *The Hour Glass*—also interested Stella for their combination of simplicity and mystery. For the time being, however, she chose to do that autumn W. L. Courtney's *Undine*, an adaptation of the classic German *märchen* by Fouqué, which tells the story of a beautiful water sprite who tries to win a human soul through the love of a mortal, and fails. To accompany Undine's songs, she commissioned Arnold Dolmetsch to make her a psaltery, and for costumes she went to her old friend Graham Robertson.

A dispute arose almost immediately when Robertson showed her his sketches for the underwater scene which would feature two mermaids, immobile because of their tails.

"Their tails?" said Stella dreamily, then turned on Robertson. "And what about *my* tail?"

"You are not going to have a tail."

*"No tail?"*

"No. Certainly not."

But Stella was roused. Two lovely tails for mere supers, and no tail for the star? "I'll have a tail," she said, meaning it.

"You will *not* have a tail! *Never* will I design a tail for you!"

"Then I shall design a tail for myself. Anyone can design tails."

It was almost a quarrel: they glared at each other across the heaps of drawings. Robertson rose, pale and determined.

"Then I will have nothing more to do with that scene," he announced.

"I'll have a tail!" cried Stella.

But when the curtain rose on *Undine* at the Shakespeare Theatre, Liverpool, the last week of September, Stella was tailless. She played *Undine* for a week with *Tanqueray*; but she was, as she had told Murray, very tired, and began to think of treating herself to Christmas in Dresden with Stella. At first it had looked as if Beo would be home by Christmas, forfeiting the cricket matches and parties he had enjoyed while stationed at Wei-Hai-Wei for a return via Vladivostok, Hakodate, Singapore, and Hong Kong. But Beo did not come, and Stella chose the less-loved daughter. "Darling," bubbled young Stella, in raptures over a letter announcing her mother's visit, "I daren't believe it *too* much in case something happens to prevent your coming. Oh! it would be lovely. . . . at first you must be regularly lazy and thoroughly rest yourself and lie down a lot, and go for long drives to the woods—they look so lovely just now, all shades of brown and green. And then, when you are quite rested, I must take you to the beautiful statues and pictures and old jewelry and to see Weicke act. Oh, darling, it will be glorious. . . ."

Stella came to Dresden, a center in that first decade of the twentieth century for study and gracious living, and put up at the small, elegant Savoy. Between visits with young Stella and to the statues and pictures, she became in her impulsive way very interested in an American woman, Mrs. Hobson, who was also staying at the Savoy with her children, one of them a friend of young Stella's. Twelve-year-old Henry Hobson was struck with the charm of the "great lady" who often had her meals at their table, although the tiny dog gobbling off her mistress's plate was even more interesting. Eventually, however, Henry had cause to regret the glamorous new eruption into his life. They had all been invited to a party for the young people, and Henry was eyeing the delicious-looking supper being laid out on tables at the end of the room when Stella descended upon him, crying, "Henry, are you not going to dance with me?" That was awkward enough, but after a few whirls Stella said, "Henry, Pinkie is not feeling well; I need an escort to take me back to the hotel; I want to take her back to our room." The tall, shy, polite Henry looked longingly across the room at the imminent supper, but "Never mind," said Stella winningly, "we'll be back in a short time." Off they went in a horse cab to the Savoy, where Stella told Henry she would be down in a moment. She was not. Tormented with visions of the supper he'd waited for all evening, Henry counted the minutes, seething with resentment. At last Stella descended, all apologies; darling Pinkie had not wanted to settle down. By the time they rejoined the party, Henry's fears were realized. Supper had been served and eaten; the tables were empty. Mature years later Henry forgave her. "I enjoyed Mrs. C. and Pinkie Panky Poo," he remembered. "She was a great lady."

Assured that her daughter was becoming a finished young lady, Stella returned to London to face the new year. She had agreed to do a play called *The Queen's Romance* with Lewis Waller in February. Perhaps, as she'd remarked to Murray, the public would come. But she still needed a special play, another *Tanqueray* or *Ebbsmith* that she could stamp as her own. Such a play did not seem to be forthcoming.

# TWENTY-THREE

## *1904–1905*

$\mathcal{S}$INCE *For the Crown* days Stella had liked John Davidson, and now admired his blank-verse adaptation of Victor Hugo's *Ruy Blas*. As Dona Maria de Neubourg, Queen of Spain, she had such heady exchanges as

> QUEEN: Oh, thanks, and thanks again! I saw and heard
> The lightning of your eye, your voice of power.
> Like a destroying angel on their heads
> You poured the certain terror of the truth!
> Whence came this strength, so regal, so divine?
>
> RUY BLAS: Out of my love for you. The overthrow
> Of Spain which those unhallowed Councillors
> Blindly prepare, involves your piteous ruin;
> And I would save the world to save your heart
> One throb of pain, one moment of dismay.
>
> QUEEN: Is this not madness?

And so forth. As Queen of Spain, Stella also had an inflated costume. Graham Robertson (forgiven the tail) was called in, to find the current designer in despair. "It's so difficult to get the women to wear the stiff Velásquez dresses," he complained. "They manage to give them a modern look directly they try them on. You'll *never* get Mrs. Campbell into those hoops."

Robertson did have misgivings, but went round to where Stella was trying on at Mrs. Nettleship's. Stella studied herself at length in the mirror, then told Robertson exactly what she thought of the costume, as well as exactly what she thought of him. Then she threw herself upon the floor and lifted her voice in woe.

"But—but I look such an absolute *fool! Don't* I?"

"You do," agreed Robertson, who knew it always paid to be candid with

Stella Campbell, "but I don't suppose you mean to play the Queen of Spain on all fours. Won't you get up and look again?"

There was a dangerously tense moment before Stella picked herself up off the floor and examined herself in the mirror again. To her surprise, she found that she looked very lovely.

"In the end," said Robertson, "she swept on to the stage like a magnificent frigate with all sail set; and the other ladies, who had at the last moment reduced hoops and abated stiffenings, reaped their reward in looking limp and characterless."

Lewis Waller, her opposite, was currently the most popular actor in London. Handsome, virile, with a thrilling voice, Waller commanded a fanatic following of females who banded themselves together into the K.O.W. (Keen on Waller) Brigade and packed the pit, welcoming their idol with delirious screams and storms of applause. Waller himself would rather have played Shakespeare, but was condemned to dashing roles. His method was the antithesis of Stella's intimate, natural style; and although they both liked Davidson's play, they approached their parts from different points of view.

The resulting disharmony was not lost on first-night critics at the Imperial on February 11, 1904; the histrionic methods of the two lovers were called "absolutely distinct." Stella had her own explanation: Waller, she said, "addressed his blank verse to the universe," whereas she addressed her blank verse to him. But chiefly it was Davidson's version of Hugo that critics attacked. In the original, Ruy Blas (disguised as Don Cesar) achieves gradual promotion at court, gradually becomes the Queen's favorite, patiently masters the techniques of statecraft. But Davidson plucked six months out of the drama, making the improbable wildly impossible and the impossible utterly ineffective, said Archer. Even Max Beerbohm could not be kind. "I do not say that [Davidson] could have done his work better. I do say that he ought not to have done it at all": blank verse was no medium for "the jolly headlong unreality and monstrosity of Hugoesque romance." "The critics found it tedious," said Stella. "They called it a piece of literature, rather than a stage play. This was tragic for John Davidson, who had put some of his best work into the play. The public, unfortunately, do not think it is their duty—though the play be the work of a distinguished author, produced by a recognised management, and played by artists of quality—to come and see it, and judge for themselves."

Apart from the failure of her play, Stella experienced a deeper sadness these weeks. Henry Tanner, only sixty-one but suffering from chronic Bright's disease, was very ill—dying. For Stella it meant the loss of a man who had been a father without a father's repressive authority. Unselfish, uncompetitive—never more than a private secretary in the City—her uncle had been content to applaud her rise to fame, and Stella loved a sympathetic audience. Night after night Lewis Waller drove her to Chelsea after the theatre so that she could be more quickly at his side. Her engagement at the Imperial ended on March 3 after twenty-four performances, and still Henry Tanner lingered, suffering. When he finally died on March 29, it was not Stella, however, who was with him, but Edwin, who had also comforted John Tanner in his final illness. Stella was devastated.

"Thank you for your dear sympathy," she wrote Gilbert Murray. "For the first time in my life I have seen great great sickness—and Death—and I have lost the dearest friend I have in the world—& it seems to me there are thousands & thousands of years added to the age of my soul—& my understanding. . . ." "Looking back now," she would write years later of the adored uncle of her childhood, "I feel my youth was spent at court in the presence of a king."

Then a disturbing letter came from Beo. She had thought him set firmly on the right track. Previous letters had charted his career: following his current tour there was to be six weeks' leave, the Channel Squadron for two months, then Greenwich, and finally a distinguished career in the Royal Navy. Now, however, he wrote her urgently from Port Said: "Darling mother, you must withdraw me from the service: bodily, nobody could be better suited to it than myself, but in mind I am miles from it. . . . Don't think this letter is written on the impulse of the moment; I have been wanting to write it for a year and a half, but I have waited to see if I changed, but I did not. Mind you see about it. With all the world, sun, moon and stars full of love and kisses . . . P.S. The Diplomatic Service is the one I should like most of any *service.* . . . So do, do, do take me out now, at once."

Stella's chagrin was considerable. Beo's ship arrived, and Beo returned to 33 Kensington Square, which now contained, besides Pinkie, "the children": a black monkey named Venus, a Siamese cat, and a parrot. Stella sent him to his old schoolmaster R. M. Pearce for a talk, and Beo confessed that he wanted to go to Oxford or perhaps write plays. "The boy has character and determination and has made up his mind," Pearce told Stella; "better withdraw him." Stella did withdraw Beo, feeling she had failed.

Then more unrest in Dresden. Although young Stella loved doing German with Fräulein Nachtigal and going to *Tristan and Isolde* with Lady Elcho and seeing Weicke perform, Stella opened her latest letter to find, "I am not despondent, but the only thing I really would care to do, is—act. But, of course, if you think I have no talent, I shouldn't want to—but *do* give me a chance." This was harder to accept than Beo's dream of Oxford,

Stella as a young actress

Stella as Mrs. Tanqueray, painted by Solomon J. Solomon

Portrait by Prince Troubetskoy

Stella as Eliza Doolittle in the 1914 production of *Pygmalion*

with which she could hardly quarrel. The last thing she wanted for her daughter was an acting career. She sent back a flat no, telling Stella she could come home to a London "season," but not to the stage. Almost eighteen now, young Stella did come home, and plunged into a round of dances, luncheons, and supper parties. It was arranged that Edith Lyttelton present her the following summer at Court.

Fourteen years had passed since Lady Horner and Edith Balfour disguised themselves as actresses to mock Ben Greet's troupe at Wilton; both had since become close friends of Stella's. Edith, now the Hon. Mrs. Alfred Lyttelton, was one of the most interesting members of the progressive set headed by Lord and Lady Lytton; her home at 18 Great College Street in the shadow of the Abbey and Houses of Parliament had become a salon for the intellectually and politically liberal. "D.D. Lyttelton is among the friends I love who neither spoil nor flatter me," said Stella. "She never hesitates to tell me my faults." "I wish, Stella darling," D.D. would say, "people did not call you 'difficult'; but they do, and you are; do be careful" —or, "Stella, you are so absolutely ignorant of the world." Stella found her extraordinarily generous, capable of taking endless pains to help someone in trouble, impatient with affectation. She loved the theatre with more tolerance than Stella, and would go alone in a cab on a wet night to sit in the pit and applaud indifferent actors in mediocre plays.

Now she had written a play of her own, and Stella was to produce it and play the part of Theodosia Hemming, a downtrodden fitter at Madame Stephanie's dressmaking establishment. Stella thought *Warp and Woof* "an excellent little play"; D.D. was a dear friend; Stella was currently out of plays and inspiration. Besides, she had discovered that producing an intelligent play by a friend was far more exciting than producing Shakespeare. If a Shakespeare play failed, it was the actor's fault; if it succeeded, the credit was Shakespeare's. Every word, every scene was known beforehand; there was no thrill of surprise; every movement was steeped in sacred tradition. And then the playwright himself was not there to blame, praise, or please— while it was such fun and happiness helping a friend to success. Finally, Stella liked experiment, and the topic of sweated labor offered relief from refined adultery.

Like most things Stella touched, the first night of *Warp and Woof* on June 6 took place in a blaze of publicity. She had taken the large, handsome Camden Theatre in unfashionable Camden Town for an opening that was really a social event. Word had got out that *Warp and Woof* was the effort of the wife of a distinguished politician, and that the fashionable world would be there. By eight o'clock three or four thousand people were milling about the theatre entrance trying to get a look at the arriving "nobs."

Finally, mounted police had to be called out to keep back the crush of the curious from the door. "What a first night it was!" laughed Stella, who could act her best on the news that a lord or lady was out front. The fact that tonight society was gathering to hear itself condemned by one of its own members made the occasion all the more piquant.

Not surprisingly, the *Westminster Gazette* had to report the next day that society had been "hardly enthusiastic." Many critics concluded, however, that while *Warp and Woof* was technically amateurish, the author's intention was admirable; and Archer wished there were more plays like it.

J. T. Grein, that pioneer of Ibsen and the New Drama, was, predictably, the only real enthusiast. "The miracle of miracles!" he exclaimed. "Here we have upon the London stage a play that sets both heart and mind in motion; a play that is pretty nearly a faithful reproduction of life; a play open to deep reflection, to heated controversy; a play, lastly, to command the world's respect." Finding Stella "at her best," Grein deplored the fact that *Warp and Woof* had seen the light away from London's center, concluding his glowing review, "May the new dramatist have come to stay." The *Westminster Gazette* was among the dissenters. Given the amateurish quality of the play and the limited opportunities for Mrs. Campbell, "it becomes clear the experiment was injudicious."

Judiciousness was not Stella's long suit. Had it been, she might not have responded to a telegram of April 29, "VOULEZ-VOUS M'ENVOYER PELLEAS ET MELISANDE," by agreeing to appear with Madame Sarah on July 1 at the Vaudeville, where *Warp and Woof*, transferred from Camden Town, had just ingloriously died. In London for her usual summer season, Sarah announced herself ready at last. Still, she had misgivings, asking her companion, Suze Rueff, one day whether she had seen La Patrick act Mélisande. Suze hadn't, and expressed surprise that Sarah would risk an English actress. But Sarah thought that the English accent, if not too pronounced, might serve to emphasize the dreamlike quality of Mélisande—"and then, she is so beautiful!"

Shocked by her own daring to act in French, Stella nevertheless arrived nonchalantly at the first rehearsal with the tiny black monkey Venus perched on her shoulder—and had she not been "so beautiful," Sarah might have cancelled the production right there, for once Madame began to work, she worked in dead earnest. La Patrick seemed to treat the whole thing as a joke, as did Venus, leaping on to her head and distracting everyone with its antics. When it became clear that Sarah was not amused, Venus disappeared; but then there was trouble with the French. Stella had been priming with Mademoiselle Drouin, Lady Eden's governess on loan to Kensington

Square for two weeks, and had scribbled a lot of notes in her prompt book to remind herself that *dans* was pronounced *don* and *cependant, ce/pen/dant*. Actually, she spoke quite good French, but without much attention to the liaison and the mute *e*. Although Maeterlinck's play was in prose, the lines flowed, and if Stella did not say *davantage* as *davantage-uh*, then Sarah was tripped out of step and unable to find the right intonation.

"It was all very worrying, and rather surprising," said Suze Rueff, "for Mrs. Pat had an excellent ear; she was very musical (a first-rate pianist), but somehow she wasn't trying, and there were some stormy episodes." One morning when Suze looked in at rehearsal, Sarah suddenly summoned her onstage, thrust a copy of the play into her hands, and told her to take La Patrick and march her through her lines. There might have been an explosion, but Stella was all graciousness and for several days took Suze home to lunch with her, where they went patiently over Sarah's corrections. Only once did she protest, inquiring ironically whether, if they took the play on tour, Sarah would let her come along without her teacher.

Graham Robertson, friend to both Stella and Sarah, had been called in to help with production, but wisely limited himself to agreeing with both women on all points. Stella was to wear "the gold umbrella case" designed by Burne-Jones, but Sarah needed something to transform her into Pelléas; and Robertson produced a light surcoat of chain-mail that lent a semblance of manliness to her slight figure. Robertson noticed no strain in the relationship; he had never seen Sarah more unruffled. At one rehearsal, for example, she had leaned out of a window into what was supposed to be velvet-black night but, by a technician's error, turned out to be brilliant noonday. Robertson waited for the blow-up, but Sarah merely glanced back over her shoulder and murmured, "Rather a *fine* night, isn't it?" "I think she regarded the performance as a little holiday," said Robertson; "she liked Mrs. Campbell, who interested and amused her, and a peace that really passed all understanding remained unbroken." Sarah herself was in the midst of a strenuous season, playing *La Sorcière* often twice a day, rehearsing *Pelléas* mornings, and giving flying matinees at outlying theatres on spare afternoons. Robertson observed to her son, Maurice, that she was working very hard: were the matinees really necessary? "Well," said Maurice, "what *is* mother to do in the afternoons?"

Even more than for Stella, the theatre was Sarah's whole life. She took her work with passionate seriousness, never clowning onstage, never walking through a performance if she did not feel like acting that day. "The immense care for detail in this greatest of all artists always seemed to puzzle Mrs. Campbell a little," said Robertson. "One evening I was sitting with

Madame Sarah in her dressing-room at the theatre, watching her make up. . . . This evening Sarah was gradually resolving into Cleopatra, and, as final details were being added, Mrs. Campbell entered.

"Sarah was absorbed for the moment and could spare little attention: she was painting her hands, staining the finger-tips and palms with the dusky red of henna. Mrs. Campbell watched with some impatience; she had business to discuss and was in a hurry.

" 'Why do you take so much trouble?' she said at last. 'What you are doing will never show from the front. Nobody will see it.'

" 'I shall see it,' replied Sarah slowly. 'I am doing it for myself. If I catch sight of my hand it will be the hand of Cleopatra. That will help me.' "

Robertson felt that Stella, on the other hand, took her art and her own great gifts too lightly. "She would lose interest in a part and play with it instead of playing it, she played with her public (a most dangerous amusement), she exasperated managers, who found that they dared not rely upon her. The very qualities which had brought her triumphantly to the front, the super-sensitiveness, the fastidiousness, the habit of seeing both sides of most things and the ridiculous side of everything (and everybody), actually hampered her later on in her career." But now all was peace and goodwill. Stella took over most rehearsals, and Sarah altered nothing her *"délicieuse amie"* proposed, only asking permission to turn her back to the wall in the window scene so that Stella's hair might fall over her face.

Surprisingly, Stella's and Sarah's audacious partnership worked. The theatre was crowded; critics generally praised. The youth, innocence, and poetry of Sarah's Pelléas seemed miraculous; Stella's Mélisande was even more childlike, poetic, and beautiful than before. Max Beerbohm, however, chose to stay away. He had suffered torments five years earlier over Sarah's Hamlet, concluding that "the only compliment one can conscientiously pay her is that her Hamlet was, from first to last, *très grande dame."* The thought of Sarah, now sixty, playing the boy lover Pelléas depressed him even more. He was, as he eventually wrote in the *Saturday Review,* perfectly ready to give the play the benefit of the doubt. "I love the play too well, and am loth that my memory of it as performed by Mrs. Campbell in her own language, with Mr. Martin Harvey as Pelléas, should be complicated with any memory less pleasing. I am quite willing to assume that Mrs. Campbell speaks French as exquisitely as she speaks English, and that Sarah's Pelléas is not, like her Hamlet and her Duc de Reichstadt, merely ladylike. But the two facts remain that Sarah is a woman and that Mrs. Campbell is an Englishwoman. And by these two facts such a performance is ruled out of the sphere of art into the sphere of sensationalism. If Maeterlinck were a sensationalist, that would not matter."

During the run of *Pelléas*, Sarah threaded her way through the crowds of people in Stella's dressing room and handed her a little silver casket containing twenty £5 notes. "She said how grateful she was to me—the simple graciousness of her act! Did she ever know, I wonder, how my heart almost choked me?" Laughter choked Stella on another occasion. There had been trouble at rehearsals over the first scene in Act II, the scene in which Mélisande and Pelléas enter together, and Mélisande sits down on the edge of the fountain in the park, her hair trailing in the water, and starts tossing and catching the ring Golaud has given her until it falls into the water and is lost. Sarah could not be satisfied: Stella wasn't giving her words the right intonation, the two of them were out of tune. Finally discouraged, Stella complained that the small fountain was nothing like the beautiful one in the English production—how could she be inspired by "that silly fishpond"? Sarah held her tongue, but did not forget. Seizing Suze Rueff before a matinee one day, she pressed a half-sovereign into her hand and instructed her to bring back as much fish as the money would buy—"just ordinary, common fish, *avec des têtes à faire peur!*" Suze returned with the most hideous fish she could find, and Sarah directed that it be installed in the fountain. In the second act Stella innocently entered, sank down on the edge of the stone basin, and bent to gaze dreamily into the imaginary water. Suddenly her shoulders began to heave with laughter; it was several seconds before she could recover enough to speak her first line, *"Je voudrais toucher l'eau."* Sarah had her revenge for the "silly fishpond" at last.

Before parting, they agreed to a tour with Maeterlinck the following summer. And now there was nothing for Stella but a return to America. On this third trip she would be accompanied by her daughter. During a long social summer young Stella had not given up her desire to act. Although she had fallen in love with Ego Charteris, he had not proposed, nor had any other eligible young man. In any case, she might have refused them if they had. She was unimpressed with the life her mother wanted for her; quietly but stubbornly she begged to act. But Stella would not hear of it. Her daughter could go along and see for herself the gruelling life her mother led; she would meet the rich Americans who vied to entertain Stella wherever she went; but there would be no acting. And, in fact, a headline announced upon their arrival in New York that September, "MRS. CAMPBELL DETERMINED HER DAUGHTER SHALL NOT FOLLOW IN HER FOOTSTEPS."

Stella was back with Charles Frohman, and had one play, *La Sorcière*, written by Sardou for Bernhardt and played by Sarah the past summer. She, young Stella, and Pinkie put up in a suite on the fourth floor of the Hotel Seville, and Stella began to rehearse at the New Amsterdam Theatre on

42nd Street west of Broadway. Interviewers crowded round, as usual. As usual, what did she think of America? "I do not approve of the big, ornate theatres," Stella answered promptly, "the as-good-as-you servants, the expensive dressmakers, and most theatrical press agents." She also had failed to find any romance in America, and "Without romance life would not be worth living."

"Is there common sense in its place?" asked a reporter.

"Why not say commonplace sense?" quipped Stella.

One interviewer reported her wearing "a creamy-white waist of bronchitis-defying cut, and a dark, swishy skirt which snaked after her like something trained." A reporter from the *Herald*, on the other hand, was struck by the starkness of her appearance: lustreless hair, white face without a trace of make-up, no jewels—she might have been a nun. Smoking perfumed cigarettes, cuddling Pinkie—old now and almost blind—she discussed *The Sorceress* in her beautiful, low, measured voice with its perfect enunciation. She hoped audiences would like her Zoraya in Louis N. Parker's translation. Certainly Zoraya was different from anything she had played before.

*The Sorceress* opened on October 10. Although Max had deplored Sarah's performance as "art without life—a dead thing galvanised," Stella made a success with the melodramatic tale of warring Moors and Christians in medieval Spain, and of the forbidden love of a Moorish woman for the Spaniard Don Enriquez. She played thirty-six performances at the New Amsterdam, transferred to the Harlem Opera House, and then went on to the familiar Montauk Theatre in Brooklyn before leaving New York. "Everywhere the showy, splendid production, and the brilliantly theatrical *rôle* of 'Zoraya' delighted the audience," said Stella. "The statement that had often been made—that most of the women I played were alike—subsided." Critical reaction was mixed, however. William Winter in the *Tribune* almost outdid himself, calling Sardou's drama "a prolix medley of pretentious nonsense." But it was the actress he was after. "Mrs. Campbell, who is nothing if not abnormal, offered a variant of the old, familiar type of female crank, so frequent in Sardou's melodramatic concoctions, and so useful to performers who mistake singularity for genius and delirium for inspiration, and she offered it in her customary style, of affected embellishment and vapid eccentricity. . . . Mrs. Campbell's acting imparted nothing beyond revelation of a morbid personality. The actress, nevertheless, had her audience—for in America there is an audience for everything." The *Evening Post*, on the other hand, lauded her "personal charm and emotional eloquence"; the *Stage* called her Zoraya "wonderfully fascinating"; the *Times* reported that "In the more refined and gracious aspects of the part Mrs. Campbell was most satisfying. . . . High-bred and intelligent she seemed in the extreme degree."

Stella went on alone to Philadelphia; young Stella, she told reporters, had been overcome by the fatigues of travel and had gone to stay with friends in Canada. In Philadelphia, where she opened at the Broad Street Theatre the day after Christmas, she received one of the more intelligent criticisms of her version of Sardou. The play was old-fashioned, noted the reviewer; the company played it with the natural method of the most modern school of acting; discords were inevitable. Yet such a complaint was really a compliment to Mrs. Campbell's interpretation: Sardou must seem false and theatrical to an actress whose power lay in subtle detail and understatement. She played Zoraya as such a woman would be in real life—but alas! concluded the reviewer, Sardou's melodrama was as far removed from reality as is the equator from the North Pole.

Then on January 3, 1905, there occurred an event that press agents had not contrived. At twenty minutes to eight, as the audience was already filing into the Broad Street Theatre, Stella prepared to leave the St. James Hotel at 13th and Walnut Streets with Martha Waldron, a member of her company. She had Pinkie under one arm, her muff and some books under the other. A brougham was waiting. Stella put her foot on the step, mounted, and slipped suddenly on the ice-covered ledge. Dropping muff and books, but clutching Pinkie, she fell heavily forward into the brougham, striking her knee hard on the iron bars at the foot of the carriage door. Martha hurried to help her, but she could not move. Bellboys and clerks came running. They lifted her on to a chair, her knee somewhere near her chin, her leg dangling, and carried her to her room. Doctors were summoned while at the theatre the waiting audience was dismissed. They ruled a transverse compound fracture of the kneecap and two broken tendons. Stella's first thought was of her mother: she asked Martha to cable a message. As she dictated, "DO NOT BELIEVE EXAGGERATED ACCOUNTS IN PAPERS. NOT ANYTHING SERIOUS," Dr. Martin broke up a wooden hatbox to make a splint, pulled the leg out straight, and bound it to the wood while Martha looked away, unable to bear the sight of Stella's face. Then they lifted her up. Passing a mirror on the way to the elevator, Stella wondered why her face was blue. "Breaking the knee-cap is the most painful thing in the world," explained the doctor.

Downstairs they put her into a carriage with Pinkie, Martha, and a collection of friends. Throughout the long drive to the University of Pennsylvania Hospital, Stella chatted calmly, though still in great pain. Fifteen doctors gathered in the operating room as Dr. Martin removed four splinters of bone and finally set the knee in a plaster cast with weights tied to her foot to keep the leg from shortening. She was then wheeled to her room, but without her black silk stockings, which someone had filched for a souvenir. "MRS. CAMPBELL MAY BE LAMED FOR LIFE," shouted the papers next day.

Young Stella came hurriedly from Canada and took up her post at her mother's bedside. Flowers, bonbons, books, and cakes began to fill the room. Members of Stella's company paid anxious visits (she had been, the papers noted, "kind and amiable" to her cast on this tour). Fashionable Philadelphia began to call. Mrs. John Groome was forced to cancel a tea in Stella's honor. Mrs. Spencer Ervin wondered whether she would have to cancel an opera party for the actress. Young Stella began to answer dozens of letters of inquiry. "She really hurt herself in her attempt to save Pinkie from being killed," the daughter wrote Harriett Carolan, a San Francisco friend, "but she won't let us blame Pinkie!" Beo wrote lovingly: "Poor you! How it must have hurt. I can't bear being so far away from you, and you ill. . . . They have huge placards up, bigger than when Port Arthur fell. I wish I was with you to comfort you."

Besides the danger of her being lamed for life, there was the financial disaster. The press spoke of a loss of perhaps $50,000; she was already losing $3000 a week. Richard Mansfield telegraphed, offering to take her company if it would help her; but instead, many of the actors contracted to Frohman were put into other productions. Dr. Martin came, shook his head, and pronounced her case a *ne plus ultra.* "*Knee* plus ultra," corrected Stella brightly. But he was reassuring. He told her that if she could control her nerves and realize that only her knee was sick, she would not need crutches and could act again in less than five weeks.

At first it was all rather pleasant. Miss Marion Smith, the matron, found time to mother both Stella and her daughter, making them feel almost as though they were at home. Visitors showered Stella with attention, spoiling her. It was fun to send flowers and a charming little note to a Miss Elizabeth Robinson down the hall when she heard that she too was suffering an injured knee. It was sadly moving when a dying man asked to see Pinkie and in his delirium cried, "Oh, the little dog, the little dog." It was gratifying to receive a note from the novelist Ouida venturing to thank her for the "admirable example of affection" she had demonstrated for her dog. She did enjoy the lovely book of Keats's verse from Harriett Carolan. But after two weeks Stella became very depressed. Her leg was out of the cast, but she could not move it. The thought of all the money she was losing sickened her, as did the fear that she would never walk normally again. She grew so severely depressed, in fact, that one night at nine o'clock Dr. Martin was sent for. Stella immediately launched into a catalogue of woes, but Martin cut her short. "Oh, well, if you are feeling like that, you must come to the ball tonight," he said. "It is *the* ball in America, the Philadelphia Ball. Dress her, make her look beautiful," he told the nurses, "and I will come back for her in an hour." The nurses helped Stella into a black velvet gown embroidered with gold, aides carried her downstairs and laid her in the carriage with Dr. Martin and a nurse; she was carried into the ballroom and installed on a couch, and there she stayed until five in the morning, laughing, chatting, gorging on hothouse grapes, and forgetting all about her knee.

By the third week she was hobbling up and down corridors with a young intern on either side, all three singing glees. On February 9, her fortieth birthday, she was able to tell Harriett Carolan that "On March 6th I open in the 'Sorceress' for a tour of eight weeks. Today is my birthday. 24!!!!!!!" Her age had become another cause for worry. The long hair was still black, the curiously opaque skin unlined, the white throat still glorious. But an Italianate fulness had begun to flesh out her frame. To think that her appeal had been a haunting, almost painful, thinness; that boys had once teased her with "Skinny be be." These days one carried the chin higher to preserve the famous sweep of throat; one drew the stays tighter; one studied the mirror. Perhaps one even discouraged one's elegantly slender young daughter from an acting career for reasons other than social ambition. "The young people do have a time in this country," she complained to D.D. "No one takes any notice of me. Why don't people fall in love with me? I am not *so* old." And yet Stella did nothing to preserve her looks. She adored food and ate enormously. She powdered carelessly. She and exercise were deadly enemies.

Finally she was well enough to leave Philadelphia, where she had come to find the people more simple, home-loving, and caring than anywhere else and could count dozens of friends. On March 5 she arrived in Chicago to start "screaming and falling about in Sardou's silly play" for two weeks at Power's Theatre. The next night a doctor was in the wings to monitor her condition after two months of inaction. When she came off after a good deal of screaming and falling, he took her wrist. "Normal," he pronounced. "Few artists come off the stage with a normal pulse; you are all right, my dear, knee and head." Although the knee continued to pain her, she was able to move onstage with all her former suppleness. As for her acting, the scholarly critic Hutchins Hapgood found Sardou "uninspired, sensational, base material," but decided that "Mrs. Campbell plays with a distinction that never leaves her an unsympathetic and relatively meaningless role. There is no more distinguished actor or actress on the English or American stage than she; none who acts more intelligently—few who have as much talent, intellect, and beauty."

Having ordered Oscar Wilde's *De Profundis*, which everyone was calling wonderful, Stella went on to Milwaukee for a performance at the Davidson Theatre on March 22, announcing there that arrangements had been concluded for a tour with Bernhardt in *Pelléas et Mélisande* that summer. Then it was Toledo, where the *Blade* reported that "Miss Stella shows no leaning towards a stage career, but is exceptionally fond of society, where she has gained a reputation for wit, distinction of manner, and what is termed smartness." In Davenport, Iowa, there was trouble over the theatre. An enemy of steam heat since her first American tour, Stella always ordered all heat turned off in her hotel rooms and theatres. In Davenport, however, the manager decided not to co-operate; it was reported that he turned on the steam heat and padlocked the doors. Whereupon (it was also reported) Stella seized a chair and broke every window pane in sight. Back in Boston at the Hollis Street Theatre on April 11, she took her audience rather than the theatre by storm, although the *Globe* decided she was *not* beautiful— only striking, commanding, and impressive.

Just as Stella impressed America as being either abnormal or beautiful, or not beautiful but intelligent, America variously impressed her. Every town, she noted, seemed to have a park, and she and her daughter loved to drive through them in an open brougham, even in freezing weather. In Pittsburgh there had been a long sidewalk hanging precipitously above the steel mills. No handrail, no fence between her and the two-hundred-foot drop. A dense black fog billowed up from the fumes and smoke—"a boiling hell," thought Stella, peering over. Trains were all abominably overheated, but train officials, she discovered, could be managed. "No dogs allowed in this car," one of them said severely, catching sight of a wet nose poking out of her furs. Stella drew herself up. "DOG?" she demanded with a Siddonian sneer. "It's a *Verberduna.*" The conductor hesitated, scratched his head, looked again at the expensively dressed woman and the wet nose. "Better keep it in a cage," he muttered, and moved on down the aisle.

When the time came to return to England, Pinkie again presented a problem. This time Stella could not pretend ignorance of quarantine laws or get away with an uninspected Gladstone bag. She therefore bought a parakeet shortly before their departure in May. "I thought if the sailors heard Pinkie bark I could say it was the parakeet," explained Stella. "Unfortunately I told this to Lord Charles Beresford, who was on board, and he amused himself by asking people if they had heard Mrs. Campbell's remarkable parakeet 'bark.' People began to suspect." Unwilling to chance customs at Liverpool, Stella decided to make a break at Holyhead. When the "donkey" came up to the side of the ship, there was a woman waiting to disembark. Down the ladder she went, her friends and daughter watching anxiously, a small black silk bag under her coat cradling a little dog. At

Holyhead she found a hotel and the next morning took the train the 224 miles back to London. But she had not evaded the law: everybody knew Mrs. Pat had smuggled in Pinkie Panky Poo. Bouchier Hawksley appeared in court for her. He pleaded that the dog was fifteen years old, blind and toothless, and that Mrs. Campbell had broken her leg in Philadelphia rather than drop her. The judge inquired what fine Mr. Hawksley saw fit to impose. "In view of the circumstances," said Hawksley gravely, "thirty shillings." Stella heard the verdict with relief. She had understood that evader and ship's captain would each be fined £100.

All in all, it had been a Pinkie tour. The accident cost her some $20,000, money which she could ill afford to lose, particularly since Frohman had disappeared without offering her a contract for another American tour. Of course there were the weeks with Sarah to look forward to. "HEUREUSE D'ALLER AVEC VOUS JOUER NOTRE CHER PELLEAS," Sarah had wired on May 19. She would pay her English friend £240 a week, £35 for each additional performance, and all travelling expenses. Dear Sarah, who sent "MILLE TENDRES BAISERS," was quite her favorite leading man.

# TWENTY-FOUR

## *1905–1907*

*B*ACK IN LONDON, Stella was approached by Eleonora Duse, who asked if she might borrow her *Tanqueray* scenery for a London production of *La Seconda Moglie*. Stella replied that she would be honored and turned the scenery over promptly, only requesting a box for the premiere. The ticket arrived, accompanied by a bill for four guineas. Surprised, Stella paid and was present and applauding in a box at the Waldorf Theatre on the evening of May 23. During the first interval a page boy approached with a large box of gardenias and laurel leaves. A charming token of gratitude, thought Stella, but modestly asked whom the flowers were for. "Please throw them on to the stage after the second act," instructed the boy. "I thought this was going rather far," Stella complained to Arnold Bennett afterwards, blaming Duse's manager, however, not Duse. "I lent the scenery for nothing. I paid for my box. And then they wanted me to throw flowers at her!" Her wry summation: "In *The Second Mrs. Tanqueray* Duse made a tour de force; but I was forced to tour."

On Sunday, July 9, Stella boarded the train at Euston with Sarah and her French company, and they set out to test their hermaphroditic impersonation on the provinces. They made, in Stella's words, a brilliant success. Stella's Anglicized French proved no drawback; in Birmingham, in fact, a young orchestra member named Eric Coates, playing the Fauré for their matinee at the Theatre Royal, found himself terribly disappointed in the divine Sarah and madly in love with Mrs. Pat. He innocently thought she spoke French better than Bernhardt, not realizing that he could understand her better simply because of the English accent.

The tour was also a test of their friendship. The two had a good deal in common. Both were strongly attached to their sons. Once Sarah had pleaded with American customs officials not to open a small bundle she had tucked away in a large handbag; they did, only to discover white patent-leather baby shoes and a tiny shirt. Both were also mad about animals:

Sarah's bizarre pets were legendary. Both had fierce tempers. Both were candid. Both possessed great courage.

There were differences, of course. One night Stella and Sarah sat up late discussing flirting—in French, since Sarah spoke no English. Sarah hated it. She argued that it stirred physical passion simply *pour passer les temps*. That was immoral, and something characteristic of English men and women. French women, said Sarah, loved and gave themselves—*c'est tout*. Stella disagreed. Flirting was not immoral in itself; its effect depended solely on the moral character of those flirting. Sarah shrugged, unconvinced. She told of her first visit to England, when a supper was given in her honor and she was treated like and felt like a queen, until the host, seeing her to her carriage, stole a kiss. It was *abominable, abominable!* It showed the man had no respect for her. She had not spoken to him again for years.

They differed chiefly in their attitudes toward their art. Members of Sarah's company warned Stella that Madame had never been known to laugh or clown onstage. To Stella that was an immediate challenge. One day she caught sight of a tobacco pouch shaped like a fish in a tobacconist's window. She bought it and, carrying on the fishpond joke, painted the pouch with gills and scales, took it to the theatre, and tied it to a bit of canvas at the bottom of the fountain. Pelléas entered in the second act, paused by the fountain, suddenly spied the fish, and, bursting into a poetic improvisation about *les poissons là*, bent gracefully to scoop it up and nearly lost her footing.

"When the curtain fell Sarah did not allude to what had happened, neither did I. The next day when we lunched together she had a strange, preoccupied expression on her face. Later, at the matinée, when we came to the Cave scene, at the point where she tenderly takes my hand and helps me over the rocks, she took hold of my hand, hard—squash—she held a raw egg in hers.

"I did not smile, but with calm dignity I went on with my part. I can see now the tears of laughter trickling down her cheeks, and her dear body shaking with merriment as I grew more and more dignified to the end of the scene.

"Her company told me afterwards, almost with awe, that Madame must love me very, very much."

The ice was very thin, but Stella skated recklessly on. The raw egg must be revenged. During one performance, as Sarah reached up to caress Mélisande's hair, Stella, under the cover of her long tresses, slipped a live goldfish into Sarah's hand. With complete calm Sarah continued her lovemaking, concealing the goldfish in her fist for the rest of the scene. Again nothing was said. But if Sarah had contemplated a Paris production of *Pelléas* with Stella to follow this tour, she now thought better of it.

Offstage they got along happily. One night when Stella found Sarah in a rage over a hotelkeeper who had charged her for forty bottles of beer for her servants, some English tactics were called for. "What matter *how* many bottles of beer have been drunk, how *dare* you contradict Madame!" thundered Stella, completely intimidating the man, who scurried from the room. Another morning, in Liverpool, Stella heard terrible growls and rough voices raised in anger. Hastening to Sarah's room, she found her in an altercation with two toughs who had just delivered Madame a tiger in a large iron cage. Sarah was demanding they open the cage; the men were demanding £30 and a quick exit. Stella took charge and, rapidly persuading Sarah that a cat of that size was something too much of a pet, muscled the angry men and the cage out of the room. Eventually Sarah admitted that a tiger might have proved rather troublesome on tour.

There were quieter moments. One evening in Blackpool they were to have dinner together, and Stella went to knock on Sarah's door. *"Entrez,"* said Sarah. Stella went in and found her sitting in front of the bay window looking out at the great stretch of sand and sky bathed all red and gold in the setting sun. Stella sat down silently next to her. After a few moments Sarah turned toward her and said, *"Les morts sont toujours avec nous,"* and Stella felt she understood.

They played twenty cities in all, including Dublin, Belfast, Glasgow, and Edinburgh, from July 10 to 29. It was an exhausting schedule that called for them to leave Newcastle at 1:10 a.m. after a matinee and an evening performance, arrive in Glasgow at 6:25 the morning of the twenty-eighth, play a matinee and an evening performance the same day, play two performances in Edinburgh the twenty-ninth, and leave for London that night to arrive at eight in the morning so Sarah could return to Paris the same day. They had been received everywhere with great enthusiasm. "Only in Dublin," said Stella, "did one critic demur. He wrote: 'Mrs. Campbell played Mélisande, Madame Bernhardt Pelléas; they are both old enough to know better.'" Sarah at any rate knew better than to attempt another round with the irrepressible Stella. But they remained friends, and Sarah had picked up enough English to wire from Dakar on August 13, "LOVE YOU DARLING."

A month later an event occurred that marked the end of a theatrical era. Playing a farewell performance of *Becket* in Bradford against all medical advice, Sir Henry Irving collapsed upon return to the hotel after the performance and died. The news reached Ellen Terry in Manchester, where she was acting Barrie's *Alice Sit-by-the-Fire.* That night she managed to play almost until the end, when she came to the lines, "It's summer done, autumn begun. Farewell, summer, we don't know you any more. . . . I had a beautiful husband once, black as the raven was his hair"—here she broke down and wept for her former partner and lover while a respectful audience filed silently out of the theatre.

It was summer done in more than one sense: the day of the great actor-manager was drawing to a close. As an actress, Stella had found herself frustrated by that male tradition. Yet she had Irving's temperament—the egocentricity that wanted to manage, direct, dominate. Like him, she belonged to the Victorian actors' theatre rather than to the new authors' theatre promoted by Shaw, Archer, Grein, and Granville-Barker. Like Irving, she was a star; the vehicle was secondary—audiences came to see the performer, not the play.

The following February, on the eve of her fifty-ninth birthday, Ellen Terry began rehearsals at the Court Theatre of Shaw's *Captain Brassbound's Conversion*, her capitulation to the authors' theatre she found so alien. Shaw had wooed her with the play since 1899, but "it's not the sort of play for me in the least," Ellen had objected. If he had written it for anyone, "it is surely for Mrs. Pat. *Not* for me." Eventually Ellen softened toward the play and gave it a copyright performance, as Stella had given *Caesar and Cleopatra*. But Ellen was used to Shakespearian spectacle and continued to consider *Brassbound* closet drama. Her consent to play it in 1906 meant not so much a love of the part, but rather an acknowledgment that the Court Theatre under the direction of J. E. Vedrenne and Harley Granville-Barker was the most interesting playhouse in London, and Bernard Shaw London's most provocative playwright.

Stella might have taken a hint from Ellen's capitulation or from Forbes-Robertson's American success with *Caesar and Cleopatra* that year; but she was only forty-one and still unexcited by the author theatre of Shaw. She also deplored the playwright's shallowness, as she saw it. "It's that journalistic cleverness of his that I detest in anything but a daily paper," she had written D.D. Lyttelton from Philadelphia. "If he'd just give one real sob— then he might play the ass for a thousand years." Instead of *avant-garde* drama, she plunged into three experiments which brought her, on the one hand, some pleasure with no profit and, on the other, some profit with no pleasure.

On May 23, 1906, handling the production herself, she opened at the Criterion playing the Countess of Ellingham in a translation of Henry Bernstein's *La Rafale*. It had been successful in France; as *The Whirlwind* it fell flat in England. Desmond MacCarthy, a young critic making his debut in the *Speaker*, looked around at the sparse and tepid first-night audience and came away wondering what had misfired. "The personages belong to 'the gay, adulterous world,'" he mused. "That ought to draw. There is plenty of conventional law-defying passion in it. That promises success. The hero is a fascinating aristocratic gambler, who has never been known to turn a hair under tremendous losses; the heroine is the sort of woman who is the source of many aphorisms about women; these you would expect to be good guarantees. But no; there was something fatally wrong with it." Shaw would have analyzed it this way: "A modern manager need not produce The Wild Duck; but he must be very careful not to produce a play which will seem insipid and old-fashioned to playgoers who have seen The Wild Duck, even though they may have hissed it." With *The Whirlwind* Stella played the first act of *Undine* as a curtain-raiser. Walkley dismissed her as "a mournful and sententious Undine in, to tell the truth, a mournful and sententious little play." Both disappeared on June 9 after twenty-one performances.

Stella followed this failure ten days later with amateur night, playing Margaretta Sinclair in D.D. Lyttelton's *The Macleans of Bairness*. D.D. had succumbed to the temptation of writing a play about Bonnie Prince Charlie, and "Whom the gods wish to destroy," Anthony Ellis wrote sardonically in the *Star* after the disaster, "they first impel to write a play about Prince Charlie." Although Stella had liked D.D.'s play when she read it in America, even thinking that Frohman might produce it there, she had again under a mistakenly generous impulse sold her own powers far short. "There is an absence of effective emotional stress," complained Walkley. "This is a misfortune for the play, and a positive calamity for Mrs. Patrick Campbell, whose tremendous talent for depicting emotional stress is to all intents and purposes wasted. She looks very beautiful, with her fine eyes, her raven tresses, and her air of 'petitionary grace'; but opportunity for acting, passionate or pathetic, she has none or next to none." But, of course, it was such fun to help out a friend and do Society a favor. This particular favor lasted five performances.

"Then came what to me was a nightmare," said Stella, "—*The Bondman* at Drury Lane, by Mr. Hall Caine." Caine had managed to convert his immensely popular novels into equally popular stage successes with dramatizations of *The Deemster*, *The Manxman*, and *The Christian*. *The Bondman* was a gigantic, cluttered play, clogged with action that veered wildly between a Manx farmyard studded with live cows and chickens to a sulphur mine in Sicily. Knowing that Frank Cooper and the popular Henry Ainley would steal the show as Jason and Michael Sunlocks, Stella did not really bother to study her part of Greeba, who has little to do or say. She would have loved to walk out on the whole thing, but after the failures at the Criterion she desperately needed the £230 a week she'd been offered.

"I remember one or two things about this play—the blowing up of a sulphur mine to 'Rachmaninoff's Prelude,' Miss Henrietta Watson and I squashed up against the wall in the dark, like flies, quite certain that the next moment we would be killed by the most awful 'business,' 'properties,' sulphur fumes, rushing and screaming 'supers,' 'property' walls, earth, and stones hurled about. Also there were real cows that I had to lead across the stage. I had a short-sighted dresser of the 'hook-scratching-down-the-back-for-eye' kind. My own dresser, Julia, was engaged elsewhere, and was unable to come to me. I remember saying I could not act, I could not live, I could not breathe in the din and misery. . . . I remember, too, at the rehearsals of this play getting into great trouble because I suddenly asked, 'Whose are these children? Are they *mine?*' Lots of children were about me, catching hold of my hand and my skirts. I had not read the book, and I could not grasp the plot of the play. I believe now they were my brothers and sisters, but I do not remember."

On opening night, September 20, 1906, Stella got into great trouble again. Finding Hall Caine backstage white and trembling with nervousness, Stella felt a rush of sympathy and blurted impulsively, "Is this your first play?" "I have been wickedly accused of saying it on purpose, and of being heartless, which was just what I was not," said Stella. "Ignorant, impulsive, yes; for, had I stopped to think, I should have remembered his many successes."

A. B. Walkley said all that needed saying critically about *The Bondman.* Confessing he suffered from "Caineblindness," he mused that "Mr. Hall Caine must be a great writer, for everybody else says so. . . . His plays seem to us of poor intellectual texture, crude in method, garish, and as noisy as a brass band. . . . Panting geography toils after [the characters] in vain as they whirl round the globe. . . . They have hearts, abnormally developed hearts, thumping, palpitating, bursting or broken hearts. They have consciences—everything but life." Yet, concluded Walkley, "We would much rather see Mrs. Campbell in a part unworthy of her than in none at all." The unworthy *Bondman* settled in immediately at Drury Lane, however, playing nightly to £700 houses.

A young woman named Dorothy Burroughes bought a ticket one night and fell immediately under Mrs. Campbell's spell. She went back again and again, and then, "like a stage-struck loon," sent a fan letter to the actress. Stella answered graciously in her dashing, almost indecipherable hand, and Dorothy agonized over the message. Had Mrs. Campbell written "*Someday*

you must come and see me" or "*Sunday* you must come and see me"?
Dorothy felt sure it was *Someday*, but by squinting hard could turn the
word into *Sunday*. She wrote an eager acceptance.

"I shall never forget my first sight of the little white house in Kensington
Square with the green door," said Dorothy; "and years after when I stood
upon that step, grown up and with my knees no longer trembling under me,
I still felt an indescribable tenderness for it. Perhaps it was because when I
first saw it I was so young and romantic, and that green door seemed to me
like an opening into an enchanted world. That house had an atmosphere of
excitement. There were always people coming and going and telephoning
—great people, too, with wonderful names.

"At our very first meeting she said, in that lovely deep resonant voice
which I already knew so well in the theatre: 'How beautifully you seal your
letters! How do you do it? The seals are so *fat!* After tea you must teach me
how to make such seals!' " After tea with the daughter whose smile Dorothy
thought dazzlingly lovely, "She found every bit of sealing-wax in the house
and sat down eager as a child, and I knelt beside her and we had a lovely
time making seals. Then she asked me about myself, and when she heard I
was training to be an artist she said: 'You must come and draw me.' And
she showed me her lovely original Burne-Jones, and told me thrilling stories
about him as if he were a human being whom she saw every day, and not a
god who lived in the Holy of Holies."

Encouraged, Dorothy went back again and again to Kensington Square.
She got to know the actress in all her moods—"and they were many." Too
unsophisticated to appreciate it fully, she still felt Stella's wit, always a little
malicious but turned as readily against herself as others. "With the greatest
affectation of simplicity," said Dorothy, "her great eyes wide open like
those of a child, she would make astounding comments which were not in
the least childlike. For example she referred to one famous actress as 'an
inspired housemaid,' and these observations were not merely malicious—
they had almost always a ghastly grain of truth in them."

Dorothy decided that animals were the only creatures that the actress
loved absolutely. One day she arrived to find that the cat had just had
kittens in Mrs. Campbell's best hatbox. "There was a new hat in it, too,"
said Stella, and then, indulgently, "But never mind—she has taken a fancy
to it!" On another occasion they decided upon an outing in the park. Exquisitely gowned in yards of tulle and wearing elbow-length, biscuit-colored
gloves, Mrs. Campbell entered a fishmonger's shop in Kensington High
Street and in superb, resonant tones demanded, "A bag of *sprats*, if you
please!" They then proceeded with great dignity to the Round Pond in

Kensington Gardens, where Stella amused herself by flinging sprats into the air while the gulls circled and swooped.

Stella liked attention from adoring young girls, attention at all times. Visiting Sargent's studio one day, she found young Cynthia Charteris sitting for a charcoal drawing. Cynthia was feeling shy and Sargent shy with her when Stella surged in. "Oh, you are going to draw my golden frog!" she sang in her vibrant, dusky voice. "Isn't she Batrachian? Mind you, get the preposterous width between her green eyes. They're so far apart that if a fly wanted to go from one to the other he would have to take a fly—I mean a cab." Cynthia giggled, but Sargent frowned, not liking his studio quiet violated.

Another visitor proposed that Cynthia looked more like a large, semi-wild feline. "No, no, no!" trilled Stella in low register. "She-is-the-great-frog-of-the-western-world." Fumbling in a flowing sleeve, she then produced a new distraction—something too canine to be a mouse, yet hardly a dog. "Wouldn't you like to draw my Pinkie Panky Poo?" she wheedled, holding up the dog appealingly in Sargent's face. "Isn't she be-yoo-ti-ful? She's got Wemyss's whiskers, Balfour's nose, and Marjorie Manners' eyes."

Sargent regarded Pinkie with distaste. "I like *big* dogs," he said.

"If you were a real artist, you would draw my lovely Pinkie Panky Poo instead of that plump, pale frog," Stella warbled, undeterred.

Sargent pointedly drew out his watch, but Stella ignored it, going to peer at the portrait. "But, my dear man, you mustn't make my golden frog's hair *black*," she cried. "Can't you see it's the color of the best marmalade?"

*"Demons! Demons! Demons!"* spluttered Sargent. "Since the er—*medium* in which I am *trying* to work is black and white, how can I make Miss Charteris' hair look er—um fairer, without making it er—um appear to be *white!*"

The irrepressible Stella was finally maneuvered out gently, but it was not their last encounter. Finding herself seated next to Sargent at a dinner party one night, she wheedled him to paint her. The more morose he became, the more she coaxed, pressing her hands together, praying, "Oh, Mr. Sargent, *do* paint my portrait." Sargent finally looked her straight in the eye. "I cannot paint beautiful women," he said with finality.

While cows bellowed and mines exploded on the stage of Drury Lane, Stella planned an excursion in December to the Court Theatre to investigate the New Drama of Shaw. They had reopened correspondence that month after a five-year silence, Stella replying to his "delicious letter," "I dread seeing my photographs—the days of dewlaps have arrived! God help me and all women! Oh that I had mislaid countless sons and daughters and that they would all turn up today or to-morrow and prevent me accepting an offer to tour in America, that is lying on my table—20 weeks at so many dollars a minute! . . . I see your play Friday afternoon next. God bless you for the smiles you make us smile and forgive you for your literary lack-of-taste misdemeanours that make us squirm." "Dearest Princess with the Six-teen Chins," Shaw replied familiarly, ". . . You will be delighted with the Doctor's Dilemma if they are in a good vein on Friday. The death scene, a miracle of my lack-of-taste (Stella, Stellata, Stellatissima: ora pro nobis) is the most touching and beautiful one in all dramatic literature, because, Princess, it is *inspired*."

*Must* she tour? Shaw asked in the same letter; and it was perhaps at his instigation that Stella was invited to do seven matinees of *Hedda Gabler* at the Court Theatre after *The Bondman* exploded for the last time in Febru-ary 1907. "I was delighted," said Stella, unaware of Barker's and Vedrenne's passionate authors'-theatre stance. "I felt sure if I could play 'Hedda' with success the play would run for months. I spent on Hedda's wardrobe well over the salary I would receive." She had taken a long holiday from Ibsen, put off by the cliquishness, as she thought it, of the Ibsenites. Archer, she told D.D., had "lied so terribly about Miss Robins' art [as an actress] & he & she buzzed so on the wheel of Ibsen's genius & thought themselves so fine—perhaps I am prejudiced." Now she found herself excited by Ibsen and her role and spent a fortnight studying Hedda into the early hours of the morning. She knew her Italianate beauty had little to do with Ibsen's concept of a cool, unruffled Hedda with steel-gray eyes and plain brown hair, but felt she could overcome that handicap. Rehearsals with Laurence Irving playing Eilert Lövborg went with comparative smoothness, and although the "basso-relievo" methods of Barker and Shaw (who sometimes sat out front) irritated her, they left her pretty much alone.

When Stella wanted to play magnificently, she did, and her Hedda Gabler proved one of her greatest creations. Desmond MacCarthy consid-ered her Ibsen's bored, sulky, power-hungry heroine to the life. *People* said she played with "a sinister yet fascinating intensity of realism absolutely unique upon the English-speaking stage." Max Beerbohm found her read-ing of the character "perfect from first to last"; her only fault beyond her control: she was physically too beautiful; Hedda should be *mesquine*. In-terestingly enough, Stella did not consider Hedda either sinister, sulky, or power-hungry. She believed her to be essentially a good woman—proud, intelligent, well-bred; a vital person stifled by the commonplace, acutely and tragically unhappy with her baffled instinct for beauty, her warped sense of honor, and her hatred of being pregnant with the child of the ridiculous Tesman. Yet when Stella played Hedda, she played her with a malignancy that made audiences shudder.

The packed theatre and the outstanding notices made Stella confident that *Hedda* would be held over for a long run. But the Court management had discovered with Ellen Terry that the star system did not pay: the combination of a small theatre and a high-salaried actress did not make them money. Besides, they were committed to the idea of repertory—not the kind of repertory Stella had tried to practise at the Royalty by giving audiences a variety of experimental plays still dominated by one star, but repertory with balanced casts and regularly alternating plays. One afternoon, therefore, Barker found Stella in her dressing room and announced that, while she could have the translation to take to America and the provinces, the play would end with the seventh matinee. The fact that he quickly added, "What beautiful hair you have!" did not comfort Stella. "I went in misery to Mr. Hawksley, asking if anything could be done. He pointed out that my contract was for seven matinées only. Mr. Heinemann, who held the acting rights, made every effort, but Messrs. Vedrenne and Barker were adamant." Stella thus lost a second round with Barker, *Hedda* came off, and Stella exited with an acting triumph but less money than before.

She could not afford to take a theatre, and no actor-manager would have her. "Waller is used to being the be-all & end-all on his stage," she had explained to D.D., anticipating her difficulties on returning to London from America, "& I don't think he wants me there again." As a be-all and end-all herself, she had no choice but tour the provinces before returning to America again. Even with provincial theatre managers taking on average fifty per cent of her profits, she could still make more money on tour than in her own theatre. She added *Hedda* to her repertoire, and young Stella and a new leading man, Ben Webster, to her company. Webster, after playing Captain Ardale in the original *Tanqueray*, had vowed he would never act with the maddening Stella Campbell again; but here he was, he could not say why: somehow the magnetism was irresistible, and then, one forgot the pain.

Stella had resigned herself to an acting career for her daughter, and found herself even glad of her presence. "If Stella can do well, life will be much more interesting for me," she wrote her mother at Gensing Lodge, "for I am very tired of being alone in my work." Stella Pat was rehearsing Ellean beautifully, to her mother's surprise, and was "wonderfully obedient and quick," and saw her mistakes in a flash. Yet the disappointment was there. They had gone to Katharine Horner's and Raymond Asquith's wedding, then to Viscountess Gladstone's reception, then to the Asquiths' ball, where Beo and Stella danced reels until three in the morning. The fashionable wedding reminded the mother that her hopes for young Stella had not included her playing Ellean.

Or her son playing Eilert Lövborg in *Hedda Gabler*. Beo had gone up to Oxford for the fall term of 1905 and started reading for an honors degree. He registered to enter Christ Church College, then decided on Hertford, where he showed promise as a middleweight boxer. But academic life suited him no better than life in the Navy, and he began to think of a secretaryship in Africa that Mr. Hawksley might get him, or if that fell through, doing some work with a man who was making torpedo boats, or if that didn't turn out, consulting the Lytteltons, who had heard of one or two things that might suit him. Meanwhile, he lived lavishly off his mother: "Please send £1000," he could wire from Vienna, "girls and bonbons expensive."

Then in the summer of 1907 Beo decided that his mother's life might suit him best, or at least be the easiest way to earn a living. He caught up with the company in Edinburgh, and Stella capitulated. She would take him to America, where there were hundreds of influential and interesting people to meet; he could take care of her and Stella Pat on the tour. Still, Beo was not quite satisfied. "Beo cannot quite make up his mind," Stella explained to her mother, "because he first wanted to be an 'Admiral' and then a 'Prime Minister,' and just an actor seems a 'come down' to him. I am so grateful to the stage, I cannot feel as he does; we talk together about it at night. I think Stella's success has encouraged him." For Stella herself the stage had been an entry into society; for Beo, brought up with the Asquiths, Charterises, and Horners, it was a tall step down. He took it, but lightly enough, appearing one morning for early rehearsal with a mackintosh flung over pyjamas. "Well, Mother, I overslept," said Beo, his eyes twinkling in anticipation of her indulgence, although her face was severe, "and I thought it would worry you more if I was late."

From Edinburgh the company went to Dublin and Belfast, then wound back down to London. Ben Webster's dread had been groundless. Not only had Stella treated the company generously to sandwiches and beer, but she had been quite amiable, only telling Webster playfully that he had such a sweet smile and such a *good* face that he made her Agnes Ebbsmith look ridiculous refusing his Lucas Cleeve—enough so to make her pull the play out of the repertoire. Lulled by the charm, Webster resolved to paint on a truly lecherous lip, since he very much wanted the part in the forthcoming American tour.

Like Webster, George C. Tyler had sworn he would never deal with Stella Campbell again. Yet here he was, in the midst of negotiations (he couldn't quite say how), and they were already at each other's throats over the question of repertory. Tyler objected that it was hard to book one-week stands with a handful of old plays—the public wanted something new. Finally a Mr. MacCullough came over to London to settle the difficulties in person. They arranged that she would make a twenty-six-week tour coast to coast playing *Tanqueray*, *Ebbsmith*, *Magda*, and *Hedda Gabler*, and have her own private train ("Brass bedsteads, dressing room, observatory room —so you can see miles down the railway line. Imagine it!" she wrote her mother). Then came a cable from New York asking her to produce Hugo von Hofmannsthal's *Electra* at the Garden Theatre along with a one-act Japanese play called *The Moon of Yamato*. This she agreed to, meanwhile conducting exhaustive rehearsals in preparation for the tour. "Remember all you want to ask me, darling, for it will be many months before we meet," she wrote her mother; then made a flying visit to St. Leonards to find Louisa Tanner unwell and much more frail than Stella had ever seen her. Then home to oversee the packing of the endless trunks. Beo had gone absolutely delirious at the idea of America and of sailing on the luxurious *Lusitania*; she was finding it impossible to manage him.

On November 3 they sailed: Stella, Beo, young Stella, a manservant, a maid, Mr. MacCullough, and the aged Pinkie. While the company crossed in the plain *Philadelphia*, Beo and young Stella revelled in their regal suite on the sunny side of the upper deck, the gorgeous salons, the orchestras, and the sumptuous food. Stella was perfectly aware of the added responsibility. She had two young people to teach to act; as she'd told her mother, "If I haven't learned enough patience by the end of the American tour it will be a strange thing." Yet from the days of her first tour with Greet, Stella had always been anxious about her babies, and now she too was happy. "They were safe, beautiful, full of eager life, and my heart was full of pride and hope," she said, "and above all, they were *with* me."

# TWENTY-FIVE

# *1907–1908*

*D*O WE HAVE to submit to this kind of thing?" demanded Stella, surrounded by reporters in her sitting room at the Plaza. She was at the height of her fame, and knew she did. "A good woman is a dramatic impossibility," she replied crisply to the eternal curiosity about her choice of roles. "I succeeded because I had to," she answered another inevitable question. Interviewers jotted down the fact that Stella Patrick Campbell was both acting as her mother's stage manager and making her New York debut in *Mrs. Tanqueray.* In the midst of the commotion Beo wandered into the room. "I say," he drawled, "it looks like a game . . . haven't had my dinner," and strolled out again. Getting her own dinner downstairs later, Stella lit one of her perfumed cigarettes. A shocked *maître d'hôtel* hurried to her table. She must put the cigarette out immediately. Ladies did not smoke, and the Plaza catered only to ladies. Stella stared, blew jets of smoke through her nostrils. "Oh, you old silly-billy," she laughed. "Don't be such a puritanical Mayflower teapot!" A compromise was finally reached. Waiters shrouded her table with a tall screen, and Stella finished her dinner and her cigarette behind it.

The next day she gave an interview about Bernard Shaw, whose reputation had been made in recent years by Court Theatre productions of *Candida, Man and Superman,* and *Major Barbara.* Smarting, perhaps, over the "princess with the sixteen chins" or perhaps told by D.D. that Shaw had called Pinkie "a cheese maggot under a microscope," Stella was critical. "Shaw is quite out of it in London," she told the *Telegraph* interviewer. "One scarcely hears of him now. Shaw offends good taste. When one meets an Irishman like Yeats—an Irishman of truly cultured taste—one sees that Shaw has no taste. Shaw seems to have been left quite to himself. The Irish won't have him because, as they say, he's not a true Irishman, and the English won't have him for various reasons, and so, I suppose, he'll have to be called an American, if he is to be called anything." Having implied that

Americans lack taste, Stella then condemned *Major Barbara* as particularly offensive. "No, it was not much of a play—are any of Shaw's, for that matter? His characters are not characters—they are merely mouthpieces of Shaw's views. And one grows tired of mouthpieces, doesn't one?" Stella was not talking behind Shaw's back. Sharing a box at the Court Theatre that year with him and Charlotte, she had duelled with G.B.S. "I do not like your plays because there is no beauty in them," she challenged. "Well, you see I have had to live without it all my life," replied Shaw. "But there must be God in art—there is no feeling of God in your plays," insisted Stella. "Ah," said Shaw, "but you see, *I* am God"—upon which Stella dismissed him as a clown.

She opened on November 11 at the Lyric with Ben Webster as leading man. As the week progressed, she found again that audiences were enthusiastic and critics divided. The *Evening Sun* called her Hedda "listless, bored, and boring" except for the last scene, when "she woke up and played splendidly." The *World*, on the other hand, congratulated her for a "merciless, cold performance" so realistic that "Mrs. Campbell's Hedda seemed to have nothing in common with the stage." Stella herself felt her Hedda was received with much acclaim. But again her repertoire was condemned: "The assortment of females that she has chosen to represent is particularly obnoxious. . . . A more disgusting mess than Mr. Pinero's play on this subject has seldom been deposited on our stage." Critics also complained that her company was "too English": their accents were obscure and Mr. Webster's waistcoat particularly annoying. As for Stella Patrick Campbell's performance as Ellean, critics decided that she was "at present unsuited." She won some praise as Magda's sister Marie, but was unable to continue as Mrs. Elvsted in *Hedda Gabler* because of illness.

After a week at the Lyric, Stella, Beo, Stella Pat, two English servants, a black cook, four black servants, four English stage staff, the entire company, and Pinkie boarded the train and set out on a gruelling series of one-night stands. The private car engaged for Stella at a cost of $350 a week still could not compensate for her dislike of travel, inability to sleep on trains, and loathing for steam heat. In Waterbury, Connecticut, they were shunted alongside a factory, where the car sat for hours. Stella made the best of the situation by distributing candy and cigarettes among the curious factory workers. In Worcester, Massachusetts, where they pulled onto a siding to spend the night, the pounding of seventy-odd passing trains made the layover hell. Smoking oil lamps gave them all sore throats. The cook turned out to be unreliable: Stella was furious when she discovered that he was using her specially cured reindeer tongues to make sandwiches for "the boys." In Rochester, as she was dressing for a performance of *Magda*, a freight train with thirty loaded cars jolted her coach, sending everything not bolted down flying. If that was not enough, the station master that night, thinking she might be cold, sent 180 pounds of steam pressure into the radiator above her head. That was the last straw, and in Ottawa she fled to a hotel, where she could throw open the windows and get some sleep. George Tyler duly received all the complaints and realized that it was going to be *that* kind of tour. The Royal Tigerine, he christened her.

Ben Webster meanwhile cursed himself for having been lured back into Stella's orbit. "Mrs. Pat is playing vilely—codding half the time and querulous the rest," he wrote to his wife, May, who was making her own tour of the States; "she attacked me after the 3rd Act for bullying Paula instead of being gentle, and at the end of the play said it was hopeless and went into long dissertations—I wasn't at all in the humour. . . . I can see myself being very rude to her in a brace of shakes but will endeavour to keep myself within bounds. But much depends on what happens to-night. I think it's only just her policy to make everyone around her feel small and uncomfortable, but it doesn't add to one's enjoyment."

Had Webster been rude to Stella, she would have laughed and backed down. His wife got along "famously" with her: she was Irish and gave as good as she got, and Stella respected her for it. But Ben failed to take the example; when Stella came down the aisle of the coach at two a.m. exclaiming in ringing tones, "Oh! Is everyone asleep?" he hadn't shouted, "Not now, damn you!" as he felt like doing, but only hissed "Shh!" And so Stella tyrannized and he suffered.

What he hated most, though, was the way she betrayed her own gift. "Oh! how I hate acting with her!" he wrote May from snowy Hamilton, Ontario. "She hasn't been finding faults so much lately, but she will make comments on the audiences and things generally while one is playing a scene with her, and it makes me mad. She said I was a snob because I played Lucas so well before the Governor of Canada. Last night she amused herself by inventing Royalties in front while I was speaking. 'Play up—Prince Louis of Battenberg is in front!' and so on, and as this amused her mightily it must have been very obvious to the audience and must have helped them understand the character of Agnes considerably! No wonder they cracked peanuts in the gallery till it sounded like a hail-storm on a conservatory roof! Can you see what my liver is like this morning? Dear heart, forgive me. . . ." And then when she was not amusing herself by whispering, "You look so funny!" under her breath in the midst of his most critical speech, she would play listlessly. It really was maddening, because she could be magnificent whenever she chose: in the last act that night she had played Hedda with banked-down fury and the desperation of a trapped animal, and even her piano-playing offstage had been "vibrant with despair and doom." So Ben raged as the tour prepared to head south to Detroit, where they would not act, but spend a week rehearsing *Electra* for New York in February.

The company continued to grumble about the bad theatres, the wretched trains in which they either stifled or froze, and the pitiless grind. In Detroit they swore that rehearsals for *Electra* were scrupulously arranged so that no one would have any free time. They howled when informed that the whole *Electra* cast would have to buy their own sandals at eighteen shillings a pair. Battles raged between the Royal Tigerine and the cast, who were under personal contract to her, and between the Royal Tigerine and George Tyler. Company managers joined at Oshkosh and resigned in Peoria. Tyler was breathing hard. "The life of the stage is a hard one," Stella would write years later in understatement; "the sacrifices it demands are enormous. Peaceful normal life is made almost impossible by the ever over-strained and necessarily over-sensitive nerves—caused by late hours, emotional stress, swift thinking, swift feeling, and that odd *reculer pour mieux sauter* which comes upon all public performers." Webster noted that even though Stella was exhausted she would sit up talking until four in the morning on night journeys, "which will kill her shortly I imagine." Strained and sensitive nerves taxed them all.

On Christmas Day they played a matinee and an evening performance at the Valentine Theatre, Toledo, to a tremendous evening attendance. On New Year's Eve in Kalamazoo, Michigan, when Stella tried to send a cable, she was assured that there was no one at the post office since practically the whole town had turned out to see *Hedda Gabler*. Then came Chicago, where they opened at the Garrick on January 6, 1908, and where Stella made instant news when she insisted on a frigid stage and no heat in the dressing rooms. Wrapped in ulsters, the stagehands grumbled; but when she ordered them to wear rubber shoes so they would not tramp about during performances, they positively rebelled.

In Chicago even Ben Webster cheered up. He lunched with Mr. and Mrs. McCormick and told May he found the American rich ever so much more jolly than the English: "they never make you feel their wealth in the way English 'maggots' would." There was an evening at the home of Mrs. Marshall Field (Marshall Field had married Delia Caton after her husband's death, and died himself in 1906) to hear Fritz Kreisler play. Then Webster gave a return luncheon at the Chicago Club for twelve; the newly fashionable cocktails, good wine, and four courses of elegant food cost him $37.

And again fashionable Chicago welcomed Stella and now her children as well with open arms. Stella herself gave a dinner party to twenty-five for her son's twenty-third birthday, with Beo making a speech and toasting his mother of "twenty-one." "Beo and Stella's power of enjoyment is extraordinary," Stella wrote her mother happily. Certainly for Beo Chicago did prove exceptional. Helen Bull, a debutante from a good though not wealthy Quincy, Illinois, family, was invited to balance a table of the younger company members at a dinner given in Stella's honor. If Mrs. Bull had not been prostrated with a nervous attack, her daughter would never have been allowed to attend a party with actors; but Mrs. Bull *was* prostrated and Helen crept out with her sister Margaret for the adventure. "Quaking ecstatically," they were introduced to Mrs. Campbell and the charming Stella Pat and then to a man over six feet tall with "meltingly expressive eyes, beautiful hands, and a voice to charm the Middle-Western birds out of their twangy trees," thought Helen. She did not catch his name, and guessed he was either the husband or the son-in-law of the star until they sat down to chat. Then she discovered that the melting-eyed one was Mrs. Campbell's unmarried son, that he'd been a midshipman in the British Navy, had taken part in the Boxer Rebellion in China, had come over to America "on a lark," and was trying the part of Frank Misquith in *The Second Mrs. Tanqueray.*

The next day Helen was not surprised to open a note from Beo begging her to make one of his party next Friday at one o'clock. *"Do come,"* he wrote. "At the next table will be my mother, my sister, Mrs. Herbert Stone, and 'motley crowd,' but as I started to get [my table] up first I am determined that we shall be 'the observed of all observers'—so *do come.* I am simply existing till Friday week when, if I receive an invitation, I am coming from OSSSKOSSSHSH back to Chicago for the Assembly Ball." Thrilled, Helen accepted and that Friday gorged herself on caviare, mushrooms *sous cloches*, English pheasant and bread sauce, enormous hothouse asparagus, and, for the sweet, a Trojan horse made of spun sugar and filled with giant red strawberries. She found herself quite intoxicated with the handsome and evidently rich young man, never dreaming that Mamma paid all the bills. Before the Campbell party left, Helen saw Beo again with her sister chaperoning, and solemnly received his itinerary with a letter that said a great deal between the lines: "It was charming having you both to tea. . . . I feel quite homesick and a 'throat-lumpy' feeling at the thought of leaving Chicago, or rather the *people* in it. . . . I am full of hope. Please don't forget me, and if you ever find time to drop me a line, do. Oh, I wish, I wish, I wish it wasn't Leap Year and I wish Oh, such a lot of things—but that's no good so I am going to try to work to materialise my wishes. I suppose you think I talk pretty good drivel."

The company left Chicago with rave notices but without young Stella,

who, her mother decided, was worn out and better off staying a week with
Mrs. MacVeagh at her beautiful Lake Shore Drive home, where she could
rest, eat regularly, and be charmingly amused. The fact that Eames Mac-
Veagh had shown enough interest in Stella to deny their engagement in the
papers had not escaped her attention. Mrs. MacVeagh had taken all the
Campbells in charge; now she invited Helen Bull to luncheon with Ethel
Barrymore and Madame Paderewska, scrutinized her, and approved. As
increasingly frequent letters arrived from Beo, Mrs. MacVeagh became
Helen's chief confidante and supporter. Finally one day when Helen was
upside down in a basin shampooing her hair, the phone rang. Although it
was currently twenty-three below zero in Minneapolis, Beo was warm.
Would she marry him? She would, of course.

In February they were all back in New York for joint performances of
*Electra* and *The Moon of Yamato*, a one-act tragedy written for Stella by
Viscount Robert d'Humière. Stella was very apprehensive about undertak-
ing both plays and wanted her daughter to do *Yamato*, but Liebler refused.
She had wanted to do *Electra* ever since seeing it performed in Germany,
and in 1906 had negotiated for Gilbert Murray's translation of Euripedes'
classic. But she had her own vision of the play, and it did not coincide with
that of Vedrenne, Barker, and Murray himself, who insisted that if she
played *Electra* in America, she play it exactly in the Court Theatre version.
"I am so sorry," she wrote Murray after attending a performance, "—you
made me feel you were vexed at what you thought was my want of appreciation & respect. Indeed I wasn't 'talking' I was 'exclaiming' which is a very
different thing. Truly I was a little disappointed here & there. Perhaps the
rhythmic beauty of the lines had to go a little. Then again I had a dream of
dignity & poise—& a colour scheme. I love the play more than I knew I did.
After all I did want to take it all over the world & you & Vedrenne-Barker
wouldn't trust me! Someday when you are an old man & 'Vedrenne-Barker'
is dead with overwork the play will be done again & then you will allow a
white haired old woman to tell the young actors & actresses what she
dreamed when you read her 'Electra' 40 years ago!"

In the end she settled on Sophocles in a double adaptation—Hugo von
Hofmannsthal via Arthur Symons—that emphasized Electra's passion,
anguish, and avenging spirit. Symons's translation "put a magic mist of
loveliness upon it," thought Stella, without harming the realism of the
original. Having seen the Greek chorus done ineffectually at the Court, she
cut it from this version; she also cut many lines, not only of Clytemnestra
and Chrysothemis but of Electra as well. Worried that her inexperienced
daughter as Chrysothemis and her supporting cast were not strong enough,
she cabled to Maud Tree, and that capable actress came from London to

play Clytemnestra. Stella had herself costumed in thundercloud black and, already exhausted, opened on February 11, 1908, with Webster as Orestes to a New York crowding that year to see *The Merry Widow*, not sombre Greek dramas.

"Perhaps there are some actresses whom she does not surpass in imagination, in ingenuity of technique, or in faculty of dramatic invention," judged the *Town Talk* reviewer, "but the fact is, she accomplishes more with her art than any woman of whom I have any knowledge. . . . I seriously doubt whether there is any other woman who can hold an audience from the beginning to the end of that sombre tragedy. . . ." But critical opinion didn't matter; as Stella said, that season *The Merry Widow* won.

Five days later an interviewer from the *Globe* found her in her suite at the Plaza. She was serving tea, her shapely white hands moving among the silver urn and cups. She wore the inevitable black, sitting framed in a window through which frosted trees gleamed against a jagged skyline. On her lap, huddled in a kimono, lay Pinkie, white marbles for eyes. Mrs. Campbell fed it milk. A buxom woman sat nearby, negotiating with Mrs. Campbell for a benefit matinee to assist the crippled children's ward at her favorite hospital. Stella Patrick was there, looking (thought the *Globe*) "quaint, English, mouse-like." Mrs. Campbell was looking particularly worn out. She was weary, weary, weary, she confided, and very discouraged that New York was not coming to *Electra*. "I don't want to go back to *Tanqueray*," she sighed. "It's like post cards after Michael Angelo." Did she have any comment on the public's lack of response? "Just tell them I've worked hard," said Stella. "I wanted to do something beautiful, something noble—and I'm—I'm sorry they don't like me."

Discouraged, she invited the New York theatrical profession to a special matinee on February 18: 2500 people came. Then she broke down, and the Garden Theatre was dark. News that January that her mother was dangerously ill, the strain of her teaching her children to act, the demands of playing both a Japanese and a Greek tragic heroine eight times a week, Beo's romance with Helen Bull, the popular failure of *Electra*—all these burdens were finally too much to bear.

After the New York disappointment, the company set out again for California. On March 19 they were playing *Hedda* in Los Angeles, where Stella found the mild climate with its flowers, birds, trees, and scent of mimosa and jasmine intoxicating after the chill of New York. There the great Madame Modjeska came to see her, writing afterwards to "Mrs. Campbell—beautiful Electra . . . What a tremendous part, and what a wonderful achievement! I am so happy to have seen it, because that thing will live with me. . . . I do not know anyone who could play this part as you play it. Every pose, every modification of voice was perfect, but, what was most wonderful, the feeling, the passion, your own self animating that classic personage and making it a real—a living—suffering creature."

From Los Angeles they travelled north to San Francisco, still showing the ravages of the great earthquake and fire of 1906, although new construction jutted up here and there. They opened with *Tanqueray* at the Novelty Theatre on Monday, March 23, ending on Saturday with a double-bill matinee of *Electra* and *The Moon of Yamato* and *Magda* at night. "For the hour and three-quarters the audience sat breathless," said Stella of *Electra.* "The play appealed to their imagination—and again, as so often before, I was overpraised, spoiled, petted and fêted." In San Francisco the Royal Tigerine showed different stripes when a stage electrician fell ill and she sent immediately for the finest doctors to attend him. But then stagehands generally liked Stella and spoke of her "in a jolly sort of way," considering her "a good fellow sort of woman." Actors in her company, on the other hand, "were forever falling in love with her, suffering tortures, loathing her, forgiving her, and worshipping her once again," observed Ben Webster. Ben was not one of them, although he was not immune to her caprices. Her stage misconduct was still driving him mad. One night in *Hedda* she had the book open and calmly read from it. One night in *Ebbsmith* "I don't think she stopped her silly cackle once during the entire play; but I'm getting used to it now and it doesn't disturb me." Once during a long duologue with Orestes she simply walked off, twice for a drink of water and once for a dispute with the limelight man. Sometimes even Ben could not help laughing. In *Tanqueray* Paula is supposed to complain bitterly about the dull quiet of Aubrey's country house. During a performance in Illinois that was constantly disturbed by the rumblings and hootings of locomotives, "Why," Paula complained, "why did you bring me to live out here, right next to a railway station?"

During the week in San Francisco Stella was entertained by her close friend Harriett Carolan, daughter of George M. Pullman and heiress to his great fortune, who lived with her husband, Francis, at Crossways Farm, a modest thirty-room cottage surrounded by its own hothouses, greenhouses, tennis courts, dog kennels, stables, polo grounds, and fox-hunting trails. Then the company boarded the train again, taking with them at the last minute "a nice little man" recommended as an actor by one of Stella's friends. To their surprise, the nice little man sat up all night in the men's smoker with his overcoat neatly folded over his arm. In the morning he explained apologetically that he did not know how to get into an upper berth. Duly instructed, he clambered up the next night and promptly pulled down the iron curtain rod, cutting open his head. Stella began to scold him in public, telling him it was dishonest to take the job when he'd obviously never toured before. Webster privately agreed, but wished she wouldn't say it so often. The nice little man only bowed his head meekly. In Seattle he disappeared. Eventually they discovered that his only previous experience had been as a lay-brother librarian in a monastery.

From Seattle they set out across the Cascades and the plains, winds howling and snow driving: Walla Walla, Spokane, Winnipeg, Fargo, Grand Forks, St. Paul, Minneapolis, Chicago. Beo saw Helen again, gave the twenty-one-year-old woman her first kiss, and left her to dream of the return of the beautiful young man with the melting brown eyes. "Oh, dear," Beo wrote Harriett Carolan, frustrated at not being able to claim Helen at once, "I wish I was doing something brilliant with a steady income—at present I don't feel worthy to win and wed any woman. But I have a funny nature and I want all I can get out of love and happiness now at once." Stella also had her worries. "And now a secret," she wrote her ailing mother. "Beo has fallen in love with a very beautiful young girl, charming in every way. I send you her little note to me, which will show you what a darling, happy thing she is. She is very fair and tall. The question is, what is to be done? They want to marry. Her people haven't much money. I say nothing; he is so proud and happy, I am afraid of interfering."

In May the company was back in New York, Stella, Beo, and Pinkie to sail the seventh on the *Celtic*—Stella Pat had been called back to London early to play a part in Pinero's *The Thunderbolt* at the St. James's. In San Francisco, Lord Lowndes read of Stella's departure in the papers. Still violently in love with her and having just come into another little legacy, he telegraphed and booked himself a cabin on the *Celtic*. "Lovelit to the very monocle," he surprised her at the gangplank. Stella greeted him with joy. "Take this basket and guard it as you would my life," she said, bestowing upon the hopeful lover a ventilated receptacle. "I'm smuggling Pinkie Panky Poo," she breathed. "Nobody must know she's aboard. Nobody must know that you are my friend and savior. So don't—as once you loved me!—speak to me or show the slightest recognition until we are alone together in England." And she sailed up the gangplank, leaving Lord Lowndes to contemplate a desolate crossing in the company of Pinkie.

The ordeal was over. Stella's devil had ridden her harder than usual during these months that were to have been so happy because she had Beo and young Stella with her. She left with a wail of dissatisfaction at the "uncivil way" she had been treated in America. The country was pitifully behind the times: it had not understood her in Ibsen. The subordinate staff of George Tyler had been particularly odious. She had been absolutely driven from Liebler, and would play next season for David Belasco. And then, being Stella, she could not resist one of those quips that were becoming known as "Mrs. Patigrams." Her son, she told a reporter, was showing great promise in *Electra*. "He is letter perfect"—this with an affectation of great pride—"in his first three lines."

But George Tyler had the last word on the season of the Royal Tigerine. "Not for two hundred thousand dollars," said Tyler, "would I repeat this tour!"

# TWENTY-SIX

## *1908–1909*

*L*ORD LOWNDES succeeded in smuggling Pinkie into England, but he did not succeed with Stella. She returned to find her daughter at the St. James's in a Pinero play, but could comfort herself that Stella Pat's name had not been made overnight there. *The Thunderbolt*, in fact, was not a success; but Stella persuaded Pinero and Alexander to let her take it on tour with Stella Pat retaining her part as Helen Thornhill, the illegitimate daughter threatened with disinheritance by her dead father's acquisitive family. She herself would play the sympathetic Phyllis Mortimore, and for Ann Mortimore she engaged Florence Farr, whose recent experiments with cantillating Yeats's poetry to the psaltery and directing Greek choruses at the Court seemed to put them in the same aesthetic camp.

Relations between mother and daughter were often strained, however. Shaw telephoned Stella Pat to ask whether she would consider the part of Raina in a revival of *Arms and the Man* during the Barker-Vedrenne season at the Haymarket. Stella Pat replied that the *Thunderbolt* tour was set and the parts cast. Well, Shaw told her, she should go upstairs and read the part and think of all the disagreeable things that had happened between her and her mother in the past five years and ring him back if she changed her mind. He tried to get Stella herself on the line, but she was ill; later he broached the subject, however, and Stella fell upon him "in her most governessy mood," calling him names and preaching the bad taste of interfering in her family business. Shaw replied rudely and expected that Stella Pat would have a bad day as a result, although she might find it easier to break loose another time.

Stella had gone to see her mother at St. Leonards almost immediately upon her return, and was shocked to find her so frail. Her apprehension was soon confirmed. On August 4 Louisa Romanini Tanner died of throat cancer and heart failure at the age of seventy-three. Lulo was with her; Stella came when the news reached her on tour. "In death she looked a marble figure of a lovely girl," said Stella, "her black hair scarcely tinged with grey, in two plaits around her head. My beautiful Italian mother!" Her children, especially young Stella, had loved their grandmother; Nina, Edwin, Max, and Lulo had loved her too, but Stella believed that she had set her mother highest and loved her best, and was the best loved. "You are brave, darley, and you work so hard," her mother had always told her and, "Some people have white blood, some people have red—yours is red!" Now, thought Stella, there was no one left to call her "child" any more. For a woman who had so much of the child in her, it was a lonely realization.

The *Thunderbolt* tour ended, she played some matinees in London, then set out again, this time with *Electra* and an engagement to play Yeats's *Deirdre* at the Abbey Theatre in Dublin. Yeats had for years tried unsuccessfully to drop salt on Stella's tail, as he put it; but when Stella had asked for *Deirdre* in 1906, he hesitated. There was a new actress, a Miss Darragh, who was more capable, perhaps, of intellectual tragedy. "I feel that a change is taking place in the nature of acting," he explained to his father; "Mrs. Campbell and her generation were trained in plays like *Mrs. Tanqueray*, where everything is done by a kind of magnificent hysteria (one understands that when one hears her hunting her monkey and her servant with an impartial fury about the house). . . . A new school of acting is now growing up under the influence of the various attempts to create an intellectual drama, and of changes deeper than that." But Miss Darragh had not created a memorable Deirdre, and Yeats now wanted Stella and the prominence she would bring to a production. "Is she really going to come here?" he wrote Florence Farr in September 1908. "I have put *Deirdre* into rehearsal but I have never really believed she would play in it."

Stella arrived for rehearsals at the Abbey Theatre on November 5. Joseph Holloway, diarist and inveterate playgoer, dropped in that morning and found Yeats and Stella Campbell chatting in the scene dock, Lady Gregory talking with actors in the greenroom, and Sara Allgood practising her opening ballad. When rehearsal began, "Yeats kept busily walking up and down in front of the stage, and his gesticulation occasionally sent Mrs. Campbell off in a laugh until she finally had to tell him to sit down. She was quite nice to the players and made many suggestions in an almost apologetic way. She chaffed Kerrigan for not looking at her at all. 'You mustn't like me,' she said. Kerrigan is cast for 'Naisi,' and is much too small in stature for Mrs. Campbell's build. She has to bend down whenever she comes near him. . . . Mrs. Campbell kept going through her part in an intense, suppressed, emotional way, going over and over again some passages which she hadn't as yet quite committed to memory."

*Deirdre* was scheduled for seven performances beginning November 9. "One woman and two men; that is a quarrel that knows no mending," says old King Conchubar—and *Deirdre* is the story of a woman "with too much beauty for good luck" who loves young, strong Naisi and kills herself over his dead body rather than go to the marriage bed of his murderer, the old King. Joseph Holloway was there to comment. ". . . Most of the audience had been attracted to the theatre to see Mrs. Campbell fill the role of 'Deirdre,' and a hush passed over the house as the play commenced, and never was broken until the scene was shut out again from all our eyes. . . . The beautiful speech, exquisite posing, and delicious chanting of Sara Allgood as the 'First Musician' led up to the coming of the ill-fated pair of lovers in truly poetic way . . . so that when 'Deirdre' in the person of Mrs. Campbell appeared, the way had been perfectly paved for her great, well-won success.

"At first her mannered style of delivery and somewhat stooping form did not attract me much, but as the piece progressed one forgot her strongly marked mannerisms, and only saw the baffled woman's fight for death by the side of her loved one, slain by the order of the treacherous king who coveted her body. Her cajoling 'Concobar' into allowing her to attend to the dead body of her beloved 'Naisi' was a supreme piece of dramatic art, full of subtlety and intense emotionalism. Her savage outburst on his refusing her first request was superb in its tigerish savagery; the baffled woman let loose the floodgates of her wrath on the loveless old man who waded through crime to attain her, and annihilated him into submission. . . .

"Mrs. Campbell's 'Deirdre' grew on one until it quite captured by its sheer intensity. When the actress is moved by emotion or passion, her whole body moves in jerk-like wriggles that punctuate her every word. This eternal lack of repose in her acting, to my mind, militates against 'perfect' being applied to her creation in poetic work, where the dignity and repose of tragic grandeur is the coping stone of all classical art." Yet, concluded Holloway, "When Miss Darragh and Miss Mona Limerick filled the title role, they were out of harmony with the company who supported them. It was not so with Mrs. Campbell's rendering. It fitted in perfectly with her surroundings, and a perfectly harmonious whole resulted. She is too great an artist to let herself get outside the picture for a moment. The audience was deeply moved and applauded enthusiastically when all was over. . . . I had a word with Dr. Douglas Hyde on the stairs leading to the vestibule. It was the greatest bit of tragic acting he had ever seen."

After the performance there was a supper for Stella at the Gresham Hotel, after which Judge Ross proposed a vote of thanks to the actress and eulogized her acting in an eloquent oration. Stella responded with a few brief words she had jotted down on the back of a menu card. She said she had grown to love the Abbey company and closed with an attempt to express her thanks in Gaelic that sent the whole table into a roar of laughter. Next Yeats stood up, announced that for once in his life he had nothing to say, and went on to say it at prodigious length. Writing to his friend John Quinn a few days later, he retracted his former doubts about Stella. "*Deirdre* has been played with triumphant success—great audiences and great enthusiasm; and Mrs. Campbell has bought the English and American rights for five years. . . . There has not been one hostile voice here and I am now accepted as a dramatist in Dublin. Mrs. Campbell was magnificent."

After Dublin Stella took *Electra* and *Deirdre* on tour, winning good notices and at Southport creating a stir when a jet of flaming methylated spirit from the torch she was holding high above her head fell on her hair. Being Stella, she was struck by the absurdity of such an accident just when Electra is awaiting the death cry of Agamemnon, and only laughed. As a result, stagehands and actors watching in the wings did not rush forward to help. The audience, however, was horrified. "Will no man save her?" someone shouted, but by this time Stella had beaten out the flames and come down to the footlights. "Please sit down," she said calmly; "this stuff does not hurt." She was not calm next day when local papers reported there had been no danger since the "GREAT ACTRESS ON FIRE" had been wearing a wig. Stella was rather vain about her magnificent black hair, and the wig charge infuriated her. About the real danger she was cool. "I wasn't hurt," she wrote Harriett Carolan from the Victoria Hotel, "—just a little hair burnt and 3 holes in my dress & thank heavens I didn't lose my nerve. You should have heard the audience."

Back in London she decided to try out her Electra and Deirdre in a series of matinees beginning November 27 at the New Theatre. She had apparently become only a matinee performer in London: her repertoire was experimental and matinees were all she could afford. She was comforted to learn that Sir Charles Wyndham and Mary Moore secretly watched her conduct rehearsals from a box and for the first time (as far as she knew) credited her with some sense. Both plays were well received by advanced critics and attacked by old—"the usual reception of intellectual drama in London," noted Yeats. Heading his review "A NEW ACTRESS," Archer was enthusiastic. "Mrs. Campbell has an imagination which requires the magic spark of poetry to kindle it to a creative glow. . . . It is hard to imagine her after such performances as these, relapsing to the mannered prettinesses—the adroit evasions which have so often been her standby in the past." Walkley also acknowledged the new power: "Much playgoing, it may be, makes one callous, but it will be long before we shall think without a shudder of the 'Electra' we saw yesterday . . . a festered lily—something less than a woman, because it is the wreck of what has been more than most women."

Intellectual drama did not pay, and in January 1909 Stella was playing in *Olive Latimer's Husband* by Rudolph Besier, with the powerful and effective Lyn Harding as her leading man. The play took a realistic look at human perversity. Olive is a gentle lady with a dying husband upstairs who never appears in the play. Olive is in love with his doctor, the doctor returns her love, but they are too noble to do anything about it. Upon the husband's death, they discover that he was very much aware of what was going on downstairs and in fact has even written a deathbed note blessing their liaison. Their passion legitimized, Olive and the doctor recoil from each other in horror. But although the acting was praised, the play was too realistic for audiences and critics alike.

Beo meanwhile was doing little besides fretting for Helen Bull, whom Stella had rather hoped he would forget, given his incapacity for supporting a wife. But there was no chance of Beo forgetting. "One night," said Stella, "after an especially long talk we had, I went to his room and sat on his bed—his eyes were full of affection for me, and love and yearning for beautiful Helen; it was more than I could bear. I said, 'Perhaps I could furnish you a little flat with some of the things from here, and make you an allowance for a year—you would have to work hard, ever so hard—American girls only look up to men who work for them, and provide for them well; and for their children.' I kissed him and went back to bed. In the morning early he came to my room, with a smile—'Was it really you, mother, who spoke to me last night, or was it an angel who sat on my bed?' "

That day Beo cabled Chicago that he was coming. Despite her consent, Stella was not optimistic. "I can't refuse," she wrote Harriett Carolan, "but I'm pretty heartbroken about it." Before Beo sailed, William Bull wrote to say that he could not allow his daughter to marry on such conditions. Beo just laughed. Within a fortnight Stella opened a cable: "MARRY ON THE 25TH, MIND YOU DON'T GET A STUFFY FLAT, LOVING BEO." He had asked her—and found her willing—to get him into the Navy, out of the Navy, into Oxford, and on to the stage. Now she was to launch him on married life.

The wedding took place in Helen's grandfather's house in Quincy, with her immediate family and a few friends attending. Beo was impeccably turned out by the best London tailor; the bride wilted (it was the hottest April 29 on record) in a dark crepe-de-chine gown garnished with metallic tulle, and a picture hat of the same tulle dripping with battleship-gray ostrich plumes. After the wedding breakfast the Bulls' faithful servant

Richard drove them to the station to catch the train to St. Louis, where they would pause overnight en route to New York, to sail on May 8 for England. Beo pressed a $10 bill into the old man's hand, but he shook his head. "Better hang on to it, Mister Beo, sir. You'se marryin' Miss Helen and you're goin' to need it more'n me!"

Terrified that they would be taken for bride and groom, Helen sat apart in the observation car assiduously writing thank-you notes, while Beo, dying of the heat but refusing with British obstinacy to remove his coat or loosen his tie, sat staring out of the window. That night in St. Louis they slept on different floors of the hotel because Helen, cursed with soft, stringy hair, not only declined to face her bridegroom the next day without having spent the night in "Magic Curlers," but also declined to let him see her in those "Magic Curlers." Beo courteously yielded. The next morning Helen found a curling iron on her breakfast tray. It was Sunday and all the shops were closed, but the desperate Beo had conjured one up, having no intention of spending a second bachelor night.

There was no one to meet the boat train when it pulled into London, so they took a hansom cab to Kensington Square. While Beo went with the luggage across the Square to their new flat in Abbott's Court, Helen rang the bell of No. 33 and found an affectionate group there to meet her: her mother-in-law, young Stella, Nina Hill and her sons Roy and Francis, and Miss Morris (Morrie), Stella's devoted secretary and slave. There was no Pinkie, but an equally bizarre little beast called Georgina ("Named for Lady Burne-Jones, of course, because she's so well behaved!"). A cold meal waited, and when Beo arrived and sat down to his mutton, Stella gave Helen a tour of the house and Helen, who had expected something shockingly exotic, found herself pleasantly surprised. The dining room and drawing room on the ground and first floors each consisted of a long L-shaped room with a tiny room at the back. These boxes were powder rooms ("Nothing to do with Guy Fawkes, dear") through which, in Queen Anne's day, the family stuck their heads to be powdered. There were two rooms apiece on the top two storeys: Stella's and her daughter's bedrooms on the second, Beo's old room and a boxroom under the roof. Two or three servants slept in the basement next to the kitchen. Although every other room was heated (sometimes) by a small fire in the grate, Helen discovered that the windows were left open all year round. Stella had little patience with her chattering teeth. "Oh, you Americans!" she scoffed. "You're all alike— always blown out with steam heat and oysters!" Each room opened on to a steep and narrow staircase. The bathroom was off the drawing-room landing and Helen was soon acquainted with the sound of used bathwater gurgling noisily through a decorated lead pipe at the rear of the house to irrigate the charming walled garden. The dining- and drawing-room walls were panelled in the original white-painted wood and formed a perfect background for the Burne-Jones paintings, William Morris tapestries, Italian furniture, and Oriental rugs. A particularly cherished bust of Dante stood atop a tall pedestal. Helen thought the dining-room furniture commonplace and the stiffly starched napkins puzzling, but admired the old willow ware, the antique knives and forks with green ivory handles, and the rattail spoons.

But it was time for the new couple to see their own home, so they all trooped across the Square to Abbott's Court. Helen found the flat generously provided with Stella's things and two servants to look after them. And then they were finally left alone, except that Helen, looking about at her mother-in-law's furniture and feeling "the presence" across the Square, was not exactly sure it was *her* home that she'd come to. The new country, the new surroundings, the new British husband—above all, the formidable mother of that husband—left her feeling uncharacteristically dependent.

In the following weeks she marvelled at the immediate and warm acceptance she received in society as Mrs. Pat's daughter-in-law. Invitations flooded in: if they went out for an hour, there was sure to be a fresh batch of orange envelopes when they returned. She met James Barrie and Max Beerbohm, D.D. Lyttelton and the Mackails, Ruby Lindsay and her cousin Lady Violet Manners. Ruby and Letty were her own age and they quickly became close friends, labeling themselves "the Three Hags." The first wedding Helen went to in London with Stella was Ruby's to Major Ralph Peto; and there, too, was Mrs. Potter Palmer over as usual for the season: London accorded her the social prestige New York refused.

Helen quickly discovered that Stella loved a title and that her titled friends loved her. Helen's first large social event was an evening reception at the Duchess of Sutherland's. Following her famous mother-in-law into the room, the bride from Quincy was dazzled by the glittering tiaras and decorations. "That's Lady Marjorie Manners," said Stella, nodding at a lovely girl in scarlet chiffon who had waved. "Come—I'll introduce you. . . . No—wait! You'll have more to talk about with that pale lady in the corner —the one sitting alone. Such a dear creature! She's Mrs. Maybrick the murderess. She was released from prison only last week. It's her first big London party, so *she* feels shy, too."

Fortunately, Helen was saved by the arrival of a kindly-looking old gentleman.

"Dear Lord Esher!" exclaimed Stella. "I want you to meet my new daughter-in-law. She's American—so of course she's dying to tell you all about her bathroom *spigots*."

Inured now to jokes about American plumbing, Helen had also learned to catch Stella's bantering tone.

"How nice to meet a British plumber at last," she said brightly. "I can't wait to compare details."

"Oh, my dear!" cried Stella with a deprecating little scream. "In England we say *de*tails, not de*tails*—unless of course you meant de tail of de fish. Was that it, dear?" By this time an audience had begun to collect, alert for the latest Mrs. Paticism. "I'm having such a hard time trying to understand a word she says," Stella went on plaintively. "I wonder if any of you can translate this for me: 'Waaal, I gues Ah ken hev an ahlive in a glass of watter ef Ah waaant one!' " Laughter. "She's spent all day in her room trying to say 'vahse' instead of 'vaysse,' so she can arrange my poor flowers without killing them." Much laughter. But when the humor at her daughter-in-law's expense threatened to wear thin, Raymond Asquith, the Prime Minister's son, began to take Stella to task, telling her she was making a laughing-stock of herself, not Helen. Actually, Helen admitted, she probably encouraged her mother-in-law, since she always laughed harder than anyone else.

At supper Stella created another sensation. Asked by a footman what she would have to eat, she replied absently without looking up, "Oh, some champagne, I think—and a Belle Elmore."

The footman paled. Belle Elmore had been the wife of the notorious Dr. Crippen, who had quite recently murdered, dismembered, and buried her in small pieces under his pantry floor. (Unlike Mrs. Maybrick, Dr. Crippen was not present this evening; he had been hanged.) Hoping he had not heard correctly, the footman dared to repeat the question.

"But I've told you once, my good man," said Stella, breaking off conversation with her neighbor and looking up, annoyed. "I said a Belle Elmore. Surely you know what a Belle Elmore is! A mixed grill, of course. Marrow-bones, tongue, some liver—brains—kidneys."

The American press reported the incident coast-to-coast. Whatever her mother-in-law did, Helen was beginning to learn, became notorious overnight.

Fortunately for Helen, Stella became involved that summer in a new theatrical project. This time she agreed to produce *His Borrowed Plumes* by Mrs. George Cornwallis-West, the famous American beauty (née Jennie Jerome) who had married Lord Randolph Churchill and remarried in 1900, five years after Lord Randolph died raving mad of syphilis. Jennie told Stella that a London manager had offered to produce her play for £300. Stella pricked up her ears, read it, decided it had certain points of cleverness, and offered to try to pull it together and make a success of it herself. Stella would play the part of Fabia Sumner, a brilliantly successful novelist married to Major Percival Sumner, author of comparatively unsuccessful plays. An adventuress, Angela Cranfield, plots to steal Fabia's husband by stealing the scenario of Fabia's latest novel and giving it to the Major for a play of his own. The unsuspecting Major uses the scenario; the play is produced; the audience explodes into applause and calls for "Author!" By now, however, he has discovered the truth. He reconciles with his wife, then appears before the curtain to announce that she is the real author and that he has been masquerading in "borrowed plumes."

As Stella had hoped, the production quickly took on an exaggerated importance because of the interest royalty and society took in it. At the same time, she intended to do a professional job of it; to her disgust, however, the whole thing became a kind of game. She had put together a distinguished cast: Henry Ainley, the current matinee idol; Dawson Milward; Gertrude Kingston; Winifred Fraser; and Sara Allgood (and, not surprisingly, Stella Pat and Beo). But even the competent cast was not holding the play together, Stella thought. Some of the actors had begun calling it "His Sorrowing Blooms," a dangerous sign.

She did not show her irritation to Jennie. "The rehearsals are getting on," Jennie happily wrote her sister Leonie on June 27, "and this week there are to be two daily. Mrs. Pat has really been an angel, and the Play would not exist without her. . . . I gave a supper party at the Ritz last Friday, too successful for words. . . . Kitty, Ann, Consuelo, Juliette, Violet Rutland, and Mrs. Pat, Stella, Muriel Wilson, Henry Ainley, Yates, Hugh Cecil, Bernstein, Martha Bibesco, Maurice Baring, Milwood (my leading gentleman), Clare, Winston and Jack etc. We kept it up till 2:30 A.M. A hundred wild dances and fandangos . . . everyone taking the floor. . . ."

Despite the party-like atmosphere surrounding its birth, *His Borrowed Plumes* was ready on July 6 at Hicks' Theatre in Shaftesbury Avenue. The house was packed to the ceiling with everybody who was anybody and had found a ticket. Winston Churchill, currently President of the Board of Trade, sat with his mother and stepfather in a box, looking "profoundly nervous." In the opposite box was the Duchess of Manchester, while Prince Francis of Teck, Grand Duke Michael of Russia, the Duchesses of Marlborough and Roxburghe, Earl Howe, Lord Elcho, Lord Charles Beresford, and Margot Asquith studded the audience of celebrities and socialites. Just before curtain a very young girl followed her beautiful mother, the Duchess of Rutland, down the aisle and, before slipping into her seat, turned to face the crowded house, deliberately scanning the faces of the audience. "Ah!" exclaimed Lady Diana Manners happily, blowing kisses in all directions. "Everybody one loves best!"

The four performances were billed as "Mrs. Cornwallis-West's Matinees," Stella's name appearing on the program only in the cast. Dresses
were credited to Madame Arqua, Paquin, Messrs. Liberty, and Jays; ladies'
hats to France Marbot, Paris and London. And it was the hats that chiefly
impressed A. B. Walkley: hats in the audience as well as onstage, for the
theatre was crowded with fashionable ladies who might have written modern comedies come to enjoy the fate of a fashionable lady who actually had.
"These are the occasions that reconcile one to the theatre," wrote Walkley
solemnly. "For a sudden feminine glory invades it and transfigures it, so
that it becomes an exhibition of beauty and elegance; the very latest dialogue on the stage is accompanied by a *frou-frou* of the very latest Paris
fashions in the stalls. . . . In the presence of so many and so beautifully
complicated hats it is, of course, impossible to think of them as mere cover-
ings for the human head. They really fulfil the important office of creating
an illusion about life, like the poetry of Shelley or the music of Debussy.
With their exaggerated brims and monstrous crowns they completely shut
out the dull, the workaday, and the disagreeable. Everything, you feel, is
for the best, and looking its best, and wearing its best, in the best of all Di-
rectoire worlds."

Then Walkley dismissed hats. The most beautiful, the "most suave and
distinguished and arresting thing" in the theatre that afternoon was Mrs.
Patrick Campbell, who wore no hat but a wealth of black hair in a classic
fillet, wonderfully clinging draperies, and, as a neglected wife, the wannest
of smiles. Max Beerbohm was at Hicks' that afternoon as well, and came
away disappointed. He had long hoped that some clever person in the midst
of society would write a real play about the aristocracy. When he heard that
Jennie Cornwallis-West had written a play, therefore, his heart had begun
to thud, his pulses to throb, and his temperature to rise. Mrs. West had lived
in the heart of the *beau monde* for years, she had married one politician
and mothered another, she had that additional asset of foreign birth, which
might have lent objectivity. But alas. *His Borrowed Plumes* was good entertainment for the average playgoer, but it told one nothing real, after all,
about Jennie West's world.

Perhaps it was the rich drift of Stella's dark hair amidst the sea of tulle
and plumes that particularly arrested George Cornwallis-West that afternoon. Perhaps it was the tall, dashing figure he cut in his scarlet coat of the
Scots Guards that particularly attracted her that evening at a celebratory
gathering. According to the sharp-eyed Helen Campbell, George flirted out-
rageously with Stella that night. Helen believed that they met for the first
time at the premiere of *His Borrowed Plumes*, but a few years earlier
Jennie's older sister, Clara Frewen, had written her husband, ". . . Leonie

says Jennie seems so happy and contented, so I do hope George's little flirt with Mrs. Pat Campbell means nothing. . . ." George claimed he first met Stella in the winter of 1908–1909 when she came frequently to the house they had taken in Cavendish Square to discuss Jennie's play. Clara's words raise the possibility that "the little flirt" might have inspired Stella to produce it in the first place. Quite certainly it inspired the following exchange between Fabia Sumner (who much resembled Jennie) and a friend:

> FABIA (*discussing a visiting actress*): You think that she and my husband are too much together?
> JANE: You're so occupied you don't see what all your world does. Among snakes, that woman is a puff-adder.
> FABIA (*with a bitter laugh*): Are you so sure that I do not see—that I don't know?

The flirtation that was plain to everyone at the celebration of Jennie's play soon became something more. "I believed his life was unhappy," said Stella, "and warmly gave him my friendship and affection. . . ."

George was the son of Colonel William Cornwallis-West of Ruthin Castle, Denbighshire, and of Mary ("Patsy") Cornwallis-West—at least officially. Patsy had been a P.B.—Professional Beauty—whose picture gazed out of shop windows along with Lillie Langtry's, Ellen Terry's, and Jennie Jerome's. Like other P.B.'s, she had had an affair with the Prince of Wales. It was widely assumed that George was his child and that by standing godfather Albert Edward had acknowledged a closer relationship. The Cornwallis-Wests were one of those families with more good connections than money. Patsy had succeeded in marrying her daughter Constance to the Duke of Westminster and her daughter Daisy to Prince Hans Heinrich of Pless. George was intended for some wealthy daughter of the nobility, but upset all her plans when, during Daisy Warwick's weekend party for the Prince of Wales, he found himself overwhelmed by Jennie Churchill's considerable glamour and she found herself smitten by the young lieutenant's fair good looks and fine physique. She was then forty-three but, according to George, did not look a day over thirty; he was twenty-five, having been born the same year Jennie married Lord Randolph Churchill.

The marriage was romantic, and George continued adoring for many years. But quite apart from their difference in years, the combination of physical attraction and social ambition did not favor stability. Jennie discovered that the good-looking sport was, as a fellow Scots Guard officer described him, "a bit short on brains." His passions were shooting and fishing; she did not share them. George, on his side, found that his wife dominated him, controlled the money, which, however, she spent far too lavishly, and, worst of all, was so constantly involved in social, literary, and philanthropic schemes that he was overlooked. He added infidelity to his passion for sport. He nursed resentment: he could never be as important as Jennie; he felt emasculated. All these grievances he poured out to Stella in the months following the production of Jennie's play, and Stella was all sympathy. George failed to see that she was very much like the woman of whom he complained.

Meanwhile, Stella had contracted to appear with Beerbohm Tree at His Majesty's in *False Gods*, an adaptation of *La Foi* by Eugène Brieux, the most discussed playwright in France. Tree was cast as an Egyptian high priest, Henry Ainley as a handsome young apostate, and Stella as blind Mieris. "I was curiously uncomfortable in my work in this theatre: a disturbing mixture of domesticity and art, of Society and Bohemia, of conventionality and vagary—irritated me," said Stella. "Besides, I always felt the polite thing to do would be to give up my part to Lady Tree." She had mixed feelings for Tree himself. She thought him tiresome in *jeune premier* parts, insincere in tragedy, but the best character comedian of his day. His method often flustered her: he acted in "flashes" and between those flashes tended to be forgetful and self-preoccupied. He let things go, disappeared at a moment's notice when someone dropped in to chat, amused himself with quips at his actors' expense. When an actress in *False Gods* kept rhapsodizing about the "glorious skay"—"Oh my God!" exclaimed Tree. "Remember you're in Egypt. The *skay* is only seen in Kensington!" Confronted with another temperament, Stella controlled hers. She did not whisper disconcerting remarks under her breath while he acted, or stick pins into him to wake him up. But she could not always resist. Once at supper in the Dome, Tree had bragged expansively about his own triumphs, concluding with the assertion that no woman could be a manager.

"Now, Mrs. Campbell," he said fatuously, turning to her. "Wouldn't you like to be an artist-manager?"

"Yes, I would," replied Stella agreeably. "Would not you, Mr. Tree?"

Tree was a lavish producer, and he gave *False Gods* the full His Majesty treatment, turning it into an Egyptian extravaganza with music commissioned from Saint-Saëns, an elaborate interior set, and a large cast swathed in bandages and bronze greasepaint, posing with perpetually horizontal hands. As Mieris, Stella murmured obscurities like "Nothing is impossible to our gods, but his gods are stronger still." "Spectacle and pessimism," damned the critics, and Brieux himself was so angry at the mutilation that he did not show up at the supper party Tree gave for him in the Dome. Stella disliked both the "sadly cut" play and her part. One evening Graham

Robertson was waiting backstage to talk with Tree. "In the dusk of the wings a wonderful figure moved towards me," said Robertson, "—it was Mrs. Campbell clad in curious mummy-like swathings of black and yellow which clung closely to the shape. She looked magnificent and I ventured to tell her so."

"Nonsense," said Stella briskly. "I look like an elderly *wasp* in an interesting condition."

Following *False Gods*, Tree put on *Beethoven* with a wonderful part for himself but none for Stella. It was decided that she would appear instead as Sonja in the one-act *A Russian Tragedy*. Tree originally intended it as a curtain-raiser, but on opening night he changed his mind and put Stella last. "Following the death of Beethoven and the great Symphony, a Russian spy story was impossible," said Stella. "I was told that Tree not only made his speech, but that the orchestra played 'God Save the King,' and the critics and most of the audience left the theatre before my one-act play commenced!"

As the year drew to a close, Stella looked back on disappointment. Her acting had received familiar praise, but *Olive Latimer's Husband, His Borrowed Plumes, False Gods*, and *A Russian Tragedy* were mediocre vehicles for her powers. She continued to search for new material, however, and in November Yeats came to Sunday luncheon to read her *The Player Queen*. It was an experience that he did not easily forget. Luncheon was scheduled for 1:30, and Yeats was punctual. Toward two Stella appeared, followed by lunch at last. Afterwards she listened with great enthusiasm as Yeats read the first act, only slightly distracted by the squawkings of a green parrot. Encouraged, he launched into Act II, but then a musician arrived. Could she take ten minutes? An hour and a half later Yeats dared to suggest that he had better go and cancel an engagement for that evening. "Oh, *do,*" said Stella with effusive apologies. He returned to the battle at 6:30 to find the musician just stepping out the door but in his place a deaf man ensconced at Stella's side whose sole mission in life seemed to be the imparting of irrelevancies in her ear. Yeats finally managed to get through the second act, and Stella was still enthusiastic; but then the telephone began to ring, and after that there was supper with Stella Pat, Helen, Beo, and various distant relations. As they stood up from the table, Stella's dressmaker arrived. Would Yeats excuse her for just a very few minutes? Presently there was a great commotion overhead and a distraught helper rushed down like a messenger in a Greek tragedy to announce that the dress was a full six inches too short in front. More petitioners had meanwhile gathered in the drawing room. At 10:30 they consulted: should someone be despatched to knock at Mrs. Campbell's door? No one volunteered. The relatives began to discuss the cost of taxis. At 11:30 Stella herself emerged, all contrition: she would only be a few moments longer. At twelve Helen announced that she was leaving and did, taking Beo with her. At half past twelve Stella made a wan entrance, supported by her daughter. "This is absurd!" Yeats said quickly. "You must go to your bed, and I must go home." "No," said Stella, "I must hear the end of a play the same day I hear the beginning." Yeats began the third act, but it was no good. She had forgotten the first two and began to take the play personally, complaining, "No, I am *not* a slut and I do *not* like fools." Yeats gave up and went home to assure her by letter that, though his heroine might be a slut who liked fools, he had not suggested *she* was.

Although her professional life seemed at a standstill, there were private upheavals. From the beginning Helen had not felt in charge of her own marriage, and the impression grew stronger month by month. Stella dropped in rather often, and when she found a table moved, a picture missing, or a chair readjusted, her face would grow tragic. "Oh, dear," she would quaver, "I hoped you'd *like* my taste!" Why, she eventually began to argue, should they not come and live with her? She was so used to her beloved Beo under her roof. It was foolish to keep up two houses and two sets of servants. Beo's room was empty and crying for him. Helen dug in, knowing that they would clash at close range. She also suspected that her mother-in-law knew of the large monthly allowance donated by her Aunt Elizabeth; she guessed that Stella had a pressing need for monthly contributions to her own household, particularly since she was at present "resting." The more hospitable Stella became, therefore, the more Helen stalled, feeling at the same time that resistance was useless.

"One unlucky day," said Helen, "when I'd been using an evil-smelling depilatory in the bathroom, Mrs. Campbell dropped in for tea. She began instantly sniffing and snuffing at the pervasive stench.

"' *Leprosy!*' she cried. 'Of *course!* That poor old man on the first floor! . . . I'd know this frightful smell *any*where! . . . *Leprosy!* Oh, my precious Bimbo! He musn't sleep here another night. . . . Quick, dear—everything must be out before he gets back from golf. . . . Of *course* you can, if you don't waste time arguing. . . . Never mind *them;* just explain and give them a week's wages. . . . No, I can't stay—I shall be sick. . . . Everything's all ready for you at home. I'll have the sheets aired before you get there. . . . Hurry, dear—*hurry!*'

"I hurried. I didn't try to explain. I knew Mrs. Campbell too well by then. If I'd so much as mentioned a depilatory, all London would be told: 'So sad! My little Helen *admits* she's part gorilla.' "

So Stella had her precious Beo back where she wanted him, and he and

Helen crowded into his room under the roof. "Mrs. Campbell" became "Stella" to Helen ("Old Stella" when she rubbed her the wrong way), the sister-in-law "little Stella" or "young Stella." The mother-in-law had won, and now she set about teaching the uncouth American British manners and British idiom. "I saw Lady So-and-So on the street this afternoon," Helen might announce innocently. "I'm not surprised!" Stella would exclaim until the offender changed prepositions. Young Stella, on the other hand, was slipping out of her mother's hands. She had played successfully in *The Prisoner of Zenda* and had a solid success in Alexander's revival of *The Importance of Being Earnest* that November at the St. James's. Worse yet, she was in love, and not at all with the kind of man her mother had planned for her. Mervyn Beech, eldest son of the Reverend Howard Beech of Great Bealings, Suffolk, was a young District Commissioner in the Colonial Service in East Africa. He had come home on a fortnight's leave, met Stella Pat, and fallen instantly in love. Now he wanted to take her back to Africa to live. Hurt and angry, Stella opposed the match. She could not believe that her daughter would give up the now desirable stage career and her brilliant social connections. Most of all, she could not believe she would defy her mother. "In my anxiety for her happiness," said Stella, "I appeared wanting in loving sympathy." It was an understatement.

At the same time, she herself was growing more and more involved with George Cornwallis-West. He, in turn, was enraptured with her beauty, her comparative youth (she was only ten years his senior), her brilliant conversation and agile wit. More than this, Stella encouraged him, fortifying the ego that Jennie threatened. She urged him to write plays, novels; she would produce and star in his plays and make him famous. George recognized her as another powerful woman, but believed her supportively, not crushingly, strong. Stella recognized the weakness behind the good looks and charm, but it was an attraction.

She had not counted on the talk her liaison with Jennie West's husband would excite, however. In mid-January 1910, with no firm engagement, she suddenly decided to go to America. Leaving Georgina behind with Morrie and her daughter with the despised Mr. Beech, Stella sailed on the nineteenth with "only a strong desire to get away from England—and gossip."

# TWENTY-SEVEN

# *1910–1912*

O N MY ARRIVAL in New York," Stella relates, "I telephoned to Mr. Norman Hapgood, saying, 'Here I am. I have quite a good one-act play and a lovely frock, and I would be glad of a vaudeville engagement. What shall I do?' "

Disguising any shock at this departure from serious theatre, Hapgood told Stella to ring up Albee, head of the circuit. She did so; told him she would act twice a day and wanted £500 a week. It was a large salary, but she badly needed money and knew she could not last long playing twice a day on the road. Albee replied that she must play a week outside of New York first; if she proved a draw, he would engage her at her price for ten weeks. She played, drew, satisfied him, and opened in New York at the Colonial on Valentine's Day in the twenty-minute Russian spy drama, newly titled *Expiation*.

Alan Dale had never liked Stella, but now he capitulated. "MRS. PATRICK CAMPBELL TAKES NEW YORK BY STORM," announced that hyper-critical man. Vaudeville audiences, noted Dale, were not like theatre audiences: vaudeville audiences waited to see and had to be shown. Well, she had shown them. Physically, of course, she'd grown a trifle stout. But the shoulders were still wonderful; and the moment when she turned her back to the audience and clasped her hands above her head, making them express all her throbbing emotion—well, that had been pure enchantment. (Stella was quite aware of the power of that pose: "I can hold an audience as long as I want to with my back.") Applause swept the house at the curtain, and Mrs. Campbell appeared and made a gracious speech praising her new audience. Her conquest was the more unexpected because everyone had predicted that the great Mrs. Pat with her high notions about "art" would not last a minute in vaudeville. Interviewed by Dale, she proved totally amiable. She admitted frankly that she had joined the circuit for money. "I don't flatter myself that I will 'elevate' vaudeville; in fact, it doesn't require any elevating." Dale was impressed. Mrs. Pat was "a conversational true-penny" if he'd ever met one: she said exactly what she meant.

Stella had also brought along a one-act play by Beo called *The Ambassador's Wife*. When the tour looked as though it was going to be profitable, she sent for Beo and Helen, Beo to act the role of a revolutionary in *Expiation* and that of a condemned prisoner in his own playlet, which she decided to try out on Chicago. What she really wanted was to do repertory at the New Theatre in New York. On February 19 she lunched with Norman Hapgood and some other theatre people at the City Club to discuss a possible season in New York. But meanwhile there was the vaudeville tour, so the three packed their bags for Cleveland, Toledo, Keith's Vaudeville in Philadelphia, a return engagement at Keith and Proctor's Fifth Avenue Theatre, and then, billed as "England's Greatest Actress," Easter week in Chicago at the Majestic.

In Chicago there was a reunion with one of her most enthusiastic admirers. "Make love to me if you must," she had told critic Ashton Stevens, "but not in a newspaper—it detracts from the value of your criticism." Stevens found her now at the Virginia Hotel, lying on a divan, smoking mild cigarettes and wrapped in a gold kimono with a "border black as her stygian hair." If she felt vaudeville a loss of face, Stella was not admitting it; she praised the players as "simple, sincere, and devoted to their art," and called vaudeville itself "refreshing." Then suddenly, as one questions an old friend: "Tell me, am I at all oldish or wrinkled?" She had turned forty-five that February and was involved with a man of thirty-five. Of course Stevens protested that she was as glamorous as ever, and Stella was perhaps comforted for the moment. Yet luncheon that day might have consisted of quantities of oysters, *pâté de foie-gras*, turkey breasts, frog legs, canvasback duck, pudding, and a sweet—not precisely a diet for a woman concerned with her figure.

Leaving Beo and Helen behind, she started working her way back to Boston. "Oh, those two performances of *Expiation!*" groaned Stella. "I had to kill a man twice a day and shriek—and it had to be done from the heart—the Americans see through 'bluff'—and I was advertised as a 'Great tragic actress'!

"One day—I forget in which town—it was time to get up and think about the morning performance. I found I was unable to make any effort to move. My maid rang the telephone for the Hotel doctor—I tried to speak; it was impossible, I could only cry. 'No more acting; away to Canada, to St. Agathe des Monts, and stay there until your nerves are mended,' said the doctor.

"And I went, and there I remained alone, unutterably sad—walking about that lovely place. Canaries—sand—glorious sunsets—no paths, planks of wood—fields of large white daisies with millions of fireflies—flat patches of water reflecting the sky. . . ." Stella stayed at St. Agathe in Quebec for ten days; heard with shock and sadness of the death of Edward VII on May 6; then travelled back to Chicago to rejoin the children.

In Chicago Stella could do no wrong. Years earlier when Phil Burne-Jones's "Vampire" had been exhibited to hostile response, her loyal socialite friends had indignantly demanded its removal. Here, then, was the best place to offer Beo's play. During rehearsals at the Majestic a former protégé sought her out. Having scored solidly in plays like *Becky Sharp*, *Hedda Gabler*, and *Leah Kleschna* with Mrs. Fiske, George Arliss still had not attained stardom and actually felt in danger of fading into obscurity. Now, however, he sensed he might have something important in hand. Backed by George Tyler, the prolific and successful Louis Parker was in the process of creating a vehicle based on Arliss's own inspiration, a play about Disraeli. Arliss and Stella paused to have their picture taken with Beo, looking over the manuscript of *The Ambassador's Wife*—Stella in black walking habit, white waist, and large hat loosely hung with a black veil, Arliss with the habitual monocle screwed into his eye, and Beo modestly gazing at the manuscript in Arliss's hand.

Beo had a good deal to be modest about. It did not help *The Ambassador's Wife* that it was sandwiched between the Four Floods, Acrobats Extraordinaire, and a brilliant group of trained seals; yet, had the play had any merit, Stella's acting could have put it across. As it was, "A feeble effort," the Chicago *News* decided; "her talented offspring cannot write a play." Still, audiences and mother were indulgent. "It was quite a success in its way," recorded Stella diplomatically, "and gave them both great encouragement."

The tour over, Stella left Beo and Helen in a small furnished apartment on East 19th Street in New York, sublet to them by Theda Bara, and sailed for England with no engagement in prospect. She arrived at Kensington Square to find her daughter as determined as ever to marry Mervyn Beech, even though she continued to have acting engagements in London. Did she, Stella demanded, intend to throw everything over and go to live in Africa with savages? But the usually submissive daughter was unusually stubborn about Mr. Beech.

Winifred Beech (Mervyn's sister) had managed to win Stella over, however. "I was fascinated with her mother's beauty, her voice, and her unaccountability," said Winifred, just young Stella's age. "She was always very kind to me and loved playing with my hair, which she would twist and plait and arrange in fantastic fashion. She was to me an absorbing study, 'a bundle of contradictions, a mass of incongruities'; for one hour sweet, gentle and considerate, and during the next . . . utterly unreasonable, dismissing the servants for the slightest peccadillo and pleased with nothing." Expecting an actress to be carelessly bohemian, Winifred was continually amazed at Stella's meticulous neatness. Yet domestic details could madden her. "I can see her now," said Winifred, "entering Stella's bedroom, her great tragic eyes smouldering, and declaiming passionately—'They tell me there is no more toilet paper in the house. How CAN I be expected to act a romantic part AND remember to order TOILET PAPER!' "

Stella Pat and Mervyn had coaxed a reluctant Winifred to break the news that they intended to marry in Nairobi. It was arranged that Mervyn take Stella Pat out to supper so that Winifred would find Mrs. Campbell alone at Kensington Square. Stella was eating her own supper when Winifred arrived and cautiously broke the news. Stella regarded her with a pitying stare; then, picking up a large cucumber from the table, viciously whacked off the end as though she wished it were someone's head. She then began to point out the mad impossibility of the plan.

"Your brother," she said, "may be a very delightful and brilliant man, but you don't know Stella as I do. She is accustomed always to be the centre of the stage both in social and theatrical life. She could never take a back seat, efface herself, and help a man with his career. There is an undercurrent in Stella of which everyone but her mother is unaware. She may think her world 'well lost for love,' but she would soon get bored with the life of East Africa, pine for London, and make your brother's life miserable. It would be pure folly for her to attempt such a sacrifice—for to her it *would* be a sacrifice and not"—smiling satirically—"the crowning joy of her life as marriage ought to be. Then your brother," she continued, "has scarcely any private means—only his salary in the Colonial Civil Service. I own that it is a good one, but if anything happens to him? I can't give Stella an allowance. I have worked very hard to give my two children an exceptional education and advantages, and now . . . they must fend for themselves. I know exactly what will happen if Stella marries your brother. He will die after one week leaving her with seven babies." She carved another bit of cucumber into seven neat pieces. "Darling," interrupted Winifred, "isn't that rather quick?" Stella permitted a smile to touch her lips; then, finishing off the cucumber, moved to a comfortable chair, lit a large black cheroot, and lectured Winifred in similar strain for another hour.

Having done her duty, Winifred kissed Mrs. Campbell's rather chilly cheek and left, exhausted and depressed. Stella and Mervyn must now fight their own battle. This they did during that summer of 1910, and Stella found herself unwillingly succumbing to their enthusiasm, their romantic stubbornness, and to Mervyn's beautiful hands and smile. "But although she eventually was obliged to accept the position," said Winifred, "her attitude towards it was ever reluctant and discouraging. Always she hoped that the fires would flicker out as quickly as they had blazed into being."

As crucial as her daughter's choice of a husband was her own choice of a new play, for the summer passed and there was nothing to do in London. She finally appealed to an old admirer; Pinero replied cautiously: "I don't know what I shall turn to after I've finished a little light play upon which I am now engaged; but should I become possessed of an idea leading in your direction I should be delighted. By-and-by, when I come back to town, I will ask you to let me have a talk with you. You are now docile, you say. Well, I have never found you anything but a good comrade; and as for wrinkles, the only wrinkles I can associate with you are those which, through your great intent, you are bounteous enough to give to others."

But "by-and-by" was not very satisfactory, and so she asked Gilbert Murray for his translation of *Medea* for seven West End performances in November, and afterwards America ("Please treat this as quite private"). Then *Medea*, or the money, or a theatre was not available after all. For fun she took part in a tableau written by D.D. about St. Ursula and the eleven thousand virgins. Cynthia Charteris Asquith played the young saint, her heavy red-gold hair falling to her knees, and Stella visited her in angel wings. The pretty little performance was given several times at the Court Theatre, where young men roared applause for the aristocratic beauties and sent them bouquets and baskets. "Mrs. Campbell I loved to distraction," said Diana Manners, assigned the task of representing a thousand of the virgins. "I saw no beauty in her because she was always telling us she was 'older than God.' She had beautiful hands that liked giving. I see them fondling her horrible little griffon Pinkie-Ponkie-Poo, and snatching necklaces from her neck to put on to mine."

Nigel Playfair, who had asked her to be godmother to his first child, came round to Kensington Square, but although he might have helped, Stella was not dressed for visitors and would not come down. "I did hope you would come back," she wrote him with the frustration of an actress out of work. "Indeed indeed I don't want to go to America heaven knows, but I must 'go on' & here I am not wanted & I cannot afford to rest." Finally America was the only answer—an engagement at the Knickerbocker Theatre under Charles Frohman's management playing Fanny Armaury in *The Foolish Virgin*, Rudolph Besier's translation of Henri Bataille's *La*

*Vierge folle*. On November 2 she sailed from Liverpool on the *Adriatic* for her sixth American tour, whisking Stella Pat out of harm's way by taking her along for company.

It is better to travel in hope, goes the saying, than to arrive. Although *La Vierge folle* had been a Paris success, Stella did not like the English version. "At Mr. Frohman's request the play was much altered," she said, "the religious argument being entirely eradicated, thereby making it simply a story of a wife chasing a husband, who was enjoying life away from her with a 'foolish virgin.' At the end of the play the poor girl, overhearing the wife's appeal to her husband, shoots herself. In the French it is a fine play; the religious argument against the wilful destruction of the virgin soul, and the wife's belief in her duty to be of spiritual help to her husband, give dignity and some excuse to the ugliness of the story. The Americans disliked the play intensely."

Stella made better press appearing with her daughter and Mrs. Benjamin Guinness at a dog show at the Plaza, or pictured in *Vogue* with Georgina, or giving a thrilling recital, in a large black hat with flowing plumes, of Jean Ingelow's "High Tide on the Coast of Lincolnshire" at Maxine Elliott's Theatre—a benefit matinee for the Downtown Day Nursery and the Catherine Lorrillard Wolfe Art Students Club. And she had a better time at the Washington Square home of her dear friends the Guinnesses, or at the Hapgoods' home, the closest thing in New York to a French salon, where theatre and society people mingled for witty chat. Stella and Norman Hapgood had become good friends largely on the strength of their very different theatrical tastes. Hapgood thought Stella the essence of *fin de siècle*, nobody approaching her interpretation of that important phase of drama that had begun with Ibsen and now seemed to be drawing to a close. She was unique in that nobody else could quite fill the place she filled. Stella clashed with his championship of Shakespeare, arguing that for her Shakespeare was unreal and lacked her kind of poetry, refinement, and finesse. One night she had entered a theatre late, not sure what the play was, and heard the words "the foul womb of night." *"That,"* Stella told Hapgood in tones that evinced anything but admiration, "was Shakespeare."

It was at the Hapgoods' too that she met another personality who intrigued her because he was her opposite, a dark, rosy-cheeked young fellow whose hit play, *Salvation Nell*, had made him the lion of the season. The shy, modest Edward Sheldon and the flamboyant Stella took to each other immediately, and promptly became good friends.

Young Stella made her own headlines with the announcement of her wedding the coming June in Nairobi, to Mervyn Worcester Howard Beech. Although it was not clear where she would find acting opportunity in East

Africa, the press claimed that she would not, as previously reported, give up the stage. Stella Pat sailed back to London early, where, in February, Beo sent her good wishes from New York. He hoped to goodness he and Helen could get back before she sailed; he was just beginning to realize how much he loved and would miss her. Stella herself had given up. "I could not refuse my consent to her marriage any longer—my lovely sensitive girl," she said. But she was very unhappy with her daughter's decision: "I understood at last the cry my mother gave 28 years before."

Although Rudolph Besier's translation of *La Vierge folle* had done Stella little good, she was still interested to hear that he had written a play for her called *Lady Patricia*. Leaving failure behind, Stella returned to London in March, arriving the day before the first rehearsal at the Haymarket. Lyall Swete, who had loved her in the old days of *Tares*, was producing the comedy, her first since *The Canary*; and from the beginning the play promised success. "The Soul of Patricia," wrote Stella on the leaf of her prompt copy, and rehearsals went without catastrophe. She liked Swete; he found her patient, forbearing, and helpful. The supporting presence of Stella's friend Rosina Filippi and a tractable leading man, Arthur Wontner, also promised well, and after the first performance on March 22 everyone knew they had a hit.

She swept onstage in a gown of mist-gray chiffon over satin gleaming with moonlit beads and crystals to parody a member of the "Souls"—a female Bunthorne of exquisite sensibility. The press greeted her elegant mockery with a unanimous shout of delight. "Every bit of it flashes and sparkles," enthused the *Daily Telegraph*, "and not one of the diamonds is paste." Lady Patricia herself was "altogether joyful. Mrs. Patrick Campbell played her excellently, consummately." Mrs. Campbell, said Walkley, had not had such a chance for revelling in the comic spirit for years; she made "the most delicious, absurd, fascinating, and fantastical of mock-heroines." Not only was Mrs. Campbell in top acting form, said another critic, she looked "as graceful, young, and beautiful as when London was first fascinated by her Mrs. Tanqueray." In town for the season, Alan Dale positively raved: "At last Mrs. Pat has come into her own. . . . Lovely . . . the only thing that's kept me awake and smiling."

She was the delight of London, her Lady Patricia the word of the day, an extended run stretched before her, money was coming in steadily. But Stella had a devil. In the first week of the run she began to fool, this time picking on Athene Seyler, who was scoring a first success. Two nights running Stella threw her the line "What a pretty face!" instead of "Will you come in to dinner?" unnerving the comparatively inexperienced and comparatively plain actress. Athene waited for the third "What a pretty face!" It came the next night, and at the line she deliberately made a grimace like a naughty boy's which got a big laugh from the audience. That was enough for Stella, who was not going to feed laughs to anyone. She backed down, made a great friend of Athene, and began to invite her to her dressing room between acts, where she would read Keats and Tennyson to her "quite divinely."

She could not afford to fool. *"Private*—My dearest read this letter carefully & whatever answer you give me I BEG you to let it make no difference to the sincere & warm love I have for you—& the affection you have for me," she wrote Harriett Carolan on April 25, five weeks into the run.

"I am in *real* money troubles & I want you if you can to lend me £200 until Christmas—it's just possible I can return you half of it before Christmas—it depends a little on the success of this play. I have many dear friends who would help me if they could but they are poor—& you know how hard up everyone is over here.

"Dear Harriet—forgive me if I am presuming on your dear generous nature. It hurts me to ask you—but my salary is claimed by my creditors & my present means & Stella's coming marriage all help to make things *dreadfully difficult*. Forgive me for asking you & don't please love me less."

Stella could make or break a production. Desperate as she was for money, she perversely set about committing Lady Patricide in the coming weeks. She began to fool in earnest. Taking a sudden dislike either to Besier or to her part (he never knew which), she began to pull tricks—turning her back to the audience, keeping up a running commentary (not necessarily under her breath), walking off in the midst of another actor's speech, inventing her own dialogue. As a result, *Lady Patricia* fell to pieces and had to be withdrawn a few weeks later.

Perhaps she would have argued, with her incorrigible logic, that she wanted to be free for the festivities. In any event, she had made herself so. This June London was as lively for the coming coronation of George V as it had been sombre the previous June over the death of Edward VII. One of the most spectacular events took place on June 20 at the Albert Hall: the Shakespearian National Theatre Ball arranged by Jennie Cornwallis-West to raise funds for a Memorial Theatre. Six hundred of the cream of society costumed themselves in authentic Tudor satins, velvets, and ermines, and danced beneath a painted blue Italian sky until dawn. If George had reason to complain of Jennie's ignoring him before, he had more reason now, for Jennie had thrown herself into the task of making the ball a success and, even more, into her "Shakespeare's England" exhibition, complete with the Globe Theatre, Sir Francis Drake's ship the *Revenge*, jousting tourneys, and galas at the Mermaid Tavern. To help raise money for the cause,

Jennie asked George to approach the wealthy, widowed Mrs. Leeds for £50,000, and George found himself in the delicate position of asking his mistress to help his wife. For comfort these days he turned increasingly to the charmingly sympathetic Stella, who, after all, may have killed *Lady Patricia* so that she could spend her evenings with him.

She did not participate in one notable event—the Women's Coronation Procession on June 17, even though bands of actresses under the pink-white-and-green banner of the Actresses' Franchise League joined the more than forty thousand demonstrators for votes for women. She had not joined the A.F.L., founded in 1908 (with Forbes-Robertson in the chair) chiefly to demand equal pay for actresses, and now extending its activities in support of suffrage organizations like the N.U.W.S.S. and the Pankhursts' W.S.P.U. Even the apolitical Ellen Terry belonged to the League, drawn in by her militant daughter, Edy Craig; but Stella held aloof. Like many women who had fought their way to the top on their own, she could be ruthlessly Darwinian; she was besides an anarchist who could not be organized. In this self-imposed isolation, she then imagined that she was excluded from progressive causes, just as she had felt excluded from the elitist Ibsen movement. In a sense, she was literally excluded: since she had become a touring actress, she had little contact with West End actresses as a group. Then, too, causes were apt to be distressingly unfashionable, peopled by earnest, dowdy types who held noisy meetings in dingy halls—hardly her milieu. Yet she was capable of regretting uninvolvement. "The best thing in this world is to be a useful woman—that's what *I* am not," she could say, "—and the next best to be a kind woman, and I am not even that."

Pomp, pageantry, flares, and fireworks marked the Coronation on June 22; five days later at His Majesty's the acting world paid tribute with a Gala. Everyone finally took part, thanks to the efforts of Lena Ashwell (that "profoundly uninteresting young person," according to Pinero), one of the most militant members of the A.F.L. Discovering that the Gala program had been drawn up with parts for all the leading actors, but for only two or three actresses, Lena appealed to the Managers' Association to include out of common courtesy a play in which the actresses might appear. She got no response until she wrote and threatened to send a letter of protest to Queen Mary; then she was allowed twenty-four hours to round up a play and a female cast. Luckily, she had already produced Ben Jonson's masque *The Vision of Delight*; she found actresses eager to participate; and the masque ended the memorable Gala evening. As her contribution, Stella recited the prologue, delivering the verses "with admirable balance and sweet cadence," while Lily Brayton, Lena, Marion Terry, Evelyn Millard,

Lilian Braithwaite, Constance Collier, Gertrude Kingston, Lillah McCarthy, Evelyn D'Alroy, and Marie Löhr charmed the audience as Delight, Phantasy, Peace, Grace, Laughter, Love, Harmony, Revel, Sport, and Spring. All this and more Stella Pat missed as she exchanged vows with Assistant District Commissioner Mervyn Beech in Nairobi to become, as she discovered, "the seventieth white woman in Africa." But she had escaped Mam*ma* at last.

Having thrown away a *tour de force* in *Lady Patricia*, Stella was now forced to tour. Vaudeville had paid in America, and she signed on for an autumn tour of the music halls in a one-act play called *The Bridge*. The bridge in this case was to be blown up by Olga Weather and her Nihilist lover, Ivan, in order to wreck a train carrying a certain Grand Duke responsible for the death of Olga's husband. In the course of the destruction Stella was to run the gamut of her powers as an emotional actress. Before she left, Martin Harvey called her to the Lyceum for a few matinees of *Pelléas and Mélisande*, with Arthur Wontner from the *Patricia* cast playing Golaud. Then Stella set out for the Brighton Hippodrome to try her luck with music-hall audiences. Her reception there and at the Palace in Manchester was lukewarm, but audiences were more cordial in Glasgow, Newcastle, Sheffield, and Leeds. It was money, badly needed money, and, moreover, she had a play to come back to.

*Bella Donna*, Robert Hichens's incredibly popular novel, had been made into a play by J. B. Fagan. George Alexander had sworn he would never let Stella Campbell inside his theatre again, but now he had *Bella Donna* and there was only one actress who could play the lead. Gritting his teeth, he had Fagan send Stella the novel; she replied to Fagan that she had tried to read it, "but threw it into the slop pail." Alexander could not afford to feel relieved. He would have preferred *anyone* else to Stella Campbell, but, as Fagan's actress wife, Mary, admitted: *"There was no one to touch her."* Alexander sent her the script. Chastened by financial worries, Stella accepted and the St. James's braced for her arrival.

Fagan had made a workmanlike rather than inspired version of Hichens's exotic tale. Since Stella had thrown the novel into the slop pail, she did not know what the playscript lacked of the original. Nevertheless, she insisted at the outset that the first act be rewritten and that Hichens, not Fagan, do the rewriting. Alexander disagreed. Perhaps because the Coronation Honors List in June had elevated Alexander to Sir George, mere silence followed his refusal. Then Stella's eye fell upon Gerald Lawrence, engaged to play her millionaire Egyptian lover.

"You must try to *change* his appearance," said Stella to Hichens, glaring at the terrified actor. "You must put a *tarboosh* on his head!"

Hichens consulted the discomfited Lawrence. "Anything for the good of the play!" he laughed nervously, and was promptly fitted with the headgear.

"Good heavens!" cried Stella. "Now he looks like an ice-cream man! Take it off—take it off!"

The tarboosh came off, leaving Lawrence's hair standing on end.

"Gracious goodness!" exclaimed Stella, widening her eyes. "Now he's just like a black beetle!"

Privately, Lawrence confided to Hichens that it would rather tax him to play the lover to a lady who held his looks in such low esteem. Hichens agreed that it might, and went to Sir George. The play would be wrecked unless a new lover were found; Mrs. Campbell could not be replaced: Lawrence could. Alexander pointed out that Lawrence was under contract and that he could not afford to pay two Egyptian lovers; desperate, Hichens agreed to pay half the black beetle's salary. As a result, the handsome Charles Maude was hired, Stella accepted him, and rehearsals got under way again until Stella discovered that in the temple scene she was expected to ride off on a donkey. "You expect *me* to ride an *ass!*" she asked Alexander indignantly. Alexander ventured to point out that Jesus Christ himself had done so, but this was scarcely argument enough for Stella. The donkey left the cast.

*Bella Donna*, the story of an adventuress who tries to poison her husband but is foiled by a conscientious doctor, opened on December 9, 1911, and although the sensational play did not add to Alexander's artistic reputation, "The smart world was interested," said Stella, "and the play made a small fortune." It elevated Robert Hichens, as the *Tatler* blared, to "the Man of the Moment Who Possesses an Unrivaled Knowledge of 'The Eternal Feminine' "—which meant that Stella had lent the role all her usual enchantment.

Stella called Hichens "a man with the eyes of a devil and the voice of a curate." Forgetting his earlier raptures, Hichens labelled her "the Queen of Snobs," feeling that she always snubbed him in society. They reconciled when he took her after the premiere to supper at the house of her old friends Lord and Lady Wemyss. "She amused the company by pretending that she hated the rôle of Bella Donna and was certain that her public would think her an abominable woman because she played it so well!" said Hichens. "We all tried to reassure her, but she bemoaned her cruel fate and said that nothing but the large salary she earned had induced her to play it. 'Even Uncle Hitch,' she exclaimed, 'is beginning to believe I'm a bad woman! What a curse it is to be poor! I should like to play nothing but *saints*—but they won't let me!' "

Graham Robertson agreed with Stella about the play's merits. *Bella Donna* "was only memorable for Alexander's clever performance as the

Jewish doctor and for one of Mrs. Campbell's great moments, which occurred within two minutes of the fall of the curtain. The Beautiful Lady (a
sordid adventuress), her schemes thwarted, her beauty a wreck, her career
at an end, walked up the stage and out through a gate at the back. That was
all. What the actress did to get her effect I have no notion and I doubt if she
had. Her face was hidden, she never paused or looked round, but the
audience sat frozen—they had seen a living soul pass into hell." The exit
became one of Stella's famous moments, to rank with Paula's deliberate,
sensuous peeling of grapes—"I like fruit when it's expensive"—or the way,
as Paula, she stumbled back, loose at the knees; or the moment Magda
enters her home and sees at a glance its impoverished provincialism; or
Mariana's recital of being snatched up in her mother's arms to her lover's
urging of "Be quick! Be quick!" when, said critic James Agate, she struck
"the note of extravagant importunacy, of pleading for more than life can
hold, of childish mutiny, of animal distress" simply by the intonation of the
voice and a way of turning the head "to give the wonderful sweep of throat
and chin."

"I saw this wonderful and fascinating actress in *Bella Donna* with Sir
George Alexander," confirmed Margot Hamilton. "I could not keep away
from it—twice when I went there were screams from the dress-circle and
the gallery, the play was so realistic. . . . The last scene of all remains very
vividly in my mind. Mrs. Campbell is alone, and the scene is in mime. On
the right is the house of the Arab she was in love with. On the left through a
gate can be seen the desert, with the Nile and the dahabeeyah in the distance.
She gives an agonising look at the house and very slowly goes through the
gate out into the desert. I cannot tell you how dramatic it was."

On the other side of the curtain Stella and Alexander picked up their
feud where they'd left it, Alexander for a second time refusing to speak to
her at all. One evening, however, he was told that she was fooling away a
scene with her stage husband, so he slipped into an unoccupied box to
watch. To his horror, he discovered that all through the intensely dramatic
episode she was amusing herself by flicking chocolates at the backcloth,
punctuating the tense conversation with a series of plonks as the chocolates
hit the star-studded sky and plopped into the River Nile. Furious, Alexander forgot he was not speaking to his leading lady, dashed backstage, and
confronted her at the end of the scene. "I see you are angry," said Stella,
eyeing him calmly as he clawed the air and gnashed his teeth with rage.
"Your wife would not like me to speak with you when you are angry. She
says it upsets your digestion." Sweeping past the inarticulate manager, she
sailed to her dressing room and locked the door. He wrote her a letter;
she returned it unopened.

This last straw caused Alexander to finally reject Bernard Shaw's play about a professor of speech and a cockney flower girl. During the run of *Bella Donna*, Alexander and Shaw had met between acts. Alexander had asked for a play; Stella Campbell needed a play. Shaw had had a play in mind for her since the Forbes-Campbell partnership, and he went home now to write it. In June 1912 he was able to propose a reading for Alexander and Stella, but Alexander asked to hear it alone. When Shaw, a masterly reader, had finished, Alexander spoke. "That play is a cert, a dead cert. Now listen to me. I will get you any actress you like to name for the flower girl. I will pay any salary she asks. You can settle your own terms. But go on for another play with Mrs. Campbell I will *not*. I'd rather die." Why couldn't he work out the part of Eliza Doolittle so that some other actress could play it? suggested Alexander. But Shaw rejected the notion: if he watered down Eliza, then Professor Higgins would be simply a brute. He must have Mrs. Campbell for the sheer balance of the thing. But Alexander shook his head, and Shaw took his play away.

Offstage, life also had its tempestuous moments. While Beo and Helen were still in New York, George Cornwallis-West had found his way there, and during his stay was operated on for an internal ailment. Stella sent Helen urgent letters, asking her to visit him every day and send her progress reports. This Helen obediently did, taking hour-long streetcar rides to the hospital in the sweltering New York summer days; but avenged herself by falling in love with George's golden charms. Then Stella wrote, pleading loneliness: she wanted Beo and Helen back with her at Kensington Square. They came, and Stella learned about Helen's little hospital romance. It did not make relations between them smoother. "One day I went up to my room at the top of the house, left the door open, and screamed myself hoarse for five full minutes," said Helen. "Stella was in the room below, but she made no attempt to find out if I were being raped or murdered. No doubt she thought either would teach me a lesson."

"DOES GREAT ACTRESS LIKE SON'S WIFE?" a headline in the Denver *Post* had asked back in 1910. Stella liked Helen as much as she could like any wife of her darling Beo; but the two inevitably clashed, since Helen had a strong will and a flippant tongue of her own. Stella attempted to cow her by never letting Helen or any of her visiting American friends forget that they were not British. Shaking hands with a New York guest, for example, she disconcerted him by suddenly grasping his shirt cuff, pulling it down, and rolling it between her fingers and thumb. "The best silk," she purred approvingly. "We love you rich Americans over here." On another occasion Helen introduced her to an enormously tall young man who was blocking the sky directly in front of her. Stella scanned him. "I'm sure you couldn't possibly have such a ridiculous name as *Emery Pottle*," she said severely, "but if you have, would you mind sitting down?" (Stella found American names like Potter Palmer, Millard Fillmore, and Peabody Wetmore quite unforgivable.) With Helen, the "fun" could be cruel. One night when the Baron and Baroness de Meyer dined at the Square, Stella seized on the topic of the Baroness's remarkably slim and tiny feet, knowing very well that Helen was self-conscious about her large ones. "Oh, don't be so self-*conscious*, dear!" she cried, insisting that Helen take off her slippers and compare her "monstrous extremities" with the Baroness Olga's exquisite ones. "We all know Americans have *lovely* feet!"

If Beo had been supportive and successful, Helen would not have felt so overwhelmed by her famous mother-in-law. But Beo adored his mother and, not able to make a success of anything, allowed her to support him lavishly. There had been a hopeful period when Gerald du Maurier agreed to produce Beo's new play, *The Dust of Egypt*, at Wyndham's. Stella herself was optimistic, writing Arthur Symons, "It's very exciting about Beo's play; a lovely girl is to play the Egyptian princess, Enid Bell. Won't that be a first night!" But although the popular du Maurier played the lead and James Barrie was there with all his clothes on wrong-side-out for luck, he assured them—even his shoes—the play that opened February 3, 1912, ran only a few weeks. Not that Beo gave up. He began to dream of being a theatrical producer instead of a playwright, and Stella gave him every encouragement.

In June 1912 Bernard Shaw also sought encouragement from Stella Campbell. He had a play that was a "dead cert." He would not give up the idea that Mrs. Pat must be his cockney flower girl—never mind that she had never been impressed with his plays. He arranged that Stella be invited by D.D. Lyttelton to a reading of the play in Great College Street on the twenty-sixth. There was no guarantee, of course, that the temperamental actress would appear at all.

# TWENTY-EIGHT

# 1912

STELLA DID APPEAR at D.D.'s that Wednesday to listen to Shaw's play. She heard his vivid rendition of the coster-girl's "Aaee-ow"'s with a deepening frown. "That's not a nice sound, Mr. Shaw!" she objected. Gradually it dawned upon her that this was *her* part. Yet Shaw's reading was so mesmeric that she listened to the end. She wrote him next day thanking him for thinking she could play his "pretty slut" and inviting him to Kensington Square. He came on Friday. When she took the maidenly modest Shaw's hand, she mischievously contrived that his fingertips brush her bosom. She took him to sit on a sofa in the white-panelled drawing room; as he talked, she stroked Georgina winningly with her beautiful white hands. She suggested they visit a certain lord who might back a production of her own; Shaw went in the taxi like a lamb. Though he had begun the business with the utmost confidence in his invulnerability to her charms, before he knew it he was "head over ears in love with her—violently and exquisitely in love." He returned eagerly the next day, then went home to deny his infatuation. "Many thanks for Friday and for a Saturday of delightful dreams. I did not believe that I had that left in me. I am all right now, down on earth again with all my cymbals and side drums and blaring vulgarities in full blast; but it would be meanly cowardly to pretend that you are not a very wonderful lady, or that the spell did not work most enchantingly on me for fully 12 hours."

Stella intended to take her own theatre for *Pygmalion*, finding the money somehow; she also intended to choose her own Professor Higgins. Shaw agreed to the first but not the second proposition. The single-star system, he wrote, was all right for the provinces or America, but it was dead in London. It was the combination that succeeded: Irving and Terry, Wyndham and Mary Moore, Fred Terry and Julia Neilson, George Alexander and Irene Vanbrugh. Lewis Waller himself could not do it alone in London, Tree did not try to, and Stella solo had not been able to make the Royalty a paying proposition. If she attempted *Pygmalion* now without a strong Higgins, not even his genius could save her. She was content with worms, he charged, because worms never gave any trouble—and actually in plays that needed mere producing they made the best casts. But *his* plays needed acting, hard acting; he must have a heroic Higgins to complement her Eliza. Privately, Shaw believed that, although he could train the cat to play Eliza, he could not teach the dog to play Higgins: Higgins was the stronger part. He himself wanted the actor who had made his *Man and Superman* a great success in America, the young, handsome Robert Loraine. His letter wasn't all business. He would be fifty-six this July and he was acting like a schoolboy. He'd been telling everybody he was in love with her—Barrie had asked him the other evening in his slowest Scotch drawl, "Shall you be seeing Mrs. Campbell again tonight?" It was vile—all this ribaldry he could not help bringing down upon her head. And now he must go read this letter to his wife, Charlotte, who was unfailingly amused at his love affairs.

Stella smiled over the many pages written on green paper because their writer was suffering a headache. "I wish you weren't so early Victorian!" she replied. ". . . You must let Loraine have the play if Higgins is more important than Eliza. But he and I cannot be forced into partnership—that would never do. One knows, only too well that a 'two star' show is better than a 'one star' and that an 'all star' show is fit only for Kings and Queens! The two star affairs you quote were more or less bound by cupid! I suggest Matheson Lang or Charles Lowne—Aubrey Smith will play with joy the 2nd part and do the easier share of the business. . . . I would be very unhappy if I couldn't feel the very best had been done for your brilliant play—I would far rather lose 'Eliza.'" Of course he would want to know how secure her financial backing was, and she would know that in a few days. About the love-talk she said nothing.

Shaw flung back a reply. He was an artist: he cared nothing about finance. All he wanted was his Eliza and a proper Higgins. Lang and Lowne were impossible. If she had a heart, she would not be so obstinate; but if she would not have Loraine, then they must wait until someone she *would* have came forward. Meanwhile he would simply howl at her lack of feeling until all London knew of her cruelty. He would give the play to Robert Loraine and Cissy Loftus for America, he would write *such* a play for Lena Ashwell, who really loved him, he would—

"Oh darling what a letter!" laughed Stella. "I call you 'darling' because 'dear Mr. Shaw' means nothing at all—whilst darling means most dear and most dear means a man, and a mind and a speaking—such as you and your mind and your speech! Now please pull yourself together and tell me whether I may get on with business or no. . . . I long to get on with the whole thing and call rehearsals on Sept 1st or else get off—you know how *much* I want to work with you—and as sure as one can feel—I feel *sure*. . . ."

But Shaw did not allow her to get on with it, keeping up the pretense that he would give the play to Loraine and Loftus. Unrattled, Stella proposed H. B. Irving, and privately told D.D. that she would act with Loraine or Norman McKinnel; nothing came of either. She reported that Edmund Gwenn and Hilda Trevelyan were offering her the Vaudeville on any terms, under their management. Finally she had three Higginses she wanted to discuss, and phoned Adelphi Terrace; but Mr. Shaw, she was told, had gone out with Mrs. Shaw. She sent him a note: she would keep herself free until eight on the chance he might come. She was not being merely obstinate: "I appreciate you more intelligently & passionately than you give me credit for," she assured him. But eight o'clock came and went, and no one rang.

Shaw was incapable of keeping his affairs to himself. He turned now to D.D. Lyttelton to discuss the new entanglement, telling her he was not sure of Stella's real or unconscious motives for wanting to produce *Pygmalion*. D.D. replied that she thought both he and Stella were being terribly silly about the play, and as for motives, "What does all that matter, if she is the woman who can play your part? . . . She is the least intriguing the least worldly wise of women . . . to a degree that is sometimes maddening. I do not agree with you that her motive conscious or unconscious about her male 'supports' in acting is merely one of self-aggrandizement. The true fact is that she has *no* motive but merely a succession of violent antipathies & prejudices & contempts with moreover ignorance added—i.e. that she is quite unable to teach or to build up another person's talents. She can only destroy & that is why she is so *fatal* as a producer. She as Mr. Barker truly says 'subtly humiliates & disconcerts people.' She does not set out to do this— it just arises from the inevitable impact of her domineering personality. Believe me you miscalculate her if you think her actuated by any thought out or planned motive in these matters. By nature she is absolutely gener- ous & if you found her an actor she liked & respected she would do any- thing. I admit this is difficult—almost impossible!"

Speaking as a playwright herself, she would *never* advise anyone to give Stella anything to produce, continued D.D. But when a play was produced by some other skilled person, then Stella was "one of the fine instruments of the stage" and she thought it simply cowardly of him not to use her just because he could not have the leading man *he* wanted. Besides, Stella firmly believed that the author should produce his own play and would never stand in his way. "You would have squabbles, of course, but far from spoiling your play she would make it—produced by you," urged D.D. "Say what you like Liza is a very difficult part to play & requires great technical skill & great brilliance & intelligence. All these Stella will give you."

"Her motive for going in for management has nothing to do with [her] fear of star casts," continued D.D. later. ". . . She has never been able to save a penny in her life. . . . She knows what has been made by Alexander over Bella Donna. She also understands that as managers take big risks they cannot afford larger salaries. But she wants to throw her work & prestige into an enterprise where *she* can gain the profits. She does not want the worry & care of management. . . . But she wants not greedily but prosaically to provide for her old age & her children. I really & seriously think given this condition that you produce yourself & are strong enough to insist upon your own way, that play would have enormous success & I do hope you will take up your courage & throw aside misgivings & go ahead. Tell her quite simply that you produce your own play *entire*. Of course she does not see the play as a whole . . . what great actor does—but *you* do & that is the important thing. If you don't do this I shall know that it is for the same reason I should hesitate myself: i.e. that you do not feel sure you could stand up to her in spite of all your conceit. . . . Dont be a craven over it."

Before Shaw could decide whether he could brave Stella or not, the battle over *Pygmalion* came to a sudden halt. As Stella rode in a taxi one day with Georgina on her lap, the driver suddenly swerved to avoid a boy on a bicycle and collided with another taxi. Stooping to snatch up the pitched-off Georgina, Stella felt a blinding blow as her head went through the partition window. Dazedly she noted that someone picked up the boy and carried him off and that her hatpin had been broken in two. She herself hailed another taxi and went on to the St. James's. Her dresser's eyes widened as she came in. "What is the matter, Madam, you look so funny!" Julia exclaimed, and hurried out. Alexander came a moment later. "I'm all right," said Stella, condescending to speak, "and I'm going to play." "Look in the glass," said Alexander, also breaking vows of eternal silence. She looked, saw her head raised six inches higher than normal and great bruises beginning to swell her eyes and jaw. A doctor was sent for; she was ordered home to bed with ice bags on her head. Sir Alfred Fripp, M.D., arrived. Stooping for Georgina had saved her face, he told her; she had missed death by a hair's breadth. She was begged not to talk, but could not stop. Tiny threads of cotton seemed to be pulling her head up into the air.

Fripp assured her that she would be acting again in a week, but *Bella Donna* came off on August 1 after a thirty-four-week run before she was able to return. She tossed restlessly in bed. Her face was black and blue, her eyes invisible. At length, although still ill, she decided to go with Sir

Edward and Lady Stracey to Aix-les-Bains in their Rolls-Royce. Before leaving she wrote Shaw, hurt at his hesitations over *Pygmalion*: "Indeed I wont even bother myself for one instant again about 'Liza.' I so absolutely *believe* in Cissy Loftus and Loraine for the parts." Shaw too was going on holiday. She hoped he'd have a lovely time and leave his cap and bells and bladder-whacking at home.

"Stella, Stella: all the winds of the north are musical with the thousand letters I have written to you on this journey," replied the irrepressible Shaw from Bad Kissingen. ". . . I solemnly protest that when I went into that room in Kensington Square I was a man of iron, insolently confident in my impenetrability. Had I not seen you dozens of times, and dissected you professionally as if you were a microscopic specimen? What danger could there possibly be for me? And in thirty seconds—oh Stella, if you had a rag of decency it *couldnt* have happened. I always thought that if I met you I should ask you to play. I looked at the piano; and I said, 'Good God! fancy listening to *that* when I can listen to her.' Is this dignified? Is it sensible? At my age—a driveller—a dotard! I will conquer this weakness, or trade in it and write plays about it. . . . Still, O Stella, I kiss your hands and magnify the Life Force for creating you; for you are a very wonderful person."

Stella opened the letter at the Hotel Mirabeau. She did not attempt to answer in the same tone. She was perfectly aware that Shaw was attached to Charlotte, with whom he was travelling. She suspected he was courting her for the prestige and publicity she would lend his play. She suspected that he was afraid of her, and was using love-talk to disarm. She herself was very attached to George, who, unlike Shaw, needed her. Still, she loved music and poetry as well as flattery, and Shaw could draw singing words of adoration out of his pen like a magician. "Perhaps someday, if you are very good and behave properly at rehearsal I will write you a love letter," she encouraged. "Love letters!" retorted Shaw. *"Sancta simplicitas!* When did you ever write me anything else?" But that was bravado.

She intended to stay at Aix three weeks, taking the baths to heal her aching body, but found after a week that bathing made her very ill. So she went on alone to Chamonix, where she clambered about the mountain without a guide in Louis XV heels, lace stockings, long skirts, and floating veils. Then an offer to tour in America brought her back quickly to London, where Beo, who had been staying in the country, met her at Kensington Square. He looked into her face. "Mother," he said, "you are ill; I'm going to sleep here." He sent for Helen, and Stella went to bed, where she still talked plays. Barrie had written one especially for her called *The Adored One*; Shaw was still holding out *Pygmalion*. "Do something quickly," she wrote him at the beginning of September, "or I shall have vanished to America. I am not going to live much longer and I must tidy up!"

Illness always hit Stella hard, as though her great vitality recoiled violently upon itself in revenge. Now she collapsed entirely. Doctors were summoned. Lying inert, she could hear whispers of "brain . . . blind . . . paralysed . . . sinking fast." Candles were held to her face, her eyelids lifted by careful fingers. In the room below she could hear the murmur of voices consulting. She only knew that she cared about nothing and need not trouble about anything any more. Out in the streets headlines shouted that the famous actress's condition was deteriorating . . . "little hope for recovery" . . . "near death." In the Square straw was laid to deaden the noise of ceaseless carriages arriving with friends anxious to inquire or offer help. Stella only wanted peace. Occasionally, when Beo or Helen tiptoed into the room or a cable arrived from young Stella in East Africa, she would rouse herself, but she soon sank back into indifference. One day Helen put her head around the screen and whispered as though she could not believe the news, "You are going to *live!*" Stella heard and was not comforted. To live meant getting to her feet again, meeting the face of a woman of forty-seven in the looking glass, deciding what dress to wear or what hat to put on. To live meant picking up all the senseless threads of life, going to the stage door again night after night, pushing on a career. To live meant worrying about George and his unhappiness. To live meant facing the terrible bills of this illness. Why? she wondered listlessly. So much easier simply to escape. She closed her eyes and for weeks made no effort to live.

Eventually her strong constitution and the devotion of friends pulled her back. Madeline Wyndham wrote her gratitude for years of dear, faithful friendship and prayed she would be well. D.D. came to sit by her bedside almost every other day. "My dear, I'm so sorry you are ill—I knew nothing of your accident!" wrote Ellen Terry. ". . . Do get well—and keep on being lovely Patricia Campbell." Mrs. Rosa Lewis, the celebrated proprietress of the Cavendish Hotel and a favorite of King Edward's, came to the Square bearing silver dishes of Stella's favorite snails exquisitely cooked as only she knew how. She did not mind at all when one day a visiting marchioness swept disdainfully past her. "Me in me sinful sables," she murmured happily, giving her furs a little pat as she laid them aside, "and 'er in 'er virtuous cat!" And one morning Sarah arrived in mole-skin and sables. Beo helped her up the steep, narrow flights of stairs to cries of *"Ah, mon Dieu! Ces escaliers! Vertige! Vertige!"* and ran to fetch brandy and vinegar salts so that the actress could comfort her ailing Mélisande. Downstairs, Helen dealt with a crush of fashionable visitors and streams of gifts, giving the callers tea and trying to remember which lord had sent what brace of game.

So many baskets of snipe, woodcock, grouse, and pheasant piled into the house that the kitchen had begun to look like an aviary. Stella was indifferent to game, but confessed herself pleased with six pheasants shot by the King because now, she said, she could put "BY APPOINTMENT" over her larder. Nina came constantly with strong beef tea. Baskets of pears appeared and disappeared (Stella loathed pears). Flowers heaped the invalid's room. Servants threatened to quit under the incessant demands for refreshments for all visitors at any hour, and it was only Helen's "beastly American amiability" (as Stella rather ungratefully termed it) that kept the house running during the long weeks of recovery.

But no one eventually brought Stella more comfort than Bernard Shaw. At first he had declined to believe her ill, but when letters came from Helen in October saying that the doctors were greatly encouraged and hoped that in another week or two Stella would be able to sit up, he began to take her condition more seriously. One way to cheer her was by flattery, and he filled letter after letter with paeans to her womanhood: "I kiss your hands and praise Creation for you . . . O beautiful illustrious . . . O sweet of body and kissable all over . . . O glorious white marble lady. . . ." These could be smiled over. Occasionally a line flashed out with sudden seriousness. "I shall never quite get over it," Stella read in late October; ". . . I mean the falling in love. I havnt been quite the same man since."

The metamorphosis worried Shaw because he was both sexually repressed and fundamentally loyal to his wife. It was safer to turn temptation into a play. This he had done the previous July, writing *Overruled*, a one-act farce about adultery immediately inspired by the sign TRESPASSERS WILL BE PROSECUTED on D.D.'s gate. How nice it would be if there were no signs, thinks Shavian hero Gregory Lunn—if married couples were free to pursue sexual adventure without the absurd punishments of jealousy and divorce. Yet Shaw's hero is as terrified as he is attracted by the seductive goddess Mrs. Juno—Stella, of course. He wants to desire her, not to possess her. "Don't be alarmed," Shaw has Gregory tell Mrs. Juno: "I like wanting you. As long as I have a want, I have a reason for living. Satisfaction is death." "Yes," replies Mrs. Juno with Stella's wit; "but the impulse to commit suicide is sometimes irresistible." Gregory protests. "Danger is delicious," he argues. "But death isn't. We court the danger; but the real delight is in escaping after all."

To assure themselves an escape route, both Stella and Shaw discussed their romance with D.D., who was flattered and amused to be in the middle, though she did not take the affair seriously in the least. "And you need not be afraid," she wrote Shaw, "—you can dance round each other for a long time yet—both pretending a great passion, both knowing perfectly well that you each have a foot firmly caught in the kitchen door. And you will never have to break with Charlotte however little you cool. . . . So please go on dear Mr Shaw—I would say this even if there were danger—the more, in my earnest opinion. Go on seeing & writing to her & amusing her, for I fear she has many many weeks yet on that [weary] bed."

D.D.'s chief concern was for Stella. "I wish she would get well now," she continued, "but she won't just yet. For a long time I have felt that some smash like this must come, but I did not know what form it would take. She has been ill through & through—body & mind & spirit—a regular cataclysm it has been—& severe just in proportion to the strength vigour & richness of her temperament. What she will get up to I don't know, but she will be different & if possible still more dear to me & I hope to you."

Encouraged, Shaw brought his new play, *Androcles and the Lion*, to Kensington Square to read to Stella, but did not find his goddess alone. He was in no mood to perform before D.D., Beo, and Helen, but complied, rearranging furniture and lights before launching into his "bawling, shouting, roaring, bustling, brutal" Christian-martyr play. In the end he read too long and stayed too long and talked too much; and saw Stella become restless and annoyed. With her temperature soaring from the fatigue of the visit, Stella apologized the following days: "Oh darling! I think D D and I behaved like ungrateful savages, and you so good, and so gentle with us—and so kind to come and see me at all and honour me by reading your *brilliant* play. . . . I send you my love and I am sorry I was a churl and you had no tea and your hands were cold." But Shaw's relentless loquacity tired her. "—Oh dear me," she sighed, "—it's too late to do anything but *accept* you and *love* you—but when you were quite a little boy somebody ought to have said 'hush' just once!"

Yet Stella was charmed in spite of herself. She tried to write three times within the week, but had to give up when her temperature "went up to the moon." Shaw had replied to her rebuke, "My shyness and cowardice have been beyond all belief"; she refused to believe in either. "I see you," she answered, "—as sensitive as Keats—as timid as a lamb—and that 'want of taste' we grumbled at, is a sort of Swank. . . . These letters of yours are traps—traps like your Irish accent. There is a tract called 'Led on step by step'—that's what's happening to me! . . . I'll whisper something—'I'm afraid of the Keats, and the lamb.' "

Stella could not be more afraid of the lamb than Shaw was terrified of the tigerine. "Shut your ears tight against this blarneying Irish liar and actor," he promptly responded. "Read no more of his letters. He will fill his fountain pen with your heart's blood, and sell your most sacred emotions on the stage. He is a mass of imagination with no heart. He is a writing and talking machine that has worked for nearly forty years until its skill is devilish. I should have warned you before; but I thought his white hairs and 56 years had made his philanderings ridiculous, and that you would beat him at his own game and revenge his earlier victims. I pray still that you, great actress as you are, are playing with him as he is playing with you. . . .

"But don't cut him off utterly. He is really worth something, even to *you*, if you harden your heart against him. . . . Oh dont, dont, DONT fall in love with him; but dont grudge him the joy he finds in being in love with you, and writing all sorts of wild but heartfelt exquisite lies—lies, lies, lies, lies to you, his adoredest."

"You didn't *really* think that I believed you came to see me because you were interested in *me*," Stella countered. But then Shaw came to the Square again and behaved in such a "bewilderingly charming way" that she was quite beguiled again—even if, with all her teasing, she could never lure him into being late for dinner back at Adelphi Terrace. "I haven't said 'kiss me,'" she wrote after one heady encounter, "because life is too short for the kiss my heart calls for. . . . All your words are as idle wind—Look into my eyes for two minutes without speaking if you dare! Where would be your 54 years? and my grandmother's heart? and how many hours would you be late for dinner?" Shaw himself felt the impact of that encounter. "I dont understand it. I am not terrified," he wrote the same day. "That's what ought to terrify me; but it doesnt. Still, nothing has happened as I thought it would happen. And thats odd. Am I going to learn something?"

Helen Campbell watched the romantic progress with something less than enthusiasm. "It was during Stella's illness that Mr. Bernard Shaw came into the picture," said Helen, "—and came, and came, and came." The tall, lathy playwright knocked almost every afternoon at the same hour, when it became Helen's duty to entertain him in the drawing room until Stella's current visitor left, or until she had made herself ready to receive him. At first Helen found the task a privilege and a delight; but as the months wore on, she found Shaw's lessons in relaxation and the therapeutic value of raw carrots decidedly less fascinating. She was perfectly aware that he too regarded her simply as a stop-gap. When the nurse would finally come down to say that Stella would see him at last, "he would leap into the air," said Helen, "beard flying, and gallop up the stairs three steps at a time." She would sigh with relief and go downstairs to encourage all the other visitors who had been herded into the dining room.

Then came days when the door was barred to Shaw and no letters passed between the Square and Adelphi Terrace. Stella had had a severe setback. "Most dear man of brass, full of grindstones and things!" she was finally able to write on December 2, "—it's a sad woman that's writing to you—

for the doctors tell me that in 6 weeks I have made no improvement and they cannot let me lie here much longer—and—Oh, but I am not going to tell you—I was such a green sick skeleton those days I didn't write. . . . I think if you don't come and see me rather soon there won't be me to see. . . ." Shaw came immediately and enchanted her again, leaving her with thoughts of Blake's "Bend not a joy towards yourself and spoil the winged world." "This week is going to be a bad week," she wrote soon after he left. "—I won't be able to write for a few days—my friends must fold their hands for me—My eyelids are heavier than I tonight—I am glad we met."

For several weeks doctors had recommended an exploratory operation, but were baffled by Stella's stubborn "Not unless you tell me first exactly what's the matter with me!" Shaw entered the dispute. She should first have an X-ray; the power of the X-ray itself must arrest the malignant routine her system had fallen prey to. More important, he wished to come and see her on December 10 to put to her "a very indelicate question" on a matter of business. Stella guessed he wanted to ask about her salary. "I played for the Irish people for nothing," she replied, "—for Trench for what he could afford—for Tree for all I could get, for Alexander what he offered—for you—for love." She had passed on his X-ray suggestion to her doctors and they had been indignant. She was desperately ill, they told her, and only *acted* well for her friends. The operation was necessary; she was going to a nursing home. Shaw hurried to the Square and asked her frankly about her financial situation. Stella was indignant: not even D.D. had dared to ask how much she was in debt all these years. After he left (he had come secretly, the doctors having forbidden visitors), she thought over his kindness and the folly of his infatuation.

"Bless you—you were brave," she wrote that evening, "—and now I'll tell you a great secret—I know as much about Blake as would fill a thimble —and I know six little pieces by heart for the piano and if you heard me play one of them you'd box my ears—and when I come out of that 'home' it's to be Mrs. P.C. and Mr. Bernard Shaw." Then, relenting: "Thursday coming perhaps you might telephone up and ask how I am—I think I leave here Wednesday—I wish I was dining with you at the Ritz tonight both of us 21!—and you in evening dress and I looking lovely too! Oh no, I mean I wish it was a wet night in the park and you were speaking and I was giving away pamphlets and leading the applause. . . . I wish I had all your words and your beloved Irish accent to dress my dreams and then someone would listen to me—and I *did* have something to say—it's too late now. . . ."

But Shaw was not to be put off from talking either money or love. He realized that she was recklessly extravagant. "We had better dress up as beggars and go to Stella's door," he told D.D., "and what we collect may keep her until she gets another engagement." Now he presented her with the hard facts. She'd made £116 a week through the run of *Bella Donna*. Half of that had gone to her bankers for debts, leaving her £58 a week to her credit—a mere nothing considering her expenditures. Nothing saved. No one to turn to, except perhaps Lord Savile or D.D.—and she was far too proud. The rent to pay, the Christmas quarter, Christmas boxes, bills, nurses, doctors. He knew she was desperate: just the thought that there might be a bill of sale on the piano cut him like a dagger. He cursed his cowardice in not bringing with him yesterday a new £1000 note to crackle under her nose. She could have snatched it and burnt it before his face if she'd liked; only he would have had the immense satisfaction of offering it. He knew she'd never take it, "Only, dearest, if you ever want anything ever so little, remember, crackle, crackle, crackle, crackle."

Money was not his only theme. He had just seen *Troilus and Cressida*, and as Troilus loved Cressida "with such a strained purity," so he loved her. ". . . And I love you for ever and ever and ever, Stella. And I agree that when you are well we shall be Mr. Bernard Shaw and Mrs. Patrick Campbell; for Stella means only Stella; but Mrs. Patrick Campbell will mean my treasure, my darling, my beloved, adored, ensainted friend of my very soul.

"Oh, before you go, my Stella, I clasp you to my heart 'with such a strained purity.' A thousand successes, a thousand healings, a thousand braveries, a thousand prayers, a thousand beauties, a thousand hopes and faiths and loves and adorations watch over you and rain upon you. Goodnight, goodnight, goodnight, goodnight, my dearest dearest."

In his genuine anxiety over her circumstances, Shaw appealed to D.D. "You touch me at once when you talk about her future," she replied. "Hasn't it always haunted me & haven't I tried over & over again to get her to save & to put by. But as you know by now she is not merely extravagant but a terribly glad giver. She has kept & still keeps all sorts of obscure retainers & relations—she simply has not saved because she has given & given. . . . I see nothing for it but that you & Barrie & Pinero should each write a play for her (you have already) & that you men should find a man or a syndicate ready to put up the money to run her & a company in those plays, she having a share in the profits as well as a salary. Then those profits ought by arrangement with her to be invested for her at once & held by trustees. Could not something of this sort be managed. She will never take money from any of us unless at the last gasp."

Although Stella could ask Harriett Carolan for money, she was still proud with her English friends and would not listen to the "crackle, crackle, crackle, crackle" of Shaw's £1000 note. Her situation, however, was something worse than he imagined, she told him. Her "banker" was Saunders the

Jew at 10 Savile Row; his terms fifty per cent: he lent her as much as she liked. But "now to business," she continued, dismissing the topic. "Four doctors have just left—3 knights—and they tell Helen she must search at once for the man I love and bring him to me, and he must be told that he is to obey me entirely—and that if I am tired of my bed I must sit in his lap with my arms round his neck in an armchair by the fire all night—and that when I want to be kissed he must kiss me *at once*—any hesitancy might kill me immediately, and that if I want to go to sleep all night with my head on his breast, he musn't move for fear of waking me, because if I wake up I might start wanting to be kissed again and that would spoil my night's sleep. That directly I am well I must be taken to Italy by him and be shown all the beauty that dwells there, and that if I talk nonsense and betray the ignorant fool I really am he must shut his eyes tight so that I never see that he knows, and all his other duties in life must be put aside and this *only*, said the Knights, will cure me. Poor Helen said she didn't know the man so how could she fetch him? I wonder what sort of man he is. . . ."

She might well wonder. Shaw could offer wonderful words, a play, even £1000, but no more. George Cornwallis-West would lean upon her. Still, that was comforting in its way. One day he had come to see her. They had not met for a long time. He seemed deeply moved and unhappy as he sat by her bedside. "Live, Stella," he had pleaded; "live and help me." The words had profoundly touched her. She had offered him hope. Just before Christmas, therefore, George quit his and Jennie's house in Norfolk Street, leaving behind a letter of goodbye that Jennie answered the next day. She had been prepared, but the blow was still hard. If the separation and divorce were really to take place, it couldn't happen too quickly now—they would both be happier when it was over. She had, thank God, the courage and strength to fight her own battle in life.

Stella also had courage and strength. As she prepared to face the operation that now seemed inevitable and the long weeks of recovery in a nursing home, she thought more and more of George and of his need for her. And George began to think more and more luxuriously of placing his hurt ego, frustration, and debts in the lap of the generous and sympathetic Stella. Yet she spent New Year's Eve with Helen and Beo and the other George, so intoxicating him that although he was expected for a little celebration at Barrie's that same evening, Shaw did not arrive there until one. "This is a terrific romance, and at last Shaw can blush," noted Barrie. "But which of them it is that listens I can't make out."

# TWENTY-NINE

# 1913–1914

O N JANUARY 12, 1913, Stella was taken to a nursing home in Hinde
Street and deposited in the care of Sister Dove. "No nurse comes to
your room unless you ring, which will be very convenient if I am able to ever
again flirt with Shaw," she scribbled to Helen next day. "Don't worry about
me, there's a darling. Being carried up the stairs yesterday was the worst
part of all. . . . Do you and Beo feel happy and have some fun, and thank
you darling for all your goodness."

The exploratory operation was scheduled for the next day, Shaw having
persuaded Stella to have his Dr. Bowlby in attendance, since, like D.D., he
did not trust her doctors. In his kindly, meddlesome way he wrote Helen
advising her not to worry: "Stella, saving your ladyhood, will not give a
damn for the whole business, so don't be afraid of being harrowed." She
had more strength in her little finger, he thought, than all the doctors put
together. And in fact Stella faced the ordeal calmly, and was able to tell
Helen two days afterwards that they had found no malignancy: "Well,
darling, I am getting on all right. My cough is a nuisance and wrenches—
and I took DREADFUL. They evidently banged me on the jaw and gagged
me, because my mouth is sore and my jaw blue. . . . Stella must have her
cable—Operation successful Mother getting on splendidly. . . ."

After four and a half months of baffling illness she now began to recover.
There were three weeks ahead in the nursing home, but she had already
turned the place into a reception room. D.D. came and proposed her home
at Wittersham for recovery; Lady Hamilton pressed Malta; Lady Charles
Beresford recommended Brighton. (Given her disastrous financial state,
Stella felt it more likely she'd be convalescing twice daily at the Hippodrome instead.) Lady Horner, Lady Jekyll, Lord Ribblesdale, and Lord
Savile were frequent visitors. Clarkson the wigmaker sent her white hyacinths. Barrie and Max Beerbohm called, and Max played her games of
chess. Shaw sent his novel *Cashel Byron's Profession* to "his most agitating

heart's darling" and tried to work a visit to Hinde Street into his frenetically busy schedule.

That month he finally told Charlotte what all London seemed to know: that his afternoons that fall and winter had not been spent at committee meetings and the theatre, but at the bedside of Stella Campbell. Although he claimed that Charlotte was unfailingly amused at his philanderings, she was devastated by the revelation. Others took the romance with varying degrees of interest, amusement, or contempt. Forbes had been "very nice" when Shaw told him, but seemed to expect he couldn't stand it long. Barrie, himself captivated by Stella, wryly decided that she loved them both for the plays they might write her. Shaw's closest friend, Sidney Webb, usually only bored with women, had detested Stella when Lady Elcho had brought her one day to tea; he now branded Shaw's love affair "a clear case of sexual senility." Ellen Terry had once been the recipient of Shaw's ecstacies herself; she thus replied carefully to his announcement. *"I'm* in love with Mrs. Campbell too," said Ellen, "or rather I'd like to be, but something tugs me back. She is amusing and was nice to me in America." But at Adelphi Terrace the hurt, angry Charlotte turned overnight from an amiable wife, Shaw told Stella, into "a domestic fiend."

This did not stop Shaw either from writing or visiting whenever he could get away or she would receive him. He came on January 29 and they played chess and he enjoyed himself immensely—she was such "a jolly playfellow" and such "an old-fashioned child" he'd like to spend an hour with her every day in the nursery. But Stella, now that she had left that bedchamber where magic spells had worked, began to look at Shaw more objectively, and many of his qualities rankled with her. No matter how fervently he protested his devotion, for example, he never let that devotion interfere with his work. His egotism also irritated her, his maddening consciousness of his position among the immortals. "The British Museum indeed!" she chided, "how this trick of yours annoys me, thinking everything appertaining to yourself will eventually find its way to the British Museum." She thought him treacherous too and "no gentleman": "What a vile habit to read my letters aloud," she complained. She scorned his hesitation to put words into action. "I adore and at the same time detest your fears and tremblings and bewitching timidities," she wrote, "—'late for dinner,' 'not fit to work,' unmanned 'if within a fortnight of a public appearance you shake the hand of a sick widow you professed to love!' If only you'd eat red steaks and drink beer your spirit would be meat, I mean meet to mate. . . ." And Shaw purposely emphasized his timidity as protection. "I scribble in great haste," he apologized, "—going out with Charlotte to try a car, and darent be an instant late. Oh why, why, why did I fill up this afternoon? If only I could steal a minute before dinner; but I darent, darent, darent: youd make me late and then—"

But if Shaw flaunted Charlotte for Stella, she too had "one foot in the kitchen door," as D.D. put it. Writing on February 3, she asked him to postpone his visit until 7:45 because, "At 6 o'c someone who is troubled, and who troubles me deeply will be here." The someone, of course, was George. On January 20, Jennie had filed a divorce petition, charging desertion; and George sought out Stella for comfort and reassurance. George was becoming "dearer to her than her bones." But he did not have Shaw's wit, playfulness, and imagination; so that Stella, even while priding herself on the iron will that resisted blandishments, often found herself hungering for a temper to match her own. "Darling Mr. Mouse," she wrote Shaw on one of those occasions, "—I love you so much and yet I have no 'christian' name for you—'Darling,' 'Tenderness,' 'Most sweet love'—those I have. Oh Mr. Mouse, I wish cheese wasn't in traps, and cats everywhere. I want to sit in a hayfield with you—and the sun shining—I want to have upon my feet laced up boots and walk with you around the world whilst you tell me all the mistakes people are making, and what a heavenly world it will be when there are no more traps—and cheese everywhere—and cats eat roots and don't mew. Oh my Mr. Mouse I've gone silly in my heart and head— what shall I do? Oh Mr. Mouse what SHALL I do." And then her better judgment would take hold. "I think I have fallen into a hornet's nest," she scribbled at the end of February, "—I think you are mad! I think I am pretending to be what it amuses you to think I am . . . . You are all right for Charlotte. You'll do for Barker. . . . But the Italian peasant must have a blue sky, and a saint to worship—and Oh! oh! oh! 'the emerald *must* keep its colour'—and Stella must be loved by a King among men who will lift her up beside him on a white horse and ride away with her to the moon."

Perhaps all her dissatisfaction could be summed in her conviction that Shaw was all brain and no emotion. He had sent her a revised edition of his *Quintessence of Ibsenism* and asked her to jot down her criticisms of his critique of *Hedda Gabler*. Stella did not jot ("I should write myself an ass on every page"), but she did rebel against his version of the play. ". . . Not one little bit do you understand Hedda—your interpretation of 'do it beautifully' positively made me scream—her love—her shame—her physical condition—her agonizing jealousy—even the case of pistols—you're wrong at all points—did you think about it at all—or is it just your adoration for bl—dy plain facts that makes you so indifferent to all the poetry, the universal truths and beauty that lie behind and beyond? . . . And with whom are you quarrelling? Be calm, dearest, be gentle with fools. . . . The fact is you have too much brain—you tumble up against it. . . . I knew by instinct what Ibsen and the rest of them *taught* you. But then I had a father who only read and talked Darwin, and a mother who loved only Dante—and whose soul was steeped in beauty."

Shaw felt the dissatisfaction. "I shall be at a loose end tomorrow between half past five and seven," he wrote; "but I wont call without encouragement; for I believe you hate me as much as ever *really.*" When he could snatch an hour or two for a visit, he often found her now with her titled friends. Then in early March she left the nursing home with Helen for Brighton, and in spirit seemed farther away than ever. He knew her world—motor rides with dukes, champagne and oysters with duchesses, late suppers with earls. He knew how little taste she had for his socialist and feminist friends, or for the causes he championed. She classified his wife, Charlotte, rather contemptuously as a "suffragette"; he doubted whether she'd heard the name Marx. "I tried to read *The Case for Socialism*," she admitted, "but I heard a thrush singing all the while." Nor, apart from her friendship with Barrie and her respect for Pinero and Ellen Terry, did she have much to do with the theatrical world. "Acting," she could say, "is no profession for a *man.*"

Stella felt the discord of their worlds. "My dear old Earl!" she wrote, after Shaw had taken tea one day with her and Wemyss. "I hope you will forget his prejudices & like him. I was a girl when I first met him—he helped me to trust myself—in art & in life. I loved him for that. . . . The people in my own profession terrify—stifle—confound me. These others are my *friends.*" Titled or not, they were friends who often disliked what Shaw stood for, and she listened to them. Laurence Tadema, daughter of Sir Lawrence Alma-Tadema, came to Brighton to see her, and warned her against Shaw: "Part of the scourge that is in the air . . . He walks into your heart with his muddy goloshes and then walks out leaving his muddy goloshes behind him. . . . Don't give him affection—he will surely hurt you." Shaw had better not come to Brighton after all, Stella told him; she was not brave enough to face him after hearing that.

Taunting him, even, with their differences, she described her convalescent days there. Lord Savile had filled her room with flowers from Rufford. A delightful luncheon with Lady Charlie Beresford. Many rendezvous at Cheeseman's Oyster Shop with the Duke and Duchess of Rutland and their daughter the Marchioness of Anglesey. Motoring with Savile . . . Yet with a few tender words she could whistle him back in a moment. "I want my plaything that I am to throw away," Shaw complained as days passed and she did not summon him. "I want my Virgin Mother enthroned in heaven. I want my Italian peasant woman. I want my rapscallionly fellow vagabond. I want my dark lady. I want my angel—I want my tempter. I want my Freia with her apples. I want the lighter of my seven lamps of beauty, honor, laughter, music, love, life and immortality. I want my inspiration, my folly, my happiness, my divinity, my madness, my selfishness, my final sanity and sanctification, my transfiguration, my purification, my light across the sea, my palm across the desert, my garden of lovely flowers, my million nameless joys, my day's wage, my night's dream, my darling and my star."

"Your letters," replied Stella, capitulating, "—a carnival of words—how can I answer with my poor whining beggars?"

Had Stella trusted Shaw, she could have heard something of more value to her than the carnival of words: his common sense. She was in great financial difficulty after eight months of not working and was even being forced to contemplate giving up 33 Kensington Square. Shaw guessed the crisis and wrote her in a solicitor's mood. "Your calm instinctive attempt to deceive me about your house—the certainty that you will hire a flat at about three times the rent you will get for 33 (that is what always comes of attempts to economize)—your hints about Australia . . . the knowledge that you *must* be hideously in debt after this ruinous illness—your entourage of society people who are always offering their friends everything and giving them nothing except motor rides that cost more in tips than taxis, and meals and hospitality—that can be had at half the price at a hotel . . . your ridiculous idea that you can always be a goddess to me (or that you could ever be anything else) and must therefore never exhibit yourself as a mortal with cares and anxieties and worries . . . all these things stimulate my meddlesomeness to the highest degree. . . . Two heads are better than one when a situation has to be considered. Always hear what a committee has to say, even if you dont accept the conclusion."

Stella listened, then went her own way. Barrie's play *The Adored One* was ready for her and Shaw still offered *Pygmalion*, even though she believed he meant it for any actress but herself. Shaw urged her to secure Barrie's play under Charles Frohman's management for the Duke of York's in September. His play could wait; and not only would Barrie be offended if she slighted his, but his play was the surest and most lucrative. But Stella had a third offer. Having sworn he would rather die than act with her again, George Alexander now came forward and offered to revive *The Second Mrs. Tanqueray* for her that summer at the St. James's. It was the act of a gentleman—and a masochist. It was also the act of a manager who had made £25,748 from *Bella Donna* and £21,342 from *Tanqueray* and recognized the part Mrs. Patrick Campbell had played in those successes. To her astonishment, Alexander was positively amiable, inviting her and Helen to Pont Street to discuss the revival, giving them cake and wine and showing them his baby picture. Stella also wanted *Pygmalion* for the St. James's that summer with Alexander as Higgins, but Shaw refused to put his play up for a short off-season run. He also chided her for throwing away *The Adored One* and *Pygmalion* for the St. James's, but Stella replied indignantly, "Did you think I ever meant to let either part go if I could help it? It's taken me 20 years to make you or Barrie think I was worth speaking to far less writing for—that fine play *Belladonna* at last convinced you!!!!" She was impatient that Shaw did not seem to see that she needed money immediately, not in September.

Although disappointment in him became her main theme, Shaw did not cool toward Stella that spring. She returned to Kensington Square in early April and began to venture from her bed. She found that she had to learn to walk again, and Shaw was her teacher, taking her in a hansom to Richmond Park and making her jump up repeatedly onto a park bench, a method that had once cured Charlotte. On the first day of spring he came to the Square and spent what seemed to him a deliciously domestic evening. Afterwards she delighted him by driving with him to King's Cross, where he caught the train for his country home at Ayot St. Lawrence, having bribed the cabman to go very slowly with his precious cargo on the way back to the Square. The next evening at ten he was able to snatch another hour; the next afternoon they went to a matinee; the following day he appeared at the Square for tea. But word that he had given *Pygmalion* to Germany for its first production disgusted Stella, as did his continued reluctance to meet her openly more often. "So there's to be no theatre to-morrow," she wrote in May. "Coward!" Barrie had taken her out to supper and then to a play, she told him; and she had had lunch in a restaurant with a man who did not mind being seen with her and did not think her undignified.

This last was George. In March Jennie had requested an order for the restitution of conjugal rights; George had not complied. That same month he took a necessary step, registering for four days as "Captain and Mrs. West" at the Great Western Railway Hotel at Paddington with "a woman unknown," making sure to be noticed by the chambermaid. Divorce proceedings were going along smoothly, and Stella and George began to be seen together in public. "Well, George evidently has a penchant for brunettes," remarked Jennie. "I'm always taken for a gypsy, but as for Mrs. Pat—why she's nothing more or less than an ink bottle!"

Although Stella accused him of cowardice and now quite openly preferred George, Shaw continued his romance, which, by his standards, was quite reckless. "Oh dearest Danger, I must love thee less/ Or plunge into a

devil of a mess," he had concluded a sonnet to her; and at Adelphi Terrace
he was frequently in a devil of a mess with Charlotte. "I am all torn to bits,"
he wrote after one telephone call to Kensington Square; "you dont know
what it is to me to be forced to act artificially when everything has just been
freshly stirred in me. . . . But the worst of it is that all our conversation
was overheard; and the effect was dreadful: it hurts me miserably to see
anyone suffer like that. I must, it seems, murder myself or else murder her.
It will pass over; but in the meantime here is a lovely spring day murdered.
. . . And believe that you cannot possibly have wanted a run through the
lanes with me this summer day more than I. I throw my desperate hands to
heaven and ask why one cannot make one beloved woman happy without
sacrificing another."

"Poor you," replied Stella, unmoved by his predicament. "It's quite
stupid nothing can be done to prevent your suffering." Now that George
clearly wanted her, she began to wish for more openness with Shaw. She
would have liked to know the wealthy, green-eyed Charlotte, about whom
she was most curious. From the beginning she had wanted Charlotte to
acknowledge her by leaving her card at the Square; it would have lent
respectability to the otherwise hole-in-a-corner romance. She wanted Shaw
to make up a theatre party with Charlotte, D.D., and herself. She wanted to
lend Charlotte her copy of *The Crock of Gold*. She could not understand
why Charlotte should not love her ("That shows some good in her," said
Charlotte grimly). "Stella may not be greatly interested in your plays, but
she is deeply interested in Charlotte—or so she assures me," D.D. had
informed Shaw at the start of the romance. Now Stella wanted both Shaw
and his wife to attend a party celebrating the first-night revival of *Tanqueray* on June 4. "It's not going to be a bohemian merry making," she
assured him. "The supper is now going to be given by Lady Wemyss, at 23
St. James Place. George West and his party come on then with Ribblesdale
and the rest—so with the exception of my poor self the company would
have been fit for your lady. If you won't come—it will make me unhappy—
but that doesn't matter, does it?"

Shaw and Charlotte refused, and Stella celebrated a revival which many
thought better than the original with her titled friends and George. Then on
June 9 she suddenly invited Shaw to Kensington Square to confide that she
was thinking of marrying Cornwallis-West. In the train to Ayot that night
Shaw wrote, pleading. She must not talk to him of marrying George because, with his farsightedness and objectivity, he could immediately see all
the worldly reasons why she should. He could also see himself putting
himself aside and driving her into George's arms, just as he had put *Pygmalion* aside and driven her into the arms of Barrie. "But that cost me

nothing," he continued, "whereas this would turn me into rusty iron and cut me off for ever from what is common and young in my humanity. Therefore, though I like George (we have the same taste) I say he is young and I am old; so let him wait until I am tired of you. . . . It is impossible that I should not tire soon: nothing so wonderful could last. You cannot really be what you are to me . . . a figure from the dreams of my boyhood. . . . I will hurry through my dream as fast as I can; only let me have my dream out."

To hasten his waking, Charlotte took him to the Continent in June. He continued to write Stella letters which he hastily stuffed in his pockets at the sound of his wife's footsteps; when he returned to London, he hurried to the Square. He found a distant and saddened Stella. Alfred Lyttelton had been taken ill and was sinking, the children had been called to the nursing home, and her heart was aching intolerably for D.D. in her grief. Shaw's failure to honor her mood further alienated her. When he came again, she was formal and shut the door on his visit with an exclamation of relief. "Stella: don't play with me," Shaw protested, hurt. ". . . When you shut the door on me the other day with a forced smile, and said 'Ouf!' when it slammed, I said, 'So it has lasted only a month after all!' And then I remembered that it began in the middle of summer, and lasted a whole year. I have been a saint for your sake for a whole year. Or perhaps I must confess to two little sins, because you know about them; but one was at Brighton, which is outside the pale of saintliness, and the other, though it profaned your temple, you forgave. That is a very clean slate for you, as slates go. And not until the year was out did you say 'Go and love somebody else and don't bother me.'" Of course, he was such a man of brass that she could not really hurt him; yet later, coming upon Blake's drawing "He shall take from thee the desire of thine eye," he had been torn with an unforgettable pang at the realization of his loss.

Stella thus abandoned the world of dreams in which she and Shaw had played at being children, and he had made her laugh until she named him Joey for the clown in the pantomime, and he had whispered delightful words of love to her, his goddess, mother, and darling. She returned to the theatre—to the "old Tank woman," as she called the play that now thoroughly bored her; and to those "dear pleasant spooks of do-nothings," as Shaw called her aristocratic friends. During the run of *Tanqueray* she appeared at the Duke of York's to rehearse Barrie's play, the "temperament" quite restored.

Dion Boucicault would produce the Stella-inspired story of a woman, Leonora, who pushes a man out of a railway carriage because her little girl has a cold and he won't shut the window, and who, because of her charm and fascination, is ruled "Not guilty" at the murder trial. A great artist and producer, Boucicault could be officious at rehearsals. Ellen Terry had once listened to his minute explanation of how she, England's foremost actress, should play a scene. "Yes," said Ellen sweetly after the lesson, "and then I just add that indescribable something of my own for which you pay me all that money." Now Boucicault tried the same technique with Stella; he dared put his arm around her waist and tell her, "No, my dear, you go here, and then you turn there, and you say your line like this." Stella grew "silent as doom, cold as the snows on Fuji-Yama." Sensing danger, Barrie left the stalls and strolled onto the stage, pipe in mouth, hat on the back of his head. "I think perhaps she will do better," he said softly in his slow Scottish burr, "if you leave her alone."

Barrie was among the few who could manage Stella. With amusement he watched her courting both himself and Shaw for plays. "He and I live in the weather house with two doors," teased Barrie, who lived opposite Shaw in Adelphi Terrace, "and you are the figure that smiles on us and turns up its nose at us alternately. However, I would rather see you going in at his door than not see you at all, and as you are on elastic I know that the farther you go with him the farther you will have to bound back." He was wary of the temperament, however, having run up against it more than once. To another playwright who complained that his chances had been ruined when, in the midst of reading a first act to Mrs. Campbell in her dressing room, Pinkie had become violently sick, Barrie replied comfortingly: "I shouldn't worry, I've read a play to that dog myself!" But Stella loved and admired "Jim," and was all enthusiasm over his play and the part of Leonora, which fit her, she thought, like one of her own long white gloves.

Nigel Playfair offered her his cottage near Ramsgate on the coast of Kent, and she decided to retreat there and prepare quietly for the opening of *The Adored One* on September 4. Before leaving, she paid a series of visits with Shaw to his invalid sister, Lucy, and Lucy found herself delighted with Mrs. Pat. One day Stella brought along Sara Allgood and all three of them gave her a concert, Mrs. Pat playing the piano better than most professionals, thought Lucy, and Shaw singing in "a throaty baritone" while Mrs. Pat made fun of him. The afternoon ended with the three dancing a Scotch reel to "Wee Macgregor" on the gramophone. "Amongst my most frequent visitors is Mrs. Patrick Campbell," Lucy was able to boast to a friend; and Shaw appreciated Stella's amiability, telling her, "You brought out a nice side of Lucy that I haven't seen since she was a girl."

His dream was still not out, and he proposed joining her at the seaside. A tender letter from him had again kindled some feeling, but Stella refused. She left the second week in August with Georgina, her maid, Prosser, her chauffeur (she had purchased a motor that summer), a mountain of luggage, and Barrie's play. Ordering Prosser to unpack, she threw off her hat, gazed about the cottage, and prepared to discover relaxation and renewal. Playfair had privately bet she would not stand the solitude four hours; actually, it was a full twelve hours later that Stella burst out of the cottage and made for the nearest luxury hotel. That same evening the Playfairs' housekeeper answered a knock at the door to find a tall, silver-whiskered gentleman in walking boots and knickers, looking quite done in from his expedition across the sands. Informed that Mrs. Campbell had departed suddenly for the Guilford Hotel at Sandwich Bay, he spun on his heel and strode off into the night.

Stella's reaction on finding Shaw a fellow guest at the Guilford was less than enthusiastic. She unwillingly accepted his company for two days. As if to make up for her half-heartedness, Shaw radiated zest, adventurousness, and high spirits. Stella yawned. Finally she wrote him a note: "Please will you go back to London to-day—or go wherever you like but don't stay here. If you won't go I must—I am very very tired and I oughtn't to go another journey. Please don't make me despise you." Stella was ultimately respectable: to share a week with one man (at a hotel notorious for fashionable liaisons) while she had decided to marry another was not to her taste.

Shaw did not leave; she did not appear. That night he went out to look for her on the flinty beach where the lights of Ramsgate twinkled to the north. She was not there. When they finally met, she explained that she had been occupied in a frantic search for Georgina, who had lost herself in the tall grasses that thatched the dunes. They shared a nightcap. "You've paid your bill, and gingerbeer one shilling," said the waiter to Stella, and as Shaw paid, she wondered whether he understood. She noted with annoyance that he was terribly sleepy, perhaps in self-protection; but she did not want lovemaking now, had he offered it. "Let us bathe before breakfast, at a quarter to eight," said Shaw. "No, at eight," replied Stella. "Too late," protested Shaw: "a quarter to eight." "Please not before eight," she begged. The next morning she rose at six, wrote, "Goodbye. I am still tired—you were more fit for a journey than I," and by 7:30 her driver was speeding her south in the rain with Georgina, Prosser, and the luggage along the coastal road to St. Margaret's Bay. Since all hotels were full, however, they went on to Littlestone-on-Sea, where she found large rooms with a balcony overlooking the sea.

Cries of rage reached her there next day. Had he seemed sleepy? asked Shaw. A tactful retreat in the face of her obvious boredom. *He* had been ready enough. "Bah! You have no nerve: you have no brain: you are the caricature of an eighteenth century male sentimentalist, a Hedda Gabler titivated with odds and ends from Burne Jones's ragbag: you know nothing, God help you, except what you know all wrong: daylight blinds you: you run after life furtively and run away or huddle up and scream when it turns and opens its arms to you . . . you are a one-part actress and that one not a real part: you are an owl, sickened by two days of my sunshine. . . . Go then: the Shavian oxygen burns up your little lungs: seek some stuffiness that suits you. You will not marry George! At the last moment you will funk him or be ousted by a bolder soul. You have wounded my vanity: an inconceivable audacity, an unpardonable crime."

"Oh, my rancor is not yet slaked," she read, opening a second letter the same day. He had not pressed her into love; he was not greedy; there were to have been seven days, and he had wanted the last to be the best. But she knew nothing but an erotic sentimentality that wanted to be forced because it could initiate nothing. He had proposed freedom and fellowship; her soul had not been large enough to embrace them. A third letter arrived the next day. Pain had replaced outrage. "Another day that might have been a day!" she read. "What have I shrunk into? . . . How could a human heart deal another such a—such a kick?"

"You lost me because you never found me," Stella retorted. "I who have nothing but my little lamp and flame—you would blow it out with your bellows of self. You would snuff it with your egotistical snortings—you elegant charmer—you lady-killer—you precious treasure of friendship— for you do I keep my little lamp burning for fear you may lose your way in the dark. . . . Do you think it was nothing to me to hurt my friend?" Still another pained protest reached her. "You are trying to break my heart with your letters," she defended herself. "You know I did *rightly*. What other thing was there for me to do? I had to behave like a man—and a gentleman hadn't I? I will see you Monday or Tuesday."

Trying to forget the unhappy man at Sandwich (she did not think him fatally so), she sat in the sea to bathe, took sunset drives along the coast to Rye, played with Georgina on the sands. There were miles of sea all round, sea that came right up to the green in front of her lodging house; miles of heather and sky. On Friday, however, she found herself looking about for him, half expecting that he might have come after her. That night she found no letter, so she wrote him the next day. "I have studied—I have rested—I have slept—I have thought a great deal—and I am ready for four months hard work. I leave at 2 o'c today and arrive at 7 this evening." Shaw himself had been back in London "from the land of broken promise" since

Wednesday. "You could not argue your case half as well as I have argued it fifty times," he told her, still stinging from the rebuff, yet wanting to excuse her. He *knew* he would telephone her when she returned.

But the Guilford episode proved decisive. Even though they continued to meet, Stella was somehow irretrievably lost. When he left for the Continent again with Charlotte, he continued to write faithfully, but his style was subdued. He was horribly unhappy every morning, he told her; he welcomed the inevitable business of travel that would occupy him for the day. Stella herself was occupied with *The Adored One* and seldom wrote.

Rehearsals were "miserable," even though she had great faith in Barrie's play. She had liked it from the moment he read it to her; she found it funny and charming that a mother should push a man out of a railway carriage and that the solemnity of a murder trial should be burlesqued. And that she liked it was all that mattered to Stella; she never judged a play by commercial or any other ordinary standards. Yet Frohman was also delighted to have a play by the popular Barrie, and everyone looked to the magic ingredients of Barrie, the lucky Duke of York's, and the inimitable Mrs. Pat to combine in a huge success. Her friends too were profoundly relieved that Stella had this means of financial recovery—for when it came to borrowing money from them, said Denis Mackail, she "had the conscience of the most obstinate and determined man."

On the first night of *The Adored One* the magic ingredients failed. The curtain rose on a crowded house; the man refused to shut the carriage window; Stella opened the door and pushed him out. But instead of the expected laugh, the audience gasped. Was this a joke? Was this what Barrie thought of mother love? Then between the acts the heavy courtroom scenery jammed. Waiting out the long interval, the audience found time to decide that spoofs of murder were not funny. The trial act was devoted to proving that Leonora possessed so much charm that she could get away with murder. The audience was not convinced. When the curtain fell, Barrie—for the first time in his life—was booed.

He appeared in Stella's dressing room to tell her that no one had ever worked so beautifully for him before; then in desperation went to consult Boucicault about saving the play for her and Frohman. At length he returned wearily to his flat in Adelphi Terrace, and there Stella, Beo, the Countess of Lytton, and Viscountess Gladstone eventually found him after supper at the Savoy. Barrie hid his fatigue and disappointment, so that Stella found him, as usual, gentle and dear; but in the next days he quickly turned the trial scene into a dream sequence, added a love scene, and finally some nightmare effects to show that there had been no murder at all. More rehearsals; another first night; but failure was too much in the air, and the play ran ten weeks instead of the four months Stella had expected.

She comforted herself a little by buying her baby grandson, Patrick, his first shoes and stockings before Stella Pat and Mervyn took him back to Africa along with a nanny who was looking forward rather apprehensively to living in a mud hut. As Stella had predicted, her daughter was not happy. Mervyn often went on safari, leaving her alone in the tiny village of Ngong. She longed for England. That autumn too Stella was deserted by Beo and Helen. Lord Savile had become an intimate of the family since the death of his wife, Violet, a close friend of Stella's; now he offered to make Beo's dreams of becoming a theatrical producer true. With Savile's signature, Beo was able to borrow the enormous sum of £10,000, rent an office in Mayfair, buy a likely light comedy called *The Night Hawk*, engage a competent cast, and hire Lady Duff-Gordon to make the fabulous costumes. There was so much money that the couple could move from the bedroom under the roof at Kensington Square to a small furnished flat in Berkeley Street. When Stella was terribly hurt, there was the excuse that Beo needed to be near his office and the theatre. Helen also found herself deserted as Beo became a man of affairs; to console her he gave her a valuable Japanese spaniel, WuPu, which he had accepted in payment of a debt. As the opening of *The Night Hawk* approached, however, Beo was not only busy, but oddly withdrawn and sombre. He denied that anything was wrong, but Helen grew increasingly worried. Then one day, going through the laundry hamper, she discovered that all of Beo's evening shirts had baize-green cuffs.

It would have been strange if Stella's son had been able to manage money, and stranger if the spoiled young man who wanted everything right away had not turned to gambling as a way of getting it. Helen had known Beo gambled; she did not know that Stella had paid thousands of pounds of Beo's gaming debts. Confronted with the shirt-cuffs, Beo confessed. A group of professional sharpers had heard of his £10,000 windfall, and had fleeced him of every penny. None of the production expenses had been paid; Beo was not only cleaned out, but in disgrace.

This left Savile with a bad debt of £10,000 and only one choice: to take over *The Night Hawk*, pay all costs out of his own pocket, and hope for a success. He succeeded in hoping, but the play was loudly booed and collapsed in less than two weeks. Since New York often welcomed London failures (and vice versa), it was decided that Beo go to America to find a producer. Whether he succeeded or not, Helen and Beo agreed that she would follow in a last attempt to save their disintegrating marriage. Her patience with her handsome, irresponsible husband was almost at an end. Beo perhaps had his own discontents: there was evidence that the wife who had chosen to spend her wedding night alone in hair curlers had not improved dramatically since. On December 14 Beo sailed for New York, leaving behind a mother exhausted with his shiftlessness, and a disenchanted wife.

That fall Stella had cast Shaw in the role of marriage counselor to herself and George. "There are rocks ahead," she told him, "—you are wise and clear sighted. . . . Be quite serious in your friendship for me—I am so troubled just now, and must put aside trimmings and prettiness." One of the rocks was the ten-year difference in their ages. She had gone to a play and wept like a baby when the slim-as-a-pin leading lady said goodbye to her silly man. To think what she would be ten years hence; to realize that now was the golden hour and still be afraid to seize it. Another rock was George's precarious financial situation. He had quarrelled repeatedly with Jennie about her extravagances which he could not support, but his own style of living had done as much to put him deeply in debt. His style was matched by Stella's. She was spending the Christmas holidays at the Berkeley Hotel in Eastbourne; the manager had made reductions for her, but the cost was ruinous, nevertheless.

Brooding, on these familiar themes, she was reminded that Shaw had promised her his play. She'd heard he had talked with Tree about *Pygmalion* at His Majesty's. "I know you made yourself out a fine fellow," she wrote him on December 20 from Eastbourne, "—but what did you make of me? I was told today that you wanted me to play 'Eliza' for the joy of making a fool of me. A Merry Christmas."

Shaw ignored her distrust. He himself was staying alone in a hotel at Ilfracombe, estranged from Charlotte. He answered with a last burst of emotion for the year that had been and was gone:

New Years Eve. O night of all nights in the year—of my most immemorial year! Do you remember last New Years Eve? I am actually asking you do you remember it? Was it anything to you except that you were ill, and were determined to prevent me from seeing the new year in with Lillah and Barrie? *I* remember it: it tears me all to pieces: I believe we were both well then, and have been ill ever since. . . . I think of it with a frightful yearning, with a tragic despair: for you have wakened the latent tragedy in me, broken through my proud overbearing gaiety that carried all the tragedies of the world like feathers and stuck them in my cap and laughed. And if your part in it was an illusion, then I am as lonely as God. Therefore you must still be the Mother of Angels to me, still from time to time put on your divinity and sit in the heavens with me. For that, with all our assumed cleverness and picked up arts to stave off the world, is all we two are really fit for. Remember this always even when we are grovelling and racketing and drudging; for in this remembrance I am deeply faithful to you—faithful beyond all love. Be faithful to me in it and I will forgive you though you betray me in everything else—forgive you, bless you, honor you, and adore you. *Super hanc Stellam* will I build my Church.

And now let us again hear the bells ring: you on your throne in your blue hood, and I watching and praying, not on my knees, but at my fullest stature. For you I wear my head nearest the skies.

"Such a wonderful beautiful letter," replied Stella, awed. ". . . If I could write letters like you, I would write letters to God."

# THIRTY

## *1914–1916*

*B*Y FEBRUARY of 1914 negotiations that had begun the previous November when Shaw read *Pygmalion* to Tree in the penthouse dome at His Majesty's were all but complete. Stella had never been the terror at His Majesty's that she was at the St. James's; Tree was too absent-minded to remember unpleasantness anyway; and besides, every actor-manager knew that Mrs. Pat was the only actress on the stage who could (if she wished) carry a play to success on her shoulders alone. Still, Tree protested when she asked for £130 a week, full salary for matinees, and 2½ per cent of the receipts with an eight weeks' guarantee. Stella replied that her best offer was 2 per cent after the first £700, and left him to fight it out with her solicitor, Bouchier Hawksley.

"You are wonderful at rehearsal," she wrote Shaw enthusiastically on February 21, "and we'll all shed our blood for you." As it turned out, a great deal of blood was shed during the following weeks. Shaw was a tactful director, but insisted that his plays be interpreted his way: "I like an empty head for my ideas," he told Stella. He remembered, too, that D.D. had thought him too craven to handle Stella and was determined not to be intimidated. Tree could be directed by no one. Despite her promise to be "tame as a mouse and oh so obedient," Stella throve on conflict. The three geniuses met head on. "It will be AWFUL if in the end I find even Bouci-cault easier to work with than you Joey!" Stella warned, only three days after the "wonderful rehearsal."

Actually, Stella worked enormously hard on Eliza Doolittle, wanting to please Shaw even while she fought him. One of the best jokes of *Pygmalion* was that it had the "Queen of Snobs" playing a barbarous-tongued cockney guttersnipe badly in need of delousing and a bath. Stella sweated over the challenge of "Te-oo baynches o' violets," "Never yeow moind, young men," and "Thenk you koindly, laidy"—and experimented with "Loiza Deowlit-tle" or "Lawza Deulittle" as the better rendition. Phonetic pencillings in her prompt copy alternated with propitiating little scribbles to Shaw: "Bless you for your pretty compliments"; "My hand is held out Joey"; "I'll do my level best to be exactly what you want"; "Your delicious play needs real greatness sympathy & intelligence"; "gentle Joey." When she could wrestle his rehearsal notebook away from him, she scribbled "Darling" and "beloved" and "dear DEAR Joey" in the margins.

Had she been able to study it at more leisure, she might have been less amiable. Shaw sketched her in feather boa and straw hat looking all her forty-nine years. "Dreadfully middle-aged moments," he jotted at the point where Higgins chucks Eliza under the chin and says, "Youre not bad looking." Stella did her own sketches of him in her copy, and—very self-conscious about her middle-aged profile—drew it, then wishfully cancelled the dewlaps and redrew a young line. It did not help when Shaw called up from the stalls, "Good God: you are forty years too old for Eliza; sit still and it's not so noticeable!"

The thoughtless Tree often wandered away from the stage in the middle of a scene, missed his lines or had not learned them, and was so forgetful that once, when the slippers Stella was required to pitch at him hit him square in the face, he collapsed, totally shattered, forgetting it was part of the business. His vagueness drove the efficient Shaw almost as wild as Stella's pig-headedness. Accustomed to writing little notes to guide his actors, he now penned Tree a lengthy missive. "I will not go so far as to say that all people who write letters of more than eight pages are mad, but it is a curious fact that all madmen write letters of more than eight pages," mused Tree. "It's splendid of Tree to accept with gentle indifference letters that would have made a frenchman 'call you out,' " scolded Stella. "Why did he? because none of us can spare the time to take that side of you that *hurts* seriously!" As Shaw's commands and directives grew more frequent, Tree took him aside. Plays, he suggested, had actually been produced at His Majesty's once or twice in the past without G.B.S.

Rehearsals blew up with amazing regularity. Once they were halted while Tree recovered from Shaw's "I say, Tree, must you be so treacly?" More often it was Stella and Shaw who collided. "Some day you'll eat a pork chop, Joey," Stella challenged from the footlights, "—and then God help all women!" Sometimes when they clashed over her rendition of Eliza's cockney, she refused to continue until he left the theatre. Upon these occasions Shaw would gather up his notes and make a reproachfully dignified exit. Once, however, she did not let him get out of the dress circle before launching into her lines. Shaw wheeled. "Accursed woman," he cried, "can't you wait till I am out of earshot?" Tree also cursed. "Why do you always turn your back to me at this point!" he fumed. "But it's a very nice back, isn't it?" purred Stella, getting a chuckle from Shaw. Often her conduct sent Tree screaming from the stage; for days they communicated through an intermediary. One morning Philip Merivale, cast for Colonel Pickering, was waiting in the wings. "That there Patrick Campbell," confided a hand, eyeing the stage, "'e was a lucky man!" "Why, yes," agreed Merivale, "she's still a handsome woman." "I don't mean that, I mean 'e got 'isself killed in the Boer War!" "I never could bring myself to hit [Tree] hard enough," sighed Shaw, "whereas no poker was thick enough, no brick heavy enough, to leave a bruise on Mrs. Campbell." Stella did not agree. "I hope you will make heaps of money Joey and keep your gay belief that you and your play alone did it and that without you there would have been but failure and fools," she wrote in April, exhausted by Shaw's "ceaseless teasing and braggarting." "Any more directions you have for me give me through Bell."

On Monday, April 6, Jennie was granted a decree nisi, dissolving her marriage to Cornwallis-West. ". . . I understand that you are going to be married on Tues.," she wrote George. "You need not fear what I may say, for I will not willingly speak of you. . . . I am returning you my engagement and wedding rings—I say good-bye—a long, long good-bye." At the last moment George's sister Daisy, Princess of Pless, wired Jennie without success not to make the decree absolute, evidently panicking at the thought of an actress for a sister-in-law. Stella and George did not even wait for Tuesday. Two hours after the decree was granted, they were married at the Kensington Registry Office, Stella's lawyer, Bouchier Hawksley, accompanying them. Stella wore a black silk dress trimmed with plaid ribbons under a white net vest, and a black hat. George fought back hysteria at the sight of the two witnesses, who, except for white ties, looked exactly, he thought, like mutes at a funeral. Outside, photographers tried to snap them as they emerged. George saw red, grabbed their cameras, stuffed them into his car, and drove off to Kensington Square, where Stella had preceded him. Then the couple set off in George's car for Crowborough, a breezy golfing resort near Tunbridge Wells. The honeymoon was necessarily brief, since Stella had disappeared from His Majesty's without a word and *Pygmalion* was due to open in five days.

"We were happy at last," said Stella, "—I with my belief in the love I had struggled against for so long—convinced that George had been a very unhappy man—that his unhappiness had been the fault of others—and that I could help him." Privately, she rejoiced in "the deep deep peace of the double bed after the hurly-burly of the chaise-longue"—or of Shaw's frustrating bedside timidities. Others were less optimistic about the marriage which had earned George the nickname "The Old Wives' Tale." "His people must love him because of his 'expression,' if nothing else," Violet, Duchess of Rutland, wrote Stella ambiguously, "and if they love him they must be glad to know how happy he is." Jennie's brother-in-law Moreton Frewen was more blunt: "So that beauty George West is to be married on Tuesday to Mrs. Pat Campbell. . . . Full Fathom Five they dive to a joint folly."

She did not think so now. Sweeping into His Majesty's in time for dress rehearsal at six o'clock on Thursday, she ignored Tree's inarticulate fury, explaining only, "George is a GOLDEN man!" Tree's temper was not improved by Shaw's suggesting to him at the Friday rehearsal that he might share some of the spotlight he'd been hoarding for thirty years. "I've stood your insults long enough. I'll have no more of them!" cried the outraged Tree. "Ah, now, don't lose your temper," cajoled Shaw. "If you could just forget that you are Sir Herbert Beerbohm Tree for a moment and step into the part of Professor Higgins, we'd get along splendidly." Shaw also had last-minute advice for Stella, hurling her a directive the day of opening:

### FINAL ORDERS

The name Nepean is in two syllables, not three. . . . If you have ever said to Stella in her childhood "I'll let you see whether you will . . . obey me or not," and then inverted her infant shape and smacked her until the Square . . . rang with her screams, you will . . . know how to speak the line "I'll let you see whether I'm dependent on you." There is a certain dragging intensity, also used in Act IV in "YOU thank God etc," which is wanted here to re-establish your lead after Higgins' long speech about science and classical music and so on. The author took care to re-establish it by giving Eliza a long and energetic speech in reply to him; but the ignorant slave entrusted with the part thought she knew better than the author, and cut out the speech as useless. Now she has got to do it the other way. . . .

At the end when Higgins says "Oh, by the way Eliza," bridle your fatal propensity to run like Georgina to anyone who calls you, and to forget everything in an affectionate tête à tête with him. Imagine that he is the author, and be scornful. . . .

That smile on "More friendly like" is developing to excess. It should be the ghastliest wannest thing, because you are just about to burst into tears; and the smile must be that sort of smile. . . . Make that smile an inch wider, and you may as well stand on the points of your toes and raise your arms gracefully above your head.

I give up in despair that note of terror in the first scene which collects the crowds and suddenly shews the audience that there is a play there, and a human soul there, and a social problem there, and a formidable capacity for feeling in the trivial giggler of the comic passages. But until you get it I shall never admit that you can play Eliza, or play Shaw.

The danger tonight will be a collapse of the play after the third act. I am sending a letter to Tree which will pull him together if it does not kill him. But a good deal will depend on whether you are inspired at the last moment. You are not, like me, a great general. You leave everything to chance. . . . I could have planned the part so that nine tenths of it would have gone mechanically even if your genius had deserted you, leaving only one tenth to the Gods. Even as it is, I have forced half the battle on you; but winning half the battle will not avert defeat. You believe in courage: I say "God save me from having to fall back on that desperate resource," though if it must come to that it must. I dont like fighting: I like conquering. You think you like fighting; and now you will have to succeed sword in hand. You have left yourself poorly provided with ideas and expedients; and you must make up for them by dash and brilliancy and resolution. And so, *Avanti!*

"Dear Joey," Stella replied meekly. "All success to you to-night. It's nice to think of your friendship and your genius—I'll obey orders faithfully, I am so thankful you carried through your giant's work to the finish."

Thanks to Shaw's and Tree's genius for showmanship, the forthcoming production of *Pygmalion* had been boomed to an incredible extent. The newspapers were full of puffery and photographs, especially of Stella, including one of her in *The Trumpet Call* with the caption, "This dress fell off on first night." One paper featured a daily column about the play; another sponsored a contest to guess what the "naughty" word Eliza speaks at the end of the third act was going to be, raising expectation to fever pitch. Tree piled interview on interview, Shaw did the same, and the advanced booking soared to almost £4000. The press had played up Mrs. Pat as a cockney, reporting that she'd had lessons from a real *h*-dropping flower girl. On Saturday morning flower girls by the dozen gathered around the statue of Eros in Piccadilly Circus, then marched to His Majesty's and queued at the gallery door. Tree had arranged for one particular flower girl to be at the theatre door at ten a.m. dressed like Eliza—dark woolen shawl, canvas apron, rolled sleeves, button boots, plain shiny black "beater" straw hat skewered with an enormous hatpin, a bottle of spirits clutched in her hand. The whole district was patrolled by photographers. Hurrying to His Majesty's at Tree's request at three o'clock that afternoon, Shaw found himself being snapped as far away as the National Gallery. When he arrived, he found Tree agonizing over an issue of the *Daily Sketch* that demanded *Pygmalion* be stopped before its language could profane the theatre of Shakespeare. Tree begged Shaw to withdraw the "bloody," or at least substitute "ruddy." Shaw refused.

That evening he dined with friends, then went on to the theatre. Charlotte did not accompany him. Ill, estranged, and alone in London much of the previous winter, she was unaware that her husband's romance with

Stella had collapsed. As plans shaped for an April production, she decided that she preferred not to face a play which seemed to her a public testimony to her husband's infatuation, and sailed for America on April 8, two days before the *Times* announced the marriage of Stella and Cornwallis-West.

Shaw found the theatre crammed, as expected. His protest against the immoderate laughter which he felt often wrecked his plays was read aloud, and the audience seemed disposed to behave itself. Then he sat back, dog-tired, to watch the play that had begun as an idea for Forbes and the young Mrs. Pat and had finally fought its way through to a production seventeen years later.

From the moment the curtain rose on Tree under an umbrella in Covent Garden with "real" rain falling, to Eliza's triumphant exit in a taxi, the first act went smoothly, delightfully. No one noticed that Stella was thirty years too old to play Eliza; "sword in hand," she conquered them. During the sustained applause Shaw hurried round to tell Tree that the play was safe until the end of the third act, and found him as happy and excited as a child.

In the second act Geraldine Olliffe played very well as Mrs. Pearce and Edmund Gurney as Doolittle was, thought Shaw, "a colossal success." He was glad to see that although there was plenty of laughter the action was not being seriously interrupted. The applause at the end of the second act was long and happy. During the third act, however, the house could hardly contain itself. Stella played the tea-party scene magnificently, ravishing the audience almost to delirium. But the moment Shaw dreaded was approaching. "Are you walking across the Park, Miss Doolittle?" asks young Freddie. "If so . . ." Stella lifted her chin. "Walk!" she exclaimed, and then with the most elegant diction, uttered the *word:* "Not bloody likely." There was a great gasp from the audience, an intake of breath that could have been mistaken for a hiss. Then the house began to rock with laughter. Shaw sat aghast as the audience roared and cried themselves into such total abandon that he doubted whether the play could continue. Tree's stage manager timed the delirium with a stopwatch: it went on for an unparalleled minute and a quarter.

Shaw believed that the difficulty would come now with the inevitable letdown after Stella's performance in the third act. But there was not only a letdown, thought Shaw, "writhing in hell" through Acts IV and V; the perverse Tree was going just opposite to his instructions and descending further and further into absurdity every moment. Not Stella, however. She was magnificent, playing way over Tree's head and saving the whole fourth act. In the fifth she cleverly played to Tree, letting him emote and "firing off broadside after broadside" for him to meet. She had done—to Shaw's amazement—virtually everything he had instructed her to do, whereas Tree seemed to be doing his best to thwart him. The last thing Shaw saw as he hurried from the theatre to avoid the calls for the author was Tree wooing Eliza like a Romeo, completely ignoring Shaw's direction that he occupy himself affectionately with his mother and coolly fling Eliza's commission to buy ham over his shoulder as an afterthought.

Surely, thought Stella, no first night had ever gone with more success and joyousness than that first night of *Pygmalion*. She herself had not met with such universal acclaim since the first night of *Tanqueray*. "Mrs. Pat held audience spellbound . . . Mrs. Campbell's Eliza is a delicious thing," raved the critics. "Those who saw the first night of Pygmalion at His Majesty's theatre in 1914," wrote George West long after he might have been accused of partiality, "will remember how, despite the brilliancy of the play, it was her personality which carried it to success. The late Sir Herbert Tree, never famous for remembering his lines, forgot many of them that night, and this made her task the more formidable." It had all been worthwhile—the quarrels, the directives, the insistence that Shaw was master and she the ignorant slave.

The next day Stella, George, and his huge black retriever, Beppo, motored down to Ayot St. Lawrence, where Shaw gave them lunch and tea to make up for avoiding congratulations and dressing-room kisses the night before. Both Stella and George were very amiable and very happy, and treated him like a beloved uncle. Or so he told Charlotte in a letter that day, adding that she *must* in future consent to receive Cornwallis-West in the country. In the same letter he expressed doubt that *Pygmalion* could succeed. The farcical success of the first three acts and Stella's acting in the last two might save the play; at any rate, nothing would persuade him to sit through another performance.

In coming weeks Shaw grew increasingly disgusted with the whole business. Proofs of photographs showed him looking "like an old dog who had been in a fight and got the worst of it." He suppressed them, but sent one to Stella inscribed "Aren't you ashamed?" and to Tree "This is your work." He was even more disgusted that the "Not bloody likely" pushed every other critical consideration of the play into the background. As the wildly successful production continued to run, he was still further harassed by letters from Tree complaining that the play was too long and that Stella did not change dresses quickly enough. Counter-complaints came from Stella: "Tree takes 5 minutes between each word and each bite of the apple in Act 4. I have facial paralysis from trying to express some sort of intelligent

Stella as Fanny Armaury in *The Foolish Virgin*

*Above and below:*

*Deirdre* at the Abbey Theatre with J. M. Kerrigan, 1908

Stella and Sarah Bernhardt in *Pelléas et Mélisande*, 1904

In *The Sorceress*

Stella in the first production of
*Mr. and Mrs. Daventry*

As Electra, 1908

*The Bondman,* 1906

George Cornwallis-West          Sir George Alexander

*His Borrowed Plumes*, 1909. (From left to right beginning with third figure) *back row*: Winifred Fraser, Henry Ainley, Mrs. Patrick Campbell, Dawson Milward, Stella Patrick Campbell; *front row*: Annie Hughes, Mrs. George Cornwallis-West, Gertrude Kingston

George Arliss, Beo, and Stella in Chicago

George Bernard Shaw

Stella, photographed by Bernard Shaw

Cartoons by Max Beerbohm
*Left*: Mrs. Campbell and Mr. Shaw as they respectively appeared to themselves
*Right*: Mrs. Campbell and Mr. Shaw as they respectively appeared to each other

Stella as Eliza Doolittle

From *Pygmalion*

The first costume sketch for Eliza
Doolittle by Charles A. Buchel

Sir Herbert Beerbohm Tree
in *Pygmalion*, 1914

*Madame Sand,* 1920

Madame Rosalie La Grange
in *The Thirteenth Chair*

*Ghosts,* with John Gielgud

Stella, 1926

In *The Sex Fable* with Ronald Squire and Anthony Ireland

Mrs. Pat on the occasion of her United States
radio debut with the NBC Radio Guild
in *The Second Mrs. Tanqueray*

As Mrs. MacDonald in *A Party*

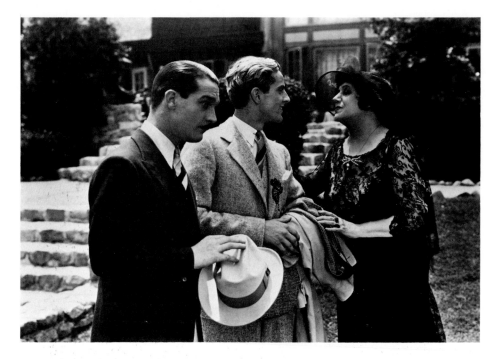

In *The Dancers*, 1930

With Norma Shearer and Moonbeam in *Riptide*, 1934

*One More River* with Jane Wyatt, 1934

As the old pawnbroker in *Crime and Punishment*
with Marian Marsh and Peter Lorre, 1935

Hollywood.
*Standing*: Elizabeth Allan, Tai Lachman, Ivan Lebedeff, Loretta Young
*Sitting*: Anna Sten, Marlene Dietrich, Mrs. Patrick Campbell

Elsa Lanchester, Stella, and Charles Laughton
at the Trocadero

Stella Campbell. Photograph by Cecil Beaton—New York, 1919

feeling so now I hide my face until it is well again. . . . Come soon," she warned, "or you'll not recognize your play."

Shaw did not come. "Your play *goes* every night most wonderfully," Stella coaxed at the end of April, but she had finally discovered that Tree had the better role—hers was "a mere masquerade." Both Tree and she were genuinely hurt that Shaw had washed his hands of the production; Tree's only ambition in the world was that Shaw should be pleased with his Higgins. But Shaw did not enter the theatre again until the hundredth performance on July 15. Then he discovered that the incurably romantic actor had contrived to throw a bouquet to Stella just before the fall of the curtain, leaving no doubt in the audience's mind that Higgins and Eliza would wed. Shaw had himself subtitled the play "A Romance in 5 Acts," but romance for him meant the baffling of sexual passion, not its fulfilment. He left the theatre indignant. "My ending makes money," protested Tree; "you ought to be grateful." "Your ending is damnable," replied Shaw; "you ought to be shot." The playwright's indifference to his performance and the strain of playing with Stella soon discouraged Tree. At the end of June he announced that *Pygmalion* would come off in July. "It is quite absurd that the notice should go up at the end of a £2000 week!" complained Stella with justice. But Tree was immovable. Summer had inevitably thinned the houses; he wanted a holiday; and having netted £13,000 from the production, he left for Marienbad at the end of July.

Alexander then offered Stella the St. James's for *Pygmalion*, and she began negotiating a move, making her husband manager-in-chief. George turned to Shaw, whom he quite liked, and proposed that he and Shaw find the capital for a new production. Shaw was not unwilling, but advised that the cast from His Majesty's must be salvaged as much as possible, even though Stella would want to turn the St. James's into "a casual ward for all the unfortunates who want engagements." He would not produce again, but would tutor Philip Merivale as Higgins, trying for a crisp performance instead of Tree's "tedious slovenly one." As for Stella, she would continue to draw, amuse, and fascinate—but there would be no poor, dirty flower girl and therefore, in his opinion, no play. To let George in on an important professional secret, Stella was no actress at all, simply an enchantress, and her success at enchanting made her, for his purposes, "a complete idiot." He would help rearrange the enchantress's cave, although he expected that even this gesture would create storms.

But *Pygmalion* was not produced at the St. James's because no one seemed disposed to lend George money, and Stella rejected an alternate proposal: "Barker & the Kingsway & all the superiority of the lot of you would stifle me dead as mutton." Besides, events triggered by a shooting on June 28 somewhere in Bosnia were beginning to precipitate ominously. Although Ned Sheldon, visiting London, found that the recent divorce of Lady Randolph Churchill and her former husband's immediate marriage to Mrs. Campbell almost equalled the shock of the Archduke's assassination, there was growing realization that July that Europe was edging toward war. Americans began to flee Europe, jamming steamers. Sheldon lingered, seeing Stella often, cementing the friendship that had begun in New York two years before; but when chance offered a convenient passage home, he took it. Soon after, Stella and George left for Ireland with servants, dogs, and fishing rods, and an agreement with (yes) George C. Tyler for a fall production of *Pygmalion* in New York. And then on August 4 England declared war.

Stella cabled Beo in New York the same day to "COME AND HELP." His cable anticipated hers: "HAVE ARRANGED, SAILING." Beo had been unable to find a backer for *The Night Hawk*, and his marriage was over. Upon returning to England, he submitted to an operation so that he would be able to pass the medical board. War seemed an answer to his aimless existence. George rejoined the Scots Guards and was made a Lieutenant Colonel Commander a few weeks later; headlines announced that "MRS. CAMPBELL SENDS HER MEN TO WAR." Stella was scheduled to sail for New York on the *Lusitania* on October 3, hating to leave but, "As usual I had to make money." Although she always insisted, "I like porters, not sentiment, at railway stations," this time she was genuinely unhappy. "I hate leaving my responsibilities, my beloved George and my dear dear children," she told Shaw, who came to the boat train to see her off. "You have Charlotte to look after you." It was true, and she left sadly with her maid, Mills, and WuPu.

WuPu? In New York, Helen Campbell picked up her newspaper to find a front-page photo of a smiling Stella descending the gangplank of the *Lusitania*, a little dog cuddled against her cheek, and the headline "MRS. PAT BACK IN U.S. WITH NEW DOG." Furious, Helen immediately guessed what had happened. Stella's trademark was a small dog. She could not bear to put Georgina in six-month quarantine. On the pretense of restoring WuPu to Helen, then, she had left her beloved Georgina behind with Morrie and taken WuPu, who would have to face quarantine on return to England while Stella went home to a rapturous Georgina. Giving Stella the benefit of the doubt, Helen waited for the knock on the door and the restoration of her pet; but no word came from Stella at all.

*Pygmalion* opened on October 12, three days after Stella's arrival, at the

Park Theatre in Columbus Circle. On the eve of production, Shaw sent off a letter of warning to Tyler—as though Tyler needed warning about the Royal Tigerine. Tyler would find that her change of dress took longer than the change of scenery: he must find her a dressing room on stage level. "If you cannot give her a room on the stage level she will agitate for a tent (she had one at His Majesty's here); and when SHE starts agitating don't argue but surrender at once, even if it involves rebuilding the theatre; you will find it cheaper in the long run." The play had run until 11:30 in London, but that was because Tree was so abominably slow—Merivale would beat his time by forty-five minutes. Now, Stella would still want the play cut, "partly because its length hurries her dressing and interferes with the de-lightful levees she holds in her dressing-room, and partly because she thinks that Mrs. Pearce and Doolittle are insufferable bores and should be cut down to two or three lines apiece." But though he must agree with her in everything, Tyler must not cut a line. "It is no use arguing; she is clever enough to talk your hair grey; but she has no more judgment than a baby, and will spoil the play if you will let her. She does not know where the interest of the play really comes; and does not care twopence about the part, to which she has never given five minutes' serious thought, except as an excuse for fascinating and a joke. . . . She can give a charming per-formance if she likes, and if she sticks loyally to the text and does not gag or play for silly laughs. . . . The moral of all this is, that, for her sake and for your own, you must stick to me and to the play, and resist all her wiles . . . if mortal man can resist such a siren—which I rather doubt."

*Pygmalion* was played uncut; Merivale did beat Tree's time by forty-five minutes; and the ignorant slave again ravished her audience, even though she delayed the fourth act by a delightful levee. After the triumph the audience remained standing, calling her back again and again. No other actress (thought first-night critics) could have achieved the irony and depth of feeling, have been at once so comical and pathetic. Stella finally answered the tumult with a speech. Her voice was sad; she spoke of the war and of a world that was changing before everyone's eyes, seeming, thought one critic, the "most melancholy of mortals." Then she went to despatch a cablegram to Shaw. "FROM ALL APPEARANCES YOUR PLAY IS A GREAT SUCCESS. YOU ARE," she added with a straight face, "A MADE MAN."

She was far more concerned about the other George. On landing she had received the news that he had been shot in the courtyard of the Ritz as a spy. More believable reports told of his escape from Antwerp in one of the first bunglings of the war. Churchill as First Lord of the Admiralty had realized Antwerp's strategic role as the bulwark of the Pas-de-Calais and had sent a brigade of two thousand men of the British Royal Naval Division on October 3 to relieve the besieged city. But it was too late, and with the retreat of the Belgian Army, the hopelessly outnumbered British were at the mercy of the Germans. Some of the shockingly untrained division broke and bolted into Holland; others stayed and fought their way out through the Germans. George was one of these and, though privately feeling he would never make it, managed to find his way through Denmark and eventually back to England. "Churchill is very much blamed," Shaw told Stella, who was intensely frustrated by lack of news from England. "Altogether George could hardly have had a harder job, or one bringing a higher proportion of kicks to halfpence." In England rumors that George (whose sister Daisy was married to a German) had been shot as a spy persisted until, enraged, he got his solicitor to send a letter to the *Times* declaring that he was alive and exceedingly annoyed by vicious rumors to the contrary.

All this news reached Stella through Shaw, who was being violently condemned for his anti-war stance back in England. "This war is getting too silly for words," he wrote her in frustration: "they make no headway and produce no result except kill, kill, kill. The Kaiser asks from time to time for another million men to be killed; and Kitchener asks for another million to kill them. . . . Do we two belong to this race of cretins?" Other news was that Forbes-Robertson had beat by £500 her first week of *Pygmalion* with *Caesar and Cleopatra* in Chicago—it served her right for having just yawned and pinched Forbes's leg the day he read it to them both. And Stella junior, back in London for good without her husband, had quite lost her old woodenness onstage and gave a distinguished performance of a too easy part in *The Flag Lieutenant*. And she: did she ever ask herself what had become of his sonnets?

But Stella was too ill and busy to reply. From the Park Theatre she had transferred to the Liberty; on November 30 she began a week at Wallack's; on December 11 she gave a benefit matinee of *Tanqueray* for her sister-in-law the Duchess of Westminster's hospital, raising £500. Altogether she gave eleven performances her last week in New York—ten of *Tanqueray* and a tableau of Mélisande. On December 13 the *Pygmalion* company set out on tour, arriving via Pittsburgh in Detroit on the seventeenth. There, for the first time, the company realized that America too was worried about the war, though still not in it. Attendance was poor on opening night; seventy-two people turned up the second night; the third night Stella let her understudy face the empty house. They were not the only ones in trouble: on December 18 papers announced the failure of Liebler and Company, ruined by a disastrously expensive and equally poor production of Ned Sheldon's *The Garden of Paradise*. The *Pygmalion* crew were lucky enough to be bailed out by four performances to mammoth audiences during

Christmas week and good business at the Star Theatre in Buffalo on New Year's Eve. They began the new year trekking the Midwest—Cincinnati, Indianapolis, Louisville—and by the time they reached Lima, Ohio, Stella again had George, who had contrived three months' sick leave to join her.

She had been suffering from severe colds and a cough, but grew well and happy with his arrival. In Lima, however, there was trouble of the kind that George seemed adept at getting into. The local paper not only repeated the old but still juicy story that he had divorced Lady Randolph Churchill, twenty-three years his senior (an exaggeration—she was a mere eighteen) to marry Mrs. Pat hours later, but went on to declare flatly that his King and Country needed him more than did the American stage. George did not take this quietly. He blustered into the newspaper office and, although the editor had him firmly put out, drew another headline the next day: "GEORGE CORNWALLIS-WEST—FAR FROM THE FRONT—VERY FAR FROM THE FRONT—DECLARES WAR IN THE NEWSPAPER OFFICE." It did nothing for George's ego either when the New York *Sun* reported him employed by his wife as ticket-taker; actually, Stella had put him on the payroll as company manager.

At the Blackstone Hotel in Chicago, Stella worried about her own publicity. "Oh, the old ——!" the Chicago *Herald* had reported her as exclaiming over Shaw's demand for ten per cent on *Caesar and Cleopatra*. "There was a horrid interview in the paper here the other day," Stella explained hastily on February 3, her first letter to Shaw since mid-October. She was afraid of his formidable business sense (he had netted £16,595 the past year); she knew also that *Pygmalion* was now her bread and butter. ". . . Should you see the interview please pay no attention—it's all lies—never mentioned your % or offered any opinion." He was much loved in Chicago, she went on to assure him; only people *would* take his most "topical badinage" as "deepest and eternal truths." George was looking after her splendidly, as well as her side of the business. George was an angel—a most beloved man. She did not see how she could let him go back to that "crazy vulgar accursed war"—it was like a dream having him here. No, she did not miss Shaw's sonnets. Looking back at their love affair, she only regretted that he had betrayed himself hopelessly to her by poisoning Charlotte against her with his infernal mischief.

The company stayed a week in Chicago, but it was not like old times. "Where are all the people in Chicago I know?" Stella complained. "They're never here when I'm here." Relatively immobile at the beginning of the century when she had first exploded into the city's affections, wealthy Chicagoans had now discovered Palm Beach and Southern California and wintered elsewhere. The same was true when she arrived in Philadelphia: ten years, the automobile, and now the war seemed to have changed everything.

With George she observed her fiftieth birthday in Philadelphia happily enough, even though the fact that she was too old to play Eliza continued to torment her. She had lost weight with illness and the fatigue of the tour, however, and with the new slimness and her hair plaited around her head and a short jacket with a high neck, she hoped she gave some illusion of youth. And she continued to be happy with the courtly, handsome, sensitive Philip Merivale, whose playing of Higgins was so *alive*. Her own worries were temporarily silenced by a cable on February 19 from her darling Sarah in Bordeaux: "DOCTOR WILL CUT OFF MY LEG NEXT MONDAY AM VERY HAPPY KISSES ALL MY HEART." Pitou's cable four days later announcing that "MADAME IS AS WELL AS POSSIBLE" scarcely dulled the shock.

They went on to Washington, where a Mrs. Stotesbury lent Stella and George her mansion, her servants, and her motor; when Stella asked the housekeeper for a bill after a fling of entertaining, she was told, "There are no bills." Baltimore, Charleston, Boston: by then George's three months were up; he sailed for England on March 30. Toledo, Cleveland, Milwaukee the last week in May, Minneapolis, and a generous agreement from Shaw authorizing a summer tour from June 1 to September 30 and allowing her, besides her salary, half his author's fees every week that the gross receipts did not exceed $4000. Shaw was not all business. He had found George looking well and Georgina looking immensely fat. And when he had seen D.D. at the Albert Hall, where Sir Thomas Beecham was giving nightly concerts to make up for the suspension of all opera, his breast had welled with affection for those old times, a burst of sentiment dampened by Charlotte, who sat conspicuously studying her program.

Stella did not answer. The company crawled across the West in sweltering heat, playing to nearly empty houses. People thought *Pygmalion* highbrow and wouldn't come; her other standby, *Tanqueray*, had been done to death by the movie version and every little stock company in America. Even her cheap summer company did not save money. She arrived in San Francisco in mid-July, $7750 out of pocket, but was comforted by George's reappearance if not by the reason for it: financial embarrassment made his absence from England temporarily desirable. In San Francisco at the Columbia, though business picked up splendidly for two weeks, her manager felt she couldn't last the summer without a third play. George suggested something called *Searchlights* that he'd liked in London; of course, if George liked it, that was reason enough. But her part was too trifling—

the public always wanted her guts—and *Searchlights* lasted for seven performances.

George was very much enjoying himself, however. She had taught him the roles of Orreyed in *Tanqueray* and Doolittle, and he had the lead in *Searchlights.* But then he inconveniently collapsed; three of San Francisco's best doctors diagnosed "brain fag," and she sent him to the mountains to recover for six weeks. He stayed two, came back to act, moped about still unwell, so Stella sent him away again, this time to Glenwood Springs, Colorado, on a fishing trip. J. W. Austin, who had joined and opened as Higgins in San Francisco, had a different version of George's breakdown: he got tired of acting and went fishing.

Young and unafraid—two invaluable qualities if one were to act with Mrs. Campbell—Austin observed his new employer with amusement and awe. She was not exactly sylphlike, but had lost none of the superb fluid artistry, he thought. He found her tremendously outgoing, tremendously interested in all kinds of people, and generous to the extreme in helping them. He dared to ask whether the stories told about her were true. Stella denied that she was ever intentionally cruel, but admitted an irresistible urge to prick the balloon of vanity. When she confided during a rehearsal of *Tanqueray* that "Alexander looked like a waiter in his dress clothes," Austin understood how the prick could sting. Alexander was the most fashionable actor in London's most fashionable theatre, but Mrs. Pat had correctly spotted that he was *too* got up. "She had an Iago-ish sense of devilment," he concluded.

He endured the temperament onstage. He watched her fool away a whole act until the audience was restive, even hostile; then watched her come back, give her all, and have them eating out of her hand. Only once, during one of Higgins's long speeches, did her teasing get to him, and he walked off—he could do it, being Higgins and in his own house. He waited for seconds that seemed like hours, then returned to find Mrs. Pat rather white, arranging and rearranging her flower-girl feathers. She never mentioned the incident. On the other hand, he had never met anyone with a greater reverence for the art of acting. "It isn't the opinion of the many that counts," she would tell him, "—it is the opinion of the very few who know"; and—wisely, he thought—"To be a great actress you must have a bit of the gutter in you." "Her own acting was fascinating," said Austin. "Sometimes as Aubrey Tanqueray—a prig of a part—I'd give up and just watch her expressions and gestures and the large eyes which said much more than dialogue."

From the coast the company worked their way back toward the South. In

September Stella finally wrote Shaw from St. Louis. "I have grown quite plain and my hair is getting gray," she mourned. But it was not only the fatigue of touring—anxiety about the war set nerves on edge. The newspapers in America were enough to make them all maniacs, she told him; a few weeks ago there had been an enormous headline: "BRITISH NAVY SUNK." She had been very anxious about Beo. He got ill in the trenches at Gallipoli and was sent to Alexandria. Only three men left of his platoon; only two hundred of George's brigade—it made one sick to read it. And now she'd had a cable that Beo had returned to the front; no more news except five thousand casualties in the big engagement of August 29: "O the enormity and eternal bloody error of this war!" George's financial affairs were an added and continual worry, and somehow Shaw's common sense and sanity seemed particularly appealing now. "I miss you," she told him simply; "I wish you were here."

Louisville, New Orleans, Charleston—a blur of hotels, dressing rooms, theatres, and audiences that came, more or less, and applauded, more or less. The tour finally ended on October 26, and Stella and George fled to White Sulphur Springs, West Virginia, to recuperate. The next day she wrote D.D. the accumulated news of months.

Nina's youngest son Francis wounded, no word from Roy for weeks and weeks. Young Stella, her nurse, and baby Patrick living at the Square; Stella—with war making serious theatre in London impossible—very hard up. Her maid, Mills, too worried about her wounded fiancé to stay in America, back at the Square as housekeeper and cook for Stella. Helen unable to get her decree nisi because Beo was at the front. Stella still furious with Helen for an article she'd got published in *Harper's Bazaar* making fun "in vile taste" of Beo, friends, servants, and especially of Stella herself. (Stella also furious because one night in New York Helen had stolen into her dressing room and abducted WuPu, and she'd not been able to say a word.) George earning £30 a week, saving her £20, as a substitute for the actor who had cost her £50. (But George costing her hundreds of pounds a week to support.) Herself wanting to come home, but knowing that as long as she stayed away she was sending money back to George's creditors. *Pygmalion* unfortunately not appealing to the masses, or she would have made a fortune.

There was compensation as long as George was with her, but in January 1916 he was compelled to return to England to face bankruptcy charges. Desperate for £3000 to stave off his creditors, Stella set out on a series of one-night stands in Brooklyn, Newark, and Albany, swinging westward to Ohio and Indiana before returning for another circuit through upstate New York. She did not succeed.

"Harriet dearest," she wrote from Olean, New York. ". . . What I am going to say seems like madness & a wild dream! I want to know if you would lend me £2,500! I will hand you my Life Policy today full paid up for £3000 to hold until I have paid this debt to you. I could surely pay £1000 this autumn and the balance next year. I feel I wouldn't rest in this world or the next if I didn't make a supreme effort to help George. I can read between the lines of his letters how he is suffering. . . . Bankruptcy is a crushing despair to an Englishman—he has to leave all his clubs—many friends he must lose. I can't bear to think of my darling happy George— *crushed*. Harriet darling if there were anyone else in the world who had any money & cared a straw for us—I wouldn't ask you to help. . . . Darling cable me 'Yes' or 'impossible.' . . ."

Four days later George's creditors met at the London Bankruptcy Court under the receiving order made against him, finding that he had liabilities of £15,866 and assets valued at £969. The defendant attributed his failure to the war and to his having to pay large sums on behalf of a third party. This time he could not say, as he once had upon receiving a second speeding summons, "There isn't a sportsman among you; you ought to be shot."

On March 22 Stella wound up a tour that had lasted seventy-five weeks. She was too exhausted to drag on, and she had failed to save George. Back in New York, she hired a masseuse who declared she could *feel* Madame's inflamed nerves. When she lay down, she could not get up again; when she sat up, she could not lie down; when she laughed, she cried. The second week in April she sailed for England. On board, the holiday atmosphere of previous voyages was distinctly lacking; there were inevitable thoughts of the *Lusitania*, sunk without warning by a German submarine the previous May. She was provided with a lifebelt and instructions. Large stencilled letters on her cabin wall directed her to the nearest lifeboat; the lifeboats themselves bulked uncovered on deck. "I look about New York to make plans for this autumn," she had written Harriett, "& then I return to sad London *for a little*." But it would be eleven years before she saw America again.

# THIRTY-ONE

# *1916–1919*

*A*FTER SPENDING two restless days on board ship in Falmouth harbor before being permitted to land on April 19, Stella found a telegram from George asking her to wait for him there. She found rooms in a lovely inn overlooking the bay and filled them with daffodils for his arrival that evening on the night express. It was an emotional reunion, for that day he had faced the public examination of his affairs. He'd had to confess that he'd been borrowing heavily from moneylenders since 1901, and that since coming of age he'd raised £132,750 on mortgage of his reversion. As an officer in the Scots Guards he'd contracted debts of nearly £8000. Now, he had told them, he was only anxious to have the proceedings wound up so that he could go back to the Army. Stella soothed and petted her "golden pheasant," as she liked to call him. They had "three divine days" in Falmouth in the sunny rooms, eating fresh eggs and Cornish cream for breakfast and strolling about the town. Then George's mother wrote that they must come to Ruthin, and there, at the renovated red brick castle that dominated its steep, ancient village, Stella relaxed at last.

It was heaven, she told D.D.—lawns and meadows covered with primroses and daffodils, old-fashioned gardens and dungeons and secret passageways and a soft green hollow where the moat had been. Singing birds, blue, blue hills—more than a thousand acres of loneliness and peace. During the day they fished and hunted plovers' eggs and took tea with neighbors miles away; at night they slept in the very room where her beloved George had been born. The weather was splendid: mists at night and glorious mornings, and in the woods the blue hyacinths were coming out. George was so wonderful to her, and they understood each other. And he was writing a play. How he found time to do it in the midst of all his troubles, she did not know; but she thought it had a good chance: its bones were straight. What with his acting and writing and soldier work at Antwerp, George was, as the Americans would say, "some man."

She did not have to apologize for Beo, who these past long months had filled her with pride. He was commanding the Brigade Mortar Battery against the Turks in Gallipoli. He'd been extraordinarily lucky—hit all over his body, but always by spent bullets or stray fragments of shrapnel; one young chap had had his head blown off by a shell right next to him. How long his luck would last rested with the gods, but everyone felt that no one would get off the Peninsula with a whole skin. He was very lucky in his job: his commanding officers seemed to think he *counted*. He loved getting her photographs and Gladys Cooper's; they made his dugout cheerful and reminded him that there were other things in the world besides corpses, explosions, lice, and stench. Another reminder was the key to 33 Kensington Square that was always in his pocket. "Darling, what wouldn't I give for a long talk with you like we used to have," he wrote. "I wish I was with you and working for you, and helping to make all a success. I get many spare moments to think over my life, and I feel so heartbroken at all the worry I have caused you." One day Stella had opened a packet to find he had sent her his Croix de Guerre. He did not feel it good enough: "I do hope I get an English honour, for your sake, Mother dear," he told her. "I only want it for you." Triumphant, she wrote to D.D.: "I have always felt Beo's worth, & in the blackest days of worry felt he would win out all right: his heart is so simple & *warm* & he was always so ready to love everybody & think everybody was *good*—a child's nature. If Helen had only loved him & understood him."

The long, beautiful days at Ruthin drifted by. It would have been quite perfect except for the newspapers. One came down to breakfast never knowing what horrors would leap at one from the page. Ego Elcho—handsome, eligible Ego, whom she had thought of for Stella but who had married Lady Violet Manners instead—wounded and missing. His younger brother Yvo dead. Mary Charteris's husband, Tom Strickland, missing. It was dreadful, these young people's hearts torn like this; and yet, "It's only when the sun goes down that one thinks of these things," she told D.D.; "the day is too lovely."

In London, Alexander had been thinking of reviving that sure hit *Bella Donna*, and asked the young actor Hesketh Pearson, on leave in London, to suggest a lead. "Mrs. Pat is the only actress who can play it," responded Pearson promptly. "Out of the question!" Sir George shot back. "She's quite impossible in the theatre, and makes my life a hell!" He had been slow at coming to terms with what the war had done to London theatres. Spy melodramas, musicals like *Chu Chin Chow*, and revues ending with spectacular defeats of the Germans had become the only money-makers; Alexander had produced five plays between the autumn of 1914 and the summer of 1915, and all five had lost money. He needed a success; he wanted *Bella Donna*; there was only one actress who could play it and draw the public. Perjuring himself once again, Alexander approached Stella about a revival to begin at the end of May. "Trashy *Bella Donna*," as she called it, again proved a hit, running through the summer. In London again, Pearson dropped in to chat. Was Mrs. Pat still impossible and his life a hell? "She is," replied Alexander with a gesture of despair. "It is." Yet the impossible Stella made possible his first successful season in some years.

Now that she was back in London, Stella tried to see Shaw. She sent him photographs: "You'll see by the enclosed I am not too fat and ugly to be spoken to"; she tempted him with the news that Alexander might do *Pygmalion* in the fall. But Shaw proved strangely indifferent, positively gloomy. "I assume that you are in London," he had written in May; "but I dont care. I never felt so morose in my life. Lucky for you to make money by *Pygmalion*. I must have lost by it; for my income is down by nearly half. . . . I am old and finished. . . . Everything has gone to the devil. . . . This is a rotten world. George looked tired when he came back: I do not think he has long to live. You must be feeling very old and feeble. Your handwriting is improved but there is always some little rally before the end. I wonder which is the easiest: charcoal, morphia, or prussic acid. Well goodbye: we shall probably never meet again." Eventually Alexander decided against *Pygmalion* for the autumn, and Shaw dispiritedly agreed; with his unpopular stance against the war, it was not safe to produce him for the duration.

Stella's alternative was producing a one-act play written for her by the author of the despised *Bella Donna*. In *The Law of the Sands* Hichens again called up the brooding ambience of the mysterious East, and again Stella unleashed the requisite combination of torrid and tragic fascination. Played at the London Opera House at the head of a variety bill—the only kind of entertainment these grim days—it was successful, and Stella took it on tour that autumn, impressing the provinces. No, she was not (as Shaw suggested) chatelaine of Ruthin Castle these days. Although George's father had died in July, there was only hard work for her ahead. George himself was in France as Assistant Provost Marshal in the 57th Division. And darling Beo, now in France with the Light Trench Mortar Battery, Howe Battalion, Royal Naval Division, had captured more than four hundred Germans with only eight men and a tank, and made news (anonymously) as a "gallant officer" in the London papers. "That's more than I have ever done as an actor!" laughed Beo.

There was more occasion for pride in the new year, 1917. Beo won the English honor for her, receiving the Military Cross and then the bar in January. He came home for the investiture at Buckingham Palace, and

Stella, longing to be there, denied herself the pleasure, knowing that her presence would turn the event into a photographic orgy over "Mrs. Patrick Campbell and Her Brave Son." "Where were you?" asked Beo, handing her the case and hugging her hard. "A poor old woman came up to me and said, 'Bravo, my son'—everyone thought she was my mother!" That night she heard him coughing in his sleep (he'd explained he'd been "gassed a bit") and giving what she thought must be orders to his men in a strong, deep voice. And then she gave him back to France and the trenches.

Another family member that January also made news. Four columns in the *Times* of January 4 told the shocking story of George's mother's overly warm interest the previous year in a young soldier convalescing at a home in Denbigh. Mrs. Cornwallis-West, it seemed, had visited the home frequently, dispensing cheer and chocolate. To Patrick Barrett, "a reticent boy of 27," the sixty-three-year-old former P.B. had not only dispensed cheer, but had obtained him a commission, invited him to Ruthin Castle, and later pursued him with letters that "alarmed the invalid greatly." "I could not look Colonel West in the face again after your kissing me," Barrett protested. "I don't want you to teach me poetry. I just want to serve my God and King. Your note frightens me very much." The singularly humorless young man asked to be transferred; suspicion was aroused; a Court of Enquiry pounced upon the scandal; Second-Lieutenant Barrett was exonerated and Mrs. Cornwallis-West informed that she had acted in "a highly discreditable manner." Poor Patsy—she had chanced on a young man with a conscience. Stella and her mother-in-law were fond of each other, and Stella promptly invited her to stay at the Square, where they could ride out the storm together. Later she publicly defended Patsy in the *News of the World*. Was the public aware, she asked, that the defendant was sixty-three, one of the most loved of mothers, and a dearly loved wife? That she was an impulsively warm-hearted Irishwoman who wept at the sight of wounded soldiers and called them all "darling Tommies"? Surely it was a pitiable affair: who, after the court's decision, could feel a fine fellow? Of one thing Stella was sure: no one could prevent her mother-in-law from sentimentalizing over wounded soldiers or alter the poor chances an Irish heart had when it was up against a British middle-class one. She might have added that, had Colonel Cornwallis-West been alive, a court would have thought twice about bullying his wife.

Stella also encouraged George these months, to the extent of producing and acting in his one-act war play *Pro Patria* at the Coliseum in February. This time she was cast as Therese Bonnet, a passionate Alsatian widow unaware that her house is being used by German spies and that her son is their chief; in a melodramatic climax she thwarts his machinations. It was not badly received, but that spring she approached the more lucrative Shaw again and again, attempting to entice the vegetarian to the Square with a menu of vegetable soup, macaroni, salad, cheese, Devonshire cream, fruit, and brown bread prepared with her own hands, since she could no longer afford a cook. She wanted to tour with *Pygmalion* (the fourth act and a few lines cut). Shaw replied that Charles Macdona had *Pygmalion* for the provinces, but that he would recommend that Macdona hire her. "If you will write to him," replied Stella, "and not make me feel an absolute *brute* ousting the other lady whom I am sure looks and plays Eliza better than I did, or ever could—and get me enough salary to pay for Eliza's two smart frocks—my hotels—keep 33 Ken S. going for the 5 weeks I am away and for 4 or 6 months afterwards—until Stoll gives me another 3 weeks at the Coliseum—I shall be eternally grateful." But then she hung back, so that in August Shaw was forced to remind her that she had *Pygmalion* reserved for her in six big cities, and that she *must* go if she did not mean to retire and leave George to starve. But Stella chose to tour with *Pro Patria* instead, George (back from France) playing her traitorous son.

While Shaw was willing to let Stella have *Pygmalion*, he was determined not to risk his other plays, even though she was the actress who had inspired him more than any other and *Pygmalion* had made more money than any other of his plays. He had just completed *Heartbreak House*, a sober drama about England's perilous drift toward destruction, and the character of the dark-haired siren Hesione Hushabye was again—undeniably—Stella. Reluctantly, he consented to a reading. "I have *no* hesitation in feeling that I listened to a very fine play," Stella wrote afterwards; "the first act delights me—you beget your dramatis personae like a God—but as you went along you lost respect for their bones. They didn't always stand steady on their feet. Your pen makes you drunk. You look for the keyhole with your hat! You become unkind—you lose respect of persons . . . the people become mere mouthpieces of the general scheme—without bones flesh or blood—I feel *disorder* where you would probably feel 'there I was inspired.' Ah but you think me a fool. . . . I wish I was a man and old enough for Captain Shotover." They were the same complaints she'd always had about his plays. Shaw heard them unmoved: he had no intention of submitting either his play or his nerves to another bout with Stella Campbell.

"My beloved Beo is in great danger and my heart aches and the hours are heavy," she had told him. Certainly these were dreary months. She forced herself to learn recitation to pick up a little money, practised a blood-curdling poem called "The Hellgate of Soissons" on Cynthia Asquith and friends, bringing tears to their eyes, then "nearly died of fright" herself doing it for some soldiers in hospital. She accepted a part in W. L. Courtney's drama of ancient Greece, *Simaetha*, but although it featured a fire in which she was spectacularly burned to death, its run at the Coliseum was brief. Nightly now, sirens wailed the approach of the dreaded Zeppelins. All normal living had come to an end. At the Square, food and servant shortages were daily news, air-raids the evening's entertainment. The suspense of waiting for and facing the casualty lists in the papers day after day was all but intolerable. Every night when Stella left the theatre and stepped into the darkened streets, she had to pass the long gray line of ambulances waiting at Charing Cross to pick up the newly arrived wounded. "By Jove, I'm glad I'm an Englishman," Beo had rejoiced back in July 1916. "The Hun is a beaten man. . . ." But the autumn and winter of 1917 arrived, and the Hun had refused to lie down and die.

Then, as so often in the past, but less often now, she found herself in a play that clicked. This was *The Thirteenth Chair* by Bayard Veiller, a whodunit about a murder committed at a country house during a séance. Originally, Veiller had conceived the spiritualist Madame Rosalie La Grange as a little Irishwoman of about fifty (but old for her age), quaintly dressed, who drops curtsies and bad grammar indiscriminately. By the time Stella got through with her, Madame La Grange had turned into an Irishwoman of about forty (but young for her age), dressed simply but well, who bows graciously upon entering the room and speaks impeccable English. Thus Campbellized, *The Thirteenth Chair* opened at the Duke of York's on October 16 and immediately proved a diversion for war-sick audiences. Cynthia Asquith came with her mother, Guy and Frances Charteris, and Mary Strickland on the twenty-seventh. Cynthia, who had once had a tremendous *culte* for Mrs. Pat, had been disenchanted of late. She looked, thought Cynthia with the heartlessness of youth, exactly "like a leg of mutton," and then, too, she was so embarrassing with her young husband—terribly arch, indulging in love badinage, and even kissing him on the nose in front of people. But Mrs. Pat onstage was not Mrs. Pat embarrassing one at Kensington Square, and Cynthia found *The Thirteenth Chair* "a really admirably exciting play" with Mrs. Pat excellent as the medium. Afterwards they all went round to her dressing room and found her in great spirits. Her happiness, thought Cynthia again, had disfigured her—it kept her too fat; but, after all (relenting), it was wonderful that she should have found happiness to such an extent. They took her back to Catherine Street for tea, and of course she gushed a great deal about her "golden pheasant."

Steady money came in again at last. One of the first things Stella did with the new riches was to send Cynthia's son Michael a beautiful golden tortoise-shell cat named Algy that delighted him. Another was to buy a dozen silver teaspoons for Edith Sitwell because she had hurt Edith's feelings. Well acquainted with Lady Ida Sitwell, Stella was also friendly with her children, Osbert, Edith, and Sacheverell—though at the sight of tall-as-a-crane Edith she invariably exclaimed, "You'll never have your mother's beauty, poor child! But never mind! You look at one in such a nice way, it doesn't matter." Commiserated with once too often, Edith finally learned to jump in first: "How d'you do, Mrs. Campbell. Yes, I know I shall never have my mother's beauty, but I look at you in such a nice way, it doesn't matter!" During the war years Edith came to London and worked at the Pensions Office, renting a humble little flat in Bayswater. Here, with Osbert (home on leave), Stella had come to tea. But—"Why have I not got a silver teaspoon?" Stella had demanded incredulously as tea was handed round; "*Why*"—wind rising in her voice—"have I not got one?" "Because I'm poor and can't afford it," said Edith finally. Stella quieted down immediately, and now a dozen silver teaspoons arrived at Edith's flat. If Stella Campbell hardly ever said a kind thing, reflected Osbert, she never failed to do one.

Or almost never. Stella Pat and her young son were still living at the Square, but between Stella and her daughter there was a fundamental quarrel. Stella, who lavished affection and gifts not only on Beo and George but on countless friends, relatives, and followers, could not be generous with her daughter. The competitive struggle had gone on for years, of course, but now it reached a climax with Stella's refusal to let her daughter resume the name "Stella Patrick Campbell," under which she had made her stage reputation. On her return from Africa, Stella Pat had applied to London managers, but found them extremely reluctant to hire the unknown "Stella Mervyn Campbell." Cynthia Asquith bicycled over to the Square that November and stayed for lunch and a long talk with the frustrated daughter. "Poor thing," she recorded later in her diary, "it is a terribly hard life! She is trying to live on about four pounds a week, with a child and her husband's bills to cope with. Her stage career seems very hand-to-mouth and her luck very bad, as the plays she is in nearly always come off at once after they have let her into all the expenses of a season ticket, gloves, stockings, etc. For some inexplicable reason, her mother won't allow her to use the name Patrick Campbell, which deprivation greatly reduces her salary. An amazing woman—she threatened her own daughter with legal proceedings."

The reason was explicable enough: an aging actress's jealousy of her daughter and possessiveness toward the name that she alone had made famous. The strain of living under one roof could not last long, and Stella Pat moved into a flat at 52 Hogarth Road with little Patrick and her faithful

Nanny, who stuck with them even though she got no pay. Between acting jobs she worked in a factory that made aneroid batteries; war work was not unrespectable. She did not resent the love that was poured out upon Beo; she saw his weaknesses clearly, but liked him. She also accepted the fact that her mother loved little Patrick and did not speak against his grandmother to her son. Not that Stella would allow anyone to call her "grandmother"—she was known in the family as "Mother Beatrice" or "M.B."

Stella's current affluence was also felt by Beo. Cigarettes for his mates, tins of kippers and haddock, a thousand of the Christmas cards he'd designed printed up for his men to send to loved ones. Beo had been scrappy and optimistic at the beginning of the war; he had changed. "We out here see the Boche as he is, with the veneer of civilization off, and there is only one thing to do—*kill him!* as quickly as possible. . . . None of us really expects to come out alive—least of all a Trench Mortar man. . . . The gassing I got last November is beginning to tell on me. . . . I'd give a lot to be able to have forty-eight hours' sleep in dear old thirty-three." He also felt terribly anxious for her with the air-raids and all the shortages at home. "My own darling Mother . . . George tells me you are not well and are suffering a great deal. Do please take care of yourself—it makes me more nervous than all the shells and bombs in the world." But as the incredible blood-bath continued, there was finally no possible stance but optimism, whether one felt it or not: "I am so afraid we shall be in the trenches for Christmas, and I expect the Boche will attack again, but we are ready for him. He has never driven the old R.N.D. back a foot, and never will while any of us old 'uns are alive. The *esprit de corps* is fine, and I flatter myself the Battalion is in as good fighting trim as it has ever been; but it has been hard work training the new men and lecturing and putting new morale into them—eight solid hours a day, and the weather abominable. . . . My own darling . . . my own darling Mother. . . ."

Early on the morning of Sunday, December 30, as Beo and his commanding officer were standing at the top of the stairs of their dugout talking and laughing in the biting winter air, a shell burst beside them, killing them instantly. Four days later, returning to her dressing room after a matinee of *The Thirteenth Chair*, Stella was told that her son was dead. Her first reaction was disbelief: death was not something that could happen either to herself or to Beo. She went home, missed the evening performance. The next night she was back at the theatre. "My beloved Beo is killed," she wrote Shaw. ". . . I feel he is asleep, and will wake and come to me if I am quite strong and calm."

The letters of condolence that meant everything and nothing began pouring in. Testimonies from officers to Beo's gallantry, popularity, pluck, splendid character and leadership. From Mary Wemyss at Stanway, who had lost both Ego and Yvo, a cry of pain: "I know how you adored Beo, and Beo is associated with our happy past. . . . You have joined the band of those who mourn for heroes—and Beo was a glorious soldier." From Shaw outrage: "It is no use: I cant be sympathetic: these things simply make me furious. I want to swear. I *do* swear. Killed just because people are blasted fools. A chaplain, too, to say nice things about it. It is not his business to say nice things about it, but to shout that 'the voice of thy son's blood crieth unto God from the ground.' . . . Oh damn, damn, damn, damn, damn, damn, damn, damn, DAMN DAMN! And oh, dear, dear, dear, dear, dear, dearest!" Of all the messages, Stella probably found Jim Barrie's the most comforting. "How good that you have had a son who stood the supreme test of manhood," he wrote. Stella felt the same. "I, who hate war with a hatred that makes me feel a fiend," she said, "learned through war I had brought a *man* into the world—that is enough——"

*The Thirteenth Chair* ran four months through blackouts and raids. London seemed a kind of hell as the endless lists of dead and wounded mounted. Still numb with grief for Beo, Stella went to visit the actor Allan Pollock in the hospital. He had been frightfully injured—his face shot away; and now surgeons were grafting what amounted to a new one. Stella demanded that he remove the bandages and let her see his ravaged face. Pollock refused. "I've lost a son in this war and I have the right to look," she insisted. Pollock shook his head; the sight, he told her, would be too horrible. "Nonsense, man," retorted Stella, tears channelling her face powder, "I have just left Lady Tree."

Finally she escaped London for Ruthin Castle, to be quiet and think over what had happened to her. At first the grounds and garden and quiet were as soothing as ever, but then the days became long and wretched until George finally arrived with fourteen days' leave. Quite naturally, she looked to him for love and comfort. But he was not the same George who had hunted plovers' eggs and slept happily with her in his childhood room two years before. He did not respond to her endearments as he used to. She had always dreaded that she would become too old for him; she knew that her weight and waist had lost their magical proportions years ago. Another woman? She could not believe it. She did not understand what was happening, only sensed a change. "About six months after my sorrow," she wrote with retrospective restraint, "life began to teach me its hardest lesson, which must be learned if we are to comprehend in any measure the grace of God. That there can be a fundamental gulf of gracelessness in a human heart, which neither our love nor our courage can bridge."

Having spent her salary lavishly—most of it on George—Stella faced hard reality upon returning to London: she could no longer afford to keep 33 Kensington Square. "I am free on the 29th for Eliza if anyone wants me—tour or otherwise," she wrote Shaw that autumn; but Macdona did not want to handle the unpredictable Mrs. Pat—a bit of "dowdy wariness" that made her yawn. She planned a three-week tour of Birmingham, Manchester, and Liverpool with *The Thirteenth Chair*, but it was not enough to save Number 33. A Mrs. Wedgwood replied to her advertisement, and they met over tea to talk terms.

Mrs. Wedgwood called her little girl, Veronica, into the drawing room and she came, timid but eager to see the great lady. She first spied something soft and furry on the great lady's lap that might, she thought, be a muff (but was, of course, Georgina); then she lifted her eyes to the actress's face. "This is my little girl," said Mrs. Wedgwood. Stella studied her. "Do you know who I am?" she asked slowly in a voice that sounded to the girl like the pouring of heavy cream. "Yes," whispered Veronica; "you are Mrs. Patrick Campbell." Such moments softened a little the blow of leaving Kensington for 15 Tedworth Square in Chelsea.

No matter how grim her personal circumstances, Stella always kept a brave face. Nothing that she did was ever shabby, and she had the new place extensively renovated while she stayed temporarily in Savoy Court. "Quite nice," she told Shaw, "and a room for George's big retriever 'Sylvie' (poor Beppo has gone) and his golf sticks and fishing rods—and a marble floor to the drawing room—very low rent."

That November, after four years, the carnage of the Great War officially ended. The conservative estimate of ten million dead and twenty million wounded appalled even the idealists. Virtually a generation of British men had been wiped out. At Christmas, Stella Pat and her son came to Savoy Court; the first Christmas after Beo's death would have been too hard for Mother Beatrice to bear alone. She had had plans with George for a shooting party at Newlands, the Cornwallis-West place in Hampshire, but it had fallen through, and George went to Newlands alone to spend (so he said) Christmas with his mother.

Early in 1919 they moved into 15 Tedworth Square with Morrie, Georgina, Sylvie, and Sally, the newest little dog. George, however, was frequently absent. Since his duties as Assistant Provost Marshal could not account for all the hours that Stella was forced to spend alone, he explained them away as visits to friends, fishing and shooting expeditions, or bachelor weekend parties; and Stella wanted to believe.

Lonely and humiliated, she turned to Shaw, though she said nothing about George's desertion. "I wish you were near—perhaps soon I'll be going to Cork. George is A.P.M. there—and I believe loving it. He writes today he wants me to come—I'm too old for Eliza—I may go to America quite soon—I'm not wanted here—I have offered to take 10% to 12%—they call me 'England's greatest actress'!—but there it ends." But it was to the sympathetic Ned Sheldon that she poured out her troubles. "STELLA, DEAR, I LOVE AND BELIEVE IN YOU," Sheldon cabled from Los Angeles in July. "WISH I WAS THERE. SURE THIS CANNOT CONQUER YOU. YOU ARE SO HIGH ABOVE THEIR REACH. TENDEREST THOUGHTS AND AFFECTION." She replied, and he sent an answering letter: "I wish courage and wisdom could keep you from suffering. I know they can't, but they will carry you *through* it, anyway. . . . One thing I am sure of, you have made no mistake in keeping your ideals high as the stars. Even what you are going through now wouldn't bring you as much suffering as trying to lower them. That is the sort of person you are, and you can never change, thank God!" Sheldon himself was suffering the trauma of a steadily crippling arthritis. During these months the two drew more and more upon each other.

Finally there could be no more pretense. Where had he been? she demanded after one prolonged absence. Unable to meet her eyes, George mumbled something about golfing. "Your golf sticks are *there!*" cried Stella scornfully, pointing to the bag of clubs that had stood in the hallway all weekend. "I would rather be in hell than live in the same house with you!" shouted George. They battled until December. Then, "Forgive me, forgive me, darling, I have been mad," said George one day. Two days later he left Tedworth Square for good.

A week or so later Daisy Pless advised Stella to go down to Newlands to talk with him. Stella went with the faithful Morrie and put up at a hotel at Milford-on-Sea. She arranged to meet George on the cliffs. There he told her that he had been living with a woman at Newlands. Stella responded appropriately. George seized her by the throat and cried that he would throw her over the cliff. His face was hideously distorted, his grin positively evil. She gripped his arm tightly. "Don't think of me as your wife," she urged, "but as a pal who has come down here to help you. Let me speak with her." He grew more quiet and released her, and she walked unsteadily back to the hotel. The next day she met the woman, who told her, "We have been lovers off and on for twenty years." Stella returned to London sick and bewildered. During the following week she learned that the woman was married and had three children, and that all George's sporting weekends had been spent with her.

Stella had been the responsible financial party for the five years and eight months of their marriage. George had borrowed on her credit throughout; they had told themselves that he would eventually repay. In the following days she discovered that a bank had been pursuing him for a large sum of money borrowed on false security, a debt that the other woman had recently paid. She found that before leaving he had arranged for their incomes to be taxed separately, although in the past she had paid all taxes. She realized too that he had taken away all his furniture after she had given up much of her own to make room for his. She also discovered very quickly that he had left her with bills of well over £9500. She was almost fifty-five, alone, and unemployed. For comfort she had the farewell letter George had left with the parlormaid to be added to the hundreds of love letters which he had written to her and she had saved. "I am dross," George had written; "you are gold."

# THIRTY-TWO

# 1919–1922

*S*TELLA SPENT Christmas at Tedworth Square with Morrie and D.D., who came for four days. Together they went to watch Stella Pat play Raina at last in Shaw's *Arms and the Man*. "You have done wonders with Stella," the mother told Shaw, one of the last agreeable words she had for him in the months to come, for a revival of *Pygmalion* at the Aldwych soon set them at each other's throats.

This time C. Aubrey Smith would play Higgins. The eccentric and beloved Tree had forgotten the furor of 1914 and was boyishly eager for a revival, but he had died suddenly in July 1917. Since Aubrey Smith was incurably amiable, there could be no fight with him: the contestants this time were Stella, Sir Herbert's daughter Viola Tree, the manager, and Shaw the producer. "Poor Viola has already got that dreadful look on her face that Boucicault had when you were rehearsing Barrie's play," Shaw groaned as business got under way the third week in January 1920. "How *can* you? . . . Now we shall quarrel for the next month. Oh Stella, Stella, Stella, why did God afflict us with one another?" Her reply, "You make a fine mistake if you think I am out for quarrelling!" did not reassure him.

Shaw quickly adopted the tactic of divide and conquer. On the one hand, he comforted Viola by calling Stella an anarchist, too great a fool to learn anything, a shameful clown, a tramp, a disgraceful incompetent, an idiotic amateur, and a malicious devil. He advised her to stay out of the way and let him handle Stella: he would jump on her with impunity. To Stella he wrote, "Belovedovedest: Viola will be the death of me. . . . Viola is a darling unprofessionally; but as a manageress she is a spoilt child playing with dolls, and gives every reason for her whims except an artistic or business reason. . . . Viola [is] playing all sorts of tricks, and interfering on the stage at the most difficult moments." Another ploy was simply to keep them both out of the theatre as long as possible. "Do not dream of coming until

Monday at the very earliest, and not then unless I tell you it is safe," he warned Stella, at the same time telling Viola, "I think you had better keep out of the way for the next few days." But on February 4 the battle was joined: Stella, after hurling every possible accusation and insult at his head, made a magnificent exit speech banishing him from her affections and esteem forever, stormed to her dressing room, locked the door, and played the piano for hours while the cast (who could not proceed without her) listened entranced. Shaw was not entranced; he responded with a written ultimatum advising her that if she continued to play Eliza her way and not his, the play would not open.

Stella did not have the courage to open this scorcher. She felt strongly that Shaw was deliberately setting Viola against her ("Viola darling . . . Joey set us by the ears"). Her age also tormented her: in a few days she would be fifty-five; Eliza stubbornly remained nineteen. Her self-consciousness was not helped by the presence of her old enemy Marion Terry in the cast, playing Higgins's mother, nor by Shaw telling her that Viola "declares that Marion Terry's movements are so beautiful that she must keep walking about the stage, which means that there is going to be a beauty and youth competition between Mrs. Higgins and Eliza. . . . [Marion] has not the slightest intention of playing a matron; and Viola will abet her."

"Of course I look 60," Stella flung back, "—of course I have a hideous 'gin and misery' voice, and of course I can't give any kind of a performance to compare with a pretty young girl's. . . . Please don't write me any more letters. I *have* letters from you that will be read out at my funeral oration, but these you are sending me render me witless." She begged him not to mistake her "brilliant impertinence for insolence," nor her "desire for individual radiance . . . for uppishness." She was, of course, an anarchist; but she also believed that her great success with Eliza gave her certain privileges with the part. Shaw did not agree. He fumed over the liberties she took—her tendency to play for laughs, and the costumes that displayed Mrs. Patrick Campbell while eclipsing Eliza. "Final scene rotten," he scribbled savagely in his notebook, "—no delicacy or pathos—hugging Higgins at the end—serve you right, you ungrateful devil."

When the curtain rose again on *Pygmalion*, however, Stella's performance had all the old fascination. Arnold Bennett saw the revival and noted in his journal that "*Pygmalion* is on the whole poor. Most of the characterization is quite rotten, and wilfully made so for the sake of art and eloquence. The last act is foozled. Mrs. Campbell was superb. There is still nobody else to touch her." The young Anthony Asquith came to a matinee and reminisced years later after directing the film: "I remember Mrs.

Campbell's Eliza vividly—and no one else whatever. I can even remember how she added two words—'as how' in the famous funny passage just before 'not bloody likely,' the line: 'But it's my belief *as how* they done the old woman in!' I noted this at the time, and when it came to making the film I added the words 'as how' though they are not in Shaw's text." The play, said Stella herself, went with all the old merriment; but she and Shaw remained deadlocked—he for his play, she for her interpretation of Eliza.

During the run Stella hired a car and made visits to Shaw's dying sister, Lucy. She tried to convince Shaw to go with her; she wanted to heal the wounds inflicted during rehearsal, writing, "Don't be angry with me any more. Life has taken some skins off me and I can't battle with your jibes and jests—though I admit the memory of your golden heart washes all away like waves of the Sea—and I do love you." She was impressed with the little house Shaw had leased for his sister: perhaps when she was too old and decrepit to act, he would let her die there? It was a common theme these days. Shaw continued to reserve *Pygmalion* for her in the six big towns, but again refused her *Heartbreak House* and—her latest inspiration —*Pygmalion* for the cinema, even though she pleaded that a film would keep her out of the workhouse. Shaw knew better. "Alas! alas! nothing will keep you out of the workhouse. All the enchantresses end there. Serve them right, too, mostly!"

*Pygmalion* drew £1554 weekly through February, returns that with good management would obviously yield a handsome profit, said Shaw. By March he was telling Viola that unless she could flood London with a very clever poster or persuade Stella to play Higgins (which she could do very well), he did not see how it could last the season. Eventually *Pygmalion* was transferred to the Duke of York's. Shaw came to look at it in May and went away disgusted. "You have now got the play as nearly as you like it as you will ever get it," he wrote Stella the next day. He admitted she *looked* a hundred times better: someone had evidently persuaded her to give up that terrible American front spot lighting that made her face like a kitchen clock covered with make-up and flattened out her figure to twice its natural width. But as for the play, "It is now really good Victorian drawingroom drama, pleasant and sweet, and in what you (bless you!) call good taste. You are not a great actress in a big play or anything disturbing or vulgar of that sort; but you have your heart's desire, and are very charming. . . . I enjoyed it and appreciated it in its little way. And that was magnanimous of me, considering how I missed the big bones of my play, its fortissimos, its allegros, its precipitous moments, its contrasts, and all its big bits. My orchestration was feeble on the cottage piano; and my cymbals were rather disappointing on the cups and saucers. Still, you were happy; and that was something. And Higgins was not brutal to you, as I was. A perfect gentleman. . . . I almost slept."

The receipts, moreover, were so appalling that he doubted the public knew the play was on again. A procession of sandwich men might help—only he couldn't afford them. Fortunately, Stella was already rehearsing the title role of Philip Moeller's *Madame Sand*—a "thunderingly difficult" part, she told Shaw; "—if I don't get stink bombs on the first night I will on the second!" She was startled the day before the June 3 opening with a note from him wishing her luck. "Why Joey that was kind of you," she answered, pleased. "I didn't expect your good wishes. To get out of Eliza into this minx in four days wasn't easy! . . . *any* night there is a box waiting for you—I would love to hear your fun about it."

Shaw came and was among the few who recognized that she gave a remarkable performance. Many critics condemned the portraits of Liszt, Heine, Chopin, and Musset as caricatures—as though some American tourist had wandered through the Latin Quarter and misunderstood everything. Stella's George was dismissed as "Mrs. Patrick Campbell in breeches," while others laughed at the trousers and wondered how George's "trick cigar" was made to puff real smoke—innocence that made the veteran smile. But Rudolph Besier considered her performance "pure genius—like everything you do," and her severest critic fumed at the illiteracy and stupidity of a British public that could not recognize a great performance when they saw one. "What induced you to imitate Oscar Wilde?" added Shaw. "It was an inspiration, and amazingly like the original." He found the play weak, however, and intended to tell Moeller to rewrite it because "your lovely performance is too good to be thrown away: it is a repertory part. Why can you not act as intelligently as that for me, devil that you are?"

Following the closing of *Madame Sand*, Stella accepted a fortnight's engagement for September to play *Pygmalion* in Cologne to the British Army of Occupation, with Esmé Percy as Higgins and members of the Army's dramatic company. "I was over-praised, over-entertained, and over-photographed," she commented succinctly. On her return she went straight into rehearsals for a production of *Macbeth* at the Aldwych opposite the American tragedian James K. Hackett. She had never conquered Lady Macbeth, but discovered now that playing her opposite Forbes had been cream compared to acting with Hackett. It was immediately apparent that the American actor regarded Macbeth as the solar system, recognizing her existence only as his cues. "Whenever he opens his mouth he spits at me, and whenever I speak he clears his throat," complained Stella. She also complained during rehearsals at having to sit on a green log in a puce dress while Macbeth did all the talking. "Well, well," murmured the director, anxious to keep the peace, "I'll ask Mr. Hackett to *pat* you once or twice." Stella turned melancholy eyes upon him. "I *hate* being patted!" she moaned.

As frequently happened when necessity conflicted with inclination, she became ill and played opening night on November 2 with influenza. "*Macbeth* last night at the Aldwych with the American actor Hackett and Mrs. Patrick Campbell," noted Arnold Bennett. "He has good diction. Mediocre as a whole and largely bad. Mrs. Pat inaudible. Witches appalling. Music ditto, besides being much too slow and besides being played in darkness." Most critics agreed with Bennett. "Oh, I am such a failure in it!" cried Stella to a nameless young admirer who had come backstage to tell her he thought her "a pale and wonderful apparition." Shaw did not wholly agree. The night he saw her, she had played Hackett off the stage and made only a few blunders, chiefly when she forgot she was Lady Macbeth and tried to be "a Paffick Lidy." Archer had told him that she pecked at the part, Massingham that she sleep-walked through it. He had not understood the sleep-walking until D.D. told him that someone had told her that Lady Macbeth should be seen through a sheet of glass. "I wish I had been there with a few bricks: there would not have been much left of your glass. . . . However, what is the use of talking to you? Or at least of *my* talking to you? Something silly, like the *Thirteenth Chair*, will turn up for you presently. Or some nice man will come and talk about sheets of glass."

"What abominable letters you do write me Joey dear!" replied Stella. She preferred listening to Jack Mackail, who had suggested the sheet-of-glass effect. "Archer, and the other men never realize that I *chose* to be an amateur, and not a professional!" she defended. Shaw scoffed: she did not want to be an amateur, but a lady, and so underplayed Lady Macbeth, like "the celebrated decayed gentlewoman who had to cry laces in the street for a living but hoped that nobody heard her."

Through it all Stella maintained her reputation for irrepressibility. One night after a particularly troublesome performance she confronted Hackett backstage. "I wish by all that's holy, sir," she boomed, "you would have your catarrh when you are off-stage, or at least during your own speeches and not mine!" She was also in good form when Dame Madge Kendal came onstage after a performance and, taking no notice of Stella, fell to gushing profusely over Hackett. Stella listened impatiently to the torrent of flattery. Then—Hackett had made her play the sleep-walking scene on the ramparts instead of in the antechamber—she interrupted, "And how did you like my *street*-walking scene, Mrs. Kendal?" The stately and puritanical actress's mouth twitched; she deigned to invite Stella to luncheon the next day, but Stella knew better than to go.

The year ended with Stella breaking down and being ordered to bed. Barely recovered, she injured an ankle in February and was ordered to lie up on the sofa. Although she had worked more or less regularly during the past year, she had often had to settle for poor salaries since she was in constant financial difficulty and could not afford to hold out for better terms. Now temporary inaction was not only difficult but disastrous. During the year George had applied for an order of discharge of bankruptcy. In his petition he blamed his insolvency on the failure of his firm, the extravagance of his first wife, speculative losses in copper, on the Stock Exchange, and on a patent rifle of his invention, and, lastly, on himself. Stella attributed her appalling debts to George. Nothing had been done about a divorce. Desperate, Stella hit upon the idea of raising a little cash with a book of memoirs. There was only one person who knew all about such things, so "Joey—I have had a letter from a publisher that I would very much like your opinion upon. . . . The letter is in the form of a contract and I am afraid of it . . . He gives me two weeks to decide and I want to hear your views. . . . Please be a little kind to me. I have stood your unkindness and your grumbling so bravely." She also put in another request for *Heartbreak House.*

Shaw demanded she send him the letter at once and receive any publisher's ultimatums thumb to nose. "This new stunt about you bearing my unkindness bravely takes my breath away," he marvelled. "I am the greatest playwright in the world; and I have been treated by an actress as no dog was ever treated by the most brutal trainer. . . . Belovedest: I *can't* put you into the cast of H.H. You have intimidated me far too completely. . . . And the rest of the cast, the manager and the backers, would go on strike at once. What *I* dare not face, nobody else with any sense is likely to take on. You must take a theater, write your own plays, and train a company of orphan apprentices to act with you."

Stella obediently forwarded the letter from Constable and set to work on the memoirs, which she wanted to title *The Life of Mrs. Patrick Campbell by Beatrice Stella Cornwallis-West.* The task terrified her—she could not organize and her only notion of punctuation was a hyphen—but the prospect of the workhouse was a strong incentive. Shaw came to call on February 25, and she jotted down his advice to pass on to her lawyer, Mr. Chantrey, so that he could renegotiate with Constable. At home Shaw wrote to Otto Kyllmann of Constable in his kindly but meddlesome way, explaining that Stella wanted the £1000 advance in a hurry since the wolf was at the door, but that they might consider the prudence of advancing it since she was also thinking of taking a stop-gap engagement at the Palace which could interfere with her completion of the manuscript. He had no trouble convincing Kyllmann that he knew much more about Stella's business than she did, with the result that Kyllmann in turn confided his negotiations with Stella and Chantrey to Shaw. The lady's lawyer put forth so many suggestions and alterations, Kyllmann told him, that he feared there might be even more difficulties after she signed. The lady had asked for money on signing, but now they were uncertain that she could be trusted to finish the manuscript. They had indeed some misgivings about the disruptive engagement at the Palace Theatre. And, finally, Constable understood that the lady would be guided entirely or largely by Mr. Shaw's advice, hence their troubling him once more with the matter.

"I felt absolutely humiliated by the letter to you from Kyllman which you sent on to me," Stella wrote Shaw. "As for Chantrey, he has only put forward the points from your own letter of advice to me and the three notes I took of what you said the last time I saw you. It was after Sadler heard a chapter of the book that he wrote his letter embodying Constable's offer, which letter made me definitely decline Butterworth's offer. Constable now sends a contract to Chantrey of a totally different nature. Kyllman has evidently been advised that I am a beggar, and an unreliable one!—Its a pity. . . ." She promptly changed publishers, signing with Hutchinson instead. "I never after that most atrocious letter of Mr. Kyllmans to you had the courage to think of trusting him with my poor Babe."

Against doctors' advice, she had undertaken to "make a fool of herself" for £200 by reciting a prologue and epilogue to a biblical film called *The Dawn of the World* and, accompanied by a virginal, "The Song of Solomon." She performed three times a day for four weeks, thankful to be making money; then caught a chill, broke down again, had to refuse an offer to tour in *Macbeth* with Hackett, and was ordered into the country for six weeks' rest.

She went away to Rusper in west Sussex and tried to relax. There in June she heard that Jennie Churchill's leg had been amputated. They had met once face to face at a party at Ned Lathom's just after Stella's marriage to George—she and George, and Jennie escorted by Chips Channon. There had been a tense moment, then Jennie had swept on with no word of greeting. "I wish in some way I could tell her how sorry I am for her," she wrote D.D. now on June 22, little dreaming that a week later Jennie would be dead. She herself was "not very happy," but much better and able to be up a few hours each day. She was reading—light books, deep books; they all seemed to say the same thing. Schopenhauer's *Studies in Pessimism* made her laugh, Nietzsche seemed a friend to shake hands with, Bergson made her think of the nurse who emptied the baby out with the bathwater. She liked Samuel Butler and expected Shaw had got a good deal from him. The wicked men in the novels she read were mostly like George, and the silly women mostly like herself. The whole world seemed to come out of one nutshell. "I don't feel I ever want to live again," she sighed. "If I could take George's hand & feel I was *helping* him I believe I would." On the other hand, she had decided that George's love for her was a joke. "I am restless beyond words unless I am lying flat. I take my medicine once a day not 3 times or I drowse—& feel horrid—in a cage."

At last, with a £500 advance from Hutchinson, she decided to give up acting for a while, give up the flat in Tedworth Square, and make a long retreat into the country somewhere to finish her memoirs. Ned Lathom, a young dilettante lord who lived in foolish extravagance at 47 Cumberland Place and at Blythe Hall on his Lancashire estate near Ormskirk, suggested that she lease Ashfields, a cottage on his grounds. In September she did play for a fortnight in Liverpool in Clemence Dane's one-act drama *The Terror*, getting half a dozen calls each night; but she grew more and more absorbed in her book and in the unfamiliar pleasures of country living. The privet hedges were full of birds, and the sunken rose garden in front of her sitting-room window and the jasmine vines tangling the cottage promised spring beauty. Pear trees hung heavy with fruit, Irish ducks preened in the pond, hens cackled contentedly in the courtyard. To the east faraway hills, to the west fields and ploughmen with their horses and dogs, crows and seagulls feeding on the newly turned earth, and the wind blowing from the sea fourteen miles away. She invited her poor brother Max to live with her, gave him a spade for the garden and a hatchet to chop wood. She had helped him all these years: paid to have his worthless music published; played the piano to amuse him; challenged him at chess. But Max had gotten queerer than before. He went about shaking his head and spluttering his lips, and when asked why he made such strange noises, whispered that it was "the spirits."

Stella dedicated her autobiography to a young girl she had encountered one night outside the stage door of the Duke of York's after a performance of *Madame Sand*. "What are you waiting for?" Stella had asked. "To see you," the girl replied. "Where do you live?" "Richmond." "How are you going to get back?" "Walk. I walked here early this morning. I wanted to get a good place to see the play, and I did: and now"—with a look of ecstacy before she vanished—"I have been waiting to see *you*."

She intended to include many of Shaw's letters, and he had unwarily agreed, telling Hutchinson that he and Stella had a gentleman's agreement that he not refuse copyright to anything of his in her manuscript. He also offered to read the book in proof, correcting obvious errors and pruning all her little snobberies—"Darling: Come to tea at Marlborough tomorrow: Alexandra: P.S. Edward sends his love."

Nothing could have been chummier, and in this benign atmosphere Stella confided to him for the first time that George had left her. "I couldn't bear to make you tell me before," replied Shaw; "but I have sometimes had occasion to wish that I knew. I nearly asked D.D. once, but couldn't quite bring myself to. You should have put an advertisement in the papers— STOLEN—*from 15 T. Sq.* A HUSBAND—*The Property of Mrs. Patrick Campbell—Anyone restoring him to the above address will receive a reward of* HALF A CROWN. Then we should all have known. I'm sorry: I ought not to be the sort of person that it's painful to tell such things to; but I suppose I am." If George wanted his freedom, Shaw suggested that she trade the marriage settlement George had made upon her for £20,000 and a divorce.

And then Shaw suddenly woke up. Whether he finally remembered the extravagance of what he had written, or whether he mentioned the coming publication to an outraged Charlotte, or whether (as Stella suspected) a conversation with D.D. had made him change his mind, he now demanded to see the letters she proposed publishing. There was nothing to do but get Morrie to make copies and send them, but she was aggrieved: there was the gentleman's agreement and, besides, when she'd asked him to read over the letters before, he'd refused. "Here are the dear letters," she wrote the day before Christmas from Blythe Hall, where she was spending the holiday with Ned Lathom. "If I inspired a little of the tenderness of their genius I am proud, not vain. . . . People talk carelessly, but nobody will *think* anything but what lovely letters and what a dear man you are. I do not fancy that Charlotte will misjudge me, or that she will see that permitting the letters to be published is other than a *panache* in her bonnet."

Stella had always stunned Shaw with her lack of *savoir vivre*. He now read the words she proposed giving to the world and hurled back a reply. She should take "that terrible wadge" and put it into the hands of any experienced person and that person would tell her without hesitation that its public exposure was utterly impossible. Why, there was one passage that would enable George to get a divorce, and other perfectly uninteresting parts about appointments and hours which would nevertheless cause Charlotte acute pain. She wished to publish them, he suggested, simply for money. He also suggested that if he allowed publication, D.D. would spit in his face.

Stella fought back. His mention of money was repulsive. D.D. had just written that she must not cut out his letters and that Charlotte knew they were going in. She would like to know the passage that would enable George to get a divorce. As for the uninteresting appointments and hours, let him cut them out before returning the "wadge" to her. "Please Joey don't put on your suburban cap," she pleaded. Why could he not be courageous and *young* and give her her way?

"Now God defend me from idiots!" fumed Shaw. "I might just as well write essays on Relativity to a female Kingfisher. Send me your proofs when you get them. I will then tell you, brutally and dogmatically, what you may say and what you may not. The situation is new to you. You have been before the public for sixty years or so; but during that time you have never uttered a word to it that has not been put into your mouth by somebody else. You have therefore never learnt the rules or acquired the sense of responsibility of authorship. And, owing to abysmal deficiencies in your nature, you never will. So you must do what you are told. Out of all patience—G.B.S."

"I have the proofs here, and I must admit your letters in print seem more of a joke against me than ever, but delightful reading," Stella replied calmly. "My book is obviously the work of an inexperienced sentimental, elderly lady—with gentlemanly feelings—and it is a little interesting and unusual. Your letters are of course its illumination." She would *not* send proofs, though she would go over them with him privately whenever and wherever he liked. She only wanted him to return to her the letters edited to prevent Charlotte's hurt and George's suspicion. "Stella, Stella," groaned Shaw: ". . . Remember: you start from the position that the publication of intimate letters that were never intended for publication is not permissible among persons of honor. If they are love letters the difficulty is decupled, centupled, miltupled. If they are love letters from a married man to a woman who is not his wife, and who is engaged at the time to another man whom she has subsequently married, the difficulty becomes a wild impossibility: if the man publishes them he is a blackguard: if the woman publishes them she is a rotter and a courtesan." The only thing he would now allow was that she send him the entire manuscript for him to cut, after which he would hand it to Charlotte to read and tell him whether she still found anything offensive in it. The alternative was to abandon all notion of publishing Charlotte's husband's letters.

Stella capitulated to the extent of sending Shaw the letters in proof with her further deletions, but still insisted on putting all the letters together at the end of the book with his photograph and a really lovely one of herself. At the same time she contacted Herbert (Beb) Asquith, reader for Hutchinson, and Sir George Hutchinson himself, breaking the news to them that her book would not contain all the letters she had promised because Mrs. Shaw would be upset. But she still trusted Shaw to return the wadge more or less intact with permission to publish: after all, there was that gentleman's agreement and he could not be quite the coward he pretended. Then she opened the returned proofs that Shaw had spent two days slashing.

"I burn so with blushes at your confounded impudence, that I don't feel the cold," she raged.

"You have spoilt my book.

"You have spoilt the story.

"You have hidden from the world the one thing that would have done it good: Lustless Lions at play—

"May you freeze in that sea of ice in Dante's Inferno—I don't care.

" 'Stolen your fig-leaf' indeed! You wear no 'fig-leaf' in your letters. . . .

"It is really sad: you creep on the ground, instead of flying in the air—through taking away those delicious letters. . . ."

Faced with the "murdered bundle," Stella cut even more, deciding that what Shaw had left misrepresented both herself and her feelings. Her accelerated pace was felt by Mrs. Whittall, the young war widow who had answered "Mrs. West's" advertisement in a London paper for help with literary work. Stella now rose even earlier on winter mornings to drag her from her warm bed for dictation and proof-correction. Morrie was not spared either; and both women were relieved when she suddenly went to London on February 19 to visit her dying friend Melicent Stone, leaving them with only Georgina and Sally to wait on. In London Stella took the cut letters to Beb Asquith at Hutchinson; back at Ashfields, she wrote in a quite pacific mood to Shaw to tell him that his massacred letters were now the only insincere things in the book and, as for his opinion of her stuff, "Of course it is amateurish and not professional—thank God."

Shaw meanwhile had been in touch with Hutchinson himself and got them to send what Stella had brought them. He discovered that his *Macbeth* letter had been hard on Hackett; that Stella had included two indiscreet letters of his to D.D. about their courtship; and that Stella had expressed an unflattering opinion about Charlotte. Hutchinson also told him that the book was amateurish. He wrote her again, adamantly refusing to let the thing be published as it stood. This was a last straw for Stella. "Well, there is nothing left for me to do but to hit you back with the poker, holding it with both my hands—having no respect for your few remaining transparent hairs—and to hit you flat dead. I *am* going to publish exactly what I like. . . ."

"There has been *great trouble*," she wrote D.D. in disgust the same day,

February 24. "Joey having heard the book was 'amateurish' and an opinion expressed about 'Charlotte' revoked—causing no end of awkward feeling between the publishers and myself. . . . Whatever it was you said, caused a revulsion—or convulsion. . . . I was *absolutely* to blame for having read any of my MS or told anybody at all, about the letters. . . . you will realise the immeasurable amount of difference to the interest in my book. So far as I am concerned, I had to learn the lesson to keep my affairs to myself, and if I haven't learnt it now, I deserve to be hanged! The book will be out quite soon—the serial rights in America first. . . ."

In early March *My Life and Some Letters* went irremediably into the hands of the publishers, and Stella went to London to stay with Colonel Guy Wyndham, Mary Wemyss's brother. After three weeks in the midst of that social whirl she moved to 6 Carlton Mews, a house let to her cheaply until May by her good friends Benjamin and Bridget Guinness. During her stay there she went to a production of Shaw's *Misalliance* (out and out the best thing he had done, she thought) at the little Everyman Theatre in Hampstead. Afterwards she walked up to the box office and declared herself available. Consequently, she received an offer of £3 a week for a fortnight's revival of *Hedda Gabler*—£3 to the actress who used to command £200 or £250. "Don't write to MacDermot saying I am an impossible woman, and that I will smash his Theatre at the first rehearsal," she with reason begged Shaw: ". . . I need that £3 a week sorely." From Carlton Mews she moved in with friends in Hampstead, then migrated to Park Lane—accepting hospitality wherever she could find it from friends who remained indulgent, even though the stout Mrs. Pat bore little resemblance to the willowy actress of *Tanqueray* fame, and even though her little dogs *would* eat off the best china. With her daughter, now touring under the name Stella Patrick Campbell in the third-rate but incredibly popular *Knave of Diamonds*, she seldom crossed paths.

During May she read the advance publicity for her book and found that Hutchinson was waving Shaw's love letters as a come-on for her "crass trash," as she dubbed it. But when the American serial appeared, she read it through with mounting alarm. It was a jumble of errors (what copy had they used?) and Shaw's "wadge" was intact. "Oh Joey—oh lor! oh Hell! I have just seen the *New York Herald*, they have put in all the letters uncut, this in spite of all their promises and the enclosed. What can I do now. . . . I feel *very* unhappy because I know how much you will mind—for myself, well . . ."

In the next weeks she tried to discover what had happened. "Beb Asquith must have let the letters go to America 'uncut'—it was very wrong—he should have told us there was a chance—and given me the opportunity of trying to get in touch with the N.Y. Herald." Then she went to Hutchinson in person and found that all the portions cut in her proof were not cut in theirs. "All the clumsy errors have come about because Beb Asquith begged me not to correct Miss Morris' rough typed proofs made from my dreadful scribblings, because I would find it much easier to correct the printed galley proofs—in the meanwhile they traded with the American representative *with* my rough uncorrected stuff. Whether this is illegal or only a breach of trust I do not know—but it is pretty infernal. The *New York Herald* evidently found my stuff dull, and they have enlivened it with a nightmare of lies and vulgarity." "Nothing matters now," replied Shaw in despair. Stella brightened. If nothing mattered now, could she put the "Dearest" in his "crackle crackle" letter and the beautiful New Year's Eve letter in the British edition? Shaw abruptly decided some things mattered after all, and refused.

Published in September, Stella's book did not create the sensation that might have been expected from the memoirs of a *femme fatale*. This was because she had not chosen to represent herself as one. She could not have been more discreet. Forbes was mentioned a few times as Mr. Robertson, and only in connection with their theatrical partnership. She included one poem, "To Beatrice," written to her in 1910 "by a well-known London manager" whose wife had given her permission to publish all his tributes—before their subsequent mysterious disappearance. She said almost nothing of the dozens of men who had loved her or of her feelings for them. She presented her family as impeccably virtuous and loving: John Tanner's folly, her runaway marriage, the quarrel with Lulo, Max's queerness, her running battle with her daughter-in-law, Beo's fecklessness, the power-struggle with her daughter, George's desertion did not exist. She emerged from her pages a good mother, an actress, and—since she liberally salted her memoirs with the titles of her aristocratic friends—a snob. Shaw's love letters were really only another testimony to her virtue—sonnets to the remote dark lady of his dreams.

The *Times* gave *My Life and Some Letters* a full column, though it admired the photographs more than the text. The *Spectator* liked it and the *Daily Telegraph* said, "She may be sincerely congratulated. Her book is interesting from beginning to end, perhaps a little over-laden with letters from various persons, mostly distinguished. But she uses these skilfully to suggest the deep impression she made in the course of her career on all those who were intelligent enough to understand that she must be judged by her own standards and not by those of other people." The American edition published by Dodd, Mead in November drew criticism ranging from "A brilliant book" to the New York *Times* verdict that "It is ill-written in every sense of the word, short of being illiterate—though Bernard Shaw accused its author even of that. And yet it is extremely interesting, quite as much for its omissions as for what it contains; for its manifest imperfections as much as for its merits."

Graham Robertson read it and allowed that the note of self-praise was not as loud as he had expected from the extracts. In several cases he thought her extremely generous to friends who had behaved surprisingly unlike friends on certain occasions. He had always noticed that she did not bear malice, but would forgive—if not forget—an injury quickly. Of one crisis in her life, when she was absolutely left in the lurch and almost ruined financially by someone she had every reason to trust, she said barely a word: Robertson considered it fine of her to let him off so easily. He also thought it right that she had said nothing negative about Beo—a curiously fascinating, irresponsible, faunlike creature, thought Robertson, unstable as water—even though his follies had left a deeper mark on her than any other of her troubles. On the other hand, Robertson found it annoying that she never seemed to attribute her failures to any faults of her own, and never, apparently, considered that she could have taken steps to remedy them. And he especially deplored letters praising her acting from Lord This and Lady That—surely the opinion of the call boy or the stage electrician would have been more valuable?

Even edited, Shaw's love letters attracted a good deal of attention—as Hutchinson knew they would. At least one critic, however, declined to believe in them. Deciding that Mrs. Campbell had "tilted the shafts of memory's cart and let the contents fall," Desmond MacCarthy found Shaw's letters one of the few treats in her "loose heap of testimonials, compliments, worries and sorrows"—but declined to believe they had been motivated by love. "They are full of dancing gaiety," said MacCarthy. "They show a most exquisite helpful regard for her. They are full of gratitude to her for having inspired such an excitement in him that, to his immense delight, he can fancy himself in love; the impulse to wild silliness is so strong. But they are not the letters of a man who *wants to be loved*, and therefore they are not love letters. Desire to be loved is itself almost a definition of being 'in love'; without that desire love is indistinguishable from sympathy." If the reader wanted a look at true love, he or she must rake through the heap and extract the letters of Mr. Patrick Campbell to his young wife. In fact, in MacCarthy's opinion, Mr. Patrick Campbell emerged from the autobiography as the only piece of gold in the rubble.

But, of course, MacCarthy had read the expurgated letters. Always terrified lest heart dominate brain, Shaw had been as near rapture with Stella as he could come. "I forgive you the letters," he wrote her finally in acknowledgment of that passion, "because there is a star somewhere on which you were right about them; and on that star we two should have been born. I told you you had never learned to live in this one; and the Titanic slavery by which I have learned has separated us. . . . I made you pretend; but do not ever let yourself suspect that I have pretended or denied."

# THIRTY-THREE

# *1922–1927*

O N MAY 20, 1922, the curtain at the Everyman Theatre rose on the grandly massive figure of Mrs. Patrick Campbell practising pistol shots alone in a darkened room. She took careful aim, counted slowly—one, two, three, four, five, six, *seven!*—dropped her hand, then lifted it again to aim. If any in the audience were shocked either at the unorthodox beginning of *Hedda Gabler* or at the bulk of the figure dominating the tiny stage, they quickly forgot their astonishment as soon as the beautiful dark voice began to speak. For then, as George Rylands (up from Cambridge) could testify, the spell began to work; the presence unlike any other—smoldering, dangerous, like a tiger ready to spring—began to play upon the senses.

James Agate went to Hampstead that May and found again "the old haunting quest for beauty, the imperious line, the importunate sweep of the throat." How triumphantly the actress disobeyed Ibsen's conception of Hedda, he thought; she wore "her black mane as it were a thundercloud," her eyes were "twin craters presaging disaster"—she filled the eye that Ibsen left empty. In the later scenes, thought Agate, she was like a proud figure of Goya: her hand on extravagant hip, the full white throat, the dark masses of hair and geranium-colored shawl. Ivor Brown, another fine critic, also found his way to the stuffy little Everyman that spring. "The size and flame of her acting consumed that humble temple utterly," he marvelled. "She must have made herself felt that night from Finchley to Camden Town."

"Some say I 'walk through,'" Stella told Shaw, betraying the fact that she did not always feel like throwing her flame. Yes, she did sweat visibly: her hair was so heavy and the steep spiral stairway up to her dressing room was torture to climb after an exhausting tragic act. She felt a freak on that little stage; only here and there did she do anything nicely. Yet, "It's a pity you don't see *Hedda*. It would be good for you—I mean, inspire you one way or another." Her remarkable performance was eventually transferred for a brief run to the Kingsway, where "those theatregoers who appreciate magnificent acting" were encouraged by the *Daily Telegraph* to go. But Shaw held aloof these days and would not come.

On June 19 she left London, "on the road for the rest of my life," having accepted £3 a week to tour with Paula, Magda, Hedda, and the popular *Thirteenth Chair*. She took with her a good company that included William Armstrong, Catherine Lacey, Walter Fitzgerald, Annie Esmond, and Chris Castor. The newcomers soon learned how erratic, how exhausting, how hilarious life with Mrs. Patrick Campbell could be. "Touring with Mrs. Campbell would have cured anyone of being too serious about anything!" said William Armstrong. He vividly remembered his first meeting with her: "She looked very majestic: voluminous: magnificent: with piercing dark eyes and dark hair parted in the middle. . . . It was a wonderful face. Her eyes were amazingly youthful. When she looked at you, you saw that they were really the eyes of a young girl. You forgot her age, her stoutness, her chins. And there was that deep, unique, throaty, husky voice. It's difficult to explain the power of her attraction, but there was *genius* in her whole personality."

Rehearsals were lively. At Eilert Lövborg's first entrance in the second act, Armstrong appeared, heavily bearded, and said very nervously and with a wistful smile, "Will you, too, shake hands with me, Mrs. Tesman?" The effect was not at all what Stella was looking for. "No, no!" she exploded. "Go back! You can't come on smirking like a Botticelli angel. You've got to come in looking *dangerous*. Now go back and come on again looking *dangerous!*" Playing opposite her Hedda could be a remarkable experience. "She was a superb actress," said Armstrong, "when she cared to take the trouble. Her acting had something electric about it—something feverish—dynamic. It was *tempestuous*, and if she were really feeling emotional and playing with intensity, it was often overpowering." Stella herself quickly grew fond of the young actor, whom she nicknamed "Fanny." She was fond, too, of Annie Esmond, who played Miss Tesman in *Hedda*; and Annie adored Mrs. Pat.

In Brighton another young actor encountered Stella for the first time. John Gielgud was introduced at a luncheon party given by Ned Lathom in a private suite at the Metropole. Stella was playing Hedda on one of the piers; Gielgud had not gone to see her, but everyone else had, and one enthusiastic guest came up to exclaim that her performance had been a *tour de force*. "I suppose," replied Stella mournfully, "that is why I am always forced to tour." She had grown fond of that line. It was Gielgud's impression that, except for the worshippers who dared stand up to her in her bad moods, her company dreaded her. He had heard of her love of rich and titled people, and how they ran after her and entertained her and gave her presents. With young actors, he saw, she was very proud, but also very generous with advice and criticism. She told him that afternoon how much she loved his great-aunt: she always spoke warmly of Ellen Terry.

In July the company swung north. "As the tour went on she got younger and younger and more and more dynamic, and we got older and older—more exhausted," sighed Armstrong. Stella needed all her stamina, for she was planning to produce a play by her longtime New York friend Hoytie Wiborg. Stella had often stayed at Hoytie's Fifth Avenue home, and Hoytie's sister Sara and her husband, Gerald Murphy, had been equally gracious; Stella was delighted, as usual, to do a friend a favor. As amateur playwrights, Edith Lyttelton and Jennie Churchill had displayed some adeptness and even George's *Pro Patria* was constructed with skill. Hoytie Wiborg's *Voodoo*, however, had little merit. That Stella could have accepted it at all indicated how far her sense of loyalty could warp professional judgment. Of course, she looked remarkable as a Virginian grandmother in black braids and crinolines—but the rest of the thing was remarkable only for its idiocy. The Virginian grandmother has a grandchild who has been stricken dumb; the darkies on the plantation believe the dumbness is a curse and responsible for a crippling drought. One slave tries to murder the child; another intervenes to save him. In the end the rains come. *Voodoo* opened in Blackpool, and that night the rains came in the form of pelting oranges, from which the bowing cast fled precipitately.

Stella had promised Hoytie to give *Voodoo* three performances. Any other manager would have tossed it out after the first night, but Stella wound up playing it three times a week for five weeks on the three best days, and losing £1500, since *Hedda* played to slimmer crowds on Monday, Tuesday, and Wednesday. "Yes, Hoyti's play was an ugly business," Stella confided to D.D., but that was due entirely to her own misjudgment. At Blackpool the manager had offered her an entire week at Plymouth the following month. Hoytie had begged that *Voodoo* be run the Plymouth week. Stella had capitulated. That meant playing *Voodoo* during the intervening five weeks or the black cast from America would not have stayed on. "What I really resent," continued Stella, "is that the words 'all salaries' in the contract had 'not including Mrs. Campbell's' written after them; therefore Hoyti considers she has no moral claim upon her for my salary for all the work I did." In the end Stella got no salary at all. When she finally cabled Hoytie that she could not go on with her play, Hoytie responded, "YOUR CHICKEN-HEARTED CABLE JUST RECEIVED." "This cable addressed to me!" cried Stella, adding (as an afterthought) that her trust in Hoytie's friendship was over.

The young black actor playing the slave who saved the child had a very fine singing voice which he was called upon to use in the part. During those grim performances that Stella forced herself to undergo, she would glide up to him and whisper in all too audible tones, *"Do* sing again—you're better than the play!" Offstage, she gave Paul Robeson much kind advice and encouragement, telling him, "You know, one day you will play Othello!" Another actor defected, however: William Armstrong handed in his notice, having accepted an invitation to go as director to the Liverpool Playhouse. Stella said nothing at the time; then one night in *Hedda*, pretending to doze during the love scene in the second act, she suddenly "woke up" and exclaimed in the audience's full hearing, "I could have made you into an actor, and you throw me out on the *trottoir* like an old *cocotte!"*

"I have been playing in all sorts of silly little towns, most expensive seats 2/6, cheapest /5," she wrote D.D. in October. "I cannot tell you how hard I have been working. The fag of it all is enough to 'drown the cry within me.'" Next week it would be Northampton, Manchester, Bolton. She bought a car, not able to bear the railways any longer. Whenever she could, she would have herself driven after the performance to Ashfields, even though it meant a long drive back the next morning. The rush of the car through the black night soothed her immensely. The company headed south again for Wimbledon, Derby, Brighton. Arnold Bennett, in love with Dorothy Cheston (a member of Stella's company and her good friend), came down to Brighton the first day of February 1923. "I saw a rather wonderful performance of a very fine play, produced with taste & without any of the West End customary exaggeration," Bennett wrote Frank Swinnerton. "Mrs. Pat. Camp. was superb (but obese) as Magda, & she produced the play herself. Full house."

Leamington, Buxton, Folkestone, Margate, Eastbourne, Hull, Leeds, Westcliffe, Southampton, Reading, Cardiff. Houses were not always full. In Belfast in March 1924, Stella was obliged to write Pinero asking him to reduce his fees to five per cent straight. Business was very bad: last week she had dropped £50, this week £60. Her running expenses were well over £200; her shares a mere £272, £220, and £186. Pinero agreed. Then finally in late March she was able to come back to London, if not to the West End, playing *Magda* and *Tanqueray* at Croydon. There she telegraphed Shaw on the opening of his new play, *Saint Joan*, with Sybil Thorndike and her old friend Lyall Swete.

"Then you still live!" replied Shaw promptly. "After reading your telegram I went to Lyall Swete's dressingroom to give him a final word before the curtain rose; and he began to rave about you as the greatest actress in the world, swearing that you are as beautiful as ever, and that you had

trained a perfect company to support you in perfect performances of Hedda
and other plays; he having seen you lately. The man must be crazy.

"God intended you to play the serpent in *Methuselah*: I wrote it for
your voice. When I told Edith Evans that she would have to enter bald-
headed, old, half naked, and in rags [as the She-Ancient], in a bevy of
youths and maidens made as pretty as the stage could make them, and that
in that ghastly condition she would outfascinate them and play them clean
out of existence, she believed, and did it. Sybil Thorndike for a whole
month never let me doubt for a second that she regarded me as far superior
to the Holy Trinity as a producer. And now Siddons and Rachel were never
so praised and exalted as these twain. If you had only had faith as much as
a grain of mustard seed!

"Well, are you quite well? and are you making plenty of money? and
have you still the cottage at Ormskirk? and has your virgin loveliness really
come back? and do you remember Tristan and Isolde and forget all our
stupid conflicts? and did the book get you out of debt? and—and—and—
and—what sort of life are you having generally?

"I shall be 68 in July: that is about all MY news, except what you may
read in the papers."

"Dear dear Joey," Stella answered happily. "Your letter at the theatre
gave me strange pleasure—all the dreariness vanished.

"I have owed you a letter for a long long time—I did write to you very
many months ago, but never sent it.

"It's two years next June since I started to clear £6000. It's nearly cleared
up now, but it has been a mighty, an almighty job!

"The book brought in about £2500. I believe, and there is still more to
come in.

"I started my tour on £15 with 'Hedda Gabler.' . . .

"I have a car. I couldn't stand waiting about in cold stations, and I must
have air—a bedroom in station hotels couldn't be borne for nearly two
years. I spend most of my day in the car, that is a joy. Next year I mean to
drive it myself. It is a six-cylinder Buick, that can be shut or open, and has
done 24,000 miles without a rattle.

"Yes, I still have my cottage at Ormskirk, with its lovely garden. I have it
on a twenty one years lease. Ned Lathom is no longer my landlord, the
local grocer is.

"I have an excellent cook-housekeeper, a gardener with one leg and four
fingers—blown up in France—I was persuaded by the local clergyman to
take him in—for my sins!

"And there is a little step-niece by marriage on the Campbell side, who
lives there and we have happy times together. She is twenty two. I found her

in Edinburgh; her brother of nineteen killed in the war, her sister of sixteen a few months later died of influenza, and the child was alone when she discovered her father with a gas-pipe in his mouth—dead. Her mother has seven children and not a penny....

"I wonder if you remember my brother Max, who was very strange. I have taken care of him for over three years, and he is now quite well which delights me....

"Dear Lyall Swete loved me when Beo was four years of age, and wrote pretty poems to me, one entitled 'The Child of the King.' He would have me believe I haven't disappointed him, but I daresay you are right in saying 'he must be crazy.'

"Will you take me to a matinee of 'Saint Joan' this week? That would make up for a great deal. I have read your praises with so much pleasure....

"Sixty eight indeed? Twenty two—and I your grandmother.

"I never forget Tristan and Isolde—and you twenty one—I seventeen—harps in the air...."

But Shaw neither replied nor took her to a matinee, and after Croydon Stella set out again. If Lyall Swete was crazy to think she still played magnificently, he was not the only madman. A young actor named Ralph Richardson went to see her several times in one week at Portsmouth, and thought Mrs. Campbell the greatest performer—in fact, the only truly great performer—he had ever seen, an opinion he would maintain through the years. Cecil Beaton went more cautiously to *Tanqueray* at the Pier Theatre at Bournemouth that April 1924, interested to compare Mrs. Campbell's vintage performance with the lovely Gladys Cooper's 1922 version of Paula. "But it was frightfully badly acted to-night," he recorded in his diary, "especially by Aubrey Tanqueray: he was stiff, prosy, and absurd. Mrs. Pat was incredibly huge and terrible. It's tragic that she should be appearing at this stage of her life in the part that 'made' her in the heyday of her beauty. Poor old thing, she does look awful now! Repulsive! She was twice as large as any man on the stage. She has a wonderful voice, though, and has certain very splendid little tricks, a laugh 'Ho, Ho, Ho, Ho,' deep and unusual, which she brings into play each time she's getting upset. She gives out a long, breathy sigh, 'Ooorrrr, I'm so happy!'; and she has an effective sniff.

"The truth is she is still a great actress with a compelling command; her performance was much quieter than Gladys Cooper's, but it was not as convincing. I suppose that was because Gladys looked so marvellous. Mrs. Pat appeared like a terrible old landlady with her insolent ways and untidy black hair about to fall down. Gladys's cockney flashy bravura added to the character. Molyneux made dresses for Cooper that were staggering in their

Byzantine beauty, whereas poor old Mrs. Pat had on some pea-soup creations and old washed-out shawls with which she was continuously
meddling. It was distracting to see her pulling her bodices from falling off
her shoulders.

"Mrs. Pat was horribly to the front each time she was on stage—even
when she ought to have faded into the background. Instead of quietly
playing the piano, she strummed so loud that no one could hear a word that
was being said by others. She was late for her cue twice. Once she kept the
stage waiting for about three minutes—the old brute. I've heard crowds of
stories of her beastliness to other actors and her jealousy. But she knows she
is a monster and is the first to laugh at herself. She is most amusing, the old
brute, when she takes her call. She waddles to the footlights and leans
forward, holding up her skirt with one hand, and bowing with a terrible
sneer on her face." After the performance young Cecil Beaton went home
and drew himself naked in the mirror, vastly pleased, no doubt, at the
difference between the reflected image and the old brute who had entertained him that night.

Chester, Luton, Bedford, Carlisle, Dundee, Glasgow, Edinburgh,
Sheffield, Hastings, Worthing, Southport . . . On October 9 the company
descended upon the Papworth Village Settlement in Cambridgeshire, where
Max had been in residence since July, to give a charity matinee of *Magda*.
Max had settled in very well, the matron of the colony for treating and
rehabilitating tubercular patients assured her. He enjoyed listening in whenever good music was broadcast, and so far there had been no "spirits" at all.
Stella provided £1 a month pocket money, and paid part of the £2 a week
for expenses. The whole colony turned out for *Magda* and afterwards Stella
distributed her flowers among the men in the wards. Letters of appreciation
followed her to Ashfields. "I wonder if even you can realise just what it
meant to take several hundred isolated people who, for the first time, under
your spell completely lost themselves in you & your art—this is a feat that
only a great genius could accomplish," wrote Head Matron Katie Borne
gratefully. Less gratifying news followed some months later. "Do you think
your brother could get on with less stout?" a matron inquired anxiously in
December. "That runs away with money."

In 1925 the tour went on: Dunfermline, Aberdeen, Gennock, Perth.
Stella celebrated her sixtieth birthday as she usually celebrated birthdays—
with a performance, this time at the Royalty in Chester. "Is there a more
energetic, high-spirited woman in the world than Mrs. Patrick Campbell,
who is preparing a new play for the provinces, and then for London?"
wondered *John O'London's Weekly*. "What is her age? She has no age! . . .
She has retained her beauty and an intelligence that makes most men seem

like half-wits." Stella was deep in negotiations over the new play by Frederick Witney called *The Adventurous Age*. She thought her part as an elderly woman vainly trying to recapture her youth ironically amusing, but was dissatisfied with other aspects of Witney's work. Surely he could be amusing without being indecent, for example; and surely he could provide three pages of brilliant dialogue for the last scene. She continued to pepper him with suggestions for alterations and additions—things he would see immediately if he could watch them rehearse, while Witney grew more and more sullen under her tutelage. An opening was finally arranged for Swansea in May; the play went very well. Yet Stella still had objections to it. "After the very clever scenes with father and son and mother and daughter the scene with the butler and children is bad," she wrote to Witney frankly in July. "1st it isn't particularly funny. 2nd the plan is never carried out. 3rd it is far better for the curtain to come down with the audience wondering what will be done instead of the butler being dragged in there. The idea is *old*. It would be angelic if you would see to this. . . . I hope some fees come your way soon. You broke your promise about sending me that play to read. I have quite made up my mind that you are not a very agreeable man—or perhaps it's just me you dislike. Warm regards." But in Exeter that August the play was "going splendidly," and she planned to tour with *The Adventurous Age* and *The Thirteenth Chair* in the fall.

Manchester, Chatham, Ipswich, Woolwich, Brixton, Chester, Luton, Bedford. During brief runs up to London, Stella managed at last to find herself a flat at 64 Pont Street, a curve of Victorian red brick and white trim. Ashfields was proving too expensive and difficult to maintain. From her bow window in town she could look across the street to the former home of George Alexander, dead of consumption at fifty-nine, two years after the revival of *Bella Donna*. While in London she managed to get brief engagements in October at the Grand Theatre, Croydon, and the King's Theatre, Hammersmith. It was at this time that Lord Lowndes, now an immensely wealthy widower living in Florence, saw the announcement of her appearance in the *Daily Mail*. At the sight of the magic name, the old passion stirred. Impulsively he left his villa and came to London, where he hired a roofless Rolls-Royce, loaded the back seat with orchids, and drove unannounced to Hammersmith. There in an inconspicuous part of the darkened theatre he waited for the entrance of the woman he had loved vainly and might now win.

"But when Stella came on, what was left in my heart sank," Lowndes sadly wrote to his good friend Ashton Stevens. "She was old, Ashton; she was—I loathe to use the word—fat; and I was cured. I left the flowers and I left the theatre before the first act was over. I wish I hadn't seen her that way and I shall never see her again." (Years later Stevens told the story of Lord Lowndes's baffled quest to Ethel Barrymore. Her eyes brimming with tears, Miss Barrymore replied, "Never tell that again to an actress over forty.")

Carlisle, Dundee, Glasgow, Edinburgh. By this time Stella and Frederick Witney were feuding openly. He wanted her to play *The Adventurous Age* in London; she replied that no one wanted it in London—not her fault. If he wanted a London production, he should find the capital; undoubtedly he could succeed where she had failed. She found his letters most disagreeable. She did *not* "dragonize." She did not understand what he meant when he wrote that "Everyone is thanking God they have a sense of humour—the worst of bad signs." She had not "choked off" George Tyler: he wanted her to play *The Adventurous Age* in America along with another play, but not *Tanqueray*—but *Tanqueray* was her biggest money-maker. As it was, she had substituted his play for *Tanqueray* in Dundee, Glasgow, and Edinburgh—and was losing money on it. "You baby you!" she scoffed. It was the sad case of a disappointed playwright and a great actress in hard times, scuffling over a third-rate play.

Since the wonderful dark voice could still beget dreams, Stella took a few engagements during these years reading scenes from *Cyrano* and *Pelléas* and reciting "High Tide on the Coast of Lincolnshire" over the air for the B.B.C. And then at last the offer of a London engagement at £100 a week brought the grinding road work to a halt. "The theatrical world is interested in the return of Mrs. Patrick Campbell to London," the press announced glibly, ignoring the intervening struggle for survival. "She has been touring the provinces for the last four years, and intends to appear shortly in an amusing comedy by a new writer. Those who have followed her career know what a rich vein of comedy lies hidden in her greater talent for emotional acting, and are looking forward to the pleasure of seeing this famous actress condescend to make us laugh."

Stella prepared for H. F. Maltby's *What Might Happen* by losing weight, then by taking a step far more drastic. "The other night I dined at the Benjamin Guinnesses to find Mrs. Patrick Campbell threatening to bob her hair," said Brian Howard, a young do-nothing about town. "I believe she's done it by now. She'll look like some nonconformist cook who's stayed too long in the kitchen. *Dreadful.* Marvellous hair, it was." "SHORN OF HER TRESSES," announced the *Daily Graphic* in May; Mrs. Campbell had joined the great army of the shingled, sacrificing a glorious head of hair so long she could sit on it. Stella professed to have no regrets. Samson obviously knew nothing about haircuts: *she* felt stronger than ever.

Quite hearty enough, in fact, to sabotage any play she did not like—and she did not like Maltby's farce about a post-war social revolution which finds the aristocratic upper classes down-at-the-heel and dropping their *h*'s, while a one-time office boy has made enough money out of the war to send his son to Harrow and Cambridge. It was her first engagement in a West End theatre since *Macbeth* at the Aldwych nearly six years before. Perversely, proudly, she chose to ignore that fact. The play was excellently cast: Fred Kerr from the old *Daventry* days, Lilian Braithwaite, Edmund Gwenn, and Stella playing Countess Strong-i'-th'-Arm, a *nouvelle-pauvre* aristocrat. "Everything should have been ring-a-rosy, but it wasn't, and the fly in the ointment was Mrs. Campbell," fumed the angry author. "That extraordinary woman from the outset took exception to a certain member of the cast; she wouldn't come out into the open, and she wouldn't resign; she just sulked, lost all interest in the production, made no attempt to learn her lines and deliberately went out to wreck the whole show." "Oh, what a bad girl I am, aren't I?" Stella would exclaim, widening her eyes, when Braithwaite, Kerr, or Gwenn insinuated that rehearsals might improve if she knew her lines. "I really *must* learn them!"

*What Might Happen* opened on June 10, 1926, at the Savoy. "My dear Lilian," purred Stella after the first night, "if I had known you were such a good *prompter,* I wouldn't have bothered to learn *any* of my lines!" Out in front, however, critics had a different view. The *Daily Mail* called the piece splendidly acted, and rejoiced that Mrs. Patrick Campbell was back in London, "a much younger 'Mrs. Pat' than she has appeared for years past." In the *Sunday Times* James Agate regretted that "Mrs. Patrick Campbell should make one of her rare West-End appearances in a part which revealed her talents only by their misappropriation." Stella agreed, thereby making an enemy of Maltby, who believed that she and she alone had wrecked his play. "There has been a lot of rubbish written and spoken about Mrs. Campbell," he wrote later. "She was never a great actress, not even a very good one; she had a wonderful personality, voice, figure, appearance and eyes, but she never rose above the standard of a gifted amateur." Maltby confided this opinion to Pinero during the run. "So you've found *that* out, have you?" replied the older dramatist. "I knew that when she was playing Tanqueray and Ebbsmith. If she is *absolutely* fitted in a part, she can wear it—but she can't wear anyone else's."

Stella held a complementary opinion of Maltby's talents. "Our ridiculous play comes off in a fortnight," she told Witney on July 17. Unfortunately, her salary stopped with the play. "I wish I had an Inn," she wrote her business manager, Arthur Bertram, that August, "—anything I would be content with rather than acting." She'd been *out* of work for seven months and now *in* for only six weeks. It was quite dreadful. Impossible. She couldn't get people interested. She needed his help.

With time on her hands Stella took an interest that September in a much talked-about dramatization of Margaret Kennedy's *The Constant Nymph* starring the remarkable young actor and playwright Noel Coward. The day of dress rehearsal she rang Noel and implored to be allowed to come. It was rumored that stalls were going at £10 and she, an old, unwanted woman, couldn't afford a first-night seat. Of course Coward said yes; and Stella appeared in the front row of the dress circle rather late, cuddling a Pekinese that yapped incessantly through the quieter scenes. At the final curtain she accosted producer and co-author Basil Dean, who had been trying to avoid her, being more than a little afraid of what she might think of the piece. "Beautiful play, Mr. Dean," murmured Stella in her most winning tones. "Beautiful play, and how bad Noel is! I *must* go and tell him."

Coward had already experienced critical reaction from Stella. "Mrs. Patrick Campbell came one night in a box, and great excitement reigned behind the scenes," he recalled of a November 1920 production of *The Knight of the Burning Pestle*. "This excitement waned towards the end of the play, when it was discovered that she had been sound asleep since the beginning of the first act. I sent her an outraged message through a mutual friend, and the next night there she was again, in the same box, but far from sleepy. She wore long white gloves, and applauded wildly every time I stepped on to the stage." Now, on the morning of *The Constant Nymph*'s opening, Coward's phone rang and he picked it up to hear Stella's beautiful, sympathetic tones. The fair girl had been *quite* good, but why, oh, why was he playing Lewis Dodd? "You're the wrong type, darling!" she moaned. "You have no glamor and you should wear a beard!" "An example of her delight in perverse judgments," commented Basil Dean, "for Lewis Dodd turned out to be the best performance in character that Noël had yet given."

Stella had in the meantime decided to take *The Adventurous Age* to America without a firm commitment from Tyler, a bold step. "Cheer up," she wrote Witney that September, "—it is an awful push up the hill." "I have lost patience," Witney retorted in October, but by November Stella had made arrangements to sail. "I will do my level best for you," she promised.

The sea on that crossing was very rough, and few passengers dared the deck. During calmer moments Stella would emerge and sink into a deck chair next to Osbert Sitwell, who was braving the weather heavily muffled against the winds. She appeared, said Sitwell, "with a little the air of a luminous-faced seal," mournfully enduring the agony, but her tongue as wicked and bubble-pricking as ever. "What she most enjoyed in conversation was to see how far she could go," decided Sitwell, "like a child playing Tom Tiddler's Ground, without being caught—without being hurt. Sometimes, however, she hurt others in the process." The best tactic was to startle her by agreeing with her in an unexpected way. Thus when she asked a mutual friend earnestly, "Norah, were your eyes *always* as far apart as that?" if Norah could answer, "No, Stella: didn't you know? They had to be *dragged* apart"—then the encounter ended in a burst of laughter. Yet Sitwell was struck again during the voyage by her kindness and spontaneity, and later would be much impressed in New York with the way she tried to help visiting English writers and painters establish themselves.

If Stella mourned the difference between the Mrs. Pat who had conquered New York in 1901 and the stout, shingled Mrs. Pat of today, she tried not to show it. "I'm out of a job," she informed reporters on landing. "London wants flappers, and I can't flap." She headed for the Barclay Hotel on East 48th; there was no little dog this time to cause trouble. There were still friends in the city: the Hapgoods, Hoytie Wiborg (*Voodoo* unaccountably forgiven), the Murphys, and the Guinnesses, whose lovely home in Washington Square with its ceiling of birds in flight painted by Bridget herself was home away from home to countless Britishers. Most of all, there was Ned Sheldon. In the autumn of 1922 he had moved into a spacious penthouse fourteen stories above Madison Avenue at 48th Street. Paralyzed now and blind, he was one of the most sought-out people in New York, entertaining visitors one by one from his brocade-covered couch, offering them delicate sympathy, counsel, and encouragement. He was the one person to whom Stella could confide the heartbreak she hid from the world; he had always been completely frank with her and, as a result, she trusted him. She confided to him now the apprehensions of an aging actress trying to reconquer a city that had forgotten her.

She and the long-suffering George Tyler finally agreed on a production of *The Adventurous Age* at the Mansfield Theatre. "Oh my God what a business it has been," she wrote Witney on January 7, 1927. "I cannot *begin* to tell you but you *must* admire my temerity! The play goes on here in 3 weeks & if a success until the 2nd of May & the management has an option on my services in your play as a 'road tour' until December. . . . You should now make £50 a week for 8 months with any luck—and if you will get out a scenario for a good movie I will go to California June, July, and August & do it. . . . If you will send me any play or plays I will do my utmost to get them done for you here. My energy has put me in touch with the right people. . . . I do hope things haven't been too difficult for you," she added less optimistically. "I have been nearly crazy. . . ."

Stella fought gamely for what was to prove her greatest disaster. She had changed, theatre had changed, audiences had changed. No matter what her reputation, an overweight, aging siren in a dated British farce could not interest a New York that worshipped jazz, cocktails, and roadsters, and had installed the fast-living, hard-drinking Scott and Zelda Fitzgerald as its idols. Stella not only failed to convince; she was tragically misunderstood. British audiences had known she was spoofing the character of the over-sexed matron, Adela Rivers. New York audiences thought they were being treated to a grotesque exhibition of the actress playing herself. "HAPLESS RETURN," mourned Alexander Woollcott; "a recklessly ill-advised and acutely embarrassing evening. She has changed in outward semblance be-yond all recognition." The reigning critic, George Jean Nathan, was remorseless. "Mrs. Patrick Campbell is still a skillful comedienne," said his kindest sentence, "but what chance does mere skill at trivial comedy stand against the recollection of a once lovely woman become fat and yellow?"

A year later Nathan looked back at the debacle more philosophically. "In the third act of the piece, the action called for Mrs. Campbell to crawl down a short ladder from the window of a house. Upon her negotiation of the feat, not without considerable visible effort and audible puffing, a great wave of applause broke over the auditorium. Though plainly unintentional, that applause was so ironically insulting that it would not have surprised me in the least had Mrs. Campbell, were she not the well-bred woman she is, thereupon stepped to the footlights and in very polite terms bidden her audience to go to Hell.

"The pathos and significance of the incident should not be lost upon us. Here was an actress who in her heyday was a celebrated beauty; here was a woman who, aside from what acting talent she possessed, was once a slim and sightly creature to stimulate men's fancy, to turn the heads of countless cavaliers, to make tom-toms of innumerable masculine hearts, aye, even to cause the very dogs in Hyde Park to chase their tails with an unwonted pruritus. And what had time wrought of her? A Brünnhilde creased with the years, an old woman plainly strapped in to the point of discomfort, whose mere climbing down a few rungs of a little ladder without collapsing created a gaping astonishment in her audience. That way lay the pathos. And this way lies the significance: that no woman such as Mrs. Patrick Campbell was should, when the decades have stolen her physical splendors, risk longer the kindly derisions of an ever essentially cruel theatre.

"There is nothing more sad and nothing more ridiculous than the specta-cle of an ex-beauty fighting it out on the old line."

"I don't know whether it isn't better not to send you the vile notices," Stella wrote Witney on February 10. "I send you only the best. The audience saw nothing at all funny in the play & during the boy & girl scene in IIIA many of them walked out. The first night house was

| | |
|---|---|
| Mon. 7th | $1,154 |
| Tues. | $ 229 |
| Wed. M. | $ 236 |
| Wed. E. | $ 183 |

and I hear to-night—Thurs.—there is nothing. We ought to have over $1000 a night to make any profit. You can guess how heartbroken I am for you—& for myself. . . . It was all done lavishly & the scenes beautiful & on the whole the company played very well. . . . I had made up my mind we were going to have such a success. They want things so strong here—so daring & so full of *punch*."

*The Adventurous Age* closed after six weeks. If anything was needed to add to her distress, it was the cable from D.D. advising her that her daughter was very ill and that she should return at once. She was deep in debt without a penny for passage. She wrote Shaw, asking for a large loan. Marvelling at her thriftlessness, he nevertheless sent her a check for £1000; she booked immediately.

Two years later when an American reporter came to Pont Street to interview her, Stella had not forgotten. She gestured him to a seat in the carelessly tasteful drawing room littered with worn Orientals, books, and autographed photos. "I think I shall never visit your country again," she told him. "My last visit was a bitter experience. There were unkind things said, and they hurt. I played the part of an elderly woman trying to recapture youth, and I played it too well. The New York critics were crushing. One said it was time for me to retire to a cottage with my scrapbook. That was the cruellest thing anybody ever said of me."

# THIRTY-FOUR

# *1927–1930*

*I*AM THREE PARTS a fool," Stella was fond of saying, and it was this knowing innocence that both created her difficulties and enabled her to survive them. She did not give up after a disheartening failure, but rather decided that since her figure had deteriorated while her voice had not, she would join the lecture circuit. In London, therefore, on the afternoon of July 7, 1927, she stood behind a lectern and spoke to an audience on "Diction and the Dramatic Art." She could not remember a time, she said, when she had not loved words and wanted to render their music perfectly. Diction was an art that should be loved and studied; beautiful speech should be the habit of a lifetime. One should be as proud of one's English as one would be if someone said, "How beautifully you speak French."

Then her tone became critical, reflecting the defeat in New York. The plays of today were not written for fineness or for beauty of language. Speech had become talk, and talk chatter. The craft of acting had been forgotten. "Natural" acting—the watchword of today—often simply meant "commonplace." Actors were not given great lines to speak. What could even a Mrs. Siddons make out of a bit of dialogue like "I say, darling, don't be a rotter" or "Don't cheek me, sweetie"? Emotional scenes seemed quite impossible on the stage today; passion unthinkable. The stage was peopled by pretty walk-abouts with barely covered knees and Eton-cropped hair: pretty puppets who did not get the chance to voice the great independence, courage, and humor of our time. But she felt confident the day must come quite soon when young actresses would sit up all night, as she and her generation had, to get a sentence, a phrase, or even a word beautifully right; for poetry and truth, imagination and romance, radiance and glamour were things that could no more pass away than the sun, the moon, and the stars.

"We spent a glorious hour with Mrs. Patrick Campbell as an orator," Stella was pleased to find J. T. Grein declare next day in the *Sketch.* "And no sooner did she appear, a majestic figure, full of spirit, than we felt that she is not only a great actress, and a skilful writer, but a speaker of rare quality. Witty she was too. The audience rose to Mrs. Campbell at her every demonstration. . . . The discourse should be repeated in every city of the realm." Agreeing, the *Sphere* called her "that greatest of all actresses of our day . . . the possessor of the most wonderful and fascinating voice in the world, and the complete knowledge of how to use it."

But critics like Grein belonged to the old school. There were other critics present that afternoon who decided that Mrs. Campbell was simply mourning an age that was dead. If plays no longer boasted "fine language," it was a matter for rejoicing: naturalness was preferable to the "stilted and antiquated back-chat of a Pinero play." In modern plays young girls would look extremely odd in long skirts, and if there were no emotional love scenes in the West End these days—well, undoubtedly few modern people made love emotionally. To quote the rather vulgar old song, "What you've never had, you'll never miss"; inadequacies on the modern stage were surely noticed only by an actress who admitted to being a grandmother. "Mrs. Campbell is the latest scold," agreed the *Daily Mail*.

Stella chose to listen to Grein and take her lecture on tour. She could not avoid knowing that to the public she was an actress who had been at her height in the nineties. She was already a legend, a subject for nostalgia. The previous December two playgoers writing in the *Sphere*, for example, had reminisced about her Paula Tanqueray: "My word, how wonderful it seemed! I can remember the dress 'Mrs. Pat' wore. It was cerise velvet; and I remember the air—no one excelled George Alexander in that sort of thing—with which he removed her cloak from her shining shoulders. What a precise, haunting articulation she had. All the young men were in love with her. . . ." "Yes . . . I saw 'The Second Mrs. Tanqueray,' it must have been in 1893, from the pit, with a man who has since become famous. We were incredibly moved. I remember after the fall of the curtain, we walked for half-an-hour without speaking. . . ."

That was thirty-three years ago, but Stella stubbornly refused to wither and die. Her zest for life was unquenchable. "Mrs. Patrick Campbell and Komisarzhevsky came for lunch—in order to meet each other," Arnold Bennett recorded that September. "Komi said very little. Stella talked tremendously, and very well. Her ideas are exceedingly sound, and in spite of all that I have heard about her naughtiness, she seems to me to be fundamentally good-natured." In December Stella was back again, negotiating with Bennett to produce and act his play *Flora*. She arrived for tea at 5:30 and "made a terrific outpouring." "If you want to keep me quiet give me a cigar," she said. Bennett gave her one, without much effect.

"Later, she went out into the Square smoking it. Her energy seems quite unimpaired."

The energy did indeed appear limitless. "A sensation was caused at Mrs. Benjamin Guinness's ballet party last night," reported the press in November, "by the appearance of a stout elderly gentleman . . . dressed in check trousers, a long green coat, a striped waistcoat, a yellow top hat, yellow gloves with a red beard and eyebrows, a red rose, a loudly patterned handkerchief, and a huge cigar." Although his two "Hungarian" companions were quickly identified as Lady Churston and Miss Cathleen Nesbitt, no one guessed that "the electrician of the Moscow Theatre" was Mrs. Pat. Professionally, too, she kept at it, trying out her lecture; appearing in *Madame Kuranda* in the provinces, a play about a psychic that was slated for London but never made it; and writing an article for *Pearson's Magazine* on "What Matters Most in Life" (it was, said Stella, "a sound mind and a courageous spirit").

Some friends had fallen away, some had died; but some remained—not only old friends like the Guinnesses, Lady Horner, Ned Sheldon, and D.D., but the admirers and protégés that every famous actress inevitably collects over the years. The most devoted of these was still Morrie, whose fidelity far exceeded her secretarial wage. She had begun as a fan throwing bouquets of violets; through violent storms and dismissals she had hung on, adoring her employer. Once after Stella had shown her the door, she had turned up, incredibly, onstage in the midst of a performance that same night, her head poking out of a prop fireplace, her hands clasped, her eyes pleading forgiveness. Of course she was back at the Square the next day. Another devoted admirer was Mary Hand, a young artist who had begged to draw Stella in *Pygmalion* days. When she had called, Stella had treated her warmly, sweeping a hand at a life's accumulation of treasures and urging, "Please, take anything you admire." Naturally, Miss Hand had not, although she found the impulsive generosity touching. In 1925 she had begun to collect Stella's flattering reviews, copying them exquisitely by hand on large cream sheets in colored inks. The friendship would endure twenty-five years.

Stella was also good pals with her grandson, Patrick. Although her daughter had told her "You needn't have come" when she hurried back at D.D.'s cable, Stella Pat was still at Pont Street recovering, and Patrick, now fifteen, came on holidays. His childhood had been divided: wretched digs with his mother on tour and heavenly summers at Stanway with Michael Asquith. Some summers Barrie would take Stanway with Lady Cynthia as his secretary, and Cynthia would invite her friend Stella Pat. The young people would all play croquet ("the great activity"), or take part in the once-a-year cricket match between the house and the village, or listen to the stories Barrie would come upstairs at night and tell. Other times Mother Beatrice had taken him on holiday to Ruthin Castle, where he revelled in an enormous baronial hall studded with animal heads and hung with two-handed swords, and magnificent dungeons. When he returned to school at Winchester House, M.B. would send him £5 notes, although she never came to visit. She liked him, and he liked her—the tall, thick-set, rather overpowering grandmother with the square face, white skin, and beautiful hands who carried herself like a queen.

Shaw too had not deserted her, writing to his "Dear Unforgotten" the last month of 1927. He had been silent for almost three years, but if she knew the trouble those unlucky letters had made for him, she would understand many things. He did not regret it now, but it must not happen again until they both were dead—then they could be added to Heloise and Abelard and the lot of them. He picked up what news he could of her from D.D., Lady Horner, and Dorothy Cheston-Bennett, who all said she was recovering her good looks. When, he demanded, had she lost them? And why did she not finally divorce George and marry some duke? In the new year, 1928, he began to advise her again about her career. He saw no reason for her to hesitate for a moment over Bennett's *Flora*. "Either you are in business as an actress or you are not. It is now, I take it, a case of 'Mrs. Patrick Campbell at liberty. Matrons, heavies, comedy, character: 64 Pont Street.' Well, here you are offered a leading part in a play by an eminent author. Of course you take it without any fuss, as a taxi driver takes a fare, and glad to get it. It is of great importance to you to get into the routine of the theatre as leading Old Woman, and break with your starry past. . . . And if it comes off, *do* behave yourself, dear Stella, if you can. Dont begin to do everybody's business except your own, especially the producer's. *That*, as you very well know, is what is standing in your way."

Stella dug in her heels. He did not understand. *Flora* was not a gift: she would have to find money to produce it. "If I may make an excuse for my bad name it is this," she continued stubbornly, "—I am—in a small way—an imaginative artist, and there is my difficulty. Sometimes I cannot learn my words until I know what the others are bringing to or taking away from their words. . . . I search for the spirit whilst the producer is struggling with the letter—this reads as *banale* but it is simple and true for me." It was quite stupid of her, she knew, but she could not think of herself as an old woman who had arrived at matrons and heavies. "I see myself as an un-wanted child just as I see you, not as an old gentleman, but as a brilliant adorable Irish lad whom I love with ardour." To this string of romanticisms

Shaw sent back "a scorcher." Stella drew herself up. "I know where Satan has gotten you Joey," she replied, "you are *brain proud!*"

Yet she admired the brain more than she would ever admit, always returning for the advice she seldom took. She had been asked to play Mrs. Alving for the Ibsen Centenary, she told him in February. He had bashed and beheaded her so often, he must do it once more if he thought she would ruin the play—she could still get out of it. Shaw evidently did not think so, and she reported to the little Gate Theatre in Villiers Street to rehearse *Ghosts* with the young actor she had met at Brighton, John Gielgud. She brought with her an exercise book into which Mary Hand had copied out her part in large letters, and the latest Peke, Kwei-Li. She dropped down heavily into her chair, adjusted Kwei-Li, and the company went through their parts. When anybody else read, Stella would lower her exercise book and gaze mournfully and intently at the speaker.

"We soon found that she knew far more about the play—and every part in it—than any of the rest of us," said Gielgud, cast as her son Oswald. "Mrs. Campbell could have been as fine a producer as she was an actress. She helped me enormously with the emotional effects of my difficult part, couching her advice in graphic terms. In the scene where Oswald tells his mother of his terrible disease, she said, 'Keep still. Gaze at me. Now, you must speak in a Channel-steamer voice. Empty your voice of meaning and speak as if you were going to be sick. Pinero once told me this and I have never forgotten it!' " If she knew more about the play than anyone else, she did not, however, seem to know a line of her part. "My dear," she groaned to Gielgud during rehearsal in the loudest *sotto voce* in London, "it's all like a very long confinement!" Between practices Gielgud often took her to lunch at the Escargot Restaurant in Greek Street, discovering there that the full figure was no accident as Stella greedily devoured snails by the dozen. Yet she constantly bewailed her fate. "My face looks like a burst paper bag," she would moan; or, when the beautiful singer Madame Marguerite D'Alvarez made an entrance, "Ah, yes—*me* in a spoon."

At the dress rehearsal, when everyone expected her to be late, temperamental, and inaccurate, she astounded the cast by arriving on the minute, word-perfect, and in full command of her brilliant talents. A special Sunday performance initiated the series; but for the critics Stella performed unevenly. Although one declared that "her art and personality are as fascinating as ever" in the most satisfactory performance of *Ghosts* he'd seen, and another that "Mrs. Campbell gave a most wonderful performance," James Agate disagreed. "Mrs. Campbell's performance fell below her own standard because one felt that in the first two acts her body and soul were not in it. It was the third act alone which enabled one to say confidently: 'There, young people, is the great acting we are always telling you about!' "

Leon M. Lion undertook to give eight more performances, but chose Easter week, when everybody was out of town. "Mrs. Campbell was very cross that the house was so poor and that none of her Society friends had bothered to turn up," said Gielgud. "She dearly loved a Lord. She would say to me out loud during a scene, 'The Marquis and Marchioness of Empty are in front again!' " The theatre *was* full of very serious young people come to see the legend. To foil them, Stella walked through the first acts, which in the foyer they ecstatically declared great acting; then, laughing in their faces, she showed them in the third what great acting could be. She had not tired of playing with her audiences.

"She was an extraordinary, fascinating woman, and we became great friends," said Gielgud. "I was very flattered that she seemed to like me, because I knew how difficult she was. She was losing her friends and she had hardly any money, though she refused to take any notice of that. She was defiant about her unpopularity both with managers and actors who appeared with her." He came to Pont Street expecting a flamboyant gypsy atmosphere; he found instead Morris wallpapers, a fine rosewood grand piano, a bust of Dante enshrined with flowers. "She could be wise and even affectionate," said Gielgud, "and why she had to be so ill-behaved, sometimes even common and rude, it was difficult to tell. A kind of demon seized her and she could not resist being unkind to people, making cheap jokes at their expense. Yet she could also be witty, very ladylike and gracious." Gielgud had heard about the bad behavior from his great-aunt Marion Terry. Once in Dublin Stella and Marion played a scene from *Lady Windermere's Fan* together, but Stella was not on speaking terms with Marion and stood throughout with her back to the audience. "How did you play the scene?" marvelled Gielgud. "*I* spoke all her lines," said Marion. Sensitive, kindly, and unafraid, Gielgud won Stella's affection. He did not think her an old brute. She looked romantic, he thought, and had nice ankles.

Under the defiance Stella's heart was often sore; but she could admit it to only a very few chosen friends. She would like to come and sit by his bedside, she wrote James Agate, who was ill, that May, but "It can't be done, you would either look upon my jokes as tears, or my tears as jokes. . . . And I cannot be funny," she continued, "—eight years and the only engagement offered me in London was 'What Might Happen'! I suffered agonies, but crossings are not swept, and bootlaces are not worn, and £100 a week was too tempting to resist. And then Mr. Grein's one performance of 'Ghosts' came along. When I asked him for my two guineas fee, which all the other artists had received, he said he did not like to offer it to me, I was too majestic. . . . I hope some afternoon when you are well again you will come and have tea with me here, where the desire to open my heart would not be so great as by your bedside. . . . You know quite well I couldn't burst into flames until the third act of 'Ghosts,' " she concluded, defending herself against his criticism, "with all those conversations around the happenings of twenty four years ago—except that one silly word 'Ghosts.' You can't do anything with that word, unless your eyes pop out, or your hair is white."

That May eight theatrical societies gathered at the Hotel Cecil to pay tribute to the man who had been chiefly responsible for introducing Ibsen to England in the nineties. Stella presided over a distinguished gathering, reading aloud a tribute to J. T. Grein from Shaw. It was a time for looking back. "I am better; very well, in fact," Pinero wrote her that month. "But I don't care much for the theayter in these days, knowing that I shall meet upon the stage no troublesome Mrs. Campbell (who was never troublesome when she and I worked together), nor anybody else with a tithe of her charm and power. . . . When I return we will meet and you shall tell me all your hopes and aspirations. As long as those survive we are in the spring of life. I kiss your hand."

Stella refused an offer from Nigel Playfair to play Mrs. Crummles ("So you're the one turning the somersaults for Nigel that I wouldn't," she said to Miriam Lewes, former acrobat, who took the part), but did consent to play in *John Gabriel Borkman* at the Q Theatre in October. Jack de Leon, young manager of the Q, was asked to tea at Pont Street and told there that she would play not Mrs. Borkman (as de Leon had in mind) but Ella Rentheim; that she would accept £50 for the week; that at twenty-five he was too young to be managing a theatre; and that it was interesting that Nancy Price would play Mrs. Borkman and Victor Lewisohn her husband. "But do you think I could manage Miss Price?" she demanded. "Is she *strong?*"

Miss Price turned out to be that; the two immediately locked horns. Rehearsals got under way, directed by the noted Ibsen actor Rupert Harvey. This did not stop Stella. "Mr. Harvey," she boomed, "I have *forgotten* more about Ibsen and about acting than you will ever *learn!*" "You have indeed forgotten it *all!*" cried Mr. Harvey and stalked out, never to return. A deputy appeared and launched into action which Stella soon brought to a halt. "It's no good having a *producer* who insists on *producing!*" she exclaimed. "We are getting on very well, don't you agree? Miss Price doesn't need production, and Victor will let *me* help him!" By the time the play opened, there had been three producers. Stella and Nancy Price feuded with each other and with everybody else. Miss Price demanded a pink spotlight, Stella a straw-colored one. The embattled technician had to keep one in pink and one in straw and not let the lights cross. But although they opposed each other onstage, they secretly admired each other and there were many touching reconciliations. After one terrible scene during which Stella stormed off the stage—through the fireplace—she repented and hurried to Nancy's dressing room to apologize. She was appalled to find it locked. "Nancy!" she wailed desolately. "Nancy!" The door opened.

Onstage, however, they remained enemies. "I saw her play Ella Rentheim in *John Gabriel Borkman* in a little repertory theatre at Kew Bridge," said Gielgud. "Her dressing-room was so small that she could hardly move in it. She gave a marvellous performance in the second and fourth acts, and a disgraceful one in the other two. Mrs. Borkman was played by an actress called Nancy Price whom Mrs. Campbell disliked. They refused to take any notice of one another, which was something of a drawback since the first act consists almost entirely of a duologue between Mrs. Borkman and Ella Rentheim. The two ladies sat in large armchairs on either side of the stage (with two prompters as near as possible in the wings) looking straight into the audience, and speaking their lines without taking any notice of each other at all. Then the second act began. Mrs. Campbell liked Victor Lewisohn, who played Borkman, and thought him a fine actor. So she suddenly blossomed and gave the most wonderful performance. She only acted to please herself, with no sense of responsibility towards an audience or her fellow actors. Yet she came to see me act quite often and used to give me wonderful tips."

The first thing to be noted about the revival, wrote the recovered Agate in the *Sunday Times*, was that the theatre was packed to the doors at every performance; the second was that, when she liked, Mrs. Patrick Campbell was still the best tragic actress in the country. If acting were considered as a marriage of spirit with the technical ability to convey that spirit, Mrs. Campbell had no rival on the stage. In the first act, he admitted, she had been maddeningly perfunctory; then, paired with Lewisohn, who was that unmistakable thing, an actor, she came to life. Lewisohn caught fire from his great partner, and the emotion rose to the heat at which it first fuses into a whole, then consumes clean away the very means of its representation. Tragedy burned up the lamp that held it and flamed like a star, unconditional and absolute.

Practically speaking, Stella had to pay for her gowns and taxis to the theatre and made no money from the production at all. "Doesn't your conscience prick you—you with your daily fortune pouring in—and I a beggar—I cannot think how I can go on loving you as I do!" she had written Shaw back in February. In November, Shaw came up with a suggestion. A bookdealer, Gabriel Wells, was making a special business of buying up Shaviana, and Shaw was advising friends to sell every scrap of his writing in their possession while the craze lasted. "No. No; I just couldn't bargain with your lovely letters," protested Stella. "The really ladylike thing for me to do would be to hand them back to you." She did not do the lady-like thing, however; and she did begin to contemplate the value of Shaw's signature. He had given her a handsome set of his complete works for a wedding present. Eventually she sold the volume of *Plays Unpleasant*; the dedication "To Beatrice Stella Cornwallis West, from the author, whom she despised in those days, only to find twenty years later that he was a Great & Good Man" made it worth £100. She did not give up the idea of acting in his plays either, particularly when she heard that he was using her again in his latest, *The Apple Cart*.

"I can't read plays to a starving woman," Shaw replied to her invitation to Pont Street. "What are we to do about you?" She had ruined D.D., Nancy Astor had other uses for her spare thousands, Bridget was in the south of France, and he had a financial partner (Charlotte) who wouldn't allow him to throw money into the sea. What about a benefit? Sybil Thorn-dike had said there were plenty of artists who, like herself, adored Stella and would do anything for her (obviously, they had never acted with her). Perhaps a Civil List Pension. Or if the telephone and electric-light people were threatening to cut her off, why not send their bills to him? "This letter is only to draw your fire," Shaw added. "D D thinks you will be indignant if I breathe a word to you."

"Years and years ago Alfred Lyttelton said to me: 'Don't tell D D anything you don't want repeated,'" replied Stella. "I am not starving—I eat more than you do—my electric light burns brightly—and my telephone is in order—and there's a good fire in my grate. . . . I don't want a Benefit. I sent a cheque for £25 to Ellen Terry's (which she acknowledged with a letter beginning: 'Dear Sir'—she had not deciphered my signature!). A Civil List Pension, indeed! My love to you and your merrymaking." She only wanted him to come and read his play.

Although denying she wanted a benefit or any other favors, Stella at heart felt neglected, as Stella Moore sensed. Blond, pretty Stella Moore was Stella's godchild and namesake, daughter of the young woman driving the pony trap whom Stella had met at Malvern more than thirty years before. With her gift for encouraging friendships, Stella had remained close to Ginny Moore. Now Ginny's daughter wanted to be an actress, and Stella took her in as protégée and companion while she studied at the Royal Acad-emy of Dramatic Art. Stella Moore came to know the actress well during these years, and guessed that beneath the proud display of indifference lay hurt. Forbes-Robertson had been knighted during his farewell London season in 1913, a deserved tribute to a fine classical actor. Du Maurier had become Sir Gerald in 1922, and although Stella would have been the last to begrudge the honor, she considered him an actor who had been content to play in slight comedies, never realizing his potential. Women were slower to win equivalent recognition, of course. Ellen Terry had not been made Dame Grand Cross until 1925—a shocking slight to the great actress who had flourished in the 1880's. Madge Kendal, who had made her debut as Ophelia in 1865, was not recognized until 1926. Stella had for long been called England's greatest living actress, but no honors came her way; and she rejected a benefit, too conscious of how she had alienated the acting world to rely now on its generosity.

Stella Moore discovered a great deal more about her godmother during these years. The actress had violent partialities that nothing could shake, and as violent antipathies. Gerald, William Armstrong, and Ernest Thesiger were perennial favorites. Her negative verdicts were decisive: "If you prick her," Stella said contemptuously of Marie Tempest, "sawdust comes out." She was capable of "whiplash cruelty." She could be generous with the younger generation of actresses: "There's a clever little girl," she purred approvingly, putting her finger under Cathleen Nesbitt's chin. She had what Shaw called "pothouse humor," replying solemnly to a visitor admiring her frilly lampshades, "Oh, do you like them? I cut up my drawers!" She loved babies and children; she idealized mother love. On the other hand, "Oh, darling—the *animal* in man you wouldn't believe!" The one class of people she never insulted was the aristocracy—"No one could call me a *snob*, darling, but I do have a duchess and a princess for sisters-in-law!"

"I was under the impression that the great battle of life was fought in our youth," Stella wrote Shaw, "—not a bit of it—it's when we are old, and our work not wanted, that it rages and goes on—and on—and on." In March 1929 she was at the height of a financial crisis, considering cashing in her life-insurance policy to pay back current loans from friends and wanting to take elocution pupils except that her landlord would not allow them at Pont Street. Then an offer came to play Anastasia Rakonitz in G. B. Stern's *The Matriarch*, an adaptation of the author's novel *The Tents of Israel*. Stella accepted the role reluctantly. "The 'Jewess' will disgrace me if I make a success of her, and I will never get another engagement if I make a failure," she told Shaw, reluctant as ever to play matrons and heavies. Nevertheless, she took the "Jewess charade" seriously, listening to recordings of cantors in an attempt to render lines like "Perhaps you can count, yes, Wanda? without you disturb us with a bee in a haystorm!" with some authenticity. Not that she would admit the records. When congratulated for the extraordinary voice she assumed for Anastasia—how did she do it?—Stella replied brightly, "My dear, nothing could be easier, I simply copied King Edward!" "Who will remember my Mélisande?" she wailed as the May 8 opening approached.

The theatre was the Royalty, where twenty-eight years ago she had reigned as actress-manager. Now Stella found the stairs from the dressing room to the stage too rickety to support her bulk, and sent off a letter to the London City Council advising that, as she was suffering from *globis invectus* and found the stairs excessively difficult to negotiate, they would have to be reconstructed. "What is *globis invectus?*" asked one of the cast, surveying the new stairs. "I haven't the slightest idea," said Stella.

As the matriarch, Stella triumphed. While Stern's play was voted a very flawed piece of work, everyone rejoiced that it had brought Mrs. Patrick Campbell back to a West End theatre. "A remarkable performance," said the *Evening Standard.* "To put it bluntly," said the *Daily Telegraph*, "when you go to see 'The Matriarch' you will not, if you are wise, set out with the idea of seeing a fine play. You will go to see, first and foremost, one magnificent part, magnificently played." Agate disagreed only in finding the part weak, but "how much weaker, then, must it seem when it is made to carry the full freight of Mrs. Campbell's genius, personality, and, may one say, legend." Desmond MacCarthy did not like the play, "Yet it has one great merit; it shows off a small segment of Mrs. Campbell's talent. I wish I could say that it exhibited its orb, but that would be a magnificent compliment and it deserves nothing of the kind. Still, the slip of the full moon it does reveal is so bright, that it is well worth the while of amateurs of acting to go and see it."

Many people did crowd to the Royalty, aware that something special was happening there. Augustine Birrell voiced the nostalgia that Stella's presence in the West End called up among many playgoers. The surface of society had in the last decades somehow become smoothed, Birrell mourned—a characterless plane. Similarly, in the theatre there were only a few tyrannical personalities left from the great age. Mrs. Campbell was one of them—and London needed her very badly on its depleted stage. "The best acting on the London stage just now is coming from two actresses whose combined ages total 129 years," agreed the *Daily Mail*, "Mrs. Patrick Campbell and Miss Marie Tempest. . . . The case of Mrs. Campbell is the more remarkable in that of late years she has acted comparatively seldom. She is one of the few remaining feminine links on the stage with the great days of George Alexander, Pinero, and Tree. As for her performance at the Royalty, it is constantly being quoted as one of the—if not the—best pieces of acting in town. . . . It is a brilliant comeback. . . ."

*The Matriarch* settled in for a comfortable-looking run, and Stella was in funds again. Instead of Pinoli's, where one could get marvellous hors d'oeuvres (and lots of them) for only 2s./6d., she could now afford the Savoy again. She took her grandson there after the play for a treat. Mother Beatrice, as Patrick already well knew, was just as much onstage in a restaurant as in the theatre. The meal was a performance, and he cringed as she imperiously summoned a waiter to cut up chicken livers for Swizzles, one of the current kennel. She had to be surrounded by gray people, he decided—doormats. You had to extinguish yourself or be extinguished by the larger-than-life personality of M.B. Not that he was in any danger; yet it was probably best they saw each other only at holidays.

Stella's *Matriarch* salary did not prevent her from disposing of the rest of Shaw's wedding gift to Gabriel Wells to lift "a load of debt," though she *hated* parting with them. She had been told that in America Shaw's letters were worth £200 each—and she had ninety-three: £18,600. She also had an idea of their value in print. Sell them, Shaw told her; but any further publication during Charlotte's lifetime was absolutely out of the question. Her main business with Shaw now, however, was *The Apple Cart*. D.D. had told her that she figured in the play as Orinthia, the mistress of King Magnus, who, however, will not leave his wife, Jemima, for her. He *must* come to Pont Street and read her the play, or she would have him up for an illegal act. But Shaw slipped away to the Adriatic on holiday that spring, promising to read her the scene when he returned.

During his absence Stella was not calmed by a chance encounter with Edith Evans at the Selfridge Ball, where Edith gazed eagerly into her face, explaining that she was going to play her that summer in Malvern, Birmingham, and London. Indignation was fueled by Bridget Guinness's "the infamy of it," D.D.'s insistence that only she had the right to play herself, and Morrie's lifting her hands to heaven and calling the travesty "a national calamity." By the time Shaw returned in late June, Stella was on fire. "My dear Stella," he placated: ". . . Edith Evans guessed, of course. D.D. knows; Bridget knows; Nancy [Astor] knows; perhaps half a dozen others know; (or think they know! for only you and I will ever know); but the Press must never get hold of it." He added that the first rehearsal was scheduled for July 1. "You should have sent me your play to read," replied Stella, dismayed at the *fait accompli*. "You are out of tune with friendship and simple courtesy."

Perhaps agreeing, Shaw came to Pont Street on July 11. It had been many years since their last meeting. He was shy about his seventy-three years, wary of her temper. He was greeted by a maid in a voluminous white cap and then Stella herself, the little dogs yapping at her heels. If he was appalled at the change in his gypsy, playmate, Mother of Angels, he did not say so, but read her the play in the lilting Irish voice that had charmed her seventeen years before in D.D.'s drawing room. It did not charm her now. She did not like King Magnus's "dreadfully commonplace and vulgar" criticisms of Orinthia. She did not like Orinthia's jibes at King Magnus's wife, finding lines like "Heaven is offering you a rose; and you cling to a cabbage" or "Oh, drown her: shoot her: tell your chauffeur to drive her into the Serpentine and leave her there" terribly crude. As he sat there reading out what he had done to their beautiful romance, she thought that she knew him for the first time. A mountebank—and she had trusted him like a child. Of course, some lines seemed to have a ring of truth, such as Orinthia's "You are the King of Liars and Humbugs" and "Magnus, you are a molly-coddle." Yes, those were well enough. But the rest was all terribly pedestrian and disillusioning.

Shaw went home and altered a few of the passages she had complained about loudest. He could not take out overt allusions to Basil (Beo), even though he did delete "the morals of a tramp," and changed the lines "Orinthia: It is out of the question: your dream of being queen must remain a dream" to "Orinthia: We are only two children at play; and you must be content to be my queen in fairyland." But Stella was not satisfied. "Tear it up, and re-write it with every scrap of the mischievous vulgarian omitted, and all suburban back-chat against Charlotte and suggested harlotry against me, and the inference of your own superiority wiped out. . . . Please do as I say—you will feel strangely relieved." But Shaw had no intention of tearing up the Magnus-Orinthia interlude of *The Apple Cart*. Besides, it soon became clear that Stella wanted it both ways: she was furious at being identified as Orinthia and furious when he suggested altering the likeness. She was a fool—such a fool—and yet, after all, he owed her a great deal. ". . . Of course we are a pair of mountebanks," he wrote a few weeks before *The Apple Cart* opened at Malvern in August; "but why, oh why do you get nothing out of me, though I get everything out of you? Mrs. Hesione Hushabye in *Heartbreak House*, the Serpent in *Methuselah*, whom I always hear speaking with your voice, and Orinthia: all you, to say nothing of Eliza, who was only a joke. You are the Vamp and I the victim; yet it is I who suck your blood and fatten on it whilst you lose everything! It is ridiculous! There's something wrong somewhere."

Stella was the more touchy about her private affairs being aired on the stage because of the reappearance that summer of George. She had answered the telephone one day to hear him asking for a divorce. He was in love—not with the previous lady, whose fortune would have disappeared had she married him, but with an unconditionally wealthy woman. He wanted to marry her. He wanted his freedom. Stella did not leap to give it to him. Instead, she reminded him that he owed her £4500 for debts she had paid after his desertion. When he paid it, she would consider that he had a right to happiness with someone else.

George immediately set about soliciting the help of D.D., Bridget, Lady Astor, and Shaw. His appeal had been the topic of the day at Cliveden, where Shaw and D.D. spent the weekend with Nancy Astor; they had all agreed that now there was a chance of providing for both herself and George and of getting rid of him, Stella should leap at it. Shaw passed along their recommendation to Stella, reminding her that George was living precariously by his pen and that if it failed, she would have to support him. Why not let someone else do it, meanwhile accepting his offer of £800 a year in repayment of the debt?

"You must not believe all that George says," Stella answered coolly (a remark that Shaw passed on to George). He did not, Shaw replied. But the situation was unhappy. Chains bred hatred. Was she herself quite sure she never wanted to marry again? And did she enjoy the knowledge that no man dared approach her for fear of being named co-respondent? "Interference and advice without frankness is without excuse," retorted Stella. "I know what George is capable of both saying and doing, and can listen to no word prompted by conversation with him." She was truly angry, not only at Shaw's aiding and abetting George (as she thought), but at the still rankling use she believed he had made of her private life in his play.

Shaw tried to set the record straight on both counts. Since Tedworth Square he had seen George just three times and had read a play of George's which Shaw judged worthless. "He may be the most abandoned reincarnation of Barry Lyndon on Earth for all I know; but as you keep all the blarney he ever wrote to you, and you do not seem to mind being his wife, I cannot help suspecting that he is just George and nobody else." As for Beo, he had never gossiped about him, or learned anything about him beyond what he observed for himself and heard from his "Mother of Sorrows." For her sake, he would let him go in *The Apple Cart* as a beautiful child. Beo didn't deserve it, but since he had suffered for the sins of others, perhaps the balance of justice was struck. As for the rest of the play, Orinthia's husbands were not Pat Campbell or George, but just men like any others who bite off more of what dazzles them than they can digest. She must admit she was impossible to live with.

She did not admit it. "When a man cannot meet his wife's eye, the poor phrase 'rather be in hell than live in the same house with you' helps him, and seems to justify him to his friends. So it was spoken to me and it was agonizing. I am not yet old enough to look back upon it as a joke. Please me and cut it. And why the lie 'both husbands ran away'—is it necessary for your wit—look to it please."

"How troublesome you are!" sighed Shaw. "Very well . . . I have changed it to 'he said no man could call his soul his own in the same house with you.' I admit it is an improvement. . . . Stella, Stella, don't you KNOW that you are so exacting, so exciting, so absorbing, so incessant that only a wooden Highlander from a tobacconist's shop could bear the enormous strain of living with you? Can you blame your runaway husbands? Poor Patrick flying to South Africa for sleep (you told me you had kept him ecstatically awake for years) and finding it there from a Boer bullet, or George pretending to fly from the police (so you now tell me): dare you pretend that Orinthia is Candida?—that I have lied?" He also urged her again to accept a cash settlement from George. If fourteen years had passed since George absconded, he probably owed her (principal and interest) about £7000. Interest on £7000 at five per cent was £350 a year. George was offering £800 per annum—a generous settlement. And, since she had married George with eyes wide open, would she please not strike any more moral attitudes? He would only laugh.

"Cash has nothing to do with it—£800 or £8000: neither does repayment come into it," Stella answered coldly. "No woman's eyes when she loves are open until she is cheated." And with that she closed the conversation.

On October 30 Frank Vernon and Jose Levy, the producers, gave a party onstage at the Royalty to celebrate the two hundredth performance of *The Matriarch*. Stella was the center of attention, receiving the congratulations of Arnold Bennett, Gerald and Muriel du Maurier, Nigel Playfair, Norman McKinnel, Lilian Braithwaite, Sheila Kaye-Smith, and the author. More difficult to accept was the praise of Constance Collier, for it was she and not Stella who would be taking the play to New York—a blow to Stella, even though she had not wanted the role. "She'll never succeed," Stella predicted mournfully; "she *is* a Jew." Eventually *The Matriarch* ran for 249 performances; but although it was Stella who created its success, the Shuberts did not want her for America. Nor did anyone act on Desmond MacCarthy's suggestion that, having been reminded of how great their finest actress was, someone should take a hint and write her a play. Her reputation had become too formidable; she had made too many enemies.

In December, and January of 1930, therefore, she toured the provinces in *Ghosts*, devastating Dublin with her performance and causing the Irish actor Anew McMaster to exclaim that he would not have forgone the horror and pleasure of working with her for anything. Then, with nothing else to do, she decided to take her lecture, revised and retitled "The Art of Acting and Beautiful Speech," to America on tour.

Before leaving, she made an appearance at the cocktail party John Gielgud threw to celebrate his brilliant first Shakespeare season at the Old Vic. Arriving in Upper St. Martin's Lane in unbecoming white with black polka dots, she toiled up three flights of steep steps to his flat. At the top, gasping for breath, she paused at the door, awaiting recovery and an entrance. Then she sailed into the crowded room. "Who is there here," she cried in that dark contralto, "who still *loves* me?"

# THIRTY-FIVE

# *1930–1934*

*H*AVING EVIDENTLY recovered from the shock of a matronly Mrs. Pat, New York critics handled quite gently the actress who swept onto the stage of the Guild Theatre in black velvet and entertained them for an hour on the subject of speech and acting. Staying at the Ritz-Carlton, Stella gave three lectures at the Guild that February 1930. Some critics found her talk under the hard lights touching and melancholy, an echo from a noble tradition that had almost vanished from the stage. Another found the actress who said "beeen," "figger," and "velly" charming, interesting, but oh so English and not a little condescending. Perhaps John Mason Brown liked her best. "With ease Mrs. Campbell ranged from the formal coloring of the Twenty-Third Psalm to the childlike noises of Mélisande, from the flavorsome cockney of Eliza Doolittle to the sibilant tones of Lady Macbeth's sleep-walking scene, from the sardonic coldness of the first line that Hedda Gabler speaks to the sincere affection that must shine through the first of Paula Tanqueray's speeches. . . . In short, within that brief hour at her disposal Mrs. Patrick Campbell cast her old spell over us once more."

Stella included another diversion in her lecture: a scene from *The Matriarch* "as Constance Collier would play it." Collier's one weakness as an actress was a shrill monotony of delivery. After showing audiences her own impressive range, Stella then altered her voice to a toneless whine—it was a funny and devastating parody that effectively sabotaged the forthcoming production. Meanwhile G. B. Stern was in Hollywood trying to convince studios that a motion picture should be made of *The Matriarch* with Mrs. Campbell in her original role. But the Hollywood project died after Constance Collier flopped in the New York production—another instance of Stella's ill-timed mischief, for a movie success in *The Matriarch* might have changed the course of the next years.

John Mason Brown met Stella at a luncheon party. Sunlight was streaming into the room and, "Dear Mr. Mason Brown," said Stella immediately, "please stand over here and let me turn my back to the light. I do not wish to have you look too closely upon my ruined face." The ruined face had become an obsession. "As a matter of fact, Mrs. Pat, though overblown, was still as much of an event as a person," thought Mason Brown. "The footprints of beauty remained on her face, her eyes were glorious, and her wit, her quickness of mind, and her ability to seem soothing while being naughty, or even cruel, were all as they must have been in her Paula Tanqueray days."

Footprints of beauty did not console Stella; yet the agony was off-record. "Behold! a woman of glorious middle-age who has no desire to be young again!" bubbled a New York interviewer as Stella turned sixty-five that February. "She is Mrs. Patrick Campbell, the darling of the Victorians, for whom Shaw and Barrie wrote play after play and to whom countless men wrote passionate love-letters. . . . 'If one has youth and good looks,' she said today, 'nothing else is essential. But I would rather not be young. It is not so boring to be old. When you're young no one pays attention to anything except your looks.'" Well, it was no crime to lie to those frightful reporters.

Stella announced she had come to New York primarily to consider *Ladies of the Jury*, a farce recently acted by Minnie Maddern Fiske. She did not find it suitable and instead took her lecture on tour, accompanied by Woosh Woosh, a tiny Peke she was keeping for a friend. "THEN AS NOW THE WORD IS FASCINATION," approved the Boston *Transcript*, going on to describe the scene at Jordan Hall: a neutral curtain rather the worse for wear, footlights up, lighted reading desk, the inevitable pitcher of water. The audience waited five minutes, then the hangings parted noiselessly and the actress moved (walked was not the word) toward the desk, clad throat to heel in black velvet, pearls banding throat. A long moment of silence, a gust of applause. A gracious bow without condescension. Raven-black hair fluffing either side of her forehead, eyes pools of light and dark, figure unbent, step firm and free.

With little variation Stella repeated that scene again and again that spring and early summer, insisting that "Beautiful speech is a habit of mind—an art and a personal matter," and reliving her great stage moments for generally appreciative, if specialized, audiences—women's clubs, Ivy League colleges, elocution and oratory schools. Her appearances were as much social as artistic events, usually accompanied by receptions, dinners, luncheons, or teas at which Stella shook hundreds of hands and played Greatest Living British Actress with flair. There was only one problem with the lecture circuit: it paid little.

Since 1912 when Shaw had written "Nobody who has not seen you move . . . has the faintest idea of your fascination. . . . It would be well worth

Pathé's while to pay you £5000 for a film," Stella had not been able to get the idea of making a movie out of her head. She decided now to go to Hollywood, partly with the notion of convincing some director or other to film *The Matriarch*, partly with the intention of teaching graceless starlets the art of beautiful speech. Before leaving, she returned to New York, where, at a party at Mrs. Reginald de Koven's, she came face to face with her former daughter-in-law. Helen was now the Marchesa Spinola, married to an impoverished Italian nobleman and running a little gallery on East 54th Street, where they sold antiques from the households of equally impoverished Italian noblemen. They had not seen each other since Helen left Beo; and if Helen had not heard that Stella was in New York, she might not have recognized the carelessly made-up woman, quite thirty pounds heavier than she remembered her. But Stella got her licks in first. "Oohh," she moaned, fixing her eyes on Helen's throat, "how *sad* to see a young thing *withaw!*" the accent adding, Helen felt, millions of crepy wrinkles to the offending neck. "It was just like old times," said Helen, and the ice broke immediately. The next day Stella came round to meet Ugo and the children, who immediately adored "Auntie Stella" and her imitations of a goldfish. She urged Helen to come to Hollywood with her, and, although she should have known better, Helen agreed because it meant a chance to see her mother in Pasadena.

They shared a stateroom on the Twentieth Century Limited a few days later, and trouble was not long in brewing. Otis Skinner and his wife were on the same train, bound for Hollywood to make the film *Kismet*. Though aging, Skinner still had the vestiges of matinee-idol charm, which he made the mistake of using on Helen instead of Stella. The more assiduous his attentions to the younger woman, the more acidulous Stella became. When they reached Needles, California, simmering in hundred-degree heat, Skinner made the mistake of alighting and returning with a single ice-cream cone, which, kneeling, he offered to Helen with a courtly flourish. Just then the train lurched, throwing him off balance. Stella gave a compassionate little scream—"Oh, the *poor old man!*"—and rushed to help him to his feet with twitters of solicitude.

They stayed at the Ambassador Hotel in Los Angeles, where a photographer shot them the next day in the glaring sunlight of the garden. Stella did not share Helen's laughter at the result: "It only makes my battle harder." It *was* a battle. Producers and agents hesitated; what name did a great actress from the past cut in Hollywood, 1930? The film colony was more gracious: Stella and Helen lunched with the Louis Bromfields and dined with the Leslie Howards. Helen's mother arrived, and Stella made great friends with Mrs. Bull, even though she couldn't resist an occasional jibe: "Oh, my dear," watching Mrs. Bull go through her exercises one day, "are you *sure* that's not terribly dangerous at your age!" But Stella and Helen could not stand each other long. The day came when Helen packed her bags and fled the Ambassador, a desertion that Stella insisted on attributing to the Great Cheiro, a palm reader who had said to her of Helen, "I wonder how you have stood her so long!" and must have made the same remark to Helen. Helen's place was taken by Stella Moore, whose transportation and living expenses Stella paid in return for companionship in the frightening world of Hollywood.

For, no matter how much insolent courage Stella might summon, flashy, celluloid, heartless Hollywood was no place for an aging stage actress. Well, not quite heartless; one day George Middleton was called to Winfield Sheehan's office at First National, where they were turning a dated English play called *The Dancers* into a film. Middleton was told to make a place in the film for Mrs. Campbell as somebody's aunt or something—two or three scenes would be enough. Her name would help sales in England; besides, Sheehan knew she was broke. They were giving her $8000. Middleton should do his best.

For Middleton, a playwright turned screenwriter, it was an emotional moment. As a college student he had worshipped the glamorous Mrs. Pat. Now he was to pry open a mediocre script and fit in some silly part for the actress who had made Pinero's name, played with Bernhardt, and been loved by Shaw. He did it, but with a heavy heart. Fortunately, the studio gave her star treatment: limousine service, flowers in her dressing room.

A day or so before she had to face the camera, Stella came to Middleton's office. She was on the defensive, he noted, at the same time that he noted her pale, strangely unlined face, the raven-black hair, the eyes full of worldly wisdom, and the voice he would have known from a thousand others. She was aloof, and it was not until he mentioned theatre connections and friends they had in common that she unbent. Then he ventured.

"Mrs. Pat, I want to tell you about a young college lad I once knew who loved the theatre. He hadn't much money [but he] wrote to the theatre to reserve a single seat in the gallery for each of the five plays in your announced repertoire. When the doors opened he was first in line at the box office. He eagerly asked for the seats which were to be reserved in his name. For weeks he had saved out of his allowance and lunch money. His heart had been set on seeing you. But his letter had never been received. He insisted he had written it. The line behind grew impatient. He stood there stubbornly demanding the seats. Tears filled his eyes and probably got into his voice; for the manager, in the back of the office, heard his plea. The lad got those seats. I'm that lad, Mrs. Campbell."

As he spoke, Middleton's eyes again filled with tears at the memory of all that the theatre and the actress had once meant to him. Stella smiled, but did not, he thought, grasp what he was feeling. Instead, she recognized the handwriting of Pinero and Shaw in framed letters hanging on Middleton's wall. *"Dear Pin,"* she purred. But when he mentioned Shaw, she laughed. "Here I am broke, and I have in my safe deposit all those letters he wrote me—a hundred and twenty-five of them. Of course I can't be a cad and sell them, can I?"

Shooting began. ". . . I can never forget how cruel it was to watch this great lady, through necessity, do this triviality so many routine screen actors could have done better," said Middleton. "She didn't make anyone happy at rehearsals—she was not openly contemptuous, and she tried hard to adapt; but she was used to an audience, to moving majestically about, and she could not handle herself in the narrow confines of a camera's angles. She knew nothing of the medium, whose ABC's our star had at her fingertips." It further depressed Middleton that, besides himself and Sheehan, no one on the set had ever seen Mrs. Campbell onstage, and the little "star" had never even heard of her.

"But what is there about her that is so wonderful?" she asked, wide-eyed. How could words convey to someone who had never seen Mrs. Campbell act the sheer force of her personality, her power to hold and fill a stage?

"She has the one thing that nearly all screen actresses lack," answered Middleton: *"breadth."* The little star's eyes grew larger. Breadth? It wasn't something, evidently, that had anything to do with films.

When *The Dancers* was finally put together, most of what Stella had done was bad. "Yet there was one moment," said Middleton, "—a second or two—when she read a totally unimportant speech. But from it radiated a thousand meanings. It was a moment as unforgettable as the last time Isadora danced. I used to have that scene run just to recapture a flash of the old Mrs. Pat: an arresting, fascinating woman, a queen I had once bowed to."

Whether or not Stella realized that her part in *The Dancers* had been largely a charity, nothing else came her way as she lingered in Hollywood after finishing the film in September. Friends continued to fete her royally, particularly new friends Gwendolyn Seiler and Harry and Tai Lachman, and Stella continued to alternately charm and outrage the film colony. The flagrant youth of Hollywood continued to depress her: at one party where young actress-mothers continually gushed over their babies, Stella interrupted wearily, "Why, you know, I myself have the most charming little girlie of forty-five!" But the $8000 dwindled rapidly, and in October the press announced that she would make a five-month lecture tour of the United States and Canada beginning in January 1931. In November she got Los Angeles and San Francisco engagements to play Mrs. Alving in *Ghosts*. In Los Angeles she made headlines: "MRS. PAT CAMPBELL ROWING WITH ACTOR OUT ON THE COAST; *Star Slaps Stage Manager and Fires Leading Man; May Face Suits.*" A new leading man was rushed from New York to replace Lionel Belmore, but Stella denied that she had socked the actor in the heat of an argument over his poor performance, or the stage manager either. Whether or not she had, it was an unfortunate story.

She began her tour in the Midwest. In Chicago she was engaged by Samuel Insull, a public-utility magnate and opera patron, to give a private recital to fifty friends in his spacious, top-floor apartment in the Opera Building. Ashton Stevens was there with his young wife, and after the performance, which he found "magical," guided his wife across the room for an introduction. The wife, however, protested. "You've told me what she said to Laurette Taylor the night London hissed her opening: 'Did you ever consider that all this hubbub may mean merely that the audience doesn't like you?' And I certainly don't want her to say anything like that to poor little me!" But Ashton pushed her over to Stella. Stella did not say anything at all for fully thirty seconds following the introduction. She gazed at the girl with great, humid eyes, and as she gazed, she blushed as Stevens had never seen a woman blush before, the color flushing her cheeks and throat and flaming in her lace-edged bosom. Then she turned to him. "Oh, Ashton," she pleaded, "have I grown so old?" "My wife cried when we got home," said Stevens; "she would have preferred a licking."

From Chicago she worked her way east, arriving in snowy Toledo, Ohio, on January 30 to be met by the shivering manager of the Valentine Theatre. "I shall need two taxis," Stella announced promptly. Flora Hineline looked about for a retinue, but the actress was quite alone. Then around the corner of the shabby waiting room came dozens of Red Caps bearing bags. Stella busily counted twenty-three as two taxis pulled up. "No, sit with me," she commanded; "the other one is for the bags." At the hotel an amazed doorman kept shouting "Front! Front! Front!" as bellboys poured out to bear away the luggage. Finally, up in her suite, the boys had all been tipped and dismissed. "Now," said Stella, "I want to go shopping immediately." Miss Hineline timidly inquired what she wished to purchase. "A bag," said Stella; "a big one."

They set off to the best store Miss Hineline could think of, where, however, Stella rejected piece after piece of elegant luggage. "Isn't there a cheap store somewhere?" she asked outside. There was, and she chose a huge, ugly leatherette carry-all that they took turns lugging back to the hotel. "I am travelling for the first time without a maid," Stella explained as they stumbled along. "I know nothing—absolutely *nothing*—about packing! In each city I jam my bags chock full until they will hardly close and I still have things scattered about which I cannot conceivably get into any of them. So I need this bag for the things left over. It should last me two or three cities before I have to buy another."

The theatre for the ten a.m. lecture the next morning was packed. Stella made a regal entrance in trailing velvet, and the audience rose. Having decided, evidently, that Toledo deserved her profile, she posed herself sideways and lifted her chin. Although no one could possibly have heard anything behind third row center, thought Miss Hineline as the talk commenced, the audience sat as if spellbound, watching the no longer young but ineffably glamorous actress relive a lost tradition. That evening Stella was entertained in one of Toledo's finest upriver homes. She gazed about the palatial rooms, then leaned toward her host. "They tell me you made it all in ——! Why couldn't I have thought of that—it's so simple." The millionaire's wife gasped, expecting the worst, but her husband only threw back his head and roared. Well, thought Miss Hineline, she could still get her man—"poor wonderful, successful, unhappy, aging Mrs. Pat Campbell." Stella replayed this scenario more or less exactly until May, booking usually for $400 and train fare, her collection of bags steadily growing. But it was not a living. The Depression thinned audiences, and she spent as much as she made.

That spring George again asked for a divorce, and Stella replied again that she expected "decent behavior"—payment for the release of the marriage settlement and compensation for twelve years' desertion—before exposing herself to the unpleasantness of a divorce at her age and in her position. Back in London in June, she found Shaw again involved in the dispute, an intrusion she refused to tolerate. A few days later George announced that he was dropping the matter entirely. "I cannot imagine how the question was ever opened up again if he was not prepared for personal sacrifice in proof of the sincerity of his wish to behave decently," she told Shaw. To which Shaw replied that she and George could take their ignoble domestic squabble to some dreary circle of Dante's hell and waste eternity in recrimination. It was nothing to him.

His next sentence made Stella sit up and take notice: "This year my correspondence with Ellen Terry will be published for the benefit of her estate. . . ." If the Shaw-Terry letters proved popular, he said, a demand might arise among maniac collectors for *their* whole correspondence. She should therefore (if she could afford it) keep the letters together and will them to Stella junior, or, if she was forced to sell, sell in bulk. He had heard that Benjy Guinness would give £4000 for the letters. If true, he might offer to throw in hers (yes, he had kept them: a pitiable weakness) if Benjy would give her £5000 in brewery shares or even cash—although he knew she would either spend the cash in a week or take a theatre and produce a wretched play. Stella laid down the letter thoughtfully. Shaw's and Terry's letters in print . . . her Joey going down to immortality with Ellen and not herself. No—she was not going to sell to Benjy Guinness. Just the other day a publisher had valued Shaw's letters at £10,000 and publishing rights at £20,000. "What arrangement can we make, you and I?" she wrote back. But Shaw wanted no arrangement.

Just after she had returned to London that June, she had been offered the part of "a horrible Countess with pince-nez looking for a Gigolo" in New York. She did not want it. Shaw was writing a play, she'd heard—couldn't he save her? No, he could not; there was nothing in *Too True to Be Good* but two flappers and a ridiculous old woman. So Stella prepared to pack her bags again—more sadly now, for her beloved Swizzles had died that July. In September she paid a flying visit to her old friend Graham Robertson and provided him with so many chapters of the autobiography that must never be written that his head spun. "My word, what a best-seller it would be!" exclaimed Robertson, finding Stella still "very wonderful and witty." Then on September 19 she sailed on the *Aquitania* to fulfil an engagement for a fifteen-minute part in something called *Le Sexe Faible*, which a translator who was either incompetent or dishonest had translated as *The Sex Fable*.

On the afternoon of October 31, 1931, she was interviewed at the Hotel Barclay. She was wearing a simple black satin dress with a faded rose tucked in the belt; she was not easy to talk to, the interviewer decided: her mind was so swift, her personality so compelling, and she kept one in such constant gales of laughter. "I wish he wouldn't use the word *veteran* of me," she complained of the critic John Mason Brown. "It makes everyone think your eyes are glass, your hair a wig, and your legs wooden! And my hair is *not* a wig and I won't be a *day* over forty. Of course, I have a daughter who's forty-six, but what of that!" She was asked about the much discussed Shaw-Terry letters. "There is absolutely no comparison between Shaw's letters to Ellen Terry and his letters to me," she replied quickly. When and if she published, "I shall write my *own* preface to the edition, not Mr. Shaw, as he did in the Ellen Terry letters. I do not intend to give him the opportunity to say the last word. I don't trust him enough."

The crashing failure of *The Sex Fable* that evening, for which she was in no way responsible, only stimulated her appetite for publication. It was not the money—she could have sold the letters for as much as $350 or $500 apiece at any time; it was the compliment Shaw's published adoration would pay to her badly wounded pride. "Dearest Joey, what objection can there be? Letters written so long ago, and all three of us on the verge of the grave! . . . When you wrote these lovely letters, some whisper in me of my beautiful Italian mother inspired you, awoke the impersonal ideal, set your genius on the plane where angels and poets pass the time o' day." If this plea did not move him, of course, there was a "savage" alternative. She could publish and let him sue her. It might provide a little amusement in these miserable times.

NO, replied Shaw. For one thing, his and Ellen's letters were literature, while his best conversations with Stella had been *viva voce*. "You would not come out of it with a halo like Ellen's," he warned. "I should come out better, because, though I amused you handsomely, you kept your head and were never enchanted as I was. Perhaps you have written love letters, but not to me. . . . You had no confidence in me; really small blame to you, Stella: do not think I am reproaching you. . . . As to all your threats, dear Stella, you were not born to be a blackmailer; that is why you do it so badly. No publisher would dare touch my letters without my authorisation. . . . I have to disregard the money aspect of the affair ruthlessly. Unless the rumor that B.G. left you £500 a year (which would last you a week) is true, you must be starving. Very well: starve: everybody is starving. You can sell my letters; and you can sell George; the divorce court is not worse than playing Lady Godiva with me as the horse, if you make it a matter of delicacy. With the proceeds you can marry a multi-millionaire and make his life so unbearable that he will be only too glad to give you a million or so alimony. . . . At all events for me you are an insoluble problem; and I have callously given it up, as there is no use making myself unhappy about it."

Shortly after the run of *The Matriarch* ended, the Guinnesses had begun to make Stella an allowance of £500 a year, tax free, paid quarterly. With it she supported herself, sent money to Max, hired a maid when possible, and paid interest on £600 that D.D. had lent her when George left. Of course she spent each quarter's £125 long before she had it in her hands. She had begun to trim her shabby hats with nail scissors; the rose in her belt was still more faded. In January 1932 another brief engagement bailed her out temporarily—playing Clytemnestra to Blanche Yurka's Electra for four

matinees of Sophocles at the Selwyn Theatre. The ladies clashed tempera-
mentally and stylistically. "Look at Blanche," Stella would murmur at
rehearsals in a stage whisper that hit the back of the balcony, *"Yurking
away at it."* Stella went her own way, playing Clytemnestra for sympathy
and ignoring the stark realism Yurka was trying to achieve. "You really
*liked* it, darlings?" she asked friends and admirers gathered in her dressing
room after the first matinee. "Fancy! How could you possibly?" The production won little critical praise, John Mason Brown reporting with some
amusement that Yurka played Electra most unclassically· on all fours. "I
love my roses and the thorns—and I adore you for writing so sincerely
about my work," Stella wrote the critic. J.M.B. and Stella appreciated each
other. He remembered how she had shocked his sweet little scrubbed-faced
serving girl at a luncheon party by booming out in her great voice Lady
Macbeth's "I have given suck, and know how tender 'tis to love the babe
that milks me!" Another time the talk had turned inevitably to Shaw, and
Stella had become so excited that she whisked him back to her own apartment, where she seized copies of Shaw's letters, settled in a stuffed chair
next to a roaring fire, set her spectacles on her nose, and read out the letters
magnificently, often interrupting to convulse him with malicious comments.

But times were very hard, and not helped by another message from
George asking for his freedom. She again refused unless he paid, having
discovered (so she thought) the real reason for his desertion. "I knew it
wasn't another woman in his heart," she told D.D.; "he must have had
offers coming in for his estates—and then there was the sale of his pictures
at Christies—the old armour and silver—the lovely pictures he sold . . . for
£12,000 . . . and Ruthin brought £160,000 and Newlands £12,000 and
then there was Arnwood and all the furniture and other things. . . . It's
like an Irish play by Lady Gregory. George knew nothing could be parted
with according to the Marriage Settlement without my 'consent in writing,'
and then the money would have had to go into the Trust Fund—the creditors would have come first—liabilities contracted before his marriage to
me—and then he could only touch the interest on all monies until my
death. By leaving me as he did he somehow got everything into his own
hands. . . . It isn't a pretty story, and when one thinks how dreadfully I
suffered—it's absolutely shocking to think I could have been such a fool."

William Rollo, her lawyer, agreed that she should not divorce George
unless he paid his debts to her, at the same time advising her to begin
proceedings for a decree nisi. In the six-month interval Cornwallis-West
could settle his financial liability. Should he not, she would still be in control and could refuse to make the decree absolute. But Stella rejected this
"common bargain," refusing to take any step until George paid. "I do not

like standing in the way of other people's happiness," she told Rollo; "on the other hand, I feel deeply that righteous indignation demands fair play and decent behavior."

These years were increasingly restless. In April Stella returned again to England for a brief tour of the old *Thirteenth Chair*. While she was there, Ivor Novello's *Party* opened in the West End, a skit about one of those mad theatrical bashes that people pretend to despise but would give a year of their lives to attend. The presiding personality at this party was Mrs. Mac-Donald, a character inspired by none other than Stella herself. Lilian Braithwaite attempted it, and Stella came one night to watch Lilian play herself. "Lilian, darling!" she exclaimed backstage. "You make me so much *nicer* than I really am!"

Friends came to the rescue again, this time the Murphys, who lent Stella a lovely little farm at Cap d'Antibes, set in an orange grove, with paved courtyard, open fires, and nightingales. There in that corner of the Riviera where "everybody is either mad or asleep or Anglo-Saxon," she entertained Ford Madox Ford at "a Mad Hatter's tea-party," presiding over the table, thought Ford, "like a great black Alice" as she simultaneously rehearsed a beautiful blond New York actress in the "Bells of Ender" and pressed upon him "vast slices of ham, pickles, rose-leave conserve, tea, wines of the country, iced mandrake juice," demanding all the while from beneath the largest black hat he had ever seen WHAT HE HAD SAID ABOUT HER IN NEW YORK. There too Diana Forbes-Robertson was brought by the singer Madame Edvina to lunch. Stella set out to charm this youngest of the four daughters of Forbes and Gertrude Elliott, whom she had never met; she succeeded. As they were leaving, Stella took Diana's hand and buried it in her ample blue-velvet and pearl-roped bosom. "Dear child," she purred, "do please remember me to your dear"—a perfectly timed pause— "*mother.*"

But the pleasures of sun and British society were overshadowed by the thought of another lecture tour ahead: the endless trains, the packing and repacking, the shaking of hands, the fatiguing hours on the platform for a very modest fee, ten per cent of which went to her agent, ten per cent to British income tax, and seven and a half per cent to American taxes. There was only one person who could save her. She had an offer from a magazine for the Shaw-Campbell letters: $25,000 with an advance of $5000. "Do put fear on one side, and send me that telegram to enable me to cancel my cruel American lecture tour, and settle down here to write," she again begged Shaw. "The moment is a very grave one for me, much graver than appears in this letter." Shaw was adamant. "There are certain successes that cannot be repeated and certain sacrifices that cannot be made twice. . . . I know how exhausting the lecturing road is in America; in fact, I know everything better than you do. And I haven't a scrap of unkind feeling about you. But as to the letters: N O. The Fates, not I, decree it."

Rescue from the road did come, from another source. John Gielgud was producing Rodney Ackland's *Strange Orchestra*, a modern play about young people living in a Bloomsbury flat owned by a slovenly Bohemian woman with a heart of gold. Mrs. Lyndon was a tremendous part, and much of the play's success would depend on who played it. Gielgud badly wanted Stella. She read the script at Cap d'Antibes and disliked it—another "whoopee sort of thing, but not funny—untidy"; but she had no choice but to take it. The taking created another problem: Woosh Woosh and the quarantine. At Folkestone on August 28, just before customs, Stella ripped open the lining of a hatbox, tucked her charge in, and repinned the lining, covering the bulge with five large hats. But when she became unaccountably nervous and conspicuously reluctant to have the hatbox searched, an official distracted her attention while another rummaged through the box—and there was the tiny Peke. She was forced to surrender the pet to a cage in the Quarantine Department.

Aware that Mrs. Pat was apt to treat a producer "as dust beneath her chariot wheels," Gielgud awaited her appearance at the St. Martin's Theatre with apprehension. She was late the first morning, and pretended that she did not understand the play. "Who are all these extraordinary characters?" she demanded. "Where do they live? Does Gladys Cooper know them?" She continued to be late on subsequent mornings; she persisted in threatening, "I am leaving in a fortnight; you must get someone else to play this part." Every afternoon she went to sit for two hours next to Woosh Woosh's cage, murmuring comfort. She also managed a return visit to the Savoy, where Ashton Stevens saw her surrounded by admirers. Her eyes gleamed as he approached. "Don't tell me—I know you—don't tell me: William Winter!" In fact she was rehearsing splendidly and knew all about the play, wisely advising Gielgud when he wanted to cut a certain actor's line, "You know, his whole character is in that line; I shouldn't cut it if I were you." And then she threw the whole thing over, reclaimed the Peke from the Quarantine Department, paid the fine of £10 7s., and sailed for America, where there were no evil laws to torture poor dogs—and no prospect of anything but the lecture circuit again, either.

She arrived in the States slimmer and more relaxed, and in the coming weeks disguised whatever fatigue and dreariness she might have felt. The routine was now familiar. "Long ago—1933, I *think!*—this lovely creature came to my then school, Ethel Walker's, Simsbury, Connecticut, as a visiting lecturer," remembers Juliette Hollister. "We were all in drabs—dreary uniforms in a convent-like atmosphere—*grim!*—when this glamorous dazzling creature appeared before us! What she said I haven't the foggiest idea. But that we schoolgirls would not forget her fifty years later is a tribute, I'd say." Julia Child, then at Smith College, had the same impression. "Mrs. Campbell came and stayed at President Nielson's residence, and gave a reading. She brought her little dog with her, who had to eat dinner out of silver salvers furnished by the Nielsons, and her reading was very dramatic. She was dressed in a voluminous long white gown with a large white scarf. And she had lots of black hair which, as she moved about, kept coming undone—it was supposed to be a bun at the back of her head. She had a large black bone hairpin which she would use to gather up her hair and pin it with a great sweeping gesture. There was so much movement going on that I don't think anyone had any idea what the dramatic piece was about, but it certainly was an event that I remember with tremendous amusement."

William Lyon Phelps had seen Stella's Magda in 1900, and the memory of that magnificent performance was still vivid. He now persuaded her to give a lecture at Yale. She still had her glorious voice, and she recited Browning's short poem "Wanting—is what?" in a manner, said Phelps, that was better than a hundred annotations. Staying as a guest at his house, accompanied by Woosh Woosh, she smoked big cigars and declared that she would love to hear him lecture. Afterwards she remarked, "Why, you *love* people. It is unmistakable, in the way you look at the audience, in the way you talk." They said goodbye the next day. "You *are* going to kiss me, aren't you?" asked Stella.

Then in July came news that New York wanted her, and Stella quit the road, returning to the city in August. "Trailing clouds of authentic and arrogant glamor, heroine of a saga of wit and charm and insolence, seventy [*sic*] but emphatically of the younger tradition of the stage, Mrs. Pat Campbell is on the town," wrote Lucius Beebe, "and Manhattan, from Madison Avenue to the East River, would be aware of it even if her name were not printed in letters three feet high all over Mr. Brady's Playhouse as the leading woman in Ivor Novello's 'A Party.'" Her press coverage, always good, soared. Bosley Crowther attempted an interview at the Barclay on the hottest day of the summer, and found her in the dining room.

"Well, go ahead," said Stella. "I'll try to tell you anything you want to know—" but at that moment the *maître d'* placed a menu before her. "Oh, bring me a bit of madrilenne and a salad—you know, one of those delicious salads you have here."

Crowther pulled out his notebook expectantly, but Stella had begun to gasp. "I say," she cried, "can't we have a bit of air in here? This is positively stifling!" Waiters made vague motions. "But you go ahead and ask me a question," she told Crowther affably.

"Well—" began Crowther.

"I say, really, I can't possibly endure this any longer! I'm sure I shall faint. Waiter, will you have my luncheon served in my rooms? Come!"

In her suite it was rather cooler, and Stella flung off her hat. "Now what was it you were asking me?"

"Well, are you happy about the present-day theatre?"

"Really, I do think that a rather silly question," said Stella brightly. With a sweeping gesture she indicated her companion, Helen Arthur. "You'll answer that for me, won't you, dear?"

Crowther listened for a long time to what Helen Arthur thought Mrs. Campbell thought. Stella meanwhile got on the telephone. Would they send lunch up immediately: they were busy people. Soon two waiters arrived with a table.

"Please don't say that I relished my food!" Stella exclaimed with a smile. "Say that I 'toyed with my madrilenne' or something like that. And be very careful what you say about me. If you have a delicate pen you'll know exactly how to put it."

Crowther had to admit that at this point he did not know exactly how delicate his pen might be. The interview was clearly over, and as he took his leave, Stella sprinkled powdered sugar over her cucumber-and-lettuce salad, wet it down thoroughly with French dressing, and fell to.

Another reporter found her in a red gown with trailing sleeves and a large picture hat. The day was again terribly warm, and Stella comforted herself by ordering watermelon heaped with ice cream and blandly attacking the combination. She served it to her guest on a dime-store plate: "I went in to buy things because I've already discovered that everybody in America has gone cheerfully Woolworth. It's delightful." Interviewers could be less delightful. "They keep asking me about the past," she complained, "but I'm living in the present. I'm glad to be back. One always is. The only thing about New York is that every year is a new year. One must always begin all over." Yes, *A Party* was supposed to be about her. Lilian Braithwaite's performance had been "simply lovely, courteous, beautiful, and full of charm. When I do the part here, however," said Stella, "I must play it with humor—the only way I know by which an actress can imitate herself."

Audiences had fun at the *Party* when it opened on September 4, but critics found fault with a plot that dealt with nothing more than the rivalry between two famous actresses—Mrs. MacDonald (Mrs. Campbell) and

Miranda Clayfoot (based on Tallulah Bankhead)—and the determination of the latter to catch a lord before the party is over. Miniature vaudeville acts by the "guests" filled the gaps: Cissy Loftus doing imitations, Stella reciting a speech of Hecuba's from *The Trojan Women*, Gertrude Niesen singing torch songs. Pretty tenuous and feeble, the reviewers decided. But everyone loved Stella playing Stella. Puffing a long black Havana oscuro, a miniature white Peke tucked under her arm, she reigned over the festivities. "It was, of course, Mrs. Pat Campbell who was the life of 'A Party' at the Playhouse last night" . . . "Mrs. Patrick Campbell is one of those actresses who could bring majesty and subtlety to an Earl Carroll blackout" . . . "The best thing about it is the return of Mrs. Patrick Campbell. . . ." John Mason Brown found Stella more than an actress. She was a character in her own right, one of the most diverting and arresting characters the modern theatre had ever produced.

If Stella was the best thing about *A Party*, the best thing about the play for her was Moonbeam, the little white Peke. Having returned Woosh Woosh to its owner, Stella was dogless, and the attraction was instantaneous. "I fancy Moonbeam felt sure I was his mother," murmured Stella, "and that the other mother he had known was just a dream." There was a terrible moment at the end of the run when a little man came to her dressing room to tell her that Mr. Brady had only bought Moonbeam for the play. "I just looked at him and said 'Is it?'" said Stella. "Just like that, knowing that it didn't make any sense, and the little man went away." Officially it was announced that Mr. Brady had presented Moonbeam to Mrs. Campbell as a gift. Not since Pinkie Panky Poo had a dog so quickly become identified as its owner's trademark, and Stella seemed to love Moonbeam better than all the rest. Strollers in Central Park began to catch frequent sight of a large lady in a big, floppy hat presiding over the cavortings of a tiny white creature. "Moonbeam, Moonbeam," the large lady would admonish lovingly, "no madness now!"

During the run of *A Party* Stella did all the things she did best. She sat with Ned Sheldon in his darkened room. She dined at Mrs. Nathaniel Bowditch Potter's with Mrs. McLean and the Hope diamond on one side and the Grand Duchess Marie three places away in front of the lobster aspic. She spoke about the theatre in a suite so crowded with pots of orchids that there was hardly room to sit down: there had been no new movement in the theatre since Ibsen, she declared, whose reputation in England she gave herself some small credit for establishing. She successfully maintained her reputation for guilelessly saying the wrong thing—in this case to a famous and nearly bald gentleman who found himself presented to Mrs. Campbell for at least the ninth time. For the ninth time she failed to recognize him. At last he took the liberty of expressing his annoyance. Her voice filling with tears of mortification, Stella blurted, "I'm so sorry—I think it's because you do your hair differently!"

She also had dinner with Alexander Woollcott. As he waited for her taxi to arrive, Woollcott felt he must be dreaming. Mrs. Campbell at dinner seemed as likely as the boy at the switchboard calling up to say "Lady Macbeth is on the wire" or "Will you speak to Lucrezia Borgia?" The critic had had several fearsome encounters with her. One had occurred when Stella, Theda Bara (whom Stella admired immensely), and Mrs. Leslie Carter all appeared in Katharine Cornell's dressing room after a performance of *Dishonored Lady*. Stella caught sight of Woollcott. "Ah," she exclaimed, pouncing on him, "you're a famous critic! Tell me, who *should* have played *Dishonored Lady?*" Woollcott tried to mask this terrible remark by a series of introductions. Surely Mrs. Campbell knew Mrs. Leslie Carter, the only other famous "Mrs." actress of their generation? "Honored, honored!" boomed Stella; then, without relinquishing Mrs. Carter's hand, she turned to Woollcott and in the least confidential whisper in New York murmured, "I thought she was *dead!*"

But this evening Stella arrived with Moonbeam in her arms and proved disarmingly mild. She talked of her autobiography, regretting now that she had included so many critical bouquets. Woollcott protested that the only thing wrong with the book was that it gave no idea of her genius for disconcerting speech. Stella objected immediately: never, never did she say such things. Woollcott pointed out that even in her extremely cautious narrative the cloven hoof was occasionally visible.

"But, my friend," replied Stella with a gusty sigh, "that cloven hoof—it's on the foot I have in the grave."

Then it was time for her to leave for the theatre. Woollcott put some slices of chicken in an envelope for Moonbeam, whose usual reward for his scene onstage with Stella was a meagre chicken bone. "It will be enough for both of us," said Stella, gathering up her Peke.

"I put her in a cab and thought as it went racketing off up the street how tremendous a woman she was, how negligible were most of us beside her, how many and how terrifying were the citadels she had stormed in her long and tragic day, how bright in the afternoon sunshine was the banner that flew ever in her heart," sighed Woollcott. An hour later the taxi driver found him. "Say," he said, "I didn't like to bother that lady friend of yours, but see what she paid me with." In his grimy palm lay two coins of the realm, but not—Woollcott saw—of this realm. He redeemed the shillings gladly and went to enshrine them on his desk.

Woollcott too had been touched by Stella's first encounter with Hollywood. "What enchanted me was her unwavering and ingenious rudeness to everyone there who could possibly have been of assistance to her. She would encounter Harold Lloyd or Ruth Chatterton at a party, and murmur, 'Now tell me, what do you do? Are you connected with the cinema?' Her failure to be politic took on the proportions of a magnificent gesture. She was like a sinking ship firing on the rescuers."

In December 1933 Stella got a chance to fire another round. M-G-M offered her a contract, and again she boarded the Twentieth Century Limited for Los Angeles. In the coming months she took care to keep up the old façade of insolent indifference. George Cukor threw a party for her; everybody who was anybody came. "You are a very *beau*-tiful young man!" she purred to the well-known Joseph Schildkraut: "why don't you make a film?" "But, my dear Mrs. Campbell," replied the young actor, "my name is Joseph Schildkraut!" Stella winced, but rallied. "Then why don't you *change* it!" She repeated the gag down the line. "If you don't know who I am, I'd better fire my press agent!" exclaimed Douglas Fairbanks. Colleen Moore, another victim, watched the progress and found it hard to believe that the great actress had ever been a beauty—dyed hair (she guessed), fat, lots of teeth. On Stella went until Bebe Daniels came along. "You're so *beau*-tiful," said Stella predictably, "you should be in the movies." "And what did you say your name was?" asked Bebe. Stella drew herself up. *"I* am Mrs. Patrick Campbell." "Oh," said Bebe guilelessly, "—Campbell soup family?"

Her behavior, seemingly so self-destructive, was on the contrary a courageous fight for survival. Even though Stella had given half a dozen interviews declaring that seventy was just the right age to launch a film career (she was nearly sixty-nine), she must have suspected she had little chance against the merciless camera. Witty insolence guaranteed her attention, at least; and she kept up the game. Viewing her first screen test, she quipped that she'd rather imagined herself looking like Rossetti's Blessed Damozel leaning out of heaven, but found herself looking like Mussolini's mother instead. Crew and cast had been instructed to treat her with the deference due a legend, but not everybody got the message. "Hullo, babe!" a cameraman greeted her one morning as she reported to the set. "What's the little dog's name?" "Tittiebottles," Stella replied austerely.

She was cast as a partying auntie in *Riptide*, directed by Edmund Goulding and starring Herbert Marshall, Robert Montgomery, and the queen of M-G-M, Norma Shearer. Although Stella considered Shearer one of the sanest of movie stars, she had less than endeared herself to the film star at a screening of a Shearer film at Shearer's house. She had watched in apparently appreciative silence; when the lights went up, Irving Thalberg asked how she had liked his wife on the screen. "Oh, charming, charming," bubbled Stella. "Such tiny little eyes!" Norma had her innings in *Riptide* when Stella had to deliver lines like "I wish I felt as well as she looks," and a string of babble that generally poked fun at her age and weight, although she did portray a woman of some wit and spirit.

But filming was terribly difficult for Stella, just as it had been for Ellen Terry when as an old woman she had made a few movies. Accustomed to acting a whole play from beginning to end, Stella was now handed a bit of dialogue out of context and told to jump in. She felt fragmented, and had great difficulty learning her small part. More difficult still was trying to empty herself of expression. The emoting powers that were her trademark —the widened eyes, sulking brows, toss of the head, sweep of arm—looked grotesque on film, which demanded a smooth face and miniature gestures. Then she wanted an audience, and she did not want direction. Hardest of all was not commanding center stage. Uneasily she mingled with a crowd at a bar, or hung on the edges of a group of houseguests. Most of her scenes ended up on the cutting-room floor.

She managed to bring to the filming her own brand of mayhem, however. The most solemn moment of *Riptide* is the moment Norma Shearer listens to Herbert Marshall tell her he has discovered her infidelity and cannot be a husband to her any longer. Menthol tears trickle down Norma's cheeks; she bows her head; she is the epitome of beautiful misery. Then, after a long pause, Herbert Marshall gazes into her eyes and in a deep, passionate, thrilling voice says, "Let us go to the zoo." Stella had not seen the previous shot in which both parents had promised their little daughter a trip to the zoo for her birthday, and did not realize, therefore, that Marshall's words signalled forgiveness. The zoo line reduced her to hysterics, bringing all action to a halt as she staggered off the set to her dressing room to dissolve into helpless laughter.

Eventually the director insisted she have her own menthol tears. "May I not express my sympathy and my tears by the tone of my voice and the expression of my face?" asked Stella with stage instinct. No, that was not the Hollywood way. The camera began to grind, the false tears trickled down her cheeks. Her nose began to itch, she broke into giggles, and there she was again—keeping all sorts of important people waiting while she wiped her eyes and tried to recover. In another scene she was to make a regal exit after refusing to be photographed. Just at the door, however, a photographer was to snap her ample rear, at which Stella was to exclaim "Oh!" and execute a bump and grind. She went through the charade a dozen times, shot from every angle, till she felt that the gods themselves must be howling "Shame!" When it was finally over, she flopped into a chair. "Bang goes my chance of being buried in Westminster Abbey!" she exclaimed ruefully to an appreciative audience.

*Riptide* was not a good movie, and the most one could say about Stella's performance was that she looked out of place. Yet she did so for the best of reasons. Her dark hair was messy but, unlike Shearer's plastic ridges, real. She had texture—real white skin, frowsy black velvet dress, shapely hands —compared to Shearer's glossy celluloid perfection. Her make-up was bad, but the eyes large and expressive. One could almost smell her—a mixture of stale powder, tobacco, and violet cologne. But reality was not what M-G-M wanted, and *Riptide* only proved that Stella was unknown to film audiences. "Hardly a ripple of interest has been aroused by the appearance of Mrs. Patrick Campbell in one of the principal roles in Norma Shearer's *Riptide,*" reported the press, "although a few years ago the presence of this celebrated English actress in any picture would have called for considerable comment."

M-G-M used her again for one scene in *Outcast Lady* with Constance Bennett and Herbert Marshall and, in a minor part, the fine English actor Robert Loraine. Sir Cedric Hardwicke wandered onto the set and watched Stella blow her lines repeatedly as take followed unsuccessful take. At the close of the day's shooting she seemed no closer to remembering her words than at eight o'clock that morning.

"What's the time, dear?" she asked Hardwicke with weary brightness.

"Five o'clock."

"No, in London, dear."

"It's eight hours ahead there. That would make it one a.m."

"As late as that?" exclaimed Stella, registering dismay. "No wonder I'm so tired."

M-G-M lent her to Universal for *One More River*, an all-British cast playing the Galsworthy story: Diana Wynyard, Frank Lawton, Colin Clive, Reginald Denny, C. Aubrey Smith. Her maid and Moonbeam were given bit parts, and Stella had third billing as an eccentric, aristocratic aunt. And then there was nothing more. She packed her bags and headed for New York, putting up again at the Barclay. A letter from Daphne du Maurier found her there: she was writing a portrait of her father, Gerald; could Stella help? Stella responded with enthusiasm: dear, dear Gerald—so loyal and courteous and amusing. His gentleness and *joie de vivre* belonged to an age that was past. She would send Daphne his letters. Reminded of that past, perhaps, Stella decided to return to England.

There was only one problem: Moonbeam and the quarantine. Arriving at Dover in August 1934, she bravely handed the Peke over to officials, who put him in a hamper labeled "Rabies." She travelled with him in the baggage van to London, taking him out of the hamper when the guard was not looking. Arriving at the quarantine home, they passed through a gate with a big iron bell. At its ringing, Stella heard the voices of hundreds of dogs and cats lifted in the vain hope (she thought) that their owners had come for them at last. Moonbeam's cage was stowed among dozens of others. Stella stayed with him until nightfall, finding the noise, the grief, and the smell of the caged animals almost unendurable.

When she returned after thirty-six hours, Moonbeam's joy was heart-breaking. Impulsively, she demanded his release and took the train with him back to Dover. There she cabled her housemaid, Maggie Keefe, to meet her. They caught the boat to Boulogne, three men—were they detectives?—escorting her on board. In Boulogne she left Maggie and Moonbeam at the Hotel Meurice and returned to London to dispose of the flat at 64 Pont Street. (Morrie had gone in 1932.) During her brief stay in London she also made her will. Then she returned to Boulogne to wait there a fortnight for a boat back to America. She was not only a lonely old woman now, but an exile as well.

# THIRTY-SIX

## *1934–1938*

$\mathcal{I}$N OCTOBER 1934 Stella returned to 605 North Elm Drive, the pretty house she had rented in Beverly Hills set among roses and orange, lemon, fig, and mulberry trees. She had no prospect of employment. Occasionally someone would suggest something, but none of the suggestions ever came to anything. Whenever she rang her agent's office, a girl's cheerful voice told her, "Sorry, he's out." "Oh, *do* say something different," Stella finally exclaimed; "say he is dead, or married, or having an abdominal operation!" The girl laughed sympathetically—*she'd* tried to get into pictures herself. Calls to the studio drew similar results: M-G-M was "thinking of her," but "nothing suitable had come along."

There were still luncheons, dinners, and cocktail parties—but it took courage to mingle with glamorous stars who talked incessantly about their current films. There were concerts and books to read, often until two or three in the morning. There were her canaries and finches—she had a lively feeling for birds and knew their ways—and the lovely garden. There was Moonbeam. She tried her hand at writing plays, but was too restless to accomplish much. As months dragged by, she became increasingly discouraged, convinced that no one would give her even a small part, much less a starring role.

Finally, one evening at a party, she met Josef von Sternberg and was struck with his unusually sympathetic and intelligent manner. He seemed genuinely concerned that she was not working, and promised to consider her. The result was an invitation to play the old Pawnbroker in Columbia's *Crime and Punishment*, which starred Peter Lorre as the young murderer Raskolnikov. "During these three days' work, I grasped fully how foolish I had been to imagine for one moment that there was going to be any intelligent pleasure in working even with this man," said Stella. "He wanted merely obedience and silence to get his own effects. Anything in my face and figure that wasn't ugly enough, he made into a Camera distortion. The

Director and the Cameraman together did the 'acting' of my short role, helped, I suppose, in the cutting room. When I saw the rushes, I knew beyond question that no Director asks for imagination, gift, or experience from the Artist. I had myself wished to put the necessary horror and ugliness into my face, voice, and movements, but instead it was achieved through the exaggeration of every shadow in the face, and even of the pores of the skin. . . . I managed for only a short moment to introduce a little sinister atmosphere."

As an artist who had always controlled the image she presented to an audience, Stella could not forgive the dictatorship of the camera. Actually, her performance is effective—however little she liked the looks of it—reminiscent of the Matriarch as she fingers a brooch, calculates its price, and grudgingly pays. But the film itself—the "Russian" actors clad in pin-striped suits, afternoon dresses, and chic berets—was ludicrous. Though her part was negligible, Stella was the only authentic-looking character in it.

Shortly after her appearance in *Crime and Punishment* she was interviewed by *Movie Mirror*. Arriving for the assignment, Harry Brundidge found a tall and stately figure in the garden who looked so young for the woman of seventy he expected that he told her he had an appointment with her mother. "If that is true, I would advise that you begin making your arrangements with the good St. Peter," said Stella with a smile. She took him into the living room, poured him a whiskey and soda and herself a ginger ale. He was still astonished. "Many, many years ago I made a serious mistake," agreed Stella. "I told my correct age at a time when I could have lied about it. Now it is too late and I must be content with old lady parts because everyone knows my daughter is forty-eight."

The interview as usual dwelt mainly on the past: her rebellious childhood, her tragic marriage to Pat Campbell, her father's whispered "Mrs. Tanqueray" as he died, her son's death in France. "Deep down, I'm a dignified woman," Stella insisted. "My life has been a tragic one. I'm funny only on the surface." Yet, she added, she had much to be thankful for. Many at her age vegetated at the seaside in wheelchairs; she herself was moving along toward eighty, seeking her eighth or ninth fortune, doing quite well, thank you. She had a big new Packard, money in the bank, and was off to Carmel for the weekend. Was there any message, asked Brundidge, that she would like to relay to old and new friends? Stella thought. "Sure there is," she slanged. "Tell them all I am going to have my face lifted—at eighty-five."

"I think Mrs. Pat Campbell is one of God's noble women," enthused Brundidge. "I'd love to have hundreds of thousands of words to write about her—and the subject would be forever new." The intimate of Bernhardt, Maeterlinck, Pinero, Forbes-Robertson, Arliss, Tree, Barrie, Shaw—England's greatest living actress, and now starting a new career in films. "More than seventy years old, this woman? Impossible! Yes, laughable," thought Brundidge. She was young, she was vital—she could not fail.

*Crime and Punishment*, however, was Stella's last picture. In April she was forced to give up her Beverly Hills house and move into an apartment in Sunset Tower on Sunset Boulevard. Charlie Chaplin promised to cast her as a prima donna in his new movie, then rewrote the part into a minister's wife with hiccoughs—a role she was not sorry to lose. She was "almost promised" a part in *Marie Antoinette*, but then Norma Shearer started a baby and the film was indefinitely postponed. Stella of course had been spending as if the part were assured. In April 1935 she wrote to Shaw. She had actually turned down a chance to act Prola in a Theatre Guild production of his *Simpleton of the Unexpected Isles*—luckily, as it turned out, since the play flopped commercially. But now she did not want a play. ". . . Hollywood and the Camera have taught me humility—deep humility: nobody need be afraid of me anymore. Thirteen weeks work in *16 months*—think of that misery—it has almost broken me up.

"The studios say I am too celebrated for small parts, and too English to 'Star'—that Kalamazoo, Bute Montana, and Seattle, would not understand my English style and speech. . . .

"Bridget Guinness—dear Bridget—did attempt to keep me from *mourir sur la paille* but her money isn't enough for Hollywood. In retirement in Florence it would be ample—but the urge won't be silenced . . . yet! . . .

"I couldn't accept the rather large cheque George's lady offered me through her lawyer for George—somehow—somewhere sacred nerves rebelled—it isn't reasonable I know—but I fancy you may understand.

"It's odd too that I don't mind brazenly cadging you. . . . I am in a very nasty jam—I can go on for 6 weeks perhaps, but it will be six weeks more before my allowance comes again, and then it won't be enough to put me straight. . . .

"Will you—I would sell my shoes for you—help me? I want you to cable a cheque to the Security First National Bank, Beverly Hills. . . . You helped me long ago when Stella was ill and D D advised me to return to England (my Stella greeted me with: 'How silly of you to come'). . . . Meanwhile if a contract turns up I will let you know. I won't say 'How much'—I am ashamed—besides you know most things and will guess."

Shaw was a rich man but no longer in the business of bailing out Stella. She tore up his "rude horrid letter" of refusal.

Meanwhile the parties continued, the endless cocktail parties that began at five and ended at five the next morning. They were beginning to feel like nightmares—fifty or a hundred and fifty guests all rushing in at once, all with lovely teeth, all with perfect manners, all talking brightly and lacing their patter with the Americanisms Stella found so ugly: "bunk," "phoney," "uh-huh," "earful," "blah," "yep," and "oh, how cute!"—there was nothing, she discovered, not even God's beard, that couldn't be called "cute." At ten there would be a lavish buffet, at one the champagne still flowed, at five in the morning lovely, bedraggled starlets danced alone in corners humming their own accompaniment, reeling actors tripped over rugs, and the beautiful leading lady vomited into the toilet off the cloakroom.

Stella kept up her act bravely. Did she, a gentleman asked her across the table with a leer, object to nudists? "No," said Stella promptly, "only to fig-leaves: they attract my attention." A local bigwig heard that one of Mrs. Campbell's sisters-in-law was a princess and the other a duchess. How was it that she was not a snob? "It isn't necessary," murmured Stella. On spotting her elusive agent among a crowd of tuxedos at a party: "Please introduce me to that young man. He looks quite intelligent." Enthusiastically, to a famous actor who was bellowing Hamlet at a party: "You know, you would be quite good if you took a few lessons!"

Friends assured her that she must keep her name before the public. She tried to assemble her own interviews from scraps of questions asked at old ones. But no one found her manifesto—"I would like to play in a Picture in which the Director gives me my head a little—to write a book that people don't find too dull to finish—to carry my age with grace, and at the end to close my eyes with composure and fold my hands"—catchy enough to print. She managed to get on the air; the drama critic Edwin Schallert interviewed her on May 22, 1935, over KMTR. Her "Good evening, Mr. Schallert—tell me, do we get paid for this?" was to the point, but no film contract followed. She tried a plant in the papers announcing she was leaving for England. It netted three dinners, one cocktail party, and two luncheons to wish her *bon voyage*—and, finally, a test for a "good part" with Gary Cooper.

She was sent five pages of anonymous script at ten p.m. and stayed up all night struggling to memorize "Toodle-oo, you adorable young man, my name is Madame Pomponi, have you ever heard me sing? If you haven't you haven't lived, I can still sing rings around the yowling cats today." She reported for the test next day, was called "Honey" by the make-up man, felt her lines going. "Don't worry," a sympathetic actress reassures her, "your words will come to you directly you begin." Stella seizes her arm. "Do you know what this play is about?" she asks hungrily, thinking that if she knows, the part might begin to fall into place. "Oh, yes: I've read

the book." "What!" says Stella. "Is it possible it is a *book?*" A strange
gentleman with blue eyes addresses her. "I still have the panama hat your
son gave me," he says, taking her hand. Beo! Tears fill her eyes, but she
remembers her make-up. A voice calls for places. She is terrified when the
camera begins to turn, misses a page, blurts out, "He'll be a riot, don't let
any of those other squaws get at him. Doodle-oo—I mean Toodle-doo—oh
no, no, no, no!" "Please don't stop, Mrs. Campbell," shouts the director,
"—go on." She goes on, repeating the same nonsense seven times. "Please,
Mrs. Campbell: face the camera!" "We can't see your face at all." "Speak a
little quicker." "Please try and remember your words!" At last it is over.
She goes back to her dressing room. It seems a hundred years since she has
left it. She wonders why she feels so ill. Hunger? Or is it just that she feels so
insulted she'd like to die? Eight days later her agent reports, "You were not
fair or fat enough for the part."

Finally Stella had had enough. After a determined search she found a
small log cabin in the San Bernardino Mountains, a hundred miles from the
now detested valley of the pitiless sun. In three rooms more than a mile
above sea level she found virgin pine forest, snow-capped horizons, silence.
There was nobody about except the families of five maintenance men living
in cottages down the road, and a general store. They brought her wood for
her stove, preserved peaches, fresh eggs. They were kind for the sake of
kindness, not self-seeking; they did not mistake sex for love; they were
better-looking than movie stars. She tried the rugged life—tramped about
on snowshoes and (because all the other dogs ran free) made Moonbeam a
leash two yards long. He was not deceived, however, and sat ashamed in the
road until she released him. She grew to love the solitude so much that the
projected construction of a millionaire's lavish home nearby angered her
more than it did the natives: it was as though "a brass trumpet blew death
and destruction"; she could feel the vulgarity creeping in, the lovely corners
of the forest being cut away, the rhythm of a deer path being destroyed. The
daily newspapers brought enough of the world's ugliness as it was—war,
greed, lust, incontinence. Nobler things were chronicled as well, but the
print was small.

Stella recorded these reflections in a sheaf of reminiscences called
*Chance Medley*, pouring out her bitterness against the place that had rejected her, idealizing rugged isolation. Her sincerity was unmistakable. But
she did not really have the bucolic temperament. Besides, the high altitude
played tricks with her blood pressure, bringing on fainting fits. After seven
months she relented and retreated to Laguna Beach on doctors' orders.
Lonely and displaced, she felt suicidal there; she headed for New York, the
only place, it seemed, where she might still find work.

John Gielgud found her there in 1936, living without a maid at the Essex House. She had been laid up with influenza for nine weeks, and the room was littered with clothes and papers. The actor's eyes filled with tears. Stella eyed him. "All the Terrys cry so easily," she murmured. When she recovered, she took him to meet Ned Sheldon. Gielgud saw a man lying rigid in bed wearing a bow tie and a soft shirt. His smooth jaw was carefully shaved, a black mask hid his eyes, and his hands lay concealed under the brocade coverlet. Stella arrived ten minutes late in a complaining mood. She pouted, she put Moonbeam up to Sheldon's face to be loved, she moaned that nobody wanted her now that she was old and fat. Sheldon grew very quiet. Immediately she changed and began to talk at her most brilliant and fascinating clip. After they left, Gielgud told her how much he appreciated the initiation and how delightful she had been. "Ah," said Stella, "one has to be at one's best with Ned. After all, we are all he has left. Think of it. There he lies in that room up there which he will never leave, and here we are walking in the street in the sunshine." "I never loved her more than on that day," said Gielgud.

He was in New York playing Hamlet. "Give me the beauty I long for," Stella had begged him. But, invited to a party afterwards, she was her tactless self. "Why do you sit on the bed?" she asked Judith Anderson, who played the Queen. "Only housemaids sit on the bed!" "Why has the ghost got mumps?" she complained to the director (the ghost had worn a large mask). On December 11 Gielgud took her to the film *Rembrandt* starring Charles Laughton, a player whom Stella had long wanted to act with, just as she had always wanted to play King Lear in a beard. When they came out, the man who had been King Edward VIII was broadcasting his abdication speech from Fort Belvedere. They went into the Plaza Hotel to listen. Stella burst into tears. "Let's send him a telegram," she urged. Gielgud pointed out that they did not know the ex-King, and that at any rate he would have left Fort Belvedere by this time. "Oh, yes—we must, we must," cried Stella and dragged Gielgud off to find the nearest post office. "Isn't this wonderful?" she exclaimed to the clerk. "The greatest thing since Antony gave up his kingdom for Cleopatra." Gielgud finally persuaded her to transfer her congratulations to Mr. Laughton, telegraphing their appreciation of his film.

In those days, Gielgud recalled, she trimmed her floppy hats with nail scissors and wore an old black coat littered with Moonbeam's hairs, yet could still sweep regally through a hotel lobby and into a waiting taxi. She could still exit regally from a taxi as well. On one occasion a driver waiting for his fare looked over his shoulder and saw a spreading puddle on the rear floor. "All right," he snarled, "who's responsible for this?" Stella clutched

Moonbeam to her bosom. *"I am!"* she said loftily, flung open the door, flounced from the cab, and sailed away. She was still perfectly capable of putting anyone in his place—Clifton Webb, for example, at dinner at "21" with Gielgud and Gladys Cooper. "Not doing much in Hollywood, are you, old girl?" asked Webb, who had yet to make his film success as Mr. Belvedere. "Not doing much yourself, old boy!" countered Stella; then, turning to Gielgud: "Not quite top drawer, do you think?" she confided loudly. She would be amusing until her bluff was called. Noel Coward sat at the next table. As they were leaving the restaurant, Stella halted beside him. She had called Noel "a three card-trick mentality," but now she wheedled, "Why don't you write a play for me?" "Because you're impossible," Coward said bluntly. Stung, Stella became loud and abusive. It was sad, thought Gielgud, who tried to hurry her away.

The admiring James Agate came to visit her in May of 1937, and took her to lunch at Voisin, her favorite restaurant. "Didn't notice what we ate or drank, and don't remember paying," said Agate. "Probably very good. After lunch went for a drive across Washington Bridge. This also I dare say is very nice, but my attention was entirely taken up by Mrs. Pat, who radiated quicksilver." That afternoon Agate listened to Stella expound on everything from Moses to Schnabel. There were only ten commandments, Stella decided, because Moses must have said to himself, "Must stop or I shall be getting silly." Schnabel's playing of Beethoven was like "the winds of the air and the waves of the sea, without shape." The George Washington Bridge was "the world's greatest piece of architecture after *Hedda Gabler.*" "She is the great lady of the American stage," she confided of a famous actress. "Her voice is so beautiful that you won't understand a word she says." "Flight" in acting was the first quality of an actor, and she discussed it at length. About Agate's latest *Ego*, crammed with communications from his famous friends: "I did so enjoy your book," bubbled Stella. "Everything that everybody writes in it is so *good!*"

Then she reminisced about Sarah. Stella had dined with her three nights before she died on March 26, 1923. Sarah had been wearing a dress of pink Venetian velvet with long sleeves. Incredibly, just a year before, the seventy-eight-year-old actress had appeared in London playing the part of a young man in Verneuil's *Daniel.* That night Sarah sat with a white face, eating nothing, yet infinitely gracious. Her paralyzed son, Maurice, was there, fed by his wife. Sarah knew she did not have long to live. At the end of the meal she was carried upstairs in her chair. At the bend of the staircase the chair paused; Sarah kissed one finger and held it out. They both knew they would never see each other again.

The rest of the ride was punctuated by Stella's melodious disputes with the cabby, who failed to convince her that a certain monument was not Grant's Tomb, and by their futile pursuit of the *Hindenburg*, which they had spotted prowling majestically between skyscrapers. "I think I have never been in contact with a mind so frivolous and at the same time so big," said the dazed Agate. "When I got back to the hotel I found I was holding a velvet geranium which, in one of the altercations with the taxi-driver, had become detached from Mrs. Pat's headgear. We had chattered and chunnered for four hours."

"That man Agate!" exclaimed Stella to Shaw, "acceptable only to heaven because of his great love of horses! . . . I was his guest—it was a mean trick to turn my nonsense into 'copy.' *He* started luncheon with two cocktails. . . . Then a bottle of champagne followed, and he finished up with a double brandy. I had to amuse *him!*" She did amuse. "One remembers the great wit," said Rebecca West, who saw her in New York during these years. "One laughed all the way home." She did not understand why people thought Stella's beauty such a wreck. "She was wholesomely massive," thought West, "like Renaissance royalty." She would later pay Stella even higher tribute: "She was as beautiful among women as Venice is among cities, and all her beauty was at the service of a genius as remarkable."

Eventually the Essex House too became expensive, and Stella moved into the Hotel Sevillia at 117 West 58th Street, where she had a furnished bedroom, sitting room, bathroom, kitchenette, service, electricity, and a bellboy who occasionally took Moonbeam out to the curb or fetched her a piece of tongue from the delicatessen nearby—all for $83 a month. A new hat was an event. Now and then she got an engagement reading chapters of *Chance Medley* or one of her own plays, *A Movie Kiss*, to women's clubs. Then in July and August came two summer-theatre offers to play *The Thirteenth Chair* at Milford, Connecticut, and Cohasset, Massachusetts.

Although Marcus Merwin officially managed the Connecticut Players, Stella ran the show from the moment she stepped on the stage of the Plymouth Playhouse. "She was indeed impressive, but a bit tatty," remembers Charles Kebbe, a young actor Stella plucked from a minor part to play the head of the great English country house. "She was without funds and earning her keep trying to teach two Connecticut Wasp-Debs to be ladies. They hung around and were dull. We paid her $400 that week. She held court after rehearsals and at night after the show we all sat at her feet while she rumbled on about Bernard Shaw. She used to carry around a small, dirty-white Pekingese named Moonbeam, and a sight for natives was several of us with Mrs. Pat and dog crowded into a booth at the big Howard Johnson on the Milford Turnpike having pigs-in-blankets, wonderfully large hot dogs, wrapped in bacon and broiled, then covered in luscious sauce and bedded in large toasted buns. She loved them, and Moonbeam got his share.

"Her entrance I remember. Family and guests in tails and long dresses. Butler announces Madame La Grange. We all turn facing stage left and remain stock-still. I can see Mrs. Pat in the wings slowly counting up to ten on her fingers. Then she swept on stage to the rabid delight of her audience —swept as if she had come down a grand flight of stairs. Are there any actors who can accomplish that feat today? She was a hard worker, very hard. She knew every letter, every comma of that play. The cast quickly learned that as we spoke our lines on stage we would hear them echoed quietly by Mrs. Pat in the background. The audience didn't hear this, but we did, and it kept us on our toes. Another way she would keep us alert was by suddenly turning to an actor if she felt his attention lapsing, and asking *sotto voce*, 'Did you want to say something?'" Was she a great actress? Kebbe wondered. Perhaps not by today's confident standards. By the standards of her day—indubitably yes. By all-time standards, probably not. She was, however, that compelling, encompassing personality called a star. Nobody cared what she played in, it was she alone they came to see. "She was in some ways a trial—had one magnificent flight of raging temper at the dress rehearsal, but was worth it all," confirms Marcus Merwin. "After her opening performance the audience rose to its feet and cheered and shouted. I never really expected to see a thing of that sort, but the old girl got to them and they couldn't help themselves. And after five years away from the stage, past seventy-two, but still as brilliant an artist as ever. I admit it was pretty exciting. She had to make a speech to stop the tumult."

"An ovation, calls, and a cry for a speech each night were comforting so far as these things go," Stella wrote Shaw that August back in New York. Now eighty-one, Shaw had packed up her letters in six envelopes "with infinite labor and a little heartbreak" and returned them to her. Not that there could be any publication before his and Charlotte's ashes were scattered, but the joint correspondence might eventually be a valuable literary property—if not to herself, then to Stella junior. With no faith in the future, Stella still pleaded: "In 50 years time life will be lived in the AIR. Nobody will read books—only those on gas and engines and screws and light-signals and such things. Books of wit and wisdom and beauty and drama and history and poetry will only be read aloud by cripples on the radio, and nobody will listen." The time was now; she would not sell the letters to a dealer before they were edited and published. But again Shaw refused. The pieces of paper on which he had written his words were hers; his words were his own.

Although Stella scoffed at Shaw's constant protestations of decrepitude, the death of Barrie that August of 1937 shocked her into a realization of her own seventy-two years. So many were gone: Tree, Alexander, Ellen Terry, darling Gerald. The knee she had injured so long ago in Philadelphia became inflamed; she found it painful to climb into taxis or up a flight of stairs. Another torment was the knowledge that since she could not afford the storage bill, Harrod's would soon be meddling with her beloved possessions—the Morris table, the books, the grand piano. Then she missed her family—her Stella; Patrick, now grown and married, and herself a great-grandmother. A number of years ago she had reopened communication with Lulo, in 1929 sending her £20 for doctor bills ("I am *so glad* to be able to help, I think of you both unceasingly"). In 1931, when Lulo could no longer afford her current house, Pilgrims, Stella proposed taking over the mortgage rather than letting her sell it at a loss, and with that security providing Lulo with a supplementary allowance of not less than £3 a week for the rest of her life—a piece of generosity she herself could ill afford. Although Lulo bridled at the suggestion as an infringement of her freedom, Stella had meant it kindly. Pretty Stella Moore was out of reach, having married Guy Coltman-Rogers in 1934. Stella had fought vehemently against the marriage: giving up a career to marry a man twenty years older with grown children was utter folly. When her goddaughter had gone ahead, she had relented and with characteristic generosity given her her own maid. The parting of so many ways had left Stella lonely, although her exile was of her own choice.

Stella was never without friends, however. Katharine Cornell called quite often, and Sara Allgood, and all kinds of English actors who were passing through. And in 1937 she met a comfortably wealthy widow named Jennette (Jane) Cutler Curtis, an inveterate theatregoer who enjoyed spending money on travel, books, and people. Hearing that Mrs. Campbell was in New York, Jane telephoned to ask if she might call; they met, and Mrs. Curtis was instantly captivated. She decided that she desperately needed acting lessons, for which she would pay handsomely. Stella was not fooled, but accepted the assignment. "That was no more a lesson than my hat," she wrote after payment arrived for a session that was really a social call. ". . . I wonder why you like to try & make me swindle you. . . . I shall never feel I have earned it." Between lessons Jane sent flowers, delicacies from her kitchen, and wool kneecaps for the arthritic knee. She also sent Frances.

In the following months young and pretty Frances Tompkins became errand girl, secretary, maid, dog-walker, and confidante on loan from Mrs. Curtis, twice a week for two or three hours at a time. Her most difficult assignment occurred when Stella insisted on being taken to Macy's to shop for Christmas presents for her daughter, Patrick, and her great-grandchild.

The taxi crawled downtown in a crush of holiday traffic; Macy's itself was a madhouse—the throngs, the noise, and the heat were overwhelming. Stella, clutching Moonbeam, could not get near a counter, could not attract the attention of the harried clerks, could not even glimpse what was on display. Frances finally fought their way to an exit, certain that any moment her pale and shaken charge would collapse; desperate, she bullied their way past laden shoppers into a cab. "Stella scraped together some money and sent it to her daughter so they could buy what they wanted in London," said Frances. "She worried constantly about her daughter and family. I often wondered if they worried as much about her." Whatever the source of that money, it was not John Gielgud: Stella returned the Christmas check the kind actor sent her that year.

In the new year Cecil Beaton, now a famous photographer, asked to photograph the old brute who had disillusioned him at Bournemouth fourteen years before. She arrived for her sitting in the inevitable black velvet, wearing ropes of artificial pearls and carrying Moonbeam. "In appearance, Mrs. Pat seems a prototype of a stage duchess," said Beaton. "But, after the hot lights had played on her for a while, she began to disintegrate. There was something ghastly about her dirty white gloves, her fallen chins and the tragic impedimenta of age. She bellowed like a sick cow, throwing her hands to the skies, 'Oh, why must I look like a burst paper bag? Why must I have all these dewlaps? Why can't I be a beauty?' "

Beaton was not too repulsed to take her to her favorite Voisin, where she proved in good form. She trounced Orson Welles's production of *Julius Caesar*: "They have no reverence, those boys. They speak the lines as if they had written them themselves. . . . Mr. Welles's Brutus is like an obstetrician who very seriously visits a lady in order to placate her nerves." (She had evidently forgotten her own cavalier treatment of Lady Macbeth, when, said Gielgud, she entered like the Queen of Hearts about to have the gardeners executed, and read out Macbeth's letter with ill-concealed contempt.) "Lillian Gish may be a charming person, but she is not Ophelia. She comes on stage as if she'd been sent for to sew rings on the new curtains." Kirsten Flagstad, on the other hand, "walks meaninglessly around the stage, like a wardrobe in a seance." Beaton found her judgments canny and clear.

They both mourned the recent death of Violet, Duchess of Rutland. "She was the most beautiful thing I ever saw," said Stella of her old friend. "In my day, beauties were poetic-looking. They wore long, pre-Raphaelite tea gowns. They moved and spoke very slowly, giving the impression that they had just been possessed."

At that moment Stella spotted Noel Coward at a wallside table and sailed over to join him, the late unpleasantness forgotten. Beaton watched the pantomime and thought Coward seemed ill at ease. "He wants to put me in his new play," Stella announced on return. "I refused. I could never talk like a typewriter. I couldn't tap out, 'Do you love me? Don't you love me? I don't love you.'" Beaton laughed, but wondered how she could turn down a play when she hadn't had a chance for years. But Stella always could—in this case, *The Lyons Den*, a play about Tallulah Bankhead into which Noel had been persuaded to fit Stella. "Tallulah is always skating on thin ice," Stella liked to say. "Everyone wants to be there when it breaks"—except, in this case, Stella herself.

On the street they said goodbye. Stella quoted a line of Swift's to Vanessa: "You have taught me to distinguish and you leave me desolate." He left her standing in the snow, "a monument in black velvet."

He sent her his proofs and she returned a few days later, swathed in furs, a feathered hat, and the usual trailing black. She had brought along some old photographs. "Look at the beauty of that neck, at that line of cheek," she moaned. "And look at me now, all wind and water." Beaton looked at a face so lovely that it was almost frightening to compare it with Mrs. Campbell today. "Oh, God," whimpered Stella, sensing his reaction, "how can You be so unkind as to do this to me? Why must we all become ugly? I don't know how some women stand it. Why don't they commit suicide?" Yet she thought Beaton's photographs quite wonderful, and offered him $40. Beaton remonstrated—he thought the pictures ordinary and anyway had made them as a tribute. "It's rather affected of you to go on like this, you know," said Stella, unmoved. "I shall give you *thirty* dollars, then. I can afford it. I have a rich pupil now." She invested the words *thirty dollars* with Shakespearian grandeur, thought Beaton, making it seem as though she were bestowing gold coin, lending the whole transaction dignity.

The next time Beaton saw Stella he was a pupil himself, having been appalled at the nauseating smugness of his recorded voice. He found her in two stuffy, overheated rooms. Moonbeam curled in a basket. Every bit of furniture covered with remnants of brocade, the radiator swaddled in a snood of red brocatelle, photographs and water colors spotting the room, bags of all descriptions hanging from lamps. The lesson proved a revelation. Stella recited Tennyson's "Come not when I am dead, to drop thy foolish tears about my head," a poem which it was impossible to patter through with smug, fashionable nasality. Beaton listened in amazement to "the turtledove-richness of her cooing." Trying it himself, he recognized how "light and murderous" his own rendition was. At his second attempt, "You've done it!" cried Stella. "You've altered the pitch of your voice." She proceeded to demonstrate some secrets of her stage technique. When she moved, for example, her foot preceded any other part of her body; if she did no more than turn to look out a window, her foot turned first. Her arm movements too were unusual. "No, no, you cannot open your arms with elbows close to your sides. You are not a Jewish comedian. You must show the best part of your arm, the inside. Now, raise the palms of your hands and push outwards as if you were parting the winds!" The head must become a gracious extension of the body. "In moments of anxiety, you must never throw your head from side to side. It is foolish and restless. Raise the head and clasp it still; no, not with your hands, with your spirit! Now you're learning all my tricks!"

He was with her on the ninth of February, her seventy-third birthday. Happy returns were few. "Some gardenias and a cablegram from England paid homage to her great character, to an actress who had been loved by Shaw, who had brought a new influence to the theatre and was now a waning one. The young ballerinas across the street were doing their arm exercises. . . . Moonbeam, who would never be in quarantine, snoozed contentedly in his basket."

Shortly afterwards Stella was forced to bed, where her aching knee confined her until June. She waited for offers during the long months, but none came. A last flicker of hope died when a part she had expected from Guthrie McClintic did not materialize. She finally announced her intention of leaving for Boulogne to the amiable Jane Curtis, who immediately and quietly set about paying up Stella's dressmaker and hotel bills and also, thought Frances Tompkins, at least part of Stella's passage on one of the smaller French liners. Jane gathered together friends and Frances, and they all went to give Stella as gala a send-off as possible from Jersey City. A Mrs. Sykes, a friend of Jane's who was going on to London, would watch over her on the voyage. And so Stella was carried on board, since she could not walk, and waved off by Frances and dear Jane. She had chosen Boulogne because it was as close as she could get to England and its insufferable quarantine kennels, and because (she reasoned), should any offers come, she could always hire a maid to stay with Moonbeam and cross the Channel to act again in her native land.

# THIRTY-SEVEN

# 1938–1940

*S*HE SPENT the long crossing in bed, only crawling out once or twice to sit on a chair in the corridor. At Boulogne she was carried off the boat by three strong men: "Thank God there were no reporters; I *did* feel an ass!" She tried a resort at Wimereux for rest and economy, but the sea was too rough and the terrain only rock and sand, so she returned to Boulogne, putting up at the Hotel du Pavillon Impérial. It was pathetically under-staffed, she decided, although there was a boy to take Moonbeam out to the curb. As for herself, it took her twenty minutes to buckle her shoe. "I could shriek at the squalor of not being able to take care of myself properly," she complained to Jane. "I am *sure* I ought to have a sort of maid nurse . . . I just *cannot* go on like this. I don't sleep—and I don't like to take any more of Dr. Bliss's sleeping draughts. I couldn't throw them off at all, & 'stared at the carpet' for five days afterwards. . . . Thank you for everything dearest Jane. I *know* you helped me just as much as you could & I am very grateful —indeed—indeed."

She lingered in Boulogne three weeks, hoping that her knee would permit her to cross to England so she could see her little granddaughter, Jennifer Stella Sigrid; she would not be carried on and off trains. It did not heal, and late that July she left for Sirmione, Lago di Garda, where her friend Naomi (Micky) Jacob, a writer and former actress, had a villa. She reached Milan after a roastingly hot train journey, was met, and after a four-hour automobile ride collapsed into bed at the Hotel Catullo and stared at the ceiling for five days. When she got up, she found the place bewilderingly beautiful: a peninsula with lake around as far as the eye could see, the Scaliger Palace backing a charming piazza, flowers, vines, and little white iron tables and chairs in a garden with three stone steps down to the lake. But although she should have felt better in the Italy she had always romanticized, the heat oppressed her; she felt nervous, restless, and often wanted to scream. The presence of Micky and Gwen Richardson Blake, who had acted with Terry, did not help much. She feared she would have to escape into the hills, but eventually moved instead to the Hotel Sirmione, where there were mud baths for her knee. She tried to discipline herself into giving up all thoughts of returning to America, where she was not wanted, or to England, from which she was banned. But she could not give up the hope that someday—somewhere—anywhere—she would act again.

There was another Englishwoman at Sirmione. Agnes Claudius was in her late thirties, a sometime writer under the name Claude Vincent, like Micky Jacob a lesbian, and one of those professional fans whom actors attract. John Gielgud had attracted her, to his misfortune, since he found her hideously ugly, pretentious, tiresome, and addicted to sending imperative notes demanding to see him, always (it would turn out) on trivial matters. But she had virtues. Now, when Gwen told her that the great lady was not happy, Claudius took the boat to Desenzano to try and find something that would cheer her, and returned with a great bunch of Pre-Raphaelite–looking tuberoses which she sent to the Hotel Sirmione. The next day she received a summons.

"It was not a small woman who lay against the pillows," said Claudius. "Her face was dead white, the texture of the tuberoses, and her Piero della Francesca eyes stared appraisingly at me. As for the rest of her, she seemed to be carpeted over by several yards of completely black, tangled hair."

"So you are the Claude Miss Jacob has been telling me about," intoned Stella mournfully. "Well, you've got a Pharaoh's face—I shall call you Egypt. . . . It was kind of you to send me those tuberoses, though their scent is *rather* too strong at night. I wonder how you found them—one doesn't seem to be able to get ANYTHING here! Perhaps you could be clever and get me another spunnnnnnnge? Miss Jacob has sent me hers, but it's made of wood! And I need some *more* mutton chops for Moonbeam. I'm told that all one has to do is to take the boat to Desenzano—could you do that for me, otherwise he won't have any lunch. Oh, and perhaps you can find a bank where you can cash a cheque for me while you're over there. . . ."

"Who could resist that voice?" Claudius asked herself. She could not, and found in the next days that she had fallen under the spell of a terrible and wonderful witch. "Very soon we were all at her beck and call. Mickie cooked her a chicken stuffed with grapes as no one else knew how; the Overland didn't dare break down in case something was needed from further even than Desenzano; Gwen's beautiful niece spent hours with Stella who could never look long enough on beauty; I shuttled back and forth to other Garda towns, seeking such improbable objects as screws for her noiseless typewriter or lace for the chemises with which she dressed her bed lamps in any hotel in any part of the world."

Everything connected with Stella became an adventure. She wanted to go to Brescia, where her grandfather had been born, but before going she must have her hair washed. "But they *must* use *only* pure Marseilles soap, Egypt. I wouldn't think of letting them use their shampooooooohs. Who can tell what they really put in those bottles!" So Egypt went looking for *sapone di Marsiglia* and finally persuaded a hairdresser on the piazza to risk an encounter with the great actress and her hair, grown back since the bob to luxurious length. Stella drove all of the one hundred yards to the piazza in a taxi with Moonbeam, and submitted her head to the chosen hands. It took nearly four hours to dry the yards of black hair while the whole piazza looked on and marvelled.

It was the first sign of her recovery. After that, she began to venture out more frequently, using a silver-knobbed cane that had been Beo's, Moonbeam tucked under an arm. Egypt found every excursion touched with Stella's magic: a visit to a little monastery, where quite ordinary birds seemed to sing angelically for the occasion; a luncheon in the hotel garden with her doctor, at which she made them all rosy on Lambrusco; an encounter with Robert Penn Warren, who found her, to his surprise, able and eager to discuss his works as well as those of Allen Tate and Cleanth Brooks. "Of course you're all too learned for me," she protested on the drives they all took together, "but you aren't being abstruse just for the fun of it. It's Art for Art's sake with a vengeance." Egypt thought that no other actress of her generation had the same critical acumen, not even Eleonora Duse. She was absolutely captivated by Stella, and would have been cruelly hurt had she known that Stella wrote Jane Curtis that she had met no one interesting at Sirmione.

In the August heat, however, the magic began to wear thin. Claudius had come to Sirmione after a serious accident ("Why does Egypt have such a *worried* walk?" Stella would ask, but get no answer), and found she could not keep up with Stella, whom radium treatments and mud packs had quite cured. So she went away to the tiny lake of Tenno above Riva, promising to return shortly; then sent Stella great bunches of cyclamen and announced that she would stay another two days. Those two days happened to coincide with the arrival of a London publisher to discuss with Stella the possibility of editing the letters, should the chance ever arise—Shaw was, after all, going on eighty-three. Stella had warned Egypt that when he came she would be expected to be there to take thorough notes; and she was not. When Egypt returned to Sirmione, Stella was all gracious reproof and the climate had cooled between them. Egypt felt ashamed: she had failed her queen when she had been most needed.

The publisher had brought Stella flowers and had actually stirred her virgin heart—"20 years a virgin anyhow!" she told Jane Curtis. She professed herself "almost entirely in love with him," without naming his name. She was also full of plans. Harry Lachman, one of her closest Hollywood friends, was making a picture in Paris and had promised her a part. She thought too she could perhaps act at the English Theatre there. She had sent two chapters of *Chance Medley* to *Town and Country*, and was waiting to hear. "I don't ever seem to *want Peace,*" she told Jane, "I want to battle on & on—now that I have both my knees." When *Town and Country* accepted the chapters with an advance, she left for Paris. Egypt, who could not keep up the pace and in any case would not accept the payment for her companionship that Stella insisted on, returned to England.

In Paris Stella settled at the Hotel Brighton in the Rue de Rivoli. She had a cosy sitting room with open fire, a huge bedroom, a fine bath, service, sun all day, and a lovely view over the Tuileries for a hundred francs a day. A daily maid got her breakfast and tea; she went out to the good, cheap little restaurants in the vicinity for supper. The Duke and Duchess of Windsor were in the neighborhood and the Lachmans were there—Harry and his beautiful Chinese wife, Tai—and she dined with them often, although the film project had evaporated. Cecil Beaton turned up and took her to a cocktail party. Her old friend William Armstrong came over and met her for lunch at Rumpelmeyer's. "Oh, don't kiss me, Fanny!" boomed Stella as heads turned. "The French are such gossips!"

She was not quite forgotten professionally. Robert Stevenson came over from Ealing Studios with a script. She read it, but it turned her stomach: a wooden duchess to play opposite Seymour Hicks's dancing, singing, tipsy duke, with just enough lines to feed the other actors. She refused it. There was nothing at the English Theatre, however, and no broadcast work or pupils. That December 1938, therefore, she wrote Shaw. She had heard that his film *Pygmalion* was making him a fortune. He must have forgotten how she had taken the play to Tree and begged him to read it after Alexander had turned it down, how she had stood his bullying at rehearsals, how she had spilled her heart out trying to make his Eliza human and beautiful. Had he remembered, surely he would have sent her a Christmas box! There were so many things she wanted the money for: a long talk with her daughter in London, tickets to his play *Geneva*, lunch with James Agate again. She would like too to see what England's popular actresses were doing, and see after her precious belongings at Harrod's, and see *him*. Shaw was unmoved. There was her captive George and his ransom. While she had that diamond in her safe, no one would believe she was not rich. Or he could tell her how to make a fortune—she should write the true story of *Pygmalion*; the dismal string of lies in her last letter was not worth tuppence.

This refusal opened the last skirmish between them. In a long and heated reply Stella defended herself to the man she thought had always misunderstood and condemned her even while she fascinated him. And that, Stella declared, was what made him so vindictive: he had not had the courage to take her in his arms and kiss her, so he had bullied and maligned her instead. "To this day you haven't forgiven me—you have written to me—spoken to me—branded me as an 'impossible woman in the Theatre.' I have remained calm and watched role after role being covered in green baize that I could have made sing down the ages. The Portuguese Jew [Pinero] knew there would have been no 'Mrs. Tanqueray' if he had interfered with the amateur. Some people recognize and can manage a 'blood 'orse,' some cannot. . . ." As for George, she had no George to sell. Years ago she had expressed her willingness to divorce, and had received no reply. Still, with all his maddening perversity, she could not think of him as anything but Joey—the tragedy of baffled sincerity. She sent her love and prayers, and hoped that he continued well.

"Your consciousness is so entirely imaginary that I give you up as hopeless," replied Shaw. ". . . If only you could write a true book entitled WHY, THOUGH I WAS A WONDERFUL ACTRESS, NO MANAGER OR AUTHOR WOULD EVER ENGAGE ME TWICE IF HE COULD POSSIBLY HELP IT, it would be a best seller. But you couldnt. . . . I havent any money. . . . As to bringing you over, I had as soon bring the devil over. You would upset me and everybody else. You dont know how I have blessed that wretched little dog. . . . Joey was the cleverest thing you ever invented, by far, by far, by far."

Stella fought back. "This last letter of yours is full of craziness, and unbelievable unkindness. . . . *Six* engagements with Alexander . . . *Nine* engagements with Robertson—until Hamlet and his pretty wife left no place for me. *Four* plays with Gerald du Maurier. . . . *Two* with Hare. *Four* with Tree. . . . And you dare to accuse me of humiliating people! Since you first dipped your pen in the ink-pot what else have you ever done? . . . I believe you have eaten your own heart. . . . 'Goodbye' unless you ask me to write again." Yet she mentioned the Christmas box again, and even enclosed a copy of one of his letters in an attempt to soften the heart he might not yet have swallowed. She still could not bring herself to sell them, though she threatened to do so again and again. She carried them with her in a large black hatbox, a reminder that she had a last resource, but even more importantly, a reminder that she had once been powerful and adored.

She got a little Parisian sempstress to reline an old cloak for the winter; her furs had somehow been left in New York. At Christmastime she wrote her "Beloved Ned: Each day I have hoped for some happy news to give you. Each morning I have wished that I could have come and sat by your bed. . . . This Christmas you will be nearest to my heart, for I verily believe I love you better than anyone in the world, and I also believe that God has made in you the bravest and finest man that ever lived. I believe in God's patience because I have witnessed yours. I believe in God's sympathy and understanding because I have known yours, and I believe in God's goodness because he has spared you to us that we may see to what unselfish and noble heights a man may attain. I wish you knew how you help us all. Christmas blessings upon you, dearest Ned."

By the end of December she owed her hotel four weeks' rent because she had thought that *Town and Country* would take four short stories and had spent the anticipated advance; but *Town and County* had not. The hotel people were beginning to be dreadfully rude; she held her head high against their sneers, but loathed the indignity. She would receive her allowance on January 6, but it was already mostly spent; she had never yet stretched it through a quarter. To make things worse, her grandson's wife, Gunnell, and daughter were coming to visit. She would naturally pay for their week at the hotel, ashamed she could not afford to have them stay longer, and had even promised to send them on a visit to Gunnell's home in Norway. And so, sitting on a bench with Moonbeam in the Tuileries one day, she thought of the only help available and went to cable Jane Curtis for $100. At the same time she informed the hotel that she must move. The management considered, then replied that "for the prestige of her name" they could arrange a smaller, cheaper apartment, but still very nice.

In February 1939 she came down with influenza and an abscess in her throat that grew larger and larger until she was wild with pain, although she refused a doctor or a nurse as long as she could because of the expense. The care and the medicine ruined what was left of the first-quarter allowance, of course. She finally cabled Gabriel Wells, offering him Shaw's letters at his price; but, unaccountably, nothing came of the offer. "My heart feels like a tomb that hasn't even a corpse in it," she wrote Sheldon wearily. People were telling her "Go back to England," not realizing that living there was three times as expensive as living in France, and that she was desperate. When her next allowance came on April 6, all but £50 would go to clear debts—£50 to live on for the next three months: impossible! "Why am I alive—what for?" she wrote Jane on May 20. Yesterday she had gone to the English Theatre, praying she might be of some use to them. There had been six people in the audience downstairs and twelve up; she'd not had the heart to go backstage after that. She was almost demented from having no work. Desperate plans kept rushing through her head . . . it was wild, but a little house with a garden in the South of France with paying guests in season. All up in the air, but could Jane possibly spare $200 without taking bread out of the mouths of babes or thinking her an adventuress or depriving herself? ". . . I know well that to people of integrity borrowing money is something quite ugly and a mild form of swindling," Stella argued. ". . . I have never felt like that myself because I never had any of the respect for money that comes with inherited wealth to nice people—the money I had, I *earned*, and my *joy* was giving it and helping, and I must own, spending it carelessly. Now I see—now that I am old—that [age] without money is a dreadful thing—instead of giving to those you love you have to take. It is a *hell* that and needs a lot of strength to bear. . . ."

On May 27 James Agate wired her flowers in memory of the first performance of *The Second Mrs. Tanqueray* forty-six years before. In June the hotel was desolated to inform her that they must raise her rent to eight hundred francs for the summer tourist season. An s.o.s. brought Agnes Claudius to Paris to help her move to cheaper quarters at the Hotel de Calais in the Rue des Capucines, one room, with the bath on the next floor. "I am very grateful to you to have enabled me to cut down my expenses," she wrote after Claudius had returned to England. To Jane: "I had to come to this dreadful little Hotel . . . the bathroom downstairs one flight—that does choke me—and the place is full of stuffy stinks and sounds." She did not know how long she could stand it—or Paris. She felt she was choking there, not well enough to walk about, not energetic enough to meet old friends or look for new. She was becoming more and more solitary day by day—horrid, unfit for company. She ached to be taken care of. She ached most of all to get away to the South of France, remembering the heavenly little farm the Murphys had lent her at Antibes; it did not matter if one was shabby there. Still, one of the brightest moments in her dreary days had come when she had stopped in front of a jeweller's window to admire three ropes of enormous pearls. The jeweller had come out, and she had asked him the price. "A million francs," he had told her, "but I would make an arrangement for you." She'd laughed and said she had no money, but the jeweller had smiled gravely and, bowing, said: *"Madame, je connais les gens."*

Quite apart from Stella's urgent desire to get out of Paris, events were taking shape that would disrupt everyone's lives. Not that she was unaware of the storm warnings that flew in every paper and announced themselves from every kiosk; she followed the daily news avidly, though she knew no better than most what to make of it. "I have said all along that we must be friendly with the Dictators," she had written Jane the previous autumn (it was by no means an uncommon view). "Their people like them—just like we like that silly George and Elizabeth—and you like your cheerful President." Yet she was astonished when King George sent Hitler congratulations on his fiftieth birthday—was it policy or what? "It is very bewildering about Hitler and the Jews. . . . When one thinks how the Jews all over the land hate Hitler almost to distraction, one feels sure, unless he frightened or rather terrorized them with punishment over the Rath Assassination, the lives of Dictators and their followers would not be worth a cent." She *was* sure that if England did not want war, it would have to swallow Hitler for the present, and she did not worry excessively about the Jews. Why did they not leave countries where they were not wanted, and found their own, and put their brains to work? "I shouldn't be surprised if they rule the world in the end," she wrote Jane comfortably in one of the last months one could be comfortable about anything going on in Europe.

That summer of 1939 she had a week's holiday at Sables d'Or, courtesy of Sara Murphy; but the wretched weather caught her sciatic nerve and she was bedridden for nine days in excruciating pain. The birth of a second great-grandchild, named in tribute Angela Beatrice Rose, cheered her a little. Then Shaw, whose bark was always worse than his bite, wrote to say that *Major Barbara* was to be made into a film by Gabriel Pascal, and that Pascal wanted her for the part of Lady Britomart, Barbara's aristocratic mother. Was she still seriously in the field?

"Yes: I am still 'seriously in the field,'" replied Stella on June 28, "but you know not as cannon fodder." She had turned down the English Theatre's offer of a part as a Jewish mother whose lines consisted chiefly of "Oi, oi, tch, tch." She was getting used to poverty and discomfort. "There is no reception room here, so don't ask Pascal to come & see me. I would be ashamed of my shabby little bedroom," she ended indefinitely. Hearing nothing from her, Pascal eventually gave the excellent chance to Marie Löhr. "He gave you up because you would not be separated for six months from your dog," wrote Shaw. "For Heaven's sake, when that wretched animal perishes . . . buy a giant panda or a giraffe or a water buffalo or a sea lion, any of which you can take with you anywhere." He was keeping away from Malvern that year, he told her, although his new play about Charles II was enlivening the Festival. But he had given up producing: "I am too old, too old, too old." Yet it was not Moonbeam that prevented Stella from accepting Pascal's offer, since she had always planned to leave him in Paris if a chance arose. It was terror of the camera and certainty that she could no more make a film successfully in England than she could in Hollywood.

And then it was too late to think of England. The personnel of the Hotel de Calais were called up, the French government requisitioned all the bedding, the residents fled, and in two days the place was a military stable. Stella fled too, to the Josse Hotel at Antibes—a twelve-hour journey, herself lame and Moonbeam grumbling all the way like an old husband. There were four other guests and four officers quartered at the hotel, and soldiers and cannon in the field nearby. "Oh, dearest Jane," she wrote on September 7, in the week Hitler attacked Poland, and England and France declared war on Germany, "everything that is going on in the world seems like an awful dream—from here it is unbelievable. . . . It's agony—all news is censored and the papers are 3 days old—and the radio is in empty gaps and you FEEL all the important things are left out." News did come of the possible evacuation of Antibes, giving rise to vivid pictures of her hobbling down some road carrying Moonbeam and a bottle of drinking water, and collapsing as the enemy thundered nearer. Italy was impossible since no English money could be sent there; France the only solution, although she wanted to be near the border in case France fell. She decided upon Pau, a resort city at the foot of the Pyrenees.

Shortly before leaving Antibes, Stella was sitting alone at an open-air café when she caught the attention of two Englishwomen at another table. Mrs. Whittall and her daughter, Dorothy, could hardly believe that the large woman in black woolly pants with hair piled up like a black mountain above a purple bandeau was the former tenant of Ashfields. Mrs. Whittall had had to go to law for the £50 in overtime that the actress had forgotten to pay and be content with a recommendation that said she was very good at proof-correcting and making coconut icing. She'd last seen her in *The Matriarch*, an intensely enjoyable performance and so like herself, thought Mrs. Whittall. Now she and Dorothy went over and Stella was all graciousness. She at once began to coax the nineteen-year-old girl to accompany her, a lonely old woman, to Pau. Magnetized, Dorothy agreed.

She began to regret it almost as soon as they boarded the train. Soldiers kept pouring into the compartment and, before she could stop him, a particularly large one sat on the black hatbox containing the Joey-Stella letters that Mrs. Campbell seldom let out of her grasp. That indignity was succeeded by the equally insulting spectacle of soldiers teasing Moonbeam, who snapped and snarled quite unpatriotically. Arriving at Toulouse at midnight, they were told there would be no train to Pau for another twelve hours. Stella did not spend them quietly. She talked incessantly and exhaustingly about the theatre and about music; she prowled restlessly among her luggage, which consisted of numerous bags, a typewriter, several walking sticks, and, of course, the large black hatbox. After forty-eight hours they finally reached Pau and a hotel. "*Do* stay on with me, my dear," Stella pleaded, "—I'll give you the *moon*." They had not been in the hotel room an hour when the bed she was sitting on—still talking at full pitch—collapsed. The staff was summoned and execrated in French that was not

Mélisande's. In the dining room, waiters grew mutinous as she insisted on veal cutlets for Moonbeam. Finally on October 22 they were able to move into a mews flat above a disused stable connected with the Pavillon de Madrid in the Avenue Château d'Este. There were five rooms and a balcony, polished floors, solid old furniture, but no adequate bathroom. Having settled her in, Dorothy proposed leaving for England; but Stella pleaded, gave her stockings and shoes, and promised her the rope of pearls if only she would stay on. Privately, Stella considered Dorothy the most uncultured person she'd ever met (Dorothy thought that Beethoven was a painter) and could not understand her lack of devotion to Moonbeam, yet she did appreciate her enthusiasm for washing, ironing, and cooking. Dorothy in turn thought that the woman who got up in the middle of the night to make herself a cup of tea, talked irrepressibly, and sent her on dozens of errands, "eccentric in her habits." After about a month Stella could no longer ignore Dorothy's discontent, and let her go.

"My dear," she wrote on November 12 with her typical combination of warmth and plain speaking, "—I am so pleased to get your letter—especially the words 'Happy to be at Home.' . . . I knew I was right to make you go. You must not think for a moment you were not of great use to me. YOU WERE. I could never have got here without your help. And without your shopping and cooking I would have surely died. I have quite a heap to be grateful for, believe me. But never in this world will you make a tidy clean mildly obedient (old) lady's companion—never in this world. And you must thank God for it. But I am sure all that and a great many more things you will be as a loving and happy wife. And there is always your very pretty face to enchain and inspire affection. Bless you! To-morrow I see about the bath being put in, and having my hair washed—also having the leaves swept up in the Parc so that Moonbeam can walk and run there happily. . . . My thanks and all happiness. I hope your life pans out as the cards said."

In Pau she finally wrote to Agnes Claudius, who had been pursuing her by mail the last months in vain. She had a wonderful view of the Pyrenees, she told her, but the roads were hard to walk on. The bush outside her window had turned brightest gold and splashed the walls of her room. The air was bracing. Once in a while she could afford to rent a car, and the scenery was breathtaking. But she was very lonely and had no friends. She intended to go see the English clergyman and arrange for a place in the cemetery and also ask him who in Pau loved dogs. She had two spare bedrooms at the *pension* and "Someday you must come to me for a month or two . . . I would beg you to let me defray all your expenses."

This was not possible, but Claudius sent the papers, books, and magazines she requested. "Why are all distinguished men and women photographed *smiling?"* Stella demanded after opening a parcel. "I don't see anything to smile at. . . . It is all a mean and bloody business this war game . . . it's madness and savagery running in circles . . . all wrong—all wrong— unforgivable for ever. . . . I believe in the SHARING AND BROTHERHOOD OF MAN and I have no scrap of sympathy for Imperialism in any form what- ever." She requested books to clear her mind, for "Man has gone mad." She read violently these years: Eve Curie's *Madame Curie*, Maurois's *Disraeli*, T. E. Lawrence's letters, Dorothy Parker's verse, Shaw's *In Good King Charles's Golden Days*. She reported some of her reactions to Claudius: H. G. Wells she found clever, a little vulgar, without humor; C. Day Lewis's "Fourth Georgic" was a jewel; Hugh Walpole was interesting on Henry James, although "H.J. always terrified me, he looked at me as though he were sure I were a fool and it was agony to me when he stuck at a word."

That Christmas of 1939 she spent alone with Moonbeam, she wrote Claudius. They'd sat down to turkey, spinach, and applesauce she'd made herself. The Pyrenees were buried in forty feet of snow. It was so cold she'd knitted herself a tummy-band, and she slept in her dressing gown with two hot-water bottles. She had her bath standing in a tub surrounded by boiling kettles. She *must* have a decent bath installed, but the cost was far too high, and there was no use staying on at the Pavillon de Madrid under such circumstances. What was Egypt doing for Christmas in her little cottage in Essex? Behind every word was the unspoken message, *I am lonely, I am lonely, I am alone.*

On January 18, 1940, she moved to the Hotel Pavillon de Navarre, just off the great Boulevard des Pyrénées, where she had a large, high-ceilinged bedroom with three enormous windows, and a bath. She was three minutes from a lovely park filled with tame peacocks that intrigued Moonbeam. But the people in the place were cheerful and dumb, she told Claudius—a dreadful combination unless one played bridge. She very much wanted Egypt to come and stay in a nice little room in an adjoining house—as her guest, of course. She had an electric stove and made her own *petit déjeuner* and afternoon tea. A little maid, Paulette, came in the mornings to do her washing, ironing, shopping, and mending, and would be glad to wait on Egypt too. But oh—would Egypt get any happiness out of coming? She was a dull sort of dog these days.

Back in England, Claudius called on D.D. with a letter Stella had en- closed. What was to be done about the languishing, heartsick woman in Pau? Could her daughter go to her? Without going into the mother-daughter relationship, D.D. explained that Mrs. Beech had an important job in the Censorship; it was best not to approach her. Claudius herself went to the passport office. "Surely you know there is a war on?" she was told there and everywhere else she tried. Finally she found an official who remembered Henry Irving and had heard of *Pygmalion*. He could not promise, but for Mrs. Patrick Campbell . . . She wired Stella.

It was wonderful to get her telegram, Stella replied eagerly on February 27. She would send nine hundred francs for Egypt to extricate a trunk, a big tin box, and two parcels from the hotel she had left so precipitately six months before, and she would be grateful if Egypt could pick up a few more little things on the way. "I am feeling *much more* cheerful. I am sure it's at the thought of seeing you." Burdened with boxes of the very best oatmeal for porridge, lavender soap from Guerlain, a large tin of Johnson's baby powder, and the Paris luggage, Claudius finally staggered into Pau on the first day of March as the sun was setting over the Pyrenees, and taxied to the Hotel Pavillon de Navarre.

"She was waiting at the door," said Claudius. "Her dark hair made a floppy crown round her head; her face was the white of the untinted face powder she still insisted on using. She stood very erect—a Lady Macbeth who had somehow acquired a Peke without being in the least ridiculous. . . . She was still as romantic as Burne-Jones had painted her—and in the twilight she was immensely dramatic, though her eyes shone with joy. That evening a star really danced. . . . It was she who held out a rescuing hand to the tired traveler—the beautiful hand still as young and smooth as when Mrs. Wyndham had modelled it." "Come up to your room at once," said Stella, and before Claudius could stop her, she led the way upstairs and, out of breath but triumphant, pulled Egypt into her room. She had made her a rose-sprigged blotter, tablecloth, and chair cover, and a petunia-colored chiffon bed cape, and set her own alarm clock on Egypt's bedside table— and had wanted to show her these things herself.

That evening at dinner she asked about friends, and about the success of Micky Jacob's latest book. She'd grown to dislike Micky a great deal, though she only laughed when Claudius told her that Micky had put her into her book. Then she turned solemn. "Of course you know you've come to bury me, Egypt."

"Nonsense, Stella, what rot you do talk sometimes," laughed Claudius; but the words had been said.

D.D. had sent Maurois's biography of Shelley along with Claudius, and Stella read it through the night: "groaned aloud over his sufferings—his tenderness, his sensitiveness, his generosity, his wonderfully affectionate and sympathetic nature." "Darling D.D.," she wrote her friend, "It is a joy to hear about you." Claudius was a clever creature, a good talker, and a kind listener but, Stella guessed, had found her much older and could not understand her inertia. "I collapse every day and have to lie down in silence for an hour or more. . . . It is wonderful of her having come to me and I am tremendously grateful . . . she likes the people in the Hotel. We have a delicate french poetess, and a very charming and very well educated Dutch lady and her Austrian husband, and a singer who has lost her voice, and two grandmothers with their grandchildren whose fathers and mothers are away . . . and a little countess de Montfort whose husband has left her here with two babies whilst he is at the front. . . . I wish to heavens I had kept my strength as you have. I think if my Stella had been able to get close to me—and we had shared Pat, I would not be quite so dead—so wilted & uninterested. Claudius seems to find me amusing—but I fancy it must be my spirits skelleton bones that tinkle. . . ." It was her last word to her friend of more than thirty years.

For a week or so everything seemed to go well. They went for drives and as the flowers came out Stella insisted on stopping and picking them to take back to her room. Egypt never ceased to be amazed at her keen and lively eye. She missed nothing—an old peasant woman in black, silhouetted at her spinning wheel; tiny wild cyclamen and orchids growing low under the grass through which a stream gurgled; the coppery green spray of a vine that gleamed like metal against a white distempered wall. They would have tea and scones in a little English tea room with the French poetess, Moonbeam drinking tea from a saucer and making a mess of his face, but he *would* drink tea. And Stella actually gave orders to have a new-fangled brown suit made up, sent Egypt out to find a matching bag, and was magnificently contemptuous about the one she chose.

She began too to show Egypt what an actress she had been. When Egypt came to her room mornings, she would sit up in bed and suddenly begin a whole scene—word-perfect—from *Tanqueray*, *Ebbsmith*, or *Hedda Gabler*. "My dear," she would complain over and over, "they only *behave* nowadays, they don't seem to want to *act*." She could not say it of John Gielgud, whose affectionate, anxious letter reached her at Pau; but then she had taught him a great deal about Oswald when they had played together in *Ghosts*. "But I was very bad as Mrs. Alving," Stella now judged. "I was so taken up with his part that I never gave myself time to study my own. I'm sure I could do it better today."

There were two Stellas, and one could be unkind. Claudius learned to gauge the temper of the room by whether Moonbeam took her for granted or began to snap. "Oh, Egypt, *why* don't you come into the room properly?" Stella might complain on Moonbeam's snappish day. "You've got to come through the door mentally long before you put your hand on the knob. . . . I suppose it's lack of money, I don't know—but no one will pay attention to you as they did to me!" But then there would be a little note for

"My Egypt of the magnolia face" attached by a ribbon to a beautiful silver milk jug on her breakfast tray.

Easter week marked the end of their spring. The weather turned deceptively sultry and Stella, always imprudent, tore off her scarf as they drove out into the country, although an icy wind still swept down from the Pyrenees. When she got back, she had caught a cold. Nothing serious, so she took no precautions. By Good Friday she had bronchitis. Despite the war, Pau still had a capable doctor—he suggested suppositories and an injection. "I *won't* have people sticking things into me that I don't know about," Stella protested indignantly. "Besides, you alter the dose when it suits you, don't you, Doctor?"

The weather then turned around: Stella's large, high bedroom grew dark and chill. She became restless, insisted Claudius telegraph her daughter, Gerald Murphy, and Gielgud. She complained she wanted a change of air, and Claudius dutifully went to see what arrangements she could make in St. Jean de Luz, even though all the hotels Stella would have liked were closed. When she returned on Friday, March 29, she was met by Denise, the French poet, who said gravely, "I don't think Mrs. Campbell will be able to move." Claudius found Stella in high spirits, but her flushed cheeks signalled a temperature of 104 degrees. She could not be kept under the bedclothes; she was reciting poetry and needed her hands. Dr. Aris shook his head. "She is going to be a difficult patient. Why won't she let me give her an injection?"

Next morning she insisted she was better. She sat up in bed in her cowl-necked nightdress, her tangled hair falling about her shoulders, and in a high, young voice began to recite the balcony scene from *Romeo and Juliet*. Claudius's eyes filled with tears. How could she possibly look after her?— and Stella had no more idea of how to look after herself than if she had really been a young girl of fourteen. Again Egypt telegraphed Stella Beech in London. The reply was cool: her mother had the constitution of a horse, and in any case no one was free to come; there was a war on—one must not cry wolf in the midst of war. Claudius opened the message on the day the doctor diagnosed *congestion pulmonaire*. Madame's condition was grave. She must go to a hospital.

But Pau in wartime was not equipped for such emergencies. The only modern nursing home was booked full of maternity cases; the hospital looked like the Bastille. She could not be moved to Paris. The only thing was a nurse. An ancient crone from the First World War—or was it the Crimea?—turned up, full of goodwill. Claudius engaged her.

"Oh, Egypt, how *could* you? She's so *ugly!*" whimpered Stella. But there was nobody else. Claudius herself took the night shift.

And then, in response to the notice in the local paper, a charming little fuzzy-haired woman appeared at the hotel, a fully trained nurse on leave, and very sympathetic to the idea of nursing an actress. "Sarah Bernhardt was my godmother," said Madame Lescaux. Claudius took her to Stella at once; the old crone disappeared. "I acted with your godmother long ago," Stella told her happily. "I still have the telegram she sent me on the day her leg was amputated. . . . You won't find me less brave than she was."

Stella had never slept well; now she slept hardly at all. During the long vigils by her bedside Claudius began to realize what an incredibly lonely life she had led. Acting was all she had had, and she who had been so essentially of the theatre had had to live out her old age without it. Now she called out—not to the dukes and duchesses and the earls and the countesses whom she had once adored, but to her own people: to Tree and Forbes, Gerald and Joey, Gielgud and Barrie, Ellen and Sarah. She talked to them all as though Claudius were not there. It was not delirium, thought Egypt. Her hot hands pulled at the sheets, and when Claudius tried to still them and cover her, she thrust her away, threw off the bedclothes as though they would suffocate her, and once more called for Joey and Barrie and Tree.

A Madame Boudouresque came as night nurse. She knew her job, but Stella's money could not cover her wages. Desperate, Claudius leafed through Stella's address book and telegraphed Gerald Murphy in New York. He wired a sum immediately, but the bank informed Claudius that the money had been sent in Stella's name. A bank clerk arrived at the *pension* with the paper for her to sign. Madame was in fever, he was told, bordering on delirium; but nothing but Stella's signature would do. They put her spectacles on her nose, they tried to make her hand grasp the pen. She kept dropping it, she could not see the dotted line. She wept and tore at her nightgown in distress as she tried futilely to scrawl the famous dashing signature. They tried to guide her hand. *"C'est impossible,"* said Madame Boudouresque. But the bank demanded her signature and would accept nothing less. Egypt had not the presence of mind to practise an innocent forgery.

On Wednesday, April 3, the directress of the *pension* made it clear that all bills must be settled when delivered.

"What shall we do?" Claudius asked the doctor.

"It's almost as though she doesn't want to live," he said. She had been drinking a little champagne. Claudius must go out and buy more; perhaps it would disguise the pills she refused to swallow. But the glass grew tepid by Stella's bedside; she had tasted something peculiar, and now she glared at Claudius as though she too had joined the conspiracy against her.

Then the bird came. "What's that bird doing in here—that *bird!*" Stella cried in pain and high fever, cowering as though she heard the beating of wings. Claudius tried to frighten it away, but it came back. There were faces too—angry faces—the powers of darkness massed against her in every corner of the night. She fought against them, tearing her nightgown in distress. Then suddenly she would become very quiet. Was someone near her? wondered Claudius. Beo, her beloved son, whose death she had never, never gotten over? His silver-tipped cane stood against the wall. She would not use it again.

On April 4 Claudius sat down to answer Jane Curtis's letters. "I am writing for Stella Campbell. She is very ill alas, & cannot write answers to your 2 lovely letters. She would like to, but it just isn't possible. She has pneumonia or rather, inflamation of the left lung. And she refuses the medicines & piqûre so it *is* hard to treat her, but we are doing everything possible. I have wired her family & Mr. Murphy in New York. I do not know what else to do except have a very good doctor come in twice a day, 2 good nurses one day, one night—and take care of her to the limit of my strength too. She is in great pain and is terribly weak. But she loved your letters & thinks you so wonderful to do so much, while she has to lie there in her bed—with Moonbeam sitting on it. Forgive a note, we are very busy." On April 7 she sent another telegram to Stella Beech.

On the morning of April 8 the doctor took Claudius aside. "There is nothing more to do," he said. "It's a question of hours. You should let her family know." But, face to face with the dark bird at last, Stella fought back desperately. Now she called for the doctor, now she begged for an injection. He gave her camphor for her heart, but said to Claudius, "Too late, I fear."

A second check arrived from Gerald Murphy, this time in Claudius's name. Word somehow had got out that Mrs. Patrick Campbell was dying: the phone jangled with calls from the Paris press. But it was all too late. As Shaw had said, she was not a great general: she did not plan, but relied on last-minute inspiration. Now there was no more. As the day faded, they knew the struggle was almost over. Stella lay in semi-consciousness on the bed, Moonbeam huddled against her. Claudius waited with the two nurses, who would not leave, counting seconds, minutes, hours. It was past midnight when suddenly in the half-light she felt the unmistakable flash of a wing through the room. As it passed, she instinctively jumped to her feet and drew her hand through the air over Stella's head. Stella lay very still. Moonbeam told them it was over. His tears fell onto her sheet and he clambered crookedly off the bed.

Madame Boudouresque plaited the heavy black hair into a shining coronet and dressed her in a black velvet gown embroidered in crimson and gold. She tucked cotton wool in the mouth to preserve its lovely shape. The doctor who came to certify the death in the morning insisted that the woman lying on the bed could be no more than fifty-five. Only when Claudius showed him Stella's passport would he certify that Beatrice Stella Tanner, spouse of George Cornwallis-West, had died at the age of seventy-five on the ninth of April 1940 at Pau.

The next day they took her in a very simple oak coffin to the little English church, where a small group of friends from the *pension* watched through the night. Stella would have scoffed. "All this nonsense about people sitting up two nights to make a pall," she had told Gielgud at Ellen Terry's funeral in 1928. "When I die, I shall tell them to put me on a pyre on the seashore and Stella can put a match to me." Claudius used Gerald Murphy's money to buy a small plot in the Cimetière Urbain with ten years' upkeep. Though far from England, it faced the beautiful Pyrenees. The service was very simple. The clergyman knew only that he was burying a Mrs. West—and, indeed, Stella's death certificate had stated *"sans profession."* The British actor Matheson Lang, happening to be in Pau, sent a wreath. Claudius threw rosebuds as the strangely small coffin was lowered, saying, "These are from your great-grandchildren, Jennifer and Angela Beatrice Rose." There was no stone to weigh her down—there was not enough money—and Claudius was glad anyway: Stella had fought so hard in her illness to be free. Let others place a stone, later. She told the sexton to plant blue-purple violas and Peke-faced pansies on the grave. "In any case, the ground must settle, Mademoiselle," he murmured, "but give me her name so I can mark the place...."

And then she remembered Moonbeam. She could not take him back to face quarantine in England—Stella would haunt her forever. Gerald Murphy had wired her to ship him at once to New York, but how could she get him from Pau to Cherbourg in wartime and make sure he really caught the boat? She thought furiously, but it seemed hopeless. And then:

"I shall always believe that it was Stella herself who came back to attend to this piece of unfinished business. For the next day without warning the practical night nurse, dressed in her best, came to see me. She opened a large leather bag and took out a snapshot of a fox terrier."

"Perhaps you don't know," said Madame Boudouresque, "but I'm really retired. I only take on cases when they really interest me. To nurse Madame was one thing—but I shall do very little more. This was my companion—an English dog. When he died I never wished for another.... But, as you may have seen, Moonbeam did not snap at me. Perhaps he would like to come and live with me?"

"Shall we see how he feels about it?" said Claudius cautiously, mindful that Moonbeam's temper was almost as uncertain as his mistress's.

A week later Claudius returned to Pau unannounced and paid a visit to Madame Boudouresque. There in the sunny garden was Moonbeam, bathed at last, his eyes bright, his tail hoisted like a white plume. "I promise you," said Madame, "that if the war reaches Pau and we are rationed here, I will share my meat with him. He shall have the best mutton chops; even lamb, if I can get it." And so, satisfied that Stella would have been satisfied, Claudius left him kinging it over the little French garden.

The war did not reach Pau. In the distance the Pyrenees gleamed white, the sexton planted the violas and pansies, Moonbeam played in the garden, and Stella, reunited with the company she had called for, slept at last.

# *Epilogue*

STELLA'S FAMILY was not as indifferent as it seemed. Patrick Beech, lance corporal in a volunteer territorial organization at Bristol, applied for compassionate leave in order to visit his ailing grandmother, got it, came up to London; but was stopped there on his way to Pau by the German invasion of Denmark and Norway and the imminent invasion of France.

Stella Beech made no attempt to contact her mother, however. There was between them, said Patrick, a fundamental quarrel. Opinion about Stella Beech is quite consistent. Cynthia Asquith thought her profile astonishingly lovely and her conversation trite. Bernard Shaw advised her to rid herself of excessive ladylikeness by descending the stairs every morning before breakfast standing on her hands. Stella Moore Coltman-Rogers found her rigid, with "a vein of steel." Sir John Gielgud calls her "dull and not a good actress." Patrick Beech recognized that the stage was important to her because it allowed her to release emotion that she stifled in private life. Joe Mitchenson, an actor when she taught at R.A.D.A. in the thirties, is an exception in considering her a good teacher, a better actress than her mother, and a witty woman. Clearly, the daughter suffered from the mother's dominating personality and middle-class sense of propriety, as well as from her obvious preference for her son.

At any rate, Agnes Claudius was left to deal with the winding up of Stella's affairs alone. She had kept precise accounts of all expenses incurred while nursing Stella—oranges, ice, champagne, rubber sheet, backrest, medicines; she also made note of all monies received. Some of the final details proved ludicrous. A local corset-maker arrived with a mystifying pink satin object made to Stella's specifications. No one else would buy it: Claudius must. Then the tailor demanded full payment for the brown suit. Claudius felt the fittings had not gone far enough, however, and finally called in the British Vice-Consul to negotiate a settlement.

Then instructions arrived from Stella Beech that she was to preserve the

Shaw correspondence, but give everything else away. Claudius did not obey these orders. She packed Stella's papers and typewriter in the tin box, and some books, a few bibelots, pictures, lamps, and hand-made lamp covers in a carton and sent them *petite vitesse* by rail, Pau-Boulogne-London—the only form of transportation she could afford. She never saw either box again.

Before the *scellés* were affixed to the door, she took from Stella's room—along with Moonbeam—Stella's wallet, passport, and a little cream georgette bag that held the remnants of her jewelry: the Pekin and baroque pearl rings, a marquise ring depicting a little griffon dog, a Jason brooch, a rope of inexpensive pearls. She also took, of course, the black hatbox containing the letters. These she would carry back personally to London. She informed Gerald Murphy of Moonbeam's whereabouts ("One cannot think of them apart, even in death," Gielgud told her approvingly), and evaded the landlady's request for money on the plea that she would have to redecorate Madame's room.

In his diary Shaw recorded in shorthand Stella's death on the ninth. With the exception of the deaths of Charlotte and her sister, Stella's was the only death of a personal nature that he would note. When Stella Beech appealed to him for help, he promptly sent her £100, which she sent to Agnes Claudius to pay for her mother's burial and Claudius's fare home. Shaw subsequently tore up her small checks toward repayment as they arrived, reassuring her when years later she discovered the generous deception: "You must not feel distressed about what you call your debt: you have paid it honorably to the uttermost farthing. But I had my rights and duties in the matter too. I was her best friend: you were only her daughter, a whole generation removed. It was for me, not for you, to render first aid. So everything is just as it should be."

Eventually Claudius got to Paris and went to the Ministère de l'Air, which promised to find her a place on a plane, although it could not say when. She waited in war-confused Paris until May 4, then flew to Gatwick, and finally put up in a quiet hotel just behind the gardens of Buckingham Palace.

There in the following days, as Germany invaded Holland and Belgium, she began to sort Stella's papers. She panicked to find one of the famous Shaw letters missing, sighed in relief when she found a copy and a note in Stella's hand saying she had sold it to Gerald Murphy. Notes came from Gielgud, Edith Lyttelton, Stella's dressmaker, Stella Beech, and Shaw's secretary saying he would see her on his return to London. Then she was summoned to the offices of Stella's lawyer, B. F. Guedalla, of Bartlett and Gluckstein in Piccadilly, where she turned over her accounts, the French documents, and the little georgette bag. She was told she must hand over the letters to Stella's daughter.

Calling first on Edith Lyttelton in Great College Street, she returned the beautiful fern-traced compact, a gift from D.D., that Stella had loved, and presented her with a photograph of Stella in black velvet. She found Mrs. Lyttelton as stately as a Tudor carving and much kinder than she had any right to expect. At Madame Handley Seymour's she found an early portrait of Stella installed in the place of honor. Sipping madeira, she heard Madame tell of her love for the beautiful actress and how she had never tried to dress her in the fashion of the day, but rather in the sumptuous velvets and furs that enhanced her glamour. Then Chris Castor, who had toured with Stella for eighteen months, came to tell her how "practical and exacting a professional Stella had been; contrary-minded and hard to follow, but always intrinsically right." Of course, she had been totally uninhibited, and some actors had found her outspokenness hard; but Chris was uninhibited in her admiration of Stella. And Claudius met the faithful Morrie, who, she knew, would have handled things so much better than she in Pau.

Then she went to see Shaw in Whitehall Court, very uncomfortable, remembering how he had refused money in those last years and said he would rather bring the devil over to England than Stella Campbell. She found the eighty-four-year-old Shaw springy, alert, pink-cheeked, dressed in impeccable tweeds; she also found him charming. He seemed moved when she told him how Stella had called so often for Joey during long, sleepless nights. He promised her that the grave at Pau would be maintained in perpetuity. As for the letters, he'd said it a hundred times: the paper they were written on belonged to Stella's family; the copyright was his; they would not be published during Charlotte's lifetime.

Claudius studied him as he spoke. "Of course, Egypt," Stella had said one night as she lay in bed, "everyone wanted to know whether we'd tucked up together—as if it mattered." Looking at the spry, virginal Shaw, Claudius knew that "tucking up" had never been a part of that love game. Did he sense her thoughts? He could not resist a sudden dig. Cornwallis-West had told him that once Stella had almost run him off a balcony and that he had all but jumped to escape her wrath—"a balcony like this one," said Shaw, pointing. At this moment the door opened and a presence made itself felt even before a gray head appeared unobtrusively and a soft voice said, "Luncheon." Suddenly Shaw began to jeer. Stella had been so proud of her father because he'd been in government service, but "He was in the *customs*, you know," said Shaw, as though Mr. Tanner had been in haberdashery. And then for *Pygmalion*, "We had to nail the furniture to the stage, you know, during the rehearsals; she would swish it upstage with her as she went, and change all the other actors' positions by it!"

Yes, thought Claudius; and yet he had got Cleopatra and Mrs. Juno and Hesione Hushabye and the Serpent and Orinthia and Eliza out of her. He had been magnetized by her as a critic, yet he had sent her a letter after the dress rehearsal of *Pygmalion* that a graduate of R.A.D.A. in her first part wouldn't accept today. It was as though he could not admit how much he admired her, even while he talked of her, talked of her. But in the air was that spoken word "Luncheon" and, realizing that she was not to meet Charlotte, Claudius rose to go. Shaw courteously escorted her to the lift and waited until it came. He spoke of Stella's great-grandchildren. The letters would eventually bring them money for their schooling.

Carrying the hatbox, she paid her final visit—to Stella Beech in Vicarage Court. She did not at all know what to expect, although they had corresponded. The woman of fifty-three who opened the door was as tall as Stella herself, dark-haired, handsome. But the presence, thought Claudius, the tremendous vitality of Stella was not there at all. Stella Beech was kind, fair, and patient, but withdrawn, detached—an Iseult seen through carved glass. She took the letters, some papers, a photograph or two for the grandchildren, then handed back the hatbox with the rest of its contents. Her mother's furnishings would be sold at auction. She would like Miss Claudius to have some of them, but they had to be sold by the executors; they would let her know when the sale took place. Claudius said goodbye; a few days later a gracious note from Stella Beech arrived enclosing a miniature painted by Henry Tanner of the favorite griffon, Pinkie Panky Poo.

On Tuesday, April 16, a week after her death, there had been a memorial service for Stella at Holy Trinity in Sloane Street. The verse on the cover of the memorial program was from Dante:

> Una donna soletta che si gia
> E cantando e scegliendo fior da fiore
> Ond' era pinta tutta la sua vita.*

John Gielgud, exhausted from his first night of *Lear* at the Old Vic, read the lesson to friends and admirers. Gielgud also paid tribute to the actress he had loved and admired in a letter to the *Times*: ". . . I hope that she will be remembered by the public not only as the legendary figure of comedy—the deep-voiced prima donna uttering brilliant witticisms, and driving authors

---

* A lady who all alone and singing went,/ And as she sang plucked flowers that numberless/ All round about her path their colours blent.

and managers to despair—but also as the generous, warm-hearted, creative artist, shrewdly critical, passionately fond of beauty and eager to find it wherever she might be. As with all really great artists, it was a joy to see her move and hear her speak. On the stage she expressed poetry with every gesture of her hands, and the objects which she touched in playing a scene suddenly seemed to gain immediate significance and life. A curiously complex sense of humour seemed to disturb her concentration, and tempt her in later life to a perverse desire to clown in a serious part and to wish to find tragic opportunities in a comic one. But in some lectures which she gave in London not many years ago, when she held the stage alone for over an hour, speaking wisely and wittily about acting, and giving many wonderful excerpts from her famous parts, she showed to many of those who loved her a beauty and a mystery which I for one will never forget. 'There's a great spirit gone.' "

The day before the memorial service to his dead wife, George Cornwallis-West had married Georgette Hirsch, the wealthy widow he had courted since 1929. He was sixty-six, still dabbling in writing, living at good addresses, belonging to good clubs, and, as Stella had always put it, passionately murdering birds. Eleven years later in 1951, sitting up in bed recovering from an illness, he took his own life with his shotgun.

Never willing or able to ransom George, Stella died insolvent, though nearly all her debts were subsequently paid by the sale of her possessions. Agnes Claudius attended the auction, hoping to buy some of Stella's prompt books, but could not afford to make many bids. She came away with Mrs. Wyndham's cast of Stella's lovely hand, telegrams and letters concerning *Pelléas*, and the typescript of a Maurice Baring play Stella had meant to perform. She did not know what happened to the costumes, the Burne-Jones letters, the Beardsley and Beerbohm drawings, the dozens of other precious possessions. A theatre patron, Gabriella Enthoven, bought up numerous prompt books to donate them eventually to the Victoria and Albert Museum. All of Claudius's bids on the furniture were too low: "Stella's taste was completely vindicated. For myself I wept—till I remembered how Stella herself had for years wandered without her belongings from hotel to hotel and yet had managed to make every room a mirror of her own personality." Eventually the setting for the marquise ring arrived in the little georgette bag, another kind gesture from Stella Beech; for the next twenty years they went everywhere with Claudius. In 1943 another sale of Stella's belongings at Sotheby's gave her a chance to buy copies of Stella's theatrical agreements, which she in turn donated to the Victoria and Albert.

As for the letters, Stella's copyright and interest in them were held in trust until the eventual income from publishing could be paid to Stella and

Patrick Beech or their survivors. ". . . AND IT IS MY DESIRE," Stella had declared in her will, ". . . that the Bernard Shaw letters and poems which are now in the custody of the Westminster Bank be published in their proper sequence and not cut or altered in any way, that they should be published in an independent volume to be entitled 'The Love Letters of Bernard Shaw to Mrs. Patrick Campbell' so all who may read them will realise that the friendship was 'L'amitié amoureuse.' . . ." She did not think hers worth publication: "My letters are worth 2*d.*—yours 50 quid," she had told Shaw.

In October 1943 Shaw invited Patrick Beech to visit him at Whitehall Court. Beech found him a hale eighty-seven, but a recent widower: Charlotte had died the previous month. Shaw now wanted to square the matter of the letters. He had been very much in love with Mrs. Campbell, he told Beech; she was as charming and irresistible as she was temperamental and difficult, and fond of telling him he was "no gentleman." He thought of her as a mixture of Italian nobility and English middle-class, each side predominating in turn. Of course, they had never been intimate "in the technical sense." He'd always told her to sell George, but knew she never gave up hoping that he would come back to her. When he'd told that to George, George had declared that, given the choice of going back or jumping out a fifth-floor window, he would choose the window. As for his letters, Shaw intended to settle the copyright in them for the benefit of Beech's daughters, Jennifer and Angela. He had not been able to make the arrangements before because Charlotte knew the contents of his will; and he had suffered so much for his infatuation for Stella Campbell that he would never remind Charlotte of it under any circumstances. Now, however, he was writing a new will, and the gift of copyright he had always promised Stella would be made.

Stella's and Shaw's letters were finally published in 1952 (following Shaw's death in 1950) as *Bernard Shaw and Mrs. Patrick Campbell: Their Correspondence*. It was not the title she had wanted, yet it was fairer to herself. Alan Dent, secretary to James Agate, was the official editor. Actually, the letters were edited by Stella Beech, who had no trouble deciphering her mother's impatient handwriting, who had the knowledge to provide headnotes to the letters, and who at any rate wished to suppress numerous passages and letters, some of which were never shown Dent. She was finally persuaded to cut comparatively little, chiefly portions dealing with Cornwallis-West and some dalliance she thought subject to misinterpretation. The correspondence received as wide attention as Stella could have desired and Shaw feared. While she did not emerge with a halo like Ellen Terry's, she proved she could hold her own against a master of English prose with spirit and aplomb, even while he branded her "a Monster of illiteracy." But, as Shaw had said, the best that passed between them had been immediate and *viva voce*.

Two years before publication of the correspondence, in November 1950, a few people gathered at 33 Kensington Square for the unveiling of a plaque bearing the legend "MRS. PATRICK CAMPBELL 1865–1940 ACTRESS LIVED HERE." "I am so dreadfully distressed to know you are still in London and could have come to 33 on Saturday," wrote actor Ernest Thesiger, responsible for the tribute, to Helen Spinola, who had attended both Cornwallis-West's marriage to Georgette Hirsch and the memorial service for Stella the next day. ". . . I had the greatest difficulty in tracing people who ought to have been there, and 'little Stella' only got my letter after many readdressings, as I didn't know where she was either. However, some of the old friends turned up and I am most pleased that there is at least some recognition of the fact that a very great actress lived in that dear little house."

Agnes Claudius did not forget Stella, but began to collect material and contact people for a biography of the woman she had known briefly but well. She also worried about Stella's grave: Shaw had promised her he would purchase the plot in perpetuity, but when she contacted his former secretary, Blanche Patch, she did not remember Shaw having given any instructions. "I cannot ask Mrs. Beech or Pat Beech," Claudius told Nancy Price, "—they have given strict instructions that I am never to be mentioned in connection with Stella." A biography was finally brought out in 1961 by Alan Dent, a compilation of stage facts, quotations from Stella's autobiography, and anecdotes from people who had known her. Although Claudius claimed she had answered Dent's plea with a long letter detailing the last months of Stella's life, Dent barely acknowledged her. Again, when Jerome Kilty made a successful play out of the correspondence, Claudius was hurt at lack of recognition: she credited herself with having saved the letters from destruction at Pau. "Jerry had taken my name out of his 'Dear Liar' play based on the letters, in obedience to the Beech family," she told Nancy Price; "that too had shaken me—not from the publicity point of view, don't misunderstand me, but because until then their animosity against me was something no one had told me about." Whatever the source of that animosity (if it did exist) and whatever her potential skills as a biographer, Claudius's notes and letters in the Enthoven Collection suggest that she was genuinely interested in Stella Campbell as an artist.

It is an artistry that is lost except as words have the power to evoke it. The debate about the greatness of Mrs. Patrick Campbell persists. Does she rank with Bernhardt and Duse? Some do not think so; some do; others say that whenever she wanted to, she did. "In my life I have seen six great actresses," said James Agate, who neither used the adjective often nor misapplied it, "and six only. These are Bernhardt, Réjane, Mrs. Kendal, Ellen Terry, Duse, and Mrs. Patrick Campbell." Desmond MacCarthy, on the other hand, believed that she wilfully destroyed her chance of being ranked with the greatest by refusing to act when she did not feel like it. Still, he admitted her power. "What was most remarkable was her personal magnetism, and the extraordinary ease and grace with which she achieved her effects. Byron once compared himself to a tiger which if it missed its spring went back growling to its den. Her spring was magnificent, but with her, too, it was hit or miss. She could be piteous and—at moments—tender; she could be magnificently fierce, crushingly insolent, and also enchantingly mocking. She could open the door of dreams." Ivor Brown suggested both her limitation and her strength: "Her acting best suited plays of stormy weather. It had a tremendous emotional ground-swell. . . . I have never forgotten her performance of Hedda Gabler at the Everyman's Theatre in 1922. The size and flame of her acting consumed that humble temple utterly." Yet there was hardly a critic who had not raged at the way she could deliberately, mockingly, throw away a whole scene or act when the mood took her, just as there was hardly a critic who could resist her when she chose to act.

No one was more conscious than Stella herself of the ephemeral quality of her art. Although she deplored Shaw's confidence that every word he wrote was destined for the British Museum, she envied the permanence of his achievement. "I shall go down as a footnote to your life," she prophesied. The source of their professional quarrel was just that: Shaw as writer wanted an empty head for his words to fill; Stella as an actress wanted to create from his words something personal of her own.

It is perhaps the fundamental quarrel between playwright and actor. At her best, Stella Campbell won the struggle and triumphed as an actress whose greatness, emerging paradoxically through the words of others, has not totally been lost.

# Selected Bibliography

MY MAJOR SOURCE for this biography has been Beatrice Stella Campbell's own letters and memoirs. Part of this material is published: *My Life and Some Letters* (1922) and *Bernard Shaw and Mrs. Patrick Campbell: Their Correspondence*, edited by Alan Dent (1952). Unpublished memoirs, letters, and acting notes are listed here in order of importance to this biography: (1) The Tanner Collection, containing approximately 115 letters from Stella Campbell to her sister Louisa Tanner, 122 letters addressed to either Louisa or Stella from family and friends, and miscellaneous diary fragments, clippings, certificates, etc. (Margot Peters); (2) *Chance Medley* (originally titled *Random Reminiscences*), a memoir written in 1935 dealing chiefly with Stella's Hollywood experiences (Burgunder Shaw Collection, Cornell University Library); (3) Stella's annotated prompt books: *Bella Donna, Beyond Human Power, The Canary, Electra, The Joy of Living, Lady Patricia, Magda, The Masqueraders, Mr. and Mrs. Daventry, The Notorious Mrs. Ebbsmith, Pelléas and Mélisande, Pygmalion, The Second Mrs. Tanqueray, The Thirteenth Chair* (Enthoven Collection, Museum of London), and *Deirdre* (with Yeats's alterations when Stella played the part at the Abbey Theatre in 1908), *Fedora, Hedda Gabler, Little Eyolf* (Stella as Rita Allmers), Anastasia's part in *The Matriarch, Pelléas et Mélisande* (the 1904–1905 production with Sarah Bernhardt), *The Second Mrs. Tanqueray* (copied from the St. James's Theatre production for the first American tour, 1902), and *Undine* (Patrick Beech); (4) unpublished letters from Stella to Bernard Shaw (Frederick R. Koch Collection, Harvard Theatre Collection), Edith Lyttelton (Churchill College Library, Cambridge), Agnes Claudius (Burgunder Shaw Collection, Cornell University Library), Mrs. Jane Curtis (Frances Tompkins), George R. Sims (Hoblitzelle Theatre Arts Collection, Humanities Research Center, University of Texas at Austin), Frederick Witney (Houghton Library, Harvard University), Gilbert Murray (Bodleian Library, Oxford), Harriett Carolan (Regenstein Library, University of Chicago), and Arthur Bertram (Burgunder Shaw Collection, Cornell University Library); (5) three brief scenarios for films written by Stella during the Hollywood years.

Also of great value to this biography were Agnes Claudius's unpublished memoir, *The Death of the "dearest Liar"* by "Claude Vincent" and the notes she made during the days of Stella's last illness (Burgunder Shaw Collection, Cornell University Library); the originals of Bernard Shaw's letters to Stella (in the Special Collections of the University Libraries, State University of New York at Buffalo); Dame Edith Lyttelton's letters to Bernard Shaw (British Library); and the clipping files of the Enthoven Collection, Museum of London; the Harvard Theatre Collection; the Billy Rose Theatre Collection at the Performing Arts Research Center, Lincoln Center, New York; and the Theatre Collection of the Free Library of Philadelphia.

Agate, James. *Buzz, Buzz! Essays of the Theatre.* London: Collins, 1918; reprnt. New York: Benjamin Blom, 1969.

————. *Ego 7: Even More of the Autobiography of James Agate.* London: George G. Harrap, 1945.

Archer, William. *The Theatrical "World" of 1893–1897.* 5 vols. London: Walter Scott, 1894–98.

Arliss, George. *On the Stage: An Autobiography.* London: John Murray, 1928.

Asquith, Lady Cynthia. *Diaries: 1915–1918.* London: Hutchinson, 1968.

Baring, Maurice. *The Puppet Show of Memory.* London: Heinemann, 1922.

Barnes, Eric Wollencott. *The Man Who Lived Twice: The Biography of Edward Sheldon.* New York: Scribner, 1956.

Barrie, Sir James M. *Letters of J. M. Barrie.* Edited Viola Meynell. London: Peter Davies, 1942.

Beaton, Cecil. *The Wandering Years: Diaries 1922–1939.* London: Weidenfeld and Nicolson, 1961.

Beerbohm, Sir Max. *Around Theatres.* London: Rupert Hart-Davis, 1953.

————. *Last Theatres: 1904–1910.* New York: Taplinger Publishing Company, 1970.

————. *More Theatres: 1898–1903.* London: Rupert-Hart-Davis, 1969.

————. *Sir Max Beerbohm: Letters to Reggie Turner.* Edited Rupert Hart-Davis. London: Rupert Hart-Davis, 1964.

Behrman, S. N. *Conversations with Max.* London: Hamish Hamilton, 1960.

Bennett, Arnold. *The Journal of Arnold Bennett.* New York: Literary Guild, 1933.

————. *Letters of Arnold Bennett.* Edited James Hepburn. Vol. III. London: Oxford University Press, 1970.

Brown, John Mason. *Seeing Things.* New York: McGraw-Hill, 1946.

Campbell, Beatrice Stella. *My Life and Some Letters.* London: Hutchinson; New York: Dodd, Mead, 1922.

Cecil, Lord David. *Max Beerbohm.* London: Constable, 1965.

Channon, Sir Henry. *Chips: The Diaries of Sir Henry Channon.* Edited Robert Rhodes James. London: Weidenfeld and Nicolson, 1967.

Cooper, Diana. *The Rainbow Comes and Goes.* London: Rupert Hart-Davis, 1958.

Cornwallis-West, George. *Edwardian Hey-Days.* London: G. P. Putnam's Sons, 1931.

Coward, Noel. *Present Indicative.* Garden City, N.Y.: Doubleday, 1937.

Dean, Basil. *Seven Ages.* London: Hutchinson, 1970.

Dent, Alan. *Mrs. Patrick Campbell.* London: Museum Press, 1961.

Du Maurier, Daphne. *Gerald: A Portrait.* New York: Doubleday, Doran, 1935.

Edel, Leon. *Henry James: The Treacherous Years.* Philadelphia: Lippincott, 1969.

Edgar, George. *Martin Harvey: Some Pages of His Life.* London: Grant Richards, 1912.

Farmer, Henry George. *Bernard Shaw's Sister and Her Friends.* Leiden: E. J. Brill, 1959.

Forbes-Robertson, Diana. *My Aunt Maxine: The Story of Maxine Elliott.* New York: Viking, 1964.

Forbes-Robertson. Sir Johnston. *A Player Under Three Reigns.* Boston: Little, Brown, 1925.

Ford, Ford Madox. *Provence.* Philadelphia: J. B. Lippincott, 1935.

Gielgud, Sir John. *An Actor and His Time.* With John Miller and John Powell. London: Sidgwick and Jackson, 1979.

————. *Distinguished Company.* London: Heinemann, 1972.

————. *Early Stages.* London: Heinemann, 1974 (first published 1939).

Gregory, Lady. *Seventy Years: Being the Autobiography of Lady Gregory.* Edited Colin Smythe. Gerrards Cross: Colin Smythe, 1973.

Gwynn, Stephen Lucius. *Experiences of a Literary Man.* London: Thornton Butterworth, 1926.

Hapgood, Norman. *The Changing Years: Reminiscences of Norman Hapgood.* New York: Farrar and Rinehart, 1930.

Hardwicke, Sir Cedric. *A Victorian in Orbit: The Irreverent Memories of Sir Cedric Hardwicke.* As told to James Brough. Garden City, N.Y.: Doubleday, 1961.

Holloway, Joseph. *Joseph Holloway's Abbey Theatre.* Edited Robert Hogan and Michael O'Neill. Carbondale: Southern Illinois University Press, 1967.

Isaac, Winifred. *Ben Greet and the Old Vic: A Biography of Sir Philip Ben Greet.* Published by the author, printed London: The Greenbank Press, 1964[?].

Jones, Doris Arthur. *Life and Letters of Henry Arthur Jones.* London: Victor Gollancz, 1930.

Leslie, Anita. *Clare Sheridan.* Garden City, N.Y.: Doubleday, 1977.

MacCarthy, Desmond. *The Court Theatre 1904–1907: A Commentary and Criticism.* London: A. H. Bullen, 1907.

————. *Portraits.* London: G. P. Putnam's Sons, 1931; reprnt. MacGibbon and Kee, 1955.

Mackail, Denis. *Barrie: The Story of J.M.B.* New York: Scribner, 1941.

Maltby, H. F. *Ring Up the Curtain.* London: Hutchinson, 1950.

Mander, Raymond, and Joe Mitchenson. *Lost Theatres of London.* London: New English Library, 1976.

Marcosson, Isaac F., and Daniel Frohman. *Charles Frohman: Manager and Man.* New York: Harper, 1916.

Martin, Ralph G. *Jennie: The Life of Lady Randolph Churchill.* 2 vols. Englewood Cliffs, N.J.: Prentice-Hall, 1971.

Mason, A. E. W. *Sir George Alexander and the St. James' Theatre.* London: Macmillan, 1935; reprnt. New York: Benjamin Blom, 1969.

Maude, Cyril. *Behind the Scenes with Cyril Maude by Himself.* London: John Murray, 1927.

Middleton, George. *These Things Are Mine.* New York: Macmillan, 1947.

Moore, Colleen. *Silent Star.* Garden City, N.Y.: Doubleday, 1968.

Morley, Sheridan. *Gladys Cooper: A Biography.* London: Heinemann, 1979.

Mount, Charles Merrill. *John Singer Sargent.* New York: Norton, 1955.

Murray, Gilbert. *An Unfinished Autobiography.* Edited Jean Smith, Arnold Toynbee. London: Allen and Unwin, 1960.

Nathan, George Jean. *Art of the Night.* New York: Alfred A. Knopf, 1928; reprnt. Fairleigh Dickinson University Press, 1972.

Noble, Peter. *Ivor Novello: Man of the Theatre.* London: Falcon Press, 1951.

Orme, Michael. *J. T. Grein: The Story of a Pioneer: 1862–1935.* London: John Murray, 1936.

Pearson, Hesketh. *Beerbohm Tree: His Life and Laughter.* New York: Harper, 1956.

————. *The Last Actor-Managers.* London: Methuen, 1950.

Peters, Margot. *Bernard Shaw and the Actresses.* Garden City, N.Y.: Doubleday, 1980.

Phelps, William Lyon. *Autobiography with Letters.* New York: Oxford University Press, 1939.

Pinero, Sir Arthur. *The Collected Letters of Sir Arthur Pinero.* Edited J. P. Wearing. Minneapolis: The University of Minnesota Press, 1974.

Robertson, W. Graham. *Time Was.* London: Hamish Hamilton, 1955 (first published 1931).

————. *Letters from Graham Robertson.* Edited Kerrison Preston. London: Hamish Hamilton, 1953.

Robins, Elizabeth. *Theatre and Friendship.* New York: G. P. Putnam's Sons, 1932.

Rothenstein, Sir William. *Men and Memories.* New York: Tudor, n.d.

Rueff, Suze. *I Knew Sarah Bernhardt.* London: Frederick Muller, 1951.

Shaw, Bernard. *Collected Letters.* 2 vols. Edited Dan H. Laurence. London: Max Reinhardt, 1965, 1972.

————. *Our Theatres in the Nineties*. 3 vols. London: Constable, 1931.

————, and Beatrice Stella Campbell. *Bernard Shaw and Mrs. Patrick Campbell: Their Correspondence*. Edited Alan Dent. London: Victor Gollancz; New York: Alfred A. Knopf, 1952.

Sitwell, Osbert. *Laughter in the Next Room*. London: Macmillan, 1949.

Spinola, Helen. *Nothing But the Truth*. London: Victor Gollancz, 1961.

Terry, Ellen, and Bernard Shaw. *Ellen Terry and Bernard Shaw: A Correspondence*. Edited Christopher St. John. New York: G. P. Putnam's Sons, 1932.

Tyler, George C. *Whatever Goes Up: The Hazardous Fortunes of a Natural Born Gambler*. Indianapolis: Bobbs-Merrill, 1934.

Wearing, J. P., ed. *The London Stage: A Calendar of Plays and Players*. 4 vols. Metuchen, N.J.: The Scarecrow Press, 1976, 1981.

Webster, Margaret. *The Same Only Different: Five Generations of a Great Theatre Family*. New York: Alfred A. Knopf, 1969.

Wharton, Edith. *A Backward Glance*. New York: Scribner, 1964 (first published 1934).

Wilde, Oscar. *The Letters of Oscar Wilde*. Edited Rupert Hart-Davis. London: Rupert Hart-Davis, 1962.

Winter, William. *The Wallet of Time*. Vol. II. New York: Moffat, Yard, 1913.

Yeats, W. B. *The Letters of W. B. Yeats*. Edited Allan Wade. London: Rupert Hart-Davis, 1954.

Yurka, Blanche. *Bohemian Girl: Blanche Yurka's Theatrical Life*. Athens: Ohio University Press, 1970.

# Acknowledgments

I WOULD LIKE to acknowledge the assistance and encouragement I have received in my work from both individuals and institutions, with thanks first to the University of Wisconsin-Whitewater for awarding me a State Research Grant for this biography, as well as released time for writing. I am grateful to the staffs of the following libraries and collections for supplying and granting permission to quote unpublished material: the Bernard F. Burgunder Shaw Collection, Cornell University Library; the Harvard Theatre Collection; the Frederick R. Koch Collection, Harvard Theatre Collection; the Enthoven Collection, Museum of London; the Billy Rose Theatre Collection, Performing Arts Research Center at Lincoln Center, New York; the Humanities Research Center, University of Texas at Austin; the Hoblitzelle Theatre Arts Collection, Humanities Research Center, University of Texas at Austin; the Poetry/Rare Books Collection of the University Libraries, State University of New York at Buffalo; the Mander and Mitchenson Theatre Collection, London; Churchill College Library, Cambridge University; the Bodleian Library, Oxford University; the British Library; the Rare Book and Manuscript Library, Columbia University; the Houghton Library, Harvard University; the Regenstein Library, University of Chicago; the Theatre Collection of the Free Library of Philadelphia; the Archives for the Performing Arts, Mill Valley, California; the State Historical Library, Madison, Wisconsin; Mugar Memorial Library, Boston University; the Newberry Library; the University of Victoria Library; and the Bibliothèque Municipale, Pau, France. Special thanks to James Tyler (Cornell University Library), Ellen S. Dunlap (Humanities Research Center, University of Texas at Austin), Jeanne T. Newlin (Harvard Theatre Collection), Robert Bertolf (Rare Book and Manuscript Library, SUNY-Buffalo), Kenneth A. Lohf (Butler Library, Columbia University), and Jennifer Aylmer (Enthoven Collection).

I am also grateful to the following persons or firms for permission to quote from unpublished materials: Bartletts, de Reya, Solicitors (Mrs. Patrick Campbell and Bernard Shaw); The Society of Authors on behalf of the Bernard Shaw Estate; Diana Forbes-Robertson Sheean and Maxine Forbes-Robertson Miles (Sir Johnston Forbes-Robertson); Viscountess Caroline Chandos (Dame Edith Lyttelton); Lance Thirkell (Margaret Mackail); Miss M. Lamb (George R. Sims); Mrs. C. Phillip Miller (Mrs. Patrick Campbell); Anthony Parker Tull and Campbell, Thomson, and McLaughlin, Ltd. (Louis N. Parker); and Cora A. Read and Diana P. Read (Arthur Symons).

Without the generous co-operation of British correspondents, many pages of this biography could not have been written. My thanks to Mark Baker, Roger Beacham, David Bell, P. J. Bottrill, Viscountess Caroline Chandos, T. J. Clodington, J. W. N. Dudgeon, S. Duro, T. M. Egan, A. E. Eldon-Edington, Alan Gill, Mrs. Greenwood, Miss J. Grove, Loel Guinness, Shelagh Head, Roger Highfield, Mrs. Diana Kay, A. J. McMillan, Mrs. M. J. North, Mrs. R. M. Popham, the Rt. Hon. the Lord Saville, Mr. T. Scragg, Diana Forbes-Robertson

Sheean, D. H. Simpson, Margaret Slade, Pearl Taylor, E. Turnhill, Miss D. F. Vincent, Dame Veronica Wedgwood, J. R. Wood, and Roma Woodnutt.

Thanks, equally, to American correspondents who contributed to this book: J. W. Aldrich, Karl Beckson, Gail T. Boatman, Julia Child, Harry P. Clark, James Coakley, Fitzroy Davis, Jonathan Dodd, Geraldine Duclow, Robert Eddison, John M. Fuhrman, Frances Goudy, Gene Graves, Mrs. Nelson Hagan, Allan Harrison, Russell Hartley, the Rt. Rev. Henry W. Hobson, Julliette Hollister, Nancy Jordan, Charles Kebbe, Eleanor Hobson Mackenzie, Jane Connor Marcus, Herbert S. Nusbaum, C. Pewter, Joan Reardon, Evelyn W. Semler, Wilma Slaight, and Warren B. Wickliffe. Particular thanks to Frances Tompkins, whose reminiscences of Stella Campbell and contribution of letters helped so materially with the later chapters of this book.

Again, I am grateful to Dan H. Laurence, Literary and Dramatic Advisor, Estate of George Bernard Shaw, for continued assistance and fellowship in matters Shavian and Campbellian.

My research in England was generously furthered by conversations with Sir John Gielgud, Mrs. Stella Coltman-Rogers, and Raymond Mander and Joe Mitchenson: I am very grateful. Very special thanks to Lindsay Mackie of the *Guardian*, who led me to the owner of the Tanner letters, William Sheridan; and my gratitude to both Mr. Sheridan and Mrs. Judy Brown, to whose friendly co-operation this book is greatly indebted. To Ray Ruehl of the American School in London my warm thanks for hours spent more or less cheerfully on the trail. In France my way was smoothed by Professor Gabriel Merle and the resourcefulness of Mme Suzanne Bordenave, librarian of the Bibliothèque Municipale in Pau.

My thanks to Donna Lewis and Patrice Olday for their kind assistance with typing and copying.

To Robert Gottlieb, my editor, who believed in *Mrs. Pat*—my best thanks.

An especially warm word of gratitude to Patrick Beech, whose wonderful generosity in supplying materials and memories contributed inestimably to this biography of his grandmother.

I cannot thank enough Peter Ridgway Jordan, my husband, who joined me enthusiastically in the search for Stella, and whose skill, wit, and scepticism made this a better book in every way.

# *Notes*

## ABBREVIATIONS USED IN THE NOTES

CL      Bernard Shaw: *Collected Letters*
Dent    Alan Dent: *Mrs. Patrick Campbell*
MLSL    Mrs. Patrick Campbell: *My Life and Some Letters*
OTN     Bernard Shaw: *Our Theatres in the Nineties*
TC      *Bernard Shaw and Mrs. Patrick Campbell: Their Correspondence*

Document collections cited in the Notes are listed in Acknowledgments, pages 473–4.

### PROLOGUE

Material for the Prologue derives from the following sources: Alan Dent's *Mrs. Patrick Campbell*: Chapter 58 (hereafter Dent); *Bernard Shaw and Mrs. Patrick Campbell: Their Correspondence* (hereafter *TC*); unpublished letters from Stella Campbell to Bernard Shaw kindly lent to me for this biography by Patrick Beech, Mrs. Campbell's grandson, now in the Frederick R. Koch Collection, Harvard Theatre Collection; Sir John Gielgud's reminiscences of Lord Lathom and Lathom House (or Blythe Hall): Lord Lathom was the person who introduced him to Mrs. Campbell; and the present resident of Ashfields, Mrs. Greenwood, whose thorough knowledge of the history of the house during Mrs. Campbell's residence there and generosity in imparting it proved most helpful during my visit to Ormskirk and the Lathom estate.

### CHAPTER ONE: 1865–1881

The material in this chapter is drawn from Stella Campbell's autobiography, *My Life and Some Letters* (hereafter *MLSL*): Chapters 1 and 2; from Bombay baptism, marriage, burial, and census records; from family records and letters belonging to Patrick Beech; from census and property records in the Kensington Library; from Dent: 68, 72; and from John Tanner's and Stella's letters in the author's possession, hereafter called the Tanner Collection.

The Tanner Collection of letters was found in 1974 by William Sheridan, a porter at the Onslow Court Hotel, London, in one of the hotel dustbins. They are letters preserved by Stella's sister Louisa Tanner and are addressed chiefly to her. Lulo had evidently once lived at the Onslow Court Hotel, a "residence for decayed gentlewomen," and either died there or left the letters behind (the Onslow Court Hotel's records do not go that far back).

The hotel held them for a time, finally bundling them into a paper bag and discarding them in 1974. The group of approximately 240 letters (fragments make the number difficult to ascertain) and a dozen pieces of miscellany includes some 115 letters from Stella Campbell and twenty-six from John Tanner to Lulo. John Tanner's letters are headed by the date and place of residence in Texas. Stella's letters are seldom prefixed by the complete date and place of writing; the approximate time and place can usually be deduced from their contents, however.

Bombay records and family papers owned by Patrick Beech make it possible to somewhat correct and expand Stella's comments on her family in *MLSL*. Angelo Romanini, her mother's father, was born in Brescia and died in Benares, India, in 1870; his wife, Rosa (née Polinelli), was born in Milan and died in Bombay in 1893. Romanini, a political activist with the Carbonari, left Italy to become the master of a travelling equestrian company. Stella claims he was a count; he did tell a relative that Romanini was not his real name, which would only be revealed after his death—an unfulfilled promise. Maria Luigia Giovanna (Louisa or Lu) was born in Trent, the capital of the Italian Tyrol, on July 7, 1835, and married John Tanner on her seventeenth birthday when he was twenty-two. He was born in Bombay on December 25, 1829. John's parents, John and Anne Mary (née Davis) were married in Bombay in 1823; Anne died in 1847, having borne ten children. Stella's brothers, Edwin Augustus and Edmund Vivian (Max) were born in London on May 23, 1862, and April 2, 1864.

This is the place to note that Stella Campbell's handwriting is notoriously difficult to read, as well as notoriously lacking in the conventions of punctuation, although her spelling (with the exception of proper names) is surprisingly accurate for one who flouts almost all other conventions. I have generally avoided quoting from passages that contain illegible words; when my reading is uncertain, I have indicated the fact in the chapter notes. As for amending the mechanics of Mrs. Campbell's letters: Mrs. Campbell was an actress, not an author. It does not seem necessary to me, therefore, to regard her texts as sacred. Where lack of punctuation and other conventions such as the apostrophe and capitalization interfere with comprehension or even ease of reading, I have silently provided them, while still trying to preserve the dashing and telegraphic flavor of her style.

CHAPTER TWO: 1881–1884

Material for this chapter comes from *MLSL*: Chapters 2 and 3: Stella prints Ridley Prentice's letter of September 25, 1882 (28–9), and Henry Tanner's poem (30–1); from records of Wellington College, kindly transmitted to me by archivist Mark Baker; from records of the Oriental Bank Corporation in the archives of the City of London; and from certificates of marriage and the birth of Alan Urquhart Campbell on record at St. Catherine's House, London. There is no record of Beatrice Stella Tanner's attendance at the Guildhall School of Music, although their records go back to the first year of the school, 1881. According to *MLSL*, Stella attended after her return from Paris when she was sixteen, and left at the end of the fall term in 1882. Neither is there mention of Stella in the Guildhall School of Music Scrapbooks, a collection of newspaper notices of recitals, performances, prizes, etc. Thomas Ridley Prentice does appear in the school records, however, as well as in Grove's *Dictionary of Music and Musicians*: Prentice was a pianist, organist, composer, and promoter of musical events of some note.

Most of the information in this chapter comes from Stella's letters to her sister Lulo, 1882–1884, in the Tanner Collection. The letter about Mrs. Gifford forbidding her her house is dated "Tuesday," and is probably 1883. The letter describing Patrick Campbell was written after she left the Guildhall at the end of the fall term in 1882, probably in early spring of 1884, since she states that she will be a poor man's wife. The letter ending "All my love for music is quite dead" is dated "Friday, April 4th [1884]." The letter asking "Is it madness to marry Pat on £200 a year?" is dated "Friday afternoon" and was obviously written after April 17 and before June 21, 1884. The letter describing wedding presents from Owney Urquhart is dated "Wednesday, June 18th, 84." The letter beginning "Everything is arranged for to-morrow" is, of course, dated June 20, 1884. The note written on her wedding day, June 21, 1884, is headed "Waterloo Station 12.25 a.m.," although "p.m." would seem more likely, since the wedding took place at 11 a.m. and since they would not wish to arrive at Staines-on-Thames in the early morning hours. The letter beginning "It is so grand here" is headed "Pack Horse Hotel, Staines-on-Thames" and was written during the honeymoon, June 22–25. The Tanner Collection contains a bill for £3 17s./5d. from the Pack Horse Hotel, John Bright, Proprietor, for June 24 and 25. Since it was among Lulo's papers, perhaps she paid it.

The footnote to a letter dated "Thursday" and quoted at the end of the chapter is partially illegible. It could read "When Pat first cared for me," "When Pat first came after me," or "When Pat first loved me": I have chosen the first reading.

Stella's account of her meeting with and marriage to Patrick Campbell in *MLSL* (Chapter 3) is, for obvious reasons, factually false. She states that they eloped within four months of their first meeting. Her letters to Lulo, however, indicate that the courtship began sometime in 1882, and she herself betrays the four-month story by suggesting in her autobiography that it was because of Campbell that she left the Guildhall School of Music in the late fall of 1882, and by stating that she was seventeen when they met: she was seventeen on February 9, 1882.

CHAPTER THREE: 1884–1886

Again I have chiefly drawn upon letters in the Tanner Collection. It is uncertain when Stella returned from Bournemouth, where she had gone after the honeymoon at Staines-on-Thames. The first post-honeymoon letter in the Collection is dated September 1, 1884, from 17 Milton Road, Herne Hill; there is nothing in her autobiography to fill the gap. The last letter to Lulo used in this chapter is dated only "Tuesday," but from internal evidence the time of its writing can be pinned down to three weeks after the birth of little Stella on September 27, 1886. In the Tanner Collection are five letters from Patrick Campbell to Lulo. The detailed account of Alan Urquhart Campbell's birth on January 14, 1885, is taken from Pat's letter of January 18 headed "Sunday, Brixton." The births of the children are on record at St. Catherine's House, London. There is a gap of more than a year in Stella's letters to Lulo, from the summer of 1885 till after baby Stella's birth. Little Stella was taken ill on Sunday, October 10, 1886.

Stella tells of the impression made upon her by Pailleron's *Le Monde où l'on s'ennuie* in *MLSL*: 25. The concluding episode of this chapter, the night when she found new courage, also comes from this source. She says little about her marriage until the account of that experience.

CHAPTER FOUR: 1886–1889

Stella gives the bare facts about her early acting experience with the Anomalies in *MLSL*: 37. Reviews from the *Era* and Liverpool *Citizen* are quoted in part in Dent: 22, 34. Stella prints Pat Campbell's letters, the letter from the *Tares* company, and Katherine Bailey's letter in her autobiography: 39–45, 45–8. Letters to Lulo and to Henry Tanner, chiefly undated, are from the Tanner Collection.

Stella's letter to Lulo ("I am just writing you one line my darling before going off to rehearsal") is a biographer's dream and nightmare. To find *the* letter revealing that her ambition has always been the stage is fortunate; to have that letter prefixed only by the monogram "Stella" and the day "Tuesday" is frustrating. Since her debut in *In His Power* took place on a Thursday, the letter cannot refer to that play. The contents of the letter also suggest strongly that she is getting paid for this performance, so that it might be with some kind of professional company. The letter cannot have been written after Pat left England in October 1887 because he has just asked an uncle for money and been personally refused. Therefore, the time of writing must be after November 18, 1886, and before October 1887. In a brief description of her career, the *Theatre* of June 1, 1893, says that before November 1889 she had had "a flattering local success as Alma Blake in '*The Silver Shield*' to which slap-dash person, however, her subdued and gentle style hardly permitted her to give suitable expression." The *Theatre* also says that she played Marie de Fontanges in *Plot and Passion* in June 1890 as an amateur; but since she was playing professionally with Ben Greet in June 1890, this seems unlikely. Stella herself mentions *The Silver Shield* in another letter to Lulo, also undated. It reads: "Darling—I may as well let you have one line. The Committee have changed the play—we are going to act 'Duty' adapted from Victorien Sardou's play 'Les Bourgeois de Pont Arcy.' Our next piece is the 'Silver Shield' which I believe you have seen. I am feeling very unhappy. Write to me darling—Your loving Beatrice." The word "Committee" suggests an amateur group, yet her only amateur experiences on record are for the Anomalies in *Blow for Blow, The Money Spinner, The Palace of Truth*. I have been unable to trace any early records of her acting in any other company, either professional or amateur; yet her letters to Lulo suggest that she did.

Stella's remembrance of how she got her first engagement with Frank Green's company is faulty. Letters from F. W. Macklin and Harrington Baily in the Enthoven Collection, now in the Museum of London, and a letter to Lulo written after her first interview on September 20, 1888, indicate that she was not offered an engagement immediately after the "drowned kittens" episode, as she states in her autobiography, but that the negotiations extended from September 20 to October 2, a contract finally being delivered on October 16.

Stella's whereabouts during these years becomes increasingly difficult to trace. None of her letters written on tour prefixes more than a day of the week. The contract from Mrs. Bandmann-Palmer dated April 15, 1889, is addressed to "Mrs. Patrick Campbell, Newcote, Wolfington Road, West Norwood"; Henry and Louisa Tanner must have recently moved from 14 Acacia Grove, Dulwich, to West Norwood. After the *Tares* engagement Stella spent many weeks at Newcote.

CHAPTER FIVE: 1889–1890

It is interesting to compare Stella's account of her seasons with Ben Greet in *MLSL* with her letters to Lulo written on tour. She does not mention the quarrel, for example, in her autobiography, but says only, "I do not think Ben Greet ever shook my faith, that some day I would be able to act well, and that the public would love me, and if it were necessary, I should be able to educate and provide for my children." Her letters contradict this; yet, considering that she made it up with Greet, who managed her London matinee of *As You Like It* (1891), her autobiography could be said to give the long view.

Some of the material in this chapter is drawn from *MLSL*; most of it comes from letters to Lulo in the Tanner Collection. Since these letters cover two tour years with Greet and are largely undated, it has been impossible always to connect dates with places. There is no record, for example, of Greet's company acting *As You Like It* at Merton College, Oxford, according to College Librarian Roger Highfield; yet it was Greet's custom to take his Woodland Players to both Oxford and Cambridge. Similarly—despite the research efforts of David Bell, librarian of the Ashridge Management College (formerly Ashridge

Park), and Shelagh Head, local-studies librarian, Hertfordshire County Library—I have been unable to discover the date that Greet's company performed for Lord and Lady Brownlow at Ashridge Park, although it is likely that the year was 1890 and that the Ashridge Park performance was inspired by the appearance of Greet's troupe at Wilton House that July.

I began with two firm dates for the summer of 1890: the London performance of *A Buried Talent* on June 5 and the performance on July 14 at Wilton House (program in the Enthoven Collection). Because of the generous research efforts of Roger Beacham and J. R. Wood (Cheltenham Library), Mrs. R. M. Popham (County Library of Dorset), P. J. Bottrill (County Library of Devon), and Miss D. F. Vincent (States of Jersey Library Service), I was able to chart the progress of Greet's company from Cheltenham, where they arrived on July 7, to Stella's breakdown on Jersey after the evening performance on Thursday, July 31. A local St. Helier newspaper reported on August 5 that "In connection with the Saturday afternoon performance of 'As You Like It,' the character of Rosalind was taken at short notice by Miss Violet Raye," indicating that Stella did not act again after Thursday.

P. J. Bottrill sent a thorough account of the company's stay at Torquay, where they performed July 21–29, including the fact that on July 24 they played to an audience that included several hundred seamen belonging to the Fleet, which compliment was returned when Vice-Admiral Sir Culme-Seymour and the officers of Her Majesty's Ships in Torbay gave their patronage to the Saturday evening performance. The performance on Tuesday, July 29, at Pilmuir, taking place "by the kind permission of Mrs. Houldsworth, was an exceedingly pretty, highly realistic, and most finished performance, the Rosalind of Mrs. Patrick Campbell being admirable. The audience included the Dowager Lady Haldon, the Hon. Edward Palk and many leading residents and visitors, all of whom were alike gratified with the performance and the charming surroundings."

Letters from Stella to Lulo after her breakdown are headed "Cromarty" and "Clovelly," a fact that was initially puzzling, since I was sure she could not be either up in Scotland or on the Devon coast. Mrs. Popham solved the riddle by reporting that a Mrs. Amelia Urquhart (Owney's mother) appears in the Bournemouth directory for 1890 at Cromarty, West Cliff Road, and that a Dr. Geoffrey Frost, L.R.C.P., M.R.C.S., lived at Clovelly, Suffolk Road, Bournemouth.

I am also grateful to P. R. Gifford (Essex County Libraries) for establishing the date of Laura Johnson's debut in *The Hunchback* at Colchester when Stella made such an impression, and for sending a review of the performance from the Essex *Standard* of January 18, 1890.

Louis N. Parker recalled his impressions of Stella in *Music-Master's First Adventures in Drama*, extracted in *T.P.'s Weekly* (October 27, 1928).

CHAPTER SIX: 1890–1893

Stella quotes Pat Campbell's letters in her autobiography (Chapter 4), as well as the Earl of Pembroke's letter to Ben Greet and the list of patrons for the matinee of *As You Like It*. Three unquoted letters from Pat to Henry Tanner detail his hopes for the "Stella Syndicate" and the "Beatrice Reef" (Patrick Beech).

The Tanner Collection contains Lulo's letter to Mr. Hogarth about financing the matinee, a copy of the Countess of Pembroke's letter to Stella, and letters—evidently copies—to Stella from Lady Brownlow and Lady Alice Gaisford dated March 17 and 18, 1891. Although she heads the letter "Stranraer," Stella's letter to Lulo about securing the Prince of Wales's for her matinee appears to have been written on the train. She makes her purpose for the trip quite clear: "I will do my best with old Campbell."

Dates and casts for the plays in this chapter are taken from *The London Stage: A Calendar of Plays and Players*, edited by J. P. Wearing, an extremely useful reference work in four volumes. At the last moment the names of two of her heroines were changed: Bertha to Astrea (*The Trumpet Call*) and Clarice Berton to Belle Hamilton (*The Black Domino*). Dent says, "It is a headache to the biographer . . . that Mrs. Campbell, looking back, insists on calling . . . the heroine of *The Black Domino* 'Clarice Berton' whereas all the contemporary newspapers and reviews call the character 'Belle Hamilton'"—but Stella rehearsed the role under that name. Dent discusses her early career in Chapters 1, 2, 4, and 5, quoting from Robert Hichens's autobiography, *Yesterday*: 19–20.

The Tanner Collection contains twelve letters from John Tanner to Lulo written between July 27, 1891, and March 11, 1893, each recounting his bad health and rejoicing over Stella's successes. Lulo kept him informed regularly, sending reviews. Stella wrote much less often, but did keep in touch and sent photographs.

An unidentified newspaper clipping in the Tanner Collection gives an account of the Michaelmas holiday: The sun refused to shine for the outing, "but we managed, after an excellent luncheon, to perform a few daring feats in small boats, which quite put Miss Tress Campbell Purvis's gallant expedition to the wreck into the shade. On this occasion Tress didn't seem quite so eager to row herself as she always is at the Adelphi. She was quite satisfied to take a back seat in a punt with Miss Sybil Millard Garfield. . . . When we had collided with everything on the river, we were all received with open arms by the gallant skippers and fair skipperesses of that hospitable houseboat, the Tiriwhickle, where we took tea and had our photographs taken sitting on the damp grass and more or less on each other." The day ended with a dinner hosted by stage manager E. B. Norman featuring a huge Michaelmas goose, before the company "staggered to the station and boarded the train for the 'lights of home' with regret for a happy day ended."

There are forty letters, some fragments, and ten telegrams from Stella to George R. Sims (letters undated but written in late 1892 and in 1893 and signed "Pickles") in the Hoblitzelle Theatre Arts Collection, Humanities Research Center, University of Texas at Austin. Lulo saved twelve letters from Sims, all headed "12, Clarence Terrace, Regent's Park," none of them dated, but written between the period immediately after Stella's collapse (which can be approximately dated from the running of the Cambridgeshire at Newmarket) and early January 1893. Sims obviously wearied of a correspondence begun only on account of Stella. One letter, perhaps the last, says dismissingly, ". . . I have been ill and overworked. I will take up the question of dog muzzles anon." His first letter says that he and Augustin almost rushed immediately to Dulwich on hearing of Stella's illness: Augustin is presumably Augustin Daly, theatrical manager.

Stella gives an account of her illness in *MLSL*, from which I have quoted. Her letter to Lulo from Bournemouth is undated, but is probably late December, since she is quite recovered and speaks of coming home soon, presumably to rehearse for the opening of *The Black Domino* on January 4, 1893.

CHAPTER SEVEN: 1893

I have taken the story of Stella and *The Second Mrs. Tanqueray* from contemporary sources that conflict on some minor points (the exact words Pinero spoke to her after the first act on opening night, for example) but are in essential agreement. Stella tells her version in *MLSL*: 82–97. What piece she actually played with her left hand is uncertain: in her autobiography she says it was a piece written by a girl friend; in a letter to Lulo she says it was something written by her brother Max; in a Hollywood interview she said it was a fugue for the left hand by Bach. Graham Robertson tells of discovering her at the Adelphi in *Time Was*: 247–60. Cyril Maude gives his version of the rehearsals in *Behind the Scenes with Cyril Maude by Himself*: 85–7. Margaret Webster draws on Ben Webster's memory of the *Tanqueray* production in *The Same Only Different*: 158–60. Letters from Pinero to George Alexander written between October 28, 1892, and April 12, 1893, chart the search for the right actress to play Paula: *The Collected Letters of Sir Arthur Pinero*: 137–43. A. E. W. Mason's sympathies are with Alexander in *Sir George Alexander and the St. James' Theatre*. J. M. Bulloch's reaction to the first night of *Tanqueray* was printed in the London *Times* of September 15, 1937. The incident of the "two young men" is taken from an unsigned article about Stella in the Boston *Transcript* (January 18, 1930). Always helpful are Raymond Mander's and Joe Mitchenson's books about London theatre, in this case *Lost Theatres of London*, which gives a historical account of the St. James's Theatre.

The Enthoven Collection, currently in the process of being transferred from the Victoria and Albert Museum to the Museum of London, has Stella's prompt books of *Bella Donna*, *Beyond Human Power*, *The Canary*, *Electra*, *The Joy of Living*, *Lady Patricia*, *Magda*, *The Masqueraders*, *Mr. and Mrs. Daventry*, *The Notorious Mrs. Ebbsmith*, *Pelléas and Mélisande*, *Pygmalion*, *The Second Mrs. Tanqueray*, and *The Thirteenth Chair*. Her book of *Tanqueray* is bound in gold and blue with "Stella" and a star on the cover in gold. She jotted in a number of directions like "come downstage," "laugh," "sit," and "go up to Aubrey"—rather basic notes. She has misdated the play, writing in the book "27 May 1892," and filled the copy with drawings of hearts, flowers, crowns, and perky-looking birds laying eggs.

CHAPTER EIGHT: 1893–1894

Stella's letter of May 29, 1893, to Pinero is quoted in Dent: 60. Stella prints Bessie Hatton's letter in *MLSL*: 97. Maurice Baring's reminiscence of *Tanqueray* was published as "Mrs. Patrick Campbell" in the *Fortnightly Review* (November 1922). John Tanner's letters to Lulo about Stella's success are dated June 13 and 26, 1893, from "706 [instead of 704] Nolan Street." Whether or not Stella used her father's "little preamble" is unknown, but in early interviews, when asked why she went on the stage, she usually responded, "By choice and a love of hard work." In her autobiography, however, she states plainly that she went on the stage to support herself and her children.

Stella discusses the year of her *Tanqueray* sensation in Chapters 5 and 6 of her autobiography, quoting letters of congratulation from Myra Pinero, J. W. Mackail, Philip Burne-Jones, Pembroke, Oscar Wilde, and others. Unfortunately, in the Tanner Collection there are no letters from Stella to Lulo during the first months of her success, quite probably as the result of her hard feelings about Josephine Jones. Stella alludes to the quarrel in two undated letters written from 53 Ashley Gardens, both referring to Pat's presence, so written after his return in March.

William Rothenstein recorded his meetings with Stella in *Men and Memories*: 258. Solomon's portrait of Stella currently hangs in the Arts Club in Dover Street, London. Constance Beerbohm's comment on Stella's "devil" is cited by Lord David Cecil in *Max Beerbohm*: 12. Stella quotes Pembroke's letter of advice in *MLSL*: 110–11.

Patrick Campbell's letters are taken, again, from Stella's autobiography: 119–20. Edwin Tanner's letter to Lulo about John Tanner's death is dated September 16, 1893; in it Edwin enclosed a lock of his father's hair. I am grateful to Dan H. Laurence, Literary and Dramatic Advisor, Estate of George Bernard Shaw, and resident of San Antonio, for providing me with the dates of Tanner's death and funeral. Dora Cumins's letter to Lulo is dated October 3, 1893. Stella's undated letter to Lulo ("I think somehow he would have mentioned it if Papa had been in need") is prefixed "73, Southampton Road." As usual, her whereabouts are hard to trace. Evidently she moved from Duchess Street after her *Tanqueray* success to 73 Southampton Road, then to 10 Manchester Street, the address from which she telegraphed Pat on March 12, 1894.

A. E. W. Mason provides statistics of Alexander's profits in *Sir George Alexander and the St. James' Theatre*: 63. Stella says in her autobiography that Alexander increased her salary from £15 to £30; copies of agreements in the Enthoven Collection, however, report her hired for £20 a week originally. Ben Webster's complaints about Stella on tour are reported by Margaret Webster in *The Same Only Different*: 161. The statement that Marion Terry was "a terror but behaved beautifully" is Sir John Gielgud's to the author.

Stella's version of the quarrel with Alexander can be found in *MLSL*: 116–18. She says that she went to Uncle Harry's to find Beo ill at twelve midnight after two performances on Saturday, December 23. J. P. Wearing's *The London Stage*, however, reports that there were no performances at the St. James's between December 21 and 25. One of them is wrong.

Stella's letters to George Sims quoted in this chapter can safely be assigned to this period from internal evidence and occasional place names, although the actual date of their breaking off is uncertain. Sims continued his successful career with *Two Little Vagabonds* (1896), *Dandy Fifth* (1898), etc. In 1901 he married Florence Wykes.

CHAPTER NINE: 1894–1895

Stella describes Pat Campbell's return in *MLSL*, Chapter 6. Dent prints Alexander's letter about *The Masqueraders* to Jones: 95. William Archer's review of *The Second Mrs. Tanqueray* appeared in *The Theatrical "World" for 1893*. Stella's copy of *The Masqueraders* is in the Enthoven Collection, sewn into a green-velvet-spined cover of flowered brocade. The cover bears the words "Beatrice Stella Campbell, Strictly Private and Confidential, Dulcie Larondie, 39 Somerset St. Portman [?]." She has made notes in the book and underlined in red ink. As in her *Tanqueray* copy, her additions chiefly describe action: "draws beer," "hands on hips," etc. Stella prints Henry Tanner's letter on the last performance of *Tanqueray* in *MLSL*: 122. None of Stella's letters to Lulo quoted in this chapter are dated, but their approximate time of writing can be deduced from their contents. Clement Scott's review of *The Masqueraders* is the only one Stella included in her autobiography: 124–5. William Archer on *The Masqueraders* can be found in *The Theatrical "World" for 1894*. Stella includes Pembroke's and Burne-Jones's letters about *The Masqueraders* in *MLSL*: 127–8. Henry James to Elizabeth Robins about Stella: Elizabeth Robins, *Theatre and Friendship*: 152.

Stella herself tells the anecdote about laughing at Alexander: 125–6. The description of Stella's flat at 53 Ashley Gardens comes from an interview by M. Griffith in the *Strand Magazine*, "Illustrated Interviews" (1895): 260–6 (Harvard Theatre Collection). Irene Vanbrugh records her visits to Ashley Gardens in *To Tell My Story*, quoted in Dent: 80. Ripley Court at Ripley, Surrey, was founded in 1893 by R. M. Pearce, whose name occurs frequently in letters and on checks in the Tanner Collection. I am very grateful to the present headmaster, J. W. N. Dudgeon, who sent a school prospectus as well as the *Ripley Court Magazine* (Michaelmas Term 1900) containing the following item in the "O.B. [Old Boys] Intelligence": "A. U. Campbell's name appeared fifth on the list of successful candidates for admission to the 'Britannia' in July, 1899." Beo entered the school in 1894 and left for *Britannia*, the British Naval College in Dartmouth, after June 1899, the normal month for sitting the Common Entrance Examination.

Stella's contract with Beerbohm Tree is in the Enthoven Collection. Scott's and Archer's reviews of *John-a-Dreams* are quoted by Dent: 98. Pinero comments about his difficulty with *The Notorious Mrs. Ebbsmith* in letters to William Archer (October 5, 1894) and Henry James (December 31, 1894): *The Collected Letters of Sir Arthur Pinero*: 160–1, 164–5.

## CHAPTER TEN: 1895

Stella discusses her playing Agnes Ebbsmith at greater length than any other of her roles: *MLSL*: 128–33. Her prompt copy in the Enthoven Collection again has very few directions pencilled in, although it is liberally decorated with hearts, crowns, and birds. Edmund Gosse's and Jack Mackail's letters are quoted in *MLSL*: 131–2. Maurice Baring's comments on *Ebbsmith* come from *The Puppet Show of Memory*: 157–8. Bernard Shaw's reviews are collected in *Our Theatres in the Nineties* (hereafter *OTN*)—*The Notorious Mrs. Ebbsmith*: I, 63–9. Shaw to J. T. Grein about casting *Mrs. Warren's Profession* in the *Collected Letters* (hereafter *CL*): December 12, 1893, I, 412–13. Shaw to Charles Charrington about the casting of Ellean: February 9, 1895 (Humanities Research Center, University of Texas at Austin). Stella quotes Myra Pinero's letter: 132–3. Pinero to Stella: May 1, 1895 (British Library).

The anecdote about Beo in church was told to me by Stella Moore Coltman-Rogers, Mrs. Campbell's goddaughter, namesake, and protégée, who lived with Mrs. Campbell for a number of years and knew her intimately. Stella Patrick Campbell's remark about being frightened of her mother was related by Joe Mitchenson, who, as an actor, studied under Stella Beech at the Royal Academy of Dramatic Art in the 1930's. Stella's letter to Lulo is without date or address, making it very difficult to date accurately; the summer of either 1895 or 1896 seems likely. Herbert Beerbohm Tree to Maud Tree is quoted by Hesketh Pearson in *Beerbohm Tree*: 86–7. Stella's contract for Juliet is in the Enthoven Collection, dated "1895. 20 May. London Drama Syndicate. Juliet. No. 53 Ashley Gardens, Victoria Street." Stella gives the Countess of Pembroke's letter in *MLSL*: 138–9.

## CHAPTER ELEVEN: 1895

Stephen Lucius Gwynn reminisces about Stella's Rosalind in *Experiences of a Literary Man*: 115. Stella's letters to Lulo about her Juliet are not dated, but their time of writing is fairly evident. The address from which she wrote them—54 Parliament Hill Road, Hampstead Heath—is puzzling, since she was currently living at 53 Ashley Gardens. Perhaps she retreated during the difficult rehearsal days to the house of a friend. Sir Johnston Forbes-Robertson discusses his initiation as a manager in *A Player Under Three Reigns*: 175–6. Stella prints Diane Creyke's memory of the Lyceum first night in *MLSL*: 137–8. A. B. Walkley reviewed *Romeo and Juliet* in the *Star*, the *Speaker*, and the *Album* for October 7, 1895. Clement Scott's criticism is, of course, from the *Daily Telegraph*. Archer's two articles are collected in *The Theatrical "World" for 1895*: 284–301. The Harvard Theatre Collection has a considerable number of American newspaper clippings about Stella; Arthur Warren's "LONDON IDOL IN DANGER" comes from that source. Shaw's criticism of *Romeo and Juliet* is in *OTN*: I, 207–14. Shaw began to write to Ellen Terry about *The Man of Destiny* on November 1, 1895, when she was touring with Irving in America. His "I will go to the beautiful Mrs. Patrick Campbell" was written March 9, 1896: *CL*: I, 608–10. Ellen to Shaw ("Your letter!") was written from Indianapolis, Indiana, March 24, 1896 (British Library), and is printed in full in Margot Peters's *Bernard Shaw and the Actresses*: 167. Shaw to Ellen ("*Anybody* can play Shakspere"), November 1, 1895: *CL*: I, 564–5. Stella comments on her Juliet in *MLSL* (133–40), ending, "What matter, *Juliet* was over for me, forever!"

### CHAPTER TWELVE: 1895–1896

Stella tells her side of *Michael and His Lost Angel* in *MLSL*: Chapter 8. In *A Player Under Three Reigns* Forbes-Robertson says only that the play was not well received, although he had great hopes of it. Before his death Henry Arthur Jones charged his daughter Doris Arthur Jones to give a full account of the episode, and her *Life and Letters of Henry Arthur Jones* includes letters exchanged between Jones and Forbes-Robertson, as well as Stella's letter to Jones upon resigning Audrie Lesden: 172–80. H.A.J.'s letter to Stella of January 1, 1896, is in the Rider Haggard Ms. Collection, Columbia University Libraries. Shaw's review of January 18, 1896, is collected in *OTN*: II, 15–22, and was followed by a defense of religious subjects on the stage on January 25.

Stella comments on *For the Crown* in *MLSL*: 142–5. Her letter to Gabriella Enthoven, dated "February 1896" from 53 Ashley Gardens, is in the Enthoven Collection. Dent quotes Robert Hichens on *For the Crown*: 130, and Gwynn's comment comes again from *Experiences of a Literary Man*: 115. Shaw reviewed the play on March 7, 1896: *OTN*: II, 63–70. Stella's letter to Lulo from Paris in the Tanner Collection is undated, but written soon before *For the Crown* opened. She mentions seeing Réjane in the afternoon, and Réjane played a matinee on February 18. She also tells Lulo she went to Paris to look at a play (unnamed) for herself, but found it "too spicey for London."

Stella's *Magda* copy is in the Enthoven Collection, inscribed on the cover, "Return to III Deanery Street, Park Lane W": she was evidently in the habit of staying away from Ashley Gardens a good deal—perhaps to study, perhaps to meet Forbes-Robertson. She prints some reactions to *Magda* in *MLSL*: 145–50. Shaw's review of June 6, 1896: *OTN*: II, 152–6.

This time Stella recorded many changes in her prompt book, some of which seem to have been made at rehearsal. The first act, in which Magda does not appear, was cut entirely. Perhaps at Stella's suggestion, dressier words were occasionally substituted for plainer: *father* for *papa*, *trembling* for *giddy*, *little one* for *baby*. Many speeches were pared down: Magda's speech in the last act, for instance, was changed from, "Would to God I had never come home! Do you hound me out already? I drove him to his death—surely I may bury him!" to simply, "Would to God I had never come home!" Occasionally awkwardnesses were reworked. Originally, for example, Magda replies to Heffterdingt's "Why did you come home? Was it homesickness?" with

> No. Well, perhaps a wee bit. I'll tell you. When I received the invitation in Milan, to take part in this Festival—I've no idea why they did me the honour—a singular feeling began boring into me. Half curiosity—and half shyness—half tender regret, half defiance. And it whispered: Go home unknown.

Evidently realizing that four halves added up to more than one feeling, Parker altered the lines to

> No. Well, perhaps a little. I'll tell you. When I received the invitation in Milan, to take part in this Festival—I've no idea why they did me the honour—strange feelings came over me. Curiosity, shyness, tender regret, defiance. They whispered: Go home.

### CHAPTER THIRTEEN: 1896–1897

Stella comments briefly on her Lady Teazle in *MLSL*: 150–1. Walkley's review in the *Star* is quoted by Dent: 133. Shaw's review of *The School for Scandal* appears in *OTN*: II, 174–81. Max Eliot's "CAN SHE ACT?" comes from an unidentified newspaper, dateline

"London, June 1896" (Harvard Theatre Collection). Stella gives Henry Tanner's and Margaret Mackail's letters in *MLSL*, Mackail's dated September 20, 1896: 151–2, 365–6. Stella's "pongers" remark is cited by Sir John Gielgud in his *Distinguished Company*: 17.

Shaw's and Terry's remarks about Stella are quoted from *Ellen Terry and Bernard Shaw: A Correspondence*: 35, 44, 47, 59.

Stella describes her *Little Eyolf* experience in *MLSL*: 152–4. Shaw wrote three articles about the production: "Ibsen Ahead!" (November 7, 1896), "Little Eyolf" (November 28, 1896) and "Ibsen Without Tears" (December 12, 1896): *OTN*: III, 251–3, 269–76, 285–92. Charles Ricketts's remark was recorded by "Michael Field" (Katharine Bradley and Edith Cooper) in *Works and Days* (unpublished MS, British Library). I give a more complete account of the production in *Bernard Shaw and the Actresses*: 173–6, 198–205. Stella includes William Heinemann's, F. J. Harris's, and Archer's letters about her Rita Allmers in *MLSL*: 153–4.

Stella's reaction to Ellen Terry's Imogen comes from a letter in the Tanner Collection to Lulo (June 27, 1897), preceded by "I am glad you tell me about Sarah [Bernhardt]. I wonder what your mind was—whether you went to criticize or enjoy—so much depends on that." She describes Ellen's lapse of memory in *MLSL*: 436–7. Ellen's letter to Stella, thanking her for her kind message about Imogen, is dated "Sunday 27 September"; it was loaned to me by Patrick Beech. Ellen's daughter, Edith (Edy) Craig, went to *Little Eyolf* and reported that only Janet Achurch could act. But she made friends with Stella. "Edy is going to act with Mrs. Pat," Ellen wrote Shaw on December 8, 1896, "& is quite amused by her."

"Morning Calls: Mrs. Patrick Campbell" appeared in the *New Illustrated Magazine* for May 1897: 28–31 (Harvard Theatre Collection). Stella's letter to Lulo is undated, but written during the run of *Nelson's Enchantress*. She does not mention where the new rooms are, but the last letter to Lulo quoted in this chapter when her breakdown is coming on is written from 10 Mandeville Place, West. Shaw's diary also notes an appointment with Stella on February 18, 1897, at 10 Mandeville Place, West. Archer's review of *Nelson's Enchantress* appears in *The Theatrical "World" for 1897*: 31–7; Shaw's in *OTN*: III, 50–6.

## CHAPTER FOURTEEN: 1897

Most of the information and quotations in this chapter come from letters in the Tanner Collection. Except for letters written during the first weeks of Stella's rest cure at Rasta, few of the letters are completely dated, although their time of writing is generally clear from their contents, and from corroborating letters from Forbes-Robertson and Margaret Mackail. The Collection contains two notes from Margaret to Pat Campbell (June 6 and 11, 1897) and six to Lulo (May 6, 9, 14, 20, 26, and 30, 1897). After Stella entered Rasta, Forbes-Robertson was in continual touch with Lulo, through his sister Ida Buchanan, who lived at 22 Bedford Square, and through wires, letters, and meetings with Lulo. The Tanner Collection contains eleven letters from Forbes to Lulo written from Bedford Square and on tour. They are of considerable interest, since little evidence survives of the intimate relationship between Stella and Forbes.

A packet of twenty cancelled checks written by Stella between March 21 and June 19, 1897, also provides clues to her whereabouts and expenditures. Six checks written to Mrs. Evelyn White, Brighton, for a total of £36 3s./8d. between April 17 and May 6, for example, prove that just before she entered the nursing home at Bournemouth she was staying in Brighton, a fact for which there is little other evidence except her statement to Lulo about Wrighton: "I shall never forget how good to me she was at Brighton." To herself during this period she wrote checks totaling at least £35 10s. (some checks are missing). The total sum of the twenty checks is £170 4s./4d.

Stella does not mention the name of the nursing home in *MLSL*, and although I guessed

"Raste" from difficult-to-read headings of letters to Lulo, it was not until Mrs. R. M. Popham, Librarian, County Library of Dorset at Bournemouth, sent me photocopies of an advertisement in Mate's *Bournemouth Illustrated* (1907) for the Rasta Nursing Home that I could be sure of its identity. The original Rasta was in Chine Road; Miss Stewart evidently left Chine Road in 1906, relocating Rasta at 10 Undercliff Road, Boscombe. Today Chine Road is called Durley Chine Road, and No. 6 (Rasta) is the Clairville Hotel, writes Mrs. Popham, enclosing an advertisement for the Clairville in the Bournemouth *Official Guide* for 1982. Mrs. Popham also reported an 1899 directory entry for Dr. Dennis C. Embleton, L.R.C.P., M.R.C.S., St. Wilfred's, St. Michael's Road—Stella's doctor.

Although told the picture was in the Tate Gallery, I have been unable to locate Philip Burne-Jones's "The Vampire": the Tate has no record of it. Reproductions of the picture occasionally preface volumes of Kipling's poems, and I am grateful to Margaret Feeley for letting me photograph the reproduction in her volume. An article in the *New England Home Magazine* for October 1898 (Harvard Theatre Collection) features a sensational story by Henry P. Marston about "The Vampire," Kipling's verses, and Mrs. Campbell—was Burne-Jones in love with Mrs. Campbell, did he buy her diamonds, furs, carriages, was the painting spite, etc.?—indicating that the painting created considerable comment. The *Illustrated London News* noted the painting on May 1, 1897.

Stella's letters evidence her attempts to support Lulo's acting career. The Tanner Collection contains a program of Ben Greet's series of Shakespearian revivals beginning May 10, 1897, at the Olympic Theatre, opening with *Hamlet* followed by *Romeo and Juliet, The Merchant of Venice*, and *Macbeth*. Lulo's name heads the list of walk-ons: "Misses Eleanor Tanner, Beresford, Richardson, Tate, Young, Townshend, etc." At least she wasn't an "etc." and, as Stella noted, she had a line. Archer reviewed the revivals in the *World*, finding the *Hamlet* "highly meritorious" and commenting on the minor players, "I did not notice any very striking talent in the other performers, but they were all well up to their work."

Shaw's letter to Ellen Terry of May 13, 1897, about his interview with Forbes-Robertson appears in *CL*: I, 762–3; the interview apparently took place on May 10 when Forbes was in London for the day. Stella's reference to Robert Louis Stevenson's and W. E. Henley's *Admiral Guinea* is puzzling, since it opened at the Avenue Theatre on November 29, 1897, with Elizabeth Robins; perhaps the reference is to a copyright performance. It was Henry James's custom to go abroad summers, but in 1897 he went instead first to Bournemouth, where he met Stella walking on the sands, and from there to Dunwich. As a friend of Elizabeth Robins, James knew something of Stella Campbell, though they were not more than acquaintances. He knew, for example, that it was Stella who, visiting Elizabeth one day, pounced on a bundle of proofs or manuscript in her flat and discovered that Elizabeth was the author "C. E. Raimond." Unable to keep a secret, Stella shared her discovery with the world, and Elizabeth, the most secret of individuals, was forced to admit her clandestine career.

CHAPTER FIFTEEN: 1897

As in the previous chapter, most information comes from Stella's letters to Lulo, written from Kensington Cottage, Great Malvern, from Bath, and finally from Hatch House. Lady Queensberry's letter to Lulo about turning Hatch House over to Stella for August is dated July 2, 1897 (Tanner Collection). The Collection also contains three letters from Lewis Vernon (Loulou) Harcourt, British politician and son of the well-known liberal politician William Harcourt; they are dated May 14, June 3, and July 7, 1897. Stella included Henry Tanner's letter and her answer and Pat's note about acting in London (signed, as usual, "Daddy") in *MLSL*: 156–8. I am indebted to Stella Campbell's goddaughter Stella Moore

Coltman-Rogers for telling me about her mother's meeting with Stella at Malvern when she was a young woman in her twenties. Ginny Moore later ran a hotel, the Grosvenor, at Malvern, and remained friends with Stella Campbell the rest of her life. Mrs. Pat was incredibly generous to her and her family, said Mrs. Coltman-Rogers. Forbes-Robertson tells of his decision to play Hamlet in *A Player Under Three Reigns*: 182–6. There is one letter from Josephine Jones to Lulo in the Tanner Collection, headed "Fairseat, Wrotham" (Kent), undated, but written in August 1897 shortly before Lulo visited Stella at Hatch House.

CHAPTER SIXTEEN: 1897–1898

Ellen Terry wrote Shaw about pulling the new Hamlet out of bed on September 7, 1897: *A Correspondence*: 183–4, and Shaw wrote Terry about Forbes's tribulation with Hamlet on July 27, 1897: *CL*: I, 788–9. Forbes-Robertson mentions Shaw's letter of advice about playing Hamlet in *A Player Under Three Reigns* (183); unfortunately, he reports that the letter is lost. He also says that at that time he did not even know Shaw by sight; however, Shaw had already read *The Devil's Disciple* to Stella and Forbes. Shaw told Ellen Terry of the "west end gentleman" and "east end dona" play in a letter of September 8, 1897: *CL*: I, 803. Archer discusses applause in his review of *Hamlet* in *The Theatrical "World" for 1897*: 254–8. Forbes describes Irving's congratulations in his autobiography: 184. Shaw's *Hamlet* review appears in *OTN*: III, 210–18. Ellen Terry objects to Stella's Ophelia in a letter to Shaw, October 1, 1897: *A Correspondence*: 189. Forbes-Robertson's letter to Shaw about the latter's *Hamlet* critique was written October 4, 1897 (British Library).

Stella's whereabouts during the summer and autumn of 1897 is, as usual, difficult to ascertain. Apparently she and Pat had taken rooms at the Mandeville Hotel, Mandeville Place West, where the children visited on weekends and holidays; or Pat may have lived alone at the Mandeville Hotel, Stella keeping rooms at 10 Mandeville Place. *Who's Who* for 1897 and 1898 gives her address as Milford, Surrey; a few letters from this period (Tanner Collection) are headed "Rake Mill, Milford, Surrey." "This in itself creates something of a mystery," writes Pearl Taylor, Librarian at Guildford, Surrey, "since by 1897 [Rake Mill] would seem to have been going to rack and ruin if not actually demolished. My suspicion is that she is referring to a nearby cottage which might have been the mill owner's house, or that she is confusing Rake Mill with nearby Enton Mill, which was converted to an exceedingly picturesque dwelling at about that time. That or she was staying at Rake Manor itself, which in 1897 was being restored by Lutyens. . . . There are no entries in any contemporary directories so presumably she might have been staying with friends, or renting a house which appears under the name of the owner or landlord. In 1899 the owner of Rake Manor was Mrs. Cavan-Irving and Enton Mill was owned by a Mr. A. E. Whitbourn." In the fall of 1897 Beo (now twelve) went to Ripley to school; Stella's letters from Milford mention going over to visit him. By Christmas 1897, according to a letter from Lulo, Pat had moved to 96 Queen Street; he and Stella do not seem to have lived together with any regularity after 53 Ashley Gardens. A letter from Henry Tanner to his niece Hildegarde von Jasmund mentions the inhabitants of 8 Glebe Place, Chelsea.

Forbes-Robertson describes the tour to Germany and Holland at some length in his autobiography: 186–96. Henry Tanner sent a letter of encouragement to reach Stella in Berlin a few hours before curtain time; she includes it in *MLSL* (239–40) along with her brief description of the Kaiser: 162–3. In the Tanner Collection there are a telegram for Lulo at Berlin ("LOVE AND BEST WISHES FROM MOTHER AND UNCLE"), where she had a small part in *Hamlet*, and a German poster from Hanover announcing *The Second Mrs. Tanqueray* presented by "*der Englischen Schauspiel-Gesellschaft*" on March 17, 1898, "*unter Direction von Mr. Forbes Robertson und Mitwirkung von Mrs. Patrick Campbell*." Stella relates the dispute over producing *Pelléas and Mélisande* in *MLSL*: 163–4.

CHAPTER SEVENTEEN: 1898-1899

Stella recounts the *Pelléas and Mélisande* experiment in *MLSL*: 162–76. George Edgar discusses Martin Harvey's love of the play in *Martin Harvey: Some Pages of His Life*: 212–21. The drawing of Gabriel Fauré and Stella by John Singer Sargent is owned by Mrs. Stella Coltman-Rogers, as is one of the drawings of Stella by Violet, Duchess of Rutland. Stella quotes Madeline Wyndham's letter upon the death of Sir Edward Burne-Jones: *MLSL*: 167. There are twelve telegrams from Sarah Bernhardt to Stella in the Enthoven Collection: June 28, 1898; July 15, 1903; April 29, 1904; May 12, May 19, June 4, and August 13, 1905; March 20, 1913; February 19 and February 23, 1915; April 19, 1917; and August 16, 1921.

The break with Lulo apparently came in 1898, since there are only a dozen or so letters to her sister in the Tanner Collection after that year and none between 1898 and 1901, compared to a hundred before. Stella mentions the quarrel finally in a letter to Lulo, undated but, from its black border and the address 33 Kensington Square, unquestionably written shortly after the death of Patrick Campbell.

Stella quotes Walkley's review of her Lady Macbeth in *MLSL*: 185–6. Max Beerbohm's theatre criticism is collected in *Around Theatres*, *More Theatres*, and *Last Theatres*; his review of *Macbeth* appeared in the *Saturday Review* of October 1, 1898. Max's anecdote about "It's a first-class thing" appears in S. N. Behrman's *Conversations with Max*: 237–8. I have taken the backstage encounter between Graham Robertson and Stella during *Macbeth* from his lively account in *Time Was* (252–3), a memoir to which this biography is very much indebted.

Shaw began *Caesar and Cleopatra* on April 23, 1898, and finished the play on December 9. Forbes was interested from the beginning; Stella does not mention the play. Shaw's letter to Max Hecht appears in *CL*: II, 78–9. Raymond Mander and Joe Mitchenson have said that when Stella and Forbes broke up management in 1899, they divided the spoils, Stella keeping *Caesar and Cleopatra*; it was Forbes, however, who produced the play with his wife, Gertrude Elliott, as Cleopatra.

Today 33 Kensington Square bears a plaque designating it as Stella's residence (see Epilogue). The Square preserves its quiet dignity although it is just south of thronging Kensington High Street. In the summer of 1981, Number 33 was up for sale. An affable resident, emerging from one of the fine houses on the north side and seeing my husband and me ringing the bell in vain, provided a description of the inside of 33, which he knew well, and said there had been few changes since Mrs. Campbell's time. Stella's daughter-in-law, Helen Bull Campbell Spinola, also describes the house in *Nothing But the Truth*.

Thirty-three letters from Stella to Gilbert Murray are in the manuscript collection of the Bodleian Library, Oxford. She was interested at this time in another play of Murray's, *Andromache*, and tried to arrange a reading on April 4, 1899, at Southport, but she was forced to bed there for a week with influenza and the reading did not take place. She was not the only person who found *Carlyon Sahib* interesting: Archer told Charles Charrington, "It is the most original and powerful play I have ever come across in ms.": Gilbert Murray, *An Unfinished Autobiography*: 157. Murray's comment to Archer about Stella's refusing to act is from the same source. After the failure of *Carlyon Sahib* she continued to encourage Murray, admonishing him during the run of *The Canary* in 1899, "What are you doing with the dramatic gift the lord has given you?"

Stella and Forbes are equally taciturn about the last days of their partnership in their autobiographies: *MLSL*: 187–9; *A Player*: 198–201. The quoted report of its dissolution appeared in the Boston *Evening Transcript* for December 13, 1899 (Harvard Theatre Collection). Admitting that theirs was an important and effective collaboration, Diana Forbes-Robertson in *My Aunt Maxine* is sympathetic to Forbes-Robertson, her father

(148–50). One of her statements, however, is inaccurate: "By correspondence, she played off Forbes-Robertson against G. B. Shaw; she loved to keep them both dancing, and she damaged Forbes-Robertson far more profoundly because she was trifling with a man whose love was not given lightly . . ." (149). But the famous Stella-Shaw love affair did not begin until 1912; during her years with Forbes, Stella met Shaw once on business and sent him one or two business letters. What kept Forbes (and other men) dancing was that Stella would not divorce Patrick Campbell. "That little woman I was living with—that Ophelia" comes from Mander's and Mitchenson's vast stock of theatrical lore.

### CHAPTER EIGHTEEN: 1899–1900

A copy of the agreement between Miss Santley and Stella for Stella's lease of the Royalty is in the Enthoven Collection. Stella gives Pat's undated letter in *MLSL* (200–1); Pat's letter to Lulo, the last of five, is in the Tanner Collection. A useful account of the formation of the Imperial Yeomanry and the South African War is Thomas Pakenham's *The Boer War* (New York: Random House, 1979). Details of the Prince of Wales's inspection of the Imperial Yeomanry come from an article in *News* (April 9, 1900) in the Harvard Theatre Collection. The movements of the Bucks Company of Lord Chesham's 10th Imperial Yeomanry before arriving in Africa are reported in the London *Times*.

Louis N. Parker wrote Stella about her Magda on May 9, 1899 (Rider Haggard Ms. Collection, Columbia University Libraries). George Arliss talks about his connection with Stella in *On the Stage*: 178–220. Graham Robertson praises Stella's Magda in *Time Was*: 255. He explains his preference for her Magda: Bernhardt was too much the superwoman for Magda: you felt she never could have sprung from such humble beginnings. She acted brilliantly, but you knew it was acting. Duse simply re-created her favorite character once more—the "noble, oppressed, misunderstood Martyr"; but that character had nothing to do with Magda. Stella includes Rosina Filippi's letter in *MLSL*: 150.

Arthur Symons reports his first-night experience after *Magda* to Rhoda Bouser (Wednesday, February 21, 1900). The series of letters from which this and subsequent information about his translation of *Mariana* is taken is in the Lohf Collection, Columbia University Libraries. I am grateful to Professor Karl Beckson, Brooklyn College, for drawing them to my attention.

Information about Patrick Campbell's death comes from Lord Chesham's letter to Stella (*MLSL*: 196) and from newspaper accounts in the London *Times* and in American newspapers. Stella gives her own account and prints numerous letters of sympathy in *MLSL*: 192–201. Her undated letter to Lulo is in the Tanner Collection. The story of Henry Tanner's visit to Bedford Square is told by Diana Forbes-Robertson in *My Aunt Maxine*: 149–50. Stella's "Men made love to me": *MLSL*: 107.

### CHAPTER NINETEEN: 1900

William Lyon Phelps published his appreciation of Stella's Magda in his *Autobiography with Letters*: 116–17.

I have drawn substantially on Dame Daphne du Maurier's account of Stella's and Gerald's relationship as she tells it in *Gerald: A Portrait*: 78–85. Stella contributed to this memoir, writing Dame Daphne from New York in July 1934: "I will be in England again very soon & then I will look through old letters & sit & remember & send you what I find that may please you & be of use to you. . . . I send you his last letter to me and I will send you a letter written years & years ago asking me to marry him. Someday we must meet and you question me & that will help me to remember all those things you would like to know" (Frederick R. Koch Collection, Harvard Theatre Collection). "REAL LOVE OF HER MAKES DU MAURIER'S ACTING REAL": unidentified newspaper clipping, dateline "London 5 January 1901" (Harvard Theatre Collection).

In the Bodleian Library there are nine letters from Stella to Gilbert Murray written during the 1900 tour, chiefly in September, all regarding the play or plays he was trying to complete. She was worried about the success of *Daventry* and evidently wanted a curtain-raiser to play with it.

Stella's prompt book of *Daventry* is in the Enthoven Collection, typed, with many additions and deletions, not all in her hand. H. Montgomery Hyde has provided an excellent account of Wilde, Harris, and *Mr. and Mrs. Daventry* in his introduction to the play (London: The Richards Press, 1956): 7–43. Another source is *The Letters of Oscar Wilde*; besides correspondence with Harris, the collection includes Wilde's letter of October 24, 1898, to Horace Sedger, assigning him sole and exclusive performing rights on the understanding that he would try to procure Forbes-Robertson and Mrs. Campbell for the leads: 762. In his journal for October 21, 1912, Arnold Bennett describes a conversation with Harris at Romano's during which Harris told him "more fully than ever before the story about Oscar and Mr. and Mrs. Daventry": *The Journal of Arnold Bennett*: 467. A. E. W. Mason's account of *Daventry* in *Sir George Alexander and the St. James' Theatre* strongly condemns Harris as a plagiarizer: Harris's play "not only had the screen scene in just the same position as it occupied in Wilde's letter to Alexander, but the rest of his scenario too, the same characters, the same *dénouement*. No doubt the play would have been a totally different thing if Wilde had written it. But the story and characters which made it live were Wilde's from the beginning to the end. Frank Harris adds an appendix to his book [*Life of Oscar Wilde*] which does not succeed in diminishing his debt and does not make any greater acknowledgment of it. He is not to be trusted": 90. Dent (176–7) cites an "unimpeachably honest source" for the assertion that Harris tried to make Stella his sleeping partner during their collaboration. Given Harris's character, there is no need to doubt he tried; given hers, no reason to doubt she refused.

The episodes of the Prince of Wales almost falling out of the royal box, Stella's and du Maurier's generosity in helping him exploit the role of Keane, and Stella's insisting her actors make up with blue chins are all related by Arliss in his memoir: 199–206.

Forbes-Robertson gives an account of his engaging Gertrude Elliott in *A Player Under Three Reigns*, as does Diana Forbes-Robertson in *My Aunt Maxine*: 150–1. Shaw tells Ellen Terry that her portrait has replaced Stella's in Forbes's study in a letter of October 28, 1900: *A Correspondence*: 278.

CHAPTER TWENTY: 1900–1901

Stella wrote Gilbert Murray about *Andromache* on November 15, 1900. However, Ellen Terry told Shaw on June 13, 1900, "I have bought Gilbert Murray's Andromache. . . . It's fine": *A Correspondence*: 274. *Andromache* was eventually performed by the Stage Society twice in 1901. The play "Mithue"(?) that Stella refers to apparently never materialized.

Max Beerbohm's play was based on his prose fable *The Happy Hypocrite* (1897). Ivor Novello eventually produced Clemence Dane's full-evening version, but it failed. Arliss quotes Max's "Vague Hints" in his autobiography: 201–3. Max's letter of December 11, 1900, to Reggie Turner from Brighton is included in *Sir Max Beerbohm: Letters to Reggie Turner*: 138–9. Max's letter to Stella about the cancelled party is dated January 1, 1901 (lent by Patrick Beech).

Patrick Beech kindly lent me a collection of Stella's prompt books, souvenir programs, and photograph albums, including autographed souvenir programs of the 100th night of *Daventry*, the 50th performance of *Ebbsmith*, and the 73rd of *Tanqueray*. Hesketh Pearson describes Lewis Waller's reaction to the Queen's death in *The Last Actor-Managers*: 44. Frank Harris blamed the demise of his play on Stella: ". . . Mrs. Patrick Campbell got rid of Fred Kerr, and so spoilt the whole cast." But Harris is often inaccurate. He also says, for example, ". . . after the period of mourning had passed my play was the only play, I believe, revived in that season, and it ran for fifty or sixty more nights . . .": *Frank Harris: His Life and Adventures: An Autobiography* (London: The Richards Press, 1947): 539; but Harris's was by no means the only play revived, and *Daventry* ran only from February 5 to 23.

Dent quotes Max Beerbohm's review of the 1901 *Ebbsmith*: 108. Pinero's letter to Stella of February 28, 1901: *The Collected Letters of Sir Arthur Pinero*: 183–4. Dent quotes the *Times* accolade of May 13, 1901: 182. The passage quoted from *Mariana* is from the translation by James Graham, published in 1895. Symons signed an agreement with Stella about *Mariana*, which was to be described as "translated by J. M. Graham and adapted by Arthur Symons"; however, when the play opened on May 23, 1901, Graham was listed as "adapter" and Symons's name did not appear at all.

Dent quotes Archer on *Tanqueray*: 179. John Davidson wrote to Stella about her Paula on September 8, 1901 (Rider Haggard Ms. Collection, Columbia University Libraries).

In a letter of October 27, 1901, Anthony Hope (Hawkins) asked Stella to consider *The God in the Car* because he was reluctant it should never see the light and because the heroine's role admirably suited her. He said he was ready to put money into the venture and become a partner (Rider Haggard Ms. Collection, Columbia University Libraries). The September 1901 exchange between Stella and Shaw is printed in *TC*: 4–6. Actually, the title of the "fairytale scheme" is not mentioned, but since Stella was contemplating *La Princesse lointaine* and since Shaw mentions Rostand, it seems likely that this was the play. Shaw's letter to Archer about the *odor di femmina*: February 22, 1901: *CL*: II, 218–19.

Gerald du Maurier's letters from the autumn tour of 1901 are quoted from *Gerald: A Portrait*: 85. Stella wrote Dame Daphne (July 9, 1934) from New York (see Notes, chapter 19); her comments about Gerald are quoted from this letter.

Stella summarizes *Beyond Human Power* and prints congratulatory letters from Shaw, Murray, Yeats, and Wilberforce in *MLSL*: 203–11. Graham Robertson reports his experience at the matinee in *Time Was*: 256–7. Parker wrote Stella his reaction on November 8, 1901 (Rider Haggard Ms. Collection, Columbia University Libraries). Stella thanks Shaw for his kind letter on November 7, 1901 (British Library). Shaw's letters about *Beyond Human Power* are quoted from *TC*: 6–9. Stella's letter to Murray about tickets is in the Bodleian Library. Interestingly, Lady Gregory's reaction to the play is expressed in language much like Yeats's: "I saw Bjornson's *Beyond Human Power* today. It is manifestly an unbeliever's account of belief." Yeats also wrote Stella that the essence of genius was precision, and that the zealous Sang had no precision. Lady Gregory: Björnson "cannot understand that the religious genius like every other kind of genius differs from mere zeal because it is perfectly precise. His parson would have occupied himself with nothing transcendental, but probably with the housing of the working classes or the like. He is even not a little vulgar, and one is not happy until he is gone from the stage. Apart from this it is a really absorbing play, and Mrs. Campbell plays it beautifully": *Seventy Years: Being the Autobiography of Lady Gregory*: 348. Obviously, Yeats and Lady Gregory talked over the play together!

Arliss discusses the casting and his last-minute hiring for the American tour in *On the Stage*: 208–10. Sailing as members of the American company were Arliss, Herbert Waring, George Titheradge, Adeline Bourne, Charles Bryant, William Burchill, A. Bromley Davenport, Mr. and Mrs. D. McCarthy, Lucy Miller, W. G. Saunders, Gilbert Trent, Florence Montgomery, Lilian Lisle, and Mrs. Theodore Wright.

*Notes*

CHAPTER TWENTY-ONE: 1901–1902

Chief sources for this chapter are *MLSL*, George Arliss's *On the Stage*, George C. Tyler's brash and lively *Whatever Goes Up*, and newspaper clippings and souvenir programs in the Harvard Theatre Collection, the Billy Rose Theatre Collection at Lincoln Center, the Regenstein Library of the University of Chicago, and the Free Library of Philadelphia Theatre Collection.

Stella discusses her first American tour at some length (212–30). She mistakenly gives the date of her Chicago opening as January 7, 1902; it was actually December 30, 1901. In these pages she quotes a letter from Arthur Bertram to Henry Tanner about her record-breaking Chicago run and several undated letters of her own to her uncle, which I have drawn from, as well as the irate "Lady and the Pup" letter in the New York *Evening Journal* (February 4, 1902), Norman Hapgood's criticism, and the "tanbark" article which I quote in part.

Stella's speech at the Fortnightly Club in Chicago was reported in the Milwaukee *Journal* (January 11, 1902), which also recorded that she was offered the immense sum of $3000 for a single matinee at the Pabst Theatre in that city on Thursday, January 9, but then (January 3, 1902) that "It is possible that Milwaukee lovers of the drama will not see Mrs. Patrick Campbell on January 9, as announced, owing to the smallness of the subscription list so far. . . ." The matinee did not materialize.

The New York *Times* (January 28, 1902) reported that on the 27th a fire exploded dynamite cartridges in a section of subway tunnel and the explosion practically wrecked the Murray Hill Hotel, ruined the façade of the Grand Union Hotel, and did minor damage for blocks around. It is possible that Stella miscalled the Murray Hill Hotel (which fronted Park Avenue) the Park Avenue Hotel, which, she said, was "blown to smithereens."

The Harvard Theatre Collection and Billy Rose Theatre Collection proved invaluable resources for Stella's first tour, which is scarcely mentioned by Dent, although many clippings gave no source other than city or date. The Mrs. Cornelius Vanderbilt story is dated "New York, 23 February 1902"; the article reporting the St. Louis reunion appeared in the New York *World* (May 24, 1902); the New York *Sun*'s "She didn't need the tanbark" appeared earlier on January 16, 1902.

CHAPTER TWENTY-TWO: 1902–1903

Information about the changes at 8 Glebe Place comes from a copy of a letter from Henry Tanner to his niece Hildegarde von Jasmund Courtney in the Tanner Collection, undated, but written shortly after Stella closed her run at the New Theatre at the end of July 1903. Stella very much blamed Lulo for abandoning their mother. In *MLSL*, however, she altered her original version of Lulo's defection from "I found [my mother] on my first return from America in apartments alone, my unmarried sister having gone to live with a girl friend of hers in the country" (the *Queen*, June 17, 1922) to "I found her on my first return from America in apartments alone, circumstances having led my unmarried sister to live with a girl friend in the country": 281. The two letters from Stella to Lulo in this chapter are undated; I have attributed them to the summer of 1902, when Stella's anger at the life Lulo had chosen was apparently renewed because of Mrs. Tanner's having to leave London.

Again, much of the information about Stella's second American tour comes from clippings and programs in the Harvard Theatre Collection, the Billy Rose Theatre Collection, and the Free Library of Philadelphia Theatre Collection. I am also indebted to Russell Hartley, director of the Archives for the Performing Arts, Mill Valley, California, for providing data about Stella's company in San Francisco. Edith Wharton talks briefly about her association with Stella in *A Backward Glance*: 167. W. de Wagstaffe's interview with Stella was published in *The Theatre Magazine* (January 1903): 22–5. Stella discusses *Aunt Jeannie* and *The Joy of Living* in *MLSL*: 230–6. Stella's exchange with Charles Frohman is documented by Isaac F. Marcosson and Daniel Frohman in *Charles Frohman*: 225–6. William Winter's virulently negative summation of Stella's American career appears in his *The Wallet of Time*: II, 338–67.

Newspapers give conflicting reports of Stella's arrangements with Frohman. One source announces that her engagement with him ended in January 1903, and that she would tour the West under her own direction, assisted by actor Frederick Kerr and managed by Carl Herbert. But in San Francisco she appeared at the Columbia Theatre under the direction of Charles Frohman; apparently they did business together until the end of her tour.

Stella's dinner-party repartee is reported by an unidentified Philadelphia newspaper clipping ("What does a cow have"); by Mrs. Claude Beddington in *All That I Have Met* (London: Cassell, 1929) ("Tell me, which would you sooner"); by herself ("Someone has made you unhappy"): 221–2; and by James Agate in *Ego* 7: 27 ("No *navy*, I suppose"). Stella reports Hildegarde von Jasmund Courtney's reaction to her acting and Henry Tanner's reaction to her touring in *MLSL*: 10–11, 242. The "Lord" Lowndes story was reported by Kay Ashton-Stevens in *Variety* (January 7, 1953). Sir Arthur Balfour's dictated answer to Stella's plea about the quarantine is dated from 10 Downing Street, May 26, 1903 (lent by Patrick Beech). *Life's* opinion that Stella was the best actress of the day on the English-speaking stage was voiced in the October 2, 1902, issue.

Stella's appearance on June 15, 1903, at Madame Jane Hading's performance of *Tanqueray* was noted in the *Illustrated London News* (June 20, 1903). Stella prints Sarah Bernhardt's birthday message and mentions the £100 loan in *MLSL*: 178. Stella's letter to Gilbert Murray (Bodleian Library) is dated only 1903, but obviously was written shortly after the closing of *The Joy of Living*. In that letter she also says, "I wonder whether you cared at all for 'Es lebe' in its English dress. I thought the men abominable." Stella's working copy of *Undine* was lent me by Patrick Beech; the play has been cut and altered, some of Undine's songs, for example, being transferred from one act to another. Graham Robertson reports delightfully the quarrel over the tail in *Time Was*: 258–9. Stella gives young Stella's letter from Dresden in *MLSL*: 252–3. I am very grateful to the Rt. Rev. Henry W. Hobson, Cincinnati, and to his sister, Mrs. Eleanor Hobson Mackenzie of Sandy Spring, Maryland, for their vivid accounts of Stella and Pinkie at the Savoy Hotel in Dresden.

CHAPTER TWENTY-THREE: 1904–1905

John Davidson wrote the three-act *A Queen's Romance: A Version of Victor Hugo's "Ruy Blas"* (London: Grant Richards, 1904) for Lewis Waller in 1901. Stella deals with the play briefly in *MLSL*: 237–8. In 1909 Davidson (whom she always admired), discouraged with his failure as a popular playwright, committed suicide by drowning. Again I am indebted to Graham Robertson for the costume dispute: *Time Was*: 258. Charles Ricketts seldom admired Stella: "If Mrs. Pat's voice is her own, and not worn like false hair, what a fungus creature she is—not a wholesome growth for blossom and fruit—well-coloured and of the abnormal-earthy.—I speak of her as shown in *Ruy Blas*" (Michael Field, *Works and Days*: British Library). I am grateful to Joan Reardon for passing on to me Ricketts's comments on Stella, recorded by Katharine Bradley and Edith Cooper ("Michael Field").

Stella tells of her uncle's death and Beo's and Stella's dissatisfaction with their lives: *MLSL*: 238–44, 249–55. Henry Tanner's death certificate in the General Register Office, London, gives the cause as chronic Bright's disease, immediate heart failure. Stella's letter, dated 1904, to Gilbert Murray is in the Bodleian Library.

Dame Edith (D.D.) Lyttelton, Alfred Lyttelton's second wife, was one of Stella's closest friends. Stella produced another play of hers in 1906, and D.D. played an important part in the romance between Stella and Bernard Shaw, as her letters to Shaw in the British Library prove. Her papers and numerous letters to her from Stella are in the Churchill College Library, Cambridge. Her son Oliver Lyttelton wrote a memoir of the Shaw-Campbell liaison called "A Staged Romance" which appeared in the *Times* (London) of October 19, 1968. I am indebted to Viscountess Caroline Chandos, widow of the late Lord Chandos, for information about the family papers.

Stella discusses her personal and professional relationship with Sarah Bernhardt in *MLSL*: 176–83. Suze Rueff describes their first collaboration in *I Knew Sarah Bernhardt*: 135–9. Stella's copy of Maeterlinck's play in French (Bruxelles: Paul Lacomblez, 1898; 7th ed.), bound in magenta silk and *galon d'argent*, was lent to me by Patrick Beech. The copy is much marked by Stella with pronunciation cues, stage business, and the usual sketches of herself in profile; and inscribed in her own hand, "Melicent Stone to her loving friend Beatrice Stella Campbell." (Melicent Stone is mentioned in *MLSL* as the dear friend who helped her negotiate her first American tour.) For the Stella-Sarah production of *Pelléas*, three scenes (I: iv; III: iii; and IV: iii) were cut. On page 49 Stella has written the name Jean Ingelow (1820–1897); she was later to make frequent recitations of Ingelow's "High Tide on the Coast of Lincolnshire." Graham Robertson describes his association with Sarah and Stella in *Time Was* (252–5); I have liberally borrowed from his account.

Sources for Stella's third American tour include *MLSL* (260–71) and clippings from the theatre collections of Harvard, Billy Rose, and Free Library of Philadelphia. The interview with the New York *Herald* reporter who found her nunlike appeared October 6, 1904; the report that she might be lamed for life in the Philadelphia *Inquirer*, January 4, 1905; comments on "Miss Stella" in the Toledo *Blade*, April 1, 1905. William Winter's verdict on *The Sorceress* is collected in *The Wallet of Time*: II, 358–61. The Regenstein Library of the University of Chicago has letters from Stella, her daughter, and Beo to Mrs. Francis (Harriett) Carolan of Crossways, Burlingame, California, a close friend of Stella whom she probably met in San Francisco in 1903. Stella relates her "knee plus ultra" quip, her fears about aging, and her "screaming & falling about in Sardou's silly play" in letters to D.D. of February 1905, written in the Philadelphia hospital (Churchill College Library, Cambridge).

CHAPTER TWENTY-FOUR: 1905–1907

Reginald Pound tells the story of Stella lending scenery to Duse in his *Arnold Bennett: A Biography* (New York: Harcourt, Brace, 1953): 300. Stella herself told it to Bennett on July 4, 1923, when he recorded in his journal, "Mrs. Patrick Campbell came for lunch and stayed until 4.30. . . ."

*MLSL* recounts her adventures on tour with Bernhardt (179–82); in the unpublished *Chance Medley* Stella tells the *"les morts sont toujours avec nous"* episode. Dent reports the live-goldfish story (158), quoting a letter from May Agate, sister of James, to the *Sunday Times* (July 26, 1953). Dent does not believe that the live-fish and painted-fish stories can both be true; yet since Stella would hardly invent the painted tobacco pouch, and since May Agate probably did not invent the live goldfish, and since the live goldfish was a likely retaliation for the raw egg (Stella never knew when to quit), it seems probable that both practical jokes occurred.

Ellen Terry at first disliked *Captain Brassbound's Conversion* and believed Shaw had written it for Mrs. Pat, since he was always proclaiming his fascination with her. She complains of the play and Shaw defends it in letters of August 3, 4, 6, 8, and 9, 1899: *A Correspondence*: 244–50.

Dent quotes MacCarthy and Walkley on *The Whirlwind* and *Undine*: 207–8. Shaw's prescription for the "modern manager" comes from a review, "Mr. Daly Fossilizes," in *OTN*: I, 171–8. Stella discusses D.D. Lyttelton's *The Macleans of Bairness* in letters to D.D. written from the hospital in Philadelphia during January, February, and March 1905 (Churchill College Library, Cambridge). Walkley on *The Macleans* is quoted by Dent: 208. Stella describes her *Bondman* experience in *MLSL*: 271–3; Walkley's comments in Dent: 209. Dent also tells of Dorothy Burroughes's association with Stella, quoting from her letter to him: 209–11. Charles Merrill Mount in *John Singer Sargent* describes Stella's visit to Sargent's studio: 276–8.

Stella's letter to Shaw of December 10, 1906, is printed in *TC*: 10–11; his "Princess with the Sixteen Chins" reply of December 12 (Boston University Library) is not.

Stella talks about playing Hedda Gabler in *MLSL*: 273–6; she played on March 5, 8, 12, 15, 19, 22, and 26, 1907. Stella said that the version she acted was William Archer's translation, but that it had been tampered with and seemed wrong in places to her. Her prompt book of *Hedda*, however (enclosed in a cover of gold grosgrain edged in blue-and-gray ribbon, lent me by Patrick Beech), is the 1907 edition for which Archer was writing an introduction as her run opened. It is not, therefore, the text she acted from at the Court, but the text she used for her own productions of *Hedda Gabler*. Text and inserted leaves are meticulously annotated in clear writing (though Stella's), with properties, lighting, movements, business, sound effects, and calls indicated. As an example:

> *Beginners*
>    *Miss Tesman*
>    *Berta*
>    *Tesman*
>    Set couch on rake
>    L lime to be on couch R
> *Hand properties*
>    Special Bouquet with card attached off L for Berta
>    Tesman's shoes in parcel off L
>    small black portmanteau off L
>    slip of paper with written address for Mrs. Elvsted
> *Important*
>    Heaps of books on stage—on tables sideboard etc.
> *No Plants or Palms*

Some dozen lines have been cut and about the same number of speeches shortened—for example, Mrs. Elvsted's "No, of course not. For that matter, he was away from home himself—he was travelling" reads in Stella's book: "No, he was away from home" (Act I). There are a few changes: Hedda's "Very handsome indeed!" to "Very grand indeed!" and Mrs. Elvsted's "Oh, heaven be praised—!" to "Thank God!" for instance. The most notable change occurs in Act III, where Stella has altered

> LÖVBORG. None. I will only try to make an end of it all—the sooner the better.
> HEDDA. Eilert Lövborg—listen to me.—Will you not try to—to do it beautifully?

to

> LÖVBORG. None. I will make an end of it all—the sooner the better.
> HEDDA. Eilert—listen.—Will you not try to—make an end of it beautifully?

Desmond MacCarthy's reviews are collected in *The Court Theatre 1904–1907*. Max's review is collected in *Last Theatres*: 279–82.

Stella's letters to her mother about Beo's and young Stella's going on the stage are included in *MLSL*: 278–83. I am grateful to Mrs. M. J. North, Librarian, Hertford College,

Oxford, for the following reply to my inquiry about Beo at Oxford: "I am afraid we have very little information about him. In our Matriculation Register he is entered as being matriculated into the University in October 1905.... There is a note that he was entered for Christ Church College, but this has been crossed out. Apart from this we know nothing about him, not even the subject he was reading. He is not listed amongst those who passed examinations (Honour moderations) in 1906–7 nor is he listed as a member of the University in the University Calendar for 1907, though he is for 1906. This suggests that he only stayed for a year and possibly took no examinations." Patrick Beech is the source for Beo's wire.

Ben Webster's account of the 1907 provincial tour with Stella is given in Dent from letters that Webster wrote his wife, May (later Dame May) Whitty: 267–9. Mr. MacCullough's negotiations for the American tour are announced in a story of November 2, 1907, cabled to the New York *Herald*, headed "MRS. CAMPBELL'S TROUBLE SETTLED," and her sailing date is given as November 3, 1907.

## CHAPTER TWENTY-FIVE: 1907–1908

Chief sources for this chapter are *MLSL* (285–99), which includes Stella's letters to her mother, the *Electra* review in *Town Talk*, and Modjeska's congratulatory note; newspaper clippings, programs, and reviews in the theatre collections of Harvard, Billy Rose, the Philadelphia Free Library, and Russell Hartley's Archives for the Performing Arts, Mill Valley, California; Campbell material in the Regenstein Library, University of Chicago; Margaret Webster's *The Same Only Different* (219–28), to which I am indebted for Ben Webster's insights; and Helen Bull Campbell Spinola's account of her meeting with Beo, his letters, and his proposal in her autobiography, *Nothing But the Truth*: 69–75. I am grateful to Mrs. Gail T. Boatman, current resident of the Bull house in Quincy, Illinois, for providing me with photocopies of this hard-to-locate book.

The interview about Shaw appeared in the New York *Telegraph* (November 9, 1907). The inconveniences Stella suffered in her private Pullman are recorded in the Chicago *Examiner* (January 5, 1908) in an article headed "NO PRIVATE CAR FOR MRS. PAT." Other newspaper accounts of November 23 (Springfield, Massachusetts) tell of Smith College girls coming to the Court Square Theatre performance of *Tanqueray* there because *Tanqueray* was "forbidden" in Northampton, and of November 25 (Worcester, Massachusetts) of Professor George Rockwood of the Worcester Polytechnic Institute restoring Stella's purse, which she lost driving through the park. Ben Webster's letters to May Whitty (November 22, 1907, and December 11, 1907) are printed in Dent: 267–9. Stella's letter to Gilbert Murray about his *Electra* is dated only 1906, but *Electra* was performed at the Court in January and February of that year. Stella's copy of *Electra* in the Enthoven Collection shows extensive cutting, partly due to the fact that it was played in a double bill. The interview at the Plaza appeared in the *Globe* February 17, 1908. I am grateful to Warren B. Wickliffe, reference librarian of the Burlingame Public Library, for providing me with information about Harriett Pullman Carolan. Mrs. Carolan eventually built the spectacular Carolands, a ninety-two-room French chateau standing on 554.32 acres in Burlingame, today a registered California landmark. Beo's letter to Harriett Carolan is in the Regenstein Library, University of Chicago. The story of "Lord" Lowndes coming to woo Stella on shipboard is told by Kay Ashton-Stevens in *Variety* (January 7, 1953); Ashton Stevens saw Lowndes off in San Francisco, and Lowndes wrote him later about his unsuccessful pursuit.

CHAPTER TWENTY-SIX: 1908–1909

Shaw mentions his telephone call to young Stella in letters of July 1 and 4, 1908, to Harley Granville-Barker (Humanities Research Center, University of Texas at Austin).

Stella says in *MLSL* that her mother died in July (299–300), but the death certificate in the General Register Office, London, shows she died August 4, 1908. Her age is given as 75; family records, however, indicate that she was 73. She is called "Widow of John Tanner of independent means of 23 Glebe Place"; Henry Tanner had evidently changed households from number 8 to 23. Patrick Beech told me that his mother adored Louisa Romanini Tanner; it was another source of rivalry between Stella and her daughter. There is an undated letter in the Tanner Collection from Stella to "Lise," presumably a lay person connected with the *pension*, about the distribution of Mrs. Tanner's possessions: the painting of "The Nativity" to the Reverend Mother; Watts's "Life and Death" to be returned to Roy Hill; Stella to have *Lux Mundi*, Marcus Aurelius, and Hudson's *Psychic Phenomena* (all of which she had given) as well as the works of Plato, Socrates, volume I of *Gleanings* by Gladstone, and all family papers and letters.

Robert Ross states that Stella played Oscar Wilde's *A Florentine Tragedy* nine times on tour in 1908; I have found no other mention of the performances (Ross to Sturge Moore, September 9, 1908, and February 6, 1909: *Robert Ross: Friend of Friends*, edited Margery Ross [London: Jonathan Cape, 1952]: 198–9). Stella also considered Wilde's *Salomé*: "Dear Mrs. Pat has reconsidered her large 'No' to Salomé and has telegraphed for the Text which has been sent to her. I do not feel hopeful, for Shannon's offer to do a drawing may have been mistaken by her for an offer from J. J. Shannon": Charles Ricketts to Robert Ross (no date): *Friend of Friends*: 126. Stella did not do *Salomé*. She comments briefly on her Electra and Deirdre in *MLSL*, quoting Archer on her London performances: 301–2. Yeats's letter to his father is dated Sunday, December 27, 1908; to Florence Farr, Coole Park (September 1908?) in *The Letters of W. B. Yeats*: 474–6, 511–12. The text of *Deirdre* that Stella acted from (London: A. H. Bullen and Dublin: Maunsel, 1907) was lent me by Patrick Beech and contains the alterations Yeats made for her performance. "There are two passages in this play as published which I always knew to be mere logic, mere bones, and yet, after many attempts, I thought it impossible to alter them," wrote Yeats in a brief preface to the alterations. "When, however, Mrs. Campbell offered to play the part, my imagination began to work again. I think they are now as they should be." The alterations occur after the song of the three musicians together (pp. 10–14) in Naisi's speech, which, changed, begins "Be silent, Deirdre," then picks up the original text. Other changes occur on page 19, from Fergus's "Why, that's no wonder" to Deirdre's "Where would you go, Naisi?" page 23. Holloway's impressions of the Dublin *Deirdre* come from *Joseph Holloway's Abbey Theatre*: 118–22. Yeats's comments to John Quinn were added to a previous letter on November 15, 1908: *Letters*: 512. The hair-burning incident was reported to Dent by several correspondents (223) and Stella mentions it in the quoted letter to Harriett Carolan of November 18, 1908 (Regenstein Library, University of Chicago). Dent quotes Walkley's reaction to the London *Electra*: 223.

Stella is brief about Beo's and Helen's courtship and marriage in *MLSL*: 303–4; the chief source is Helen Campbell Spinola's *Nothing But the Truth*: 75–8. Of interest too is a letter from Beo to Harriett Carolan written from St. Louis (Regenstein Library) that states, "I am now *the* married man & full of *a sense of responsibility*." The arrival at Kensington Square, her introduction to London society, and the leprosy episode all come from Helen's *Nothing But the Truth* (79–93), an invaluable impression of Stella in action, though the autobiography itself is unrelentingly arch.

Stella comments on *His Borrowed Plumes*: *MLSL*: 304–7. Ralph G. Martin discusses the play and critical reaction to it at some length in his *Jennie: The Life of Lady Randolph Churchill*, vol. II, and quotes Jennie's letter to Leonie of June 27, 1909. Helen Spinola records the entrance of Lady Diana Manners: 92. Dent quotes both Walkley's and Beerbohm's reviews: 224–6. A program and cast photograph of *His Borrowed Plumes* is in the Mander and Mitchenson Theatre Collection, London.

Stella's discomfort at His Majesty's (*MLSL*: 307–8) is confirmed by Graham Robertson's statement that she was "always a little ruffled at His Majesty's" in connection with the wasp story in *Time Was*: 257. Stella's retort to Tree's artist-manager comment comes from an unidentified newspaper interview in the Billy Rose Theatre Collection files, and seems to have been circulated by Stella herself during her 1905 American tour.

I have paraphrased Yeats's account of reading *The Player Queen* from his account to his father, J. B. Yeats (November 29, 1909): *Letters*: 539–41. Earlier, in October 1908, he had written to John Quinn: "I have finished the prose version of what is to be a new verse play, *The Player Queen*, and Mrs. Patrick Campbell talks of producing it. I am trying to get the prose version typed that I may go through it with her. She wants me to write, as she phrases it, with her at my elbow. I am rather inclined to try the experiment for once as I believe I shall be inspired rather than thwarted by trying to give her as many opportunities as possible. At the worst we can but quarrel": *Letters*: 512. Helen slipped out of the room fifteen minutes after Yeats started reading. "The only time I found Yeats worth listening to was when he could be coaxed out of his bee-loud glades and induced to talk about spirits and levitation," she wrote in her autobiography (104). "He solemnly swore that he'd seen a full-sized billiard table lifted six feet into the air and rooted there so firmly that it had to be *chopped to pieces* to get it down."

CHAPTER TWENTY-SEVEN: 1910–1912

Stella writes about her first American vaudeville tour: *MLSL*: 308–11. Alan Dale's reaction appeared in the New York *American* for February 14, 1910. Stella Moore Coltman-Rogers often heard Stella say, "I can hold an audience as long as I want to with my back." Ashton Stevens's interview with Stella appeared in the Chicago *Examiner* on April 3, 1910. Stella says in *MLSL* that she spent ten weeks at St. Agathe des Monts; according to dates from press clippings of her tour, this is impossible: it was probably ten days.

Winifred Beech (later Lady Fortescue) describes her mission to win over Stella in her memoir *There's Rosemary . . . There's Rue . . .*, quoted by Dent: 230–2. Patrick Beech gave me helpful information about his mother's years in Africa.

Pinero's letter to Stella of September 21, 1910, is included in his *Collected Letters*: 230; the "little light play" he was working on was *Preserving Mr. Panmure*. The date of Stella's letter to Gilbert Murray asking for *Medea* is difficult to decipher; it is perhaps October 9, 1910, which could be supported by her plan of taking the play to the States. Diana Cooper describes the St. Ursula tableau in *The Rainbow Comes and Goes*: 78–9. Boston University Library has a telegram from Stella to Nigel Playfair of October 5, 1910: "WARM AFFECTIONATE CONGRATULATIONS DELIGHTED TO BE GODMOTHER TELL ME WHEN WHERE THE CHRISTENING GREETINGS TO YOU ALL THREE"; and the undated letter ("Indeed indeed I don't want to go to America") ends, "I look forward to Monday the 31st [October]," evidently the day of the christening. Before leaving for America, Stella also attended the wedding of Clare Frewen to Wilfred Sheridan at St. Margaret's, Westminster, on October 15. Stella was a friend of Wilfred's parents, Algy and Mary Sheridan; several letters in the Tanner Collection are dated from their Frampton Court home. Stella sat between Lord Charles Beresford and his wife at the wedding ("How neat of him!" Oswald Frewen observed, noting also that "Mrs. Pat kept making the most startling remarks all through the service"): Anita Leslie's *Clare Sheridan*: 62–3.

In *MLSL* Stella confuses the times of acting *The Foolish Virgin* (New York, opened December 19, 1910) and *Lady Patricia* (London, opened March 22, 1911), putting *Lady Patricia* first and thus distorting the chronology of events during 1910 and 1911. Norman Hapgood discusses Stella's acting and their friendship in *The Changing Years*: 161–4. Eric Barnes's biography of Edward Sheldon, *The Man Who Lived Twice*, puts the date of his meeting Stella in New York as the winter of 1912. She was not in New York during the winter of 1912, but was in 1910–1911; I have thus offered 1911 as the year of their meeting.

Stella's copy of *Lady Patricia*, its few alterations indicating how well the part suited her, is in the Enthoven Collection. Stella prints a letter from Lyall Swete (whose name she misspells Sweete) in *MLSL*: "Wonderful. There is nothing left on that score for me to say. The papers have said it all with one unanimous shout of delight. Oh, but I knew they would" (dated "Garrick Club, 23 March 1911"): 311. The Souls: "the remarkable group of friends, among whom Lady Desborough, Lady Wemyss and Balfour had been leading members, their lighter activities including pencil-and-paper games which frightened their contemporaries. Lady Wemyss denied anything like a clique saying that they were 'merely a group of very intelligent, articulate people who happened to be friends and share a love of good talk; and that in so far as they were a "charmed circle," the line was drawn by those outside, not inside, the circle'": Index to Lady Cynthia Asquith: *Diaries 1915–1918*. Dent quotes Walkley's review in part (235); Alan Dale's reaction appeared in the Chicago *Examiner* (June 10, 1911). Athene Seyler told Dent about the "What a pretty face!" incident: 235. Stella's letter (April 25, 1911) asking Harriett Carolan for money is in the Regenstein Library. Rudolph Besier complained to Hesketh Pearson that Stella wrecked *Lady Patricia*; Pearson reports the claim in *The Last Actor-Managers*: 24.

Lena Ashwell discusses her activism in the Actresses' Franchise League in *Myself a Player* (London: Michael Joseph, 1936). Adeline Bourne, who had toured with Stella in America, was also very active in the A.F.L., as was Athene Seyler. Stella's "The best thing in this world" was written to Elizabeth Young, Dublin, quoted in Dent: 222. By June 17, 1914, Stella was showing some interest in the suffrage cause, writing to Shaw: "Lady Maud Parry has a suffragette meeting at 17 Kensington Square at 3 o'c today. Lena Ashwell is going to speak. I wish I could have been there" (lent by Patrick Beech).

Stella says little about *Bella Donna*; other sources say a good deal. Basing his account on Hichens's memoir, *Yesterday*, Dent tells the tarboosh and donkey stories; he also names Cornwallis-West as the source of Stella's "devil-curate" description of Hichens: 237–8. Mary Grey (Mrs. Fagan) wrote Dent about Stella's throwing the novel into the slop pail: 239. Graham Robertson assessed *Bella Donna* in *Time Was*: 250; Margot Hamilton communicated her impression to Dent: 238. A. E. W. Mason tells of Alexander's trials during the run and of his listening to Shaw's *Pygmalion* in *Sir George Alexander and the St. James' Theatre*: 202–4. Hesketh Pearson describes the chocolate-flicking and Alexander's opinion of *Pygmalion* as a "dead cert" in *The Last Actor-Managers*: 25–6.

Helen Campbell Spinola tells of visiting Cornwallis-West in New York, about her trials back at Kensington Square, and about the first night of *The Dust of Egypt* in *Nothing But the Truth*: 99, 112, 116, 121–2. Stella comments on Beo's first night in an undated letter to "Symons" (presumably Arthur), a copy of which was kindly lent me by John M. Fuhrman.

## CHAPTER TWENTY-EIGHT: 1912

The bulk of Stella's and Shaw's correspondence has been published in *TC*, edited by Alan Dent under the rigorous supervision of Stella's daughter, Stella Beech. Some letters and passages were not shown to Dent at all; some were simply crossed out with instructions that they were not to be used; some were released for the book but not for the serial rights. For this biography I have had access to Stella's original letters to Shaw, generously lent me by Patrick Beech; and to Shaw's original letters to her, preserved in the Special Collections of the Libraries of the State University of New York at Buffalo. Parts of Shaw's letters were also cut for publication. In this chapter the passage "Now to business . . . I wonder what sort of man he is" was not shown Dent; it is part of Stella's letter postmarked December 11, 1912: *TC*: 72. Lines cut from Shaw's letters of this period include "O sweet of body and kissable all over" (October 30, 1912: *TC*: 51–2); "I bless your illness for revealing the modelled reality of your beauty—you are really much lovelier than I thought" (November 3, 1912: *TC*: 52–3); and "It's all over now: I cant write any more. I dont understand it. I am not terrified. That's what ought to terrify me; but it doesnt. Still, nothing has happened as I thought it would happen. And thats odd. Am I going to learn something? I wonder——no: you have done your duty and suffered your suffering in that way. But I havnt. I must bring forth something. A sister for Liza" (November 18, 1912: *TC*: 57–8). Letters quoted in this chapter date from Stella's thanking Shaw for the reading of *Pygmalion* (June 27, 1912) to Stella's "Now to business" letter. Four of Stella's letters of this time are not included in *TC*.

*MLSL* provides another source for this period (313–21), although Stella's chronology is occasionally confusing. She suggests, for instance, that her collapse and subsequent crisis occurred immediately upon her return from the Continent; but she was writing Shaw from Kensington Square in late August and it was not until September 19 that the papers announced her near death. Stella prints Madeline Wyndham's and Ellen Terry's letters of sympathy, and also tells of Cornwallis-West visiting her and pleading with her to live.

Helen Campbell Spinola gives her perspective of the Stella-Shaw courtship in *Nothing But the Truth*: 123–7. A few years later she wrote an extremely amusing but devastatingly critical account of 33 Kensington Square during Stella's illness which was published in *Harper's Bazaar* (August 1915). Although "One Day with a Genius" does not identify Stella by name, her picture on the page with Georgina was enough. Helen loosely disguises the names of Stella's family and friends (Bingo/Beo, Auntie Minna/Nina, Dodo/D.D., the Duchess of Grammerton/the Duchess of Rutland, Lord Sefton/probably Lord Savile, etc.), calls Stella throughout "the Invalid," but calls Shaw by name. She portrays the Invalid as impossibly demanding and herself run off her feet with errands and visitors. Needless to say, Stella was not pleased when she finally read the piece, which concludes wittily, "Who was it said that a Genius has the capacity for giving infinite pain?"

Dame Edith (D.D.) Lyttelton's letters to Shaw are in the British Library. I quote from three dated July 15, 1912, Monday 1912, and December 30, 1912. I have previously treated the Stella-Shaw romance with some thoroughness in *Bernard Shaw and the Actresses*. Denis Mackail quotes Barrie on Shaw's romance in *Barrie*: 448.

CHAPTER TWENTY-NINE: 1913–1914

Helen Campbell Spinola includes Shaw's letter about Stella's operation (December 9, 1912) and two letters from Stella to herself written from Hinde Street (January 13 and 16, 1913) in *Nothing But the Truth*: 125–6, 127–8. Stella's account of her illness during this period comes chiefly from letters written to Shaw between January 16 and March 23, 1913: *TC*: 76–111.

Charlotte Shaw's diary is in the British Library. On January 7, 1913, she entered the words "GBS told me about Mrs. P.C." Shaw reported Forbes-Robertson's reaction to their romance in a letter to Stella of October 23, 1912; Barrie's attitude is expressed in a letter to Stella of September 7, 1912 (*MLSL*: 352–3); Sidney Webb's opinion is related by Beatrice Webb in *Our Partnership* (London: Longmans, Green, 1948); and Ellen Terry responded in a letter of September 16, 1912: *A Correspondence*: 328.

Stella wrote Shaw three letters on February 5, 1913, one of them the letter about *Hedda Gabler*, another the letter "Darling Mr. Mouse," which was not shown Dent. It is headed "To be read aloud to the family at meal times in Olivant[?] tones." Stella could be rather silly, writing nonsense like "Moonyetta minarna terya mina mininkins!" and "mornietta marni oooh Kovomooni," perhaps judiciously omitted from the published letters. Shaw's "I shall be at a loose end" (February 16, 1913) was omitted from *TC*. Stella's unpublished letter "My dear old Earl" (dated only "Sunday, North Cross, Windsor Forest") is important evidence of her attitudes toward the aristocracy and the acting world.

Laurence Tadema's letter (March 11, 1913) to Stella after her visit to Brighton testifies again to Stella's gift for friendship: "Darling, I am glad I had those days with you. I know hundreds of people, and like hundreds of people—but you are something apart and *near* me in some indefinable way. I love you truly. . . ." (unpublished letter lent by Patrick Beech).

D.D. Lyttelton mentions Stella's deep interest in Charlotte Shaw in her letter to Shaw of "Monday 1912" (British Library). On July 23, 1913, she wrote Shaw of her husband's death: ". . . he was not only my dearest friend & companion, but always up to the very end my lover—as fresh and ardent as he was 21 years ago. I have been wrapped all this time in love—& it is very cold without it" (British Library).

The published version of Shaw's letter to Stella of July 9, 1913 ("Stella: don't play with me") omits the passage about the two little sins: "Or perhaps . . . as slates go."

In a letter headed "Monday 11.45 p.m. summer 1913 St. James's Theatre, King Street," Stella and Alexander wrote: "Dear GBS  We the undersigned have had a meeting here and are desirous of acting your play here but we both feel that Barrie must have his 'Leonora' when the time comes—you must share this view. 'Higgins' is willing to change his girl for another 'Eliza' if this is agreeable to you. We can rehearse the play as soon as you like, & will produce it whenever you think it ready. We hope this will make you 'appy as it will us. Your BSC  George Alexander" (British Library). The letter is interesting for revealing the unusual amity that prevailed that summer between Stella and Alexander, and also because it indicates another reason for Shaw's refusing Alexander his play: the possibility of Stella's early exit.

Stella discusses Barrie and *The Adored One* in *MLSL*: 347–58. Some of Barrie's letters to Stella are published in *Letters of J. M. Barrie*. Another source for Stella's ill-fated attempt with Barrie is Denis Mackail's *Barrie*: 448–50. The man who read his play to Stella's sick dog was Dion Clayton Calthrop; the incident is reported by Dent: 251. Charles Frohman presented Maude Adams in *The Legend of Leonora* (*The Adored One*) in New York in 1914, where it was not a failure. *The Adored One* was omitted at Barrie's request from his collected plays, however.

Lucy Shaw tells of Stella's visits in a letter of September 4, 1913, to Janey Drysdale, quoted in H. G. Farmer's *Bernard Shaw's Sister and Her Friends*: 200–1.

Having long been curious about the Guilford Hotel, scene of Shaw's contretemps, I visited Sandwich in 1981 only to be baffled after hours of searching. Finally, as the sun was setting, my husband and I happened to mention our disappointment to the elderly gatekeeper of a local estate. He not only remembered the hotel, but had worked there for many years. He pointed out the former site, told tales of the elite clientele (including the Prince of Wales) who often visited on clandestine missions, and, back in his sentry box, produced postcards of the building. I am extremely grateful to him.

Patrick Beech told me of his mother's African experience. She visited England three or four times before finally returning in (he believed) either 1913 or 1914. He called her marriage "a disaster, but an escape from Mum." Helen talks about the disastrous *Night Hawk* in *Nothing But the Truth*: 132–4. One has her own words for a possible source of Beo's disillusionment: "The girl of today is often too promiscuous for my taste, but, believe me, too *much* reserve and *noli me tangere* before marriage can be as destructive to future understanding and happiness as what the young people nowadays call 'a shop-round first.' (This last paragraph came from the heart. I really must be serious occasionally . . . )."

The letters exchanged between Stella and Shaw in this chapter cover the period between January 16, 1913, and January 5, 1914: *TC*: 76–173.

CHAPTER THIRTY: 1914–1916

Two letters (November 19 and 21, 1913) from Sir Herbert Beerbohm Tree to Shaw in the British Library concern negotiations for *Pygmalion*. Tree says of Stella's interest in acting with him, "Under the circumstances, though I did not know there was any feeling on the part of the delightful Stella Campbell, yet I will not place myself in the position of receiving a rebuff." Stella's and Shaw's correspondence about the London production begins with her letter of February 10, 1914, and ends with her complaint on July 13, 1914, about Shaw's not coming to see the play again: *TC*: 174–85. Stella's prompt book of *Pygmalion*, much annotated (and often illegibly), is in the Enthoven Collection; Shaw's *Pygmalion* notebook is in the Humanities Research Center, University of Texas at Austin. I am indebted to Hesketh Pearson's *Beerbohm Tree* for several *Pygmalion* anecdotes (176–82), as well as to unidentified contemporary newspaper articles in the Enthoven Collection. I have drawn the account of the first night from Shaw's letter to Charlotte of April 12, 1914 (British Library). Among Stella's papers lent to me by Patrick Beech is a note from her to Shaw, undated but *Pygmalion*-inspired: "Damn you—bloody, bloody, bloody—loving Beatrice Stella."

Ralph Martin quotes Jennie's letter to Cornwallis-West about his remarriage (April 14, 1914), as well as Daisy Pless's cable and Moreton Frewen's comment: 329–30. Stella's "We were happy at last" and the Duchess of Rutland's remark come from *MLSL*: 373–5. Cornwallis-West comments briefly on the marriage ceremony and honeymoon in his memoir, *Edwardian Hey-Days*: 264–6; his comment on the first night of *Pygmalion* is from that source.

Shaw discusses a production of *Pygmalion* at the St. James's, summer of 1914, in a letter to Cornwallis-West of July 6, 1914 (British Library). Stella's remark about Harley Granville-Barker and the Kingsway is taken from an undated letter to Shaw written during negotiations for an American tour of *Pygmalion* (lent by Patrick Beech). Regarding those same negotiations, she says: "It was *your* silly clause that stupified both Jew and gentile. *My* contract was agreed to months ago. . . . It harms you being away from me so much you are dropping back into all your 'old gentleman's' ways of thought." Presumably the clause concerned Shaw's percentage.

Beo's cable and Stella's "As usual I had to make money" come from *MLSL* (375–6); her "I hate leaving my responsibilities" is written on a separate sheet of paper, no date, but just before sailing for America, and is among her letters to Shaw.

Helen Campbell Spinola's version of the WuPu abduction comes from *Nothing But the Truth*: 134–7. Helen and Beo met once again accidentally in the Rue Royale, Paris, while he was on leave. They talked of divorce and Helen decided, since neither was in a hurry, to postpone the final hearing until after the war. "Suit yourself!" said Beo. "It's all the same to me!" and drove away, waving cheerfully.

Dent prints Shaw's letter to George C. Tyler of October 12, 1914: 262. There are nine cables from Stella to Shaw about tour business in the Humanities Research Center, University of Texas at Austin. After the failure of Liebler she transferred to Klaw and Erlanger. With the exception of a letter of December 20, 1914, Shaw's comments about George being shot as a spy and the Antwerp business in letters of October 6 (26?) and November 13, 1914, and January 13, 1915, were not shown to Dent: Stella Beech disliked offending the Churchills. In *Churchill: Young Man in a Hurry—1874–1915* (New York: Simon and Schuster, 1982) Ted Morgan writes of the Antwerp rout, "George Cornwallis-West shouted at his men that he was ashamed of their cowardice, but they were quite out of control and intent only on escaping home to England. . . . Oc [Asquith] said that his commander, George Cornwallis-West, was incompetent and overbearing and was hated by officers and men": 430. Compare Patsy Cornwallis-West to Stella: "As for our beloved— you have made a different man of him, and his men I hear simply *worship* him": *MLSL*: 377. Shaw's "This war is getting too silly" was written November 13, 1914.

Particulars of the American *Pygmalion* tour come chiefly from unidentified newspaper clippings in the Billy Rose Theatre Collection, programs in the Milwaukee Public Library and Russell Hartley's theatre archives, and Stella's business cables to Shaw. The interview about Shaw's percentage appeared in the Chicago *Herald* of January 31, 1915; her comment "Where are all the people" is from the same source. Only three letters from Stella to Shaw during this tour survive, whereas eight from him are included in *TC*: 186–207. J. W. Austin gave his impressions to Dent: 267–70; Dent mistakenly dates the tour as 1920. Stella continued to give out interviews throughout the tour. An article datelined New Orleans, September 14, 1915, reports, "WOMEN BEAR HARDEST PART OF WAR, STATES MRS. 'PAT' CAMPBELL," and a New York paper in September quoted her in an unusually lenient mood on Shaw: "He has a mind that can simultaneously extract the humor, the pathos, the political and financial and psychological and moral value from any incident in life, and do all this so quickly that he has time to make a joke about something else while he is doing it. . . . He knows more about music than most musicians, more about politics than politicians, more about acting than most actors. . . . I think he has made me laugh more than anyone I know."

Stella wrote to D.D. Lyttelton on September 27, 1915 (Churchill College Library, Cambridge); she had the letter typewritten for her. Stella headed her letter to Harriett Carolan *"Private"*; it is dated either March 18 or 13, 1916, from Olean House, Olean, New York (Regenstein Library).

CHAPTER THIRTY-ONE: 1916–1919

Stella wrote two letters to Edith Lyttelton from "Ruthin Castle, North Wales" (Churchill College Library, Cambridge) and one to Shaw, undated: *TC*: 208–9: they describe her stay at Falmouth and the castle. All of Beo's letters in this chapter are included in *MLSL*: 382–424. Stella devotes an entire chapter to her son's military career; it is the longest in the book.

I have drawn upon Hesketh Pearson's *The Last Actor-Managers* (26) and A. E. W. Mason's *Sir George Alexander and the St. James' Theatre* (222) for the account of the revival of *Bella Donna*.

During this period of their relationship Stella pursued Shaw, who, after the *Pygmalion* battle, was wary of becoming involved again. They communicated by letter only sporadically between Stella's return from America in April 1916 and the revival of *Pygmalion* in February 1920: *TC*: 208–29. Three of Stella's letters (one of April 25, 1917, one undated, and one written on mourning paper after Beo's death, c. September 1918) were omitted from the published correspondence because they are brief and obscure. In the letter of April 25, 1917, she says she is learning recitation since Shaw will not give it (*Pygmalion,* presumably) to her for the music halls. She also says she is hankering after Yeats's *The Player Queen*. The 1918 note says only, "Dear Joey, Are you in London? I would like to see you? I am back from Ireland—are you? Stella."

Dent gives a more thorough account of Mrs. Cornwallis-West's scandal and Stella's printed defense: 259–61.

In a long letter of July 17, 1940, to Ellen Terry's daughter, Edith Craig (British Library), Shaw discusses the actresses of his day, devoting considerable space to Stella. He declares he almost died keeping his temper with her professionally, though offstage all was serene. Despite the fact that *Pygmalion* was his greatest London success, he would not, he says, trust the part of Hesione Hushabye to Stella, even though she was "exactly what he wanted," nor, later, Orinthia in *The Apple Cart* because he was afraid she would set the theatre upside down and his plays were too risky to take chances like that.

Stella's prompt book of *The Thirteenth Chair* is in the Enthoven Collection. There is much alteration of the style if not the content of Madame La Grange's lines; for example, "I get my messages from them that have passed on. I don't hold at all wid the cards nor tea leaves, nor any of them tricks. Wance in a while I give advice. If I was you, Miss, I wouldn't meet Jimmy at the Ritz at three tomorrow" is revised into the more refined "I have nothing to do with cards and tea leaves or any of those tricks. But sometimes I get a message from those who have passed on and sometimes I give advice. If I were you I would not meet Jimmy at the Ritz at three o'clock tomorrow." Cynthia Asquith records her reactions to Stella and *The Thirteenth Chair* in entries of June 16, 1916 (176), and October 27, 1917 (358–9): *Diaries 1915–1918*.

Osbert Sitwell's *Laughter in the Next Room* is the source of the account of Stella, Edith, and the silver spoons: 241–2.

I am indebted to Patrick Beech for information about the relationship between his mother and Stella, and his mother's leaving the Square. Stella Beech eventually resumed the name "Stella Patrick Campbell" onstage; her mother evidently did nothing to prevent it. In August 1919, however, acting in *Cyrano* with Robert Loraine at the Duke of York's, she was still billed as "Stella Mervyn Campbell." Patrick Beech says about his mother's acting career, "Mother had considerable talent but was much handicapped by maternal repression which made it difficult for her to 'let go.' Shaw wrote a letter to her saying she was much too ladylike, and should descend the stairs before breakfast daily standing on her hands! Eventually I think she found a psychological release in acting, which allowed her to display an emotion she would never show in private life." Cynthia Asquith records her visit to Kensington Square on November 8, 1917: *Diaries*: 363. She also writes in an entry for April 2, 1916: "Stella [Beech] arrived before lunch. She was very pleasant, if trite, and I still think her profile superlatively pretty. Beb [Asquith, Cynthia's husband] is happy with her": 149. "At one time," writes Patrick Beech, "mother resumed her old friendship with [Cynthia Asquith], and actually went to live with her for a time in Bath. But she left in rather mysterious circumstances, saying that Cynthia was 'a very odd person' and she couldn't continue the relationship. She would never enlarge on this, so I don't know what went wrong. Perhaps they were both too old to make a go of it."

Both Stella and Helen Campbell Spinola speak briefly of Beo's death in their memoirs. An unidentified newspaper clipping in the Harvard Theatre Collection states that Mrs. Campbell was told the news of her son's death after the Thursday matinee of *The Thirteenth Chair*. Stella quotes numerous letters of condolence in *MLSL*.

The source for Stella's visit to Allan Pollock is Ashton Stevens in a column from an unidentified Chicago paper (Free Library of Philadelphia Theatre Collection). Stevens said that Pollock himself told him the episode, and that Stella verified it.

I am grateful to Dame Veronica Wedgwood, London, for her reminiscence of meeting Mrs. Campbell at her mother's house at 33 Camden House Court on the occasion of Stella's selling 33 Kensington Square.

Stella is brief about Cornwallis-West's defection. She does print Edward Sheldon's cable and letter of sympathy of July and August 1919, but in an obscure context. Stella Moore Coltman-Rogers, who lived with Mrs. Campbell for a number of years, told me that Stella talked to her of George's infidelities: the golf-clubs episode is from that source. Stella talks about going to Newlands and discovering George's infidelity at that time in letters to Shaw of July 12 and August 2, 1929. Shaw had recently written *The Apple Cart*, drawing heavily on Stella for the character of Orinthia and upon their romance for the episode of Magnus and Orinthia. Stella thought he also insinuated too much about her marriage to George, and thus for the first time told him the story of their separation. These letters were omitted from the published correspondence. It is perhaps needless to add that they tell Stella's side of the story.

### CHAPTER THIRTY-TWO: 1919–1922

Curiously, Stella Beech deleted Stella's comment on her performance as Raina in Shaw's *Arms and the Man* from the published letter of January 5, 1920: *TC*: 228–9: "You have done wonders with Stella, such a plucky interesting performance and she looked lovely." The *Sunday Times* said that Stella Mervyn Campbell "drawled and droned the heroics of Raina, but was pleasingly natural in the unaffected parts"; the *Observer* that she managed to convey both Raina's idealism and her opportunism "without making the thing look ridiculous." Robert Loraine, with whom she had played *Cyrano* the previous year, also starred in the revival. Patrick Beech, who has four letters from Shaw to his mother about playing Raina, told me that his mother was in love with the handsome, dynamic Loraine.

The battle of the 1920 revival of *Pygmalion*, first at the Aldwych and then, apparently under Stella's management, at the Duke of York's, is documented in *TC*: 229–41. Eleven letters from Shaw to Viola Tree (Humanities Research Center) revealed his disgust with Stella's performance at rehearsals and in the production itself. He also chides Viola for altering the play, wondering how she could do it since she has gleams of intelligence at times. Arnold Bennett commented on the revival on March 9, 1920: *The Journal of Arnold Bennett*: 696. Dent quotes Anthony Asquith on *Pygmalion*: 271–2.

Stella comments on *Madame Sand* in *MLSL*, quoting Besier's and Shaw's approval: 426–8. She played for a fortnight in Cologne beginning September 11, 1920. During these years she continued her constant search for plays. On August 1, 1920, for example, Maurice Hewlett wrote her about a play of his, *The Queen of Scots*, that she was then considering. Hewlett chides her for not answering letters: she had wired for the play in the spring of 1920 and he had sent it promptly (letter in Yale University Library).

Stella airs her grievances against James K. Hackett in *MLSL*: 183–4, 429–30. Dent reports the "I *hate* being patted!" as having been told to him by critic James Agate, though Agate would not vouch for its authenticity; it sounds, however, likely. Stella described her confrontation with Hackett backstage to John Mason Brown, who related it to Dent: 162–5. Stella reports the Dame Madge Kendal incident to Shaw in a letter of August 25, 1937 (*TC*: 361–6), adding, "I knew in spite of Madge's dignity and her bonnet—she was a devil!" Bennett commented on *Macbeth* on November 3, 1920: *Journal*: 719. Shaw and Stella exchanged opinions of her Lady Macbeth in letters of December 22, 1920, and January 11, 1921: *TC*: 245–7.

Stella's and Shaw's battle over the inclusion of his letters in her autobiography occupies them from January 18, 1921, to January 3, 1923: *TC*: 250–96. The exchange contains a number of letters and passages suppressed in the published correspondence that deal chiefly with George Cornwallis-West, Beb Asquith, and D.D. Lyttelton. An unpublished letter from Shaw (February 27, 1921) to Otto Kyllmann of Constable (owned by Mary Hyde; a copy was lent to me by Dan H. Laurence) takes the general tone that Stella is unreliable.

The copy of Otto Kyllmann's letter to Shaw of March 30, 1921, that so offended Stella when Shaw forwarded it was lent by Patrick Beech. Stella's response of April 16, 1921 ("I feel absolutely humiliated"), was omitted from publication, as was another typed copy of a letter from Stella to Shaw of February 3, 1922, labelled by Stella Beech, "There is no original—or evidence that this letter was ever sent." This letter reiterates her complaints, beginning, "Joey, I have read carefully through these letters, and I feel you are wrong, wrong, wrong." Stella actually blamed Edith Lyttelton very much for making Shaw change his mind about the letters. In cut passages from a letter to him of April 9, 1922, she accuses D.D. of "Scotch jealousy": "She interfered *unwisely* giving you suburban convulsions and shaking your confidence in me entirely. . . . Under the influence of what she said you insulted me. . . . I was far too proud, after your madness and her disloyalty to show either of you the book," etc. At the same time, she says with obvious sincerity: "I love DD very much and have steadily and staunchly for 20 years."

There are three unpublished letters from Stella to D.D. Lyttelton from this period (Churchill College Library, Cambridge): June 22, 1921, written from Rusper, Sussex ("I don't feel I ever want to live again"); a Christmas letter (1921) written from "Blythe Hall, Ormskirk, Lancs.," in which she tells D.D. of a letter from Shaw (untraced) comparing her unfavorably with Margot, Lady Asquith (who had published indiscreet memoirs), and accusing her of simply wanting to make money off his letters; and a letter of February 24, 1922, partially quoted in this chapter ("There has been *great trouble*"). She kept track of her daughter if not in touch: the Christmas letter mentions that Stella Beech has moved in with Nina Hill, that she has lost her voice, but that little Pat is "splendidly well."

Sir Henry Channon tells of the brief encounter between Stella, George, and Jennie Churchill, although he mistakenly gives the year as 1920: *Chips: The Diaries of Sir Henry Channon*: 241.

Dent quotes the *Daily Telegraph* on *MLSL*: 278; Graham Robertson comments on Stella's autobiography in a letter to Kerrison Preston of November 28, 1922: *Letters from Graham Robertson*: 99–100. Desmond MacCarthy's comments come from his essay "Mr. Patrick Campbell" in *Portraits*: 59–62.

One reason Shaw claimed to be out of countenance about the inclusion of his letters in Stella's autobiography was that he expected the book to contain love letters from other admirers, whereas he turned out to be alone. Stella does publish one love poem, "To Beatrice" (dated August 1910), with the maddeningly discreet comment, "The following poem was written by a well-known London manager. His wife gave me permission to publish all the poems he wrote to me. Unfortunately, the book they were in has disappeared—she asked me for it and I thought I gave it to her, but she says 'no' ":

> Come in a dream, beloved, if thy feet
>    Are weary, thro' the valley of the night;
> Sure are the wings of drowsy thought, and fleet
>    To bear thee through the shadows to the light.
> Grey is the world between us, let us go
>    Far to the land where only lovers are:
> All day the hours like laughing waters flow
>    And all the night beneath a patient star.
>
> There is a garden where the echoes treasure
>    Thy footfall as an old-remembered song.
> The ilex and the cypresses will pleasure
>    To swathe thee in their shade. O, stay not long!
> The oleanders and the roses wait
>    Thy coming, and so soon the night is past,
> Come, come to-night; wide open stands the gate,
>    And Death must close it, with our lives, at last.

Enter, and wander down the winding stair
  Of moon-kissed marble, shadowy with time;
There is thy home, and thou belongest there,
  With all the beauty of the southern clime.
The night is warm as kisses to the cheek,
  Sweet to the ear as when a song is still,
Or the thrilled hush when thou hast ceased to speak
  And all the world is waiting on thy will.

O, blind me with thy kisses, let me swoon
  Into the dark, and glide into a sleep,
Till moth-white as the early morning moon
  Thy face appear, and I behold the peep
Of wonder-witching dawn within thine eyes
  And feel thy breath like soft winds from the South
Stir me to shake off slumber and arise
  And kneel and kiss the daybreak of thy mouth.

It is possible that the author of "To Beatrice" is Herbert Trench (1865–1923). In 1910 Trench was a manager at the Haymarket, where he had produced, among other successes, Maeterlinck's *The Blue Bird*. He was evidently still manager when Stella acted *Lady Patricia* there; at least she says in a 1912 letter to Shaw, "I played for the Irish people for nothing— for Trench for what he could afford"—and no other play seems likely. Trench also authored the prologue to Ben Jonson's *The Vision of Delight* that Stella spoke on June 27, 1911, at the Coronation Gala at His Majesty's. Of the 1910 preparation for that gala, Lady Gregory writes, "They had a committee meeting at which Mrs. Campbell had been so violent that no one but Trench had taken her part which he had done by saying she was known to be a hell-cat" (*Seventy Years*: 451). During the years 1910–1911, therefore, Stella and Trench were connected. Trench was married, so that he had a wife who might have given Stella permission to publish his poems. Finally, Trench was a published poet, with a style not incompatible with that of "To Beatrice."

CHAPTER THIRTY-THREE: 1922–1927

Reactions to Stella's Hedda at the Everyman Theatre by George Rylands, James Agate, Ivor Brown, and Sir Ralph Richardson, who described her opening the play with pistol practice, are quoted in Dent: 216–18. Stella wrote Shaw about her Hedda in letters of May 26 (Cadogan Hotel), June 11 and 16, 1922 (Deanery Street): *TC*: 292–3.

Dent also quotes William Armstrong's reaction to Stella: 280–1. Stella Moore Coltman-Rogers told me that Annie Esmond, a member of her touring company in these years, adored her. Sir John Gielgud told me of his first meeting with Stella, which he has also described in *Distinguished Company*: 32–3. Information about the ill-fated *Voodoo* comes from a letter from Stella to D.D. Lyttelton of February 13, 1923, Ashfields (Churchill College Library, Cambridge). Paul Robeson told Dent the "Do sing again" story after a performance of *Othello* at Stratford-on-Avon: 281. Armstrong reported another version of Stella's disappointment at his resignation: "Now you're going to be a little man who sits in an office and makes *lists*": J. C. Trewin in *Robert Donat: A Biography* (London: Heinemann, 1968): 39.

Stella's letter to D.D. ("I have been playing") from Ashfields can be dated from its contents as October 1922 (Churchill College Library). During this time Stella was negotiating to play *Magda* in London; sent Lady Alexander two checks for the London rights; discovered that Lady Alexander was not in the position to deal with the rights, which had been purchased by Frank Curzon; got a lawyer and lost the case—or so she reports in a cut passage of a letter to Shaw dated March 30, 1924 (Frederick R. Koch Collection, Harvard Theatre Collection). She also produced Henry Bernstein's *L'Elévation* on this tour, telling Shaw it was a success but too sad, so she dropped it. Arnold Bennett comments on *Magda* in a letter of February 1, 1923, to Frank Swinnerton: *Letters of Arnold Bennett*, vol. III, 1916–1931: 318–19. Stella's letter to Pinero was written from the Imperial Hotel, Belfast, on March 22, 1924, Pinero responding in a letter of March 26 (British Library).

Shaw's letter to Stella of March 27, 1924 ("Then you still live!") is included in *TC*: 297–8, as is Stella's reply of March 30 (298–300), except for the passage about the little step-niece (Frederick R. Koch Collection, Harvard Theatre Collection).

Dent quotes from a diary excerpt sent to him by Cecil Beaton about *The Second Mrs. Tanqueray*: 179–80.

The Tanner Collection contains five letters to Stella from various staff of the Papworth Village Settlement concerning both her performance there and the well-being of her brother Max. I am grateful to E. Turnhill, Estates Director of the Village, for his reply to my inquiry about Max Tanner's stay there. In 1927 Fred Hill (Nina's son) wrote to "My Dear Auntie": ". . . As a matter of fact, I know all about Max and his history during the past 7 years, and how you have been keeping him; also about Edwin, and that Roy [Hill] is now keeping him entirely, as you were unable to continue your share. You will have had my cable to say that I was sending you a cheque—enclose it herewith, for £40, which will be sufficient to provide Max with 30/ a week for 6 months, by which time I am sure that you, with your wonderful energy and power, will be on your feet again and be able to continue the whole allowance . . ." (Tanner Collection). If addressed to Lulo, this letter challenges the evidence that Stella was the family member who supported Max. It is possible that the letter is addressed to Stella: Lulo preserved letters addressed to her sister; Lulo is not known to have had sufficient funds to support Max; Lulo is not known to have possessed "wonderful energy and power"; Fred's letter mentions young Stella and her son, Pat, a subject of more interest to Stella than to Lulo.

Stella's itinerary in these years is largely established from her letters to Frederick Witney written on tour stationery. Between the years 1925 and 1927 Stella wrote numerous letters about *The Adventurous Age*; forty-four of these are in the Houghton Library, Harvard University; all letters quoted in this chapter are from this source. In 1925 an admirer of Stella's, Mary E. Hand, made painstaking calligraphic copies of selected reviews which she eventually presented to Stella in a decorated folder. These reviews—all favorable—were kindly lent me by Patrick Beech. The article from *John O'London's Weekly* of December 27, 1927, comes from this source.

American journalist Ashton Stevens was one of Stella's early admirers and wrote numerous articles about her. The Lord Lowndes story is relayed by Kay Ashton-Stevens (*Variety*: January 7, 1953), quoting from a 1946 column by Stevens.

H. F. Maltby gives his version of what happened to *What Might Happen* in *Ring Up the Curtain*: 187–8. "The theatrical world is interested" article appeared in the *Yorkshire Post* of May 24, 1926, copied out by Mary Hand. The story of Stella threatening to bob her hair comes from Brian Howard's *Portrait of a Failure*, edited Marie-Jaqueline Lancaster (London: Anthony Blond, 1968): 167.

Noel Coward talks about Stella's reaction to his Lewis Dodd in *Present Indicative*: 118. Suffering from a case of nerves (not precipitated by Stella), Coward played just three weeks, after which John Gielgud took over the part. Basil Dean mentions Stella's appearance at the dress rehearsal in *Seven Ages*: 321.

Osbert Sitwell's *Laughter in the Next Room* recounts his meeting with Stella on shipboard: 240–1. George Jean Nathan, the American counterpart of James Agate, reported on *The Adventurous Age* in *Art of the Night*: 61–3.

In a passage deleted from the original and published version but extant in a copy of a letter of March 26, 1929, to Shaw, Stella defends herself against his charge that she threw his money into the sea: "Perhaps its my own fault, I ought to have told you exactly what became of the £1000. I will send you my books if you like. The first £500 cleared up an awful situation after the £700 losses on that tour of mine. The second brought me back from America at a moment's notice—cleared me up there where I had been for 6 months with only two weeks work. Stella was very ill, and DD cabled for me. It enabled me to help Stella and live on here for a bit" (Frederick R. Koch Collection, Harvard Theatre Collection). It is unclear whether she repaid the money.

Paul Shinkman's London interview with Stella appeared in the New York *Herald Tribune* of November 17, 1929.

CHAPTER THIRTY-FOUR: 1927–1930

Stella's lecture on diction eventually evolved into her talk "Beautiful Speech and the Art of Acting" (or, occasionally, "The Art of Acting and Beautiful Speech"), a copy of which is in the Burgunder Shaw Collection, Cornell University Library. Mary Hand copied all the reviews of the speech cited in this chapter, as well as the reminiscences of Stella's *Tanqueray* in "The London Stage Thirty Years Ago" from the *Sphere* (December 4, 1926) and paragraphs about Mrs. Guinness's masquerade party from the *Evening Standard* and the *Evening News* (dated only November 1927). Arnold Bennett commented on Stella's vitality on September 27 and December 11, 1927: *Journal*: 980, 990. I am indebted to Patrick Beech for his reminiscences of his grandmother.

Shaw's "Dear Unforgotten" letter (December 12, 1927: *TC*: 300) renews an exchange that lasted this time until September 20(?), 1929 (the copy of Shaw's last letter is dated September 29 in the Frederick R. Koch Collection at Harvard). "Either you are in business": January 18, 1928; "If I may make an excuse": January 19, 1928; "I know where Satan": January 27, 1928: *TC*: 302–5.

Sir John Gielgud has published vivid reminiscences of Stella, to which this biography is indebted, in *Distinguished Company*: 31–9, *Early Stages*: 129–31, and *An Actor in His Time*: 66–8. Sir John told me the story about Stella acting with Marion Terry in *Lady Windermere's Fan* in Dublin. James Agate's criticism of *Ghosts* appeared under the title "A Great Actress" in the *Sunday Times* (April 1, 1928). In the Frederick R. Koch Collection of Stella's letters there is a typed copy of a letter dated May 19, 1928, lacking both salutation and signature, beginning, "To the right minded artist it is—First God, then 'le bon gout,' then the Critic!" Its contents make it clear that Stella wrote it to James Agate: she calls the addressee "You, the Critic" and cites his criticism of *Ghosts*, for example; she and Agate were good friends. The honorary dinner to J. T. Grein at the Hotel Cecil was reported in the *Daily Sketch* (May 1928), and in Michael Orme's *J. T. Grein*: 310; Orme dismisses the list of distinguished attendants as too formidable to cite: "I will but pause to praise the exemplary brevity and wit wherewith the great actress toasted her critic and friend." The Burgunder Shaw Collection has recently acquired the original autograph manuscript of a speech that Bernard Shaw wrote for Stella to read at the Grein dinner. From current newspaper accounts, however, it appears that Stella did not read the speech (which sketched her rise as an actress), but extracted only the remarks about Grein—crediting them to Shaw—to add to her own brief remarks. Stella was reluctant, as usual, to let Shaw speak for her, as well as unwilling to take credit for his wit. Pinero's letter to Stella (May 12, 1929) is in the British Library; it is published in a slightly different version in the *Collected Letters*: 284.

Sir John Gielgud reported to me Stella's comment to Miriam Lewes. Dent gives an account of the contretemps during the production of *John Gabriel Borkman* at the Q Theatre: 287–8. Gielgud's recollections of the production come from *An Actor in His Time*: 68. Agate's review appeared in the *Sunday Times* (October 21, 1928).

Stella and Shaw exchanged numerous letters about her financial situation during this time. "Doesn't your conscience": February 23, 1928; Shaw's suggestion of selling his letters: November 22, 1928; "No. No; I just": November 25, 1928; "I can't read plays": February 19, 1929 (references to D.D., Nancy Astor, and Bridget Guinness were cut in the published version); "Years and years ago"—cut passage from Stella's reply of February 20, 1929 (Stella Beech deleted all uncomplimentary remarks—they are few—about Edith Lyttelton from Stella's letters): TC: 308–12. In the Special Collections of the Libraries of the State University of New York at Buffalo there is a list of the twenty-three volumes with their inscriptions that Shaw gave Stella for a wedding present. One (his novel *Cashel Byron's Profession*) is inscribed to Alan Campbell. The inscriptions are usually flattering; for example, "To Beatrice Stella Cornwallis West—his Masterpiece to Nature's" in the copy of *Man and Superman*.

I am indebted to Stella Moore Coltman-Rogers for her memories of Stella Campbell during this period.

Dent discusses *The Matriarch*: 289–91. Stella commented that the role would disgrace her in a letter to Shaw of April 2, 1929: TC: 314–15. Patrick Beech told me that she did not want the part, lamenting, "Who will remember my Mélisande?" He is also the source for her use of phonograph records, for the comment about Constance Collier, and for the supper party at the Savoy. Stella's acting copy of *The Matriarch* is in his possession. An unidentified newspaper clipping in the Enthoven Collection reports the *globis invectus* episode.

Stella and Shaw battled over *The Apple Cart* in letters written between March 31 and August 7, 1929: TC: 314–35. During this time they also exchanged views about the question of her divorcing George. All these passages, as well as several whole letters about divorce, were omitted from the published correspondence. Shaw initiated the topic on June 20, 1929, announcing that he has just had a talk with George; on June 27 he assures her he does not believe George or anything the man says; on July 8 in a suppressed letter he tells her that the subject has been discussed at Cliveden. Shaw reported Stella's "You must not believe all that George says" in a postcard to Cornwallis-West on June 27; this and other correspondence between them is in the British Library. "Interference and advice without frankness": Stella: July 8. Shaw tried to justify himself ("He may be the most abandoned") on July 12 in answer to a letter of Stella's the same day accusing him of hitting below the belt. She replied, "When a man cannot meet his wife's eye" on July 26; Shaw answered, "How troublesome you are" on July 28; then Stella in a long, suppressed letter described the break-up of her marriage to Shaw for the first time. His reply of August 4 was deleted from the published correspondence except for a few cryptic lines about her "adventures." Stella closed the argument in an unpublished letter of August 7, 1929. *The Apple Cart* (incidentally) had the second longest London run of Shaw's plays—258 performances.

The *Morning Post* reported the celebration of the 200th performance of *The Matriarch* (November 1, 1929). Alan Dent witnessed and reported Stella's entrance at Gielgud's cocktail party.

CHAPTER THIRTY-FIVE: 1930–1934

Much of the material about Stella in America (1930–1935) comes from clippings in the Harvard Theatre Collection, the Billy Rose Theatre Collection, the Theatre Collection of the Free Library of Philadelphia, and the Regenstein Library. Critic John Mason Brown wrote a column, "Two on the Aisle," for the New York *Evening Post*: his reviews are from that source, and his personal reminiscences of Stella from a letter he wrote Dent: 294–6. The interview "Behold, a woman" was the last that Mary Hand copied out for Stella;

she gives its source as the London *Evening Standard* (March 14, 1930: International News Service).

The Boston *Transcript* reported her lecture on March 10, 1930. I am indebted to Frances Goudy, Special Collections Librarian at Vassar College, and to the Wellesley College librarian for sending me cuttings from their college newspapers: Stella spoke at Vassar on March 9 and at Wellesley on March 25. She spoke at the Athenaeum Club in Summit, New Jersey, on May 9, 1930 (program). Another program—"Shearwood-Smith, Inc. Has the Honor to Present Mrs. Patrick Campbell in a Lecture-Recital 'Beautiful Speech and the Art of Acting' Illustrated by Scenes from her Many Stage Successes"—gives a list of her engagements, though not their dates: The Colony Club, N.Y.; New Jersey College for Women; New School for Social Research, N.Y.; Columbia University; Junior Service League, Wellesley Hills, Mass.; Twentieth Century Club, Pittsburgh; Institute of Arts and Sciences, Brooklyn; National School of Elocution and Oratory, Philadelphia; Laurel School, Cleveland. She spoke under the auspices of the Acorn Club in Philadelphia on April 23, 1930; to the Arts Club of Chicago on February 10, 1931; in Toledo, Ohio, on January 31, 1931. While by no means a complete list of her speaking engagements, it suggests the range of her tour during these years.

Shaw advised Stella to get into movies in a letter of August 19, 1912 (*TC*: 33–9); he refused *Pygmalion* to her for the screen, however, simply because she was too old. Helen Campbell Spinola tells the story of her final encounter with Stella in *Nothing But the Truth*: 175–7. Stella Moore Coltman-Rogers told me that Stella paid her way to Los Angeles, that they stayed at the Ambassador Hotel, and that Stella tried to get her into film and theatre on the coast. I have made liberal use of George Middleton's account of Stella and *The Dancers* in *These Things Are Mine* (New York: Macmillan, 1947): 395–9. The play *The Dancers* was co-authored by Gerald du Maurier; the film version was rewritten by Chandler Sprague under the title *Play Called Life*, which was eventually changed back to *The Dancers*; the film starred Phillips Holmes, Lois Moran, and Mae Clark. The New York *Herald Tribune* (September 14, 1930) announces that Stella has completed filming *Play Called Life*. She appeared in Los Angeles for six evening performances and two matinees of *Ghosts* beginning November 17; then went to the Columbia Theatre, San Francisco, opening with Tom Douglas as Oswald Alving on November 24, 1930.

The New York *Herald Tribune* (October 5, 1930) noted that Stella would make a five-month tour with "Beautiful Speech" beginning January 1, 1931. Ashton Stevens's account of Stella at Samuel Insull's (and also at the Savoy Grill) comes from an undated column of reminiscences written after her death. He does not date the Insull gathering, but since Stella gave her Midwest lectures in 1931, I have placed it here. The description by Flora Ward Hineline of the Toledo lecture appeared as a reminiscence in the Toledo *Blade* of October 19, 1952.

In a letter of June 10, 1931, Shaw sent "a bit of blue paper" to Stella, evidently a message from or about George. She returned it unread in a letter of June 12, 1931: the exchange was omitted from *TC*. In another deleted passage she tells Shaw on June 30, 1931, that George has dropped the matter. Shaw announces the publication of the Shaw-Terry letters on June 13, 1931; Stella asks "What arrangement" on July 14, 1931: *TC*: 337, 339–40. Graham Robertson mentions Stella's flying visit in a letter of August 12, 1931, to Kerrison Preston: Letters from Graham Robertson: 256–7.

Stella was interviewed at the Barclay on her return to America on October 31, 1931. Stella's "Dearest Joey, what objection" is March 29, 1932; Shaw's "You would not come out of it" April 16, 1932: *TC*: 341–4, 344–7. The portion about the £500 a year and selling George did not appear in *TC*. Loel Guinness kindly wrote me about his parents' bequest to Stella: "So far as the five hundred pounds a year is concerned, I think the reason for this was that she had been for so long a very great friend of my parents and when she fell on rather hard times, I think she needed it, and that was why my father made it available to her. As a matter of interest, he had given me personal instructions, some years before she died, that if anything happened to him I was to continue giving it to her; then, as you know, she died in 1940 and so the matter was dropped."

Dent discusses the New York *Electra* briefly; prints John Mason Brown's criticism in part and Stella's "I love my roses and the thorns": 295–6. Blanche Yurka's *Bohemian Girl* tells her side of the *Electra* production and is the source of Stella's "You really *liked* it, darlings?"

Some of Stella's dealing with George and his lawyers during this year can be deduced from three letters in the Chandos Collection (Churchill College Library, Cambridge): copies of "strictly private and confidential" letters from William Rollo, Howard House, Arundel Street, Strand, written to Stella on February 4, 1932, and Stella's reply of March 7, 1932. These she sent to D.D. Lyttelton along with a letter from Cap d'Antibes (August 18, 1932) from which the passage "I knew it wasn't another woman" is taken. Stella does not give the source of her information, only says, "What a strange experience to realize after all these years the true cause of George's departure—why he was so weirdly excited." She also says, "I fancy my case will come on in November so I am going to be smothered in one sort of vulgarity and another"—but divorce proceedings against George were not carried out.

Peter Noble's *Ivor Novello* talks about *Party* (the play was called *Party* in London and *A Party* in New York because the American producer thought it commercially advantageous to have his productions at the head of the newspapers' listings of current plays) and cites Stella's comment to Braithwaite: 168.

Ford Madox Ford's *Provence* contains two delightfully impressionistic accounts of Stella as well as a wildly inaccurate account of her debut at the Adelphi: 190–200. I am indebted to Diana Forbes-Robertson for her account of meeting Stella in the South of France when she was a teenager. Of Stella's "Dear child" farewell, she says, "Mrs. Campbell and Mother had never met. It was masterly and terribly funny." The exchange between Stella and Shaw while she was staying first at Mougins and then at Cap d'Antibes took place on May 12 and 21, 1932, Shaw replying "N O" on June 12: *TC*: 348–52. She mentions in a letter to Edith Lyttelton of August 18 that she has been offered a play at the St. Martin's Theatre. John Gielgud recounts his experience of casting and directing Stella in *Strange Orchestra* in *Early Stages*: 129–31. Newspaper accounts from the *World-Telegram* (n.d.) and *Daily Mail* (September 14, 1932) tell the story of Stella's leaving England on account of "Wung-Wung-Wah-Wah-Woosh-Woosh-Wish-Wish-Bang"—called, reportedly, "Woosh-Woosh" by Stella. This is evidently the same dog that is also called "Wung Wung Warwah" in another source. I have called it "Woosh-Woosh," but do not pretend to know the actual name of this, the most mysterious of Stella's dogs.

I am grateful to Mrs. Juliette Hollister of Greenwich, Connecticut, and to Julia Child, Cambridge, Massachusetts, for writing me their accounts of seeing Stella perform in 1932–1933. William Lyon Phelps tells of Stella at Yale in *Autobiography with Letters*: 379. Corinna Lindon Smith in *Interesting People: Eighty Years with the Great and Near Great* (Norman: University of Oklahoma Press, 1962) also reports a Stella episode of these years: "One late autumn afternoon, my husband and I were seated before a welcome open fire in our New Hampshire home, when Mrs. Patrick Campbell walked in on us unannounced. Without introducing herself, she said she was visiting a neighbor and in wandering about had stumbled onto our place. She wished to thank the owners for the privilege of sitting alone in the two outdoor theatres we possessed. She was impressive and still beautiful as she sipped tea and talked delightfully about the stage. Somehow, the conversation got around to the sonnets of Shakespeare. 'He wrote them when he was in love, and that's why the mood is different,' she declared emphatically, and rather startled us by adding, 'The same thing was true of Shaw. No one would have thought his love letters to me were genuine if they had not been in his handwriting.' This was her exit line": 49.

Lucius Beebe's "Trailing Clouds" appeared in the *Herald Tribune* of September 3, 1933.

I have adapted Bosley Crowther's amusing "Mrs. Patrick Campbell Orders Her Luncheon" from an unidentified clipping in the Free Library of Philadelphia Theatre Collection. The "watermelon and ice cream" interview appeared in the Philadelphia *Record* with a date-line "New York, July 31." The episodes of the little man coming to take away Moonbeam and the "Moonbeam, Moonbeam, no madness now" are related in an interview with Stella by John Anderson, a copy of which (undated, no source) is in the Enthoven Collection. Anderson is also the source for Stella's gaffe with the bald man. Alexander Woollcott's appreciation of Stella appeared in *Cosmopolitan* (December 1933). Woollcott sent proofs of the article to Stella in Hollywood; she wired on January 1, 1934: "SEASONS GREETINGS DEAR MR. WOOLLCOTT THANK YOU FOR YOUR BEWITCHING INACCURACIES I AM NOT AS NICE AS ALL THAT."

Dent tells the Joseph Schildkraut story: 299. Colleen Moore describes Stella at George Cukor's party in *Silent Star*: 165. The "Blessed Damozel" and "Tittiebottles" quips are related by Stella herself in her unpublished *Chance Medley* (Burgunder Shaw Collection, Cornell University Library). Joan Fontaine quotes the "Such tiny little eyes!" reaction in *No Bed of Roses* (New York: William Morrow, 1978): 99, giving the occasion as a screening of *The Women*; but *The Women* appeared in 1939 and Stella left Hollywood for good in 1935. I am grateful to Fitzroy Davis, Putnam, Connecticut, for a long letter in response to my request for Campbell material. His comments on *Riptide*, however, seem doubtful: "In 1934 Norma Shearer had been off the screen for about a year due to the illness of her husband, Irving Thalberg, when she had taken a long cruise or something with him and their children. He wanted her comeback picture to be very prestigious and Mrs. Pat was sought to come from England and play a major part in it. . . . Mrs. Pat insisted that, in addition to first class travelling expenses, her *salary* was to begin from the moment she boarded the ship in Southampton and they acceded. What gall!" But Stella had been in America continuously since 1932. Stella talks at length about her difficulties in front of the camera in *Chance Medley*. Sir Cedric Hardwicke tells of encountering Stella on the M-G-M lot in *A Victorian in Orbit*: 228.

A copy of Stella's letter to Daphne du Maurier of July 9, 1934, is in the possession of the Frederick R. Koch Collection, Harvard Theatre Collection. Stella talks about her journey and her return in *Chance Medley*.

CHAPTER THIRTY-SIX: 1934–1938

During her seven-month stay at Skyforest in the San Bernardino Mountains, Stella wrote an unfinished memoir titled first *Random Reminiscences*, then *Chance Medley*. It contains a chapter called "Some Notes on the Art of Acting," six chapters about Hollywood, and nine additional chapters titled "Speech and Usage of Words," "Words and Odd Sounds," "On the Air," "An Interview," "A Young Man to Interview Me," " 'Jackanapes' and the Reason Why," "Mountains," "Joey (George Bernard Shaw)," and "Sir Arthur Pinero." Included with these chapters are "Serious People, An Original Sketch in Moving Picture Form —16 Scenes" and "A Movie Kiss: An Original One-Act Play," both of which she wrote in Hollywood. In Hollywood she also wrote a synopsis for a comedy, "What Are We to Do About Mother?" and took some comfort from William Hurlbut's "I think your five pages present very cleverly the nucleus from which to develop a story—stage or screen, stage *and* screen. It would interest me more particularly to make a hilarious comedy from it for the stage—you in it cavorting with your witty comedy, but I can't do it on account of my Fox contract. . . . But how convulsing you would be as that fool woman." She also sent Walt Disney a sketch for a "Silly Symphony" based on the Dionne quintuplets at sixty-five, their husbands, and their ninety-five-year-old father ("type Bernard Shaw"). Disney politely rejected it as not being fantastic enough for a cartoon and because he preferred not to caricature real people; he thought it might be suitable for a two- or three-reel short subject. These sketches are amateurish, though not without interest and humor (Burgunder Shaw Collection, Cornell University Library).

Harry T. Brundidge's interview "The Amazing Mrs. Campbell" appeared originally in *Movie Mirror* and was reprinted in *People's National Theatre Magazine* (London: Spring 1935): 27–31.

Stella wrote Shaw for money from Sunset Tower, 8358 Sunset Boulevard, on April 8, 1935: *TC*: 356–8. The passage about the check from "George's lady" was omitted, as well as the note she pencilled on a copy of her letter: "a rude horrid letter refusing [money] to me in reply. I destroyed it." There are black-and-white snapshots in the Enthoven Collection of both the house at 605 North Elm Drive and Sunset Tower; there is also one of her seated in her Packard outside a studio, and several of her cabin at Skyforest.

Mrs. Nelson Hagan (Madison, Wisconsin) told me that one afternoon Stella knocked at her uncle's door at 433 Locust Street, Laguna Beach, demanding, "Young man, what do you do with your garbage?" Unaware they were neighbors, Harold Hoffman nevertheless recognized her immediately, invited her to tea, and told her, "I have seen actors run down the stairs, walk down the stairs, fall down the stairs—but only you *glide* down the stairs." "Tell me more!" begged Stella, and stayed so long to tea that hints of supper floated from the kitchen. "What is that delectable fragrance?" she hinted. By now Hoffman was weary of the visit. "Fish," he said, in flatly discouraging tones. "But I *adore* fish!" bubbled Stella, and stayed for dinner. Her desperate strategies seem to confirm that she felt suicidally isolated at Laguna Beach.

Sir John Gielgud has written about Stella in New York in *Distinguished Company*: 34–8. I am very much indebted to these pages and to his personally related anecdotes of Clifton Webb and Noel Coward at "21." James Agate visited Stella on May 6, 1937. His "The New York Scene: A Talk with Mrs. Patrick Campbell" appeared in the *Sunday Times* of May 30, 1937, and is quoted at length in Dent. Stella expressed her reaction to Agate in a letter to Shaw of August 25, 1937: *TC*: 361–6. Dame Rebecca West's description of Stella as Renaissance royalty was given to Dent; her comment on Stella's wit to me; her "as beautiful among women" statement appeared in the *Sunday Telegraph* (April 16, 1961).

I am very grateful to two American correspondents for accounts of Stella's appearance in *The Thirteenth Chair* at Milford, Connecticut, during the week of July 12–17, 1937. Gene Graves of the Philadelphia *Inquirer and Daily News* sent me a copy of Marcus Merwin's comments on Stella that Merwin had sent him at the time—and also, not incidentally, put me on to the Theatre Collection of the Free Library of Philadelphia, where librarian Geraldine Duclow was exremely helpful. And Charles Kebbe of New York gave me two detailed accounts of his acting with Stella at Milford when he was "an amazed youngster of 24, much too young to play Roscoe Crosby—but Mrs. Pat didn't like the Lambs Club character who was playing Crosby in rehearsal, and took me out of a bit part and put me in that role."

Stella and Shaw exchanged letters in August and September 1937, Shaw informing her he had sent her her letters on August 11 and 14, Stella replying on August 25 and again on September 27 to say that she had received them: *TC*: 358–67.

Stella's letters to Lulo and to Flora, a cousin, about Lulo's financial affairs are in the Tanner Collection. Lulo's reply was apparently without sarcasm: "My dear Beatrice—What a wonderful brain you have to have thought out all this in the midst of all your own work and affairs. It seems almost wicked of me not to accept your 'suggestion' with all the kind feeling and thought and good intentions that have inspired you to make it but . . . I cannot sign away my liberty of action & freedom over my life and affairs." Stella replied September 16, 1931, just before sailing to America for *The Sex Fable*: "You would not be signing away your liberty of action, you would only be signing away the *necessity* of begging, or borrowing from Flora, Roy, Francis, Fred, or myself, or Violet, or someone else. Fred, or I, at your death would have been repaid any help we had given you. This seems to me *independence."*

Frances Tompkins of Key Siesta, Florida, replied belatedly to my advertisement for Campbell material, wondering apologetically whether the fact that she had been part-time secretary to Mrs. Campbell in the late thirties and owned thirty-one of Mrs. Campbell's letters to Mrs. Jane (James B.) Curtis written between April 1938 and December 1939 might interest me. It did; and Miss Tompkins, whom Stella called "dear pretty Frances," kindly provided me with photocopies. The batch of letters also included two from Stella to Frances, and two from Agnes Claudius to Mrs. Curtis—one written during Stella's final illness (April 4, 1940) and one after her death (May 21, 1940). Miss Tompkins also provided me with a long account of her association with the actress up to Stella's departure from New York in 1938.

One of Cecil Beaton's photographs of Stella taken in 1938 is reproduced in this book. His "A Portrait of Mrs. Pat," to which I am indebted, appeared in *Theatre Arts* (July 1961: 64, 78–90) as an excerpt from his book *The Wandering Years.*

CHAPTER THIRTY-SEVEN: 1938–1940

I have drawn on eight principal sources for the account of Stella's last years. (1) Under the name "Claude Vincent," Agnes Claudius wrote an unfinished sixty-three-page account of her relationship with Stella and, after Stella's death, her various attempts to preserve her possessions and memory, titling it first "Mrs. Pat," then *The Death of "The dearest Liar"* (Burgunder Shaw Collection, Cornell University Library). (2) A leather loose-leaf pocket notebook, engraved "S.C.," containing notes that Claudius made from Thursday, March 21, to Wednesday, April 10, 1940 (Burgunder Shaw Collection). According to these notes, Stella died on April 9 at 12:30 a.m. The French death certificate reads: *"Le neuf Avril mil neuf cent quarante, huit heures trente, est décédée en son domicile . . . Beatrice Stella Tanner. . . ."* Entries in the diary for April 9 are:

| 217.60 (francs) | teleg. New York |
| 12. | taxi |
| 54.60 | telegram London Paris letters |
| 3.90 | oranges |
| 60. | Paulette's week |
| 12.30 a.m. she goes | |

(3) Thirteen autograph letters, an autograph postcard, and thirty-one typed letters from Stella to Agnes Claudius, written between 1938, when she met her at Sirmione, and 1940, when Claudius joined her at Pau (Burgunder Shaw Collection). (4) Letters from Stella to Mrs. Jane Curtis and letters to Jane Curtis from Agnes Claudius (see note, Chapter 36) in the possession of Frances Tompkins, Key Siesta, Florida. (5) The last nine letters of Stella and Shaw, written between September 3, 1938, and August 21, 1939: *TC:* 370–85 and British Library. (6) Mrs. Dorothy Etté's account of escorting Stella to Pau: Dent: 276–7. (7) A letter from Stella to D.D. Lyttelton of March 2, 1940 (Churchill College Library, Cambridge). (8) The kind resources of Madame Suzanne Bordenave, librarian of the Bibliothèque Municipale at Pau. My husband and I made a flying trip to Pau and spent a hot, dusty, futile morning searching the Cimetière Urbain for Stella's grave. Although we found the name "Cornwallis-West" in the books, the cemetery official could not direct us to the site: our little French was not equipped to deal with technicalities of burial; he spoke no English. He could only tell us that the *tombe* was probably in the English section. Having painstakingly scrutinized hundreds of tombs, we only knew that it was not. Sometime in the early afternoon we were inspired to resort to the local library, where, of course,

we should have gone first. Madame Bordenave spoke no English, but recognized "Mrs. Patrick Campbell" immediately. Within hours she had arranged for us to obtain the death certificate (usually a matter of weeks); had got on the telephone and found Stella's *tombe* in *zone C, carré 5, rang 5*; provided us with local newspaper clippings about Stella's death; and finally led us on her bicycle through the streets of Pau to the Hotel Pavillon de Navarre, 15 Avenue Léon Say, tucked in just behind and below the long promenade, Boulevard des Pyrénées. Her help did not end there: she continued to send more information and photographs of Stella's first *pension*, the Pavillon de Madrid, and, finally, when Stella was publicly honored in December 1981 on the occasion of a performance of *Cher Menteur* at the Casino Royale, Pau, she provided me with complete photographic and news coverage of the events. *Merci, Madame.*

# Index

# Index

# Photo Credits

A NOTE ON THE TYPE

*The text of this book was set on the Linotype in Garamond No. 3, a modern rendering of the type first cut by Claude Garamond (1510–1561). Garamond was a pupil of Geoffroy Troy and is believed to have based his letters on the Venetian models, although he introduced a number of important differences, and it is to him we owe the letter that we know as old-style. He gave to his letters a certain elegance and a feeling of movement that won for their creator an immediate reputation and the patronage of Francis I of France.*

*This book was composed by Maryland Linotype Composition Co., Inc., Baltimore, Maryland. It was printed and bound by The Murray Printing Company, Westford, Massachusetts.*

*Typography and binding design
by Dorothy Schmiderer*